THE FACTS ON FILE

Companion to
Shakespeare

VOLUME II

Companion to Shakespeare

VOLUME II

WILLIAM BAKER AND KENNETH WOMACK

 Facts On File
An Infobase Learning Company

The Facts On File Companion to Shakespeare

Facts On File, Inc.
An imprint of Infobase Learning
132 West 31st Street
New York NY 10001

Library of Congress Cataloging-in-Publication Data
Baker, William, 1944–
 The facts on file companion to Shakespeare / William Baker and Kenneth Womack.
  p. cm.
 Includes bibliographical references and index.
 ISBN 978-0-8160-7820-2 (acid-free paper) 1. Shakespeare, William, 1564–1616—Encyclopedias.
I. Womack, Kenneth. II. Title.
 PR2892.B26 2011
 822.3'3—dc22   2010054012

Facts On File books are available at special discounts when purchased in bulk quantities for businesses, associations, institutions, or sales promotions. Please call our Special Sales Department in New York at (212) 967-8800 or (800) 322-8755.

You can find Facts On File on the World Wide Web at http://www.infobaselearning.com

Text design by Annie O'Donnell
Composition by Hermitage Publishing Services
Cover printed by Yurchak Printing, Landisville, Pa.
Book printed and bound by Yurchak Printing, Landisville, Pa.
Date printed: January 2012

Printed in the United States of America

10 9 8 7 6 5 4 3 2 1

This book is printed on acid-free paper.

Contents

PART III

SHAKESPEARE'S PLAYS

All's Well That Ends Well

INTRODUCTION

All's Well That Ends Well is one of the more enigmatic plays in the Shakespearean canon. Shakespeare wrote it at about the same time as some of his greatest tragedies, such as *King Lear, Othello,* and *Antony and Cleopatra,* and it bears the influence of those plays, presenting a fascinating mix of comedy and tragedy. Often regarded as one of Shakespeare's "problem plays" (along with *Measure for Measure* and *Troilus and Cressida*), *All's Well That Ends Well* closes with the resolution of the dramatic situation it presents, but not in the satisfactory manner expected of a more conventional play. We, as readers, are asked to think about what must be sacrificed to ensure a happy ending, and the play deliberately elicits questions about happiness, loyalty, and honor.

Written between 1602 and 1606, *All's Well That Ends Well* is the work of a mature dramatist and demonstrates a nuanced awareness of what makes comedy work and how closely the form can parallel tragedy. Shakespeare intertwines the two dramatic forms in this puzzling play, challenging the conventional love plots with complicated characters who refuse to conform. The assumption implied in the title—that all will end on a note of reconciliation—is never fully realized. The play ends on a note of superficial resolution, but the deep-rooted conflicts that have driven the drama until that point remain and linger in the audience's mind.

The dramatic depth of the play is further enhanced by the way in which the subject matter echoes the content of Shakespeare's sonnets. Dominated by the themes of the lure of sexual attraction and the frustration of unrequited love, both the sonnets and *All's Well That Ends Well* offer a multiplicity of meanings ready to be explored. Two hours' stage traffic cannot contain this late play, which chooses messy reality over a neat but contrived and artificial ending. In this sense, *All's Well That Ends Well* is typically genre-confounding, refusing to fit into any precise category. It lingers long after the curtain has fallen and never compromises, presenting a situation as it is rather than as we might prefer it to be.

BACKGROUND

Most critics agree that the play was written somewhere between 1602 and 1606, although a few believe it can be identified as one of Shakespeare's "lost" dramas, specifically *Love's Labour's Won,* which would mean that it could be dated as early as 1598. Topical references and echoes of Shakespeare's poem *A Lover's Complaint* and sonnets have led recent critics to suggest the date of 1604–06.

All's Well That Ends Well is one of a genre of plays often called the "problem plays," along with *Measure for Measure* and *Troilus and Cressida;* these comedies preceded the so-called romances *The Winter's Tale, Cymbeline,* and *The Tempest.* These three romances are, in fact, as perplexing as *All's Well That Ends Well* owing to their resolutions, which often raise more questions than answers, and the dark nature of their comedy. In his later career, Shakespeare showed a critical attention to genre that suggested a dissatisfaction with conventionally "happy" endings. In all of these later plays, the audience cannot help but be ambivalent toward the reconciliations that the plays offer, and more often than not, order is restored at some degree of personal cost. Shakespeare's dark comedies, another category to which *All's Well That Ends Well* certainly belongs, are complex, layered examinations of romance conventions that resist the genre's confines.

There are two widely accepted sources for the play: Giovanni Boccaccio's *Decameron* and William Painter's *The Palace of Pleasure,* which was a popular translation of Boccaccio's work printed several times during the second half of the 16th century. Written about 1350, Boccaccio's *Decameron* is a series of short tales, told over 10 days by a group of young Italian men and women who escape to a villa outside Florence to avoid the bubonic plague ravaging their city. On the third day, a young lady by the name of Neifile tells the tale of Giletta of Narbonne, who cures the king of France and is married to the reluctant Count Bertrand of Roussillon. Unlike Shakespeare's Helena, who is only with Bertram for a brief time, Boccaccio's heroine has a prolonged affair with her dispassionate husband, which results in two sons. At the end of Boccaccio's tale, Count Bertrand happily embraces his twin children—and his wife. Shakespeare drew heavily from this medieval tale and included popular romance motifs, such as the patient and self-sacrificing heroine.

Painter's translation, *The Palace of Pleasure,* was selected as light entertainment for "the virtuous minds of Noble dames," with an eye to the moral instruction that might be offered to the reader of the tale. It was tremendously well received and following the first publication in 1560, was reprinted again in 1560 and 1575. It is reasonable to conclude that Shakespeare's first encounter with Boccaccio would have been through Painter and that his audience was likely also to have been able to identify the story they were seeing onstage. Shakespeare's most

significant alteration to both texts was the choice to present Bertram in such an unflattering light. Additionally, Shakespeare emphasized the miraculous success of Helena's scheme: In *All's Well That Ends Well,* Shakespeare's heroine becomes pregnant after only one night spent with her husband.

The play's central concern with notions of honor is something that would have been familiar to Shakespeare's audience. In March 1603, the monarch of England, Queen Elizabeth I, died after a 44-year reign. Under Elizabeth, a culture of chivalry and honor had flourished in poetry, art, and courtly conduct. Elizabeth cultivated relationships with her courtiers that mirrored those of the medieval conventions of courtly love. Young men played the role of earnest young lover to an unavailable mistress, usually of higher social stature. Poets such as Sir Walter Raleigh, and Sir Philip Sidney would compose verses dedicated to Elizabeth, who was identifiable under pseudonyms such as Cynthia or Diana, goddesses of chastity and virginity. Through such fictions, political appeals were conducted, and performances of chivalric works were tremendously popular. However, as critics such as Mervyn James, and Richard C. McCoy have noted, these were widely recognized as social conventions. As we see in a character such as Bertram, nobility did not always translate into virtue. The outward display of chivalry led to extravagant fashions in clothing and placed a premium on courtly ritual, constructing images of the ideal courtier that men would try to follow to publicly demonstrate their virtue. The popularity of these elaborate displays emphasized the idea of the performance of nobility, severing the direct relationship between public image and personal characteristic, and encouraging would-be courtiers to fashion themselves as the ideal courtier as a means of furthering their political careers.

Elizabeth's successor, James I of England (James VI of Scotland), was a very different political animal. As strong minded and independent as she was, Elizabeth understood that as a woman and unmarried ruler, she was politically vulnerable and thus cultivated an image of herself as the

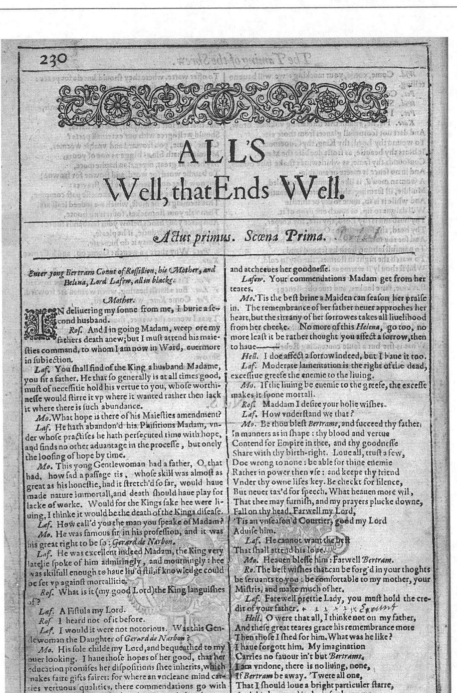

230

ALL'S
Well, that Ends Well.

Actus primus. Scœna Prima.

Enter yong Bertram Count of Rossillion, his Mother, and Helena, Lord Lafew, all in blacke.

Mother.

IN deliuering my sonne from me, I burie a second husband.

Ros. And I in going Madam, weep ore my fathers death anew; but I must attend his maiesties command, to whom I am now in Ward, euermore in subiection.

Laf. You shall find of the King a husband Madame, you sir a father. He that so generally is at all times good, must of necessitie hold his vertue to you, whose worthinesse would stirre it vp where it wanted rather then lack it where there is such abundance.

Mo. What hope is there of his Maiesties amendment?

Laf. He hath abandon'd his Phisitions Madam, vnder whose practises he hath persecuted time with hope, and finds no other aduantage in the processe, but onely the loosing of hope by time.

Mo. This yong Gentlewoman had a father, O that had, how sad a passage tis, whose skill was almost as great as his honestie, had it stretch'd so far, would haue made nature immortall, and death should haue play for lacke of worke. Would for the Kings sake hee were liuing, I thinke it would be the death of the Kings disease.

Laf. How call'd you the man you speake of Madam?

Mo. He was famous sir in his profession, and it was his great right to be so: *Gerard de Narbon.*

Laf. He was excellent indeed Madam, the King very latelie spoke of him admiringly, and mourningly: hee was skilfull enough to haue liu'd stil, if knowledge could be set vp against mortallitie.

Ros. What is it (my good Lord) the King languishes of?

Laf. A Fistula my Lord.

Ros. I heard not of it before.

Laf. I would it were not notorious. Was this Gentlewoman the Daughter of *Gerard de Narbon?*

Mo. His sole childe my Lord, and bequeathed to my ouer looking. I haue those hopes of her good, that her education promises her dispositions shee inherits, which makes faire gifts fairer: for where an vncleane mind carries vertuous qualities, there commendations go with pitty, they are vertues and traitors too: in her they are the better for their simplenesse; she deriues her honestie,

and atcheeues her goodnesse.

Lafew. Your commendations Madam get from her teares.

Mo. 'Tis the best brine a Maiden can season her praise in. The remembrance of her father neuer approches her heart, but the tirrany of her sorrowes takes all liuelihood from her cheeke. No more of this *Helena*, go too, no more least it be rather thought you affect a sorrow, then to haue——

Hell. I doe affect a sorrow indeed, but I haue it too.

Laf. Moderate lamentation is the right of the dead, excessiue greefe the enemie to the liuing.

Mo. If the liuing be enemie to the greefe, the excesse makes it soone mortall.

Ros. Maddam I desire your holie wishes.

Laf. How vnderstand we that?

Mo. Be thou blest *Bertrame*, and succeed thy father, In manners as in shape: thy blood and vertue Contend for Empire in thee, and thy goodnesse Share with thy birth-right. Loue all, trust a few, Doe wrong to none: be able for thine enemie Rather in power then vse: and keepe thy friend Vnder thy owne lifes key. Be checkt for silence, But neuer tax'd for speech. What heauen more wil, That thee may furnish, and my prayers plucke downe, Fall on thy head. Farewell my Lord, 'Tis an vnseason'd Courtier, good my Lord Aduise him.

Laf. He cannot want the best That shall attend his loue.

Mo. Heauen blesse him: Farwell *Bertram.*

Ro. The best wishes that can be forg'd in your thoghts be seruants to you: be comfortable to my mother, your Mistris, and make much of her.

Laf. Farewell prettie Lady, you must hold the credit of your father. *Exeunt*

Hell. O were that all, I thinke not on my father, And these great teares grace his remembrance more Then those I shed for him. What was he like? I haue forgott him. My imagination Carries no fauour in't but *Bertrams*. I am vndone, there is no liuing, none, If *Bertram* be away. 'Twere all one, That I should loue a bright particuler starre, And think to wed it, he is so aboue me In his bright radience and colaterall light,

Must

Title page of the First Folio edition of *All's Well That Ends Well*, published in 1623

Virgin Queen, a semidivine figure of exemplary chastity. Elizabeth's popularity was derived from her willingness to play the passive female role, even as she asserted her monarchical authority. James, however, would take an entirely different, blunt, and transparent tack. For example, in a 1609 speech to Parliament, he explained his belief in the divine authority of kings, publicly announcing that kings were God's lieutenants on Earth, likening his role to that of God's, as the giver and taker of life, and rebuking Parliament for any assumption of power that it might hold. As James's popularity waned, a nostalgia for Elizabeth grew, and the image of the Virgin Queen was cemented in the public imagination.

Date and Text of the Play

For a Shakespeare play, the textual history of *All's Well That Ends Well* is remarkably straightforward. The only authoritative text we have is from the 1623 First Folio publication of Shakespeare's plays; there are no earlier published versions. Critics agree that the text is unlikely to have been interfered with, and although some seek to examine layers of revision in the text, especially in certain stage directions and name variants, there is no evidence to suggest that the 1623 version is not the earliest draft available.

SYNOPSIS
Brief Synopsis

Bertram, the young Count of Rousillon, is planning to leave his family home in order to attend the court of the ailing King of France. Helena, who also lives in the household, is in love with Bertram, but, as she is a doctor's daughter and socially inferior, she knows that he will never love her in return. Bertram is welcomed at court by the King, who reveals that his illness is thought to be incurable. Back in Rousillon, Helena decides to use the medical skills she learned from her late father to heal the King, in the hope that it will win Bertram's affection.

Bertram watches the young men of France go off to war in Florence, quietly angry that the King

has deemed him too young to fight. Helena presents herself to the King and brings him back to health. The King offers Helena her choice of husband, and she chooses Bertram. However, Bertram is disgusted and refuses. The angry King orders Bertram to marry Helena. Bertram makes immediate plans to run away to fight in Florence and sends Helena home to his mother. He reveals to his friend Parolles that he has no intention of ever returning to his wife.

Helena receives a letter from Bertram in which he tells her that he will only acknowledge himself as her husband when she is pregnant with his child and in possession of his family ring. Helena, distraught, leaves France, telling the Countess that she is going on a pilgrimage to Spain, but instead she follows Bertram to Florence. She talks to a poor widow who reveals that Bertram continually tries to seduce her daughter, Diana. Helena reveals herself to the women and asks for their help.

Bertram attempts to talk Diana into sleeping with him. She agrees, but only if he promises to marry her and give her his family ring. They exchange rings. Diana tells him to come to her bedroom in the dark, and while there, Helena secretly takes her place. Meanwhile, Bertram's lords trap and blindfold cowardly Parolles, who instantly betrays his friends and tells as many secrets as he knows. Bertram then hears a rumor of Helena's death and joyfully returns to France, planning to marry a noblewoman. Helena, the widow, and Diana follow him.

In France, Bertram is welcomed back until he offers his new wife the ring Diana gave him, which the King recognizes as Helena's. Bertram is thrown into jail until Helena arrives, pregnant and bearing the family ring. Bertram agrees to live as her husband, and the King, delighted with the outcome, offers Diana her choice of husband.

Act I, Scene 1

We meet the recently widowed Countess of Rousillon, and her son, Bertram, the new count. The Countess and old lord Lafew lament the King of France's grave illness and express regret that Helena's father, a famous and skilled doctor, is not still alive to nurse him back to health. They leave, and Helena reveals that her sadness for her father's death is only surpassed by the misery that her unrequited love for Bertram causes her. She jokes with Parolles about the value of her virginity and then decides to try curing the King with her own medical knowledge.

Act I, Scene 2

The play moves to the French court, where the King, close to death, is deciding on the extent of his involvement in a war between the Florentines and Sienese. The King authorizes men to answer the call of war, on whichever side they see fit. Lafew, Bertram, and Parolles enter, and the young count is formally introduced to the King. The King welcomes Bertram on the merit of his late father, Count of Rousillon, who was a dear friend of the King. The men reminisce about the exemplary qualities of Bertram's father, and the King laments the rise of a younger generation who do not share the honorable principles of the older men. The King then inquires after Bertram's father's physician—Helena's father—expressing dismay upon

Lafew introduces Helena to the King in Act II, Scene 1 of *All's Well That Ends Well*. This print is from Joseph Graves's *Dramatic Tales Founded on Shakespeare's Plays,* published by John Duncombe in the early 19th century.

learning of his death. The scene ends as Bertram is formally welcomed to court.

Act I, Scene 3

The Countess and her clown, Lavatch, joke about the nature of marriage. The Countess sends Lavatch to fetch Helena, and while he is gone, the Countess's steward, Reynaldo, reveals to her Helena's love for Bertram. The Countess questions Helena on her love for Bertram. Helena confesses her feelings but admits that it is a hopeless cause. She then reveals her plan to go to Paris and try to cure the King using her father's notes and medicines. The Countess gives her blessing to Helena's endeavors.

Act II, Scene 1

The King bids farewell to a group of young noblemen who are off to fight in the Italian wars. He warns the men not to allow themselves to be seduced by Italian women. One Lord remarks that he hopes that his return will see the king in better health, but the King says he expects to be dead by the end of the war. Bertram quietly complains about being told that he is too young to fight in the war. Bertram plans to run away and join the army against the orders of the King and his friend. Lafew arrives at court and introduces Helena, who convinces the King to allow her to try her remedy. The King views her as a "blessed spirit" (2.1.175). The King tells her that if he dies under her care, she will forfeit her life, and Helena agrees on the condition that if she succeeds the King will grant her the husband of her choice. The King agrees to the bargain. He and Helena leave the court to talk further and try her remedy.

Act II, Scene 2

The Countess and her clown await news from court and exchange bawdy jokes on the nature of court manners. The clown mocks the lack of manners to be found at court and alludes to the immoral sexual behavior to be found in such places. The Countess sends him to court to pass a message of affection from her to Helena and also sends greetings to her son.

Act II, Scene 3

The scene opens with Bertram, Lafew, and Parolles marveling at the King's miraculous recovery. Lafew notes that "they say miracles are past" (2.3.1), implying how unexpected the King's return to health is. The King enters with Helena and assembles the finest noblemen in his kingdom for her choice of husband. He announces that "who shuns thy love shuns all his love in me" (2.3.72), making sure that the lords know that to reject Helena is to directly disobey their monarch. Helena addresses the lords in turn, explaining why she will not take them as a husband, as Lafew looks on, offering a commentary that seems to misinterpret the lords' willing compliance as refusal of Helena. In each of her addresses, Helena emphasizes her humble (lower-class) blood, although she does tell the Third Lord that she would be a true and faithful wife. Eventually, she turns to Bertram and humbles herself before him, telling him that she will not take him but rather offer herself to him. She tells the King that she chooses Bertram, and the King tells Bertram that he is to marry Helena. Appalled, Bertram refuses on the grounds that Helena is beneath him in class. The King rebukes him and explains that honor comes from virtue and good deeds, and offers to give Helena wealth and titles to make the marriage more socially acceptable to Bertram. Bertram bluntly replies that he cannot love Helena, nor will he even try to do so. Helena begs the King to "let the rest go" (2.3.147) and forget their pact. The King, however, is furious that his subject has so openly disobeyed him; he threatens to strip Bertram of all that he has and view him as an enemy if he does not comply. Bertram grudgingly agrees to the marriage.

The King leads Bertram and Helena off for an immediate wedding, leaving Lafew and Parolles onstage, arguing about Lafew's open disdain for Parolles's pompous character. Parolles continues to take offense at Lafew's criticism of his lowly status and superficiality until Lafew leaves, at which point Parolles boasts that he will beat the old man into submission. Lafew returns and explains that Bertram and Helena have been married. Parolles then claims social superiority over Lafew because he serves a higher master—God. Lafew becomes exasperated and vows not to give Parolles any more of his time, warning him that his arrogance will bring about his downfall. Bertram, furious, enters and decides to leave France and go to the Tuscan wars. He explains that the material rewards the King has given him for his marriage will allow him to travel to the battle, and that he would prefer to risk his life by fighting than live with his wife. He explains that he will send Helena to live with his mother and writes a letter to be left for the King once he has fled.

Act II, Scene 4

Helena is talking with the clown when Parolles enters. He brings a message from Bertram that the young count is leaving immediately and will not spend his wedding night with Helena. Bertram sends his regrets that they will be unable to consummate the marriage and asks her to leave court as soon as possible.

Act II, Scene 5

The scene opens with Lafew and Bertram talking about Parolles. Bertram assures Lafew that Parolles is a brave soldier, and Lafew asks if Bertram will help them to become friends again. Parolles enters and tells Bertram that Helena is leaving immediately. Bertram attempts to reconcile Lafew and Parolles, but Parolles denies ever offending Lafew and in doing so, offends him again. Lafew leaves, swearing that Parolles is foolish and untrustworthy. Helena enters, bringing Bertram a message from the King. Before leaving to see the King and then go off to war, Bertram tells Helena that his departure was unavoidable. He gives her two letters—one for her and one for his mother—and tries to leave. Helena asks for a kiss before he goes, but Bertram says that he is in too much of a hurry and hurries Helena away. When she has left, he tells Parolles that he has no intention of ever returning home to her.

Before leaving to fight in the Tuscan wars, Bertram hands Helena his mother's letter in Act II, Scene 5 of *All's Well That Ends Well*. Print from Charles and Mary Cowden Clarke's *Illustrated Shakespeare*, published by Cassell, Petter & Galpin in the 1860s *(Illustration by Henry Courtney Selous; engraving by A. Burgess)*

Act III, Scene 1

The Duke of Florence enters, talking with French ambassadors. He says that he is surprised that the French will not help him in the war, and the ambassadors reveal that they have no idea why the King of France will not help. They hint that young men, hungry for war, are likely to want to help, and the Duke of Florence says that such men will be welcome.

Act III, Scene 2

The Countess and the clown Lavatch enter, wondering why Bertram has not returned with Helena. The clown tells us that he no longer wishes to marry Isabel, his beloved, since his trip to court, because of the women he saw there. While he is talking about Isabel, the Countess opens the letter and reads it. Bertram has written that he has run away, and even though he has married Helena, he has not taken her to bed and has no intention of

ever doing so. The Countess is angry, but the clown jokes that by staying in the marriage, Bertram will be emasculated, so he is better off at war. Helena enters and reads her own letter to the Countess. It is revealed that Bertram wrote to her that once she can get a ring upon his finger "which never shall come off" (3.2.57) and become pregnant by him, then he will consider himself her husband, but assures her that will never happen. The Countess is furious and disowns him. Helena reads the last line of the letter, "Till I have no wife, I have nothing in France" (3.2.74), and she and the Countess complain that Bertram has gone to Florence with no one but the disreputable Parolles in tow. The Countess leaves to send Bertram a scolding message. Helena admits that in spite of his cruelty, she still loves Bertram. She vows to leave France so that Bertram can come home again.

Act III, Scene 3

The Duke of Florence welcomes Bertram, and he enters the battle, declaring himself a "hater of love"(3.3.11).

Act III, Scene 4

The Countess enters reading a letter from Helena. The letter states that Helena has taken a pilgrimage to Saint Jaques's shrine (thought to be in northern Spain). Helena writes that she wishes to free Bertram to return home so that he can avoid death. The Countess is upset that she did not have a chance to talk Helena out of leaving and writes an angry letter to Bertram, telling him that Helena has left. She hopes that once Bertram returns, Helena will. She closes the scene complaining that she is too old for so much sadness.

Act III, Scene 5

The old Widow Capilet of Florence, her daughter Diana, and her friend Mariana enter. Diana talks about the glory Bertram has won in the war, and Mariana warns her to stay away from Bertram, reminding her that for a woman, glory is to be found in her chastity. The Widow and Mariana tell

Diana that they know Parolles has been trying to win her over on Bertram's behalf and warn Diana that the soldiers are only after her virginity. Mariana tells her that many women have been ruined by affairs with soldiers, but Diana reassures her that she has no intention of being seduced. Helena enters, dressed as a pilgrim, and the Widow invites her to stay with them. Helena accepts, and the Widow invites her to watch the soldiers as they march by. She tells Helena of Bertram, who has won great honor in the war, and they talk about his rumored marriage, telling Helena that Parolles has been saying coarse things about Bertram's wife. Not knowing Helena's true identity, the women offer sympathy to the wife of Bertram, and the Widow reveals that Bertram has been trying to seduce Diana.

The army, led by Bertram and Parolles, enters. Diana says that she would like him much more if he was decent to his wife and jokes that if she were married to Bertram, she would poison Parolles for leading him astray. The Widow offers to take in Helena, and Helena asks that she and Diana join her as guests at dinner that evening.

Helena speaks to the old Widow Capilet of Florence in Act III, Scene 5 of *All's Well That Ends Well*. This print is from Malcolm C. Salaman's 1916 edition of *Shakespeare in Pictorial Art. (Illustration by H. Bunbury; engraving by L. Chapman)*

Act III, Scene 6

Bertram enters with Two Lords, discussing ways to humiliate Parolles for his general cowardice and dishonesty. The Two Lords offer to trick Parolles into thinking he has been kidnapped by the enemy to prove to Bertram that he has no loyalty. Parolles enters, and Bertram and the Second Lord stage a conversation regretting the loss of a drum. Parolles says that he will enter the enemy camp and get the drum back, and Bertram wishes him luck. Parolles leaves, and the men plan their trick. Bertram cannot believe that Parolles would brag about capturing the drum, even though he has no intention of endangering himself to reclaim it, and the Two Lords talk about how Lafew was the first to notice Parolles's lack of honor. At the close of the scene, Bertram offers to take the Second Lord to see Diana and talks about his attempts to seduce her. They leave to visit the Widow's house.

Act III, Scene 7

Helena and the Widow Capilet enter, and it is clear that Helena has told the Widow the truth about her identity. The Widow tells Helena that she was well born, and even though she is now poor, she does not want to be involved in anything that will compromise her good name. Helena swears that she is telling the truth, and the Widow believes her. Helena rewards her with money and tells her that she will help them out further once her plan has been executed. Helena's plan is to have Diana warm to Bertram's wooing and to ask for Bertram's family ring. Once he has given her the heirloom ring, Diana will make an arrangement to sleep with him, but Helena will take her place during the night. The Widow agrees to the trick, and Helena tells her that even though the plan is a trick, the seduction will be lawful, describing the upcoming events as "both not sin, and yet a sinful fact" (3.7.47).

Act IV, Scene 1

The Two Lords prepare to ambush Parolles. He enters and tells the audience that he has been leisurely walking around for three hours while Bertram thinks he is in the enemy camp looking for the drum. While the men watch, Parolles wonders what kind of excuse he can come up with for why he returned empty handed. He says that he is going to injure himself, for authenticity, and the men listen, incredulously. They attack him and "kidnap" and blindfold him. Even before they request his betrayal, Parolles immediately offers to reveal any secrets he knows about the Florentine army. One of the lords sends for Bertram and instructs that Parolles is kept blindfolded until Bertram returns to hear the betrayal.

Act IV, Scene 2

Bertram enters, with Diana. He swears his love to her and insists that he does not love Helena. Diana talks about the unreliability of love and accuses him of trying to win her with mere words. She asks for Bertram's ring, and he is reluctant to give her the family heirloom. Diana tells him that if he gives her the ring, he can take her virginity, and Bertram immediately hands it over. Diana tells him to come to her room in the middle of the night and instructs him not to speak to her while he is there. She explains that while he is there, she will put a ring on him that will be proof of their night together. Bertram agrees and leaves. Diana expresses amazement that her mother's predictions of how Bertram would woo her were so accurate. Diana decides that because men are so unreliable, she will do all that she can to remain a virgin for the remainder of her life

Act IV, Scene 3

The two French lords enter, talking about Bertram. They discuss how changed he is by his mother's letter and how unhappy the King of France is with him. They also mention that he is reputed to have compromised Diana, who is known as one of the purest women in Florence. They observe that his behavior is not noble, as he has given in to his baser human desires. It is nighttime, and the Two Lords say that they are glad not to see Bertram until later, because they want to make him realize how poorly he is behaving. They then talk about the conclusion of the war and wonder if Bertram will return to Rousillon now that Helena is gone. She has been reported as dead, from grief. They lament that Bertram will be happy to hear such sad news. The Second Lord notes that all the glory that Bertram has won in war will be countered by the embarrassment of his behavior toward women.

A messenger enters and tells the lords that Bertram has been excused by the Duke of Florence and will leave for France in the morning. Bertram enters, delighted at the turn of events: He is glad to be returning home and even more glad to learn of Helena's death. The lords remind him that he still has one piece of business left—Parolles. Parolles is brought in, after having spent the night in the stocks, and the Two Lords ask him a series of questions about the army. Parolles continues to talk and swears that he knows the Duke's military policy intimately and that he has sworn the truth. One lord asks the interrogators to talk about him, and Parolles criticizes him, mocking him as a coward, a liar, and a drunk. He also reveals Bertram's plan to take Diana's virginity, dismissing his master as "a dangerous and lascivious boy" (4.3.215). The soldiers tell Parolles that he is to be executed for the betrayal of his army, and while Parolles is pleading with them, they remove the blindfold and reveal themselves. They laugh at him and leave him alone, where he swears to follow the men and beg them to help him return by playing their fool.

Act IV, Scene 4

Helena enters with the Widow and Diana, thanking them for their help, and assuring them that they did the right thing by helping her. They are leaving together to see the King of France at Marcellus. Helena assures the Widow that she will help Diana financially and marvels at Bertram's willingness to follow his lust. She apologizes to Diana for staining her reputation temporarily, and Diana assures her that she does not mind. They leave to meet the King, full of hope that the situation will soon be resolved.

Act IV, Scene 5

Lafew and the Countess enter, talking about Parolles and lamenting Helena. The clown enters and mocks their declarations of grief. The clown describes himself as both a fool and a knave—a fool for a woman, and a knave to a man, because he would try to seduce a man's wife for his own satisfaction. Lavatch jokes that he is a follower of the devil and jokes about the hardship of following the good Christian path. The clown leaves, and Lafew and the Countess discuss the possibility of marrying Bertram off to Lafew's daughter. The clown enters and tells the Countess and Lafew that Bertram has returned, describing his physical condition, and they go to greet him.

Act V, Scene 1

Helena, the Widow, and Diana enter, exhausted, and meet one of the King's courtiers. They ask the Gentleman to help them by carrying a petition to the King, only to discover that the King is no longer in Marcellus but has returned to Rousillon. The courtier offers to take the petition ahead of the

In this 19th-century print, Helena, the Widow, and Diana ask a courtier to carry a petition to the King in Act V, Scene I of Henry Staunton's edition of *All's Well That Ends Well. (Illustration by Sir John Gilbert; engraving by the Dalziel Brothers)*

women, and they thank him and prepare to travel once more.

Act V, Scene 2

Parolles enters with the clown, who is mocking him because of the stench coming from Parolles's clothes. Lafew enters, and Parolles begs for help. Lafew refuses, telling Parolles that he has what he deserves, but agrees to feed him. As they are talking, the King arrives.

Act V, Scene 3

The King enters with the Countess, talking sadly of the marriage between Helena and Bertram. The Countess begs the King to forgive Bertram's foolishness on the grounds that he was young and impetuous. The King agrees, and they spend some time contemplating Helena's beauty and goodness. While the King's attendants leave to fetch Bertram, the King and Lafew agree on the marriage of Bertram and Lafew's daughter. Bertram had asked the King to decide on the subject, and they all agree that it is a good match. Bertram enters and tells the King that he has always loved Lafew's daughter, using that as the reason he had initially rejected Helena. Bertram offers Lafew his ring as a token of the match, but Lafew recognizes it as the ring Helena was wearing when she left court. Bertram denies this, and the King and Countess both examine the ring and declare it Helena's. Bertram lies and tells them that a Florentine noblewoman threw it out of the window at him, along with a proposition that he had declined.

The King insists that it was Helena's ring and remembers her saying that she would never part with the ring unless to give it to Bertram in bed. The King accuses Bertram of murdering Helena and calls guards to take Bertram away. At this point, the Gentleman arrives with the petition Helena had given him. It is a letter from Diana, telling the King that Bertram promised to marry her when Helena is dead. The letter claims that Diana slept with Bertram on this condition and has followed him to France to claim him as her husband. Lafew is disgusted and revokes the marriage deal.

The King calls in Bertram, Diana, and the Widow. The King asks Bertram if he knows Diana, and he admits that he does but refuses to acknowledge his promise of marriage. He tells the King that she is infatuated with him and that he used to laugh at her. He also says that he would never lower himself to have sex with her. Diana asks the King to make Bertram swear that he did not take her virginity, and when Bertram lies, Diana shows the ring that he gave her. Diana calls forth Parolles as a witness, which relieves Bertram, as he believes Parolles incapable of telling the truth.

While waiting for Parolles, the King questions Bertram about the ring, and Bertram pretends that Diana tricked him out of his ring. Diana says that they can simply return the rings they exchanged and she will leave, as she wants nothing to do with him. Bertram claims that he does not have the ring, but Diana recognizes Helena's ring in the King's hand and says that she gave it to him in bed, exposing his lie about the Florentine noblewoman. Finally, Bertram confesses that he received the ring from Diana, at which point, Parolles enters. Chastened by his recent experiences, Parolles has decided not to lie anymore and tells the King everything he wants to know about Bertram's seduction of Diana.

The King asks Diana how she came to own the ring, and she is evasive. The King threatens to throw her in prison unless she tells him the truth, but she refuses, so he orders both her and Bertram to be taken away. Diana reveals that she has something that will act as her bail and that will prove that she is either still a virgin or Bertram's wife. She sends her mother to fetch Helena. While the Widow is gone, Diana chastises Bertram for seducing her and lying. The Widow enters with Helena, who describes herself as "the shadow of a wife" (5.3.305). Helena shows Bertram his letter, which says that once he receives the ring from Helena and impregnates her, then she might call him husband. She lays claim to him on the grounds that he has her ring and she is pregnant. Bertram agrees to love Helena as his wife if she can explain how this happened, and Helena is reconciled with the Countess

and the King. The King, delighted with Helena's return, offers Diana her choice of husbands, and the play ends.

CHARACTER LIST

Bertram Count of Rousillon, later married to Helena. The son of the Countess of Rousillon. Bertram is an impetuous young aristocrat who is forced into marriage with Helena and abandons her in order to chase glory in the Florentine wars. Bertram acts on the impulse of his passions, leaving France against the King's wishes and offering his family ring to Diana in the heat of passion.

Countess of Rousillon A kind widow who loves Helena as much as her son. The Countess is a deeply respectable woman and is appalled at her son's ungallant behavior. At the same time, she thinks nothing of exchanging bawdy jokes with her clown.

Helena Helena is the daughter of a renowned physician. Helena is good, kind hearted, and extremely intelligent. She cures the King of France using her father's remedies, and she masterminds the plot to seduce Bertram and force him to be her husband. She is independent and honest.

King of France An older man, close to death as the play begins. He is loyal to Helena because of her service to him and retains great anger toward Bertram for his disobedience.

Parolles A cowardly, disloyal friend of Bertram. Parolles is arrogant, foolish, and intent on preserving himself at all costs. After being severely punished for his lies, Parolles intends to be honest, even to the detriment of others.

Duke of Florence An Italian duke who leads the army in the war.

Widow Capilet of Florence A naïve yet kind old lady, who helps Helena. Mother of Diana.

Diana A beautiful yet poor young woman, known throughout Florence for her chastity and virtue. She helps Helena, even at the risk of spoiling her good name, because of her mistrust of men.

Lafew   An old lord who is a friend of the Countess of Rousillon.

Mariana   The Widow Capilet's friend.

Reynaldo   The Countess of Rousillon's steward

Lavatch   The Countess of Rousillon's old clown. Lavatch has a dry, lewd sense of humor, and although he entertains the Countess with his critiques of the court, Lavatch espouses a dark and cynical view of the world.

Two Lords   Friends of Bertram who plot to humiliate Parolles. Sometimes known as the Brothers Dumaine.

Gentleman   A nobleman who agrees to help Helena by presenting her letter to the King of France.

CHARACTER STUDIES
Helena

Helena is the heroine of the play. An impoverished daughter of a doctor, she is a dependent of the Countess of Rousillon. Helena is well respected by all of the characters in the play except Bertram. The King of France goes so far as to imagine "in thee some blessed spirit doth speak" (2.1.175), so great is her goodness. Throughout, Helena is described in terms that emphasize her purity and inspires love and loyalty among those who encounter her. The Countess even disowns Bertram when he abandons Helena, telling her that "thou art all my child" (3.2.67) and showing the extent to which she values Helena's inherent nobility. Helena's wit and intelligence earn her respect and, more important, gain her a husband—twice.

At the beginning of the play, Helena is an outsider to the world of the French aristocracy, with no social standing to speak of. She is, in the words of the Countess, "a poor, unlearned virgin" (1.3.234). She is a ward of the Countess and deeply in love with Bertram. She is intelligent enough to know that she has little hope that her love will amount to anything and promises the Countess that "I follow him not / By any token of presumptuous suit / Nor would I have him till I do deserve him" (1.3.192–194). Helena's character is a mixture of humility and determination: She knows that she is

Helena dressed as a pilgrim in Act III, Scene 5 of *All's Well That Ends Well,* as pictured in this print from Charles Heath's 1848 edition of *The Heroines of Shakspeare: Comprising the Principal Female Characters in the Plays of the Great Poet (Painting by J. W. Wright; engraving by B. Eyles)*

too low born for Bertram but does not rule out the possibility that she might one day deserve him, and her desire to cure the King is partly driven by the idea that she might merit Bertram's love. She readily admits to the Countess that "My lord your son made me to think of" (1.3.227) attempting to cure the King.

Helena is best described as determined and intelligent. She risks her life attending to the King, agreeing to his condition that "unpitied let me die" (2.1.188) if she cannot cure him. Helena enters the court with a great amount of confidence in the face of the King's supposedly incurable malady, bargaining with him for the choice "to choose from forth the royal blood of France" (2.1.196) a husband. For a woman of the early 17th century, Helena is bold in her approach to the King and audacious in her choice of reward. She shows even more determination in her plan to force Bertram to acknowledge the marriage. Unlike Diana, Helena never dwells on the social injustices of her situation as a poor woman but is only interested in securing Bertram. The enactment of her plan requires that Bertram be accused of her murder, allowing Helena the powerful position of her husband's savior.

Yet, in spite of her aggressive pursuit of Bertram, Helena still seems vulnerable. She is simultaneously deeply pragmatic and idealistic, which makes her a sympathetic character. She opens the play weeping for her unrequited love. Her love blinds her to Bertram's shallow nature, lamenting that "though I kill him not, I am the cause / His death was so effected" (3.2.115–116). Even though the next time the audience sees Helena she will be masterminding the elaborate plan to force her husband's compliance, at the moment of receiving his letter of rejection, Helena shows us her vulnerability. She is suicidal with the thought that she might cause Bertram to come to some harm.

Shakespeare's portrayal of Helena is complex, as she can be argued to play both gender roles. She works with what critics call an "unfeminine forwardness" (McCandless 450) and takes responsibility for plots that will entrap Bertram in ways that parallel his planned seduction of Diana. She engages in a sexually suggestive conversation with Parolles and insists on the right to choose her own husband, something that is highlighted as unusual at the end of the play by Bertram's easy acquiescence to his arranged marriage. Yet, her "masculine" agency is complicated by the images that surround her as a holy maiden. Her healing powers border on the supernatural, and she is repeatedly described as a *maid* or *maiden*, terms that emphasize her virginity. She enters Florence disguised as a pilgrim, and critics note that the play preserves this image of her, by implicating Diana as the sexual subject and having her subjected to the accusations of promiscuity. Helena, on the other hand, leaves the French court a virgin and returns as a mother-to-be, and the description of how her change came about is left for after the close of the play.

Bertram

Bertram is both the hero and the villain of the play. He is the object of Helena's affection and a handsome and brave young aristocrat. Throughout the play, however, Bertram shows a lack of decorum and common decency that contradicts the general report of him as a likable young man. Bertram is the young count of Rousillon, the son of one of the King of France's dearest friends. Upon first meeting Bertram, the King talks at length of the late count's kindness and humility, telling Bertram that "who were below him / He used as creatures of another place and bowed his eminent top to their low ranks / making them proud of his humility" (1.2.41–44). Bertram begins the play in the shadow of his father, assumed by many to inherit the same virtuous character and facing the same expectations of greatness.

Bertram is defined by his youth. His mother views him as an "unseasoned courtier" (1.1.63), and Parolles dismisses him as a "foolish, idle boy" (4.3.203), both of which become evident as the play progresses. Convinced of his inherent nobility, he rashly rejects Helena before the King and plots to run away when the King refuses him permission to join the wars. Yet, he earns Helena's love and devotion, which leads many critics to suggest that there is a good in Bertram not obviously evident in the play. He draws the admiration of his fellow soldiers and earns respect on the battlefield, which perhaps hints at the man he will become once he settles down into his marriage. We might argue that Bertram reacts to the steady refusal of the authority figures around him to allow him his independence as a young man. However, Shakespeare's portrait of Bertram is unflattering, suggesting that he is unworthy of Helena, and he embarrasses his family name through his disobedience to the King and his poor treatment of women.

The Bertram witnessed by the audience is consistently selfish and openly unkind to those he

Standing before the King, Bertram refuses to marry Helena in Act II, Scene 3 of *All's Well That Ends Well*. Plate from the 1744 edition of the play edited by Sir Thomas Hanmer *(Illustration by Francis Hayman; engraving by Hubert Gravelot)*

feels are socially inferior to him. Sadly for Helena, Bertram lacks the humility and good spirits of his father. He is rash, arrogant, and dishonest. His response to Helena's request of marriage is shockingly cruel; instead of responding to Helena, he addresses the King directly, telling him that "I cannot love her nor will strive to do't" (2.3.144). He believes that by marrying Helena, "Disdain / Rather corrupt me ever" (2.3.114–115). His dismissal of Helena has no other grounds than "she had her breeding at my father's charge" (2.3.113), that is to say, she was a lower-class member of his father's household.

The dishonorable nature of Bertram's character is further revealed in his relationship with Diana. He promises her marriage, offering her his family ring, only to dismiss her as "a common gamester to the camp" (5.3.187) when Diana follows him to France to claim his promise of marriage. When talking to one of the lords, he remarks that Diana's honesty is a fault in her, showing that he is willing to make whatever empty promises are needed to gain access to her bed. Bertram is no more honorable in love than Parolles is in war, and his hypocrisy is highlighted by the juxtaposition of his scenes with Diana and Parolles's humiliation in the soldiers' camp. Later, he is entrapped in much the same way as Parolles, caught by his own dishonest behavior.

Bertram's language is dominated by lies and complaints. For Bertram, language is simply a means to an end, and the play represents a breach between his words and his actions. When he does speak honestly, particularly in his rejection of Helena, he reveals himself to be cruel and disdainful. His speeches are short and perfunctory; Shakespeare does not give Bertram an expiatory speech or eloquence to smooth his cruel actions, and because of this, he appears to many cold and unworthy of Helena. Helena never articulates why she loves Bertram, and the reasons for her devotion remain a mystery to the audience witnessing Bertram in action.

The play offers a deeply critical portrait of Bertram. In spite of the general recognition that he is a good soldier and has excellent pedigree, he appears to be fickle, devious, and untrustworthy. The King's refusal to allow him to go to war on the grounds that he is "too young" (2.1.28) can offer an excuse for his impetuousness and irresponsibility, but the play offers him little opportunity to explain or redeem himself, aside from a conditional promise of love to Helena in which he promises the king that "if she, my liege, can make me know this clearly / I'll love her dearly" (5.3.309–310). Even at the end of the play, he will not address Helena directly, recognizing his marriage as a show of duty to his monarch. Bertram embodies the play's resistance to fairy-tale endings.

Parolles

Parolles is a character who is widely considered to be of Shakespeare's invention, that is, not based on any older literary source. He is, as J. Dennis Huston suggests, "a curious mix of the corrupt and the commendable" (431). The prototype of such a cowardly and self-interested character can be found in Shakespeare's *Love's Labour's Lost* in the figure of Don Armando or even in *Henry V,* in a character such as Pistol and, to an extent, Falstaff. He is a coward and a flatterer who ultimately pays the price for his ambivalent loyalties.

Parolles, in many ways, is the natural product of a play that is so deeply concerned with the power that language can hold. Parolles, whose name derives from the French for "words," is a more extreme and potentially dangerous version of Bertram, because he demonstrates no loyalty other than to himself. Parolles is a specific type of character, known as a *miles gloriosus*, which translates

The Two Lords blindfold and kidnap Parolles in Act IV, Scene I of *All's Well That Ends Well.*

as "boastful soldier," and he is as foolish in the soldier's camp as he is at court.

Lafew notes that "the soul of this man is in his clothes" (2.5.43–44), and the play proves this assessment accurate. Parolles acts as a more slippery embodiment of Bertram, his good dress and courtly appearance masking an inherent baseness of character and lack of virtue. Even when he is roundly humiliated for his willingness to betray his company, he shows little real remorse, vowing "being fool'd by fool'ry thrive"(4.3.327). He vows to play the fool for the men as long as he can live in some degree of comfort. Instead of gracefully accepting who he is, Parolles allows himself to be shaped by his humiliation and pledges to take advantage of whatever people think of him. Parolles consistently shows a complete lack of principles and respect that make him unworthy of our sympathies, and even though the retribution he suffers is great, we do not pity him.

Countess of Rousillon

The Countess of Rousillon is the closest that Helena has to a mother. She is kind and generous, yet hardly a two-dimensional figure of extreme piety. She indulges in bawdy jokes with her clown, and shows her fury at Bertram's behavior by threatening to disown him. She is a well-rounded and human character and stands as another example of the goodness that characterizes the females of the play. She is, however, representative of an older order, one that holds no power over the younger generation and can only watch the events of the play unfold with frustration.

The Countess fits easily into the company of women in the play who privilege honor and virtue over nobility and social ranking. She reminds her son that his actions must give him the honor that his birthright presumes when she hopes that "thy goodness / Share with thy birthright" (1.1.58–59). She rejects Bertram's excuse for his rejection of Helena as "the misprizing of a maid too virtuous / For the contempt of empire" (2.2.30–31) making clear her preference for Helena's simplicity and goodness over her poor background. Her disgust with Helena's "unworthy husband" (3.4.30) even drives her to question whom she loves more—her son, Bertram, or Helena.

Throughout the play, the Countess alternates between lamentation and high-spirited joking. She is usually accompanied by Lafew and the clown Lavatch, who could be seen as representative of the two sides of her character. Even though she is traditional in her views, cherishing a world where gentle words went hand in hand with goodly deeds, she is not above a little light-hearted jesting, nor is she presented as a character living in an obsolete past. Following the news of Helena's death, she happily endorses Lafew's plan to marry his daughter to Bertram and anticipates seeing him "ere I die" (4.5.81). She is kind, yet pragmatic. Like many of the women in the play, she understands the corruption of her world and seeks to preserve the values she believes in.

Diana

Diana can be seen as the alter ego to Helena. Diana's trajectory in the play mirrors Helena's: She is humiliated by Bertram when she publicly claims him as her husband, and like Helena, she is rewarded by the King of France for her integrity and strength of character, with the promise of marriage to the man of her choosing. Diana is in similar circumstances to Helena, an impoverished young woman with no real marriage prospects due to her circumstances, but as this was the impetus for Bertram's rejection of his wife, it is what makes him so confident in his attempts to seduce Diana. Like Helena, Diana is continually likened with chastity and feminine loyalty.

Her name offers a clear indication of her character through its links with Diana, the pagan goddess of virginity and marital chastity. Diana is famed for her virginal behavior as much as her beauty, and this combination is what spurs Bertram to give up his family ring with such ease. Diana is young and inexperienced, dependent on her mother for advice on how to deal with Bertram. She reveals to the audience that "my mother told me just how he would woo" (4.2.69), illustrating her limited experiences with men. And yet, Bertram's dishonesty inspires her to swear that "I live and die a maid" (4.2.74), a promise complicated by the King's desire to marry her to a nobleman at the end of the play. Like Helena, Diana is defined by her integrity and determination. She is even willing to endure the humiliation of being publicly dismissed as a whore by Bertram in order to assist Helena. Diana is willing to act dishonestly in her manipulation of Bertram because, "I think't no sin / To cozen him that would unjustly win" (4.2.74–75). Both women recognize the corruption of the world and the way such social structures would work against them as poor women, and both use this to justify the dishonest means they use to entrap Bertram.

DIFFICULTIES OF THE PLAY

The biggest obstacle to a student approaching the play is its open-ended resolution and ambiguous genre. For years, the play has been viewed as a failed comedy because of the way in which it resists the conventions of romantic comedy: Bertram is an unworthy recipient of Helena's love, and yet she singlemindedly pursues him, subjecting him to public humiliation and potential imprisonment, in order to satisfy her desires. No character of the play acts in a manner that would consistently envoke an audience's admiration.

Technically defined as a comedy, the play offers neither uproarious humor nor a comfortable resolution that would normally be associated with the comedic form. It is difficult to root for many of the characters and to accept the sudden resolution offered in the final scene. This has led to the play being called a "problem comedy," that is, a play formally described as a comedy, which does not quite fit the genre because of its content. This title can be misleading, and in recent years, critics have opted to define *All's Well That Ends Well* as a "dark" comedy or a romance. To call the play a dark comedy is to accept the limitations placed on the resolution of the drama and to recognize that all might not be as well as it seems. To read the play in such a way is to view the title as an ironic commentary on the action of the play and to think of the title as Shakespeare's intentional commentary, framing what we see on stage.

Reading the play as a romance can be equally liberating when confronted with the conflicting messages that the text appears to present. The genre of romance was a popular medieval form and certainly one that influenced the tale by Boccaccio that was Shakespeare's inspiration. Popular examples of the romance include Thomas Malory's *Le Morte Darthur,* the lais of Marie de France, and Chaucer's "The Knight's Tale" found in *The Canterbury Tales.* Romance retained some degree of popularity into the Renaissance, finding outlet in the expressions of courtly love that Queen Elizabeth encouraged, and was the driving force in texts such as *Orlando Furioso* and Edmund Spenser's *The Faerie Queene.*

This genre often foregrounds a sense of divinely ordained propriety, a fated order to the world, and, particularly in Christian romance, much of the hero's energy is spent enduring the trials that will restore the natural order and offer him the rewards he desires, which are often in some way associated with love, security, and a sense of belonging. Elements of the genre evident in *All's Well That Ends Well* include the employment of disguise, or deceit, broad hints at supernatural powers; and the elevation of chivalric codes. To view *All's Well That Ends Well* as a romance is to consider the way in which these stories, which largely emphasized Christian values, translate onto the stage, which, by the very nature of performance, insists on a more psychological representation of character and ideals.

To discuss the play as a romance drawing largely from fantastical and symbolic generic form, then, could allow us to discuss ways in which the less believable aspects of the text, such as the bed trick and Bertram's sudden commitment to Helena, are to be viewed. Romance privileged symbolic value over emotional realism and could often be read allegorically, presenting characters as types, with great symbolic value. This might be useful in thinking about the characters of Bertram and Helena, who, at first glance, might seem little

more than two dimensional. To view Bertram and Helena as symbolic figures is to think about the codes of behavior that they represent rather than to wonder what we might do in a similar situation. Bertram is an unappealing hero, but considering him as representative of brash youth might help us understand his extreme attitudes. Although *All's Well That Ends Well* pushes us to view the world of the play through Helena's eyes, we do not have to understand why she loves Bertram; we simply have to accept that she does.

What the redefinition of genre proposes, then, is that the critic attempt to let go of the desire to empathize with, or understand the central characters, and simply accept the terms of the play as they are given. Unlike Shakespeare's great tragedies, such as *Macbeth* or *Antony and Cleopatra,* *All's Well That Ends Well* continuously pushes its audience away from emotional attachment to the characters, and while such detachment can at first appear alienating and a flaw of the play, it allows us to think through what Shakespeare is presenting and view the situation with a more cynical eye. By doing so, the perhaps ironic nature of the title is brought into sharper focus, and the ending becomes deliberately disconcerting, asking questions of the audience long after the characters have left the stage. In the epilogue the King's final request that the audience "take our hearts" (epilogue 6) asks that we decide the fate of the characters, placing the responsibility for interpretation into the hands of the audience.

KEY PASSAGES
Act I, Scene 1, 80–99

HELENA. O, were that all! I think not on my
  father,
And these great tears grace his remembrance
  more
Than those I shed for him. What was he like?
I have forgot him; my imagination
Carries no favour in't but Bertram's.
I am undone; there is no living, none,
If Bertram be away; 'twere all one
That I should love a bright particular star

And think to wed it, he is so above me.
In his bright radiance and collateral light
Must I be comforted, not in his sphere.
Th'ambition in my love thus plagues itself:
The hind that would be mated by the lion
Must die for love. 'Twas pretty, though a
   plague,
To see him every hour; to sit and draw
His arched brows, his hawking eye, his curls
In our heart's table—heart too capable
Of every line and trick of his sweet favour.
But now he's gone, and my idolatrous fancy
Must sanctify his relics.

This speech establishes Helena's character as prag-matic and romantic and underscores certain roman-tic conventions that the play will later circumvent. Helena's tears, which are supposed to be shed over her father's death, illustrate the contrast between public virtue and private desire that will later be explored more fully in Bertram's behavior. Helena feels guilty that she is shedding more tears over Bertram's departure than she did over her father's death and submits to her desire, hinting at future actions when she reveals that she would "think to wed" Bertram.

Helena's language is conflicted. She recognizes her "idolatrous fancy" as something blasphemous yet believes that her desires can sanctify the parts of Bertram that remain with her—her love is at once holy and unholy. She understands the cruelty of sexualized love—"the hind that would be mated by the lion / must die for love"—using both the sexual undertones of the medieval term *die* and the romantic notion of surrendering her will to live in a manner that echoes the conventions of Elizabe-than love poetry. Her description of Bertram's face is reminiscent of the *blason*, a popular 16th-century poetic form that dwells on the body of the poet's beloved.

Helena's speech shows her as at once submis-sive and in control of her actions. She fully under-stands that she is socially lower than Bertram, and the chances of her achieving her love are slim. Helena recognizes "Th'ambition in my love" and

thinks about how she might bring about a marriage between her and Bertram, making herself a very proactive heroine and anticipating her trip to the French court to heal the King as well as her pil-grimage to fulfill the conditions of Bertram's mar-riage contract.

Act II, Scene 2, 19–67

KING. Youth, thou bear'st thy father's face;
Frank nature, rather curious than in haste,
Hath well compos'd thee. Thy father's moral
   parts
Mayest thou inherit too! Welcome to Paris.

BERTRAM. My thanks and duty are your
   majesty's.

KING. I would I had that corporal soundness
   now,
As when thy father and myself in friendship
First tried our soldiership. He did look far
Into the service of the time, and was
Discipled of the bravest. He lasted long,
But on us both haggish age steal on,
And wore us out of act. It much repairs me
To talk of your good father; in his youth
He had the wit which I can well observe
Today in our young lords; but they may jest
Till their own scorn return to them unnoted
Ere they can hide their levity in honor.
So like a courtier, contempt nor bitterness
Were in his pride or sharpness; if they were,
His equal had awak'd them, and his honor,
Clock to itself, knew the true minute when
Exception bid him speak, and at this time
His tongue obey'd his hand. Who were below
   him
He us'd as creatures of another place,
And bow'd his eminent top to their low ranks,
Making them proud of his humility
In their poor praise he humbled. Such a man
Might be a copy to these younger times;
Which, followed well, would demonstrate
   them now
But goers backward.

BERTRAM. His good remembrance, sir,
Lies richer in your thoughts than on his tomb;
So in approof lives not his epitaph
As in your royal speech.

KING. Would I were with him! He would
  always say—
Methinks I hear him now; his plausive words
He scatter'd not in ears, but grafted them
To grow there and to bear—"Let me not live,"
(This his good melancholy oft began
On the catastrophe and heel of pastime,
When it was out) "Let me not live" quoth he,
"After my flame lacks oil, to be the snuff
Of younger spirits, whose apprehensive senses
All but new things disdain; whose judgments
  are
Mere fathers of their garments; whose
  constancies
Expire before their fashions." This he wish'd.
I, after him, do after him wish too,
Since I nor wax nor honey can bring home,
I quickly were dissolved from my hive
To give some labourers room.

This passage illustrates the generational gap that exists in the world of the play. The King of France's fond remembrances of Bertram's father look back to an older, chivalric time, which was ruled by the principles of honor, fidelity, and humility. Bertram's behavior throughout the play allows us to view the King's observation that he "bear'st thy father's face" ironically, as Bertram comes to represent none of the traits so revered in his father. The King's hope that "Thy father's moral parts / Mayest thou inherit too" is to be bitterly disappointed by Bertram, whose pledge of duty and gratitude are unfulfilled when the King demands that he marry Helena.

The King's discussion of the late count of Rousillon is a lament for a world that is lost. The play is littered with the type of characters the late count feared, such as Parolles, a man "whose judgments are / Mere fathers of their garments," and even Bertram, whose loyalties "expire before their fashions." The King's observation that the young men of today "jest / Till their own scorn return to them unnoted / Ere they can hide their levity in honor" is a disheartened recognition of the lack of seriousness that characterizes the contemporary nobility and suggests that although pride and levity have their place, now that place is at the expense of other virtues. The King admired the late count's humility, noting that "who were below him / He us'd as creatures of another place." Ironically, the humbleness that characterized the father is almost entirely absent in the son. Underlying the King's speech is an insistence that nobility is a virtue found in the character, not in the bloodlines, a point made repeatedly to Bertram throughout the play.

The King's speech is infused with a gravity that sets apart the generations of the French court. While the younger characters, such as Helena and Parolles, enjoy bickering about sex and procreation, the King, like the Countess of Rousillon, dwells on the subjects of death and decay, coloring his language with images of "haggish age" and expressing a weary sense of despair. Not only does this passage illustrate a world of values that are obsolete, but it emphasizes the nostalgia with which the past is viewed by the older generation. The King mournfully wishes that he "quickly were dissolved from my hive"—that he, too, were dead—so as not to see the codes by which he lived so willfully disregarded. The wit he observes in the younger lords of his court is style without substance, and this view determines much of the King's authoritative behavior, particularly his insistence on marrying off virtuous young women. The King believes that honor, an inherent virtue, must be privileged above life, and his insistence that he can command Bertram's hand in marriage is an assertion of power and a deeply traditional gesture that comes out of the worldview he illustrates in the above passage.

Act III, Scene 3, 103–169
HELENA. [*To Bertram*] I dare not say I take
  you, but I give
Me and my service, ever while I live,
Into your guiding power. This is the man.

KING. Why, then, young Bertram, take her;
   she's thy wife.

BERTRAM. My wife, my liege! I shall beseech
   your highness,
In such a business give me leave to use
The help of mine own eyes.

KING. Know'st thou not, Bertram.
What she has done for me?

BERTRAM. Yes, my good lord,
But never hope to know why I should marry
   her.

KING. Thou know'st she has rais'd me from
   my sickly bed.

BERTRAM. But follows it, my lord, to bring
   me down
Must answer for her raising? I know her well:
She had her breeding at my father's charge—
A poor physician's daughter my wife! Disdain
Rather corrupt me ever!

KING. 'Tis only the title thou disdains't in
   her, the which
I can build up. Strange it is that our bloods,
Of color, weight, and heat, pour'd all together,
Would quite confound distinction, yet stands
   off
In differences so mighty. If she be
All that is virtuous, save what thou dislik'st—
A poor physician's daughter—thou dislik'st
Of virtue for the name. But do not so.
From lowest place when virtuous things
   proceed,
The place is dignified by th' doer's deed.
Where great additions swell's and virtue none,
It is a dropsied honor. Good alone
Is good without a name; vileness is so:
The property by what it is should go,
Not by the title. She is young, wise, fair;
In these to nature she's immediate heir,
And these breed honor; that is honor's scorn
Which challenges itself as honor's born
And is not like the sire. Honors thrive
When rather from our acts we them derive
Than our foregoers. There mere word's a slave,
Debosh'd on every tomb, on every grave
A lying trophy, and as oft is dumb,
Where dust and damn'd oblivion is the tomb
Of honor'd bones indeed. What should be said?
If thou canst like this creature as a maid,
I can create the rest. Virtue and she
Is her own dower; honor and wealth from me.

BERTRAM. I cannot love her nor will strive
   to do't.

KING. Thou wrong'st thyself if thou should'st
   strive to choose.

HELENA. That you are well restor'd my lord,
   I'm glad.
Let the rest go.

KING. My honor's at the stake, which to
   defeat,
I must produce my power. Here, take her
   hand,
Proud, scornful boy, unworthy this good gift,
That dost in vile misprision shackle up
My love and her desert; that canst not dream
We, poising us in her defective scale,
Shall weigh thee to the beam; that wilt not
   know
It is in us to plant thine honor where
We please to have it grow. Check thy contempt;
Obey our will which travails in thy good;
Believe not thy disdain, but presently
Do thine own fortunes that obedient right
Which both thy duty owes and our power
   claims;
Or I will throw thee from my care for ever
Into the staggers and the careless lapse
Of youth and ignorance; both my revenge and
   hate
Loosing upon thee in the name of justice,
Without all terms of pity. Speak. Thine answer.

BERTRAM. Pardon, my gracious lord; for I
submit
My fancy to your eyes.

This passage illustrates the issues of honor that are at the heart of the play. The fairy-tale ending anticipated by Helena is rudely shattered with Bertram's blunt rebuttal. His plea to the King of France, to "give me leave to use / The help of mine own eyes" in his marriage shows a startling naïveté on the part of Bertram, in his belief that his marriage could be of his own choosing. Just as Laertes warns Ophelia of Hamlet—"his greatness weigh'd / His will is not his own" (*Hamlet* 1.3.17)—Bertram's assumption that he might select his own partner is an audacious one, and later we will see him happily acquiesce to the arranged marriage that will bind him to a more aristocratic spouse. For Bertram, the discussion of his marriage is between him and the King, and even when Helena begs the King to "let the rest go," Betram does not acknowledge her existence, cruelly underscoring his belief in her inferiority.

The King's first speech is preoccupied with honor, reminding Bertram that "Honors thrive / When rather from our acts we them derive / Than our foregoers." He directly contradicts Bertram's belief that to marry someone so socially inferior would "corrupt me ever" with the insistence that Helena's "place is dignified by th' doer's deed." The King insists that Helena's goodness should be its own reward and yet, sensing Bertram's resistance, offers to "create the rest" of the nobility that Helena would need to make Bertram proud. Bestowing "honor and wealth" on Helena would remove any social objection Bertram might have to the marriage, and Bertram's obstinate rebuttal that "I cannot love her nor will strive to do't" is a direct repudiation of the King's power and a dismissal of the lesson in humility that the King's speech has offered.

The scene takes on a more threatening edge with Bertram's rigid refusal to consider the King's request. Angered by his refusal, the King dismisses Helena's request to end the discord, telling her

Bertram refuses Helena's marriage offer before the newly cured King of France in Act II, Scene 3 of *All's Well That Ends Well*. This is a print from the Boydell Shakespeare Gallery project, which was first conceived in 1786 and lasted until 1805. *(Painting by Francis Wheatley; engraving by Luigi Schiavonetti)*

that "my honor is at the stake." The King chastises the "proud, scornful boy" and threatens Bertram with "both my revenge and hate" if he does not comply. His reminder that "both thy duty owes and our power claims" is a marked shift from the fatherly rebukes of the first scene, reminding Bertram of his standing in the social hierarchy of the play. Although the King insists on Bertram's willing compliance with the marriage—"speak. Thine answer."—he makes Bertram's subjugated position clear. Bertram's final acceptance of the King's orders does not illustrate any developing understanding of the meaning of honor but a forced resignation to his marriage.

Act III, Scene 7, 1–47

HELENA. If you misdoubt me that I am not
  she,
I know not how I shall assure you further
But I shall lose the grounds I work upon

WIDOW. Though my estate be fall'n, I was
  well born,
Nothing acquainted with these businesses,
And would not put my reputation now
In any staining act.

HELENA. Nor would I wish you.
First give me trust the count he is my husband,
And what to your sworn counsel I have spoken
Is so from word to word; and then you cannot
By the good aid that I of you shall borrow,
Err in bestowing it.

WIDOW. I should believe you
For you have show'd me that which well
  approves
Y'are great in fortune.

HELENA. Take this purse of gold,
And let me buy your friendly help thus far,
Which I will over-pay and pay again
When I have found it. The count he woos your
  daughter,
Lays down his wanton siege before her beauty,
Resolv'd to carry her; let her in fine consent
As we'll direct her how 'tis best to bear it.
Now his important blood will naught deny
That she'll demand; a ring the county wears
That downward hath succeeded in his house
From son to son some four or five descents
Since the first father wore it. This ring he holds
In most rich choice; yet, in his idle fire,
To buy his will it would not seem too dear,
Howe'er repented after.

WIDOW. Now I see
The bottom of your purpose

HELENA. You see it lawful then; it is no more
But that your daughter, ere she seems as won,
Desires this ring; appoints him an encounter;
In fine, delivers me to fill the time,
Herself most chastely absent. After,
To marry her I'll add three thousand crowns
To what is pass'd already.

WIDOW. I have yielded.
Instruct my daughter how she shall persever
That time and place with this deceit so lawful
May prove coherent. Every night he comes
With music of all sorts, and songs compos'd
To her unworthiness; it nothing steads us
To chide him from our eaves, for he persists
As if his life lay on't.

HELENA. Why then tonight
Let us assay our plot; which, if it speed
Is wicked meaning in a lawful deed,
And lawful meaning in a lawful act,
Where both not sin, and yet a sinful fact.

This passage encapsulates the paradox of Helena's plan. In order to force Bertram to honor his commitment, she needs to act deceptively; her definition of the plot as "both not sin, and yet a sinful fact" can apply to her and Bertram equally. Helena acquires the Widow Capilet's compliance in her plan through bribery, and when Diana's agreement is secured, through a further promise of money. The Widow, like Helena, is suffering because of her poverty, and the few doubts she has to Helena's veracity are soon resolved because "you have show'd me that which well approves / Y'are great in fortune." The Widow recognizes the importance of reputation and is reluctant to involve her child in anything that might put her name to "any staining act." Helena is at pains to emphasize the lawfulness of the plan, insisting that Diana herself shall be "most chastely absent." Diana's virtue will remain intact, and the Widow will be immune from any improper gossip, as she will have simply facilitated the consummation of a lawful marriage.

The reader's opinion of Bertram reaches its lowest point during this act because of his shameless wooing of Diana and his prior treatment of Helena. Bertram is further criticized by Helena's prediction of the ease with which he will surrender his family's ring. Helena shows an acute awareness of Bertram's personality, including all of his character flaws, and this allows her to predict his future behavior in such a way that will guarantee the success of her plot. What she reveals of Bertram's character is, at best, distasteful and, at most, repugnant, exposing him as self-centered, calculating, and impetuous. Yet, in spite of his obvious desire for another woman and the "idle fire" that leads him so easily astray, Helena's desire for Bertram never wavers. In this passage, Helena shows a startling lack of self-worth, and her deceitful bed trick has been likened by critics to her prostitution of Diana and Bertram's rape. Although the reader might question Helena's morality at this point, Shakespeare leaves little room for doubt that Bertram deserves such entrapment, which will, as Helena points out repeatedly, give "lawful meaning in lawful act" and consolidate her position as Bertram's wife.

Act IV, Scene 3, 286–334

FIRST SOLDIER. If your life be saved, will you undertake to betray the Florentine?

PAROLLES. Ay, and the captain of his horse, Count Rousillon.

FIRST SOLDIER. I'll whisper with the general and know his pleasure.

PAROLLES. I'll no more drumming. A plague of all drums! Only to seem to deserve well, and to beguile the supposition of that lascivious young boy, the count, have I run into this danger; yet who would have suspected an ambush where I was taken?

FIRST SOLDIER. There is no remedy, sir, but you must die. The general says you have so traitorously discover'd the secrets of your army, and made such pestiferous reports of men very nobly held, can serve the world for no honest use; therefore you must die. Come, headsman, off with his head.

PAROLLES. O Lord, sir, let me live, or let me see my death!

FIRST SOLDIER. That shall you, and take your leave of all your friends.
[*Unmuffling him.*]
So; look about you; know you any here?

BERTRAM. Good morrow, noble captain.

SECOND LORD. God bless you, Captain Parolles.

FIRST LORD. God save you, noble captain.

SECOND LORD. Captain, what greeting with you to my Lord Lafew? I am for France.

FIRST LORD. Good captain, will you give me a copy of the sonnet you writ to Diana in behalf of the Count Rousillon. And I were not a very coward I'd compel it of you; but fare you well.
[*Exit Bertram and Lords*]

FIRST SOLDIER. You are undone, captain— all but your scarf; that has a knot on't yet.

PAROLLES. Who cannot be crush'd with a plot?

FIRST SOLDIER. If you could find out a country where but women were that had received so much shame you might begin an impudent nation. Fare ye well, sir. I am for France too; we shall speak of you there.
[*Exit Soldiers*]

PAROLLES. Yet am I thankful. If my heart
  were great
'Twould burst at this. Captain I'll be no more,
But I will eat and drink and sleep as soft
As a captain shall. Simply the thing I am
Shall make me live. Who knows himself a
  braggart,
Let him fear this; for it will come to pass
That every braggart shall be found an ass.
Rust, sword; cool, blushes; and Parolles live
Safest in shame; being fool'd, by fool'ry thrive.
There's a place and means for every man alive.
I'll after them.

This 19th-century print depicts the soldiers as they remove Parolles's blindfold and reveal themselves in Act IV, Scene 3 of Henry Staunton's edition of *All's Well That Ends Well*. (Illustration by Sir John Gilbert; engraving by the Dalziel Brothers)

For many critics, Parolles is seen as a parallel to Helena: Both are youthful, alone, and dependent on their own initiative for survival. Unlike Helena, however, Parolles is superficial, vain, and cowardly, and this passage dramatizes his undoing. Parolles is like Helena in the way that he survives public humiliation, but he is also like Bertram in the fact that he falls victim to a plot that ensnares him. Just as Bertram's lack of honor is symbolized by the loss of a ring, Parolles's fall from grace is emblematized by the lost drum.

This passage reveals the weakness that characterizes Parolles. When threatened with torture, he easily betrays his comrades and even his friend, offering up the "lascivious young boy" to what he believes to be the enemy. In this moment of desperation, Parolles is finally revealing his honest opinion of Bertram, and despite the scene's light-hearted tone, the level of collective disgust at his behavior becomes clear when they abandon him in Italy. Parolles is willing to sacrifice his honor to preserve his life, a despicable decision for a soldier. The irony of his despair is seen by both the soldiers around him and the audience, although the scene raises further questions about Bertram's character, as his condemnation of Parolles might be seen as hypocritical.

Parolles's final speech can be interpreted as further evidence of his lack of nobility. His baseness comforts him, knowing that "If my heart were great / 'Twould burst at this" humiliation. As it is, he vows to live, thriving on his foolishness, secure in the con-viction that he can live as comfortably without honor as with. Understanding that "there's a place and means for every man alive," he vows to follow the returning soldiers, making light of his humiliation and living from the patronage of others. His speech shows that, like Helena, he is willing to endure dishonor for personal gain. Parolles is content to recognize himself as a fool, and rather than learn from the experience, he merely embraces his flaws, thinking of how to turn them into useful commodities.

DIFFICULT PASSAGES
Act I, Scene 1, 111–186

PAROLLES. Are you meditating on virginity?

HELENA. Ay. You have some stain of soldier in you; let me ask you a question. Man is enemy to virginity; how may we barricade it against him?

PAROLLES. Keep him out.

HELENA. But he assails; and our virginity, though valiant, in the defence yet is weak. Unfold to us some warlike resistance.

PAROLLES. There is none. Man setting down before you will undermine you and blow you up.

HELENA. Bless our poor virginity from underminers and blowers-up! Is there no military policy how virgins might blow up men?

PAROLLES. Virginity, being blown down man will quicklier be blown up; marry, in blowing him down again, with the breach yourself made you lose your city. It is not politic in the commonwealth of nature to preserve virginity. Loss of virginity is rational increase and there was never virgin got till virginity was first lost. That you were made of its mettle to make virgins. Virginity, by being once lost, may be ten times found; by being ever kept it is ever lost. 'Tis too cold a companion. Away with it!

HELENA. I will stand for't a little, though therefore I die a virgin.

PAROLLES. There's little can be said in't; 'tis against the rule of nature. To speak on the part of virginity is to accuse your mothers, which is most infallible disobedience. He that hangs himself is a virgin; virginity murders itself, and should be buried in highways out of all sanctified limit, as a desperate offendress against nature. Virginity breeds mites, much like cheese; consumes itself to the very paring, and so dies with feeding his own stomach. Besides, virginity is peevish, proud, idle, made of self-love which is the most inhibited sin in the canon. Keep it not; you cannot choose but lose by't. Out with't! Within the year it will make itself two, which is a goodly increase, and the principal itself not much the worse. Away with't!

HELENA. How might one do, sir, to lose it to her own liking?

PAROLLES. Let me see. Mary, ill, to like him that ne'er it likes. 'Tis a commodity will lose the gloss with lying; the longer kept, the less worth. Off with't while 'tis vendible; answer the time of request. Virginity, like an old courtier, wears her cap out of fashion, richly suited but unsuitable, just like the brooch and toothpick, which wear not now. Your date is better in your pie and your porridge than in your cheek and your virginity, your old virginity, is like one of our French wither'd pears: it looks ill, it eats drily; marry, 'tis a wither'd pear; it was formerly better; marry yet 'tis a wither'd pear. Will you anything with it?

HELENA. Not my virginity yet . . .
There shall your master have a thousand loves,
A mother, and a mistress, and a friend,
A phoenix, captain, and an enemy,
A guide, a goddess, and a sovereign,
A counselor, a traitress, and a dear;
His humble ambition, proud humility,
His jarring-concord, and his discord-dulcet,
His faith, his sweet disaster; with a world
Of pretty, fond, adoptious christendoms
That blinking Cupid gossips. Now shall he—
I know not what he shall. God send him well!
The court's a learning-place, and he is one—

PAROLLES. One what, i'faith?

HELENA. That I wish well. 'Tis pity—

PAROLLES. What's pity?

HELENA. That wishing well had not a body
  in't
Which might be felt, that we, the poorer born,
Whose baser stars do shut us up in wishes,
Might with effects follow our friends,
And show what we alone must think, which
  never
Returns us thanks.

This passage establishes the central conflation of
sex and war that characterizes the play. *All's Well
That Ends Well* enacts an ongoing battle between
men and women, and although the tone of the
discussion is playful, the substance of the banter
reveals a very real concern on Helena's part. Her
curiosity as to how she might lose her virginity "to
her own liking" shows an acute awareness of her
debilitating social status and the limitations that
are placed on her by her gender. Her light-hearted
question as to how "virgins might blow up men?"
is simultaneously an interrogation of how she
might acquire Bertram's love and a statement of
frustration at the constraints a woman's reputation
and modesty impose on her behavior.

Parolles's speech further illustrates the difficulty women find themselves in. His observation
that "the longer kept, the less worth" reveals a
superficiality that we will later see embodied in
Bertram's treatment of Diana. In fact, Parolles's
speech inspires much of Helena's later plan. He
points out that the natural outcome of surrendering virginity is pregnancy—"man setting
down before you will undermine you and blow
you up"—and outlines a lesson that Helena will
later learn about the worthlessness of virginity.
Helena learns that she cannot become Bertram's
"true" and recognized wife until she has surrendered her virginity and made herself sexually
active. To offer herself to Bertram on her virtues
alone will leave him unmoved, as "'Tis too cold a
companion."

For Parolles, virginity is a commodity, a practical fact of nature—"there was never virgin got till
virginity was first lost"—and something he considers purely in physical terms. He thinks of virginity

A page calls Parolles away from Helena in Act I,
Scene I of *All's Well That Ends Well.* This print is
from Charles and Mary Cowden Clarke's *Illustrated
Shakespeare,* published by Cassell, Petter & Galpin
in the 1860s. *(Illustration by Henry Courtney Selous;
engraving by A. Burgess)*

as a city to be stormed, an old maid, and a withered
pear. Helena, however, thinking of Bertram, cannot view virginity in such cynical terms. Her regret
"that wishing well had not a body in't" ties desires
and dreams to the surrender of her body, revealing
a more romantic view of the world that will leave
her unsatisfied until she and Bertram are bound
together in both body and soul.

Yet, the scene reveals that as idealistic and
romantic as Helena might appear in her devotion,

she is also intelligent and practical. Her discussion of Bertram's "humble ambition, proud humility" implies a sense of paradox that encourages the reader to wonder how aware she is of his character flaws. Her unabashed engagement in this banter suggests a keen mind, curious to understand the male view of the world and unoffended by Parolles's coarse dismissal of virginity as a commodity to be sold. Her response to his question "will you anything with it?" is vague, but her answer "not my virginity *yet*" implies that she is thinking carefully about when and how she might surrender her virginity. In many ways, Helena is beginning to formulate her own battle plan, and this scene suggests that her plot to lose her virginity is as well thought out and as strategic as Bertram's calculated seduction of Diana later in the play.

Act V, Scene 3, 296–334

DIANA. Good mother, fetch my bail. Stay, royal sir;
[Exit Widow]
The jeweler that owes the ring is sent for
And he shall surety me. But for this lord
Who hath abus'd me as he knows himself—
Though yet he never harm'd me—here I quit him.
He knows himself my bed he hath defil'd;
And at that time he got his wife with child.
Dead though she be she feels her young one kick.
So there's my riddle: one that's dead is quick,
And now behold the meaning.
[Re-enter Widow with Helena]

KING. Is there no exorcist
Beguiles the truer office of mine eyes?
Is't real that I see?

HELENA. No, my good lord;
'Tis but the shadow of a wife you see;
The name and not the thing.

BERTRAM. Both, both. O pardon!

HELENA. O my good lord, when I was like this maid
I found you wondrous kind. There is your ring,
And, look you, here's your letter. This it says:
When from my finger you can get this ring
And is by me with child, &c. This is done;
Will you be mine now you are doubly won?

BERTRAM. If she, my liege, can make me know this clearly
I'll love her dearly, ever, ever dearly.

HELENA. If it appear not plain and prove untrue
Deadly divorce step between me and you!
O my dear mother, do I see you living?

LAFEW. Mine eyes smell onions; I shall weep anon
[To Parolles] Good Tom Drum, lend me a handkercher. So, I thank thee. Wait on me home, I'll make a sport with thee. Let thy curtsies alone, they are scurvy ones.

KING. Let us from point to point this story know
To make the even truth in pleasure flow.
[To Diana] If thou beest yet a fresh uncropped flower
Choose thou thy husband and I'll pay thy dower;
For I can guess that by thy honest aid
Thou kep'st a wife herself, thyself a maid.
Of that and all the progress more and less
Resolvedly more leisure shall express.
All yet seems well, and if it end so meet,
The bitter past, more welcome is the sweet.

This passage offers the supposed fairy-tale ending that an audience of a romance play or comedy might come to expect; the title itself, *All's Well That Ends Well,* creates an expectation of a satisfactory ending. In this scene, Helena is reconciled with Bertram, who finally accepts her as his wife;

Parolles finds a place as the clown of Lafew; and Diana's good name is restored to her. Yet, this scene offers a series of moments of complex ambiguity that undermine any assumptions of romantic bliss that an audience might desire to harbor.

For many, the ongoing degradation that Bertram suffers throughout the final scene renders him unworthy of Helena's love. The couple's moment of reunion is short, muted, and ambivalent: "If she, my liege, can make me know this clearly / I'll love her dearly, ever, ever dearly." Like his earlier rejection of Helena, Bertram addresses his line to the King, not his wife, to whom he is pledging his love, albeit on a conditional basis. His *if* illustrates his ongoing skepticism and shows very little evidence of an enlightenment that might redeem Bertram in the eyes of his audience. His line to the king might be read as a grudging acceptance of his powerlessness or a revelation of his love for the woman who rescues him from shame and infamy, but we cannot be sure.

Helena is less equivocal: She tells the King of France that she is the shadow of a wife—"the name and not the thing"—even though she has fulfilled the criteria of Bertram's demands. She has accepted his ring and become pregnant by him. Her observation to Bertram that "when I was like this maid / I found you wondrous kind" suggests an ongoing belief in the goodness of Bertram's heart, but her devotion is not repaid with any substantial gesture by Bertram, and the couple fall silent for the remainder of the scene. Empowered by her success, Helena is willing to entertain an alternative, telling Bertram that "If it appear not plain and prove untrue / Deadly divorce step between me and you," but before he has a chance to answer, she turns to his mother, claiming her as family, without giving Bertram an opportunity to reply. Both Helena and the King ignore Bertram's conditional "if," reading his acquiescence as the happy ending they desire.

The final speech is given by the King, and offers little closure in terms of the plot. Impressed by Diana's strength of character, he offers her the same reward as Helena had received previously. Without a trace of irony, he tells her to "Choose thou thy husband and I'll pay thy dower." Diana's initial encounter with Bertram had inspired her to seek a life of chastity, and his subsequent behavior in the final scene only further confirms her view of men. Her silence to the King's offer is another ambiguous response to the happy ending of this scene.

CRITICAL INTRODUCTION TO THE PLAY

The play is set in contemporary France, mostly at the court of the French king. In terms of narrative, the structure of the play is fairly tight, rarely deviating from the main romantic plot and keeping the focus primarily on the evolving relationship between Helena and Bertram. The action of the play is driven almost exclusively by characters, and the structure insists that we keep their situation in the foreground. Even the clown subplot, which climaxes in Parolles's humiliation, is a direct reflection of the main action of the play, because of the emphasis on Parolles's soiled honor. The scene's ongoing emphasis on Parolles's deceit and betrayal draws parallels to Bertram's earlier treatment of his wife and the King's rebuking

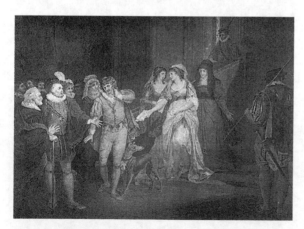

Helena presents Bertram's letter and ring to the King in Act V, Scene 3 of *All's Well That Ends Well*. This is a print from the Boydell Shakespeare Gallery project (1786–1805). *(Painting by Francis Wheatley; engraving by George Sigmund Facius)*

words. The play establishes a clear social hierarchy that is mirrored by a moral hierarchy, rectified at the climax by a community of women who bond together and offer the promise of redemption and new beginnings.

Ultimately, the play's title gives the clearest clue to the thematic issues in the play. It asks whether the ends can justify the means—whether all's well because it ends well—and appears to answer in the affirmative. The unruly Bertram is forced into a recognition of his wife's legitimacy and receives forgiveness and unconditional love, as well as the blessing of a new child to continue his family name. Helena is given a second chance to be Bertram's wife, in the fullest sense, and an opportunity to step out of the role of the shadow wife, through the consummation of their union and the exchange of rings. At the end of the play, the couple is truly married by the terms that each had defined. Diana is rewarded for her part in the bed trick with the promise of nobility and a husband, and even Parolles is offered shelter in the household of Lafew. On the surface, it seems that all has ended well, and the intergenerational conflicts, class segregation, and gender wars have all been resolved through the reconciliation of Bertram and Helen. Yet, Shakespeare's resistance to fully exploring the final conclusion accounts for the genre's instability and hints that the ideas raised throughout the play are far too big to be so easily contained.

The themes of the play are as complex and fascinating as the characters who embody them. The themes include comedy, love and marriage, sexuality and chastity, old age and youth, virtue, and honor. As well as exploring these more metaphysical and abstract ideas, the play also asks questions of a social nature, examining monarchical authority, the validity of forced marriage, the nature of nobility, and the necessity of justifying deceitful behavior on the grounds of the outcome. The resolution of the play—the consummation of the marriage of Helena and Bertram and their reconciliation—encapsulate these ideas and suggest that there is, in fact, a cure for many of these social ills, albeit a questionable one.

Many of the above-mentioned themes are portrayed on an intimate level. In spite of how little time the two central characters are actually on stage together, the play is dominated by the relationship between Bertram and Helena. And, although all may seem to end well, nothing in this play is presented without ambivalence. Bertram embodies the brashness of youth, the arrogance of nobility, and the presumed authority of masculinity. Bertram's character is illustrated by what he is not. The play's introduction to Bertram is a careful explication of the virtues of his father, virtues that he is expected to embody. The King of France openly hopes that "thy father's moral parts / Mayst thou inherit, too" (1.2.22–23). A gulf exists between what is assumed as inherent to rank and class and what is revealed through action, and the play repeatedly illustrates Bertram's hypocrisy to make this point. Bertram is continuously defined by those around him, particularly by the older generation, and only Parolles's description of him as a "dangerous and lascivious boy" (4.3.207) adequately describes what we see. In Bertram, the deliberate separation between reality and romance is most clearly established. His seduction of Diana is characteristic of this split: In her presence, it is dominated by Petrarchan rhetoric and noble promises of love, but repeatedly Bertram tells his friends that Diana's chastity "is all her the fault" (3.6.102). In many ways, the play simplistically presents Bertram as a storybook villain, and it is not until his actions are considered within the context of his wife that the ambiguities emerge.

Helena, who is widely considered to sit at the other end of the spectrum, continuously confounds expectations. Although she proves her virtue with her dedication, patience, and loyalty, the ambivalence that characterizes the play finds its central expression in her character, and, furthermore, the legitimacy of Bertram's unhappiness becomes evident in the revelation of her bed trick. Helena is variously a saint, an image of semi-divine chastity, a master manipulator, or an ambitious social climber. In Helena, for example, the play both romanticizes and condemns the fiction of love that sustains early modern marriage. The play's opening presents

Helena in a deeply sympathetic light: Although she is mourning the loss of her father, she harbors a greater sadness that her social status will not allow her to be considered a worthy match for Bertram. When mistakenly thought to be grieving for her father, Helena ruefully admits "these tears grace his remembrance more / Than those I shed for him" (1.1.75–76). And yet, in many ways, Helena's view of marriage is as cold and detached as the Countess of Rousillon and Lafew's later arrangement for Bertram. Instead of trying to secure Bertram's love, Helena simply moves up the chain of command to the King as a means of selecting her own spouse. Social mobility obviously exists within the French court, but the play hints that the conventions of courtly marriage, under the direction of an older, aristocratic generation, is outdated and constrictive.

As a ward of the French court, Bertram would have been subject to a marriage arranged by the King regardless of his intentions. Such a consideration might make for a more sympathetic reading of Bertram, forced into a marriage that he has no wish for, with a woman he has no interest in. He is frequently described as a "boy" and struggles against the authority placed upon him. The King, enraptured by memories of Bertram's father, refuses him the opportunity to go to war and prove himself, and Bertram is reduced to childish displays of autonomy, which backfire when the King, incensed by Bertram's refusal to marry Helena, is forced to "produce my power" (2.3.146). Bertram fights to be seen as a man but, in doing so, risks losing all that supplies his honor—his title and his respected name. The King's insistence that "I can create the rest" (2.3.137) necessary to identify Helena as aristocratic points to a double notion of honor, as something inherent to the nature of a person and something conferred. It is the split between the name of honor and the embodiment of honor that divides the generations in *All's Well That Ends Well.*

In the play, the constraints we see placed on the younger characters by the older generation are mirrored in the difficulties women face trying to achieve their desires within the traditional framework of female roles. The play is dominated by sexual activity. It is the frequent topic of discussion, the primary condition under which Bertram will acknowledge his marriage, and the tool to entrap him at the end of the play. Yet, the sexuality within *All's Well That Ends Well* insists on women as mothers and virgins, evidenced by the character list, which consists of widows and their virgin daughters, and the premium placed on Diana's virginity by the men of the French court, including the King. Yet, as Parolles wittily explains, "to speak on the part of virginity is to accuse your mothers, which is most infallible disobedience" (1.1.137). In *All's Well That Ends Well,* empowerment and sexuality are intricately bound together. Helena assumes a bold, unfeminine autonomy when she approaches the King and in pursuit of Bertram, but she does so in order to secure her traditional status of wife and (future) mother. Equally, Diana's chastity and integrity ensure her the security in marriage that her mother so desperately desires, but, typically for *All's Well That Ends Well,* the King's solution is not for everyone. Diana is rewarded for her integrity with the same gift as was Helena— her choice in husband—although she has already expressed an explicit desire to "live and die a maid" (4.2.75). The end of the play offers resolution, but not one that appears well for everyone onstage.

The structure of *All's Well That Ends Well* is dominated by a somewhat traditional device: the bed trick. The bed trick is a common feature of early modern drama, and Shakespeare also employs it in *Measure for Measure.* The bed trick, also reflected in Parolles's subplot, once more demands us to question. Is all well that ends well? The older generation of the play laments a decaying world, in which honor, integrity, and Christian values are secondary to fashion, self-gratification, and glory, and many critics see the bed trick as a means of restoring value to the world. By employing the bed trick, Helena, as Bertram's true wife, has saved him from himself and from corrupting both his own honor and Diana's, drawing him away from sin into lawful matrimony. Helena has taken the initiative and provided for a new generation that will be the product of integrity, determination, and adherence to the principles of marriage.

The bed trick, although a common stage convention, is morally ambiguous: Helena has either saved Diana and Bertram, or she has encouraged him to indulge in adultery and build a marriage on the basis of deception and entrapment. In this sense, she is no more exemplary than Bertram, or Parolles—just more cunning. Bertram's final acknowledgment of his marriage's validity is ambiguous, and many critics note that this is no guarantee of a change of heart. A union built on coercion and lies does not bode well for a happy marriage, and there is no guarantee that Helena will ever become more than the shadow wife of Bertram. The bed trick forces Bertram to take responsibility for his failings and acknowledge the limitations placed on his liberty. He is trapped by his situation and entrapped by his own desires. At the end of the play, Bertram, like Parolles, has no choice other than to resign himself to living as "the thing I am" (4.3.310).

There are similarities to be drawn between Helena's triumph and Parolles's denouncement. Both Bertram and Parolles implicate themselves by their eager willingness to abandon their own values of honor and nobility; Parolles is happy to betray his fellow soldiers, while Bertram shows little remorse about giving away his family ring to secure the sexual favors of Diana. Honor, like virginity, is a commodity to be traded away under the right circumstances. However, the play condemns Parolles and Bertram for such assumptions. Even Helena is roundly humiliated by Bertram when she attempts to circumvent the traditional order and sell her virginity in marriage through her service to the King. Although the deceit employed against them is cruelly humiliating, each man learns a lesson, simply that "there's a place and means for every man alive" (4.3.311). A set of values is forced upon them, as is a recognition of their place within the power structures of the French court, and at the close of the play, each man is chastened into accepting his fate. The play offers an apparently clear-cut ending, in which forces of fate conspire to restore order, even if the agents through which order is restored are less than perfect.

The conclusion of the play must be a happy one, as the play is classified as a comedy. Yet, the play draws attention to the artifice of the conclusion by the final scene's speedy close without sufficient pause to establish the authenticity of Bertram's conversion or offer the couple a speech of reconciliation that might promise hope of happiness. Bertram's ambiguous response to his wife and the new cycle of drama that is set in motion by the King's offer of a husband for Diana, in fact, suggest that little has been learned by Helena and Bertram's ordeal. Many critics question for whom the play ends well. It is difficult to readily accept Bertram's dramatic change of heart, particularly in light of his sustained resistance to Helena throughout the play. Helena, at best, is left as a wife to a chastised and unworthy husband and, at worst, an unwilling one. Certainly, the conclusion to *All's Well That Ends Well* is not the romantic ideal imagined by Helena at the beginning of the play, although Lafew's grudging acceptance of Parolles arguably foreshadows a mutual tolerance and respect between Bertram and Helena. Bertram's contrition may be real, and the King's promise to Diana may ultimately prove a blessing, but the audience must rely on no more than the title of the play to support such assumptions.

The style of the play blends verse with prose, and, as is typical in Shakespeare, the language style marks a class division. Helena, who is able to traverse class boundaries, is equally at home speaking the coarse prose of Parolles as she is in the courtly verse of the French aristocracy. Helena is the only female character in Shakespeare's comedies who is afforded the luxury of a monologue directed to the audience, perhaps indicating that we are to view the play through her perspective. Helena's language indicates her exceptional character, and frequently, she turns Bertram's cruelty into her failings, taking responsibility for his actions. Her language enacts a form of penance that is consistent with the religious imagery that circulates around Helena and hints at a larger theme of healing and forgiveness that is present within the play.

The open discussion of religion was not allowed on the Renaissance stage, yet the play is infused with a spirituality that has been argued to underpin the morality of the play. Throughout the play, Helena is described in ways that hint at her status as a semi-divine being. Aside from her exemplary patience, she has a supernatural gift for healing, and upon her rejection by Bertram, she commits to undertaking a pilgrimage to Saint Jaques le Grand. Helena is described as "the herb of grace" (4.5.17), and her status as a virgin with an uncanny ability to cure what the best of French physicians could not elevates her to what could well be a Marian (that is, a model of the Catholic icon of the Virgin Mary) level.

Yet, in *All's Well That Ends Well,* the sacred and the sexual are bound together. By marrying Helena, Bertram commits to a consummation of the marriage, and his refusal to fulfill this marital duty renders her virginity, previously the source of her strength, an icon of her humiliation. In spite of this degradation, Helena's strength of character is linked with her virginity throughout the play, and at the end, we are presented with images that are undeniably divine. Lafew's description of Helena's "dear perfection" (5.3.18) continues the Marian image of her late into the play, and her final appearance, ostensibly still a virgin, yet a pregnant wife, is deeply powerful. Diana is stained with the accusation of sexual activity, while Helena is able to make the transition from virgin to mother seamlessly. Such an image gives enormous symbolic weight to the child she carries, creating it as an emblem of hope and fresh beginnings.

Helena's ability to bring forth miracles, climaxing in the promise of a miracle birth, is characteristic of the idea of healing that is prevalent in the play. The discord that dominates the first half of the text is embodied in the sense of mourning and loss that characterizes the first scene. The sense of sickness and death finds expression in the figure of the King, the symbolic representation of his people. The King has lost hope and seeks no other cure than death. Likewise, Helena and the Countess of Rousillon are in despair for the loss of their loved ones (including Bertram). Parolles's discourse on virginity is a lively reminder of the power of renewal found in women's bodies—Parolles tells Helena that "virginity murders itself" (1.1.130)—which gives Helena the idea for curing the King and earning Bertram's hand.

The King's observation to Bertram that "it much repairs me / To talk of your good father" (1.2.30–31) suggests the curative power of a spiritually healthy state. Lavatch's retort about the quality of the men at court—"if God have lent a man any manners he may easily put it off at court" (2.2.8)—is a scathing indictment of the aristocracy, the men in whom should "blood and virtue / contend for empire" (1.1.55–56). Bertram's refusal to marry Helena could be seen as validation of the illness that pervades the world of the play. His rejection of Helena is an affront to the divine authority of the King, and his unwillingness to consummate the marriage shows the spiritual bankruptcy of the rites held most sacred to the continuation of the French aristocracy.

If we accept the reading that the imagery of healing and redemption suggests, then Helena must "cure" Bertram of his spiritual disease, as "he cannot thrive" (3.4.26) without the blessing of his sanctified wife. Like the King, and like Parolles, Bertram must be redeemed, saved from himself and his "sick desires" (4.2.36), and finds himself close enough to death to recognize and understand when redemption is offered. Bertram is offered the opportunity for recovery by the new beginning his pregnant wife promises, and his apparent aboutface might indicate a spiritual healing that comes through the submission of his body to the mysteries of connubial love.

EXTRACTS OF CLASSIC CRITICISM
William Warburton (1698–1779)   [Excerpted from *The Works of Shakespeare in Eight Volumes,* this volume from 1747. One of Shakespeare's early editors, Warburton was profoundly influential on 18th-century interpretations.]

On lines 2.3.129–131: She is Young, wise, fair; / in these to nature she's immediate heir; / And these breed honor . . .

The objection was, that *Helen* had neither riches nor title. To this the King replies, she's *the* immediate heir of nature, from whom she inherits youth, wisdom, and beauty. The thought is fine. For by the *immediate* heir to nature we must understand one who inherits wisdom and beauty in supreme degree. From hence it appears that *young* is a faulty reading, for that does not, like wisdom and beauty, admit of different degrees of excellence; therefore she could not, with regard to *that* be said to be the *immediate* heir of nature, for in *that* she was only joint-heir with all the rest of her species. Besides, tho' *wisdom* and *beauty* may *breed honor,* yet *youth* cannot be said to do so. On the contrary, it is *age* which has this advantage. It seems probable that some foolish player when he transcribed the part—not apprehending the thought, and wondring to find *youth* not reckoned amongst the good qualities of a woman when she was proposed to a lord, and not considering that it was comprised in the word *fair*—foisted in *young* to the exclusion of a word much more to the purpose. For I make no question but *Shakespeare* wrote,

　　She is GOOD, wise, fair.

For the greatest part of her encomium turned upon her virtue. To omit this therefore in the recapitulation of her qualities had been against all the rules of good speaking. Nor let it be objected that this is requiring an exactness in our author which we should not expect. For he who cold reason with the force or author doth here (and we ought always to distinguish between *Shakespeare* on his guard and in his rambles) and illustrate that reasoning with such beauty of thought and propriety of expression, could never make use of a word which quite destroyed the exactness of his reasoning, the propriety of his thought, and the elegance of his expression.

Arthur Murphy (1727–1805) [Excerpted from a theater review that appeared in the *London Chronicle: or Universal Evening Post,* November 30, 1757. Murphy was a popular 18th-century playwright and drama critic who moved in well-established literary circles. His work, both literary and critical, influenced 18th-century perspectives on comedy.]

There is not one of Shakespeare's Comedies where he has exerted a greater Share of the *Vis comica* than in this, and I do not imagine there is to be found in all that great Master's Works, if you except his Falstaff, a truer, pleasanter, and more striking Character than that of Parolles. Yet one Thing I have observed in it which I never could answer to myself: it is when, after one of his scenes with Lafeu, the Bragart in a Soliloquy [2.3.23ff.] talks of wiping off the Disgrace put upon him by that old Lord by fighting his Son, and a good Deal more to that Purpose. Every where else Parolles is thoroughly sensible of his Cowardice: why then should he just at that Instant lack that Consciousness and strive, as it were, to cheer himself into a Notion of his being brave? Besides that it answers no Purpose and breaks off the Continuity of the Character, is not this perverting the End of Soliloquies, which are in themselves but too absurd and have only been allowed for Conveniency, that by their Means the Audience may get an Insight into Characters and Designs of a Nature that require a theatrical Secrecy, that is to say, a Secrecy relative only to the Business of the Play and the Parties concerned in the Plot? This only I offer as my Doubt, and rather incline to think it my Mistake than imagine that incomparable Writer defective in that very point which was always esteemed his particular Excellence. However, that Character, even admitting that Reproach to be well grounded, is one of the greatest on the English Stage; and Mr Woodward's Exhibition of it fell in nothing short of its Beauties and Humour. As to the rest of the Parts, they are rather just than striking, and I think much may be said of the Performance.

Samuel Johnson (1704–1784) [Excerpted from *Prefaces to Shakespeare,* Johnson's seminal 1765 text. One of the first major works of Shakespearean criticism, Johnson's *Prefaces* has exerted influence in the reading of Shakespeare's plays from the 18th century until today.]

Parolles has many of the lineaments of Falstaff, and seems to be the character in which *Shakespeare* delighted to draw, a fellow that had more wit than virtue. Though justice required that he should not be detected and exposed, yet his *vices so fit in him* that he is not at last suffered to starve . . . Decency required that *Bertram's* double crime of cruelty and disobedience, joined likewise with some hypocrisy, should raise more resentment; and that though his mother might easily forgive him, his king should more pertinaciously vindicate his own authority and *Helen's* merit; of all of this *Shakespeare* could not be ignorant, but *Shakespeare* wanted to conclude his play.

This play has many delightful scenes, though nor sufficiently probable, and some happy characters, though not new, not produced by any deep knowledge of human nature. *Parolles* is a boaster and a coward, such as has always been the sport of the stage, but perhaps never raised more laughter or contempt than in the hands of *Shakespeare.*

I cannot reconcile my heart to *Bertram;* a man noble without generosity, and young without truth; who marries *Helen* as a coward, and leaves her as a profligate: when she is dead by his unkindness, sneaks home to a second marriage, is accused by a woman whom he has wronged, defends himself by falsehood, and is dismissed to happiness.

The story of *Bertram* and *Diana* had been told before of *Mariana* and *Angelo,* and, to confess the truth, scarcely merited to be heard a second time.

The story is copied from a novel of *Boccace,* which may be read in *Shakespear Illustrated,* with remarks not more favourable to *Bertram* than my own.

William Hazlitt (1788–1830) [Excerpted from *Characters of Shakespear's Plays,* his 1817 study. Hazlitt was an important thinker and literary critic, who influenced many 19th-century attitudes toward literature.]

ALL'S WELL THAT ENDS WELL is one of the most pleasing of our author's comedies. The interest is, however, more of a serious than of a comic nature. The character of Helen is one of great sweetness and delicacy. She is placed in circumstances of the most critical kind, and has to court her husband both as a virgin and a wife: yet the most scrupulous nicety of female modesty is not once violated. There is not one thought or action that ought to bring a blush into her cheeks, or that for a moment lessens her in our esteem. Perhaps the romantic attachment of a beautiful and virtuous girl to one placed above her hopes by the circumstances of birth and fortune, was never so exquisitely expressed as in the reflections which she utters when young Rousillon leaves his mother's house, under whose protection she has been brought up with him, to repair to the French king's court.

> HELENA. Oh, were that all—I think
> not on my father,
> And these great tears grace his remembrance more
> Than those I shed for him. What was he like?
> I have forgot him. My imagination

Carries no favour in it, but Bertram's.
I am undone, there is no living, none,
If Bertram be away. It were all one
That I should love a bright particular star,
And think to wed it; he is so above me:
In his bright radiance and collateral light
Must I be comforted, not in his sphere.
Th' ambition in my love thus plagues
   itself;
The hind that would be mated by the
   lion,
Must die for love. 'Twas pretty, tho' a
   plague,
To see him every hour, to sit and draw
His arched brows, his hawking eye, his
   curls
In our heart's table: heart too capable
Of every line and trick of his sweet favour.
But now he's gone, and my idolatrous
   fancy
Must sanctify his relics.

The interest excited by this beautiful picture of a kind and innocent heart is kept up afterwards by her resolution to follow him to France, the success of her experiment in restoring the king's health, her demanding Bertram in marriage as a recompense, his leaving her in disdain, her interview with him afterwards disguised as Diana, a young lady whom he importunes with his secret addresses, and their final reconciliation when the consequences of her stratagem and the proofs of her love are fully made known. The persevering gratitude of the French king to his benefactress, who cures him of a languishing distemper by a prescription hereditary in her family, the indulgent kindness of the Countess, whose pride of birth yields, almost without struggle, to her affection for Helen, the honesty and uprightness of the good old lord Lafeu, make very interesting parts of the picture. The wilful stubbornness and youthful petulance of Bertram are also very admirably described. The comic part

of the play turns on the folly, boasting, and cowardice of Parolles, a parasite and hanger-on of Bertram's, the detection of whose false pretensions to bravery and honour forms a very amusing episode. He is first found out by the old lord Lafeu, who says, "The soul of this man is in his clothes"; and it is proved afterwards that his heart is in his tongue, and that both are false and hollow. The adventure of the bringing off of his drum' [sic] has become proverbial as a satire on all ridiculous and blustering undertakings which the person never means to perform: nor can anything be more severe than what one of the bystanders remarks upon what Parolles says of himself, "Is it possible he should know what he is, and be that he is?" Yet Parolles himself gives the best solution of the difficulty afterwards when he is thankful to escape with his life and the loss of character; for, so that he can live on, he is by no means squeamish about the loss of pretensions, to which he had sense enough to know he had no real claims, and which he had assumed only as a means to live.

> PAROLLES. Yet I am thankful; if my
>   heart were great,
> 'Twould burst at this. Captain I'll be no
>   more,
> But I will eat and drink, and sleep as
>   soft
> As captain shall. Simply the thing I am
> Shall make me live; who knows himself a
>   braggart,
> Let him fear this; for it shall come to
>   pass,
> That every braggart shall be found an ass.
> Rust sword, cool blushes, and Parolles
>   live
> Safest in shame; being fooi'd [sic], by
>   fool'ry thrive;
> There's place and means for every man
>   alive.
> I'll after them.

Samuel Taylor Coleridge (1772–1834)
[Excerpted from *Lectures and Notes on Shakspere,* Coleridge's important 1818 study.]

> DIANA. The Count Rousillon:—know you such a one?
>
> HELENA. But by the ear that hears most nobly of him; His face I know not.

Shall we say here, that Shakespeare has unnecessarily made his loveliest character utter a lie?—Or shall we dare think that, where to deceive was necessary, he thought a pretended verbal verity a double crime, equally with the other a lie to the hearer, and at the same time an attempt to lie to one's own conscience?

Shaw, George Bernard (1856–1950)
[Excerpted from his review of the Irving Dramatic Club's amateur performance published in *The Saturday Review,* February 2, 1895. Shaw was a prominent 20th-century playwright and intellectual, whose influence is still felt in many of today's critics.]

Among Shakespear's earlier plays, *All's Well That Ends Well* stands out artistically by the sovereign charm of the young Helena and the old Countess of Roussillon, and intellectually by the experiment, repeated nearly three hundred years later in [Henrik Ibsen's] *A Doll's House,* of making the hero a perfectly ordinary young man, whose unimaginative prejudices and selfish conventionality make him cut a very fine mean figure in the atmosphere created by the nobler nature of his wife. This is what gives a certain plausibility to the otherwise doubtful tradition that Shakespear did not succeed in getting his play produced (founded on the absence of any record of a performance during his life-

Diana and Helena discuss Bertram as the army enters in Act III, Scene 5 of *All's Well That Ends Well.* Print from Charles and Mary Cowden Clarke's *Illustrated Shakespeare,* published by Cassell, Petter & Galpin in the 1860s *(Illustration by Henry Courtney Selous; engraving by A. Burgess)*

time). It certainly explains why Phelps, the only modern actor-manager tempted by it, was attracted by the part of Parolles, a capital study of the adventurous yarn-spinning society-struck coward, who also crops up again in modern fiction as the hero in Charles Lever's underrated novel, *A Day's Ride: a Life's Romance.* When I saw *All's Well* announced for performance by the Irving Dramatic Club, I was highly interested, especially as the performers were free, for once to play Shakespear for Shakespear's sake. Alas! at this amateur performance, at which there need have been none of the miserable commercialization compulsory at the regular theatres, I suffered all the vulgarity and absurdity of that commercialism without its efficiency. We all know the stock objection of the Brixton Family Shakespear to *All's Well*—that the heroine is a lady doctor, and that no lady of any delicacy could possibly adopt a profession which involves the possibility of her having to attend such cases as that of the king in this play who suffers from a fistula. How any sensible and humane person can have ever read this sort of thing without a deep sense of insult to every charitable woman's humanity and every sick man's suffering is, fortunately, getting harder to understand nowadays than it once was. Nevertheless *All's Well* was minced with a strict deference to it for the members of the Irving Dramatic Club. The rule for expurgation was to omit everything that the most pestiferously prurient person could find improper. For example, when the non-commissioned officer, with quite becoming earnestness and force says to the disgraced Parolles: "If you could find out such a country where but women were that had received so much shame, you might begin an impudent nation," the speech was suppressed as if it were on all fours with the obsolete Elizabethan bandinage which is and should be cut out as a matter of course. And to save Helena from anything so shocking as a reference to her virginity, she was robbed of that rapturous outburst beginning,

> There shall your master have a thousand
> loves—
> A mother and a mistress and a friend, etc.

But perhaps this was sacrificed in deference to the opinion of the editor of those pretty and handy little books called the Temple Shakespear, who compares the passage to "the nonsense of some foolish conceited player"—a criticism which only a commentator could hope to live down.

MODERN CRITICISM AND CRITICAL CONTROVERSIES

The 20th and 21st centuries have been witness to an ongoing debate over the merits of *All's Well That Ends Well,* and critical thought has never strayed far from an awareness of the play's flaws—the improbable resolution, the "bed trick" element of the plot, and the inscrutability of the central characters. Helena has been considered as both a saint and a gold-digging nymphomaniac. In recent years, Bertram has been rescued from villainy by critics who have begun to reevaluate the principles through which the world of the play is constructed and understand the character as one caught in a complex web of expectations and inflexible definitions of gender, sexuality, and class.

The first half of the 20th century saw the play suffer from neglect, at the hands of both theater directors and literary critics. With the exception of a notable few critics (including George Bernard Shaw), the play was considered a failure because of the way in which it moved along "dim, untrodden paths" (345), as Frederick Boas famously noted in his discussion of Shakespeare's "problem plays." These plays, noted earlier as also including *Measure for Measure* and *Troilus and Cressida* (some critics also include others), were problematic for their refusal to conform generically, and for the offering of a happy ending that is, at best, questionable. Frequently, these plays have been dismissed as artless and written without care by critics who read from a realistic point of view, which has led to the final act of *All's Well That Ends Well* being rejected as a psychologically fraudulent melodrama. An extreme example of the disdain the play provokes can be found in Barratt Wendell's discussion of the play: "There is no other work of Shakespeare's which in conception and in temper seems quite so corrupt as this. . . . There are other works of Shakespeare which are more painful; there are none less pleasing, none on which one cares less to dwell." (Lawrence 418). There is little of real substance written on the text prior to the late 20th century, and much of the criticism can be found in introductions to editions, which in itself, illustrates a resistance to reading the play as anything more than a failed experiment.

A notable exception to the critical consensus can be found in W. W. Lawrence's 1922 essay "The Meaning of *All's Well That Ends Well.*" Lawrence recognizes the central resistance to the play of modern critics, which has stemmed from a revulsion of the characters, from the coarse and unamusing Parolles to the social-climbing and aggressive Helena, and extended into a general dissatisfaction of the play's ending. Lawrence understands that "clearly, for us of today, All's Well perplexes more than it satisfies, and repels more than it attracts" (321). Instead, Lawrence proposes that rather than trying to understand the psychology of Bertram and Helena, we look at the play as an Elizabethan audience would have and consider the text as a product of (and reaction to) Elizabethan literary and stage conventions.

Lawrence argues that the story of the patient wife, enduring the trials that her husband subjects her to, was one that was well known to an Elizabethan audience. Beginning with the *Decameron,* Lawrence charts the many medieval and Elizabethan recountings of the story of the faithful wife and argues that we must view this play as a dramatic rendering of a well-worn tale. He says that because of the plot's well-established history, we should reject readings that attempt to define Bertram and Helena in terms of psychological realism and not attempt to seek emotional continuity in the story. He explains that the sudden and abrupt changes of heart, which we see most clearly in Bertram's acceptance of his wife, "are obviously a part of the style of the romantic and unrealistic drama, as in comedy, where all ends with general happiness" (440). He argues that the contemporary critics who condemn the play and, in particular, Helena are reading the play in isolation and imposing a contemporary morality on the characters that

simply does not exist in early modern drama, citing multiple comparative examples as evidence.

Until the middle of the 20th century, Lawrence's analysis appeared to be the lone voice defending the play. E. M. W. Tillyard's 1949 book *Shakespeare's Problem Plays,* recognized the play as a complicated and even heroic failure. In 1950, the great Shakespearean critic M. C. Bradbrook boldly stated that "all did not end well and it is not a successful play" (290). Her study, entitled "Virtue Is the True Nobility: A Study of the Structure of *All's Well That Ends Well,*" attempts to examine the themes of honor and nobility and the way in which these ideas come together, or fail to do so, in the final scene of the play. Comparing the play to *Measure for Measure,* Bradbrook explains that "the play appears more confused in purpose, more drab and depressing, if less squalid" (291). Bradbrook dismisses the characters as mere types and argues that Shakespeare fails to write a play that has gravity as a "moral history" (290). For Bradbrook, the play fails, because Bertram refuses to count himself among Helena's miracles. She explains: ". . . though Helena is wise and Bertram foolish, though she is humble and he is proud, his final acknowledgement of her would constitute a strong ending" (299). As it stands, according to Bradbrook, the play fails because the reconciliation that it promises never comes to fruition.

In 1964, Jay L. Halio identified four central issues with the play that continued to cause critical concern. He suggested that further study of the source material was needed and that critics needed to consider the role of the minor characters at greater length. He also acknowledged the central focus of the ongoing debate about the relative merits of *All's Well That Ends Well:* the character of Bertram and the question of dramatic unity elicited by the play's final act. Halio considers at length the role of healing in the play and asks the reader to focus on Helena as a woman in love, rather than a social climber, who wishes to "cure" her husband of his sinful habits. He asks, "if Lafew can accept the emergence of the 'true' Parolles, can we not accept the recovery of the "true" Bertram?" (42). However, Halio readily admits that such an assumption is difficult, as we strain to understand why Helena makes such a decision. He explains that "if Shakespeare fails to supply us with sufficient verbal clues to Bertram's character (he does not neglect them altogether), it is quite possible that he depended (if unduly) upon the implications of the plot and (more plausibly) upon the acting itself" (42). Halio concludes his study conceding that perhaps Shakespeare had finished his play "in a hurry" (43) and continuing to engage in the merit-based debate on the play's quality, but his argument that we look at the structure of the play, combining discussions of theme and imagery as a means of exploring character, is an idea that contributed to the reassessment of the play that is still continuing today.

During the late 20th century, approaches to the text diverged. Some critics, such as Robert Miola, David Scott Kastan, and James L. Calderwood, examined the structures of comedy, approaching the play as a combination of genres and comedic styles, while other critics, such as Janet Adelman, David McCandless, and Barbara Hodgdon, focus primarily on the roles of Bertram and Helena, thinking about the characters in historicist, generic, and psychoanalytic terms. Instead of attempting to ask whether the play "works," recent critics have instead chosen to look at the play as a complex interweaving of various ideas, themes, and styles. Although the label of "problem comedy" continues to be associated with these plays, many more recent critics have begun to view *All's Well That Ends Well* as a romance, which, as Alexander Leggatt suggests in his 1971 essay "*All's Well That Ends Well:* The Testing of Romance," fuses realism with the popular medieval genre of romance.

Meanwhile, in the 1985 essay "*All's Well That Ends Well* and the Limits of Comedy," David Scott Kastan proposes that we view the play as an exploration of our expectations from the comic genre and suggests that the play "makes us recognize the inadequacy of a conception of either comedy or of ethical behavior that focuses exclusively on ends" (585). If, as Kastan suggests, Shakespeare is interrogating the conventions of comedy that demand a

happy ending, he does so by drawing our attention to the instability of that ending and asking what must be sacrificed to accommodate such a resolution. Kastan considers the ongoing debate as to the value of the play by proposing that we rethink the way in which a problem comedy is approached: "if *All's Well That Ends Well* is a problem comedy, then, it is so because it sees so clearly that comedy is a problem. All is not necessarily well that ends well, and actions that end well are not necessarily comedies" (586). He proposes that we view the idea of comedy through the 16th-century courtier Sir Philip Sidney's observation that comedies reflect the errors in our life, arguing that the discomfort we feel with the ending offers us a play that is closer to realism than an audience might like.

At the end of the 20th century, Helena became a popular topic for criticism, and although critics began to examine the contrast between Helena as a sacred and a sexual being, she remained a controversial figure. In 1980, Richard Levin suggested that Helena is simply a more efficient and manipulative version of Parolles, who uses cunning and deceit to entrap Bertram, even suggesting that the audience ought not to trust her claim of pregnancy. Janet Adelman's psychoanalytic discussion of Shakespeare's late plays, *Suffocating Mothers: Fantasies of Maternal Origin in Shakespeare's Plays,* Hamlet *to* The Tempest, suggests that the play exploits a masculine anxiety over the sexualized mother, reading Helena as an extension of the Countess of Rousillon, whom Bertram is desperately trying to escape. Adelman, like many critics, implies that Helena is presented as constructed within two alternate identities, that of the Marian virgin and the deeply sexualized woman. In her 1989 essay "Sacred and Sexual Motifs in *All's Well That Ends Well*," Peggy Muñoz Simmons attempts to reconcile these two perspectives by examining the sanctity of marital sexuality. Unlike Kastan, Simmons views the play as "a typical work of Renaissance comic art that attempts to unite both the physical and the spiritual elements of human existence within a single structure of the imagination" (33). To Simmons, the play can end on an optimistic note because

Bertram and Helena have been united both spiritually and physically.

THE PLAY TODAY

Unfortunately, today *All's Well That Ends Well* remains one of the more neglected among the Shakespearean canon. Major theaters have been reluctant to stage the play, presumably due to its relative obscurity. The play was produced only once in the first decade of the 21st century by a major U.S. theater company, the Oregon Shakespeare Festival in 2009, under the direction of Amanda Dehnert. Although reviews were generally positive, almost every major theater critic noted that the play leaves the audience unmoved emotionally and intellectually unsure of the outcome. Theater critics across the board continue to approach the play as something broken, asking how a particular theatrical production intends to rectify the problems they perceive.

The play has suffered a similar fate in the United Kingdom. The Royal Shakespeare Company has mounted three major productions since 1990, one of which was a presentation in the company's Complete Works season, in 2006. *All's Well That Ends Well* received its most recent revival at England's National Theatre in October 2009, under the direction of Marianne Elliot. The more recent productions have embraced the ambiguity that characterizes the play, presenting the conflicting ideas as what makes the play modern and relevant. The thematic disunity has been embraced by productions and critics who describe the play as a fairy tale for grown-ups. The most successful productions have embraced the conflict between realism and romance, presenting a balance in productions that blend the genres in the same way that Shakespeare did, not trying to "fix" the assumed flaws. Both Dehnert and Elliot emphasized the fantastical nature of the play. Dehnert even went so far as to open her production with the announcement "Once upon a time. . . ."

Critically, there has been no clear consensus about how to approach the play. The attitude toward *All's Well That Ends Well*, however, has shifted from disdain to a recognition of the play's complexity and an embracement of the infinitely fascinating questions the text provokes. Gary Waller's excellent collection of critical essays studies at great length the way in which multiple genres are intertwined within the play, considering alternative theatrical traditions from which the play is derived as a means of breaking out of the simplistic categorization of problem comedy. Many recent critics, such as Jean Howard, Regina Buccola, and Ellen Belton have chosen to examine at much greater length the tensions between men and women in the play, looking at the presence of patriarchal authority in relationship to the aggressive women and even more aggressive constructions of masculinity. Maternity has also been a source of fascination for critics in the 20th century—indeed, a large puzzle for feminist critics of Shakespeare is the lack of mothers in the body of his work, and *All's Well That Ends Well* presents not one, but two dominant mother figures, in Helena and the Countess.

Kathryn Schwarz's 2007 article "My intents are fix'd": Constant Will in *All's Well That Ends Well*" is typical of a contemporary critic trying to wrestle with the play's history. She opens her essay acknowledging that the play suffers from an "oddly intractable image problem" (200) before attempting to understand the tensions within the play. Schwarz proposes that Helena is a character caught within a paradox: In order to be submissive, she must first assert her autonomy. She explains that the sexes within the play are interdependent, and men such as Bertram need to recognize this. She states that feminine "Constancy intervenes into masculine homosocial privilege in a way at once vital and unsettling, its guarantees securing a hierarchy that they expose as a structure of need" (202); in other words, Schwarz here is asserting that a woman, by continued patience or fidelity to an ideal, makes evident the masculine need for women to accept their given role within a power structure. Helena's status as a woman of knowledge—both in the sense of her capacity to heal the King of France and her sexual awareness—threatens to destabilize the way in which the society of the play defines itself, and this is potentially dangerous. As Schwarz puts it, "women might make men not only by incubating them but by wanting them, a proposition which, like Helena herself, serves the ends of heterosocial desire but deeply complicates the means" (220). Schwarz notes that the play must end on a note of ambiguity, recognizing that Helena's victory, when viewed from within the hierarchy of a patriarchal culture, may indeed be pyrrhic, but, like many critics today, Schwarz does not seek to discover who "wins" in *All's Well That Ends Well,* recognizing the futility of asking such questions.

The liberation of the characters from stereotypical gender constraints—for example, the historical accusation that Helena is immodest and "unwomanly"—and with the increasing acceptance of the idea that Shakespeare was not attempting to compose a realistic psychological drama have allowed for a quiet blossoming of interest in the play. At present, both criticism and theatrical production have rejected any attempts to make the play conform to ideas of what it "should" be, and such an approach has been fruitful.

FIVE TOPICS FOR DISCUSSION AND WRITING

1. **"All's well that ends well":** At the end of the play, Helena achieves her goal—she is Bertram's wife in accordance to the terms he set out in his letter. Is the resolution to the play a happy one? Critics disagree on Bertram's commitment to his marriage at the end. What evidence can we find to suggest that he will be a good husband to Helena? Does Helena get what she deserves? Does Bertram? Are Helena's actions justified by Bertram's behavior throughout the play? What does the King's response to Diana's role in the bed trick suggest that he has learned from Helena's painful experience?
2. **Gender and sexuality:** The play presents gender solidarity through the women's plot to entrap Bertram and as a general vengeance on

male dishonesty in the pursuit of sex. Does the play critique gender assumptions? Does Helena's determination and single-mindedness compromise her status as heroine? How does the play explore a view of women as simultaneously chaste and sexual beings?
3. **Honor:** Much of the play is concerned with the ideals of honor and nobility. What is honor to the world of the play? Does gender play a role in the definition of honor? Is honor anachronistic to the world of *All's Well That Ends Well.* Do any of the characters behave in a way we might define as honorable? How does the idea of warfare renegotiate the way in which honor is perceived? Is there a place for honor in this world, or is it merely a label applied to excuse poor behavior among the upper class? Are reputation and honor interchangeable in the world of the play? How are both Bertram and Helena representative of different types of honor? Can we trust these definitions of honor and virtue?
4. **Fairy tales:** The play is dominated by motifs that appear in folklore and fairy tales, from the King's miraculous recovery and gift of a husband to the success of the bed trick and Bertram's final acquiescence to the marriage. How much of what transpires in the play can we attribute to the folklorish setting. How does the play critique these so-called miracles that drive the play to its conclusion?
5. **Old age versus youth:** Are the older characters right in their perception of the younger generation as vulgar, brash, and without substance? What do the older characters, such as the Countess, Lafew, and the King, lament about the past? Are their complaints reasonable, or do they simply romanticize the past? How does this generational conflict interact with the other dominant themes of the play?

Bibliography
Adelman, Janet. *Suffocating Mothers: Fantasies of Maternal Origin in Shakespeare's Plays,* Hamlet *to* The Tempest. New York: Routledge, 1992.

Bergeron, David M. "The Mythical Structure of *All's Well That Ends Well*." *Texas Studies in Literature and Language* 14 (1972): 559–568.

Boas, Frederick S. *Shakespeare and His Predecessors*. New York: Scribner, 1904.

Bradbrook, Muriel. "Virtue Is the True Nobility: A Study of the Structure of *All's Well That Ends Well*." *Review of English Studies* 1 (1950): 289–301.

Calderwood, James L. "The Mingled Yarn of *All's Well*." *JEGP: Journal of English and Germanic Philology* 62 (1963): 61–76.

Cartelli, Thomas. "Shakespeare's 'Rough Magic': Ending as Artifice in *All's Well That Ends Well*." *Centennial Review* 27 (1983): 117–134.

Desens, Marliss C. *The Bed-Trick in English Renaissance Drama: Explorations in Gender, Sexuality, and Power*. Cranbury, N.J.: Associated University Presses, 1994.

Dessen, Alan C. *Shakespeare and the Late Moral Plays*. Lincoln: University of Nebraska Press, 1986.

Donaldson, Ian. "*All's Well That Ends Well*: Shakespeare's Play of Endings." *Essays in Criticism* 27, no. 1 (January 1977): 34–55.

Foakes, R. A. *Shakespeare: The Dark Comedies to the Last Plays, from Satire to Celebration*. Charlottesville: University of Virginia Press, 1971.

Frye, Northrop. *The Myth of Deliverance: Reflections on Shakespeare's Problem Comedies*. Toronto, Canada: University of Toronto Press, 1983.

Halio, Jay L. "*All's Well That Ends Well*." *Shakespeare Quarterly* 25 (1964): 33–43.

Hapgood, Robert. "The Life of Shame: Parolles and *All's Well*." *Essays in Criticism* 15 (1965): 269–278.

Hodgdon, Barbara. "The Making of Virgins and Mothers: Sexual Signs, Substitute Scenes, and Doubled Presences in *All's Well That Ends Well*." *Philological Quarterly* 66 (1987): 47–71.

Hunter, Robert G. *Shakespeare and the Comedy of Forgiveness*. New York: Columbia University Press, 1965.

Huston, Dennis J. "Some Stain of Soldier": The Functions of Parolles in *All's Well That Ends Well*." *Shakespeare Quarterly* 21, no. 4 (Autumn 1970): 431–438.

Kastan, David Scott. "*All's Well That Ends Well* and the Limits of Comedy." *English Literary History* 52 (1985): 575–589.

Lawrence, William W. *Shakespeare's Problem Comedies*. New York: MacMillan, 1931.

Leggatt, Alexander. "*All's Well That Ends Well*: The Testing of Romance." *Modern Language Quarterly* 32, no. 1 (1971): 21–41.

McCandless, David. *Gender and Performance in Shakespeare's Problem Comedies*. Bloomington: Indiana University Press, 1997.

Price, Joseph G. *The Unfortunate Comedy: A Study of* All's Well that Ends Well *and Its Critics*. Toronto, Canada: University of Toronto Press, 1968.

Schwarz, Kathryn. "My intents are fix'd": Constant Will in *All's Well That Ends Well*. *Shakespeare Quarterly* 58, no. 2 (2007): 200–227.

Simmons, Peggy Muñoz. "Sacred and Sexual Motifs in *All's Well That Ends Well*." *Renaissance Quarterly* 42 (1989): 33–59.

Snyder, Susan. "*All's Well That Ends Well* and Shakespeare's Helens: Text and Subtext, Subject and Object." *English Literary Renaissance* 18 (1988): 66–77.

Styan, J. L. *Shakespeare in Performance*: All's Well That Ends Well. Manchester and Dover, N.H.: Manchester University Press, 1984.

Sullivan, Garrett A., Jr. *Memory and Forgetting in English Renaissance Drama: Shakespeare, Marlowe, Webster*. Cambridge and New York: Cambridge University Press, 2005.

Taylor, Dennis. *Shakespeare and the Culture of Christianity in Early Modern England*. New York: Fordham University Press, 2003.

Thomas, Vivian. *The Moral Universe of Shakespeare's Problem Plays*. Totowa, N.J.: Barnes & Noble, 1987.

Tillyard, E. M. W. *Shakespeare's Problem Plays*. Toronto, Canada: University of Toronto Press, 1949.

Traister, Babara Howard. Troilus and Cressida, All's Well That Ends Well, *and* Measure for Measure: *An Annotated Bibliography of Shakespeare Studies, 1662–2004*. Asheville, NC, and Chandler, Ariz.: Pegasus Press, 2005.

Ure, Peter. *William Shakespeare, the Problem Plays:* Troilus and Cressida, All's Well That Ends Well, Measure for Measure *and* Timon of Athens. London and New York: published for the British Council and National Book League by Longmans Green, 1961.

Waller, Gary. All's Well That Ends Well: *New Critical Essays*. New York: Routledge, 2007.

FILM AND VIDEO PRODUCTIONS

Moshinsky, Elijah, dir. *All's Well That Ends Well*. With Ian Charleson and Donald Sinden. BBC, 1981.

—Louise C. Geddes

Antony and Cleopatra

INTRODUCTION

Antony and Cleopatra remains one of the most moving and magisterial plays in Shakespeare's canon. An intensely personal tragedy, the play exists in dramatic contrast with Shakespeare's other great tragedies, *Hamlet, Macbeth, Othello,* and *King Lear,* which are decidedly more classical narratives in which the tragic heroes' inevitable downfalls are contingent upon a series of tragic flaws and fateful circumstances. With *Antony and Cleopatra,* the sense of tragedy finds its roots in a richly interwoven tapestry that is dependent on a host of complex elements. On the one hand, the play represents an intriguing political subtext in which the divergent sociocultural aspects of Rome and Egypt are brought into brilliant relief. On the other, it traces the trials and tribulations of a love affair for the ages: the unforgettable and highly eroticized union of two of the ancient world's most storied figures.

In many ways, the play offers a living, breathing illustration of humanity's precarious fate when people are forced to exist on the political stage writ large. In this sense, *Antony and Cleopatra* provides readers with a powerful—and nearly ceaseless—study of the inherent oppositions of our private and public lives. This bifurcation results in heartbreaking clashes among the principal characters' inner selves as they grapple with their emotions in a world that judges them in terms of reason, duty, and responsibility. This notion is brilliantly depicted by the love affair between Antony and Cleopatra, a charged coupling that presages their self-destruction by challenging them to contextualize their romantic urges within the unforgiving political worlds of Rome and Egypt. Overwhelmed by their feelings of erotic love, Antony and Cleopatra attempt to maintain their political hegemony in the face of an all-consuming affair. It is an ultimately human struggle in which they must confront the most personal aspects of their inner natures as well as the inherent limitations of the physical world. In this manner, *Antony and Cleopatra* illustrates the enduring conflicts of the human self as it rages among the discrepancies between youth and age, past and present, and life and death.

Written about 1606, *Antony and Cleopatra* is often considered to be Shakespeare's last great tragedy, a narrative rife with a host of dueling subtexts and subnarratives that pit the politics of Rome and Egypt against the lustful and passionate whimsy of a romance for all time. In the play, Shakespeare brilliantly and evocatively counterpoises the political machinations of the triumvirs (members of Rome's Second Triumvirate) and Antony's military rivals with his unbridled infatuation for Cleopatra and her promises of an unfettered love. It is also a play of magnificent language at nearly every turn. As William Hazlitt famously observes, *Antony and Cleopatra* is "without doubt, one of the finest pieces of poetry in Shakespeare. The splendor of the imagery, the semblance of reality, the lofty range of picturesque objects hanging over the world, their evanescent nature, the total uncertainty of what is left behind, are just like the mouldering schemes of human greatness. Shakespeare's genius has spread over the whole play a richness like the overflowing of the Nile." With *Antony and Cleopatra,* Shakespeare affords the pure distillation of his talent—and at the height of his aesthetic powers, no less.

BACKGROUND

Shakespeare's audience was understandably fascinated by the events and history of ancient Rome. When Queen Elizabeth assumed the throne in 1558, England was in the throes of a period of great instability. The nation suffered from widespread economic uncertainty and religious disjunction. Yet, by the end of Elizabeth's reign in 1603, the kingdom had emerged as a formidable military and economic stronghold—quite arguably, the modern world's first great superpower. Shakespeare's Elizabethan audience proved itself, time and again, to be enthralled by dramatic works that explored issues related to national, military, and political power struggles. Indeed, they were interested in nearly any aspect of nationhood associated with a fledgling empire like England. Hence, the majesty of the ancient Roman civilization—and the attendant political, cultural, and social hegemony that it enjoyed during its unprecedented reign—was a subject of natural concern for the playgoers of Shakespeare's day.

Perhaps even more significant, the composition and production of *Antony and Cleopatra* roughly corresponds with the death of Elizabeth I and the coronation of James VI of Scotland as James I of England. The transfer of power and regime change in England understandably presaged a new period of uncertainty. Underneath the kingdom's Elizabethan-era expansionism and seeming prosperity existed a sense of insecurity about the nation's future—an aspect of English history that clearly parallels the breakup of the Roman Empire, which undergirds the text of *Antony and Cleopatra.*

Because Shakespeare's rendering of *Antony and Cleopatra* is an inherently dramatic work, he did not seek to constrain his narrative in terms of its absolute attention to matters of accuracy and historicity. In short, the historical reality of Antony and Cleopatra's story and the sociopolitical forces that propelled it into being are not always represented by the cold light of fact in Shakespeare's play. Nevertheless, the salient historical issues of the couple's romantic and political union are germane to our understanding of the play, as well as to the fervor behind Elizabethan England's fascination with ancient Rome.

The ancient Egypt of Cleopatra's day existed as the eastern Mediterranean Sea's most powerful economic and cultural center. Meanwhile, in ancient Rome, Mark Antony, Octavius Caesar (Octavian, Augustus), and Lepidus assumed joint control over the empire, which they divided into three provinces: Octavius controlled the empire's European holdings, Lepidus ruled its North African territories, and Mark Antony controlled its Asian provinces. Under this scheme, the Roman Empire enjoyed a vast and unprecedented sphere of influence in the ancient world. Despite its military, economic, and cultural power, however, the empire found itself increasingly vulnerable to internal civil unrest, as well as external military threats from Parthia. Antony's political life arrived at a critical juncture as the Parthians prepared to invade Syria. His efforts to provoke Cleopatra were flummoxed when the Egyptian queen attempted to establish a political alliance of her own design with Antony, as she had done with Julius Caesar in days gone by. Cleopatra succeeded in dazzling Antony by tempting his vanity. His subsequent relocation to Alexandria established a formidable Roman-Egyptian alliance, on the one hand, while leaving his provinces vulnerable to internal and external forces, on the other. It was the cause of his great undoing, as well as the heart of the tragedy of *Antony and Cleopatra.*

Shakespeare drew upon several sources for the play. The chief of these are Sir Thomas North's English version, published in 1579, of Amyot's French translation of Plutarch's *Lives of the Noble Grecians and Romans;* Plutarch's *Morals,* translated in 1603; and the 1578 translation of Appian's *Roman Civil Wars.* Shakespeare also drew on Chaucer; Cinthio's Italian tragedy *Cleopatra,* written about 1542, and an Italian life of Cleopatra written by Landi in 1551. Other sources were Robert Garnier's French play *Marc Antoine* (1578), translated into English by Mary Sidney, Countess of Pembroke (1590); Samuel Daniel's *Tragedy of Cleopatra* (1594, 1599); and the Bible's book of Revelation.

North's translation of Plutarch was used by Shakespeare for his other Roman plays, *Julius Caesar, Coriolanus,* and *Timon of Athens.* The main events and incidents of these dramas are found in North. *Antony and Cleopatra* is not an exception, and the events recorded by North, and used by Shakespeare, are

1. Fulvia and Lucius "jointing their force 'gainst Caesar" (1.2).
2. The activities of "Menecrates and Menas, famous pirates" who "Makes the sea serve them." Shakespeare makes their activities seem more threatening than does Plutarch (1.4).
3. The initial meeting between Antony and Cleopatra on the river Cydnus, magnificently described by Enobarbus (2.2).
4. The political agreement suggested by Agrippa, resulting in the marriage of Antony and Octavia (2.2).
5. Ventidius's activities amongst the Parthians (2.3; 3.1).
6. The meeting between the triumvirs at Misenum (2.7), although Shakespeare places greater emphasis than Plutarch does on the potential political conflicts among Pompey, Antony, and Octavius Caesar.
7. The activities on Pompey's galley (2.7) and Menas's suggested plot. Plutarch comments that "Pompey cast anchors enough into the sea to make his galley fast, and then built a bridge of wood to convey them to his galley, from the head of Mount Misena: and there he welcomed them, and made them great cheer." Shakespeare transforms "great cheer" into a drunken orgy.
8. The Battle of Actium, Cleopatra's flight, and Antony's following her (3.10, 3.11).
9. Enobarbus's desertion (4.6, 4.9). Plutarch places this before the Battle of Actium, but Shakespeare locates Enobarbus's flight afterward.
10. The Egyptian battles (4.7–8).
11. The death of Antony (4.14, 4.15); Cleopatra's retreat to the monument (4.15; 5.2).
12. Octavius Caesar's meeting with Cleopatra (5.2).

North's translation of Plutarch is not merely the source for these events but of various incidents illuminating personality and character. Among these are the following:

Antony as a "Herculean Roman" (1.3). In Plutarch, he is "descended from one Anton, the son of Hercules"; he is respected and popular among his soldiers (1.4). Plutarch mentions Antony's endurance and strength of character following his defeat at Modena (1.4); his superstitious character (2.3); his jealousy of Cleopatra (2.5), especially as demonstrated at the fishing incident (3.2), which Shakespeare transforms into a symbolic representation of Cleopatra and the way she has entrapped him (Antony tells Cleopatra: "You did know / How much you were my conqueror"); Antony's order that Thidias be whipped (3.13); Antony's jealousy of Octavius Caesar, for example, where he tells Octavia that her brother "hath wag'd / New wars 'gainst Pompey" (3.4), although in this instance, Shakespeare departs slightly from Plutarch, who notes that Octavius is reading Antony's will rather than his own (in Shakespeare, Antony tells Octavia that Caesar "made his will, and read it / To public ear"); Antony's obsession with Cleopatra, for example, as when Caesar tells Lepidus that Antony "fishes, drinks, and wastes / The lamps of night in revel" (1.4); and Antony's consideration for Julius Caesar and Brutus (3.2).

Cleopatra's sensuality. In Shakespeare, Enobarbus describes her on the river Cydnus (2.2): "For her own person, / It beggar'd all description: she did lie / In her pavilion cloth-of-gold, of tissue— / O'er picturing that Venus where we see / The fancy outwork nature." This transforms Plutarch's "And now for the person of herself:

she was layed under a pavilion of cloth of gold of tissue, apparelled and attired like the goddess Venus, commonly drawn in picture." Plutarch also depicts her vanity; her ability to experience extremes of emotion, such as love and hate; her tricks; and her cowardice, as, for instance, when Shakespeare writes that during the battle "the breeze upon her, like a cow in June, / Hoists sails, and flies" and Antony "(like a doting mallard) / Leaving the fight in height," flies after her (3.10).

Octavia's decency, nobility, and patience.

Octavius Caesar's ruthlessness and coldness.

Acts IV and V follow North closely. The Soothsayer's words to Antony, Antony's recognition of Octavius Caesar's better luck at sports (2.3), and the soldier's plea in 3.7 that Antony "not fight by sea, / Trust not to rotten planks: do you misdoubt / This sword, and these my wounds? Let the Egyptians / And the Phoenicians go a-ducking" almost word for word follow Plutarch. In North, a captain notes, "O noble Emperor, how cometh it to pass that you trust to these vile brittle ships? What, do you mistrust these wounds of mine, and this sword? Let the Egyptians and Phoenicians fight by sea, and set us on the main land." Yet, Shakespeare omits Plutarch's account of Cleopatra's political intrigues and her Athenian visit, Antony's negative Asian campaigns, and the detailed description of the treasure Cleopatra took with her to the monument. Octavia is a personality of considerable stature and authority in Plutarch; Shakespeare reduces her role. His focus is clearly upon Antony and Cleopatra.

Shakespeare expands, too; for example, not present in Plutarch are the whole of 1.2; Cleopatra's dream in 5.2; ("I dreamt there was an emperor Antony"); Cleopatra's talk with the Clown (5.2); Lepidus's drunken insensibility on Pompey's galley (2.7); Antony's intense anger with Cleopatra (3.13, 4.12); and Cleopatra's questioning of the messenger (2.5, 3.3).

Shakespeare drew upon Plutarch's *Morals* (1603) for the comparisons in *Antony and Cleopatra* of Cleopatra with Venus, Ceres, Juno, and Isis, the Moon Goddess. The 1603 translation of Plutarch describes Isis "as having an infinite number of names, for that she receiveth all forms and shapes, according as it pleaseth that first reason to convert and turn her." In Shakespeare, Enobarbus says of Cleopatra that "Age cannot wither her, not custom stale / Her infinite variety" (2.2).

Appian's *Roman Civil Wars* is the source for Antony's reply to Octavius Caesar in 2.2 concerning the activities of Lucius, Antony's brother who rebelled of his own volition against the Triumvirate—not on Antony's behalf. Appian is also the source for his comment that Fulvia waged war "To have me out of Egypt" (2.2). Also not in Plutarch but in Appian are Antony's reference to Pompey (Sextus Pompeius) commanding "the empire of the sea" (1.2) and his comment that the Romans "began to throw / Pompey the Great, and all his dignities / Upon his son" (1.2). Pompey's death is in Appian, not in Plutarch, and Appian notes that "There be that say that Plancus, and not Antony, did command him to die," which explains Antony's anger for he "Threats the throat of that his officer that murder'd Pompey" (3.5).

For literary handling of the Antony and Cleopatra tragedy, Shakespeare had as a model Chaucer's treatment in the *Legend of Good Women* of a highly romanticized Cleopatra and a discreet, hard Antony marrying her. There is no Octavia, and insane with despair after defeat at Actium, Antony kills himself. Cinthio's tragedy *Cleopatra* begins after Actium and emphasizes the role of Fortune. Landi's *Life* of Cleopatra is a sympathetic one focusing upon her intelligence.

Garnier's tragedy translated by the countess of Pembroke, *Marc Antoine,* focuses on Antony, has a moral emphasis and tone, and gives Cleopatra sympathetic consideration: "She is all heav'nlie." There are verbal echoes between Garnier's tragedy and Shakespeare's. In the former, there is "fat slime"; in Shakespeare, "the higher Nilus swells . . . the slime and ooze scatters" (2.7). In *Antoine,* Cleopatra's "thousand kisses, thousand thousand more" bid Antony farewell. In Shakespeare, "Of many thousand kisses, the poor last" Antony will "lay upon" Cleopatra's "lips" (4.15).

Daniel's drama *Tragedy of Cleopatra* is the foundation for material in *Antony and Cleopatra* not found in other sources. In 5.2, Cleopatra reflects on being "chastis'd with the sober eye / Of dull Octavia." Daniel also has this detail. Cleopatra's being "wrinkled deep in time" (1.5) echoes Daniel's "beauties waine" and "new-appearing wrinkles of declining." Cleopatra's determination, "My resolution, and my hands" (4.15), to commit suicide; Dolabella's love for Cleopatra (5.2); her memory, "I am again for Cydnus / To meet Mark Antony" (5.2); and the detail of her crown being "awry" (5.2), all have their genesis in Daniel. The *Tragedy of Cleopatra,* however, does not emphasize the causes of Antony's fall, though it does place Antony and Cleopatra's tragedy within a universal framework and contrasts Roman austerity with Egyptian luxuriousness. But, perhaps naively, it suggests that Antony was ignorant of women before meeting Cleopatra.

The New Testament's book of Revelation is the foundation for many verbal images and ideas in the play, whereas the other sources largely provide the framework for the plotting and its details. There are various instances of Shakespeare's use of Revelation. For instance, in the last scene of the play, Cleopatra tells Dolabella:

> I dreamt there was an Emperor Antony . . .
> His face was as the heavens, and therein stuck
> A sun and moon, which kept their course, and
>   lighted
> The little O, the earth. . . .
> His legs bestrid the ocean, his rear'd arm
> Crested the world: his voice was propertied
> As all the tuned spheres, and that to friends:
> But when he meant to quail, and shake the orb.
> He was as rattling thunder.

Revelation 10: 1–6 reads:

> And I saw another mighty angel come down
>   from heaven, clothed with a cloud . . . and
> his face was as it were the sun, and his feet as

pillars of fire . . . and he set his right foot upon the sea, and his left foot on the earth, and cried with a loud voice . . . and when he had cried, seven thunders uttered their voices . . . And the angel which I saw stand upon these, and the earth, lift up his hand to heaven.

These images of cosmic change, of "His face . . . as the heavens," of Antony bestriding the universe, and of thunder are apocalyptic in the sense that they literally anticipate change on a large scale. In the play, the old world of Antony and Cleopatra gives way to Octavius Caesar, so in Revelation, there is a vision of the end of the world. References to stars, death, and the falling of stars permeate Shakespeare's play and the biblical text. Caesar says that Antony "hath given his empire / Up to a whore, who now are levying / The Kings of the earth for war" (3.6). In Revelation 17: 1–2, there is "the judgment of the great whore that sitteth upon many waters with whom the kings of the earth have committed fornication."

In spite of the verbal parallels, the use of plot and character detail, the dependence on Plutarch, and the other sources for basic data, Shakespeare's *Antony and Cleopatra* transcends the raw material of its creation. The play centers on both Antony and Cleopatra, their middle-aged passion, and its tragic consequences. It is enacted against the backcloth of the disintegration of an empire and conveyed in unique poetry.

Date and Text of the Play

The play is recorded in the Stationers' Register for May 20, 1608, but appears not to have been published until 1623 as one of the plays in the First Folio (the first collected edition of the plays). Scholarly and critical opinions agree that the play is a relatively late one, having been written probably either in 1606 or 1607. It is in a sense a sequel to *Julius Caesar,* which was being performed in London during September 1599. Except for 1.1, neither act nor scene divisions were indicated in the First Folio. Those in modern texts largely follow the divisions into acts and scenes made by Nicholas

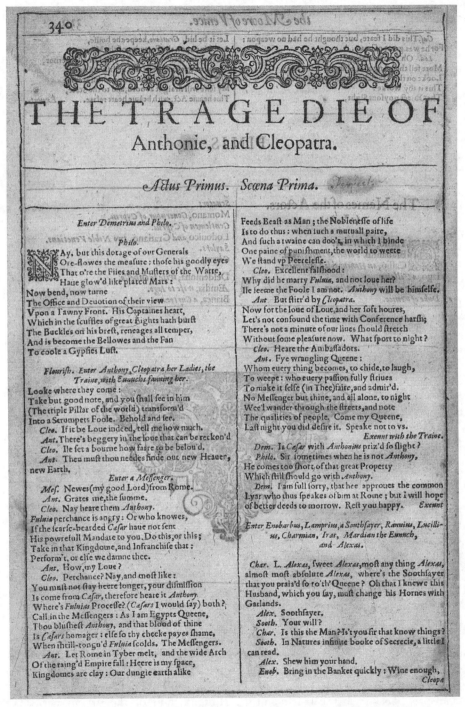

Title page of the First Folio edition of *Antony and Cleopatra*, published in 1623

Rowe (1674–1718), and the text itself contains materials introduced by editors after 1623.

SYNOPSIS
Brief Synopsis

Following the death of Julius Caesar and the defeat of Brutus and Cassius at the Battle of Philippi, the Roman Empire is controlled by three triumvirs, Octavius Caesar, Mark Antony, and Lepidus. Antony, placed in charge of the eastern provinces, has neglected his administrative duties in order to pursue a passionate love affair in Alexandria with Cleopatra, the Egyptian queen. Meanwhile, the Roman Empire is being torn apart by internal rebellions. Members of Antony's family are involved in a rebellion in Italy; there have been military defeats on the frontiers; the rebel Pompey (Sextus Pompeius), son of Pompey the Great, in control of the seas "hath given the dare to Caesar"; and Fulvia, the wife of Antony, has died. These events force Antony to return to Rome.

The triumvirs meet in Rome to patch up their differences and to unite against the threat from Pompey. Antony agrees to marry Octavia, the sister of Octavius Caesar. The marriage will cement the bond between them. Pompey and the triumvirs decide to talk and arrive at a peace treaty. To celebrate, Pompey throws a lavish party for them aboard his galley. At the party, Lepidus becomes extremely drunk. Caesar and Pompey battle, and Pompey is killed. Caesar, having used Lepidus to defeat Pompey, then gets rid of him, too. Octavius Caesar and Antony now control the empire. Antony, who is in Athens on political business, sends Octavia to negotiate with her brother on his behalf. However, obsessed with thoughts of Cleopatra, Antony returns to her and to Egypt.

Antony's return to Cleopatra and desertion of Octavia is the signal for the beginning of outright hostilities between him and Caesar. Theirs is a battle for supreme control of the empire. Cleopatra joins forces with Antony, who has control of the land but is lured into a naval battle off the coast at Actium. Cleopatra flees from the battle and is followed by Antony. Caesar pursues Antony and Cleopatra to Alexandria. Antony is defeated in battle. He commits suicide after hearing a false report that Cleopatra is dead.

In triumph, Caesar wants to lead Cleopatra through the streets of Rome. Cleopatra tricks Caesar; she has an asp brought to her in a fig basket and, with her faithful attendants, commits suicide. Caesar discovers her dead body and orders that Antony and Cleopatra be buried together and accorded dignified funeral rites.

Act I, Scene 1

The play opens in Cleopatra's Alexandria Palace. Two friends of Mark Antony, Philo and Demetrius, discuss Cleopatra's power over Antony. Instead of being a ruler, he is ruled and gives up his responsibilities for love. The grand entrance of Antony and Cleopatra serves to emphasize Philo's observations. A messenger with news from Rome is ignored; totally absorbed in each other, Antony and Cleopatra exchange views on love and faithfulness. Alone again, Demetrius and Philo observe that what they have witnessed confirms that Antony is not his former self.

Act I, Scene 2

After some talk between a Soothsayer and Enobarbus and the queen's attendants Charmian and Iras, whose fortunes are told, Cleopatra comes in search of Antony. She has remembered the messenger from Rome and has gone to find him. The messenger brings news of chaos in Italy and military defeats in Syria and Asia. Another messenger has brought news of the death of Fulvia, Antony's wife. Antony becomes aware of his responsibilities and realizes that he must depart at once from Cleopatra and Egypt. Enobarbus, not fully comprehending that Fulvia is dead, or unsure about how Antony takes the news, jests with him and comments on Cleopatra's passion for him. Antony tells Enobarbus about the seriousness of the political situation, of the disintegration of the Roman Empire, and of the urgent necessity for him to return home.

Act I, Scene 3

Cleopatra sends one of her attendants to search for Antony, with instructions that if he finds Antony happy he must say that Cleopatra is sad, and vice versa. Charmian disagrees with Cleopatra's strategy for keeping Antony with her. When Antony appears, Cleopatra continuously interrupts him and varies in her attitude and mood toward him. He tells her that he is to leave Egypt and that his wife, Fulvia, has died. Cleopatra's mood changes to a serious one, and she finds it difficult to express her feelings.

Act I, Scene 4

In his house in Rome, Octavius Caesar reads a letter from Alexandria outlining Antony's activities. Caesar comments on these to Lepidus, who tries in vain to defend Antony from Caesar's accusations. A messenger arrives with news that Pompey, a major threat to the leadership of the Roman Empire, has gained strength at sea. Octavius Caesar contrasts Antony's "lascivious wassails" (1.4.57) with his previous heroic behavior and hopes that "his shames" (1.4.73) will "quickly / Drive him to Rome" (1.4.73–74). He and Lepidus must gather together what armed forces they can in order to defend themselves against Pompey and his forces.

Act I, Scene 5

Cleopatra's obsession with Antony runs riot in his absence. She sends constant messages to him, indulges in fantasies, comparing him with some of her past lovers, and especially with Julius Caesar, whom she loved when she "was green in judgment" (1.5.76).

Act II, Scene 1

At his house in Messina, Pompey discusses the current situation with the pirates Menas and Menecrates. The main threat to Pompey comes from the experienced soldier Antony, who is languishing in Egypt. Varrius, Pompey's ally, arrives with the unwelcome news that Antony has left Egypt, returned to Rome, and joined with Pompey's enemies, the other triumvirs, Octavius Caesar and Lepidus. Menas tries to reassure Pompey, reminding him the enmity between Caesar and Antony concerning the conflict started by Fulvia, Antony's wife. Ever the realist, Pompey deduces that internal differences will be papered over in order to combat any external threat.

Act II, Scene 2

Set in Lepidus's house, this scene is divided into two sections: the first is dominated by political considerations; the second, by Enobarbus's evocative description of Cleopatra. The triumvirs meet to thrash out their differences and to try to settle old scores amicably. With great difficulty, Caesar and Antony refrain from open hostility. Agrippa suggests that Antony should marry Caesar's sister and thereby cement the bonds between the two. Antony and Caesar agree, shake hands, swear to act as brothers, and plan to defeat Pompey.

After Antony and Caesar have gone to see Octavia to get her approval, Enobarbus, Agrippa, and Maecenas remain on stage. The theme of their conversation is Cleopatra, her personality, and her power over Antony.

Act II, Scene 3

Antony tells Octavia in Caesar's presence that his public duties will take him away from her. She will pray for him at such times. Antony then confronts the Soothsayer, who tells him that in the exchanges with Caesar, Antony's fortunes will be less than Caesar's. Dismissing the Soothsayer, Antony thinks about his words and reverses his previous promises to Caesar. He then decides to return to Egypt where "my pleasure lies" (2.3.39).

Act II, Scene 4

This brief 10-line scene depicts soldiers leaving for battle. Agrippa says that shortly after Antony will kiss his wife, he will also be off to battle. Lepidus says he has things to do before joining up two days later with his allies at the mount.

Act II, Scene 5

Back at Cleopatra's court, where she is restless, displeased, and uncertain, she asks for music, then billiards, then wishes to fish in the Nile. Her mind

Cleopatra attacks a messenger after he brings news of Antony and Octavia's marriage in Act II, Scene 5 of *Antony and Cleopatra,* in this print published by Duprat & Co. in 1890. *(Illustration by Paul Avril)*

continually dwells on Antony. The arrival of a messenger from Rome seems to confirm the worst fears that Antony is dead. She threatens the messenger with dire consequences if he brings bad news but hardly gives him a chance to tell his message. She all but faints upon hearing of the marriage between Antony and Octavia. Angrily, she hits the messenger and draws a knife. Persuaded to return if, as Cleopatra hopes, his news has been mistaken, the messenger flees when her fury is once again vented on him. At the end of the scene, Alexas is sent by Cleopatra to find out from the messenger about Octavia's appearance.

Act II, Scene 6

The two warring factions meet at Mount Misenum and exchange hostages. They agree on peace terms and depart to make arrangements to "feast each other ere we part" (2.6.61). Menas and Enobarbus remain on stage, and the banter between them concerning mutual thievery gives way to serious commentary. Menas is perplexed by Antony's marriage to Caesar's sister, which will "knit" them "together" (2.6.122). Menas regards Antony as unreliable and regrets that Pompey has made peace with the triumvirate. Enobarbus believes that Antony will return to his old Egyptian love, Cleopatra.

Act II, Scene 7

On board Pompey's galley near Misenum, two servants comment on the activities of Caesar, Antony, Pompey, and Lepidus, who have gathered together for a reconciliation banquet. While the others drink and enjoy themselves, Menas attempts to draw Pompey aside. At last, he manages to suggest that Antony, Caesar, and Lepidus are in Pompey's power and should be slaughtered. The idea appeals to Pompey, but he rejects it on the grounds that his honor will be stained if the plan goes ahead; however, if he had not known about it his approval would have been forthcoming. Menas is stung by the reply and vows no longer to serve Pompey. Lepidus is removed in a drunken, insensible state. The revels continue with dancing, music, and a Bacchanalian song. The relatively sober Caesar takes his leave. Pompey reminds Antony of a dispute between them—relating to Antony's occupation of Pompey's father's house—and adds "but what, we are friends" (2.7.137), and the party breaks up.

Act III, Scene 1

On the Syrian plain, the Romans led by Ventidius (dispatched to Parthia at the end of Act II Scene, 3) have defeated the Parthians. Ventidius has killed Pacorus, the son of the Parthian king, and thus revenged the treacherous slaying of the triumvir Marcus Crassus. Ventidius resists Silius's promptings to pursue the fleeing Parthians. Ventidius is tired of fighting and does not wish to steal too much of the limelight and, hence, place his general and commander Antony in the shade.

Act III, Scene 2

At Caesar's house, Agrippa and Enobarbus mock the unity of the triumvirate and express very little faith in Caesar and Antony. Enobarbus's impression of Lepidus is very low. The triumvirate return to the stage with Caesar and Antony expressing mutual trust. Caesar is troubled in parting from his sister and asks Antony to treat her well. Brother and sister talk together, and what she says brings tears to Caesar's eyes. Enobarbus notes that tears are not appropriate to soldiers. Agrippa reminds him that Antony, too, has cried. Caesar and Octavia bid farewell.

Act III, Scene 3

This scene is a continuation of Act II, Scene 5. Cleopatra's messenger returns but is afraid of her. His report on Octavia is unfavorable. She is shorter than Cleopatra, has a lower voice, and walks more like a statue than a live person. Octavia is old enough to be a widow and has a round face and brown hair, with a low forehead. Cleopatra has a message to give to her messenger.

Act III, Scene 4

Antony is at Athens, the headquarters of his eastern command. Antony complains that Caesar has attacked Pompey and spoken disrespectfully of himself. Octavia begs her husband to think well of her brother, otherwise she will be torn between the two. Antony tells her to choose the one she feels will best look after her and takes a rather cool farewell of her.

Act III, Scene 5

Enobarbus and Eros, a slave of Antony, discuss events. Caesar and Lepidus have made war on Pompey; after the victory, Lepidus has been discarded, arrested, and held in prison. Pompey has been murdered by one of Antony's men—an action that has incensed Antony. Enobarbus is wanted by Antony.

Act III, Scene 6

The scene returns to the center of Roman imperial power, Caesar's house. Caesar catalogs for Agrippa and Maecenas a detailed list of complaints concerning Antony's behavior in Egypt with Cleopatra. Antony has divided his portion of the Roman Empire between his own sons. Caesar will allow him some of Lepidus's areas but demands in return a say in the way the lands gained from Pompey are to be portioned out. Maecenas has his doubts as to whether Antony will agree to this solution.

Octavia appears without a formal introduction, which provokes Caesar. She is surprised that Antony has returned to Egypt and that he is preparing to fight Caesar, having enlisted the support of many monarchs. Caesar offers his sister what comfort he can, but she is torn by the news, which she finds hard to believe.

Act III, Scene 7

This scene takes place in Antony's camp near Actium, where dissension emerges among his followers. Enobarbus tries to discourage Cleopatra from personally entering into the fight with Antony. Her presence will distract and unsettle him. Cleopatra ignores his advice, as does Antony when Enobarbus disagrees with his intentions to engage in a naval battle with Caesar. A soldier also urges Antony not to fight Caesar by sea. Antony will not listen and is determined to keep to his plan of attack, especially as Cleopatra has offered naval assistance. Antony is amazed by the news of Caesar's rapid advances.

Act III, Scene 8

Marching with some of his army toward the Battle of Actium, Caesar commands his forces not to fight on land until the naval battle has been decided.

Act III, Scene 9

Antony instructs Enobarbus to take the forces to a hillside position from which they can assess Caesar's naval strength and plan accordingly.

Act III, Scene 10

Elements of the opposing armies cross and recross the stage. The noise of a sea battle is heard offstage. Enobarbus tells of Antony's naval defeat; of the flight of the *Antoniad*, Cleopatra's flagship, with 60 ships. A fellow general, Scarus, enters to add that Antony has also deserted the battle to follow Cleopatra. Another general, Canidius, has seen Antony's actions and decides to turn his troops over to the opposition. Enobarbus, despite his good sense, will remain with Antony.

Act III, Scene 11

Back in Egypt at Cleopatra's palace, Antony broods over his dishonor. He offers his followers gold as payment and incentive to desert him, but they are unwilling to leave. Cleopatra enters. Antony remembers his past glories at Philippi, where he defeated Cassius and Brutus, and compares this time with his present condition. Cleopatra collapses and tries to excuse herself. Antony recognizes that she has had total power over him. Now he has to humble himself to Caesar. However, for one of her tears, the world has been well lost. He has sent their children's tutor to seek peace terms from Caesar.

Act III, Scene 12

Caesar and his forces are already in Egypt. The schoolmaster arrives in Caesar's camp to act as Antony's messenger. His presence is taken as a sign of how low Antony's fortunes have now fallen. The schoolmaster as messenger reports that Antony wishes to live in Egypt or else live as "a private man in Athens" (3.12.15). Cleopatra wishes that her heirs may inherit her kingdom. Caesar will not listen to Antony's request but will agree to Cleopatra's provided that she exile Antony from Egypt or kill him. When the schoolmaster has left, Caesar tells Thidias to try to win Cleopatra from Antony and spy on Antony's activities. Thidias is given a free hand as to how he proceeds.

Act III, Scene 13

Enobarbus is questioned by Cleopatra about what to do, and she asks if she is to blame. Enobarbus apportions the blame to Antony, who has allowed his reason to be controlled by his emotions. The schoolmaster ambassador has arrived. Antony sends him back to Caesar, challenging him to a duel, which provokes Enobarbus to wonder, in an aside, at Antony's loss of reason. Caesar must be aware that Antony is a skillful swordsman. Thidias, Caesar's ambassador, arrives with a message for Cleopatra from Caesar, saying that he knows she only loves Antony out of fear. She replies that her honor has been conquered, not defeated; she accepts Caesar's victory and places her fate in his hands.

As Thidias is kissing Cleopatra's hand in farewell, Antony and Enobarbus enter. An enraged Antony

Cleopatra greets Antony in this 1906 illustration. *(Drawing by A. M. Faulkner)*

orders Thidias to be whipped. He loses his self-control and in a jealous rage turns on Cleopatra, accusing her of various infidelities. A whipped Thidias returns, and Antony revels in humiliating him and, implicitly, his master Caesar, to whom Thidias is told to return and report what has happened.

Antony indulges in a bout of self-pity. Cleopatra, realizing that he is not himself, indulges in self-accusations. Antony, passion cooled, is reconciled with Cleopatra and makes preparations for another fight with Caesar's armies. He calls for one final night of mutual revelry. Cleopatra reveals that it is her birthday, which at least she is going to enjoy. Alone on stage, Enobarbus again says that Antony's reason has left him and that he will "seek some way to leave" Antony (3.13.205–206).

Act IV, Scene 1
Caesar reads Antony's letter and is angered by his threats, especially as they lack substance. Maecenas, Caesar's lieutenant, ridicules Antony's challenge to single combat and urges Caesar to take advantage of Antony's distraught condition. Caesar, aware that the forthcoming battle will prove to be a decisive one, intends to satisfy his army. He prepares a feast and refers to the growing numbers of Antony's former soldiers who have come over to his side.

Act IV, Scene 2
Caesar's reply that he will not fight Antony in single combat forces Antony to prepare for the next day's decisive battle. Antony bids a sad farewell to his followers, reminds them of former glories, and suggests that their supper will prove to be their last, for tomorrow they will have another master. Enobarbus warns Antony that he is fostering depression. Antony, in an effort to restore spirits, tells his attendants that he does not mean what he says and that he will join them in supper to "drown considerations" (4.2.45).

Act IV, Scene 3
This scene involves a conversation between three soldiers on duty. Rumors of strange noises are

unconfirmed; however, they agree that if the navy succeeds and the army fights well, victory will be theirs. Music is heard. A soldier regards the noise as a good omen, while another sees it as a bad omen as the sounds represent the spirit of Hercules "whom Antony lov'd" (4.3.21) leaving him. The soldiers attempt to track down the source of the music.

Act IV, Scene 4
Cleopatra helps Antony put on his armor. Her assistance is not entirely successful. A soldier arrives to tell Antony that he is expected for the battle. Trumpets sound; he tells his men that the day is a "fair" (4.4.25) one, and as a soldier, he takes leave of Cleopatra. She retires to her chamber with the thought that if only Antony and Caesar "might / Determine this great war in single fight!" (4.4.37) all would be well.

Act IV, Scene 5
A soldier greets Antony, who admits his mistake in not engaging in a land battle at Actium. The soldier tells him that Enobarbus has gone over to Caesar. Antony generously sends Enobarbus his treasures, "gentle adieus, and greetings" (4.5.16) and regrets that his "fortunes have / Corrupted honest men!" (4.5.18–19).

Act IV, Scene 6
At his camp, Caesar gives orders for the battle to commence and demands that Antony be captured alive. He also commands that the deserters from Antony's side be placed in the front lines. Enobarbus, hearing these instructions, regrets his defection. A soldier appears to tell him that Antony has sent over Enobarbus's possessions and added more to them. Enobarbus is overcome with remorse and plans suicide.

Act IV, Scene 7
This scene provides different views of the battle. Agrippa indicates that Caesar's forces are under pressure. Scarus, on the other hand, although wounded, reports that things are going well for Antony's forces.

Act IV, Scene 8

Antony sends a messenger to Cleopatra with victory news. He thanks his troops for their heroic efforts and predicts victory the next day. Cleopatra arrives. They mutually praise each other, and Scarus is personally recommended to Cleopatra for bravery. Together, Antony and Cleopatra will celebrate.

Act IV, Scene 9

A sentry and watchman talk in Caesar's camp. They hear sounds of a man in torment. This man turns out to be Enobarbus, who, heartbroken with guilt and remorse, dies. The drum sounds for the coming battle as his body is taken to the guardroom.

Act IV, Scene 10

Antony confers with Scarus. Caesar has prepared for a naval battle. Antony is prepared on land and sea. He goes to the hills near the city to engage in reconnaissance.

Act IV, Scene 11

Caesar instructs his forces to wait while Antony orders his best men into a naval confrontation. Meanwhile, Caesar's men will hold their ground in the valleys.

Act IV, Scene 12

Antony finds a high observation point to watch the battle. Scarus notes that the fortune-tellers have been negative about Antony's chances. Antony reenters with the news that he has been betrayed. His fleet has surrendered. He assumes that Cleopatra has deserted him, and when she appears, he vents his rage on her and threatens to kill her on the spot. She does not stay. He calls upon Hercules to give him the strength to take his own life and revenge on Cleopatra.

Act IV, Scene 13

Back at her palace, a frantic Cleopatra seeks help. Charmian advises her to lock herself in the tomb and to send word to Antony that she is dead. Cleopatra tells Mardian to give Antony the message

and add that his name was on her lips when she died, and to let her know how he received the news.

Act IV, Scene 14

Antony talks with Eros about his impending death, blames Cleopatra for his undoing, and contemplates suicide. Mardian, Cleopatra's messenger, arrives with the false information that she has died. This news hardens Antony's resolution to die. He asks Eros to kill him, but Eros kills himself instead. Antony, full of remorse and a sense of his own cowardice, tries to kill himself by falling on his sword. Lying wounded, he is found by two guards, who refuse his request to kill him. Diomedes appears. Cleopatra has had a premonition concerning the consequences of her false report. She has sent Diomedes to tell Antony the truth. Antony requests that as a final service his guard carry him to Cleopatra.

Act IV, Scene 15

A severely wounded Antony is brought to the monument where Cleopatra is in hiding with her handmaidens. Cleopatra, unable to leave the monument out of fear of capture by Caesar's troops, pulls Antony into the monument, helped by her maidens. She pleads with him to clear her name. Antony advises her to make peace with Caesar, but Cleopatra declares that she will never trust Caesar. Antony tells her to remember his greatness, and Cleopatra faints when he dies, for she feels that her life is no longer worth living. She tells Charmian and Iras that they will bury Antony and then imitate the Romans by committing suicide.

Act V, Scene 1

Dolabella is told by Caesar to insist that Antony makes peace. Decretas arrives carrying his sword, with which Antony had tried to kill himself, and with the news that Antony is dead. Caesar laments the loss of "my mate in empire" and "is touched" (5.1.32–43). An Egyptian messenger from Cleopatra arrives in order to discover what Caesar wants Cleopatra to do. Caesar says that she will soon find out but that he will be generous. Proculeius, the only one of Caesar's circle trusted by Cleopatra, is sent to reassure her. Caesar is worried that she may follow Antony and commit suicide. He wishes to lead her through Rome in his victory triumph. Dolabella is called for, but Caesar remembers he has been sent on another errand.

Act V, Scene 2
Proculeius arrives at the entrance to Cleopatra's monument with Caesar's surrender terms. He emphasizes Caesar's generosity if Cleopatra will submit to his authority. Gallus and his soldiers enter the monument and seize Cleopatra. She tries to kill herself but is disarmed by Proculeius. She tells him that she would rather die than be led in triumph by Caesar. Dolabella enters and takes over from Proculeius. Cleopatra gives Dolabella an account of a dream she has had about Antony and praises him. She discovers from Dolabella the fate Caesar has in store for her. Then for the first time in the play, she and Caesar meet. Cleopatra kneels before him. Caesar reassures her that no harm will come to her. Seleucus, her treasurer, after declaring that he has handed over Cleopatra's wealth, reveals that a portion has been retained, and he is driven from the stage by Cleopatra. Caesar allows her to retain the treasure and departs with reassuring words. When he leaves, Cleopatra expresses skepticism about his intentions: "He words me girls, he words me." (5.2.191)

Dolabella reappears and tells Cleopatra that in three days she will be sent to Rome with her children. Cleopatra depicts a theatrical picture to Iras and Charmian of how they will be led before the Roman crowds. She sends for her "best attires," "crown and all," (5.2.28–32) to prepare for suicide. A guard admits the Clown carrying a fig basket in which are hidden poisonous snakes. He jests with Cleopatra on the word *worm* and explains the painless way in which snake poison operates. Cleopatra puts on her robe and regal costume and is kissed by Iras, who suddenly dies. Cleopatra too takes the poison and dies as a guard rushes in. Charmian dies. Dolabella enters to discover what has happened and is followed by Caesar, who has sus-

pected that something drastic may take place. After examining the bodies, Dolabella finds a bleeding wound on Cleopatra's arm and a guard finds "an aspic's trail" (5.2.349). Caesar promises an honorable burial for Cleopatra and Antony in the same grave, orders his army to attend the funeral, then returns to Rome.

CHARACTER LIST
Mark Antony Along with Octavius Caesar and Lepidus, Mark Antony is ruler of the Roman Empire. Once revered for his prowess as a soldier and fierce leader, Antony eschews his duties in order to live in Egypt with Cleopatra. Their highly passionate and erotic love affair divides his loyalties between the Western and Eastern worlds, leaving him torn asunder between his obligations as a Roman hero and his overwhelming desires for Cleopatra, with whom he has fallen madly, hopelessly in love.

Cleopatra The beautiful and highly volatile queen of Egypt. Cleopatra's emotional nature contrasts with Mark Antony's sense of reason and duty. Seductive and cunning, Cleopatra had carried on a love affair with Julius Caesar, who was instrumental in her ascendancy to the throne, before falling in love with Antony.

Octavius Caesar Julius Caesar's nephew and adopted son, Octavius rules the Roman Empire along with Antony and Lepidus. Octavius and Antony enjoy a strained relationship, given the younger triumvir's ambition, as well as Antony's protracted stay in Egypt, for which the practical-minded Octavius accuses him of neglecting his duties.

Domitius Enobarbus Antony's faithful supporter, the cynical Enobarbus remains loyal to Antony even as he makes the damning political and military mistakes that will seal his doom.

Marcus Aemilius Lepidus Along with Antony and Octavius Caesar, Lepidus rules the Roman Empire. He is the weakest member of their triumvirate, given his precarious political position.

Pompey (Sextus Pompeius) The young soldier who enjoys great popularity among the Roman citizenry and poses as a considerable military threat to the triumvirs.

Octavia Octavius Caesar's sister, who marries Mark Antony in order to establish an alliance between the two triumvirs. Her meek disposition allows her to be easily deceived by Antony and Cleopatra.

Charmian and Iras Cleopatra's loyal attendants.

Soothsayer The Egyptian fortune-teller who predicts Antony's tragic downfall and his ill fortune in comparison with Caesar.

Dolabella One of Octavius Caesar's soldiers, Dolabella guards Cleopatra during her captivity.

Agrippa One of Octavius Caesar's officers.

Demetrius and Philo Friends of Antony.

Canidius A general in Antony's army who later defects to the service of Caesar.

Taurus A general in Caesar's army.

Silius An officer in Ventidius's army.

Maecenas and Gallus Friends of Caesar.

Ventidius A Roman soldier under Antony's command.

Scarus A young soldier who serves bravely under Antony's command.

Proculeius A traitorous soldier under Caesar's command.

Thidias Messenger and friend of Caesar.

Diomedes Cleopatra's servant.

Eros Antony's faithful and steadfast attendant.

Menas An ambitious young soldier under Pompey's command who masterminds a plan to assassinate Caesar, Antony, and Lepidus, a scheme that would result in his master's ascendancy to power.

Menecrates and Varrius Friends of Pompey.

Alexas Attendant to Cleopatra.

Mardian Attendant to Cleopatra; a eunuch.

Seleucus Cleopatra's treasurer.

Clown The Egyptian who brings the basket of figs containing the poisonous asps to Cleopatra.

Decretas One of Antony's soldiers.

CHARACTER STUDIES
Mark Antony

The opening speech of *Antony and Cleopatra* pinpoints succinctly what has happened to Mark Ant-

ony. A brave and respected general "is become the bellows and the fan / To cool a gipsy's lust (1.1.9–10)." Shakespeare in this play does not show us the young Antony (for him we must look to *Julius Caesar*) but a "Lord of lords" (4.5.17), a "huge spirit" (4.15.93) whose decline is now in progress. Antony "fishes, drinks, and wastes / The lamps of night in revel" (1.4.4–5). Throughout, Antony is described as larger than life in terms of physical prowess, military skills, character, passions, and energy. He is a "Herculean Roman (1.3.85)," an epithet not without its ironic element. Antony is called "noble" at least eight times but is rarely viewed as such. As the play develops, Antony becomes less and less in command of himself, his actions, his personal fate, and the countries he controls. Personal and public disintegration join forces. He is rational when discussing Caesar's complaints that Antony denied him "arms and aid when I required them" (2.2.93) but displays violent anger with Thidias (3.13) and Cleopatra (4.12). Thidias's kissing of Cleopatra's hand provides the flashpoint that provokes Antony's rage and is a result of his suspicion, his fear of being replaced in Cleopatra's affections, and his rash judgment. His attack on Cleopatra emphasizes physical decay; he is described as "half-blasted" (3.13.110) with images of leftover food. Antony, aware of his own weakening, attacks himself; his violence is the product of frustration at the decline of his powers.

Antony, whose "face was as the heavens" (5.2.78), and whose death is likened to the end of the universe in which "there is nothing left remarkable / Beneath the visiting moon" (4.15.68), is described favorably by his enemies. Caesar admits that in Antony "You shall find there / A man who is the abstract of all the faults / That all men follow" (1.4.8–10). He recalls Antony's bravery and courage in defeat (1.4) and admits that "the death of Antony / Is not a single doom, in the name lay / A moiety of the world" (5.1.17–19), not merely a tribute to Antony's administrative authority but to his strength. Among those close to him he inspires deep affection. The usually cynical Enobarbus calls himself "an ass, am onion-eyed" (4.2.35) when

Kyrle Bellew as Mark Antony in a 19th-century production of *Antony and Cleopatra (Photographed by Napoleon Sarony)*

he says farewell and dies of a broken heart; Eros kills himself rather than Antony. What, then, has happened to the "greatest soldier of the world" (1.3.39)?

Antony resents young Caesar's inexperience (3.13)—he is 20 years Antony's junior—and childishly and unrealistically challenges Caesar to single combat. Yet, the future is with Caesar: The Soothsayer warns Antony that near Caesar "thy angel / Becomes afeard; as being o'erpower'd" (2.3.20–21). Caesar is endowed with "natural luck" (2.3.25), and Antony's luck has run out. In the past, as Antony admits, "mine hours were nice and lucky" (3.13.184); however, "my good stars, that were my former guides, / Have empty left their orbs, and shot their fires / Into the abysm of hell" (3.13.150–152). Hercules, Antony's guardian angel, has left him: As the second soldier indicates prior to the decisive battle, "'tis the god Hercules, whom Antony lov'd, / Now leaves him" (4.3.21–22), and "Fortune and Antony part" (4.12.19).

Toward the end of the play, Antony regains some of his former virtues. He is magnanimous to Enobarbus; indeed, it is Antony's generosity that breaks Enobarbus's spirit. Antony does "now not basely die" (4.15.57) but courageously: "A Roman, by a Roman / Valiantly vanquish'd" (4.15.59–60). But, throughout the play, he is suffering from a disease, his passion for Cleopatra, which obsesses his mind and which causes him to desert his public responsibilities, leave Rome for Alexandria, and fly from the battle to pursue Cleopatra. Duty is forsaken, and in Rome, Antony confesses: "I' the east my pleasure lies" (2.3.39). Caesar's final order that Cleopatra "shall buried by her Antony. / No grave upon the earth shall clip in it / A pair so famous" (5.2.356–358) is a recognition of the inevitable and of their mutual love. Without Cleopatra, Antony's life force has gone entirely: "Since Cleopatra died, / I have liv'd in such dishonor that the gods / Detest my baseness" (4.14.56–58).

Antony is a paradox. He has sacrificed his power, authority, home, duty, and friendship for an all-consuming infatuation. Despite this, his friends remain in the truest sense his followers. Enobarbus is heartbroken. Cleopatra is obsessed with memories of him and kills herself in order to join Antony: "Methinks I hear / Antony call" (5.2.281–282); "Husband, I come" (5.2.285). Perhaps the best summary of his qualities is provided by the soldier Maecenas: "His taints and honors / Wag'd equal with him" (5.1.30–31).

The reasons for Antony's return to the East, however, are not simply boredom with Octavia, infatuation with Cleopatra, and his incapability of living without her. His spirit in Rome is dominated by the superior Octavius Caesar. He needs to leave Rome to escape his younger rival's influence. In fact, in Act II, Scene 3, it is only after a discussion with the Soothsayer about his luck and his relationship with Caesar that Antony confesses that his pleasure lies in the East. There is the suggestion that he needs Cleopatra and Egypt, that his luck has run out in Rome, which he leaves for political reasons and out of considerations of honor.

Much is learned about Antony from other characters, such as Philo, Decretas, the Soothsayer, Caesar, Enobarbus, and Scarus, among others. In the final act, Antony is immortalized in Cleopatra's poetry. We learn early on in the play that he is a creature of sexual excess, of loss of control and reason, who is not what he was. As Philo says, "he is not Antony" (1.1.57). Caesar's first words in the play condemn Antony's loss of masculinity, his excess (1.4), and Scarus observes that after Actium "Experience, manhood, honor, ne'er before / Did violate so itself" (3.10.23–24). Antony has self-awareness, reflecting, when hearing of his wife's death, that "the present pleasure / By revolution lowering, does become / The opposite of itself" (1.2.129–131), and after Actium, he tells his supporters to go to Caesar because he has "fled myself (3.11.7)"—that is, he has lost his reason.

Antony has overflowed his measure, whereas Caesar has remained full and controlled. The metaphor from a measuring cup is an appropriate one. Antony has lost his sense of self to Cleopatra. Caesar fills the vacuum left in imperial power, control, and authority by Antony's loss of self. The Roman aspect of Antony asserts itself when he rounds on Cleopatra, telling her "Though you can guess what temperance should be / You know not what it is" (3.13.126–127). Caesar says that Antony wastes time through reveling (1.4), and none of the other commentators on Antony's activities deny this. Antony is generous and is compared with Jove; Caesar is mean and controlled. Antony has deliberately chosen to lose himself. Caesar fights for supremacy of an empire, of control and self-assertion. Appropriately, Antony's friends desert him and go over to Caesar, for Antony's desire is to submerge his identity in that of Cleopatra.

Ironically, in the play, displays of the ancient Roman virtues associated with the mythological figures of Mars and Hercules come not from Caesar but from accounts of how Antony used to be, as given by Caesar. In Act I, Scene 4, Caesar recalls Antony's former heroism, bravery, and endurance; his warrior qualities. Antony accepts his rival's challenge to fight a naval battle, but not from strategic considerations. He ignores the opposition of his loyal companions to the idea: Honor probably demands that he fight Caesar at sea, and Cleopatra wishes it. Antony's motives are, as has been remarked, often unclear and at times complex. His decisions are affected, as he recognizes, by his moods. He tells his attendants after Actium to "take the hint / Which my despair proclaims" (3.11.18–19).

In Act IV, Scene 2, Antony takes farewell of his servants, thus anticipating an unfavorable outcome to the following day's battles. The scene displays his absolute honesty, interpreted by Enobarbus as mental aberration: "'Tis one of those odd tricks which sorrow shoots / Out of the mind" (4.2.13–14). Influenced by Enobarbus's objections, he then attempts to perform, to erect a facade of optimism and to "drown consideration" (4.2.45). Thus, he is easily influenced, but only too self-aware. Antony's weaknesses are admirably summed up by Pompey in Act II, Scene 1. He is a "libertine" (2.1.23) who is tied up, entrapped "in a field of feasts" (2.1.23) that "keep his brain fuming" (2.1.24). Antony's "honor" and self are being consumed; his sexual desires have led him into becoming a servant to Cleopatra. The first lines of the play indicate his lack of masculinity. Cleopatra even puts on his clothing, and in a most un-Roman manner wears "his sword Philippan" (2.5.23). Caesar comments that "the queen of Ptolemy" (1.4.6) is not "more womanly than he" (1.4.7). Antony believes that Cleopatra has emasculated him, saying to Mardian, "O, thy vile lady! / She has robb'd me of my sword" (4.14.21). Enobarbus appropriately sums up what has happened to Antony, remarking that he "only, that would make his will / Lord of his reason" (3.13.4–5).

At the end of the drama, Cleopatra, obsessed with the dead Antony, sees him as a superhuman whose "legs bestrid the ocean" (5.2.81). His physical body after his death is "this case of that huge spirit" (4.15.93). Throughout, Antony has desired to escape himself, his background, responsibilities, his time. He escapes himself through entrapment to Cleopatra. His death represents his own and, ultimately, Cleopatra's final material liberation: At the conclusion of the drama, Antony's spirit has finally soared triumphant.

Cleopatra

Cleopatra is a paradox. Her creation and conception are not without their problems. She is a mature, attractive, sensual, and complex woman. Her emotional and spiritual progress throughout the play is a central aspect of her characterization. At the beginning, she cannot endure "A Roman thought" (1.2.86), yet by the end, she dies "after the high Roman fashion" (4.15.91). Her love, Antony, is possessive, yet she, too, depends on it. When he is dead, her thoughts dwell on their past together, and her final words echo with "O Antony!" (5.2.310). We witness her experiencing diverse changes of mood, yet at the culmination of the drama, she has "nothing / Of woman in me: now from head to foot / I am marble-constant" (5.2.238–240). Variety and inconstancy, as she admits, are part of her femininity.

Cleopatra is compared with "the goddess Isis" (3.6.17), whose costume she wears is "cunning past man's thought" (1.2.150); frequently, especially with Antony and Octavius Caesar, she is shown in situations where manipulative cunning is required. She manages to trick Caesar in the end and is able to kill herself. Cleopatra is an "enchanting queen" (1.2.133), a "great Fairy" (4.8.11), a "witch" (4.13.47). She is described as "a strumpet" (1.1.13), as a "wrangling Queen! / Whom everything becomes" (1.1.49–50) and in whom "every passion fully strives / To make itself, in thee, fair and admired!" (1.1.51–52). She is an "Egyptian dish" (1.1.126) and a "whore" (3.6.68). Antony is by no means her first lover. Images of fertility remain with her, as do those of sensuality. In her, "witchcraft join with beauty, lust with both"

Cleopatra thinks of Antony in Act I, Scene 5 of *Antony and Cleopatra*. This print is from Charles Heath's 1848 edition of *The Heroines of Shakspeare: Comprising the Principal Female Characters in the Plays of the Great Poet.* (Painting by K. Meadows; engraving by J. Brown)

(2.1.22). Other characters tell us that she loves to "wander through the streets" (1.2.54); Enobarbus claims that he "saw her once / Hop forty paces through the public street" (2.2.239). When first she became Julius Caesar's lover she was brought to him rolled up in a mattress (2.6).

She appears in 16 of the 40 scenes and dominates Acts I and V. Even when absent from the stage, her presence is felt. From the opening speech of the play, we learn of her "tawny front" (1.1.6) entrapment of a great general, and "gipsy's lust" (1.1.9). Her entrance is a grand one, accompanied by Antony, "her Ladies, the train, with Eunuchs fanning her" (1.1). Her authority and command are emphasized. She dominates Antony in the opening exchanges, although her first line, "If it be love indeed, tell me how much" (1.1.14), points to the forever searching, questing, explorative nature of her personality. She teases, wrangles, and resists the definite, while playing on Antony's weak spots, reminding him of his wife and public responsibilities. Much of her power rests in her physical beauty and eroticism, suggested by the impact she has on others, by her imagery and actions, and by unspoken body language. In Act I, Scene 2, she seems to be searching for Antony, is displeased with him for his "Roman thought" (1.2.86), sends Enobarbus to find him, learns that he is approaching, and refuses to see him. She is as ever-changing as the Nile flowing through Egypt. In Act I, Scene 3, she is still searching for Antony and sends a servant to observe him and deliberately to mislead him as a demonstration of her power over him: "If you find him sad / Say I am dancing" (1.3.4–5). She is maneuvering him, playing elaborate games with him, says she is "sick and sullen" (1.3.6), threatens to collapse, rails at him, recalls their past love, denounces his falsity—all in an effort to get him to remain with her and not return to Rome. She commands the stage, leaving Antony impotently attempting to utter a few words: "my dearest queen . . . The gods best know" (1.3.17–24). Indeed, it is not until line 41 that he is able to speak at length. Cleopatra deliberately angers Antony, accusing him "of excellent dissembling" (1.3.80). However, sensing that she has gone too far and been too egotistic, she reaffirms her love for Antony and his importance in her life: "my oblivion is a very Antony" (1.3.92). Her very identity and existence revolve around him, yet such revelations of utter dependence are rare.

Cleopatra's true self and sense of self are defined through erotic encounter. She recalls her past sexual adventures with great men; she is no inexperienced girl but carries "Phoebus's amorous pinches black / And wrinkled deep in time" (1.5.29–30). She is, in other words, the representative of the eternal ancient amorous energies of sensuality, lust, eroticism, and lasciviousness. She has a dark sensuality, suggesting that she has a dark face or is mysteriously sensual. Her language and thoughts are also violent, representative of her frustration. Yet, she loyally and dutifully writes to Antony every day.

Act II, Scene 1 contains Pompey's description of her as "Salt Cleopatra" (2.1.21), as lustful with "waned" (2.1.21), pale sensuous "lip" (2.1.21). It contrasts with Enobarbus's description of her in Act II, Scene 2. Pompey draws attention to her mysterious qualities of "witchcraft" (2.1.22), which have entrapped Antony; Enobarbus focuses on her mystical magnificence, comparing her to the goddess Venus. Cleopatra is charismatic; she illuminates everything, and it is no wonder that Antony has fallen victim to her spell. Enobarbus's description follows Antony's agreement to marry Octavia and places Octavia, and Antony's politically motivated expediency, in a wider context. Octavia pales into insignificance beside Cleopatra, who is described as a paradox in nature. It is Cleopatra who animates nature with love, and not nature animating her. The waters follow Cleopatra's barge "As amorous of their strokes" (2.2.207) It is her barge that burns the water, not the Sun burning both. In a sense, she has replaced the Sun as the source of life. Her sexuality is unending, unsatisfying, for she "makes hungry / Where most she satisfies" (2.2.247–248).

Some of the negative sides of her character are displayed in Act II, Scene 5, when the messenger appears with news of Antony's marriage to Octavia. She wants the messenger to tell her what she wants to hear, deliberately bribing him with gold, almost provoking him to lie, then she will not listen to him. When she hears that Antony has married Octavia, she turns upon the messenger like a hurt, spoiled girl, curses him, and physically assaults him. Aware of her own immense power, she draws a knife on him. Her anger reflects her feeling for Antony, which has caused a total loss of dignity and self-control before social inferiors. Her vanity has been assailed: Jealous and inquisitive, she asks for pity and sends out for information about Octavia's physical features. In this scene, Cleopatra's moods have oscillated from bawdy merriment, to hopeful expectation, violent anger and rage, self-pity, jealousy, and recollection of her power over Antony.

By Act III, Scene 3, when the messenger returns with information about Octavia, Cleopatra has had time to calm herself. Naturally, the messenger is afraid of Cleopatra and in order to praise her, deliberately gives an unflattering picture of her rival. He is appealing to Cleopatra's acute vanity, especially where her physical appearance is concerned. Octavia has qualities that Cleopatra holds in low estimation—brown eyes, low forehead, low voice, undignified walk, and lack of animation. Cleopatra interrupts his description and turns it to her own advantage in order to satisfy her ego. She allows herself to be flattered, deceived, and deluded. The messenger's report, a difficult one to give in the first place, and Cleopatra's deliberate distortions of it draw attention to an important theme in the play and one directly concerning Cleopatra—the theme of truth. We do not know if the messenger's report is true, whether it has any accuracy or not. Cleopatra's rearranged report, in which Octavia is "dull of tongue and dwarfish" (3.3.16) is inaccurate. She is playing games with the messenger, with herself, and with fidelity. Such games will lead to Antony's death. Antony continually exaggerates Cleopatra's attractions, and Enobarbus's view of her as Venus is hyperbolic. What is the truth about her? Or, is Cleopatra like the Nile, ever flowing onward and changing?

Act III, Scene 7 exhibits her willful stubbornness and the assumption of qualities usually associated with masculinity. She insists on aiding Antony with naval support and her physical presence at the scene of the battle. She brushes aside Enobarbus's wise counsel that her presence will reflect negatively on Antony's masculine reputation: "Your presence needs must puzzle Antony . . . He is already / Traduc'd for levity, and 'tis said in Rome / That Photinus, an eunuch, and your maids / Manage this war" (3.7.10–15). Enobarbus's words infuriated Cleopatra into an assertion of her role "as the president of my kingdom" (3.7.17). She is a monarch with responsibilities, which at times she reveals she has by no means forgotten. The confrontation between her and Antony after Actium is a powerful one. She now has total control over him

in personal and emotional terms as well as political terms. Cleopatra's influence has resulted in the loss of her personal and political honor. The scene reveals Cleopatra's depth of feeling for him, her acknowledgement of short-sightedness—"I little thought / You would have followed" (3.11.55–56) and her commitment to the defeated Antony, now at the nadir of his fortunes, whom she could so easily have rejected. In fact, with the loss of material power and with Antony's increasing dependence on Cleopatra, their love grows stronger, and they manage to transcend themselves and merge with each other.

Cleopatra's linking of her fate with Antony's is indicated by her use of the personal pronoun *we* in her question to Enobarbus at the beginning of Act III, Scene 13—"What shall we do, Enobarbus?" (3.13.1)—and her loss of confidence contained in her remark, "Is Antony, or we, in fault for this?" (3.13.3). Her contradictory, puzzling, and mysterious nature emerges in her behavior toward Thidias in this scene: Is she exercising gratuitous power over Caesar's representative, or does she really hope to manipulate him in order to influence Caesar? Is she planning to betray the luckless Antony, enjoying her power over people; is she possibly what Antony thinks she is—a treacherous whore who is going to turn to a more powerful lover? Or, is she in this scene playing tricks, this time with Thidias in order to deceive Caesar and remain faithful to Antony? By the end of Act IV, Cleopatra is again viewed by Antony in a dual role; she is as much a victim of his moods as he is of hers. On the one hand, when he returns triumphant from battle she is Antony's "nightingale" (4.8.20) and his "girl" (4.8.21), yet by Scene 12 she has "betrayed" (4.12.10) him and is a "Tripleturn'd whore" (4.12.13) whom in defeat he blames and sends from his sight. This rage and turn of mood provokes Cleopatra into what becomes her final, fatal trick. Her test of Antony's love—at the suggestion of Charmian, she will "send him word" (4.13.4) of her "death" (4.13.10)—in fact, literally leads to her lover's death. The lie misfires and has tragic consequences that she could not have foreseen.

The last scene of Act IV and the final scene of the play (5.2) are dominated by Cleopatra, in which, through great poetry, she reveals the extent of her passion for Antony, who has become her "lord" (4.15.23) and without whom she cannot live, being forced to "come" (4.15.30) to him in eternity. In fact, her imagination takes hold of her and controls her. Antony is posthumously transformed into a superhuman figure controlling the universe—in a sense, he controls her universe. She is theatrical to the last, dying as an empress, ordering her servants—loyal to her even in death: "Give me my robe, put on my crown, I have / Immortal longings in me" (5.2.278). In the manner of her death, she is all too human. Charmian observes after she has died that her "crown's awry / I'll mend it, and then play" (5.2.316–317). Appearances have to be maintained, even after death.

Cleopatra is human and fallible, but the loyalty she has commanded lives on. In her death, she joins Antony and defeats Caesar. Cleopatra's pride will not allow her to be led in triumph through Rome. But, even in these scenes, mystery surrounds her. The episode with Seleucus, her counselor, is curious: Is she using her treasurer to convince Caesar that she has no wish to die, or does she hope to survive in the world after Antony's death? If she does, then obviously her jewels will be useful. Or, is she again playing games—perhaps the jewels will pay for her funeral expenses?

Enobarbus

Hardly noticed in Shakespeare's main source—North's translation of Plutarch—Enobarbus is transformed into a major choric character in Shakespeare's play, speaking magnificent poetry and pointed prose. He is the closest of Antony's friends and regrets the hold Cleopatra has over him, yet his great account of her shows that he is by no means unaware of her attractions. Under the pressure of Antony's defeats, he deserts him but is forgiven. Full of self-recrimination, he finds a ditch in which to die: "the foul'st best fits / My latter part of life" (4.6.39–40). His dying words are to ask Antony for forgiveness, the thought that "the

world rank me in register / A master-leaver, and a fugitive" (4.9.24–25) and the repeated "O Antony! O Antony!" (4.9.26).

Domitius Enobarbus is present at many of the most important dramatic confrontations, and his language imaginatively re-creates Cleopatra's sensuous splendor. Described by Antony as "a soldier only" (2.2.13), Enobarbus takes pleasure in his tough, skeptical "plainness" (2.6.78). An illustration of his attitudes is seen during his first stage appearance. Alexas comments, "We'll know all our fortunes" (1.2.44) to which Enobarbus tartly and aptly replies, "Mine, and most of our fortunes to-night, shall be—drunk to bed" (1.2.44). He is close to Antony yet aware of his and others' deficiencies. His choric role as cynical commentator yet lyrical poet emerges in the lengthy second scene of Act II. During the meeting between the triumvirs, his prose quips are silenced by Antony; however, at the end of the scene, he is poetically praising Cleopatra in some of the most powerful lines of the play. On board Pompey's galley, it is Enobarbus who arranges the drunken triumvirs into a circle and, when they leave the galley, warns them "Take heed you fall not" (2.7.129).

Enobarbus has considerable political and personal insight. He is aware that Pompey's days are limited and tells Lepidus, Antony, and Caesar that "you hear no more words of Pompey" (2.2.110–111). He is aware that Octavia is "of a holy, cold, and still conversation" (2.6.122–123) and that these qualities will result in Antony's return "to his Egyptian dish again" (2.6.126). He is only too aware that Antony and Caesar are on a collision course, that "They'll grind the one the other" (3.5.15), and he dares to say that Cleopatra should not interfere in the fighting, telling her correctly that her "presence needs must puzzle Antony" (3.8.10). It is he, in his choric function, who announces the naval defeat: "To see 't, mine eyes are blasted" (3.10.4). He is loath to desert Antony, and his words "an ass, am onion-eyed," (4.2.35) spoken after Antony's farewell to his followers (4.2.24–34), ironically echo his much earlier prosaic quip after hearing of Antony's grief upon Fulvia's (his first wife's) death that "indeed the tears live in an onion that should water this sorrow" (1.2.174–175).

Enobarbus may be regarded as a projection of Antony's other self. His is the cool head and military cunning that Antony has lost to Cleopatra. His meanness and cynicism complement Antony's excesses and generosity. It is not without significance that he finally leaves Antony on the night the soldiers hear music taken to represent "the god Hercules, whom Antony loved" leaving him (4.3.21). Antony's generous reaction to Enobarbus's behavior reflects his positive characteristics. Even in the heat of battle, Antony sends Enobarbus's treasure to him. It is Enobarbus who helps to bring out the best side of Antony; as a soldier remarks to the forlorn Enobarbus, "Your emperor / Continues still a Jove" (4.6.29–30).

Octavius Caesar

At the start of the play, Caesar is one of the triumvirs; by the end, he is the sole ruler of the Roman Empire. He has liquidated his three political rivals: Pompey, Lepidus, and Antony. His primary consideration is to obtain power, even to the extent of using his own sister Octavia as a pawn in his political ambitions. He gives her to Antony in return for Antony's support in dealing with rebels. Emotionally, he remains unaffected by Cleopatra, though there are hints in Act III, Scene 6 that he is upset by what appears to be his sister's humiliation: she comes "not / Like Caesar's sister" (3.6.44) and is "abused / Beyond the mark of thought" (3.6.88–89). His egocentricity is apparent from his comments and behavior. At the end of the play, his remarks regarding Antony and Cleopatra focus upon himself and "his glory which / Brought them to be lamented" (5.2.360–361). The "solemn" (5.2.362) funeral rites he affords them are a tribute to himself as conqueror.

Caesar stands in stark contrast to Antony. Octavius is young, calculating, and efficient. His soldiers are respectful toward him, not affectionate. Even Antony admires the speed with which he arrives at Actium. On Lepidus's galley, his distaste is shown by his relative silence; he only turns down Menas's murderous plan to get rid of "These three world-sharers, these competitors," because the scheme would be discovered and he would be associated with such base conspiratorial behavior (2.7.78). Antony, before the decisive battle, orders "Scant not my cups" (4.2.21); he will "Be bounteous at our meal" (4.2.9). The calculating Caesar, on the other hand, will "feast the army" knowing they fight better on full stomachs (4.1.16). He places Antony's defecting forces "in the vant, / That Antony may seem to spend his fury / Upon himself" (4.6.10).

Having chosen to make an example of Cleopatra, he uses innumerable stratagems in order to get her to Rome, sending her false messages and a party of soldiers to creep up on her. He cannot anticipate Dolabella's personal loyalty to Cleopatra or Cleopatra's insight: "He words me, girls, he words me" (5.2.191). The meeting between Caesar and Cleopatra is that between a young calculating politician and an old seasoned one in a much weaker position. His rhetoric is met by her games with her treasurer Seleucus, whom she uses as a ploy to mislead Caesar into thinking that he might be able to bribe her into being held captive to Rome.

Caesar is a practical politician, cold and calculating. His speeches contain imaginative outbursts and are usually clear and to the point. He does show some generosity to the dead Antony, admitting "that our stars, / Unreconciliable, should divide / Our equalness to this" (5.1.46–48). Even in a funeral oration, he balances life's positives and negatives.

Octavia

Although Octavia has less than 30 lines in the play, she acts as a foil to Egypt's enigmatic queen. Cleopatra has the beauty and Antony's love; Octavia is used as a go-between by her brother and Antony. Enobarbus correctly foresees that she will only provoke Antony's lust for Cleopatra. Octavia is the embodiment of Roman qualities of duty and obedience; she is torn between her husband and her brother, aware of "no midway 'twixt these extremes at all" (3.4.18–19). It is Antony's assumed mistreatment of her that further enrages Caesar against him. A rejected wife who is used by her brother as a political pawn, she leaves the play in the middle of Act III. Her brother's Egyptian campaign, not to mention Antony and Cleopatra's love, is no concern of hers. Octavia is truly "A more unhappy lady" (3.4.12) whose disappearance from the action is scarcely noted. Perhaps her one achievement is to have aroused Cleopatra's curiosity and jealousy. Cleopatra sends spies to "Report the feature of Octavia; her years / Her inclination . . . The color of her hair" (2.5.112–114). She need not fear. Ultimately, Octavia's loyalties, affections, and duties are divided. In this split state of mind, she mutters to herself: "Husband win, win, brother" (3.4.18). Further, "Her tongue will not obey her heart, nor can / Her heart inform her tongue" (3.2.48–49).

Charmian and Iras

Charmian is close to her mistress Cleopatra, to whom she gives advice even on love affairs, and it is Charmian who suggests that Cleopatra mislead Antony into thinking that she is dead. Cleopatra tells Charmian the secret of the asp and the fig basket. It is Charmian who cools Cleopatra's temper after she has drawn a knife on the messenger who brings the news of Antony's marriage (2.5), but she can go so far and no further in teasing Cleopatra (1.5). Charmian knows Cleopatra's moods, flatters her, and placates her (3.3). To Charmian, Cleopatra confides that she "might sleep out this great gap of time / My Antony is away," to which Charmian replies, "You think of him too much" (1.5.5–7).

Charmian's devotion and loyalty are tested in death. She closes Cleopatra's eyes and puts her crown straight. Her words "Your crown's awry, / I'll mend it and then play" (5.2.316–317) echo Cleopatra's previous words to her to fulfill her duty, and ironically comment upon her fate to join Cleopatra in death. She has proved the truth of the Soothsayer's words, in the second scene of the play, that Charmian "shall outlive the lady whom you serve" (1.2.32).

Charmian asks for good fortune from the Soothsayer in Act I, Scene 2 of *Antony and Cleopatra*. Print from Malcolm C. Salaman's 1916 edition of *Shakespeare in Pictorial Art (Illustration by Rev. Matthew W. Peters)*

Iras usually accompanies Charmian on stage. Her longest speech is in prose in the second scene, echoing Charmian's words about Isis, cuckolding, and fortune. It is Iras who prepares Cleopatra for death and who initially and courageously takes the poison. Iras cannot see Cleopatra humiliated: "I'll never see 't! / for I am sure my nails / Are stronger than mine eyes" (5.2.222–223).

In the second scene, the Soothsayer maintains formal verse amid the prose banter of Charmian, Iras, and Alexas, whose lively talk and suggestive remarks deflate his seeming profundities. Charmian's first words in the play contain an elaborate sexual joke relating to lust, husbands, and cuckoldry. Indeed, sexual allusions and licentiousness are never far from what she says, and they underscore the hedonistic elements of the play with its overarching emphasis on pleasure. Her opening words are a pun on the meaning of the word *know* (both to gain knowledge and to have sexual experience). At times, Charmian has a choric function. For example, she tells the Soothsayer that she wishes to "be married to three kings in a forenoon, and widow them all" (1.2.28), thus drawing attention to the motif of insatiable appetites running through the play. Hyperbolic extravagance and fantastic imaginings are by no means confined to Antony and Cleopatra. Charmian desires "a child at fifty, to whom Herod of Jewry may do homage" (1.2.29–30). She asks the Soothsayer to "find one to marry me with Octavius Caesar, and companion me with my mistress" (1.2.30–31). Her allusions suggestively relate Egypt with the birth of Jesus (specifically, the three kings; 30 years after the events of the play, Jesus was born); King Herod; lines in Matthew 2:15 ("Out of Egypt have I called my son"); and prefigure the ending of the play, for it is Octavius Caesar who is to triumph. In this way, Charmian's suggestive wit not only places the action in a historical perspective but usurps the Soothsayer's function.

Likewise, Iras's banter is not to be ignored: Its wit, fun, and suggestive lustful innuendoes also mirror Cleopatra's desires and the atmosphere of the court. Iras's lines are full of ironic phallic suggestiveness. Alexas notes that "We'll know all our fortunes" (1.2.44), to which Enobarbus replies that "most of our fortunes to-night, shall be drunk to bed" (1.2.45–46). Iras's rejoinder, "There's palm presages chastity, if nothing else" (1.2.47) is wordplay on the palm of the hand used for telling fortunes, the noted healing qualities of the palm tree, and its associations with virtue. In short, Charmian and Iras are part of the fun-loving, hedonistic, bawdy, suggestive element of the play. They mirror their mistress, her lusts, desires, extravagant imaginings, theatricality, and sheer love of life. Their fate reflects Cleopatra's tragedy.

DIFFICULTIES OF THE PLAY

For many readers, the challenges and obstacles associated with *Antony and Cleopatra* involve Shakespeare's complex—although by no means

insurmountable—use of poetry and prose. Stylistically, *Antony and Cleopatra* is characteristic of Shakespeare's later plays, in which the ideas are suggestive and densely packed together. Hence, the play's difficulties almost universally involve the playwright's usage of language games, puns, and stylistic variations, not to mention the play's sheer multiplicity of characters and political factions.

Antony and Cleopatra also offers a number of challenges based on its references, both oblique and direct, to historical events. Today's readers are unlikely to have the standing knowledge of Roman culture and history that Elizabethan/Jacobean theatergoers possessed. In and of itself, this aspect of the play can be disorienting for some contemporary readers. Furthermore, as discussed in the "Background" section, there are a number of political and historical issues that are germane to our understanding of *Antony and Cleopatra*. Students who have read *Julius Caesar* are liable to be disoriented by the character shifts in Antony from the former play through *Antony and Cleopatra*. In *Julius Caesar*, Antony is a brilliant young political orator and military strategist; in *Antony and Cleopatra*, he is a middle-aged slave to love and passion.

Perhaps even more significant, the nature and context of Shakespeare's language shifts perceptibly from *Julius Caesar* through *Antony and Cleopatra*. In the former play, readers are treated to a psychological drama involving the vexing qualities of honor, friendship, and leadership. Yet, in *Antony and Cleopatra*, the political issues inherent in the earlier play are complicated by attention to the hyperbolic aspects of romantic love, as well as by a host of equally complex social and political machinations. In contrast with the relative straightforwardness of *Julius Caesar*, the result can be beguiling, as readers must contend with a variety of different social and political contexts. In *Julius Caesar*, Shakespeare's language exists as an express vehicle for analyzing rather blunt aspects of power and nobility. In *Antony and Cleopatra*, the playwright deploys language as an infinitely more subtle device for teasing out nuances associated with politics, romance, and sexual desire—often within the same particular passage or scene. As the discussion immediately below about the play's language demonstrates, Shakespeare represents these more complicated and subtle sociopolitical contexts by deploying a wide range of linguistic and dramatic devices in order to illustrate Antony and Cleopatra's increasingly tragic plight. And, as Shakespeare so memorably reveals, the fate of the ancient world hangs in the balance.

The Language of the Play: Poetry

With *Antony and Cleopatra,* there is a tendency away from excessive use of rhyming couplets. The basic poetic style is blank verse (lines of iambic pentameter usually unrhymed) upon which Shakespeare works infinite variations. Rhyming couplets are rare, marking the conclusion of a few scenes and emphasizing aphorisms. Antony's reflections on the death of his first wife Fulvia in Act I, Scene 2 achieve aphoristic couplet expression: "she's good, being gone / The hand could pluck her back that shov'd her on" (1.2.13–32). In Act I, Scene 3, Charmian's truism "I wish, forbear; / In time we hate that which we often fear" (1.3.11–12) uses the couplet form, and the song sung by the drunken triumvirs aboard Pompey's galley utilizes this couplet form so common in Shakespeare's earlier dramatic poetry.

Shakespeare employs a host of devices in order to afford the play with its sense of infinite variety, including metaphors, similes, mythological allusions, exaggerations, contrasts, violent language, variations in rhythms, extensive use of caesuras (pauses), and end-stopped and run-on lines. Philo's opening speech (1.1.1–2) provides a useful illustration of some of these techniques at work. It starts in the middle of a thought sequence and gets no further than "Nay" before there is a caesura; the first three words *"Nay, but this"* are monosyllabic and serve to stress the implications of the next word *"dotage,"* with its threefold sense of infatuation, old age, and sleepiness. Three *o* sounds close together in "dotage of our" convey the feelings of shock, surprise, and amazement being expressed by Philo. The subject of his attention, "our general,"

is introduced at the end of the iambic pentameter line, which is not end-stopped but run on. The poetry conveys this sense—"Nay, but this dotage of our general's / O'erflows the measure"—and immediately there is the image of excess, the metaphor being taken from a liquid that has overflowed the measuring cup. These opening lines of the play are also full of repetitions, antithesis, alliteration, and assonance: "files and musters," "glow'd like plated Mars," "now bend, now turn," "bend," "burst," "buckles," "breast," "bellows."

One feature of the play is the manner in which the characters use blank verse appropriate to their personalities and situations. Enobarbus's great description at the end of the second scene of Act II should be placed in the perspective of other magnificent poetry. Caesar's lines and choice of words are careful and lucid. Alliteration is a feature of his dislikes. Thus, in Act I, Scene 4, he compares Antony's Egyptian activities to those who "Pawn their experience to their present pleasure" (1.4.32), the repetitive alliterative *p* sounds effectively expressing his distaste. On some occasions, he expresses himself by the use of appropriate assonance. He tells Lepidus, "Let's grant it is not / Amiss to tumble on the bed of Ptolemy" (1.4.16–17), with the assonantal "to tumble" gaining effect from the reference to (another) Ptolemy, the brother of Cleopatra whom she had married. Hence, in Act II, Scene 7, amid the drunken revels on Pompey's galley, he scorns Antony's toast with the words, "It's monstrous labor when I wash my brain / And it grow fouler" (2.7.97–98). The contrast between washing and growing fouler conveys his contempt for the proceedings. Caesar's rare revelations of personal emotion tend to be displayed in apostrophic invocations addressed to absent persons. In Act I, Scene 4, he calls upon the absent Antony to "leave" his "lascivious wassails" (1.4.57) and in doing so uses powerful alliterative assonance. The surprise return of his sister Octavia to Rome without sufficient pomp and ceremony receives Caesar's short, clipped, run-on lines and a chronicle-like recital of kings who have pledged allegiance to Antony. Caesar's rhythmic emphasis stresses the relative power of Antony's allies and Caesar's enemies.

Antony's verse is more varied than Caesar's and often mixes hyperbole, alliteration, and elaborate word play. In his first extensive address to Cleopatra, the effect of the cosmic imagery is heightened by the use of caesura, run-on lines, and monosyllabic forms: "Let Rome in Tiber melt, and the wide arch / Of the rang'd empire fall" (1.1.34–35). The poetic line seems to collapse with the image of disintegration. Antony's verse is characterized by the mixture of opposites: Rome collapses into its own river; the Roman Empire collapses upon itself.

At times, the tone of his verse is reflective, meditative, and idiomatic. He justifies his treatment of Caesar's messenger, telling Caesar that "next day / I told him of myself, which was as much / As to have ask'd him pardon. Let this fellow / Be nothing of our strife" (2.2.82–83). Anger takes a hypermetric, repetitive, staccato form, followed by run-on lines, explanations, and rhetorical questions. Thidias unleashes his anger, and Antony orders:

> Whip him. Were't twenty of the greatest
>   tributaries
> That do acknowledge Caesar, should I find
>   them
> So saucy with the hand of she here,—what's
>   her name,
> Since she was Cleopatra? Whip him, fellows.
>   (3.13.101–104)

In the first line, the repetitive *w* sounds, the juxtaposition of monosyllables with complex syllabic words such as tributaries that run-on across the line to "acknowledge," the use of the shortened form "Were't" with the *t* sound emphasized eight times in the line are all assisted by the length of the lines, which extend beyond the standard iambic pentameter. Similarly, the largely monosyllabic third line is reinforced by a caesura, repetitive *s* sounds, a lengthening out of the line that runs on into the next. The poetic techniques serve to emphasize changes of mood within Antony, whose

anger with Thidias is but an expression of his frustration.

Cleopatra's poetry is a reflection of her changeability, of her "infinite variety" of temperament and mood. Short sentences of dialogue at the beginning of Act I, Scene 3—"Where is he?" (1.3.1), "If you find him sad / Say I am dancing" (1.3.4–5), "I am sick, and sullen" (1.3.14)—give way to considerably larger sentences:

> Help me away, dear Charmian, I shall fall.
> It cannot be thus long, the sides of nature
> Will not sustain it (1.3.16–18).

Expressions of longing and emotion are controlled by caesura, balance, alliteration, and the use of the conjunctive "but":

> Eternity was in our lips, and eyes,
> Bliss in our brows' bent; none our parts so
>   poor,
> But was a race of heaven (1.3.36–38).

The balance of the middle iambic pentameter line achieved by monosyllabic repetitive *b* sounds is paralleled in the second half of the line by the *o* sound effects. Lengthy, reflective, almost conversational lines quickly give way to tormented, infuriated, hyperbolic utterances when Cleopatra turns upon the messenger, strikes him, and curses him in Act II, Scene 5. Lines of reflective internal monologue are found after Antony's death at the end of Act IV, and her verse fantasies concerning memories of Antony expressed in images in the second scene of Act V are but further examples of her rich, complex poetry.

The first speeches in the play by Antony and Cleopatra express their mutual fascination in a ritual-like verse chant of desire. Like two great operatic singers, they echo each other in short and long lines, rhetorical questions, self-absorption, hyperbole, and oxymoron—a familiar device of Elizabethan love poetry. Antony's assertions about their mutual love are deconstructed by Cleopatra's "Excellent falsehood" (1.1.42), which casts doubt on his values and motivation. Her skepticism gives way to his typical "Now for the love of Love, and her soft hours" (1.1.45). This note of contrast is at the heart of the poetry of *Antony and Cleopatra* and finds its clearest expression in the imagery of the play.

Prose and Its Functions in the Play

Prose in Shakespeare's plays generally represents a social—in addition to a dramatic—contrast, is frequently used by speakers from the lower social backgrounds, and is employed for comedy and parody. Found in nonformal situations, prose is used to indicate comedy and to provide comic relief. In *Antony and Cleopatra,* prose alternates with poetry and is not necessarily restricted to the comic or low-life characters. The Soothsayer uses poetry in Act I, Scene 2 to contrast with the prose ribaldry of Charmian, Iras, and Alexas. Their prose provides a tonal contrast to the Soothsayer's short staccato utterances.

The witty innuendoes serve to deconstruct the Soothsayer's role and convey a different attitude toward life, not one of foreboding, but one celebrating hedonism. Prose and verse intermingle in the same scene when Antony and Enobarbus talk. Enobarbus's speeches focus on women. Cleopatra is contrasted with the elements: "winds and waters sighs and tears . . . storms and tempests" (1.2.53). Similarly, Fulvia is contrasted with Cleopatra: She is but a tailor's plain smock that has been replaced with a new petticoat, and the "tears" (1.2.174) that Antony sheds for his dead wife merely "live in an onion" (1.2.174). Enobarbus's prose is complex, literary, and sophisticated. Its tone contrasts with Antony's lengthy poetic lines relating to his return to Rome. Enobarbus's prose places Antony's actions in their personal context, while Antony's poetry places his actions in a public and historical context in which "Sextus Pompeius / Hath given the dare to Caesar, and commands / The empire of the sea" (1.2.188–190).

Enobarbus's use of prose in Act II, Scene 2 may be divided into two sections. First, he interrupts the triumvirs with basic truths, with sharp one-liners such as "Would we had all such wives, that the men might go to wars with the women" (2.2.70). Antony's rejoinder silences Enobarbus—"Thou art a soldier only, speak no more" (2.2.113)—underscoring his percipience, honesty, and lack of pretension. Manipulating politicians do not like too much truth telling. Indeed, in *Antony and Cleopatra,* poetry is often the vehicle for preposterous suggestions and fantasies found, for instance, in Enobarbus's verse speech describing Cleopatra on her barge. This speech is prepared for by a prose exchange between Enobarbus, Maecenas, and Agrippa and forms the second example of the use of prose in this scene. These three characters are the representatives of the scheming triumvirs, who, well satisfied with Antony's agreeing to marry Octavia, have left the stage. The three less politically powerful beings take over, their statements providing a commentary and wider perspective on events. Egypt, according to Enobarbus, is "Half the heart of Caesar" (2.2.182); it's the part of the Roman Empire he desires. Enobarbus's account of the way time was spent in Egypt puns on the "light," provides a rhyming antithesis between "night" and "light," and is poetic in its implications of nonstop entertainment: "Ay, sir, we did sleep day out of countenance; and made the night light with drinking" (2.2.187).

The prose usage of Enobarbus is far from simple and contains arresting metaphors. When asked by Maecenas if it is true that in Egypt "Eight wild-boars roasted whole at a breakfast, and but twelve persons there" (2.2.189), his reply, "This was but as a fly by an eagle" (2.2.191), contains an arresting metaphor of contrast, size, and political implication, the eagle being a symbol for Roman imperial authority. Enobarbus's initial account of Cleopatra in prose before giving way to poetry succinctly summarizes Antony and Cleopatra's first encounter through the image of capturing his heart: "When she first met Mark Antony, she purs'd up his heart upon the river of Cydnus" (2.2.196). His image suggests both the closing together of the purse strings and of heart strings and conveys the persuasive power Cleopatra has over Mark Antony.

Ribald prose jokes between Enobarbus and Menas punctuate and provide a commentary on the tense confrontation between Caesar, Lepidus, Antony, and Pompey (2.6). Antony's rare intrusion into the medium is not without irony. The crocodile had the reputation for weeping over its victims: Lepidus is shortly to be a victim of intrigue; Antony, by the end of the play, will also be a victim. More conventional prose usage is represented by the servants in the banquet scene.

In Act III, Scene 5, prose conveys news and information concerning Caesar's manipulation of Lepidus. In Act IV, Scene 3, the soldiers guarding Cleopatra's palace use prose, which is punctuated by the mysterious sounds of music. In the final scene of the drama, the Clown, as befits his lowly status, uses prose that is not without elaborate punning and repetitions on worms and women. Again, his prose has a contrasting function, as it is followed by Cleopatra's impassioned verse packed with meaning and by her dramatic death.

KEY PASSAGES
Act I, Scene 1, 33–55

ANTONY. Let Rome in Tiber melt, and the wide arch
Of the rang'd empire fall! Here is my space.
Kingdoms are clay; our dungy earth alike
Feeds beast as man. The nobleness of life
Is to do thus [embracing], when such a mutual pair
And such a twain can do't, in which I bind,
On pain of punishment, the world to weet
We stand up peerless.

CLEOPATRA. Excellent falsehood!
Why did he marry Fulvia, and not love her?
I'll seem the fool I am not. Antony
Will be himself.

ANTONY. But stirr'd by Cleopatra.
Now for the love of Love and her soft hours,
Let's not confound the time with conference harsh;
There's not a minute of our lives should stretch

Without some pleasure now. What sport to-night?

CLEOPATRA. Hear the ambassadors.

ANTONY. Fie, wrangling queen!
Whom everything becomes—to chide, to laugh,
To weep; whose every passion fully strives
To make itself in thee fair and admir'd.
No messenger but thine, and all alone
To-night we'll wander through the streets and note
The qualities of people. Come, my queen;
Last night you did desire it. Speak not to us.

This brief passage presents themes, characters, and concerns that will be treated throughout the play. The opening speech contains different attitudes regarding Antony's relationship with Cleopatra; on the one hand, grand passion and infatuation are conveyed in the word *dotage,* while on the other hand, victimization and disapproval are communicated—a great Roman general "is become the bellows and the fan / To cool a gipsy's lust."

The passage is dominated by the entrance of Antony and Cleopatra, and the play immediately focuses attention on them. Their appearance emphasizes visual aspects present throughout and contrasts the somberly dressed Romans in their plate and armor with the voluptuous, "tawny" Egyptians. The contrast between Rome and Egypt, the conflict between Cleopatra and Antony, and Antony's internal psychological struggle between duty and passion are central preoccupations of *Antony and Cleopatra.*

Other important elements in the opening scene are the introduction of Antony and Cleopatra, the nature of her relationship with Antony, and Antony's worldly attitudes. Cleopatra is both dominant and skeptical. "If it be love indeed," she taunts Antony, "tell me how much." Antony, "the triple pillar of the world," is "transform'd / Into a strumpet's fool." Antony is prepared to renounce all for love: "The nobleness of life / Is to do thus."

The passage also offers a taste of the powerful, evocative imagery pervading the play. Antony wants "the wide arch / of the rang'd empire" to "fall" so that he can love. The world, the Roman Empire, can disintegrate so that Antony and Cleopatra can adhere to their romantic longings. Antony tells Cleopatra, "There's not a minute of our lives should stretch / Without some pleasure now." All is to be reduced and sacrificed for the sensual pleasure of the moment—hedonism (the pleasure principle) will predominate over duty and responsibility.

Act II, Scene 3, 10–39

ANTONY. Now, sirrah, you do wish yourself
  in Egypt?

SOOTHSAYER. Would I had never come
  from thence, nor
you thither!

ANTONY. If you can—your reason.

SOOTHSAYER. I see it in my motion, have it
  not in my
tongue; but yet hie you to Egypt again.

ANTONY. Say to me,
Whose fortunes shall rise higher, Caesar's or
  mine?

SOOTHSAYER. Caesar's.
Therefore, O Antony, stay not by his side.
Thy daemon, that thy spirit which keeps
  thee, is
Noble, courageous, high, unmatchable,
Where Caesar's is not; but near him thy angel
Becomes a fear, as being o'erpow'r'd. Therefore
Make space enough between you.

ANTONY. Speak this no more.

SOOTHSAYER. To none but thee; no more
  but when to thee.
If thou dost play with him at any game,

Thou art sure to lose; and of that natural luck
He beats thee 'gainst the odds. Thy lustre
  thickens
When he shines by. I say again, thy spirit
Is all afraid to govern thee near him;
But, he away, 'tis noble.

ANTONY. Get thee gone.
Say to Ventidius I would speak with him.
[Exit Soothsayer.]
He shall to Parthia—Be it art or hap,
He hath spoken true. The very dice obey him;
And in our sports my better cunning faints
Under his chance. If we draw lots, he speeds;
His cocks do win the battle still of mine,
When it is all to nought, and his quails ever
Beat mine, inhoop'd, at odds. I will to Egypt;
And though I make this marriage for my
  peace,
I' th' East my pleasure lies.

In this key passage, the Soothsayer can be regarded as a projection of Antony's subconscious fears about Caesar's good fortune. His presence deepens the atmosphere of the play and suggests ominous warnings of impending disaster. Antony's sudden change of mood and attitude, his decision to reverse his oaths, reflects his own insecurity, the power of the Soothsayer, and the hold Cleopatra has upon him. Note the contrasting imagery of demonology, the role of "natural luck," and an almost fatalistic sensuality. He says: "though I make this marriage for my peace, / I' the East my pleasure lies." Antony's "peace" is political, while his peace of mind and "pleasure" are personal and beyond the empire he normally controls. Where he is ruler—that is, within the Roman Empire—no personal satisfaction is to be found.

This scene is equally meaningful in terms of the manner in which it prefigures the historical, political, and social crises that lie before Antony. The ensuing political and military issues with Caesar loom large regarding Antony's fate, as does his abdication of the governance of his provinces in favor of the seductive, romantic world of Alexandria. As this passage so vividly demonstrates, Antony's mistakes, both present and future, are many, and they are largely of his own making. They are, indeed, as with the Soothsayer himself, the symbolic projection of his own most fervent anxieties and desires.

Finally, the scene also reveals the systemic failure of Antony's "better cunning" as his romance with Cleopatra evolves and deepens. Antony is clearly eschewing his duties and better judgment on nearly every level. He is ignoring the internal political issues in the empire that threaten to undo him, while simultaneously minimizing the military challenges that await him in Parthia. He is blinded by love and the pursuit of sensual pleasure to the extent that the once proud and formidable military ruler has become irrevocably weakened and vulnerable to a wide variety of threats—both internal and external, personal and political.

Act III, Scene 11, 51–74

ANTONY. O, whither hast thou led me,
 Egypt? See
How I convey my shame out of thine eyes
By looking back what I have left behind
'Stroy'd in dishonour.

CLEOPATRA. O my lord, my lord,
Forgive my fearful sails! I little thought
You would have followed.

ANTONY. Egypt, thou knew'st too well
My heart was to thy rudder tied by th' strings,
And thou shouldst tow me after. O'er my spirit
Thy full supremacy thou knew'st, and that
Thy beck might from the bidding of the gods
Command me.

CLEOPATRA. O, my pardon!

ANTONY. Now I must
To the young man send humble treaties, dodge
And palter in the shifts of lowness, who
With half the bulk o' th' world play'd as I
 pleas'd,

Making and marring fortunes. You did know
How much you were my conqueror, and that
My sword, made weak by my affection, would
Obey it on all cause.

CLEOPATRA. Pardon, pardon!

ANTONY. Fall not a tear, I say; one of them
 rates
All that is won and lost. Give me a kiss;
Even this repays me.
We sent our schoolmaster; is 'a come back?
Love, I am full of lead. Some wine,
Within there, and our viands! Fortune knows
We scorn her most when most she offers blows.

This passage illustrates a host of conflicting emotions, bitter regrets, and recriminations. The scene is undergirded by a vivid and overwhelming pathos. Antony, a man of great power, has been shamed and tamed by another. Antony is deranged and obsessed by Cleopatra. "O, whither hast thou led me, Egypt?" he wonders aloud. Bereft of dignity and reputation, Antony is now totally under Cleopatra's control. As he remarks to his beloved, "My heart was to thy rudder tied by th' strings, / And thou shouldst tow me after."

For Antony, memories of happier times give way to memories of misguided defeat and the desire for the affirmation of their love: "Give me a kiss, / Even this repays me," Antony tells Cleopatra. A host of powerful comments are scattered throughout the scene, ranging from "I / Have lost my way for ever" and "I have offended reputation / A most unnoble swerving" to "Fall not a tear, I say; one of them rates / All that is won and lost."

The scene reaches its fever pitch in its final lines, as Antony continues, tragically as it may seem, to seek out good fortune—"Fall not a tear, I say"—even as his world continues to crumble around him. He has become once and truly beguiled—"Love, I am full of lead"—and his enrapture has rendered him unable to act. "Fortune knows / We scorn her most when she offers blows," he observes, in one of his moments of great clarity in the play. And

Iras and Charmian catch Cleopatra as she falls, while Antony broods over his recent defeat in Act III, Scene 11 of *Antony and Cleopatra.* This is a print from the Boydell Shakespeare Gallery project, which was first conceived in 1786 and lasted until 1805. *(Painting by Henry Tresham; engraving by George Sigmund Facius)*

yet, for all of this realization and self-knowledge, Antony remains unable to revivify the great solder-leader of his military past. Antony's tragic fate, it seems, has been sealed.

Act IV, Scene 12, 9–49

ANTONY. All is lost!
This foul Egyptian hath betrayed me.
My fleet hath yielded to the foe, and yonder
They cast their caps up and carouse together
Like friends long lost. Triple-turn'd whore! 'tis
  thou
Hast sold me to this novice; and my heart
Makes only wars on thee. Bid them all fly;
For when I am reveng'd upon my charm,
I have done all. Bid them all fly; begone.
[Exit Scarus.]
O sun, thy uprise shall I see no more!
Fortune and Antony part here; even here
Do we shake hands. All come to this? The
  hearts
That spaniel'd me at heels, to whom I gave
Their wishes, do discandy, melt their sweets
On blossoming Caesar; and this pine is bark'd

That overtopp'd them all. Betray'd I am.
O this false soul of Egypt! this grave charm—
Whose eye beck'd forth my wars and call'd
  them home,
Whose bosom was my crownet, my chief end—
Like a right gypsy hath at fast and loose
Beguil'd me to the very heart of loss.
What, Eros, Eros!
[Enter Cleopatra.]
Ah, thou spell! Avaunt!

CLEOPATRA. Why is my lord enrag'd against
  his love?

ANTONY. Vanish, or I shall give thee thy
  deserving
And blemish Caesar's triumph. Let him take
  thee
And hoist thee up to the shouting plebeians;
Follow his chariot, like the greatest spot
Of all thy sex; most monster-like, be shown
For poor'st diminutives, for doits, and let
Patient Octavia plough thy visage up
With her prepared nails.
[Exit Cleopatra.]
'Tis well th'art gone,
If it be well to live; but better 'twere
Thou fell'st into my fury, for one death
Might have prevented many. Eros, ho!
The shirt of Nessus is upon me; teach me,
Alcides, thou mine ancestor, thy rage;
Let me lodge Lichas on the horns o' th' moon,
And with those hands that grasp'd the heaviest
  club
Subdue my worthiest self. The witch shall die.
To the young Roman boy she hath sold me,
  and I fall
Under this plot. She dies for't. Eros, ho!
[Exit Antony.]

This passage is the culmination of six scenes presenting differing viewpoints of the Battle of Actium's shifting fortunes. In the initial scenes, Antony is confident of victory, and he is reunited with Cleopatra. Enobarbus's desertion prefigures his death, and Antony's fortunes turn. Scenes 10 and 11 illustrate brief shifting perspectives, and this scene brings his fortunes to their lowest point. Antony's bitterness toward Cleopatra (based on the flimsiest of evidence, as he does not know for sure that she has cast her lot with Caesar) is related to his loss of power, sense of impotence, and sexual jealousy.

The passage teems with imagery extending from the solitary pine of the scene's opening line, Antony's vision of Cleopatra as a "Triple-turn'd whore," the vision of fawning dogs, and the tree ruined by its bark being removed to the culminating vision of self-destruction and fire. The invocation of Hercules ironically suggests a strength that has now gone from Antony, draws upon Antony's obsession with Cleopatra's infidelity (Hercules' wife was unfaithful), and the sacrifice of the innocents (Lichas the servant perhaps representing the innocent soldiers and sailors who have died, or perhaps Enobarbus).

This passage offers a powerful, destructive account of the disintegration that is beginning to overwhelm the play and its character. Antony wallows in the double betrayal of military defeat and his overwhelming suspicion of infidelity. "This foul Egyptian hath betrayed me. / My fleet hath yielded to the foe, and yonder / They cast their caps up and carouse together / Like friends long lost," he laments. On the one hand, his once proud military might has been vanquished in defeat, while on the other, his self-conscious pursuit of erotic pleasure and romantic bliss have contributed, it seems, to his most tragic and apparently indelible undoing.

DIFFICULT PASSAGES
Act IV, Scene 9, 1–23

CENTURION. If we be not reliev'd within
  this hour,
We must return to th' court of guard. The
  night
Is shiny, and they say we shall embattle
By th' second hour i' th' morn.

FIRST WATCH. This last day was
A shrewd one to's.

ENOBARBUS. O, bear me witness, night—

SECOND WATCH. What man is this?

FIRST WATCH. Stand close and list him.

ENOBARBUS. Be witness to me, O thou
  blessed moon,
When men revolted shall upon record
Bear hateful memory, poor Enobarbus did
Before thy face repent!

CENTURION. Enobarbus?

SECOND WATCH. Peace!
Hark further.

ENOBARBUS. O sovereign mistress of true
  melancholy,
The poisonous damp of night disponge
  upon me,
That life, a very rebel to my will,
May hang no longer on me. Throw my heart
Against the flint and hardness of my fault,
Which, being dried with grief, will break to
  powder,
And finish all foul thoughts. O Antony,
Nobler than my revolt is infamous,
Forgive me in thine own particular,
But let the world rank me in register
A master-leaver and a fugitive!
O Antony! O Antony! [*Dies*]

This passage's difficulty—as with so many scenes in *Antony and Cleopatra*—emerges in its subtlety, as well as the manner in which Shakespeare teases out its various strands of meaning. Enobarbus's death from a broken heart is rendered even more moving by his isolation and remorse and that his final words are "O Antony! O Antony!" The repetition of the name of the leader he has deserted, with the double *o* sounds, adds to the pathos. His final speeches combine images of melancholic depression with conceits revolving around psychological and material conditions of hardness. Alliteration and run-on lines effectively juxtapose with his self-destructing image when he remarks: "Throw my heart / Against the flint and hardness of my fault." As he dies and disintegrates, the line lengths break down and become shorter and shorter. Enobarbus's body is accorded some dignity by being borne "To th' court of guard" for "he is of note."

Of note is how such a brief scene of just over 30 lines, with an acting time of fewer than five stage minutes, conveys the passage of time. The first soldier, hearing the drums calling men to war, observes that "our hour / Is fully out." This scene is placed between Antony's anticipation of victory and his ensuing conversation with Scarus. The soldier's comment offers a double meaning: The lives of many will indeed be "fully out" before the Sun sets again.

Enobarbus's final, desperate words are the stuff of metaphor and melancholy. The very stuff of life—"a very rebel to my will"—no longer hangs upon him, and its release affords him the capacity to reveal the stolid truth of our existence, which, by its very nature, must be fleeting: "Throw my heart / Against the flint and hardness of my fault, / Which, being dried with grief, will break to powder, / And finish all foul thoughts." This powerful passage prefigures Antony's own leave-taking of this world. Will it be a heroic struggle or the stuff of pathetic and beguiling failure? Will Antony be reduced to innocuous dust and released to the wind, to be forgotten for all time? Or, can he still be a "master-leaver" of his own accord—the master military strategist whose star once shone across the Roman Empire?

Act V, Scene 2, 244–290

CLEOPATRA. Hast thou the pretty worm of
  Nilus there
  That kills and pains not?

  CLOWN. Truly, I have him. But I would not
  be the party that should desire you to touch
  him, for his biting is immortal;
  those that do die of it do seldom or never
  recover.

CLEOPATRA. Remember'st thou any that have died on't?

CLOWN. Very many, men and women too. I heard of one of them no longer than yesterday: a very honest woman, but something given to lie, as a woman should not do but in the way of honesty; how she died of the biting of it, what pain she felt—truly she makes a very good report o' th' worm. But he that will believe all that they say shall never be saved by half that they do. But this is most falliable, the worm's an odd worm.

CLEOPATRA. Get thee hence; farewell.

CLOWN. I wish you all joy of the worm.
[Sets down the basket]

CLEOPATRA. Farewell.

CLOWN. You must think this, look you, that the worm will do his kind.

CLEOPATRA. Ay, ay; farewell.

CLOWN. Look you, the worm is not to be trusted but in the keeping of wise people; for indeed there is no goodness in the worm.

CLEOPATRA. Take thou no care; it shall be heeded.

CLOWN. Very good. Give it nothing, I pray you, for it is not worth the feeding.

CLEOPATRA. Will it eat me?

CLOWN. You must not think I am so simple but I know the devil himself will not eat a woman. I know that a woman is a dish for the gods, if the devil dress her not. But truly, these same whoreson devils do the gods great harm in their women, for in every ten that they make the devils mar five.

CLEOPATRA. Well, get thee gone; farewell.

CLOWN. Yes, forsooth. I wish you joy o' th'
worm. [*Exit*]
[*Re-enter Iras, with a robe, crown, &c.*]

CLEOPATRA. Give me my robe, put on my
  crown; I have
Immortal longings in me. Now no more
The juice of Egypt's grape shall moist this lip.
Yare, yare, good Iras; quick. Methinks I hear
Antony call. I see him rouse himself
To praise my noble act. I hear him mock
The luck of Caesar, which the gods give men
To excuse their after wrath. Husband, I come.

Cleopatra commits suicide with her handmaidens in
Act V, Scene 2 of *Antony and Cleopatra*. (Illustration by
Balliol Salmon, 1906)

In this climactic passage, Cleopatra disguises her intentions from Caesar, while he attempts to conceal his plan to lead her in triumph through Rome. As with much of *Antony and Cleopatra*, the scene's challenges emerge from the multitudinous strands of meaning that coalesce in nearly every line.

In this instance, Cleopatra has won the final battle of mutual deception; she outwits Caesar (with assistance from Dolabella) and sees behind his charming exterior. The direct confrontation between them is something of an anti-climax and it is not inappropriate that their leading topic of conversation should center on finances—the symbol of power and authority. Theirs has been a political battle. Cleopatra chooses to die rather than to submit to Caesar's authority; hence, with her death, she triumphs over him. Her will has defied his wishes.

Cleopatra's memories of Antony contain images of sleep, dreams, nature, and sexual fecundity—"His delights / Were dolphin-like"—as well as the Sun and the Moon. Antony's love irradiated their universe and ennobled it:

His face was as the heavens, and therein stuck
A sun and moon, which kept their course, and
  lighted
The little O, the earth.

Cleopatra uses hyperbole to describe Antony; their conflicts are forgotten. Her memories and poetic descriptions serve to demonstrate that the imagination has triumphed over political realities. She does not attempt to ingratiate herself with Caesar, preferring imaginative over-romanticized memories of her time with Antony. In other words, reality has taken second place to dreams.

In this scene, the role of the Clown looms particularly large. The Clown with his basket is not an uncommon figure in Shakespearean tragedy. Parallels are found in the graveyard scene of *Hamlet* and the Porter episode in *Macbeth*. The Clown's prose episode acts as comic relief, a psychological release of tension; as a commentary on what is to take place (there are puns and jests on death and dying; the worm is a symbol of mortality); and as a commentary on the central themes of the play: appearance and reality, the brevity of human existence, and equality in death if not in life. Indeed, the Clown's very presence in such a climactic and important passage casts an ironic pall upon the proceedings as a lowly, comic figure dares to interrupt a scene of heightened nobility and pathos.

CRITICAL INTRODUCTION
TO THE PLAY

The historical time is 30 B.C., and Rome is the dominant power—the center of an empire stretching into Asia. It is controlled by a feuding triumvirate, the generals Octavius Caesar, Mark Antony, and Lepidus, who took over after the death of Brutus, Julius Caesar's chief assassin. The locations of the play represent several regions of the Roman Empire and the areas within its sphere of influence: Egypt (Alexandria, Cleopatra's palace); Rome (Caesar's house); Messina (where Pompey, who is challenging the triumvirs for power, holds sway); Misenum (where the confrontation between the Romans is enacted); Pompey's galley; Syria (a far-flung outpost of the empire); Actium; the surroundings of Alexandria and the environs of Cleopatra's palace; and Cleopatra's monument. Hence, the settings range from palaces and the house of Caesar at the heart of the imperial capital to outlying border posts, battlefields, ships, and Egyptian monuments. The principal location is Egypt; it is in Egypt that the Romans intrude, bringing their foreign attitudes, conventions, customs, and desires.

The Nile figures prominently, as do the Egyptian goddess Isis and the Roman mythological hierarchy. There seems to have been no scenery nor specific period costumes in Shakespeare's theater; however, in the final scene, Cleopatra asks Charmian to "cut her lace" so that she can breathe. In the opening scene, there is the stage direction "Enter Antony, Cleopatra, her Ladies, the Train, with Eunuchs fanning her," which helps to convey the exoticism of the Egyptian setting. References to cockfighting, gambling, coursing, hunting, falconry, cards, dice, and billiards point to an Elizabethan rather than a classical setting. Cleopatra uses "posts" and messengers. Banquets, toasts, much drinking, and a reference to the belief that washing in blood leads to rejuvenation all indicate the concerns of Shakespeare's contemporaries. Boy actors are mentioned in the line "some squeaking Cleopatra boy my greatness" (5.2.220), and Antony's "A haltered neck which does the hangman thank / For being yare about him" (3.2.135–136) contains an allusion to the Elizabethan habit of executing gentlemen by using the sword rather than hanging, which is reserved for the lower classes.

The setting, the historical time of the play, its social circumstances, and physical location provide the wellspring for the central antithesis of the drama: the confrontation between Egypt, which represents the values of love and hedonism, and Rome, which elevates public duty over private passion. Antony is a triumvir with administrative responsibilities; his setting is Rome and its empire, the soldiers, and the servants of the nation. His has been a background of internal intrigue and civil war, power struggles, and external threats. For him, the foundation of Roman imperial power must be maintained.

Cleopatra, too, is a ruler and a queen. She is surrounded by those who obey her every command and whim. No internal opposition to her is indicated. She has time to concentrate on personal passion set in her own surroundings and on passion having political implications. Antony, the object of her desires, is representative of Rome, the potential conqueror of her kingdom. Cleopatra's language reflects her sensuality, her desires, her longings, and her native land. Hers is a world of passions, storms, graves, flies, gnats, and the Nile.

Themes

Enumeration of some of the ideas and preoccupations exhibited in *Antony and Cleopatra* illustrates just how diverse, varied, and manifold are its themes: the limitations of the physical world, imagination, desires, inner struggle, experience, Egypt and Rome, the value of striving for power and material success, sexuality, hedonism and stoicism, the illusion that action brings results, political conflict for the control of an empire, value of the world and of love, duty against pleasure, what constitutes love, conflict, age versus youth, honor and decorum, extremes and compromise, entrapment, loyalty and desertion, power of a woman over a man, loss of self-control, truth versus lying, the past and the present, performance, theatricality, death and attitudes toward it, self-betrayal, and bungling.

Many of these themes are closely interrelated and conveyed through antithesis of character, setting, situation, images, and actions. They are enacted on the personal and private level, the microcosmic level, and on the general macrocosmic level. For instance, the age and youth theme transverses the conflict between two generals, Antony and Caesar, for supreme mastery of an empire and is associated with the past and with personal characteristics. Antony's generalship, his greatness as a military commander, is past, a memory to be recalled, as is shown in the opening lines of the play. Antony falls in the line of descent from Hercules, to Julius Caesar, to Pompey the Great. With his death dies the heroic past; the stage, the empire, is left to the uninspired, dull, younger Caesar: "there is nothing left remarkable / Beneath the visiting moon" (4.15.68–69). Antony, ironically, represents romantic hope, usually associated with youth and inexperience. With his death, "young boys and girls / Are level now with me" (4.15.67–68). It is the "scarce-bearded Caesar" (1.1.22), "the boy Caesar" (3.13.16), who opposes the love of Antony "the old ruffian" (4.1.4) for "a princess / Descended of so many royal kings" (5.2.324–325), whom "age cannot wither" (2.2.245) and who is "wrinkled deep in time" (1.5.3). Caesar spends his youthful years on the business of state. Love is related to the stupidity of old age. Antony's "white" hairs "reprove the brown for rashness" (3.2.14). Caesar personally objects to being called "boy" by Antony (4.1.1). Theirs is a personal conflict, as well as a power conflict and a fight for political dominance.

Antony and Cleopatra is a tragedy, a personal tragedy that differs slightly in degree of emphasis from classical tragedy, in which a noble person of high birth struggles against the inevitable. It is true that Antony's good luck, his protecting gods have deserted him, but his and Cleopatra's tragedy is of their own making. They sacrifice power, duty, and responsibility for love and desire. Antony is entrapped within a grand infatuation from which he cannot free himself. Cleopatra, too, is entombed with memories of Antony. Part of the tragedy is the witnessing of a once great hero defeated in a struggle for power by a younger, more calculating man. Another part of the tragedy lies in the display of self-destruction and personal humiliation by a man of honor and nobility. Caesar's messenger Thidias is whipped in order to satisfy Antony's personal frustration and sense of power over his inferiors. A brave general deserts in the middle of a battle in order to follow a woman. A great general is unable to kill himself properly and loses self-control. Dominated by a woman, he commits suicide as the consequence of a lie—a risky game of Cleopatra's. It has frequently been noted that *Antony and Cleopatra* has much in common with *Macbeth,* the Shakespearean tragedy immediately preceding it. In both, a great commander is manipulated by feminine influence and is consequently destroyed. Both tragic heroes turn on their women: Antony says, "This foul Egyptian hath betrayed me" (4.11.10). Both figures consequently achieve some measure of liberation in death.

An obvious theme of the play is the power of sexual passion over duty and responsibility—a theme expounded in the opening lines of the play: "The triple pillar of the world" (1.1.12). Antony has, according to Philo, become "transform'd / Into a strumpet's fool" (1.1.13). The play explores—through imagery, antithesis, settings, and contrasts—the nature of the relationship between Antony and Cleopatra as enacted against the background of the mystery and creative fecundity of Egypt and the Nile. At the conclusion of the tragedy, mutual suicide, the deliberate throwing off of the physical aspects of existence, brings the

Charmian covers Cleopatra with a sheet as Roman guards enter in Act V, Scene 2 of *Antony and Cleopatra,* in this print published by C. & F. Rivington in 1804. *(Illustration by Henry Fuseli; engraving by Robert Hartley Cromek)*

lovers together, reconciles them, and ensures the victory of imagination and poetry over reason and the material world.

Antony and Cleopatra enter death as lovers. Antony says, "I will be / A bridegroom in my death, and run into't / As to a lover's bed" (4.14.100–102). In the final act, Cleopatra imagines being with Antony in eternity. As she dies, she thinks she hears "Antony call" (5.2.282). He mocks "the luck of Caesar" (5.2.284), their spirits are together; "my other elements / I give to baser life" (5.2.287–

288). Her choice of suicide rather than submission shows the triumph of love and desire over physical reality. Love has ultimately triumphed.

Structure

Antony and Cleopatra's first scene identifies the central themes of the drama, including the clash between public duty and private passions; the conflict between Antony and Cleopatra, specifically, the differing values of Rome and Egypt; and the attempt to hold together a disintegrating empire. The shifting, contrasting settings illuminate these themes. Accepting the non-Shakespearean five-act division, it can be seen that a contrasting pattern emerges. The opening three Alexandrian scenes, with large casts, focus on Cleopatra and on Antony, torn between passion and the calls of Rome, then give way to the stark setting of Caesar's house in Rome. The play oscillates between these different settings, moving into short, sharp presentations of war viewed from different perspectives until the play's resolution in Cleopatra's monument. The structure reflects the play's themes: Egypt and Rome; Cleopatra and Antony against Caesar; the battle and Antony's defeat; Cleopatra's retreat into her monument; Caesar's victory; truth and illusion; the past and the present; theatricality; love, war, and death; death as unity and release; and entrapment. The world of Egypt is dominated by Cleopatra; the world of Rome, by Caesar. Antony, alas, is torn between the two.

Pointedly, Shakespeare did not expressly divide the play into acts; these demarcations were added in editions published after his death. Yet, the action of the play is divided between scenes in Egypt and in Rome. There are domestic scenes and important political ones. Crucial events are described rather than actually presented on stage. Enobarbus describes Cleopatra's arrival; for example, she does not literally float down the Nile on her barge (on the Elizabethan stage this would be an impossibility). The sea battle at Actium occurs offstage; the audience is told about it. Hence, telling is crucial to the structure. Cleopatra is not actually seen as Isis; we, the audience, are told about her habit of dressing up as Isis. We do not witness Antony's return to Egypt but learn about it from Caesar—a far from unbiased source. Structurally, groups of characters from the very opening scene of the play onward discuss the actions of other characters, usually those of the main protagonists, Antony and Cleopatra. These two appear on stage and then leave it; minor characters then appear and discuss what has happened. *Antony and Cleopatra* is the second longest of Shakespeare's works, exceeded in textual length and duration of performance only by *Hamlet.* It is rarely performed in its entirety on stage.

Analysis of act and scene and the enumeration of character appearance help clarify the play's structure. *Antony and Cleopatra* consists of some 42 scenes. Antony appears in 22 of these, that is, in just over half. Eleven of these appearances are with Cleopatra, five with Caesar. In terms of his appearances, the structural balance reflects Antony's preoccupation with Cleopatra, rather than with his Roman imperial responsibilities. Cleopatra appears in 16 scenes, only five of these being without Antony's physical presence, and even in those, he dominates her thoughts. In structural terms, then, Antony dominates the relationship. However, more than half of the action of the play is preoccupied, not with the private passion of Antony and Cleopatra, but with the power struggle for control of the empire between Antony and Caesar, as well as the attempt to keep the empire intact against internal and external threats.

The opening scenes are representative of structural principles at work throughout the play. Demetrius and Philo, hardly central protagonists, provide disparate views on the actions of the main characters. They contrast Rome and Egypt, what Antony may have become, and what he once was. After some 14 lines, Antony and Cleopatra appear, and the spotlight switches to them. The first of the eight messengers, few of whom are well treated, arrives to introduce the world of Rome, politics, and responsibility, only to be dismissed and then sought for again by Antony. Thus, repetition is a crucial pattern of the play's structure. Indeed, there is a structural principle of varied repetition represented by the messengers and their dismissal, desertion and loyalty, innumerable leave-takings, returns and departings, handshakes and the kissing of hands—so easily misunderstood (such as Antony's misreading of Thidias's kissing of Cleopatra's hand). To return to the opening scene, the lovers appear, confirm, or deconstruct what has been said about them. They leave, and at the end of the scene, Philo and Demetrius reassume their role as observers. The pattern is one of repetition, gossip, observation, and departure.

Significantly, the first three scenes focus on love. They are set in Cleopatra's Alexandrian palace, and the realities of Rome and Antony's public responsibilities intrude only in terms of the news of his wife's death and in what we are told his role was in her demise. Seemingly without transition, the action then moves to Rome and to the seat of Roman imperial power, Caesar's house, but the focus of attention is still on news of Antony's activities. There are various ways of viewing this structure, which operates on principles of contrast. Act I provides an introduction to the main characters and to Antony's conflict. Act II witnesses Antony's attempt to resolve his conflict by appeasing Caesar and accepting his Roman duties. Act III can be seen as the one in which the structural crisis occurs, for Antony is defeated at Actium—a defeat that is not witnessed, only related. Act IV sees Antony's efforts to salvage victory from defeat, his return to Egypt, subsequent defeat in battle, and death. Act V concentrates on Cleopatra and her fantasies. Throughout this organization, there emerges a pattern of central action, or the retelling of it, followed by secondary and tertiary comments on the action. For instance, the events at Actium (3.10–11) are related rather than shown. Enobarbus and Scarus comment, Canidius comments, and then Antony comments on his own actions after they have taken place. Crucial to the overall structure is observation, suggestion, and perhaps untruth. (After all, it is Cleopatra's deliberate lie to Antony, her calculated tricking of him into believing that she is dead, which directly results in his actual death.)

As the play proceeds, a change in structural procedure takes place. In Act V, the focus narrows from the previous shifting perspectives and episodic nature to concentrate on Cleopatra. There is a startling contrast between the 15 scenes of the densely populated Act IV and the two scenes that make up Act V. The last scene of the drama is nearly twice as long as the hitherto longest scene in the play: Scene 13 of Act III—also concentrating on Cleopatra and Antony—which features some 201 lines. Act V, Scene 2 has 365 lines and is dominated by Cleopatra. The setting is fixed, and she is entrapped at her monument to which even Caesar must go. Cleopatra's thoughts are dominated by Antony, whom she longs to join. Viewed in these terms, the structure of the play is episodic, contrasting, shifting in perspective, and illuminating themes. Differing viewpoints and spotlights finally focus on Cleopatra and her desire to die in order to be reunited with her dead lover. In the end, all that Caesar can do is to ensure that Cleopatra is reunited—at least spiritually—with Antony.

Style and Imagery

Imagery dominates the play. Caroline Spurgeon comments in her classic work *Shakespeare's Imagery* that *Antony and Cleopatra* is pervaded by "images of the world, the firmament, the ocean, and vastness generally. That is the dominating note in the play, magnificence and grandeur" (352). She isolates the word *world* as occurring 42 times in the play. The idea of space, of the universe, is seen as an astronomical frame of reference to the heavens, the Sun, the Moon, the stars, night and day, and to nature—the seasons, the tides, the rain, the air, the clouds. Spurgeon writes that the image of the "world" is "continually employed in a way which increases the sense of grandeur, power, and space, and which fills the imagination with the conception of beings so great that physical size is annihilated and the whole habitable globe shrinks in comparison with them" (352). Thus, the literal-minded Caesar's telling Antony in Act II, Scene 2 "if I knew / What hoop should hold us staunch from edge to edge / O' the world, I would pursue

it" (2.2.121–123) synthesizes the domestic image of the hoop—of a metal band holding a barrel together—with that of keeping together the two rivals fighting for the possession of the universe.

According to Spurgeon, a similar emotion is expressed in Octavia's "amazing picture of the gigantic gaping fissures in the round globe packed tight with the bodies of the dead" (353), conveyed in her observation on the feud between her husband and brother: "Wars 'twixt you twain would be / As if the worlds should cleave, and that slain men / Should solder up the rift" (3.4.30–32). Enobarbus has a vision of Antony and Caesar scrapping over the world as if it is "a pair of chaps, no more" (3.5.13), as if it were merely a morsel of food to be devoured. The fight between Antony and Caesar is for "the world." Antony is a "triple pillar of the world" (1.1.12), and his "sword / Quarter'd the world, and o'er green Neptune's back / With ships made cities" (4.14.58–60). In short, imagery involving the sword, destruction, mythology, and the nature of human construction coalesce throughout these lines.

Images of the heavens and nature are largely confined to the Egyptian scenes. The images of the world traverse the Egyptian and Roman settings, the exotic and the mundane. Many of Cleopatra's images are from nature and range from the animate to the inanimate worlds. Persuading Antony that she is not cold toward him, she ranges from "heaven" to "hail," to "poison" to "stone," to "womb" to "storm," to "flies and gnats of the Nile" (3.13.171). Her imagery, like that of nature itself, extends from the microcosm, the smallest gnat and fly, to the heavenly macrocosm. Natural images extend from Antony's general "Then must thou needs find out new heaven new earth" (1.1.17) to his more specific "The April's in her eyes, it is love's spring / And these the showers to bring it on" (3.2.43–44). These images include the Soothsayer's maxim—"In nature's infinite book of secrecy / A little I can read" (1.2.10–11)—and encompass Cleopatra's hyperbolic imaginative plea "O sun / Burn the great sphere thou mov'st in, darkling stand / The varying shore o' the world" (4.15.10–12). They are associated with both Antony and Cleopatra. The fecundity of nature, its diversity and richness, serves to explain their relationship. The nature of the imagery serves to pinpoint the contrast in *Antony and Cleopatra* between the competing worlds of Rome and Egypt and their conflicting sets of dramatic values.

Mythological and classical figures—Greek and Roman, Isis, Venus, Jupiter, Apollo, Bacchus, Mercury, Juno, Hercules, Dido, Aeneas, and others—are associated with Antony and Cleopatra. When Antony is dead, Cleopatra conceives him in terms of Jove. She laments, "Had I great Juno's power, / The strong-wing'd Mercury should fetch thee up / And set thee by Jove's side" (4.15.35–37). Antony is transformed in her imagination into a gigantic god whose "legs bestrid the ocean" and whose "rear'd arm / Crested the world" (5.2.81–82). Cleopatra is associated with the Moon—she is "our terrene moon," Shakespeare writes (3.2.158)—dresses up "in the habiliments of the goddess Isis" (3.6.17), and is linked with the planet Venus (1.5). In classical mythology, Venus became the lover of Mars, the Roman god of war. Antony is the representative of Rome. He is a demi-Atlas (1.5), and on three different occasions, he is cast in the image of Hercules (1.3, 2.5, and 4.10).

This brief image survey should not be concluded without drawing attention to one of the most important image patterns in the play. *Antony and Cleopatra* is perhaps Shakespeare's most sensual and bawdy drama. Clearly, images of swords rising and falling—Antony physically rising and falling and disintegrating—have sexual implications. A major theme of the drama is the passion between Antony and Cleopatra and its tragic consequences. Their passion is suggested through many kinds of images ranging from allusions to mythological lovers—including Nissus, Cupid, and Narcissus—to overt references to cuckoldry. In Act I, Scene 5, Cleopatra's desire "to drink mandragora" (1.5.4) represents her wish to "sleep out this great gap of time" (1.5.5) while her lover is away. It is also an evocation of desire, mandragora being a sleep-ing draft made from the mandrake plant, which is shaped like the male sexual organs. In the same scene, the castrated, "unseminared" slaves who surround Cleopatra represent Antony's glaring physical absence from her world.

EXTRACTS OF CLASSIC CRITICISM
Samuel Johnson (1709–1784) [Excerpted from the preface to *The Plays of William Shakespeare,* Johnson's landmark 1765 work. Johnson's remarks would inform centuries of literary critics about the nature and characterization of *Antony and Cleopatra*.]

This play keeps curiosity always busy, and the passions always interested. The continual hurry of the action, the variety of incidents, and the quick succession of one personage to another, call the mind forward without intermission from the first act to the last. But the power of delighting is derived principally from the frequent changes of the scene; for, except the feminine arts, some of which are too low, which distinguish Cleopatra, no character is very strongly discriminated. [John] Upton, who did not easily miss what he desired to find, has discovered that the language of Antony is, with great skill and learning, made pompous and superb, according to his real practice. But I think his diction not distinguishable from that of others: the most tumid speech in the play is that which Caesar makes to Octavia.

The events, of which the principal are described according to history, are produced without any art of connexion or care of disposition.

William Hazlitt (1778–1830) [Excerpted from *Lectures on the Literature of the Age of Elizabeth and Characters of Shakespear's Plays* (1817). With great skill and imagination, Hazlitt joined Johnson and Coleridge among the most deft and erudite of the Bard's early expositors.]

This is a very noble play. Though not in the first class of Shakespeare's production, it stands next to them, and is perhaps the finest of his historical plays, that is, those in which he made poetry the organ of history, and assumed a certain tone of character and sentiment, in conformity to known facts, instead of trusting to his observations of general nature or to the unlimited indulgence of his own fancy. What he has added to the actual story, is upon a par with it. His genius was, as it were, a match for history as well as nature, and could grapple at will with either. The play is full of that pervading comprehensive power by which the poet could always make himself master of time and circumstances. It presents a fine picture of Roman pride and Eastern magnificence: and in the struggle between the two, the empire of the world seems suspended, "like the swan's down-feather, / That stands upon the swell at full of tide, / And neither way declines."

The characters breathe, move, and live. Shakespeare does not stand reasoning on what his characters would do or say, but at once *becomes* them, and speaks and acts for them. He does not present us with groups of stage-puppets of poetical machines making set speeches on human life, and acting from a calculation of problematical motives, but he brings living men and women on the scene, who speak and act from real feelings, according to the ebbs and flows of passion, without the least tincture of pedantry of logic or rhetoric. Nothing is made out by inference and analogy, by climax and antithesis, but every thing takes place just as it would have done in reality, according to the occasion. The character of Cleopatra is a masterpiece. What an extreme contrast it affords to Imogen! One would think it almost impossible for the same person to have drawn both. She is voluptuous, ostentatious, conscious, boastful of her charms, haughty, tyrannical, fickle. The luxurious pomp and gorgeous extravagance

of the Egyptian queen are displayed in all their force and lustre, as well as the irregular grandeur of the soul of Mark Antony. Take only the first four lines that they speak as an example of the regal style of love-making:

CLEOPATRA. If it be love indeed, tell me how much?

ANTONY. There's beggary in the love that can be reckon'd.

CLEOPATRA. I'll set a bourn how far to be belov'd.

ANTONY. Then must thou needs find out new heav'n, new earth.

The rich and poetical description of her person beginning—

"The barge she sat in, like a burnish'd throne,
Burnt on the water; the poop was beaten gold,
Purple the sails, and so perfumed, that
The winds were love-sick"—

seems to prepare the way for, and almost to justify the subsequent infatuation of Antony when in the sea-fight at Actium, he leaves the battle, and "like a doating mallard" follows her flying sails.

Few things in Shakespeare (and we know of nothing in any other author like them) have more of that local truth of imagination and character than the passage in which Cleopatra is represented conjecturing what were the employments of Antony in his absence—"He's speaking now, or murmuring—*Where's my serpent of old Nile?*" Or again, when she says to Antony, after the defeat at Actium, and his summoning up resolution to risk another fight—"It is my birthday; I had thought to have held it poor; but since my lord is Antony again, I will be Cleopatra." Perhaps the finest burst of all is Antony's rage after his final defeat when he comes in, and surprises the messenger of Caesar kissing her hand—

"To let a fellow that will take rewards,
And say God quit you, be familiar with,
My play-fellow, your hand; this kingly
 seal,
And plighter of high hearts."

It is no wonder that he orders him to be whipped; but his low condition is not the true reason: there is another feeling which lies deeper, though Antony's pride would not let him show it, except by his rage; he suspects the fellow to be Caesar's proxy.

Cleopatra (Sarah Bernhardt) speaks to a servant in a late 19th-century production of *Antony and Cleopatra*.

Cleopatra's whole character is the triumph of the voluptuous, of the love of pleasure and the power of giving over every other consideration. Octavia is a dull foil to her, and Fulvia a shrew and shrill-tongued. What picture do those lines give her—

"Age cannot wither her, nor custom stale
Her infinite variety. Other women cloy
The appetites they feed, but she makes
 me hungry
Where most she satisfies."

What a spirit and fire in her conversation with Antony's messenger who brings her the unwelcome news of his marriage with Octavia! How all the pride of beauty and of high rank breaks out in her promised reward to him—

"There's gold, and here
My bluest veins to kiss!"

She had great and unpardonable faults, but the grandeur of her death almost redeems them. She learns from the depth of despair the strength of her affections. She keeps her queen-like state in the last disgrace, and her sense of the pleasurable in the last moments of her life. She tastes luxury in death. After applying the asp, she says with fondness—

"Dost thou not see my baby at my
 breast,
That sucks the nurse asleep?
As sweet as balm, as soft as air, as gentle.
Oh Antony!"

It is worthwhile to observe that Shakespeare has contrasted the extreme magnificence of the descriptions in this play with pictures of extreme suffering and physical horror, not less striking—partly perhaps to place the effeminate character of Mark Antony in a more favourable light, and at the same time to preserve a certain balance of feeling in the mind. Caesar says, hearing of his rival's conduct at the court of Cleopatra,

> "Antony,
> Leave thy lascivious wassels. When thou
>   once
> Wert beaten from Mutina, where thou
>   slew'st
> Hirtius and Pansa, consuls, at thy heel
> Did famine follow, whom thou fought'st
>   against,
> Though daintily brought up, with
>   patience more
> Than savage could suffer. Thou did'st
>   drink
> The stale of horses, and the gilded
>   puddle
> Which beast would cough at. Thy palate
>   then did deign
> The roughest berry on the rudest hedge,
> Yea, like the stag, when snow the pasture
>   sheets,
> The barks of trees thou browsed'st. On
>   the Alps,
> It is reported, thou didst eat strange
>   flesh,
> Which some did die to look on: and all
>   this,
> It wounds thine honor, that I speak it
>   now,
> Was borne so like a soldier, that thy
>   cheek
> So much as lank'd not."

The passage after Antony's defeat by Augustus [Octavius Caesar], where he is made to say—

> "Yes, yes; he at Phillipi kept
> His sword e'en like a dancer; while I
>   struck
> The lean and wrinkled Cassius, and
>   'twas I
> That the mad Brutus ended"—

is one of those fine retrospections which show us the winding and eventful march of human life. The jealous attention which has been paid to the unities both of time and place has taken away the principle of perspective in the drama, and all the interest which objects derive from distance, from contrast, from privation, from change of fortune, from long-cherished passion; and contrasts our view of life from a strange and romantic dream, long, obscure, and infinite, into a smartly contested, three hours' inaugural disputation on its merits by the different candidates for their theatrical applause.

The latter scenes of *Antony and Cleopatra* are full of the changes of accident and passion. Success and defeat follow one another with startling rapidity. Fortune sits upon her wheel more blind and giddy than usual. This precarious state and the approaching dissolution of his greatness are strikingly displayed in the dialogue of Antony with Eros.

ANTONY. Eros, thou yet behold'st me?

EROS. Ay, noble lord.

ANTONY. Sometime we see a cloud
  that's dragonish,
A vapour sometime, like a bear or lion,
A towered citadel, a pendant rock,
A forked mountain, or blue promontory
With trees upon't that nod unto the
  world
And mock our eyes with air. Thou hast
  seen these signs,
They are black vesper's pageants.

EROS. Ay, my lord.

ANTONY. That which is now a horse,
  even with a thought
The rack dislimns, and makes it
  indistinct
As water is in water.

EROS. It does, my lord.

ANTONY. My good knave, Eros, now
  thy captain is
Even such a body. . . .

This is, without doubt, one of the finest pieces of poetry in Shakespeare. The splendor of the imagery, the semblance of reality, the lofty range of picturesque objects hanging over the world, their evanescent nature, the total uncertainty of what is left behind, are just like the mouldering schemes of human greatness. It is finer than Cleopatra's passionate lamentation over his fallen grandeur, because it is more dim, unstable, unsubstantial. Antony's headstrong presumption and infatuated determination to yield to Cleopatra's wishes to fight by sea instead of land, meet a merited punishment; and the extravagance of his resolutions, increasing with the desperateness of his circumstances, is well commented upon by Oenobarbus [Enobarbus]:

"I see men's judgments are
A parcel of their fortunes, and things
  outward
Do draw the inward quality after them
To suffer all alike."

The repentance of Oenobarbus after his treachery to his master is the most affecting part of the play. He cannot recover from the blow which Antony's generosity gives him, and he dies broken-hearted, "a master-leaver and a fugitive."

Shakespeare's genius has spread over the whole play a richness like the overflowing of the Nile.

Samuel Taylor Coleridge (1772–1834)
[Excerpted from *Lectures and Notes on Shakspere,* Coleridge's important 1818 study. Coleridge's lec-

tures succeeded in reinvigorating Shakespeare's reputation and influence for a new generation of readers and writers.]

Shakspeare can be complimented only by comparison with himself: all other eulogies are either heterogeneous, as when they are in reference to [Edmund] Spenser or [John] Milton; or they are flat truisms, as when he is gravely preferred to [Pierre] Corneille, [Jean] Racine, or even his own immediate successors, [Francis] Beaumont and [John] Fletcher, [Philip] Massinger, and the rest. The highest praise, or rather form of praise, of this play, which I can offer in my own mind, is the doubt which the perusal always occasions in me, whether *Antony and Cleopatra* is not, in all exhibitions of a giant power in its strength and vigour of maturity, a formidable rival of *Macbeth, Lear, Hamlet,* and *Othello.* "Feliciter audax" is the motto for its style comparatively with that of Shakspeare's other works, even as it is the general motto of all his works compared with those of other poets. Be it remembered, too, that this happy valiancy of style is but the representative and result of all the material excellencies so expressed.

This play should be perused in mental contrast with *Romeo and Juliet;*—as the love of passion and appetite opposed to the love of affection and instinct. But the art displayed in the character of Cleopatra is profound; in this, especially, that the sense of criminality in her passion is lessened by our insight into its depth and energy, at the very moment that we cannot but perceive that the passion itself springs out of the habitual craving of a licentious nature, and that it is supported and reinforced by voluntary stimulus and sought-for associations, instead of blossoming out of spontaneous emotion.

Of all Shakspeare's historical plays, *Antony and Cleopatra* is by far the most wonderful. There is not one in which he has followed history so minutely, and yet there are few in which he impresses the notion of angelic strength so much;—perhaps none in which he impresses it more strongly. This is greatly owing to the manner in which the fiery force is sustained throughout, and to the numerous momentary flashes of nature counteracting the historic abstraction. As a wonderful specimen of the way in which Shakspeare lives up to the very end of this play, read the last part of the concluding scene. And if you would feel the judgment as well as the genius of Shakspeare in your heart's core, compare this astonishing drama with [John] Dryden's *All For Love*.

MODERN CRITICISM AND CRITICAL CONTROVERSIES

Contemporary critical discussions regarding *Antony and Cleopatra* take a wide variety of interpretive tacks and perspectives. Much has been written, for example, about Shakespeare's complex characterization of Antony. For A. C. Bradley, Antony is "neither a mere soldier nor a mere sensualist. He has imagination, the temper of an artist who revels in abundant and rejoicing appetites," who "feasts his senses on the glow and richness of life, flings himself onto its mirth and revelry and yet feels the poetry in all this." This vantage point runs contrary to older criticism from critics like William Hazlitt, who saw "irregular grandeur" in Antony's soul. In the play, Antony's moodiness, his self-indulgence, his irresponsibility, his depressions exhibit themselves until his final ecstatic union in death with Cleopatra. His being is determinedly hers. Yet, all is not clear, and there are actions of his that are difficult to explain—or actions pointing to serious deficiencies in his character. For instance, it can be argued that his words to Octavia are sincere and that he intends to be faithful to her. Antony may well be taken in by his own words. His action in marrying her is an adoption of the easiest line of political expediency. Or, perhaps he deliberately marries her with no intention of being loyal to her?

Shakespeare's characterization of Cleopatra has also been the subject of ongoing critical discussion. It is a critical commonplace, of course, that notions of mystery and enigma belong to Cleopatra and are part of her power. It is unclear whether she, in fact, ordered her ships at Actium to join Caesar's. Such a charismatic character has not been without her defenders. Bradley has commented on the issue regarding her deliberate betrayal of Antony at Actium: "Can we feel sure that she would not have sacrificed him if she could have saved herself by doing so? It is not even certain that she did not attempt it. Antony himself believes that she did—that the fleet went over to Caesar by her orders. That she and her people deny the charge proves nothing. The best we can say is that, if it were true, Shakespeare would have made that clear" (301). She resists formulation and characterization. On stage, Cleopatra is dominating, witty, crude, passionate, erotic, jealous, manipulating; but she is also transformed from a lover—who teases and flirts with Antony—into a tragic character dying heroically. She is accorded great poetry of memory and imagination, focused not merely on herself but on Antony. The paradox surrounding her does not disappear. Her mind is no longer fixed on the earth but has leaped into dreams of "an emperor Antony" (5.2.75). With his death, "there is nothing left remarkable / Beneath the visiting moon" (4.15.68–69). Life is no longer worth living: Antony and Cleopatra are indissolubly united for posterity.

In addition to Shakespeare's characterization schemes for the play's two principal characters, *Antony and Cleopatra* receives considerable critical attention for its complicated narrative structure and multiplicity of textual vantage points. For Anne Barton, this aspect of the play renders it a "narrative catastrophe," while for other critics it affords *Antony and Cleopatra* a taut, heightened sense of drama as the narrative's various political intrigues and machinations come to their fruition in the final acts. Indeed, the play's vexing, peripatetic structure has long been an issue of considerable critical interest. Bradley, for example, notes the relative lack of action in the opening three acts of the drama. Shifting perspectives, viewing characters from what we as an audience are told about their activities, seems to be the activating structural principle. The great 18th-century critic Samuel Johnson argued that *Antony and Cleopatra*'s episodic structure was one of its virtues: "The continual hurry of the action, the variety of incidents, and the quick succession of one personage to another call the mind forward without intermission from the first act to the last. But the power of delighting is derived principally from the frequent changes of the scene." John Dryden—the late-17th-century dramatist who rewrote *Antony and Cleopatra* and adapted it for the Restoration stage—believed that there were many irrelevant scenes in the drama. His play, entitled *All for Love, or The World Well Lost* (1677), replaced Eros, Enobarbus, and other characters regarded as minor with one figure, Ventidius, who is upgraded from his Shakespearean role in Act III, Scene 1.

Such issues continue to resonate in the present. For Frank Kermode, *Antony and Cleopatra* "ranks among Shakespeare's supreme achievements." In Kermode's estimation, the play's complex structure emanates from the romance that exists at its core. As Kermode defines it, romance offers "a mode of exhibiting the action of magical and moral laws in a version of human life so selective as to obscure, for the special purpose of concentrating attention on these laws, the fact that in reality their force is intermittent and only fitfully glimpsed." In the "reality" of *Antony and Cleopatra,* the play's multitudinous political rivalries and warring factions exist as expansive subplots of the principal characters' passionate, albeit tendentious and highly eroticized, romance. In so doing, Shakespeare establishes a feverish cauldron and sense of chaos, an uncertain world that, for the most part, inevitably leads to Antony and Cleopatra's undoing. For critics such as Marjorie Garber, this is the express result of the play's narrative structure: "The design of *Antony and Cleopatra* is to offer the audience, repeatedly, a series of set pieces describing the incomparable and indescribable lovers, against which their human (and actorly) avatars must strive

to compete, and fail." It is the inexorable tragedy of *Antony and Cleopatra* that its lovers must fall short in their quest for greatness in a world in which reason and emotion cannot possibly coexist—even in spite of our most sincere wishes that it might be otherwise.

THE PLAY TODAY

Antony and Cleopatra continues to capture the imaginations of present-day readers. As with previous generations, contemporary students of the play remain fascinated with the narrative's unbridled romance—particularly in terms of Cleopatra's lavish, unvarnished eroticism. Harold Bloom aptly describes her as perhaps Shakespeare's finest female character among his entire canon, not merely for her sensual nature, but also for her undeniably enigmatic and mysterious qualities. If nothing else, she is ineffably human in the whimsy, courage, and frailty of her identity construction. The same can be said for Antony and Cleopatra's sense of romantic desperation, and for their overriding conflict with the duty and responsibilities inherent in their regal stations—an aspect of the play that resonates throughout the ages. Not surprisingly, contemporary perspectives of the play are based on its extensive production history, especially in terms of its filmic representations. While many readers have become acquainted with the play via Jonathan Miller's 1981 BBC production of *Antony and Cleopatra* starring Colin Blakely and Jane Lapotaire, it has enjoyed an abiding sense of notoriety after the release of Joseph L. Mankiewicz's big-budget *Cleopatra* (1963). The zenith of Hollywood's "sword and sandal" epics, *Cleopatra* featured Elizabeth Taylor's searing, legendary turn as the Egyptian queen alongside Richard Burton's bravura performance as Antony. In itself, the phenomenon of Mankiewicz's *Cleopatra* is emblematic of our enduring and timeless fascination with the ill-fated lovers from Rome and Egypt. When it comes to Antony and Cleopatra—and to our larger appetites for romance and tragedy—our most fervent desires, as with those of Shakespeare's ancient lovers, can simply never be sated.

FIVE TOPICS FOR
DISCUSSION AND WRITING

1. **Reason versus emotion:** What are some examples of the overarching clash between reason and emotion in the play? Which characters manifest reason-driven and emotion-driven behaviors? How do these divergent behavioral traits among the play's principal characters affect the tragic outcome of *Antony and Cleopatra*?

2. **Personal tragedy:** Critics often describe *Antony and Cleopatra* as a personal tragedy, rather than as a classical tragedy in which a person of noble birth struggles with an inevitable downfall. What are the intensely personal qualities that contribute to the principal characters' self-destruction in the play? How do issues of unfettered self-control and infatuation clash with notions of duty and responsibility in the personal tragedies inherent in *Antony and Cleopatra*?

3. **Rome versus Egypt:** How does the play's setting impact the nature and direction of *Antony and Cleopatra*? How do the contrary political and social aspects of Rome and Egypt impact the principal characters' plights? How do these disparate settings impinge upon the characters' worldviews (and, ultimately, their fortunes) in *Antony and Cleopatra*?

4. **Sexual passion:** What are the signal roles of sexual passion and erotic love in the play? How does the intensely passionate nature of Antony and Cleopatra's love affair impact the political and personal decisions of each? How do the play's qualities of romance and eroticism ultimately affect the outcome of *Antony and Cleopatra*?

5. **The limitations of the physical world:** How do the limitations of the physical world impact the fortunes of Antony and Cleopatra—both as lovers and as human beings? More specifically, how are these limitations illustrated in the play in terms of the inherent conflicts between youth and age, past and present, and life and death, among other aspects? How do these limitations of the physical world impact the ultimate, tragic course of the play and the attendant fates of its principal characters?

Bibliography

Adelman, Janet. *The Common Liar: An Essay on* Antony and Cleopatra. New Haven, Conn.: Yale University Press, 1973.

Andrews, John F., ed. *William Shakespeare:* Antony and Cleopatra. London: J. M. Dent, 1993.

Baldwin, T. W. *Shakespeare's Five-Act Structure.* Urbana: University of Illinois Press, 1963.

Barroll, J. Leeds. *Shakespearean Tragedy: Genre, Tradition, and Change in* Antony and Cleopatra. Washington, D.C.: Folger, 1984.

Barton, Anne. "Nature's Piece 'Gainst Fancy: The Divided Catastrophe in *Antony and Cleopatra.* In *William Shakespeare's* Antony and Cleopatra. Edited by Harold Bloom, 35–55. New York: Chelsea House, 1988.

Blake, N. F. *Shakespeare's Language: An Introduction.* London: Macmillan, 1983.

Bloom, Harold. *Shakespeare: The Invention of the Human.* New York: Riverhead, 1999.

———, ed. *William Shakespeare's* Antony and Cleopatra: *Modern Critical Views.* Philadelphia: Chelsea House, 1988.

Bradley, A. C. *Oxford Lectures on Poetry.* London: Macmillan, 1909.

Brown, J. Russell, ed. *Shakespeare's* Antony and Cleopatra: *A Casebook.* London: Macmillan, 1968.

Bullough, Geoffrey. *Narrative and Dramatic Source of Shakespeare.* Vol. 5: *The Roman Plays.* London: Routledge, 1965.

Cantor, Paul A. *Shakespeare's Rome: Republic and Empire.* Ithaca, N.Y.: Cornell University Press, 1976.

Charney, Maurice. *How to Read Shakespeare.* New York: McGraw-Hill, 1971.

———. *Shakespeare's Roman Plays: The Function of Imagery in the Drama.* Cambridge, Mass.: Harvard University Press, 1963.

Clough, Arthur Hugh, ed. *Plutarch: The Lives of the Noble Grecians and Romans.* New York: Modern Library, 1932.

Deats, Sara Munson, ed. Antony and Cleopatra: *New Critical Essays.* London: Routledge, 2005.

Drakakis, John, ed. *Antony and Cleopatra.* London: Macmillan, 1994.

Garber, Marjorie. *Quotation Marks*. London: Routledge, 2002.

Harald, William Fawkner. *Shakespeare's Hyperontology: Antony and Cleopatra*. Madison, Wis.: Fairleigh Dickinson University Press, 1990.

Hazlitt, William. *Lectures on the Literature of the Age of Elizabeth and Characters of Shakespeare's Plays*. London: Dyce, 1817. Reprint, London: George Bell and Sons, 1900.

Johnson, Samuel, ed. *The Plays of William Shakespeare*. London: J. and R. Tonson, 1765.

Kermode, Frank. *Shakespeare's Language*. New York: Farrar, Straus & Giroux, 2001.

Kujawínska-Courtney, Krystyna. *The Interpretation of the Time: The Dramaturgy of Shakespeare's Roman Plays*. Victoria, Canada: English Literary Studies, 1993.

Lamb, Margaret. Antony and Cleopatra *on the English Stage*. Madison, N.J.: Fairleigh Dickinson University Press, 1980.

Leavis, F. R. *The Living Principle*. London: Chatto & Windus, 1975.

Lewis, Cynthia. *Shakespeare's Four Antonios, Their Contexts, and Their Plays*. Newark: University of Delaware Press, 1997.

Madelaine, Richard, ed. *Antony and Cleopatra*. Cambridge: Cambridge University Press, 1998.

Male, David A. *Antony and Cleopatra*. Cambridge: Cambridge University Press, 1984.

Markels, Julian. *The Pillar of the World:* Antony and Cleopatra *in Shakespeare's Development*. Columbus: Ohio State University Press, 1968.

Partridge, Eric. *Shakespeare's Bawdy*. London: Routledge, 1968.

Rose, Mark, ed. *Twentieth-Century Interpretations of* Antony and Cleopatra: *A Collection of Critical Essays*. Upper Saddle River, N.J.: Prentice-Hall, 1977.

Rosenberg, Marvin. *The Masks of Anthony and Cleopatra*. Edited by Mary Rosenberg. Newark: University of Delaware Press, 2006.

Schanzer, Ernest. *The Problem Plays of Shakespeare: A Study of* Julius Caesar, Measure for Measure, Antony and Cleopatra. New York: Schocken, 1963.

Spurgeon, Caroline. *Shakespeare's Imagery and What It Tells Us*. Cambridge: Cambridge University Press, 1935.

Thomas, Vivian. *Shakespeare's Roman Worlds*. London: Routledge, 1989.

Traci, Philip J. *The Love Play of* Antony and Cleopatra: *A Critical Study of Shakespeare's Play*. The Hague, Netherlands: Mouton, 1970.

Traversi, D. A. *An Approach to Shakespeare*. London: Sands, 1957.

Wofford, Susanne Lindgren, ed. *Shakespeare's Late Tragedies: A Collection of Critical Essays*. Upper Saddle River, N.J.: Prentice-Hall, 1996.

FILM AND VIDEO PRODUCTIONS

Antony and Cleopatra. With Pauline Letts and Robert Speaight. Parthian, 1951.

Blackton, J. Stuart, and Charles Kent, dirs. *Antony and Cleopatra*. With Maurice Costello and Florence Lawrence. Vitagraph, 1908.

Carra, Lawrence, dir. *Antony and Cleopatra*. With James Avery and Sharon Barr. Bard, 1983.

Foy, Bryan, dir. *Anthony and Cleopatra*. With Ethel Teare and Phil Dunham. 1924.

Guazzoni, Enrico, dir. *Marcantonio e Cleopatra*. With Amleto Novelli and Gianna Terribili-Gonzales. Cinès, 1913.

Heston, Charlton, dir. *Antony and Cleopatra*. With Charlton Heston and Hildegarde Neil. Folio, 1972.

Mankiewicz, Joseph L., dir. *Cleopatra*. With Elizabeth Taylor, Richard Burton, and Rex Harrison. Twentieth Century Fox, 1963.

Miller, Jonathan, dir. *Antony and Cleopatra*. With Colin Blakely and Jane Lapotaire. BBC, 1981.

Rocha, Stephen, dir. *Alexandria: The Search for Cleopatra*. Vision, 1993.

Scoffield, Jon, dir. *Antony and Cleopatra*. With Richard Johnson and Janet Suzman. ITC, 1974.

The Spread of the Eagle. With Keith Michell and Mary Morris. BBC, 1963.

—William Baker and Kenneth Womack

As You Like It

INTRODUCTION

As You Like It is usually regarded as one of the finest of Shakespeare's comedies. Its main appeal for modern readers and audiences is in the interaction between the young lovers Rosalind and Orlando. The reason this relationship retains the capacity to amuse, shock, and delight is that it is by no means certain that it always involves a young man's desire for a young woman, or a woman's desire for a man. Rather, at times, it seems to celebrate the greater attractions of erotic role-play over straightforward romance.

Leaving a performance of the play, a viewer might ask, "At what point did Orlando know that the 'male' Ganymede was really Rosalind in disguise?" It could be said that a good performance will leave that question open. In the middle of the play, Orlando makes (verbal) love to Ganymede, pretending "he" is Rosalind, and he gets obviously excited while doing so. But, is he excited about the ideal (virtuous) Rosalind of his poetic imagination, or about the pretty youth Ganymede pretending to be a promiscuous Rosalind, or about Rosalind wearing man's clothes, or, indeed, about Rosalind dressed in man's clothes pretending to be a lascivious Rosalind? The answer, of course, is "as you like it." Readers and members of the audience are encouraged to explore their own fantasies, and erotic alternatives, as freely as Rosalind and Orlando explore them on the page and stage.

Obviously, *As You Like It* has other attractions besides the relationship between Rosalind and Orlando. Touchstone, the court clown, provides comic relief in his encounters with his fellow court exiles and with various rustic characters, especially in his lustful pursuit (and attempted outdoor marriage) of Audrey, the unattractive goatherd. In another subplot, Silvius, the lovelorn shepherd, pays court to the disdainful shepherdess Phoebe. Silvius protests that Phoebe kills him with her scornful glances. Predictably enough, she shoots him another harmful look and asks why he is still breathing. The artificiality of this section might make it less engaging to modern readers, but when Rosalind intervenes, disguised as Ganymede, she breathes the life of naturalism into the scenario. Offended by Phoebe's haughtiness, Rosalind/Ganymede advises the shepherdess that she should take whatever man she can get: "For I must tell you friendly in your ear: Sell when you can, you are not for all markets" (3.5.60–61). Phoebe then falls in love at first sight with the "boy" Ganymede, despite or because of his rude insults, adding another level to the play's investigation of the role of gender ambiguity in awakening desire.

By the middle of the play, Rosalind becomes a source of fascination for many audience members and readers. Many critics regard her as one of the first convincingly "real" female characters in English literature (being, in this regard, an update of Geoffrey Chaucer's Wife of Bath). Given over a quarter of the play's lines (a larger proportion than even that awarded Cleopatra), Rosalind energizes and destabilizes every scene in which she appears, no matter how conventional the basic situation. Her remarks, delivered usually in naturalistic, con-

Publicity photo from the 1936 Twentieth Century British Fox film adaptation of *As You Like It*, starring Laurence Olivier as Orlando.

greater artistic freedom or not, in *As You Like It*, Shakespeare chose not to provide a plot full of incidents, preferring to construct his drama around a series of witty conversational exchanges. As a result of this linguistic focus, there are aspects of the play that may leave modern readers cold, in particular the sophisticated play with linguistic registers and literary genres fashionable in late 16th-century Renaissance Europe—registers such as legal language and genres such as pastoral poetry, Petrarchan love poetry, allegorical epic, and so forth. Investigation of the play's use (and parody) of these forms can be extremely rewarding, however, offering an insight into the cultural mindset of the period. In any case, the play's exploration of the workings of desire and its abundant humor still make for a highly entertaining and very accessible work.

BACKGROUND

Playgoers of Shakespeare's time, like playgoers today, expected comedies to be amusing and end happily. An Elizabethan or Jacobean playgoer, however, would also expect a dramatic comedy's main characters to come from the middle or the bottom of the social ladder. These characters would engage in amusing situations; there would probably be some confusing mix-up, with hilarious consequences. This mix-up would eventually be happily resolved, and the whole thing would not only end in marriage but also feature the social advancement of its more deserving characters. The very title of *As You Like It* implies that such expectations will be fulfilled—the play's content, especially its ending, will be as we like it—and the play will be similar to comedies enjoyed in the past.

As You Like It is not only a comedy, however. In its opening acts, the play includes generic markers that inform its audience that they are watching a pastoral play. In Act I, Scene 1, Charles the wrestler compares the Forest of Arden, where the exiled Duke Senior now lives, to "the golden world" (113). By this term, Charles means the golden age of classical myth, a time when people lived at one with nature and there was no death,

versational prose, are almost always witty and frequently possess a cynical edge. As a result, she can make other characters in the play appear relatively one-dimensional, even (or especially) Orlando. Alternatively, a powerful Rosalind can inspire the actors playing the other roles to evince comparable variety and subtlety in their own parts.

Although *As You Like It* is usually seen as one of Shakespeare's most lighthearted romantic comedies, it is also, in a sense, one of his most experimental works. The play is generally held to have been written and first performed around 1599. Shakespeare, as a shareholder in his theater company, the Chamberlain's Men, had recently become a part owner of their new theater, the Globe. This circumstance gave him unprecedented freedom as a commercial playwright. Whether as a result of this sickness, unhappiness, or evil. As the more well-read members of contemporary audiences may have gathered—based on former acquaintance with Italian pastoral works such as Giovanni Battista Guarini's *Il Pastor Fido* and Torquato Tasso's *Aminta* (published together in England in 1591) and (more probably) with English pastoral works such as Philip Sidney's *Arcadia* and Thomas Lodge's *Rosalynd* (both published in 1590)—this reference signals that the play will alternate between two settings—the court and the countryside—comparing and contrasting them as moral environments, with the court usually represented as the site of corrupt "modern" values, such as selfish ambition, jealousy and greed, and the countryside as the home of timeless, "basic human" values such as sincerity, loyalty, and humility.

The way in which Shakespeare's courtly travelers are morally improved by their encounter with the countryside and its inhabitants is comparable to the manner in which a modern city-dweller might visit a health spa for a weekend in order to undergo a course of detoxification prior to returning to work on Monday with a determination to pursue healthier habits. This analogy, however, also shows an important difference between Renaissance pastoral therapy and a modern visit to a health spa: The Elizabethans and Jacobeans were principally concerned with the moral and political health of their institutions and relatively unconcerned about their personal physical health. Major social upheavals with disastrous consequences for many families, indeed, for entire sections of society, had occurred repeatedly during the lifetimes of the people attending Shakespeare's plays. Keeping the state healthy was of more pressing concern to an Elizabethan or Jacobean playgoer than keeping one's weight down.

As a result of this very same political instability, however, the late 16th and early 17th centuries in England also represented a period when the government (based around the court at London) exercised strict control over what could and could not be said in published works and in plays performed before the public. Nonetheless, if a dramatist such as Shakespeare wished to comment on the politi-

cal issues of his day, he could do this by writing in a genre or mode that was an accepted vehicle for presenting such material in a suitably disguised form. Pastoral was one of these vehicles. Certainly, it was well known to Renaissance readers that pastoral works were a time-honored method by which authors could safely reprove the perceived failings of their rulers. In his *Apology for Poetry* (published 1595), Sidney wrote:

> Is the [shepherd's] poor pipe disdained, which
> . . . can show the misery of people under
> hard lords or ravening soldiers? And [which
> can also show] what blessedness is derived
> to them that lie lowest from the goodness of
> them that sit highest; sometimes, under the
> pretty tales of wolves and sheep, [the pastoral
> poet] can include the whole considerations of
> wrongdoing (116).

As You Like It, therefore, as a pastoral play, contains suitably disguised ethical and political content aimed at improving the moral outlook of the members of its contemporary audiences, be they royal, aristocratic, middle class, or common. Of course, reading or watching the play 500 years later it is difficult to know with any degree of certainty which particular contemporary issues are being addressed in an artfully disguised form. Knowing that *As You Like It* contains "secret messages" should not be treated as a license to speculate wildly about the "true" content of the play. Certainly, it would be prejudicial to present any one reading of the play's "hidden meaning" here as definitive background. (Specific readings of the play will be discussed in later sections.) Still, it is worth stressing that although *As You Like It* appears to be and, to an extent, is a lighthearted comedy, it also contains serious political and ethical content of which contemporary viewers would have been aware.

Finally, in addition to being a pastoral play and a comedy, *As You Like It* is also a romance. It features a poor young man, a male equivalent of Cinderella, who ends up marrying a duke's daughter. Other details in the play—such as the references to wise magicians and religious hermits, sudden changes of heart by previously "bad" characters, and the mysterious forest itself—also belong to the world of romance. In fact, the main source for the play is Lodge's popular, mixed-media (prose and poetry) pastoral romance novel *Rosalynd* (first published in 1590, with three more editions appearing before the probable date of *As You Like It*'s composition). Again, this context would have informed the response of the play's first audiences. Romances spoke directly to readers' or spectators' dreams of social advancement and helped them both escape from and overcome, if in imagination only, circumstances that were making their everyday lives disagreeable. In a romance, things can be "as you like them." Moreover, as with the pastoral mode, a writer could address social and political issues in a romance with relative safety, albeit in a disguised form.

Date and Text of the Play

As You Like It was recorded in the Stationers' Register on August 4, 1600, but was not published until 1623 as one of the plays in the "Comedies" section of the First Folio (the first collected edition of Shakespeare's plays). The title *As You Like It* was not included among Francis Meres's list of Shakespeare's plays in *Palladis Tamia,* published in 1598, which implies the play was written after that time. Moreover, the forest setting, the inclusion of noble characters disguised as outlaws, and the pointed reference to Robin Hood in Act I, Scene 1 (lines 109–111) combine to suggest that the play was written in 1598–99 to capitalize on a vogue for Robin Hood plays (the Admiral's Men had staged two popular Robin Hood plays, written by Anthony Munday and Henry Chettle, in 1598).

As You Like It is divided into acts and scenes in the First Folio, possibly by the scrivener Ralph Crane, who is known to have partitioned five of the 10 plays given such divisions in the First Folio. It is worth noting that, in Shakespeare's time, plays for the public theaters such as the Globe were not separated into acts and scenes, whereas plays performed at private theaters, such as Blackfriars,

were. (The reason for this is that music was played between the acts at private theaters.) This suggests that, contrary to what some scholars have argued in the past, *As You Like It* may have been written for a relatively affluent, seated Blackfriars audience, as opposed to a mixture of seated and standing, well-to-do and "common" playgoers at the Globe. There is no record of the play having been performed in Shakespeare's lifetime; however, a document from 1669 lists *As You Like It* among plays belonging to the Blackfriars Theatre.

SYNOPSIS
Brief Synopsis

The play begins with Orlando, the youngest son of Sir Rowland de Boys, complaining of the poor provision left him by his father's will and the brutal treatment he is receiving from his older brother, Oliver. In order to show the world at large that he possesses admirable qualities, Orlando goes to the court of Duke Frederick to take part in a wrestling tournament. While there, Orlando falls in love with Rosalind, daughter of the banished Duke Senior (Frederick's brother).

Entertaining new suspicions about Rosalind, Duke Frederick subsequently banishes her from his court. Celia (Frederick's daughter) refuses to abandon her friend. The young women decide to run away to the Forest of Arden together. Since two women travelling alone might attract unwelcome attention, Rosalind disguises herself as a martial-seeming man called Ganymede. At the same time, Orlando is also forced to leave his home. When he meets Rosalind again in the forest, she is dressed as Ganymede. Not recognizing her, Orlando admits to Ganymede that he is in love with Rosalind. Ganymede claims to know a cure for love: Ganymede will pretend to be "Rosalind," and Orlando must attempt to woo "her." Orlando is happy to spend time courting Rosalind in fantasy, so he agrees to Ganymede's project.

Duke Frederick, meanwhile, is anxious to locate his daughter, Celia. He suspects that Orlando played some part in her disappearance. Accordingly, he tells Oliver to track down his brother. If

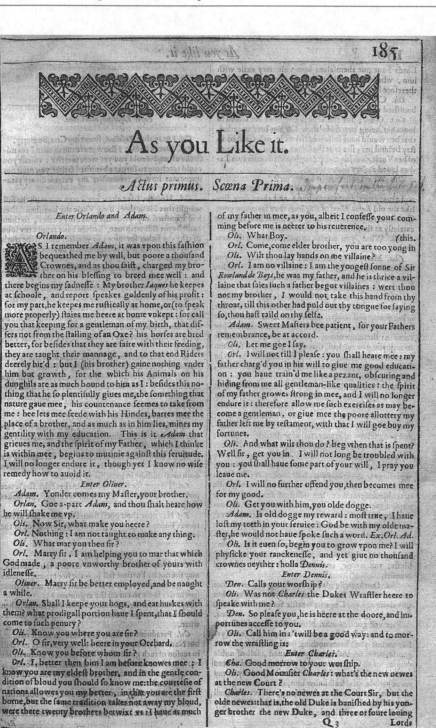

As you Like it.

Actus primus. Scœna Prima.

Enter Orlando and Adam.

Orlando.

AS I remember *Adam*, it was vpon this fashion bequeathed me by will, but poore a thousand Crownes, and as thou saist, charged my brother on his blessing to breed mee well : and there begins my sadnesse : My brother *Iaques* he keepes at schoole, and report speakes goldenly of his profit : for my part, he keepes me rustically at home, or(to speak more properly) staies me heere at home vnkept : for call you that keeping for a gentleman of my birth, that differs not from the stalling of an Oxe ? his horses are bred better, for besides that they are faire with their feeding, they are taught their mannage, and to that end Riders deerely hir'd : but I (his brother) gaine nothing vnder him but growth, for the which his Animals on his dunghils are as much bound to him as I : besides this nothing that hee so plentifully giues me, the something that nature gaue mee, his countenance seemes to take from me : hee lets mee feede with his Hindes, barres mee the place of a brother, and as much as in him lies, mines my gentility with my education. This is it *Adam* that grieues me, and the spirit of my Father, which I thinke is within mee, begins to mutinie against this seruitude. I will no longer endure it, though yet I know no wise remedy how to auoid it.

Enter Oliuer.

Adam. Yonder comes my Master, your brother.

Orlan. Goe a-part *Adam*, and thou shalt heare how he will shake me vp.

Oli. Now Sir, what make you heere ?

Orl. Nothing : I am not taught to make any thing.

Oli. What mar you then sir ?

Orl. Marry sir, I am helping you to mar that which God made, a poore vnworthy brother of yours with idlenesse.

Oliuer. Marry sir be better employed, and be naught a while.

Orlan. Shall I keepe your hogs, and eat huskes with them? what prodigall portion haue I spent, that I should come to such penury ?

Oli. Know you where you are sir ?

Orl. O sir, very well : heere in your Orchard.

Oli. Know you before whom sir ?

Orl. I, better then him I am before knowes mee : I know you are my eldest brother, and in the gentle condition of bloud you should so know me: the courtesie of nations allowes you my better, in that you are the first borne, but the same tradition takes not away my bloud, were there twenty brothers betwixt vs : I haue as much

of my father in mee, as you, albeit I confesse your comming before me is neerer to his reuerence.

Oli. What Boy.   (this.

Orl. Come, come elder brother, you are too yong in

Oli. Wilt thou lay hands on me villaine ?

Orl. I am no villaine : I am the yongest sonne of Sir *Rowland de Boys*, he was my father, and he is thrice a villaine that saies such a father begot villaines : wert thou not my brother, I would not take this hand from thy throat, till this other had puld out thy tongue for saying so, thou hast raild on thy selfe.

Adam. Sweet Masters bee patient, for your Fathers remembrance, be at accord.

Oli. Let me goe I say.

Orl. I will not till I please : you shall heare mee : my father charg'd you in his will to giue me good education : you haue train'd me like a pezant, obscuring and hiding from me all gentleman-like qualities : the spirit of my father growes strong in mee, and I will no longer endure it : therefore allow me such exercises as may become a gentleman, or giue mee the poore allottery my father left me by testament, with that I will goe buy my fortunes.

Oli. And what wilt thou do ? beg when that is spent? Well sir, get you in. I will not long be troubled with you : you shall haue some part of your will, I pray you leaue me.

Orl. I will no further offend you, then becomes mee for my good.

Oli. Get you with him, you olde dogge.

Adam. Is old dogge my reward : most true, I haue lost my teeth in your seruice : God be with my olde master, he would not haue spoke such a word. *Ex. Orl. Ad.*

Oli. Is it euen so, begin you to grow vpon me? I will physicke your ranckenesse, and yet giue no thousand crownes neyther : holla *Dennis*.

Enter Dennis.

Den. Calls your worship?

Oli. Was not *Charles* the Dukes Wrastler heere to speake with me?

Den. So please you, he is heere at the doore, and importunes accesse to you.

Oli. Call him in : 'twill be a good way: and to morrow the wrastling is:

Enter Charles.

Cha. Good morrow to your worship.

Oli. Good Mounsier *Charles* : what's the new newes at the new Court ?

Charles. There's no newes at the Court Sir, but the olde newes: that is, the old Duke is banished by his yonger brother the new Duke, and three or foure louing

Q3   Lords

Title page of the First Folio edition of *As You Like It*, published in 1623 he fails to do this, Frederick will seize his properties. While searching for his brother in the Forest of Arden, however, Oliver experiences a change of heart, repenting of his former cruelty and jealousy. Similarly, Frederick, leading an army to the forest to defeat the forces he believes are gathering around the usurped Duke Senior, meets an old hermit, undergoes a religious conversion, and restores the dukedom to his brother.

Also in the forest lives a shepherd Silvius, who is in love with the disdainful shepherdess Phoebe. When Rosalind, disguised as Ganymede, chastises Phoebe for her pride, the latter falls in love with the handsome "boy." Rosalind/Ganymede sees a way to help Silvius: She makes Phoebe promise she will marry Silvius if she cannot marry Ganymede. Thus, when the dukedom is restored to Duke Senior, Ganymede is able to reveal "his" true identity as Rosalind. Keeping her word, Phoebe now consents to marry Silvius. Hymen, the god of marriage, appears. Four couples exchange marriage vows, among them are Rosalind and Orlando and Celia and the reformed Oliver. The play ends with dancing and song as the former exiles prepare to make their happy return to the court led by the restored Duke Senior.

Act I, Scene 1
Orlando, the youngest son of Sir Rowland de Boys, feels that he is not being given the opportunities his social position deserves. Instead of providing Orlando with a proper education, as their father's will stipulated, Oliver (Orlando's older brother) treats him like one of the servants on their country estate. When Orlando complains about this treatment, Oliver responds with contempt. The brothers wrestle, and Orlando proves the stronger. Held in a tight grip, Oliver agrees to give Orlando his share of the inheritance so that he may go and take his chance in the world.

However, when Orlando has departed, Oliver talks with Charles the wrestler. There is to be a wrestling contest at the court of Duke Frederick in which Charles will fight all challengers. Knowing that Orlando plans to take part in disguise,

Oliver tells Charles that Orlando will use trickery—even poison—to win the bout. Therefore, he advises Charles to break Orlando's neck during the contest.

Act I, Scene 2
This scene takes place at court, where Duke Frederick has usurped his brother, Duke Senior. Frederick's daughter, Celia, tells her friend and cousin Rosalind, daughter of Duke Senior, to cheer up, promising that when Frederick dies, she (Celia) will restore the dukedom to Rosalind. Le Beau, a courtier, arrives and tells the two young women that the wrestling tournament is under way, and Charles (Duke Frederick's champion) has killed three young challengers. For the next bout, the wrestling contest moves to where Rosalind and Celia are standing, with Duke Frederick in attendance. Orlando is the challenger. Both women try to dissuade him from the fight, pointing out how much smaller he is than Charles. When he proves determined, however, they wish him well. Orlando defeats Charles. Nevertheless, on hearing that Orlando is the youngest son of Sir Rowland de Boys, his former enemy, Frederick orders Orlando to leave the court without a prize. Before Orlando goes, Rosalind gives him a chain from around her neck. Orlando finds himself speechless in her presence. After the women have gone, the courtier Le Beau advises Orlando to depart as soon as possible, for Duke Frederick has an unpredictable temper.

Act I, Scene 3
Rosalind admits to Celia that she feels attracted to Orlando. Duke Frederick enters and orders Rosalind to leave the court. When Celia asks why he is banishing her friend, Frederick explains that Rosalind is proving too popular with the people. When she has gone, Celia's positive qualities will be more apparent.

After Frederick leaves them alone, however, Celia and Rosalind agree to go into banishment together, joining Rosalind's father, Duke Senior, in the Forest of Arden. Also, in order to ward off attackers during their journey, Rosalind decides to disguise herself as a man, called Ganymede. They also plan to take Touchstone, the court clown, along with them.

Act II, Scene 1

In the Forest of Arden, the philosophical Duke Senior assures the lords in exile with him that he is happy living in the countryside. To entertain Duke Senior, one lord reports that he has just seen Jaques—one of their company, known for his melancholy temperament—sitting beneath an oak tree, weeping at the plight of a stag injured in the hunt.

Act II, Scene 2

Duke Frederick is furious to learn that his daughter Celia has fled with Rosalind. On learning that a servant overheard the women discussing Orlando, Frederick orders Orlando's brother, Oliver, to be brought to the court.

Act II, Scene 3

Adam, the old servant employed by the de Boys family, warns Orlando not to enter the family home. Orlando's brother, Oliver, he says, has decided to burn the house down while Orlando sleeps inside or use any necessary means to dispose of him without giving Orlando his share of their inheritance as promised. When Orlando asks where else he can go, Adam reveals he has saved 500 crowns and will give it to him. Moved by this loyalty and selflessness, Orlando asks the old man to accompany him.

Act II, Scene 4

Exhausted by their journey into the Forest of Arden on foot, Rosalind (now disguised as Ganymede), Celia, and Touchstone stop to rest. Two shepherds arrive, deep in conversation. The weary travelers overhear the young shepherd, Silvius, declare how much he loves a shepherdess named Phoebe.

Celia, Rosalind, and Touchstone stop to rest in an 1898 drawing of Act II, Scene 4 of *As You Like It. (Illustration by J. E. Pawsey)*

Rosalind then asks the old shepherd, Corin, if there is anywhere nearby where they can rest, since Celia is weak with fatigue and hunger. Corin regrets that he is unable to offer much hospitality. He looks after another man's sheep, and his master is absent; in fact, his master's cottage and his flock of sheep are currently up for sale. Celia offers to hire Corin and buy the cottage and the flock. Corin immediately agrees to the proposal.

Act II, Scene 5

The melancholy Jaques listens to Amiens and other exiled lords (disguised as foresters) singing songs.

Act II, Scene 6

Orlando and Adam now arrive in the forest. Adam is exhausted. Seeing the old man lie down on the ground, Orlando decides to carry him to a place of shelter.

Act II, Scene 7

Jaques informs Duke Senior that he has met a fool dressed in a clown's costume in the forest. Jaques then asks the Duke if he, too, might be allowed to wear a clown's suit. Dressed thus, he would be free to criticize anyone he wanted to for their immoral behavior. Somewhat annoyed by this, Duke Senior points out that Jaques himself in the past indulged in many sinful acts; therefore, in trying to purify the world with his satire, he would only spread his own corruption. At this point, Orlando appears, brandishing a sword and demanding food. If Orlando were to ask more politely, remarks Duke Senior, they would be more likely to give him what he requested. Embarrassed by this gentle response, Orlando lowers his sword, saying that he had not expected to meet civilized people in such a savage place. He mentions the old man (Adam) he has left reclining in shelter, some way off. Duke Senior tells Orlando to fetch the old man. While Orlando is gone, Jaques delivers a speech on the seven ages of man, presenting a pessimistic view of human life. Orlando returns, carrying Adam on his back. Amiens sings a song as the hungry travelers eat. Duke Senior then recognizes Orlando as the son of his old friend Sir Rowland de Boys.

Jaques explains the first age of man in Act II, Scene 7 of *As You Like It*. This is a print from the Boydell Shakespeare Gallery project, which was first conceived in 1786 and continued until 1805. *(Painting by Robert Smirke; engraving by Tomkins)*

Act III, Scene 1

Duke Frederick tells Oliver that unless he brings Orlando back to the court, dead or alive, within 12 months, his lands and all his other possessions will be seized.

Act III, Scene 2

Orlando, having written poems in praise of Rosalind, begins hanging them on tree branches in the forest.

The old shepherd Corin and Touchstone the clown argue about whether good manners are more likely to be found in the court or the countryside. In the end, Corin acknowledges that Touchstone is too witty for him, but the shepherd comes off as down to earth and sincere.

Rosalind, disguised as Ganymede, arrives, reading aloud from a poem in praise of her beauty, which she has found hanging on a tree. Touchstone improvises his own, somewhat ruder version. Then Celia enters, reading aloud another poem in praise of Rosalind. Rosalind wonders who has been leaving these verses around the forest. Celia says that she has seen the man responsible. Celia eventually reveals that it is Orlando, the young challenger they saw at the wrestling competition at court. Rosalind/Ganymede worries what to do about her male disguise, now that Orlando is in the forest.

Orlando himself now arrives, talking with Jaques. After Jaques leaves, Orlando speaks with Ganymede, unaware that he is Rosalind in disguise. Rosalind/Ganymede adopts the character of a man of the world in addressing Orlando, saying that whoever is leaving these love poems around the forest evidently needs the cure for love that "his" uncle devised. Orlando admits he wrote the poems and asks about the cure. Ganymede explains that it would work like this: Orlando should imagine that he (Ganymede) is in fact Rosalind, his beloved, and spend some time every day trying to woo "her." Ganymede, pretending to be Rosalind, will then keep changing her mood, being sometimes affectionate, but at other times acting proud, strange, or unhappy, so that in the end "her" lover

(Orlando) would be driven mad and decide to live like a monk, detached from the world. Orlando, however, says that he does not want to be cured. On the other hand, he likes the idea of engaging in this kind of role-play with such an intriguing young man, so he agrees to come to Ganymede's cottage and "woo" him as Rosalind.

Act III, Scene 3

The clown Touchstone tells Audrey, a country girl, that he has arranged for Sir Oliver Martext, the vicar of a nearby village, to come and marry them in the forest. When the vicar arrives, he points out that someone is needed to give the bride away. Jaques, who has been spying on the scene, steps forward and offers to give Audrey away. However, Jaques then tells Touchstone that this is not the proper way to get married; he should take Audrey to a church. The wedding is called off.

Act III, Scene 4

Rosalind is singing Orlando's praises to Celia when the old shepherd Corin arrives to tell the two young women that there is a scene under way that they might like to watch, involving the young shepherd Silvius and his beloved, the disdainful Phoebe.

Act III, Scene 5

Silvius pleads with Phoebe to look more kindly on him. Phoebe scorns his exaggerated praise of her and tells him to go away. Rosalind, disguised as Ganymede, steps forward and berates Phoebe for her pride. "He" tells Phoebe that she is not as attractive as she thinks she is and that, therefore, she should be grateful for Silvius's attentions. Phoebe is immediately attracted to Ganymede, preferring "his" insults to Silvius's compliments.

Act IV, Scene 1

Orlando arrives late for his first appointment with Ganymede. Ganymede, posing as a critical Rosalind, upbraids him for this. Orlando asks for pardon and attempts to woo "her," but "Rosalind" now criticizes his poetic expressions, pointing out

that no man ever died for love. At length, "Rosalind" softens her manner and asks Celia to pretend to be a priest and marry them. A mock marriage ceremony takes place, after which Orlando announces he must depart for two hours, to attend the Duke at dinner.

When he is gone, Celia attacks Ganymede for presenting the female sex in such a negative light. Ganymede, speaking now as Rosalind in earnest, declares how much in love she is with Orlando.

Act IV, Scene 2

Jaques and the other lords sing a song about awarding a deer's horns to the man who killed it. These horns are symbolic of the metaphorical horns worn by all men whose wives are unfaithful.

Act IV, Scene 3

Silvius arrives with a letter for Ganymede from Phoebe. Rosalind/Ganymede reads the letter aloud. In the letter, Phoebe declares her love for Ganymede.

A man arrives, looking for Celia and Ganymede. It is Oliver (though he does not reveal his name as yet). Announcing that he has been sent by Orlando, he shows Celia and Ganymede a handkerchief stained with blood. Orlando, he explains, had stumbled on a man in rags, sleeping in the forest. A lioness lay by the sleeping man, waiting to attack him when he woke. Recognizing the man as his brother Oliver, Orlando at first resolved to leave him there, recalling all the mistreatment he had suffered at Oliver's hands; however, Orlando's better nature prevailed: He fought with the lioness, defeating it, but receiving a wound in the process, hence the bloodstained handkerchief. The speaker now reveals that he is Oliver himself. He informs Celia and Ganymede that he has reformed his character, having repented of his former jealousy of Orlando. The wounded Orlando, he goes on to explain, took him to meet Duke Senior, where he was given new clothing. Then Orlando had sent him to this cottage, to offer Ganymede his excuses for not coming to woo "Rosalind" as arranged. On hearing all this and being presented

Rosalind, disguised as Ganymede, faints after hearing the story of Orlando's heroics from Oliver in Act IV, Scene 3 of *As You Like It*. Print is from the Boydell Shakespeare Gallery project. *(Illustration by Robert Smirke; engraving by William Charles Wilson)*

with the bloodstained napkin, Rosalind/Ganymede faints.

Act V, Scene 1
Touchstone and Audrey meet William, a country youth with a prior claim to Audrey. Touchstone bombards William with courtly wit until the youth retires.

Act V, Scene 2
Oliver and Celia have fallen in love at first sight and have already decided to get married. Orlando (his wounded arm in a sling) tells Oliver that he is surprised by the speed of this proceeding. Oliver informs him that he intends to live as a shepherd in the forest with Celia, handing over the family estate to Orlando.

When Rosalind arrives, still disguised as Ganymede, Orlando tells "him" that he is almost jealous of his brother's happiness in being able to marry the woman he loves. As for himself, he is no longer content to woo Ganymede as Rosalind; he needs the genuine article. Ganymede now reveals that "he" has studied with a magician since the age of three and can perform great things. Accordingly, "he" promises to deliver Rosalind to Orlando on the following day, when, Ganymede declares, their wedding will take place.

Silvius and Phoebe arrive. Ganymede now tells Phoebe that "he" will marry her on the following day, if "he" is able to marry any woman.

Act V, Scene 3
Two of Duke Senior's young attendants sing to Touchstone and Audrey.

Act V, Scene 4
Ganymede asks Duke Senior if he will allow his daughter Rosalind to marry Orlando if he, Ganymede, delivers her to the Duke's camp. (Duke Senior still does not know that Ganymede is his daughter in disguise.) Duke Senior gives his consent to the proposed match. Ganymede then confirms that Phoebe is prepared to marry Silvius if, for any reason, she should find herself unwilling to marry Ganymede.

After Ganymede departs, Touchstone and Audrey arrive, ready to be married. In due course, Hymen, the god of marriage, appears with Rosalind, no longer in disguise. Phoebe realizes she cannot marry "Ganymede" and consents to marry Silvius. Hymen joins Celia and Oliver and the other three couples in wedlock.

Suddenly, Jaques de Boys, the brother of Orlando and Oliver (not to be confused with the melancholy Jaques), arrives on the scene with important news: Duke Frederick, concerned that too many influential men were assembling around Duke Senior in the forest, had brought a large army to the edges of the woodland, intending to execute his brother once and for all. There, however, he met an old religious man who persuaded him to abandon his aggressive undertaking, live a quiet religious life, and restore the crown to Duke Senior.

The restored Duke Senior announces that when the wedding celebrations have been completed in the forest, they will all return to the court. The melancholy Jaques, however, declares his intention to stay in the forest, conversing with the religious convert, Duke Frederick.

Epilogue
Rosalind bids the audience a flirtatious farewell.

CHARACTER LIST
Rosalind   Daughter of the banished Duke Senior. Despite her unhappiness over the situation of her father, Rosalind remains a loyal friend to her cousin, Celia, daughter of the usurping Duke Frederick. Passionate, beautiful, witty, and flirtatious, Rosalind plays a number of different roles in the play, including that of Ganymede, a swaggering male youth.

Orlando   Youngest son of Sir Rowland de Boys. Socially ambitious, handsome, agile, and brave, Orlando feels socially and culturally stifled by his confinement to the family's country estate. Unhappy with the small sum left him in his father's will and by the cruel treatment he receives from his older brother, Oliver, Orlando remains determined to cut a heroic figure in the world.

Duke Senior   Usurped from his throne by his brother Frederick, Duke Senior lives in exile in the Forest of Arden, accompanied by a growing number of loyal lords. Adopting a philosophical outlook, the banished Duke regards his former home, the court, as the site of jealousy, greed, and selfishness. He claims to prefer his current habitat, the forest, a place where innocence and sincerity can be found.

Duke Frederick   Usurping ruler of the court. Possessed of a violent temper, Frederick is prone to sudden changes of mood. Having banished his brother, Duke Senior, and seized his throne, Frederick feels obliged to watch everyone around him with a distrustful eye.

Celia   Daughter of Duke Frederick. Mindful of the injustice done by her father to her uncle, Duke Senior, Celia is resolved to restore the dukedom to Duke Senior's daughter, her best friend Rosalind, after Frederick dies. Celia, thus, can be described as loyal, concerned with justice, and practical minded.

Oliver   Oldest son of Sir Rowland de Boys. Oliver is jealous of Orlando, his younger brother, who seems to be popular with everybody. For this reason, he abuses Orlando as much as possible until he experiences a moral awakening.

Adam   Elderly and faithful servant in the de Boys household.

Dennis   Another servant in the de Boys household.

Touchstone   A clown at the court. A master of quickfire verbal wit, Touchstone has ambiguous social status, somewhere between that of a courtier and a servant. A faithful friend and employee of Celia, he is also a sensualist, committed to satisfying his natural appetites.

Le Beau   A somewhat foolish but good-natured courtier.

Charles   Duke Frederick's champion wrestler.

Jaques   A melancholy gentleman, one of Duke Senior's followers in the Forest of Arden.

Amiens   A lord attending Duke Senior in the Forest of Arden.

Corin   An old man who is perfectly content with his life as a shepherd.

Silvius   A simple-hearted young shepherd who is hopelessly in love with the proud shepherdess Phoebe.

Phoebe   A shepherdess who is proud and disdainful toward her suitor, Silvius.

Audrey   A goatherd who has received little education and is keen to become Touchstone's wife at court.

Sir Oliver Martext   A vicar in a country village.

William   A plainspoken country youth who feels he has a prior claim to Audrey.

Audrey in Act III, Scene 3 of *As You Like It,* as depicted in a print from Charles Heath's 1848 edition of *The Heroines of Shakspeare: Comprising the Principal Female Characters in the Plays of the Great Poet (Painting by W. P. Frith; engraving by W. H. Mote)*

Hymen   A classical figure, the god of marriage.

Jaques de Boys   The second son of Sir Rowland de Boys. Jaques de Boys, unlike his younger brother, Orlando, is receiving a good education at school. Jaques does not appear until the final scene, when he delivers some important news.

CHARACTER STUDIES
Rosalind

In Act I, Scene 2 of the play, Rosalind struggles to balance her loyalties as friend to Celia and as daughter to Duke Senior. Celia asks Rosalind to "be merry" (1), for, although Duke Senior has been banished from the court where they live, at least they are together. Rosalind, however, says that "I show more mirth than I am mistress of" (2–3); as a loyal and affectionate daughter, she cannot help feeling sadness for her father's plight, but she is also making an effort to hide the extent of that sadness, out of loyalty to Celia. Furthermore, Rosalind is acting a part, pretending to be content in Frederick's court. Performing different roles is something Rosalind will do throughout the play. She is a brilliant actor.

In changing the subject from the topic of her father's usurpation, Rosalind's thoughts turn to matters of love. "I will . . . devise sports," she says to Celia. "Let me see: what think you of falling in love?" (24–25). Evidently, Rosalind is ready for a new emotional attachment. However, this concern with love could also derive from a more practical side to her nature. Rosalind may suppose her position at Frederick's court will continue to be vulnerable until she is married.

Perhaps as a result of this vulnerability, Rosalind is quick to feel pity for the disadvantaged. Seeing Orlando, as he is preparing to challenge Charles, the large champion wrestler, Rosalind tries to dissuade the young man, since the combatants are so physically mismatched. Her tact is also apparent: Orlando's "reputation shall not . . . be misprized," she says, if he agrees not to go ahead with the fight (172–173). When Orlando is victorious and fails to win a prize on account of his family background, Rosalind recognizes a fellow victim of Frederick's regime. Apparently, she has already fallen in love with Orlando, for she gives him a chain from her neck and says, "Wear this for me—one out of suits with fortune, / That could give more but that her hand lacks means" (235–236). Presumably, Rosalind sees in Orlando not only a potential lover but also a means for her to escape her current situation.

In the following scene, Rosalind's circumstances grow more serious. Duke Frederick suspects her of treachery and banishes her from his court. Her boldness comes to the fore as she forgets the mute obedience expected of women in the feudal world in which the play takes place; she dares to challenge Frederick's decision: "I do beseech your grace . . . Never so much as in a thought unborn

/ Did I offend your highness" (1.3.42, 48–49). When Frederick confirms Rosalind's banishment and exits, however, it is Celia who appears the more resourceful in suggesting that both she and Rosalind disguise themselves and flee together to join Rosalind's father in the Forest of Arden. At this stage, Rosalind is more taken with the opportunities for playacting than with the basic practical need for a disguise. She announces her intention to dress herself, not as a beggar woman, as Celia suggests, but as a man. She imagines her costume with obvious relish: "A gallant curtal-axe upon my thigh, / A boar-spear in my hand . . . We'll have a swashing and a martial outside" (114–115, 117). Acting is a passion with her. It might be thought that Frederick was indeed justified to suspect her of hiding her true feelings.

In the forest, Rosalind, disguised as Ganymede, shows more decisive qualities, suggesting to Celia that they buy a cottage and the pasture and flock that go with it. On the other hand, when she first reads the love poetry written about her by Orlando, she is girlishly flattered and impatient to learn the author's name. When she learns the poems were written by Orlando, Rosalind immediately wonders how to dispose of her male disguise. For once, Rosalind does not seem to be playing a role: She is genuinely attracted to Orlando. However, on actually seeing Orlando, Rosalind makes a crucial decision: "I will speak to him like a saucy lackey," she tells the audience, musing aloud, "and under that habit play the knave with him" (3.2.287–288). She is acting again and now with the aim of testing Orlando's love. Finding herself in complete control of her circumstances, she is able to enjoy the situation to the utmost, mocking Orlando's lovelorn declarations and recommending he undergo the cure for love that her "old religious uncle" once devised (332).

Rosalind's powers of verbal invention are not always profound. When the courtier Le Beau mentions "Three proper young men of excellent growth and presence—," Rosalind interrupts him, saying: "With bills on their necks: 'Be it known unto all men by these presents.'" (1.2.115–118).

No editor of the play allows this pun on *presence* and *presents* to pass without remarking on how poor it is. However, the "joke" is meant for Celia's ears. People regularly make deliberately bad puns, especially in front of their closest comrades. Such a poor pun, therefore, conveys the spontaneity and self-asserting nature of Rosalind's humor more effectively than would a better joke. Nonetheless, in the forest, the disguised Rosalind's powers of verbal invention blossom as she describes the love cure to Orlando. The lover, she says, was "to imagine me his love, his mistress, and I set him every day to woo me. At which time would I . . . grieve, be effeminate, changeable, longing and liking, proud, fantastical, apish, shallow, inconstant, full of tears, full of smiles" (3.2.428–432). Behaving like this, she says, "I drave my suitor from his mad humour of love to a living humour of madness" (400–401). Orlando, moreover, is now told that he must imagine that Ganymede is Rosalind and woo "her" accordingly. When Orlando proceeds to do this, using the formal language of poetic love, the saucy "Rosalind" played by Ganymede punctures Orlando's romantic dreams with sallies of pungent, conversational, yet eloquent wit: "The poor world," she says, "is almost six thousand years old, and in all this time there was not any man died in his own person (videlicet, in a love-cause). Troilus had his brains dashed out with a Grecian club, yet he did what he could to die before, and he is one of the patterns of love" (4.1.86–91).

Rosalind does more than merely have fun with Orlando in the wooing scenes. No one has ever died for love, she insists, and the poets who said they did were all liars (96–97). Thus, she implicitly tells the man she loves that when, in his poetry, he declares his love for her, he is lying, for the type of love he expresses is conventional: The virginal, ideal Rosalind he has described is a myth. Rosalind, in short, teaches Orlando to revise his notions of love. She makes him into the kind of lover she herself desires.

Rosalind also provides a credible hint as to the kind of wife she would be if married to Orlando: "I will be more jealous of thee than a Barbary cock-pigeon over his hen, more clamorous than a parrot against rain . . . I will weep for nothing . . . and I will do that when you are disposed to be merry. I will laugh like a hyena, and that when thou art inclined to sleep" (4.1.139–146). Although Rosalind later (briefly) plays the role of submissive wife and obedient daughter, declaring that she "belongs" to Orlando as his wife in the marriage vows exchanged in the final scene, it is hard to imagine Rosalind as the perpetually submissive wife of Orlando. (Notice in the speech quoted above how she imagines herself as the male "cock-pigeon" to Orlando's "hen.") Certainly, Rosalind seems to relish her independence during her time in the forest: She neglects to inform her father of her presence, despite meeting and conversing with him, disguised as Ganymede. One might have thought she would wish to put her poor father's mind at rest concerning his banished daughter (for he may well have heard news of her banishment from the court). In any case, there is nothing to suggest that Rosalind will continue in the role of submissive wife any longer than she remains in the other roles she performs.

Indeed, Rosalind not only shows herself to be a consummate actor in the course of the play; she also emerges as a powerful controlling figure. For example, she arranges not only her own marriage to Orlando but also that of Silvius, the lovelorn shepherd, to the haughty Phoebe. The source of her power is magical knowledge. "Believe me," she informs the frustrated Orlando in Act V, Scene 2, "that I can do strange things. I have since I was three year old conversed with a magician, most profound in his art and yet not damnable" (57–60). Many modern productions interpret this as Rosalind's invention, but the appearance of the god of marriage, Hymen, in Act V, Scene 4 is apparently orchestrated by Rosalind herself. "I have promised to make all this matter even," Rosalind says in that scene, about to take her leave prior to the appearance of the god. This is the language of the magician who manipulates "matter." Pointedly, Rosalind then repeats the words *make* and *even:* "from hence I go / To make these doubts all even"

(18, 24–25). Given this deliberate repetition, it is striking that when Hymen arrives, he also repeats Rosalind's magic-working words: "Then is there mirth in heaven / When earthly things made even / Atone together" (106–108). The play's stage directions leave no reason to doubt that Hymen is meant to be regarded as an actual manifestation of the god. There could be no greater demonstration of Rosalind's wonder-working powers in this closing scene.

Orlando

Orlando, in Act I, Scene 1 of the play, appears proud of his ancestry—his father, Sir Rowland, having cut a heroic figure. He complains, moreover, that being kept at home without being given any education is not fitting "for a gentleman of my birth" (8–9). His pride makes him keenly sensitive to insult, and he is quick to use physical means to resolve his problems. For example, he lays hands on his brother Oliver (51), when the latter persists in addressing him in an insulting and condescending manner and proceeds to wrestle him into submission. Later, encountering Duke Senior's party eating a banquet in the forest, Orlando draws his sword and advances, demanding food. In addition, though his attraction to Rosalind suggests a more romantic side to his nature, Orlando also reveals himself as emotionally immature when he writes clichéd Petrarchan poetry in praise of her as a perfect woman "By heavenly synod . . . devised" (3.2.147).

Orlando, nonetheless, exhibits a capacity to modify his behavior and attitudes. On learning that Duke Senior and his party in the forest are, in fact, extremely civilized, Orlando does not persist in his aggression but immediately apologizes and puts his sword away. Similarly, he is not angered when Rosalind/Ganymede teases him at length about his formal manner of praising her. Indeed, he is obviously aroused by the games Rosalind/Ganymede plays while posing as a "saucy" version of herself. Thus, Orlando reveals himself to be capable of change. This makes him worthy of Rosalind's love in her own eyes and in the eyes of the audi-

Orlando fights a lioness to save his brother, as described by Oliver in Act IV, Scene 3 of *As You Like It*. This is a print from the Boydell Shakespeare Gallery project. *(Illustration by Raphael West; engraving by William Charles Wilson)*

ence. To express the matter in language appropriate to the period, Orlando shows signs of being a perfect gentleman: strong, brave, supple-minded, sensitive, and not too domineering.

Jaques

Although famous for his speech on the seven ages of man, Jaques does almost nothing to affect events in *As You Like It*. Essentially, Jaques observes rather than participates, and he invariably finds fault with what he sees. Nonetheless, the importance of Jaques as an ingredient in the play is stressed when a long account given by Amiens in Act II, Scene 1 raises the curiosity of the audience. According to Amiens, Jaques had been sitting by himself in the forest when he saw a wounded stag. The stag was weeping, abandoned by the other members of its herd. This spectacle afforded Jaques with matter for a long moralizing discourse on the brutality of man: "Thus most invectively," says Amiens, "he pierceth through / The body of country, city, court . . ." (58–59). Duke Senior and the other lords enjoy this description of their contemplative friend, and Duke Senior asks to be taken immediately to Jaques's vicinity because he loves to speak

with him when he is in these melancholy moods. Evidently, as far as the Duke and his attendants are concerned, Jaques plays a role equivalent to a court jester, only his job is not to amuse by telling jokes and performing other humorous antics but to entertain by indulging in excessive melancholy.

Certainly, Jaques has a pessimistic outlook. His famous speech on the seven ages of man describes life as a series of theatrical roles that everyone must perform, willingly or not. This series ends in death and nothingness, in Jaques's opinion. However, for all his cynicism, Jaques claims to have a moral outlook, expressing disgust at the immoral behavior he has seen in the world at large, especially at court and in the town. After meeting the clown Touchstone in the forest and delighting at the latter's seemingly nonsensical wordplay, Jaques asks Duke Senior if he might be allowed to wear a clown's costume. Dressed thus, he would possess the license of the fool and be allowed to satirize people's immoral behavior: "I must have liberty / Withal, as large a charter as the wind / To blow on whom I please, for so fools have" (2.7.47–49). However, the Duke points out that Jaques, too, has indulged in the past in immoral activity: "Thou thyself hast been a libertine, / As sensual as the brutish sting itself" (65–66). Declining to answer this specific charge, Jaques employs the satirist's standard defense: He will not attack individuals, only the sins they commit: "Why, who cries out on pride / That can therein tax any private party? . . . What woman in the city do I name, / When that I say the city-woman bears / The cost of princes on unworthy shoulders?" (70–71, 75–76). Jaques's authority as a would-be champion of morality is nonetheless undermined by the dubiousness of his former exploits as a traveler in Europe. For one thing, as Rosalind later rightly surmises, Jaques has been profligate with his money, having "sold [his] own lands to see other men's" (4.1.20–21). There is also the suggestion that it is only now that Jaques is no longer able to enjoy certain activities himself that he seeks to criticize in others for their pursuit of sensual pleasure. Thus, Jaques comes across as a somewhat bitter, former debauchee.

Significantly, Jaques never knowingly engages in any conversation with a woman in the play. Although he does speak with Rosalind, calling her a "pretty youth" (4.1.1), it is when she is disguised as Ganymede. Moreover, when Jaques speaks with Orlando, he praises his "nimble wit" (3.2.268) and asks the handsome youth to sit with him in seclusion so they might "rail against our mistress the world" together (269–270). It is noticeable that the world, as an object of his criticism, is rendered female by Jaques. All implies that Jaques prefers male company.

Jaques criticizes Duke Senior for hunting animals in the forest, arguing that as the animals are the true natives of the woods, Duke Senior and his attendants are usurpers no less than Duke Frederick in hunting down these innocent beasts. Yet, later, Jaques enthusiastically takes part in the singing of a celebratory song over the body of a hunted stag. Although Jaques is often paradoxical, his nature as someone who enjoys criticizing the actions of others, but who himself acts in ways not always consistent with the moral positions he advocates, is readily comprehensible and familiar.

Another contradictory stance of Jaques is revealed when he mocks Amiens and the other lords for following the banished Duke Senior into the forest, "Leaving . . . wealth and ease / A stubborn will to please" (2.5.46–47). Clearly, this invites the question, Why has Jaques, too, followed Duke Senior into exile, if he regards doing so as foolish? Possibly, since Duke Senior also likes to discuss philosophy, Jaques has joined him in Arden because he is more likely to find there the type of stimulating conversation he relishes than at the decidedly nonintellectual court of Duke Frederick (at which the only pastime shown being enjoyed is a violent form of wrestling). Later, however, when the restored Duke Senior announces his plan to return to the court, Jaques declares that he prefers to stay and converse with the newly converted Duke Frederick, for "out of these convertites / There is much matter to be heard and learned" (5.4.181–182). This implies that Jaques has a sincere interest in religious matters. On the other hand, it could be

taken to suggest that what Jaques enjoys above all else is all-male company. Instead of returning to a court full of happy married couples, he prefers to stay in the forest with isolated men.

Touchstone

It might be thought that Touchstone, being a court clown, is a literary device rather than a fully rounded character. However, as James Shapiro has noted, Touchstone has 300 lines, more than any other Shakespearean "fool," and takes a more active role in the play's (minimal) plot than the "realistic" character Jaques. Thus, Touchstone has ample scope to show distinctive character traits and inform our response to the play as a whole.

To be sure, in his first appearance, in Act I, Scene 2, the clown does not seem a very unique creation. This appears deliberate, for the First Folio does not give the clown the name *Touchstone* until Act II, Scene 4. Hence, the clown of Act I, for all his clever wordplay, is dramatically redundant and (on paper) emphatically unfunny. His patter about a knight and some pancakes is notoriously tedious, occupying 17 lines (1.2.62–78). However, there may be more to such speeches than meets the eye, for the clown shows some satiric bite, observing: "The more pity that fools may not speak wisely what wise men do foolishly" (85–86). This alludes to the fact that court fools were traditionally allowed to serve a satirical function by referring in seemingly nonsensical language to official abuses of power. Evidently, in the usurper Frederick's court, this practice has been discontinued.

As mentioned, the clown begins to show nonconventional traits in Act II, Scene 4. Journeying through the Forest of Arden, Rosalind comments on the state of her "spirits," whereupon Touchstone remarks: "I care not for my spirits if my legs were not weary" (1–3). Thus, the clown reveals that he is not one for abstract notions; his physical comfort is his main concern. Refusing to join in Rosalind's sense of adventure, he declares: "When I was at home I was in a better place" (15). Similarly, when the passionate shepherd Silvius discourses romantically on love, Touchstone responds with bawdy

In this 19th-century print, Touchstone, Rosalind, and Celia meet Silvius and Corin in the Forest of Arden in Act II, Scene 4 of *As You Like It*.

innuendo, concerning a milkmaid called "Jane Smile": "I remember the kissing of her batlet . . . and I remember the wooing of a peascod instead of her" (45–48).

Since he is given to speaking in such a down-to-earth manner, it might be supposed that Touchstone is a man of the people. However, when Celia prompts Rosalind or Touchstone to buy food from the old shepherd, Corin, Touchstone rudely addresses the old man by calling, "Holla, you clown!" (63). When Corin asks "Who calls?" (64), Touchstone snaps: "Your betters, sir" (65). It appears that despite his court training, Touchstone is ill mannered and keen to assert his social superiority.

Like Rosalind, Touchstone has an extremely realistic outlook with regard to matters of the heart. Wanting only one thing from the goatherd Audrey, Touchstone summons Sir Oliver Martext, an incompetent rural vicar, to marry them because "he is not like to marry me well, and not being married well it will be a good excuse for me hereafter to leave my wife" (3.3.83–85). Yet, though they share an ability to see through romantic fictions, Rosalind and Touchstone are very different. Rosalind uses guile to manipulate Orlando (in that she remains disguised as Ganymede while encouraging Orlando to sing Rosalind's praises) and points out

the insincerity of classical poetic accounts of love, yet her guile and cynicism do not lead her to reject all sense of obligation to the feelings and needs of the man she desires. Rather, Rosalind teaches Orlando to express his own desires sincerely so that he will prove a suitable husband for her. Touchstone, on the other hand, while also familiar with classical love poetry, such as that written by "the most capricious poet, honest Ovid" (3.3.5–6), is evidently hoping to enjoy sexual relations with Audrey prior to abandoning her. By this contrast of the clown and Rosalind, Shakespeare implies that the ability to see through conventional illusions does not always accompany a lack of selfishness.

DIFFICULTIES OF THE PLAY

The majority of the dialogue of *As You Like It* is colloquial conversation, much of it in prose form, and, therefore, the language is often relatively easy to understand for a modern reader, at least compared to that of other Shakespearean plays. Nonetheless, as with modern conversation, the fast flow of witty repartee involves many cultural references, implicit and explicit, obscure and well known. Moreover, educated speakers such as Rosalind, Jaques, Duke Senior, Celia, and Touchstone flit constantly among a variety of language registers in ways that would have been entertaining to a viewer of Shakespeare's time but that a modern playgoer might fail to appreciate: There may sometimes seem to be no point to an exchange.

A good example of this occurs with the long debate in Act III, Scene 2 between Touchstone, the court clown, and Corin, the old shepherd. This duel lasts for more than 70 lines. The modern reader readily understands, of course, the humor involved in an encounter between a country hick and a sophisticated urbanite, but the joke soon wears thin if nothing else is understood to be going on beneath the surface. A contemporary audience, for instance, would have appreciated that they were witnessing an embodied pun. A simple country man at that period was also called a "clown," so in this scene a clown meets a clown. Of course, Touchstone is an educated clown who not only plays with language cleverly but also (implicitly) satirizes immorality at the sophisticated court. On the other hand, pastoral literature often represented rural characters as possessing more innate moral insight than the courtly characters who encountered them during a pastoral adventure. Thus, Touchstone may be said to be exhibiting status anxiety in this exchange in which he attempts to demonstrate that he is not only cleverer than Corin but also that the court is a better place to live than the countryside. At the same time, Touchstone appears aware that, really, the countryside is a healthier moral environment than the court, for the arguments he uses seem knowingly specious: "Why, if thou never wast at court thou never sawst good manners; if thou never sawst good manners then thy manners must be wicked . . ." (38–40). It is as though the court clown wishes to show that any case can be argued if the speaker knows how to use language well enough.

In any case, despite Touchstone's rhetorical fireworks, Corin the shepherd comes off well, expressing his own philosophical outlook in impressive tautologies ("I know . . . that the property of rain is to wet and fire to burn . . ." [22, 24–25]). Despite their amusing bluntness, Corin's utterances contain real moral force: "Sir, I am a true labourer. I earn that I eat, get that I wear; owe no man hate, envy no man's happiness; glad of other men's good, content with my harm; and the greatest of my pride is to see my ewes graze and my lambs suck" (70–74). Thus, both clowns entertain the audience by offering competing truths in comical ways. The anticipated pleasure of seeing a simple shepherd abused by a courtly wit, and the surprised pleasure of seeing the underdog hold his own, or, perhaps, even coming off better, would have entertained an Elizabethan audience and justified the length of the exchange.

In addition, this debate between Touchstone and Corin over the moral claims of life at court and in the country, respectively, may be a theological discussion in disguise. The name *Touchstone* refers to a type of stone that could be used to test the quality of silver or gold. Accordingly, some Elizabethan Protestant authorities argued that Scripture provided believers with a moral "touchstone," enabling them to test whether an action or attitude was sinful or not. Lacking an education, Corin is, presumably, not able to read. Therefore, when Touchstone insists the shepherd's "manners must be wicked," on account of his never having been at court, he may be alluding to contemporary confessional debates as to the level of education people required in order to be "good" Christians.

Again, for many modern readers, such subtexts may remain obscure. This type of problem occurs with single phrases as well. A clear instance occurs in Act I, Scene 2. The courtier Le Beau enters and begins to say that "Three proper young men of excellent growth and presence—," at which point Rosalind interrupts, saying "With bills on their necks: 'Be it known unto all men by these presents'" (115–118). There is a good chance this will be meaningless to a modern reader. As stated, this does not create large problems in terms of comprehension: The reader simply passes over the remark. However, there is the problem of appreciation: The impression is given that Rosalind is a character who makes somewhat silly, nonsensical remarks. This is not what an Elizabethan audience is likely to have thought. Rosalind is, in fact, quoting the standard legal formula of the period for the beginning of a will. Since Rosalind has lost her own inheritance (the dukedom itself) following the banishment of her father, this seemingly fatuous remark implies that she remains mindful of her dispossessed condition. She is not only educated enough to know such legal formulas but also sufficiently shrewd to insert them into conversations as harmless-seeming jokes rather than outright complaints, which would only mark her as a political enemy. The modern reader is perhaps encouraged to see Rosalind as a love-struck heroine whose most intense existence is on the emotional plane, but Rosalind is a skillful language user who constantly operates on a subtle intellectual level.

It should also be pointed out that most of the play's characters' names contain larger cultural significance readily apparent to contemporary audiences. Orlando, for example, takes his name from the titular hero of Ariosto's immensely popular Italian romance epic *Orlando Furioso* (reprinted about 90 times between 1540 and 1570). By the late 16th century, this work had acquired the status of a modern classic, being translated into English by Sir John Harington in 1591. In his *Defence of Poetry,* Sidney includes the character of Orlando in a list, along with Odysseus and Aeneas, of familiar types displaying particularly admirable virtues. Orlando, to a Renaissance reader or playgoer, is therefore the name of a brave and mighty champion of Christian heroic values, defending what his culture regarded as truth against incursions by infidels into Christendom. Furthermore, the name *Rosalind* appears to have been introduced to English literature by Spenser in *The Shepheardes Calendar* (1579). This work was based on Virgil's *Eclogues,* a series of poems which, in the Renaissance, were regarded as allegorical—affecting a surface simplicity that contains multiple hidden levels of meaning. In accordance with the way in which its classical model was read at the time, *The Shepheardes Calendar* was offered to the public as an avowedly allegorical work. Consequently, the names of its characters were expected to contain hidden significance. Rosalind, translated from Spanish, means "beautiful rose." This "rose" may be taken as a figure for natural beauty, or it could be regarded as a mystic symbol of heavenly beauty. In true romantic fashion, therefore, Shakespeare's Orlando, the champion of truth, is also a lover of beauty—spiritual and natural. When Orlando defeats a giant wrestler with ease, a modern reader might be surprised but accept it on the level of a romantic fairy tale; Orlando is the hero, so it would not make much sense if he got his neck broken in the first act. An Elizabethan audience would, on hearing the name Orlando, be prepared for him to perform marvelous feats of strength and courage. Therefore, they would be less surprised to see him throw the gigantic Charles. Although they would attribute his power to romance conventions, they would also be prepared to see in those conventions a language of allegory, alluding to hidden philosophical and mystical meanings.

In sum, *As You Like It* is by no means a difficult play to understand on first reading. It is, however, an extremely easy play to underrate, for it wears its cultural allusions and significance lightly.

KEY PASSAGES
Act I, Scene 1, 1–24

ORLANDO. As I remember, Adam, it was
  upon this fashion bequeathed me by will but
  poor a thousand crowns, and, as thou sayst,
  charged my brother on his blessing to breed
  me well; and there begins my sadness. My
  brother Jaques he keeps at school and report
  speaks goldenly of his profit. For my part, he
  keeps me rustically at home or, to speak more
  properly, stays me here at home unkept; for
  call you that keeping, for a gentleman of my
  birth, that differs not from the stalling of an
  ox? His horses are bred better, for besides
  that they are fair with their feeding, they are
  taught their manage and to that end riders
  dearly hired; but I, his brother, gain nothing
  under him but growth, for the which his
  animals on his dunghills are as much bound
  to him as I. Besides this nothing that he
  so plentifully gives me, the something that
  nature gave me his countenance seems to
  take from me. He lets me feed with his hinds,
  bars me the place of a brother and, as much
  as in him lies, mines my gentility with my
  education. This is it, Adam, that grieves me,
  and the spirit of my father, which I think
  is within me, begins to mutiny against this
  servitude. I will no longer endure it, though
  yet I know no wise remedy how to avoid it.

This opening speech explains Orlando's situation as mistreated youngest son to the audience. It also reveals the basic outlines of the youthful hero's character and introduces the theme of education, which will be explored throughout the play.

In delivering himself of this opening complaint, Orlando does not emerge as being entirely admirable at this stage in his life. This, however, makes him more interesting to the audience as a hero who possesses some character flaws. In any case, he is identifiable as a Cinderella type: an orphan abused by his older brother, deprived of what he regards as his rightful inheritance, and forced to live with the family's servants ("hinds"). Yet, unlike Cinderella, Orlando does not patiently accept these conditions. Indeed, they wound him so much because he regards them as inappropriate to "a gentleman of my birth." Moreover, Orlando, as far as can be gathered from this opening complaint, is not required to do any work—unlike Cinderella. Basically, he is complaining because he is allowed to sit around on the family estate all day doing nothing. True, he regrets his lack of an education, pointing out (somewhat jealously) that his brother Jaques (the middle son) is being "kept at school and report speaks goldenly of his profit," but it is not clear from this speech that what Orlando craves is schooling. He implicitly seems to desire a bigger allowance so he can cut a better figure in the world at large (he laments his loss of social status, claiming that Oliver seeks to undermine "my gentility"). It might be wondered why Orlando's father bequeathed him "but poor a thousand crowns." A possible answer lies in the familiarity and popularity in Elizabethan England of the prodigal son story: Orlando's father perhaps was worried for his youngest son's moral well-being if he were to have been given money to play with without any attendant responsibility.

This brings us to an important theme of the play that is clearly emphasized in this opening speech: education. What was the best way to bring up sons, especially the youngest sons of middle-class families? Do good qualities, moreover, come from blood or from breeding? Orlando seems confused on the matter: He insists that he has good qualities as a result of his pedigree but also fears they are being lost as a result of his lack of an education. The verb *feed* occurs twice in the speech: Young creatures have to be nurtured and taught proper behavior and useful skills if they are to grow into healthy, capable adults. In early modern culture, however, preferential treatment was given to first-born sons of well-to-do families. It was thought more appropriate to give the greatest share to the eldest son and relatively little to younger sons in order to preserve the family's name and position in society (daughters were to be married into suitable families). In an indirect fashion, Orlando is complaining about the injustice of that custom. And, as it is unjust, the audience may be expected to sympathize with Orlando. He has a right to complain. The audience identifies with him and hopes he will overcome his problems, improve his social circumstances, and achieve happiness. Nevertheless, the audience will also note his pride, resentfulness and lack of Stoic/Christian resignation. Accordingly, they will expect to see him receive an education in the course of the play, helping him quell these negative qualities. This suggests that the play supports the notion that true virtue is acquired, not inbred, marking it as a relatively democratic play. What remains unclear, though, is the response elicited by Orlando's use of the strong word *mutiny*. If he objects to the custom of the land, is he justified in seeking to "mutiny against this servitude"? Or, should he strive rather to subdue his own pride? The murder plot subsequently instigated against Orlando by his brother Oliver may retroactively incline an audience to agree that mutiny under such conditions is justified.

Act II, Scene 1, 1–24

DUKE SENIOR. Now, my co-mates and
  brothers in exile,
Hath not old custom made this life more sweet
Than that of painted pomp? Are not these
  woods
More free from peril than the envious court?
Here feel we not the penalty of Adam,
The seasons' difference—as the icy fang
And churlish chiding of the winter's wind,
Which when it bites and blows upon my body
Even till I shrink with cold, I smile and say:
'This is no flattery. These are counsellors
That feelingly persuade me what I am.'
Sweet are the uses of adversity,
Which, like a toad, ugly and venomous,
Wears yet a precious jewel in his head;
And this our life, exempt from public haunt,

Finds tongues in trees, books in the running
  brooks,
Sermons in stones, and good in everything.

AMIENS. I would not change it. Happy is
  your grace
That can translate the stubbornness of fortune
Into so quiet and so sweet a style.

DUKE SENIOR. Come, shall we go and kill
  us venison?
And yet it irks me the poor dappled fools,
Being native burghers of this desert city,
Should in their own confines with forked heads
Have their round haunches gored.

This opening speech of the banished Duke Senior, now living in the Forest of Arden, is an important element in the play's presentation of the pastoral mode. It should be remembered, though, that the Duke is not himself a shepherd or a native of the countryside. He describes the court as the site of sin, flattery, corruption, deceit, ambition, and greed, but the court is his own native environment. Speaking in a very ornate poetic style, Duke Senior praises sincerity, but sincerity in pastoral literature is associated with plainness of speech. Therefore, though the Duke is exiled from the court, he is also, in a sense, foreign to—outside of—the forest environment he celebrates in this speech. Hence, he may be taken to represent the division that is at the heart of the pastoral mode. Pastoral poetry first began to be written by poets in cities such as Alexandria and Rome, which had become too large for life within them to be always commodious. Thus, pastoral poetry tended to look back nostalgically on a natural way of living that the poet could never recover. The sophisticated, urban poet, therefore, in praising innocence, praises a quality he lacks. Of course, a truly sophisticated poet will be conscious of this dichotomy. Duke Senior, however, appears blithely unaware of it. Consequently, he emerges as a somewhat ridiculous figure in this exchange with Amiens, despite his studied eloquence.

At one point, the Duke appears to be saying that merely by relocating to the forest, he has regained the innocence known by Adam in Eden: "Here feel we not the penalty of Adam." It should be acknowledged that most editors of the play do not consider that Duke Senior is saying here that original sin is canceled for himself and his companions. Since the inevitability of original sin was officially a doctrine of Protestant and Catholic countries at that time, it is presumed that such a venerable figure as the Duke would not offer such a view. Hence, editors usually feel obliged to interpret the Duke's words rather loosely in their explanatory notes, suggesting, for example, that he is saying something along the lines of "Here we may feel the penalty of Adam [i.e., the change of the seasons; because it was always Spring in Eden] in the form of the winter wind, but really that is a good thing because it does not flatter us; when we feel the cold, that tells us that we are frail human creatures; this is better for our moral health." Nonetheless, it is possible to take the Duke at his word: He states that original sin is not felt "here" in the forest. (Polixenes, another elderly male character in *The Winter's Tale,* expresses the same idea in explicit terms. This proves that the view could be expressed by a character in a manner consistent with the respect due to age.) Certainly, Duke Senior's syntax is tangled in this section of the speech, which makes the sense difficult to understand. This may have been Shakespeare's method of avoiding problems with the censor, given the unorthodoxy of the view apparently expressed, or perhaps the convoluted nature of the Duke's utterance is another aspect of his paradoxical lack of simplicity in praising the simple life.

He itemizes the "perils" of the court: It is an "envious" place, where people plot against one another; he knows this to be true, for he was banished from his throne by his own brother. The court is also full of "painted pomp" (again, it is ironic that Duke Senior's speech is itself an example of "painted pomp"). Most of all, in the court, no one speaks the truth, especially to their superiors. They offer only flattery. We do not know why Duke Senior was banished. However, it appears that he is here bemoaning a lack of good advice from his former counselors. Presumably, he made some bad decisions and failed to weigh fully views opposing his own; in short, he was complacent as a ruler which, in fact, would be entirely consistent with his complacent attitude to living in the forest. He thinks it is pleasant to live in the forest, even in the freezing cold, because it "feelingly persuade[s] me what I am." This relates back to the prodigal son theme: perhaps Orlando's father chose not to give his youngest son much money so that he would be exposed to the harshness of life and become a better person as a result. In this sense, Duke Senior is correct: Adversity can be a great teacher. Nevertheless, the Duke overstates the case, saying that when the cold wind blows upon him "Even till I shrink with cold, I smile." The combination of cringing with cold and happy smiling is rhetorically unconvincing. One can easily imagine, here, the thoughts of the courtiers gathered round him ("Give me a warm house, and you can keep your self-knowledge").

Orlando will receive an education in this play; Duke Senior claims to receive one from the cold winter wind. Yet, it appears he has learned relatively little. He finds "good in everything." Thus, in the forest, there is apparently no social hierarchy, everyone is equal: Duke Senior calls his lords "my co-mates" and suggests that here he is "free from peril" of the court, as here there is no flattery. However, when Amiens (his "co-mate") next addresses the Duke, he does so in a flattering tone as to a social superior: "Happy is your grace." Moreover, Amiens seems inclined to mix a little implied criticism with his flattery, praising the duke for his ability to "translate the stubbornness of fortune / Into so . . . sweet a style." Duke Senior has merely learned how to put a positive spin on his political defeat. In addition, the reference to "fortune" points back to an earlier conversation between Rosalind and Celia; if the audience recalls Rosalind's perspicacious comments on fortune, they might be inclined to conclude that the daughter is wiser than the father.

The Duke does not respond to Amiens's flattery reprovingly, but rather, after praising the life of restored innocence in the forest, suggests they all go and kill some deer. If the peril of Adam in the form of original sin is absent in the forest, Duke Senior newly imports it in the form of death. Exiled himself, he proceeds to eject the "native burghers of this desert city." Admittedly, he claims to feel "irked" by this contradiction, but that does not prevent him from planning his next hunting trip. Again, this is evidence that for him, "doing the right thing" is a matter of style and not of modifying one's actual behavior.

In sum, Shakespeare appears to be criticizing Stoic philosophy in his presentation of Duke Senior. This school of classical philosophy was enjoying a revival along with other aspects of the classical past, but Shakespeare evidently saw in its doctrine of professed indifference to one's circumstances a lack of intellectual honesty, a failure to accept adult responsibility in dealing with the world as it is. The most serious failing that Shakespeare imparts to Stoicism (more properly it should be called neostoicism, for the Duke's philosophy contains Christian theological elements) is the self-satisfied closed-off mentality it seems to engender. By virtue of his patient acceptance of his straitened circumstances as "sweet," Duke Senior, though amiable, appears incapable of mending his faults. A more flexible philosophy is called for, this satirical portrait suggests.

Act II, Scene 7, 48–76

JAQUES. I must have liberty
Withal, as large a charter as the wind
To blow on whom I please, for so fools have,
And they that are most galled with my folly,
They most must laugh. And why, sir, must
  they so?
The why is plain as way to parish church.
He that a fool doth very wisely hit
Doth very foolishly, although he smart,
Not to seem senseless of the bob, if not,
The wise man's folly in anatomized
Even by the squandering glances of the fool.
Invest me in my motley. Give me leave
To speak my mind, and I will through and
  through

Cleanse the foul body of th'infected world,
If they will patiently receive my medicine.

DUKE SENIOR. Fie on thee! I can tell what
thou wouldst do.

JAQUES. What, for a counter, would I do but
good?

DUKE SENIOR. Most mischievous foul sin in
chiding sin.
For thou thyself hast been a libertine,
As sensual as the brutish sting itself,
And all th'embossed sores and headed evils
That thou with licence of free foot hast caught
Wouldst thou disgorge into the general world.

JAQUES. Why, who cries out on pride
That can therein tax any private party?
Doth it not flow as hugely as the sea
Till that the weary very means do ebb?
What woman in the city do I name,
When that I say the city-woman bears
The cost of princes on unworthy shoulders?

This speech contains a manifesto, or apology (defense), for satire. Jaques the gentleman courtier is (jokingly) requesting permission from Duke Senior to be allowed to wear a fool's costume. Dressed in that fashion, he would have "liberty . . . To blow on whom I please." The reference to a licensed wind may contain an allusion to John 3:8, which, in the Geneva Bible, says: "The winde bloweth where it listeth." Other Bibles use the word *spirit* for *wind*. Jaques, therefore, appears to be requesting a quasi-religious authority to satirize immoral behavior. His satire will act as a medicine that will "cleanse the foul body" of the world. In addition, he points out that anyone offended by his satire will, nonetheless, be obliged to laugh, for if they show their annoyance, onlookers will know they are guilty of the sin being criticized. This offers an explanation as to why court clowns and artificial "fools" were allowed to say supposedly nonsensical things that, beneath the surface, seemed to contain hidden attacks on people. The ridiculousness of their language allowed their victims to laugh off the attack. Presumably, these victims were supposed to subsequently mend their behavior.

Duke Senior, however, seems annoyed by Jaques's jocular request. He refers pointedly to Jaques's personal history, mentioning a time when Jaques had "been a libertine," given to indulging in "sensual" pleasures. The Duke suggests that Jaques's own nature was polluted by his former activities, and, therefore, while attempting to cure people of sin, Jaques would in fact spread worse diseases. In this manner, the Duke appears to be criticizing satirists who set themselves up as morally superior to others. Only a person who has never committed a sin should consider themselves morally qualified to criticize other people in the manner Jaques is suggesting. Otherwise, these would-be "doctors" will only make the situation worse, by spreading malice and bad feeling. There is also a veiled suggestion that Jaques is no longer able to enjoy certain pleasures himself, perhaps because of some disease he has contracted (the Duke refers to "embossed sores"). Thus, being now jealous of other people's enjoyment of those pleasures, Jaques's desire to criticize is born of resentment. Jaques makes no attempt to answer this charge. He does not deny that he had been a "libertine" in the past. In fact, his reply is entirely irrelevant to the Duke's previous utterance. Jaques answers as though the Duke had said, "Isn't it wrong to target private individuals?" If he were a licensed fool, Jaques claims he would attack sins, and not the individual sinners, criticizing "pride" itself, for example, not "any private party." This was (and is) the standard defense offered by satirists.

Act II, Scene 7, 135–166
DUKE SENIOR. Thou seest we are not all
alone unhappy.
This wide and universal theatre
Presents more woeful pageants than the scene
Wherein we play in.

JAQUES. All the world's a stage,
And all the men and women merely players.

They have their exits and their entrances,
And one man in his time plays many parts,
His acts being seven ages. At first the infant,
Mewling and puking in the nurse's arms;
Then the whining schoolboy, with his satchel
And shining morning face, creeping like snail
Unwillingly to school; and then the lover,
Sighing like furnace, with a woeful ballad
Made to his mistress' eyebrow; then a soldier,
Full of strange oaths and bearded like the
  pard,
Jealous in honour, sudden and quick in
  quarrel,
Seeking the bubble reputation
Even in the cannon's mouth; and then the
  justice,
In fair round belly with good capon lined,
With eyes severe and beard of formal cut,
Full of wise saws and modern instances;
And so he plays his part. The sixth age shifts
Into the lean and slippered pantaloon,
With spectacles on nose and pouch on side,
His youthful hose well saved, a world too wide
For his shrunk shank, and his big manly voice,
Turning again toward childish treble, pipes
And whistles in his sound. Last scene of all,
That ends this strange eventful history,
Is second childishness and mere oblivion,
Sans teeth, *sans* eyes, *sans* taste, *sans*
  everything.
[*Enter Orlando bearing Adam.*]

This speech has become famous, especially the phrase "All the world's a stage," but, in fact, Shakespeare appears to offer it as an example of studied rhetoric that sounds impressive but says relatively little. To compare the world to a stage, for example, was a cliché in the Renaissance. Admittedly, Jaques develops the notion adroitly, using a sustained metaphor related to performance ("exits," "entrances," "many parts," "acts," "last scene of all"), but all he is saying, over the course of 27 lines, is that people may like to think of themselves as unique individuals, but in fact, everyone goes through the same stages in their lives.

A depiction of the fourth age of man, as Jaques describes it in Act II, Scene 7 of *As You Like It*. This print is from the Boydell Shakespeare Gallery project. *(Painting by Robert Smirke; engraving by John Ogborne)*

In any case, Jaques's view of the human condition emerges as intensely pessimistic. It is a fatalistic vision, in which people seem to lack free will, being obliged to go through the predictable stages of life. This effect is accentuated by the scarcity of simple verb forms in the main body of the speech. Notice that in the sentence beginning with the first stage of life ("At first the infant . . ."), the subject "the infant" is not given a simple verb form for its actions. Rather the present participles "Mewling" and "puking" are used to describe its activity. The emphasis is on activity, not action. The individual does not do things in his or her life, he or she undergoes them, that being the nature of everyone's existence. It might be expected that a baby would be described in this way, but the principle is observed by Jaques in his account of the other stages of life: the "schoolboy . . . creeping," "the lover, / Sighing," "a soldier . . . / Seeking the bubble reputation." The only exception is the fifth age, "the justice," but instead of performing a decisive action, even this venerable character merely "plays his part." Moreover, this view of life is rendered even bleaker by the conclusion: Jaques sees human life as ending in nothingness. This is quite a startling declaration.

It has been suggested by some modern scholars that agnosticism regarding the afterlife did not exist as a concept in the Renaissance period, but here Jaques, in fact, expresses more than mere doubt as to whether there is life after death. He affirms there is nothing after death.

It is curious that this long speech, ending as it does in such a daring, skeptical manner, receives no reply from any of the other characters on stage. Perhaps such rhetorical performances invite applause, rather than further discussion (unless a rival orator is expected to deliver a speech presenting the opposing view). Receiving no answer from his auditors to his grand set piece, Jaques is left looking rather foolish.

Jaques however does receive an answer of a non-verbal kind. Shakespeare presents the counterargument to Jaques's pessimism by having Orlando arrive on stage, carrying the loyal old servant, Adam, on his back. Jaques's ostensibly complete catalog of human activities made no mention of such selfless actions as this performed by Orlando. Adam himself, moreover, had equally selflessly given his life savings to Orlando in order to enable him to escape his brother's jealous schemes. Thus, the long, impressive-sounding speech of Jaques is put in the scales and weighed against a single simple act of charity: a young man carrying a starving old man on his back. As mentioned, Jaques's speech receives no reply from Duke Senior, but the arrival of Orlando is met by the Duke saying, "Welcome. Set down your venerable burden."

DIFFICULT PASSAGES
Act I, Scene 2, 24–43

ROSALIND. Let me see: what think you of falling in love?

CELIA. Marry, I prithee do, to make sport withal—but love no man in good earnest, nor no further in sport neither than with safety of a pure blush thou mayst in honour come off again.

ROSALIND. What shall be our sport then?

CELIA. Let us sit and mock the good housewife Fortune from her wheel, that her gifts may henceforth be bestowed equally.

ROSALIND. I would we could do so, for her benefits are mightily misplaced—and the bountiful blind woman doth most mistake in her gifts to women.

CELIA. 'Tis true, for those that she makes fair she scarce makes honest, and those that she makes honest she makes very ill-favouredly.

ROSALIND. Nay, now thou goest from Fortune's office to Nature's; Fortune reigns in gifts of the world not in the lineaments of nature.

CELIA. No? When Nature hath made a fair creature may she not by Fortune fall into the fire?

This type of mock philosophical discussion would have been familiar to Elizabethan readers and playgoers, but to a modern reader the neatness of the equivocations can be confusing. Rosalind and Celia debate here why the goddess Fortune distributes her gifts unequally. However, before analyzing the arguments they present, it will be as well to consider how the conversation is also intended to reveal differences in the characters of the two young women.

To start with, Rosalind appears the more girlish of the two in that she introduces the topic of love, but it should be remembered that she only does this to turn the conversation away from the plight of her banished father. In response, Celia adopts a carefree, playful attitude, suggesting that love is only "to make sport withal." However, perhaps she does not like this subject of love, for were Rosalind to fall in love and get married, Celia would lose her only companion in her father's somewhat austere court. Indeed, she tells Rosalind "love no man in good earnest"—that is, not as far as marrying him. Her moral side quickly reinstates itself as she immediately realizes a dangerous implication of her words.

She adds: "nor no further in sport neither than with safety of a pure blush thou mayst in honour come off again." This seems to empty the field of any capacity for "sport" in Rosalind's mind. If it is marriage or nothing, she asks, "What shall be our sport then?" Evidently, Rosalind would be prepared to go further "than with safety of a pure blush." The two women appear to have different views on the topic of how far love can be pursued outside marriage. Hence, they will need to find a new subject of conversation if they are going to joust with each other safely.

The more sober-seeming Celia switches the talk to philosophy: She wants to mock Fortune—what a modern person would call "fate" or "luck"—because some people have much, others less. Being the daughter of a banished father, Rosalind agrees with (one imagines) a rueful smile, "for her [Fortune's] benefits are mightily misplaced." It is easy for someone like Celia, the daughter of the reigning Duke, to philosophize complacently about how unfair life can be.

At this point, however, Rosalind pursues a more surprising avenue, suggesting that Fortune "doth most mistake in her gifts to women." This might well be taken as a sort of protofeminist statement (it should be remembered that by Fortune, the two women mean "the world" or "society"). Celia does not take up this political angle, preferring to interpret Rosalind's remark as being about physical appearance: Some women are born more beautiful than others. When Rosalind points out that this is nothing to do with Fortune, who "reigns in gifts of the world not in the lineaments of Nature," Celia replies by suggesting that pretty women are more likely to "fall into the fire," that is, commit sin and go to hell. This reveals a moralistic streak in Celia. It also shows that the two young friends have a different view as to the nature of women. Rosalind sees society as unjust to women; Celia sees women as the cause of their own downfall, by virtue of their own moral weakness.

Act III, Scene 3, 12–22

TOUCHSTONE. When a man's verses
  cannot be understood, nor a man's good
wit seconded with the forward child,
  understanding, it strikes a man more dead
  than a great reckoning in a little room. Truly,
  I would the gods had made thee poetical.

AUDREY. I do not know what poetical is. Is it
  honest in deed and word? Is it a true thing?

TOUCHSTONE. No, truly; for the truest
  poetry is the most faining, and lovers are
  given to poetry, and what they swear in
  poetry may be said, as lovers, they do feign.

AUDREY. Do you wish then that the gods
  had made me poetical?

TOUCHSTONE. I do, truly, for thou swear'st
  to me thou art honest. Now if thou wert
  a poet I might have some hope thou didst
  feign.

A court fool or clown is nothing without an audience. Living in the forest, with, here, an uneducated female goatherd for a companion, Touchstone's clever remarks go unappreciated. Of course, he is also a clown on a stage delivering jokes to an audience. If his jokes are too clever, they might meet with confused silence. Touchstone, however, implicitly suggests that if the audience does not understand his humor, perhaps the fault lies with the audience not being "poetical" enough.

In any case, a modern reader might easily be confused by this exchange, in which different meanings of the words *poetical, true, honest,* and *fain/feign* are played upon. What lies behind the discussion is a moral concern with the notion that poetry (or, as we might say, "fiction") is nothing but a pack of lies. It should be remembered that the culture of early modern England was Bible-based and religious. The Bible was revered as a source of truth. Literature, including classical works such as Ovid's poetry, which Touchstone alludes to immediately before the passage given above, seemed, from the point of view of some Protestant authorities, to serve no moral purpose, having no divine

Touchstone speaks with Audrey, his future bride, in the forest in Act III, Scene 3 of *As You Like It*. This is a print from Malcolm C. Salaman's 1916 edition of *Shakespeare in Pictorial Art*. (Painting by John Pettie)

authority. Touchstone here gives the same defense of poetry that the courtier poet Sidney gave in his *Apology for Poetry:* poetry cannot be said to lie, for it never claims to be telling the truth. Accordingly, Touchstone wishes Audrey was more poetical because, in that case, when she says she is "honest"—that is, when she insists on their getting married before sleeping together—there would be at least a chance that she was lying.

Audrey asks if the word *poetical* refers to an "honest" and a "true thing." Here she uses "honest" to mean "moral, proper, upright" and "true" to mean "honest as in truth-telling." Basically, she wants to know if a "good girl" would have anything to do with whatever Touchstone means by "poetical." Though Audrey is uneducated, one has the feeling that she knows exactly what Touchstone is after, and she also knows how to keep him at bay. Touchstone, however, is addicted to wordplay to the point where he cannot resist defeating his own aims. If he is really trying to persuade Audrey to sleep with him, perhaps he should not so carefully explain that he wishes she were "poetical" because that would mean there was a chance she was really dishonest.

The play upon the words *fain* and *feign* may also be confusing. The word *fain* describes a willingness to do something, while the verb *feign*, of

course, signifies "to pretend." Touchstone adds to the difficulty by using *truest* in a particular sense, meaning "best kind of." He says: "the truest poetry," in other words, the most emotionally affecting poetry, "is the most faining," the most full of desire or longing. The audience, however, also hears the pun with *feigning*, which gives a different meaning: "the truest poetry" is that which tells the most lies (invents the greatest fictions).

At least one thing emerges clearly from all this: a further pun, buried beneath the actual language, on two meanings of the word *court*, as in "courtier" and "courtship." Touchstone is a court clown, and here he is courting Audrey, but courtly language, in its clever use of double meanings, is obviously intended to deceive. When men use language to court women, they become poets and tell lies in order to obtain what they desire.

CRITICAL INTRODUCTION TO THE PLAY
The Pastoral Mode

As You Like It is a pastoral play; therefore, it is useful to review how the pastoral mode functions. The term *pastoral* derives from *pastor,* the Latin word for "shepherd." Pastoral poetry, as written by Theocritus (ca. 316–ca. 260 B.C.) and specifically by Virgil (70–19 B.C.) in the *Eclogues,* was so-called because the main characters were shepherds. However, these poems, though set in the countryside, were not concerned only with rural matters. Virgil's shepherds, for example, frequently criticize the values of the city, describing Rome as a site of corruption, greed, and deception. The countryside thus emerges as a site of relative innocence. Moreover, then, as now, when people wished to condemn a particular lifestyle, they would describe it as "unnatural," implying that what is "natural" is inherently good. Cities, with their grand buildings, expensive fashions, rich food, exquisite ornaments, elegant language, formal etiquette, and so forth, were, by contrast with the countryside, implicitly condemned in pastoral poetry as "unnatural."

Against this, it might be argued that it is natural for human beings to build comfortable shelters and live in communities. Thus, it is important to stress that the notion that cities are sites of immorality seems to derive from the growth of the first large metropolises, such as Alexandria and Rome (the homes of Theocritus and Virgil, respectively). When people live in cities where they do not know the names of everyone they meet, there is a feeling of isolation within a crowd rather than of community. Also, the inhabitants of a large city tend not to live by a single code of behavior. Hence, people may begin to criticize unfamiliar lifestyles as "unnatural." They might then lament that things were different in the "good old days"—the "golden age"—when the city was small, surrounded by fields, and when everyone was generous and hospitable. The only place where one may find decent behavior now, they suppose, is in the countryside.

Of course, the belief that the countryside is a place where the Sun always shines, where people remain innocent and are always happy is a romantic idealization. Obviously, if the jaded urbanites of Alexandria and Rome were to spend some time in a real rural setting, they would find life there less innocent and probably much less pleasant than they had imagined. Nonetheless, this nostalgic ideal offered poets a useful way of imagining the way life should be lived. In this way, the pastoral mode provided a means of encoding discussion of political, philosophical, and theological issues that, if treated literally, might prove dangerously controversial.

The pastoral mode also contains an inherent paradox. If the countryside is a place of relative innocence, then presumably it is the case that when its inhabitants speak their thoughts, they do so not only with sincerity but also in plain language. By contrast, in the city or the court, people use sophisticated language, often with the intention to deceive in order to obtain what they desire. The paradox, of course, is that pastoral poetry is not written by shepherds but by sophisticated urban poets. Certainly, the "shepherds" in Virgil's *Eclogues* display great artistry in their songs. This makes it impossible for the reader to believe that these characters' words are meant to represent the speech of actual shepherds. From this, it can

be seen that a sense of realism is not the aim of pastoral poetry. In fact, the pastoral mode, though designed to praise the simple life, and the natural way of living, is itself not only a product but also an actual expression of an artificial manner. Nonetheless, since the pastoral countryside is described as relatively natural when compared to the artificiality of the city, then the countryside featured in a pastoral play, such as the Forest of Arden in *As You Like It*, may be regarded as an idealized zone that serves as a symbol of nature and the golden age.

In addition, in pastoral works, the countryside can function as a symbol for a person's inner being, with the city representing his or her social being. When we are abroad in our daily lives, we are obliged to behave in certain artificial ways. When alone, however, we may sit in silence and retreat inside ourselves and contemplate our "real" self. Of course, we have no access to any "real" essential self (the thoughts we have when we meditate or reflect are still, to an extent, governed by our cultural formation), but in relative terms, social life is more artificial than the reflective life.

The Forest of Arden as Symbolic Location

With this understanding of the pastoral mode now in place, aspects of *As You Like It* that might otherwise seem confusing become easier to comprehend. For example, when Shakespeare—making an addition to the story as told in his main source, Lodge's *Rosalynd*—sends a court clown (Touchstone) along with Rosalind and Celia into the Forest of Arden, it might seem that he does so only to facilitate some extra humor. However, the presence of Touchstone in the forest provides the dramatist with an adroit means of exploring the play's overarching theme—the rival claims of art and nature—for Elizabethans made a distinction between natural fools and artificial fools. A natural fool was someone born with low intelligence, while an artificial fool was someone who only pretended to be foolish. Touchstone, of course, is an artificial fool. He entertains the other characters and the audience with witty repartee whenever he appears. Shakespeare, wishing to explore the contrast between artificiality (or art) and nature, transplants this artificial fool into a "natural" setting: the Forest of Arden.

On arriving in the forest, Touchstone declares: "Ay, now am I in Arden, the more fool I! When I was at home I was in a better place" (2.4.14–15). The court clown, once removed from the court, has no function. All of his cultural training, his wit, his linguistic genius will be wasted on the native inhabitants of the forest. Thus, he is both more and less of a fool now that he is in the forest. Of course, Touchstone also means to say that he was foolish for agreeing to accompany the women to this desolate place, with no ready means of obtaining food or shelter. The artificial fool thus offers a realistic assessment of what life in the countryside is like.

Bearing in mind the aims of the pastoral mode (to juxtapose court/city values and country values), it becomes clear why Shakespeare devotes a large part of one scene to an encounter between Touchstone, the court clown, and Corin, the old shepherd, who is also a type of clown (*clown* being an Elizabethan term for country bumpkin). The artificial meets the natural in order to stage a philosophical debate as to which lifestyle is superior, the courtly or the rural. Touchstone, as might be expected, wins the argument in terms of cleverness, but Corin holds his own in terms of moral values.

The play stages other debates using the forest as a symbolic location. While the answer to the question "Is it natural for a man to love his brother?" might seem to be obviously "yes," both Oliver and Duke Frederick mistreat their brothers. Frederick banishes his brother, the rightful duke, while Oliver is jealous of Orlando's popularity and even plots his violent murder. Frederick lives at the court, Oliver lives on a country estate. Neither belong to the forest. Therefore, it may be assumed that it is their education (in other words, their upbringing) and the influence of their social environment that has taught them to forget their "natural" love for their brothers.

In the play's first scene, Oliver admits that "my soul—yet I know not why—hates nothing more than he [Orlando]. Yet he's gentle, never schooled and yet learned . . ." (1.1.54–56). Unlike Oliver, Orlando has not been "schooled" and, therefore, has not acquired unnatural vices. For his part, Frederick would seem to know, at some unconscious level, that his treatment of his brother was wrong, for when Oliver confesses that "I never loved my brother in my life," Frederick (with apparently unknowing irony) responds: "More villain thou!" (3.1.14–15). On arriving in the forest, however, both Oliver and Frederick undergo sudden conversions and perform acts of restitution to their brothers. The play offers no clear motive for these changes of heart. Modern readers, accustomed to the psychological detail of novels that carefully account for their characters' actions, might feel short changed by these miraculous conversions, or regard them as evidence of the dramatist's wish to provide a happy ending with minimum fuss. It should be remembered, though, that according to the conventions of the pastoral mode, the Forest of Arden may be a symbol of the reflective life. According to this view, the play does not describe Oliver and Frederick entering a real forest and by coincidence undergoing a complete personality change. Rather, Oliver and Frederick, having had occasion to reflect on their past actions, have undergone a change of heart. Their arrival in the imaginary forest may be a metaphorical representation of such a change of heart. Mature reflection dissolves jealousy fermented by Frederick and Oliver's respective upbringings in artificial environments and restores the brothers to a more "natural" condition of loving their siblings. Thus, these villainous characters may be said to "arrive" in the forest when they become more "natural."

The Theme of Education

Another aspect of the play's exploration of the rival claims of art and nature is its treatment of the theme of education, or nature versus nurture. The play begins with Orlando complaining that, unlike his brother (Jaques de Boys), he is not receiving an education. However, it may be wondered if education is indeed a good thing if it merely teaches people to be selfish members of a corrupt society. From the point of view of pastoral convention, in preparing for life at court or in the city, people learn to hide their true feelings and study how to use language to further their own ends. Oliver, presumably, as the oldest son in the de Boys family, has received an education, yet he does not appear to be a better person for it, as discussed previously. Similarly, Touchstone uses his courtly eloquence to attempt to seduce the simple country wench Audrey. His education has merely provided the court clown with more sophisticated means of arranging to satisfy his urges, even at the expense of others (Audrey's social position in a traditional Christian community would suffer were she to agree to sleep with him out of wedlock).

If the education provided by society is to be mistrusted, Duke Senior proposes a different type of education. Though forced to live in the forest as a result of his banishment, he claims to be happy there because the cold wind teaches him the nature of his true self. Nonetheless, as discussed in the "Key Passages" section, Duke Senior continues to speak in an ornate, artificial style and exhibits a lack of self-knowledge, which suggests his claim to be educated by hardship is more a matter of eloquence than substance. Evidently, the cold wind, a force of nature, cannot by itself teach someone to be a better person.

Conversely, Duke Senior's daughter, Rosalind, has developed a keen intelligence, along with a sharp sense of humor, as a result of her education in Frederick's court and despite (or because of) enduring a certain amount of social isolation as Frederick's "guest." The reaction of her own nature to her cultural environment and material circumstances appears to have resulted in her acquiring admirable self-control. The play thus suggests that it is philosophically naive to suppose that merely by living in the countryside in harsh conditions we will automatically become better people. A judicious combination of innate qualities, education, and lived experience is what enables people to wrestle with their flaws and acquire self-knowledge.

The melancholy Jaques, prior to the action of the play, had also sought a kind of education, selling his lands (as Rosalind surmises) in order to travel and acquire knowledge by experience. Having acquired that knowledge, he is now unhappy. As Rosalind says, this type of knowledge is dearly bought; perhaps it would be better to remain ignorant, retain one's property, and live in comfort and relative happiness.

From this treatment of the theme of education, it might be thought that the play implicitly offers a conservative message: Being content with your lot is a surer route to happiness than seeking to obtain a higher station. After all, Duke Frederick, having banished his brother and seized the throne, proceeds to live in constant fear of someone similarly plotting to usurp him. Moreover, Corin's plain-spoken speech in praise of being content with what one has instead of envying another man for his possessions is offered in a favorable light, in contrast to Touchstone's specious wordplay. Nonetheless, if the culture one lives in seemingly teaches one to aspire to wealth and to a higher position in society, then it becomes a radical, even subversive, gesture to argue that one should mutiny against the influence of such social norms and strive, not for the

Jaques weeps at the sight of an injured stag in Act II, Scene 1 of *As You Like It*, as depicted in a print from the Boydell Shakespeare Gallery project. *(Painting by William Hodges; engraving by Samuel Middiman)*

illusory, artificial happiness promised by riches and power, but rather the true contentment of being happy with one's nature and circumstances.

"Gentle" and "Honest"

The play's tradition-based radicalism informs the play's preoccupation with a group of terms related to social values. The words *honest* and *gentle* occur throughout *As You Like It* (the word *gentleness*, as Dusinberre observes, is "used more in this play than any other"). According to one of its main definitions, to be honest is to tell the truth, but the courtiers in Renaissance courts were taught to flatter their monarchs, dissemble their thoughts, and speak ambiguously—to lie, in short.

On the other hand, it should not be concluded that country dwellers are innately honest or gentle as a result of their relative innocence. Phoebe, the proud shepherdess, is decidedly ungentle in her treatment of the love-sick Silvius; hence, Rosalind-Ganymede refers to the roughness (ungentleness) of her hand ("she has a leathern hand . . . a housewife's hand" [4.3.24, 27]). Even Phoebe's style of writing is "giant-rude" and suggests to Rosalind that Phoebe is not truly female, for "Women's *gentle* brain" never wrote in such a way (4.3.33–34). Since Phoebe is ostensibly a working country-woman, some critics have taken Rosalind's comments on her rough skin as evidence of a snobbish attitude. Rosalind, though, is commenting on Phoebe's moral nature, not her physical appearance. In short, as with self-knowledge, honesty and gentleness are qualities to be acquired as a result of a combination of innate capabilities and one's response to one's environment, be it the court, the city, or the countryside.

Country Characters as Ciphers

It is not true to say that every native of the countryside is either happy or always good. Admittedly, Corin, the old shepherd, is not only content with his lot but also a hospitable host, as far as his limited means allow. However, he is almost the only country dweller in the play who is happy with his circumstances. The majority of the other rural types either have pronounced negative qualities or possess similar longings to those that compromise the characters of the courtly personages. Audrey appears to renege on a former promise to William, a country youth, in favor of marrying Touchstone, which suggests she is keen to ascend the social ladder (5.1.6–9). The shepherdess Phoebe is proud and cruel. Moreover, Silvius expresses his love in artificial, courtly terms in Act III, Scene 5 ("Will you sterner be," he asks the scornful Phoebe, "Than he that dies and lives by bloody drops?" [6–7]), this despite his being a supposedly uneducated shepherd. Hence, the play makes clear that these country dwellers are not necessarily content.

Indeed, it is not even certain that such artificial-seeming characters as Phoebe and Silvius are meant to be taken for true rural types at all. On seeing Ganymede, the love-struck Phoebe cries: "Dead shepherd, now I find thy saw of might: 'Who ever loved, that loved not at first sight?'" (3.5.82–83). The phrase is a quotation from Christopher Marlowe's *Hero and Leander*. It might be asked how the shepherdess Phoebe came to read this fashionable verse, only lately published, in 1598. Marlowe himself, of course, was not really a shepherd, which in turn suggests that Phoebe, too, is a shepherdess only in a metaphorical sense.

Pastoral drama originated in Italy as masques in which the roles were performed, not by actors, but by courtiers and members of the aristocracy. Conventionally, therefore, shepherds in pastoral plays are actual court personages in disguise. It is possible, then, to infer that Phoebe may represent Queen Elizabeth: *Phoebe* is an alternate name of Diana, the virgin goddess of the moon, one of the names used to refer to Queen Elizabeth in poetry written by such courtly poets as Edmund Spenser and Walter Raleigh. Accordingly, Phoebe's disdain for her suitor Silvius may allude to the queen's refusal to accept any marriage proposals from European royalty, no matter how worthy these suitors were as individuals.

The Theme of Marriage

Marriage is indeed another important theme of the play (as befits a comedy). Not all the characters, however, have an elevated view of this social institution. Marriage is seen by Touchstone, for example, as a legal formality. Seeking to marry Audrey the goatherd, the clown arranges for a country vicar (Sir Oliver Martext) to carry out an irregular ceremony in the forest. Somewhat surprisingly, it is the melancholy Jaques who intervenes. Indeed, this is the only effectual action performed in the play by Jaques, who normally prefers to remain a spectator of life. This fact gives the intervention a particular emphasis. "Get you to church," cries Jaques, "and have a good priest that can tell you what marriage is. This fellow [Martext] will but join you together as they join wainscot" (3.3.77–80). The use of the word *priest* and the emphasis on the necessity of being instructed as to the true meaning of marriage seem significant. Elsewhere in the play, Jaques reveals his moral disposition in his wish to criticize the sinful habits of people in the city. Here, he insists that marriage is more than a legal formality. Evidently, Jaques is alluding to the religious importance of marriage as a sacrament. Perhaps he is also seeking quietly to protect Audrey's reputation from being damaged by Touchstone's plan.

Another kind of marriage takes place in Act IV, Scene 1, when Rosalind, disguised as Ganymede, but pretending to be Rosalind, asks Celia to play the role of priest and join "her" (Rosalind-Ganymede) and Orlando in wedlock. The irony here is that this "false" marriage is, in a sense, a true one, for Ganymede really is Rosalind and Orlando does wish to marry her. Thus, the oaths "Rosalind" and Orlando exchange may be taken as a form of betrothal (an initial pledge comparable to the modern term *engagement*).

The importance of the theme of marriage is further emphasized in the play's final scene when no less a personage than Hymen, the god of marriage, appears to join four couples in wedlock. As might be expected of a deity, Hymen speaks in an extremely formal manner: "Then is there mirth in heaven / When earthly things made even / Atone together. / Good Duke, receive thy daughter. Hymen from heaven brought her, / Yea, brought her hither, / That thou mightst join her hand with

his, / Whose heart within his bosom is." Rosalind responds in an equally formulaic way, repeating the same phrase ("To you I give myself, for I am yours") to her father and to Orlando (5.4.106–115). When this formal marriage ceremony is compared with the intense mock ceremony in Act IV, it is possible to feel that, while "natural" unions may be confirmed and legitimated by formal ceremonies, they do not necessarily require them for authentication.

On the other hand, Rosalind appears, in Act V's final scene, to have lost much of her independence and subversive character and become an obedient daughter and submissive wife. However, if this ending is regarded as a relatively artificial showpiece, it is possible to imagine that the "real" Rosalind is the one who pledged herself to Orlando while dressed as Ganymede in Act IV. Indeed, this interpretation might explain a certain amount of confusion on Hymen's part, for in the first printed edition of *As You Like It* (in the First Folio of 1623), in a line quoted above, the god of marriage says not "join her hand with his" but "join his hand with his." As mentioned, there seems to be something stiff about this final joining together of souls by Hymen, as though more is being enacted than meets the eye.

"Wedding is great Juno's crown," sings Hymen, in his final speech. "O blessed bond of board and bed. / 'Tis Hymen peoples every town, / High wedlock then be honoured. / Honour, high honour and renown / To Hymen, god of every town" (5.4.139–144). The repetition of the word *honour* seems somewhat pointed (and is faintly reminiscent of the triple utterance of the word *holy* during the Catholic rite of Mass). Certainly, Hymen's claim to "people every town" might be contested: If there were no such thing as marriage, it might be supposed that people would still have children. Moreover, the pastoral mode usually represents the "town" as a site of deceit and selfish ambition, yet here Hymen claims to be the god of such a sinful realm. Perhaps, then, this ceremony of Hymen is being offered as a knowingly artificial surrogate for the "real" ceremony of the Mass, which could not be represented on stage (or, indeed, anywhere else) in England at that time.

Be that as it may, if the evident artificiality of Hymen's ceremony is read as an implicit endorsement of the earlier "mock" marriage, this would in turn suggest that the nonidealistic picture of married life Rosalind, disguised as Ganymede, described to Orlando in Act IV is a true one. When we are married, "Rosalind" there declared, "I will be more jealous of thee than a Barbary cock-pigeon over his hen . . . more giddy in my desires than a monkey. I will weep for nothing . . . and I will do that when you are disposed to be merry. I will laugh like a hyena, and that when thou art inclined to sleep" (4.1.139–146). In this speech, Ganymede imagines a male Rosalind (a "cock-pigeon" who is jealous over "his hen"), suggesting that the First Folio attribution of a male pronoun to Rosalind in Act V was intentional. More important, in this realistic vision of marriage, Rosalind is not a submissive wife but an independent individual in control of her own desires.

Critics often claim that *As You Like It* ultimately contains Rosalind's subversive, independent qualities and reduces her to a submissive wife in the final scene. However, the contrast of a genuine-seeming "fake" marriage in Act IV with a conspicuously formal "real" one in Act V suggests that readers and playgoers should not necessarily give a play's

final scene the last word. After all, when Rosalind returns in the Epilogue to address the audience, she shifts genders and expresses desires as promiscuous as ever before: "It is not the fashion to see the lady the Epilogue," she begins, making it clear that the boy actor who first played this role is still speaking as Rosalind. Later in the same speech, however, Rosalind turns into a man (or reverts to the boy actor playing her role), who imagines himself as a promiscuous female (just as, earlier, Rosalind had become Ganymede and then impersonated a saucy Rosalind): "If I were a woman I would kiss as many of you as had beards that pleased me" (16–18). The provocative spirit (named either Rosalind or Ganymede) of the play's middle section continues to exist beyond the confines of the play, despite the conventional marriage ending.

EXTRACTS OF CLASSIC CRITICISM
Samuel Johnson (1709–1784) [Excerpted from the Preface to *The Plays of William Shakespeare* (1765). Johnson throughout this work expressed forceful views with an insight that, despite their occasionally dated character, continues to make them highly suggestive.]

Of this play the fable is wild and pleasing. I know not how the ladies will approve the facility with which Rosalind and Celia give away their hearts. To Celia much may be forgiven for the heroism of her friendship. The character of Jaques is natural and well preserved. The comic dialogue is very sprightly, with less mixture of low buffoonery than in some other plays; and the graver part is elegant and harmonious. By hastening to the end of his work Shakespeare suppressed the dialogue between the usurper and the hermit, and lost an opportunity of exhibiting a moral lesson in which he might have found matter worthy of his highest powers.

Rosalind reveals herself to Orlando while Hymen looks on in Act V, Scene 4 of *As You Like It*. Print from the Boydell Shakespeare Gallery project. *(Painting by William Hamilton; engraving by Jean-Pierre Simon)*

William Hazlitt (1788–1830) [Excerpted from *Characters of Shakespeare's Plays* (1817). Hazlitt offers a romanticist emphasis on the way *As You Like It* challenges conventional moral views.]

Shakespeare has here converted the forest of Arden into another Arcadia, where they 'fleet the time carelessly, as they did in the golden world.' It is the most ideal of any of this author's plays. It is a pastoral drama in which the interest arises more out of the sentiments and characters than out of the actions or situations. It is not what is done, but what is said, that claims our attention. Nursed in solitude, 'under the shade of melancholy boughs,' the imagination grows soft and delicate, and the wit runs riot in idleness [. . .] The very air of the place seems to breathe a spirit of philosophical poetry; to stir the thoughts, to touch the heart with pity. Never was there such beautiful moralizing, equally free from pedantry or petulance.

> And this their life, exempt from public
>   haunts,
> Finds tongues in trees, books in the run-
>   ning brooks,
> Sermons in stones, and good in
>   everything.

Jaques is the only purely contemplative character in Shakespeare. He thinks, and does nothing. His whole occupation is to amuse his mind, and he is totally regardless of his body and his fortunes. He is the prince of philosophical idlers; his only passion is thought. He sets no value on anything but as it serves as food for reflection. He can 'suck melancholy out of a song, as a weasel sucks eggs'; the motley fool, 'who morals on the time,' is the greatest prize he meets with in the forest. He resents Orlando's passion for Rosalind as some disparagement of his own passion for abstract truth.

Within the sequestered and romantic glades of the forest of Arden, they find leisure to be good and wise, or to play the fool and fall in love. Rosalind's character is made up of sportive gaiety and natural tenderness: her tongue runs the faster to conceal the pressure at her heart. She talks herself out of breath, only to get deeper in love. The coquetry with which she plays with her lover in the double character which she has to support is managed with the nicest address. How full of voluble, laughing grace is all her conversation with Orlando:

> —In heedless mazes running
> With wanton haste and giddy cunning.

The silent and retired character of Celia is a necessary relief to the provoking loquacity of Rosalind, nor can anything be better conceived or more beautifully described than the mutual affection between the two cousins:

> —We still have slept together,
> Rose at an instant, learn'd, play'd, eat
>   together,
> And wheresoe'er we went, like Juno's
>   swans,
> Still we went coupled and inseparable.

Touchstone is not in love, but he will have a mistress as a subject for the exercise of his grotesque humour, and to show his contempt for the passion, by his indifference about the person. He is a rare fellow. He is a mixture of the ancient cynic philosopher with the modern buffoon, and turns folly into wit, and wit into folly, just as the fit takes him. His courtship of Audrey not only throws a degree of ridicule on the state of wedlock itself, but he is equally an enemy to the prejudices of opinion in other respects. The lofty tone of enthusiasm, which the Duke and his companions in exile spread over the stillness and solitude of country life, receives a pleasant shock from Touchstone's sceptical determination of the question.

CORIN. And how like you this shepherd's life, Mr.Touchstone?

CLOWN. Truly, shepherd, in respect
of itself, it is a good life; but in respect
that it is a shepherd's life, it is naught.
In respect that it is solitary, I like it very
well; but in respect that it is private, it is
a very vile life. Now in respect it is in the
fields, it pleaseth me well; but in respect
it is not in the court, it is tedious. As it is
a spare life, look you, it fits my humour;
but as there is no more plenty in it, it
goes much against my stomach.

There is hardly any of Shakespeare's plays
that contains a greater number of passages
that have been quoted in books of extracts,
or a greater number of phrases that have
become in a manner proverbial.

George   Bernard   Shaw (1856–1950)
[Excerpted from reviews of productions of *As You
Like It* attended by Shaw in 1890, 1896, and 1897.
Provocative, pompous, and highly amusing, Shaw's
comments achieve insight as a direct result of their
irreverence.]

If *As You Like It* were a typical Shakespearean play, I should unhesitatingly declare
[Ada] Rehan [who played Rosalind in 1897]
the most perfect Shakespearean executant in
the world. But when I think of those plays in
which our William anticipated modern dramatic art by making serious attempts to hold
the mirror up to nature—*All's Well, Measure
For Measure, Troilus and Cressida,* and so
on—I must limit the tribute to Shakespeare's
popular style. Rosalind is not a complete
human being: she is simply an extension into
five acts of the most affectionate, fortunate,
delightful five minutes in the life of a charming woman. And all the other figures in the
play are cognate impostures. Orlando, Adam,

Jaques, Touchstone, the banished Duke, and
the rest play the same tune all through. This
is not human nature or dramatic character;
it is juvenile lead, first old man, heavy lead,
heavy father, principal comedian, and leading
lady, transfigured by magic word-music . . .
You have only to compare Orlando and Rosalind with Bertram and Helena, the Duke and
Touchstone with Leontes and Autolycus,
to learn the difference from Shakespeare
himself.

What a play! It was in *As You Like It* that
the sententious William first began to openly
exploit the fondness of the British Public for
sham moralizing and stage 'philosophy'. It
contains one passage that specially exasper-
ates me. Jaques, who spends his time, like
Hamlet, in vainly emulating the wisdom of
Sancho Panza, comes in laughing in a superior manner because he has met a fool in the
forest, who

Says very wisely, It is ten o'clock.
Thus we may see [quoth he] how the
 world wags.
'Tis but an hour ago since it was nine;
And after one hour more twill be eleven.
And so, from hour to hour, we ripe and
 ripe;
And then, from hour to hour, we rot and
 rot;
And thereby hangs a tale.

Now, considering this fool's platitude is
precisely the 'philosophy' of Hamlet, Macbeth ('Tomorrow and tomorrow and tomorrow,' etc.), Prospero, and the rest of them,
there is something unendurably aggravat-
ing in Shakespeare giving himself airs with
Touchstone, as if he, the immortal, ever,
even at his sublimest, had anything different
or better to say himself. Later on he misses
a great chance. Nothing is more significant
than the statement that 'all the world's a
stage.' The whole world *is* ruled by theatrical

illusion. Between the Caesars, the emperors, the Christian heroes, the Grand Old Men, the kings, prophets, saints, judges, and heroes of the newspapers and the popular imagination, and the actual Juliuses, Napoleons, Gladstones and so on, there is the same difference as between Hamlet and [the actor] Sir Henry Irving. The case is not one of fanciful similitude but of identity. The great critics are those who penetrate and understand the illusion: the great men are those who, as dramatists planning the development of nations, or as actors carrying out the drama, are behind the scenes of the world instead of gaping and gushing in the auditorium after paying their taxes at the doors. And yet Shakespeare, with the rarest opportunities of observing this, lets his pregnant metaphor slip, and, with his usual incapacity for pursuing any idea, wanders off into a grandmotherly Elizabethan edition of the advertisement of Cassell's Popular Educator. How anybody over the age of seven can take interest in a literary toy so silly in its conceit and common its ideas as the Seven Ages of Man passes my understanding. Even the great metaphor itself is inaccurately expressed; for the world is a playhouse, not merely a stage.

And then Touchstone, with his rare jests about the knight that swore by his honour they were good pancakes! Who would endure such humour from anyone but Shakespeare?—an Eskimo would demand his money back if a modern author offered him such fare. And the comfortable old Duke, symbolical of the British villa dweller, who likes to find 'sermons in stones and good in everything,' and then to have a good dinner! This unvenerable impostor, expanding on his mixed diet of pious twaddle and venison, rouses my worst passions. Even when Shakespeare, in his efforts to be a social philosopher, does rise for an instant to the level of a sixth-rate [Charles] Kingsley, his solemn self-complacency infuriates me. And yet, so wonderful is his art, that it is not easy to disentangle what is unbearable from what is irresistible. Orlando one moment says:

> What'er you are
> That in this desert inaccessible
> Under the shade of melancholy boughs
> Lose and neglect the creeping hours of
>   time,

which, though it indicates a thoroughly unhealthy imagination, and would have been impossible to, for instance, Chaucer, is yet magically fine of its kind. The next moment he tacks on lines which would have revolted Mr. Pecksniff:

> If ever you have looked on better days,
> If ever been where bells have knolled to
>   church,
> *[How perfectly the atmosphere of the rented*
> *pew is caught in this incredible line!]*
> If ever sat at any good man's feast,
> If ever from your eyelids wiped—

I really shall get sick if I quote any more of it. Was ever such canting, snivelling, hypocritical unctuousness exuded by an actor anxious to show that he was above his profession, and was a thoroughly respectable man in private life? Why cannot all this putrescence be cut out of the play, and only the vital parts— the genuine storytelling, the fun, the poetry, the drama, be retained? Simply because, if nothing were left of Shakespeare but his genius, our Shakespeare-olaters would miss all that they admire in him.

Notwithstanding these drawbacks, the fascination of *As You Like It* is still very great. It has the overwhelming advantage of being written for the most part in prose instead of blank verse, which any fool can write. And such prose! The first scene alone, with its energy of exposition, each phrase driving

Rosalind, before she leaves with Celia for the Forest of Arden in Act I, Scene 3 of *As You Like It*. This is a print from Charles Heath's 1848 edition of *The Heroines of Shakspeare: Comprising the Principal Female Characters in the Plays of the Great Poet*. (Painting by J. W. Wright; engraving by B. Eyles)

its meaning and feeling in up to the head at one brief, sure stroke, is worth ten acts of the ordinary Elizabethan sing-song. It cannot be said that the blank verse is reserved for those passages which demand a loftier expression, since Le Beau and Corin drop into it on the most inadequate provocation; but at least there is not much of it. The popularity of Rosalind is due to three main causes. First, she only speaks blank verse for a few minutes. Second, she only wears a skirt for a few minutes (and the dismal effect of the change at the end to the wedding dress ought to convert the stupidest champion of petticoats to

rational dress). Third, she makes love to the man instead of waiting for the man to make love to her—a piece of natural history which has kept Shakespeare's heroines alive, whilst generations of properly governessed young ladies, taught to say 'No' three times at least, have miserably perished.

In spite of the beauty of the verse and the deep feeling for sylvan and pastoral scenery which pervades the play, the human part of it is excessively conventional. Like Henry V, it belongs to that moment of sympathy with the common morality and thought of his time that came between the romanticism of Shakespeare's early plays and the independent thought of his later ones.

Orlando's intelligence is the intelligence of the heart: he always comes out best as an amiable, strong, manly, handsome, shrewd-enough-to-take-care-of-himself, but safely stupid and totally unobservant young man.

Henry Sebastian Bowden (1836–1920) [Excerpted from *The Religion of Shakespeare* (1899). Basing his work on research conducted by Richard Simpson, Bowden was the first scholar to devote a book-length study to the possibility that Shakespeare's plays contained a concealed sympathy for the situation of Catholics in Protestant England.]

The pictures of the court of the reigning Duke, and of the home of the unnatural brother in "As You Like It," are drawn with such passionate feeling, that they seem not only to be wrung from the poet's own heart, but to be intended to go straight to the hearts and minds of the audience. The tyrant to whom mistrust is sufficient cause for the condemnation of a man, and mere circumstance of birth sufficient motive of mistrust, was a picture of English rulers applicable only to one party in the state. Duke Frederick says to Rosalind, whom he banishes, 'Let it suffice thee that I trust thee not,' and she replies, 'Yet your mistrust cannot make me a traitor,' and he again answers, 'Thou art thy father's daughter; there's enough.' Again, Adam says to Orlando, who had been forced to fly from the Duke for the same reasons:

> To some kind of men
> Their graces serve them but as enemies.
> . . . your virtues . . . Are sanctified and
>   holy traitors unto you.
> O, what a world is this when what is
>   comely
> Envenoms him that bears it!

Such speeches must have reminded the audience of the class of Englishmen whom the law made criminal by kind [that is, Catholics], and who were reckoned the worse subjects, the more faithful they were to their profession. In this sense must have been understood Orlando's lament over the departure of the antique world, when duty, not recompense, was the motive of service.

In the forest, Touchstone has all the privileges of his [fool's] bauble; while Jaques, who claims the same licence, fails to obtain it. His 'taxation' would not be the froth of an infirm reason, but the gall of old disappointments, stored up in the brain of a philosopher, and vented under the false pretence of extemporaneous sallies.

Among the bitters of the outlaw life the poet enumerates the being forced to live where no 'bells knolled to church'—quite a characteristic of the state of the [Catholic] recusants, who were forbidden every external sign of their religion.

Corin has known what love means, shepherd though he be, and he can open his heart to give what he has, though he serves a churlish master, who

> Little seeks to find the way to heaven
> By doing deeds of hospitality.

Here, by the way, we have the doctrine of merit laid down in clear terms.

MODERN CRITICISM AND CRITICAL CONTROVERSIES

Throughout the 19th century and into the early 20th, Shakespearean romantic comedies, such as *As You Like It,* were not always taken especially seriously by literary critics. C. L. Barber, in his influential book *Shakespeare's Festive Comedy* (1959), offered a useful assessment of the reasons for this comparative neglect. In comedies such as *As You Like It,* Barber wrote, "so much of the action . . . is random when looked at as intrigue, so many of the persons are neutral when regarded as character, so much of the wit is inapplicable when assessed as satire, that critics too often fall back on mere exclamations about poetry and mood" (4). In opposition to this tradition, Barber read Shakespeare's comedies as social commentary. In doing so, he took a cue from Mikhail Bakhtin's important study of the French Renaissance novelist François Rabelais (not published until 1965 but formulated and written in the 1930s). Bakhtin argued that Rabelais's comic novel *Gargantua and Pantagruel* was a literary manifestation of the spirit of popular carnivals, holidays, and other folk customs that challenged (albeit temporarily) the everyday world of work, rules, and laws. Applying this approach to Shakespeare, Barber suggested that in *As You Like It,* the main characters enjoy a holiday in the middle of the play, where everyday rules and customs are turned upside-down. Thus, a space is provided for subversive social commentary and provocative play. However, the play ends with the reinstatement of law and order when Duke Senior is restored to his throne. Barber concludes: "Anglican or Catholic culture allowed nature to have its day. But the release of that one day was understood to be a temporary license, a 'misrule' which implied rule, so that the acceptance of nature was qualified" (10). Thus, at the end of *As You Like It,* Rosalind discards her male disguise and becomes an obedient wife and daughter; "proper" gender roles, as well as law and order, are seen to be reestablished.

In an essay published in 1949, Northrop Frye also detected profound meaning in Shakespeare's comedies. Frye noted Shakespeare's evident familiarity with Latin New Comedy, a type of dramatic comedy produced in the third and second centuries B.C., the plots of which were concerned mainly with confused situations ending happily for the hero in marriage to the heroine. Frye, however, argued that Shakespeare "divined that there was a profounder pattern in the argument of comedy than appears in either Plautus or Terence," the playwrights most commonly associated with New Comedy (97). Shakespeare, in other words, wrote comedies that offered Christianized (and entertaining) versions of ancient rituals of death and revival. In plays such as *As You Like It,* observed Frye, "there is [a] rhythmic movement from normal world to green world and back again" (97). Death and social or natural decay are represented by the temporary removal of the main characters from their positions of security. They undergo a form of spiritual renewal in a strange location (such as the Forest of Arden) so that, by the end of the play, they are "reborn," that is, restored to their former habitat.

Like Frye, Richard Cody (1969) has insisted that Shakespeare's comedies are freighted with philosophical significance. Against the grain of critics who dismissed (and continue to dismiss) the pastoral mode as vacuous sentimentalism, Cody argues that "pastoralism may be the poetic expression *par excellence* of that cult of aesthetic Platonism which arose in Florence [in the late 15th century] and spread across Europe" (6). While acknowledging that "how deliberately Shakespeare [in his comedies] adopts the attitudes and vocabulary of Florentine Platonism remains a question," Cody nonetheless maintains that "to understand *As You Like It* as a piece of Renaissance theatre, one should look at it in the light of poetic theology" (87). Philosophical theories related to the cult known since classical times as Orphism enter deeply "into its action, plot and language" (62). Accordingly, Cody sees Torquato Tasso's Italian pastoral-allegorical drama *Aminta* as having a major direct or indirect influence on Shakespeare's play. This influence,

however, remains rarely acknowledged. Similarly, Cody's philosophical and allegorical approach to the study of Shakespearean comedy has proved less popular than more social and politically minded interpretations.

In recent decades, New Historicist critics such as Stephen Greenblatt and Louis Montrose have paid particular attention to the interrelationship between literary works and their cultural (social and political) contexts. Building upon Barber's approach, scholars loosely affiliated with this informal "movement" have tended to offer a somewhat pessimistic interpretation of early modern commercial drama as fundamentally conservative in its function. According to a characteristic New Historicist view, the revolutionary energies given expression in the middle of a play such as *As You Like It* are not really revolutionary at all. On the contrary, the play's middle represents a release of subversive energies in a safe manner, licensed by the state. These energies are ultimately contained by the play's restoration, and reaffirmation, of an only nominally altered social hierarchy in its final act.

Thus, Montrose maintained, in an essay published in 1980, that "the symbolic mediation of social relationships was a central function of Elizabethan pastoral [as found, for instance, in *As You Like It*] . . . [P]astorals that celebrate the ideal of content function to articulate—and thereby, perhaps, to assuage—*dis*content" (42). In the case of *As You Like It,* Montrose saw a particular form of social discontent being "assuaged": the problems arising from the custom of primogeniture. According to this custom, which remained standard among property-owning families of Elizabethan England, the first-born son inherited the bulk (if not all) of the family's wealth upon the death of his father. This was considered to be the best means of preserving the family's property intact and ensuring that the family's social prestige continued to increase. Thus, Orlando appears, as the youngest son of Sir Rowland, to be a victim of this custom. The play encourages the audience to sympathize with his plight as he is forced to flee his home and live in the forest. However, as Montrose pointed out, when God intervenes, in the form of the sudden conversions of Orlando's and Duke Senior's formerly wicked brothers, Orlando marries Rosalind and is promised the dukedom. Presumably, his first-born son will then inherit the throne in due course. Thus, the play allows its hero to air his complaint about the custom of primogeniture only to implicitly confirm the natural "rightness" of that custom (through its apparent divine endorsement) by the final act.

In a penetrating analysis of such New Historicist approaches to reading Shakespeare, Jean E. Howard counters Montrose's view, questioning

> whether *As You Like It* does quite the work
> Montrose assigns to it; that is, whether by the
> exaggerated nature of the conversions and
> abdications which mark the play's final acts
> the play does not in large part undo the very
> work Montrose says it does in naturalizing
> the custom of primogeniture and effacing
> its arbitrary and unjust aspects. In essence,
> Montrose sees the comic form as a vehicle for
> articulating, only to erase, the contradictions
> of a particular social formation. I would argue
> simply that a text such as *As You Like It* is more
> subversive of formulations of reconciliation
> than Montrose's reading allows (471).

This statement of Howard's will prove pertinent to later feminist analyses of the play, for from the 1970s onward, *As You Like It* began to receive particular attention from feminist scholars for its treatment of gender. Early feminist readings of the play were largely positive, applauding Rosalind's subversion of gender roles. However, later feminists implicitly aligned themselves with the New Historicist positions outlined above, arguing, as Valerie Traub observes, "that any subversion of gender is contained by the comic form which mandates marriage in the final act" (706). Traub objects to this binary either-or model, offering either subversion or containment. One way out of this rather simplistic impasse, Traub suggests, is to pay more attention to the material means by which

the alleged subversion within a play would have been enacted. In the case of *As You Like It,* this involves an awareness that in Elizabethan England, the play would have been performed by an all-male cast. Hence, a young boy would have dressed as Rosalind and then pretended to "disguise" himself as a boy (Ganymede), who then pretended to be a "saucy" Rosalind. Traub argues that the obvious outrageousness of this situation outweighs any considerations of whether the plot of the play ultimately promotes heterosexual marriage or the subversion of gender roles.

A second "escape route" from the binary model of either subversion or containment, also offered by Traub, is to emphasize, not "the fact of foreclosure" (the return to order in the play's final act), but "the *way* such containment is attained: the mechanisms and displacements set to work by the anxiety

Rosalind promises to resolve the affairs of Orlando, Silvius, and Phoebe in Act V, Scene 2, depicted here in a Herkomer Art School rendition of *As You Like It*. *(Illustration by George Grenville Manton)*

elicited through subversive action" (706). In other words, regardless of what happens at the end of the play, how do the various situations enacted on the stage feel to the audience as a result of the way the play is constructed and performed?

Howard appears to endorse such an approach in her objection to Montrose's reading, as, for example, when she questions whether "by the exaggerated nature of the conversions and abdications which mark the play's final acts the play does not in large part undo the very work Montrose says it does." With regard to the issue of gender, Howard observes that Shakespeare's Rosalind "acts out the parts scripted for women by her culture" (709). In doing so, she exaggerates them and makes them appear unnatural. Proceeding cautiously, Howard continues: "Acting out these parts does not release Rosalind from patriarchy but reveals the constructed nature of patriarchy's representations of the feminine and shows a woman manipulating those representations in her own interest, theatricalizing for her own purposes what is assumed to be innate" (709).

At this point, however, Howard appears to shift her ground. Although with regard to the issue of primogeniture Howard (as described above) contests the view that *As You Like It* is ultimately conservative, respecting the play's treatment of gender she adopts a stance equivalent to Montrose's: "The representation of Rosalind's holiday humour has the primary effect, I think, of confirming the gender system and perfecting rather than dismantling it, by making a space for mutuality within relations of dominance" (710).

Yet, as Carol Thomas-Neely has argued, at the end of the play, Rosalind, now dressed as Rosalind, continues to act out "the parts scripted for women by her culture," thereby revealing their "constructed nature" as well. As before, she ventriloquizes stereotypes (this time that of the dutiful daughter and submissive wife), revealing them to be artificial. With this in mind, writes Thomas-Neely, "the highly formalized and ritualized enactment of the weddings hints that [Rosalind's performance as bride] is just yet another donning of roles" (127).

With regard to the theme of marriage, Julie Crawford has argued that comedies such as *As You Like It* were designed to make heterosexual marriage appealing and acceptable to young people whose most common sexual urges were homoerotic. "However normative heterosexual coupling may have been as hierarchy and means of social reproduction in the period," observes Crawford, "it contradicted the likeness topos at the centre of positive ideas about union" (137). In the modern age, it is held as proverbial wisdom that "opposites attract," but in the Renaissance, on the contrary, it was believed that "like desires like." According to this view, men in the Renaissance were conditioned by the dominant ethos of their culture to find males more sexually attractive than females; while women would be more sincerely attracted to other females than to males. Carrying this notion forward in time, therefore, it could be argued that couples in modern heterosexual relationships have been conditioned by centuries of comedies such as *As You Like It* to think differently from Renaissance men and women. Consequently, Crawford argues, such plays should not be taken as either celebrating or criticizing the institution of marriage. Rather, they served to make heterosexual marriage plausible and acceptable to their spectators.

If anything, the above brief sample of modern critical views of *As You Like It* shows that the play has an inexhaustible capacity to yield material for complex social and political analyses, as well as philosophical investigations. Nonetheless, it should be stressed that for all of the fascination of the various debates summarized in this section, the play may be read and enjoyed without prior reference to them. Indeed, such an "innocent" form of reading is to be recommended, as it is always only too easy to allow a certain school of thought (New Historicist, feminist, philosophical, Marxist, or whatever) to get between us and the play, preventing us from forming our own view of its meaning. Certainly, the interpretations and analyses of critics can supplement, confirm, or challenge our understanding and appreciation of the play, but they are by no means necessary as a prelude to its enjoyment.

THE PLAY TODAY

In recent years, critics have continued to pay attention to the broader cultural context of *As You Like It*. Issues of subversion and containment, relating to gender and social order, remain pertinent, but more emphasis tends to be laid on close consideration of the significance of particular allusions. For example, the long-standing view that Jaques may be a portrait of Shakespeare's "rival," dramatist Ben Jonson (first prominently argued by Arthur Gray in 1928), has been placed in a larger cultural context in which *As You Like It* is read as a Shakespearean salvo in an ongoing "war of the theaters." In this war, the more socially inclusive and romantic strain of Shakespearean comedy (as performed by Shakespeare's theater company, the Chamberlain's Men) is pitted against a more abrasive, urban satire favored by Jonson. Some critics, however, believe the importance of this war has been exaggerated, seeing it as mainly a clever marketing ploy, intended to make audiences more interested in new plays.

On a more political note, Juliet Dusinberre has found in *As You Like It* hidden references to the earl of Essex, a once-popular figure in Elizabeth's court. For instance, the weeping stag observed by Jaques, Dusinberre suggests, may allude to the persecuted Essex's abandonment by his former supporters. Moreover, "Essex's role as a patron of drama, music and fencing . . . are reflected in *As You Like It*" (Arden, 75). Intriguingly, as patron, Essex supported not only Protestant artists but also Catholic ones. His "generosity to Catholic musicians was well known," observes Dusinberre, "and an admirable example of tolerance in a fanatical age" (76). One of the Catholic musicians Essex may have supported was Thomas Morley, whose arrangement for the song "It was a lover and his lass" is the only contemporary setting of a Shakespearean song extant. As Dusinberre notes, "Shakespeare probably knew Morley personally because they were in 1598 neighbours in Bishopsgate" (76).

Such connections may hold more importance than they appear to at first glance, for recent scholars have argued with increasing insistence that Shakespeare expressed sympathy for the situation of English Catholics in disguised fashion in his plays. Carol Enos and Peter Milward have detected evidence of this sympathy in *As You Like It*. Milward, for example, hears an echo of the Elizabethan official Lord Burghley's anti-Catholic rhetoric in one of Duke Frederick's outbursts. When Rosalind defends herself against Frederick's accusation of treason, the tyrant uses words that link treachery to Catholic notions of purgation and grace: "Thus do all traitors," he snarls, "if their purgation did consist in words, they are as innocent as grace itself" (1.3.55).

Such "confessional" readings have yet to make much impact on modern productions of *As You Like It*. When productions engage with political ideas, these still tend to be the ones explored from the 1960s onward, focusing on gender issues and questions of social order. In 1981, for example, the Cheek by Jowl theater company produced a controversial and excellent version of the play with an all-male cast. This encouraged the audience to find within the play an insistence that gender roles are cultural constructions, not "natural" givens. Crucially, this intellectual aspect did not reduce but rather added to the play's attraction as entertainment and love story.

Christine Edzard's 1992 film version attempted to make the play more obviously relevant to filmgoers' everyday experiences by transferring the action to an urban London wasteland. This certainly made for a more gritty ambience, but perhaps some of the play's exuberance was lost. More recently, Kenneth Branagh's version (2006) offered 21st-century viewers a convenient and enjoyable means of experiencing the play.

FIVE TOPICS FOR DISCUSSION AND WRITING

1. **The natural versus the artificial:** In what ways does the play contrast the natural and the artificial? Which characters seem to use more artificial language? Do any characters speak "naturally"?
2. **The theme of education:** What types of education are mentioned or represented in the

play? Does the play suggest that nature is more important than nurture with regard to the formation of a person's character? Which character has received the best education by the end of the play?

3. **The theme of marriage:** What kinds of marriage ceremony are featured (or referred to) in the play? What are the differences between these ceremonies? Which of the four marriages celebrated at the end of the play do you think will be happiest? Why? Does the play suggest that wives should be subordinate to their husbands?

4. **Gender roles:** Why does Rosalind not remove her male disguise when she learns Orlando is in the forest? Does the play suggest that women should have more freedom in society?

5. **Satire and pastoral:** Does the play engage in satire? If so, which targets are satirized? How is the pastoral mode used to criticize life in the court? Does the play suggest that life in the countryside is better than life in the court?

Bibliography

Alpers, Paul. *What Is Pastoral?* Chicago: University of Chicago Press, 1996.

Barber, C. L. *Shakespeare's Festive Comedy: A Study of Dramatic Form and Its Relation to Social Custom.* Princeton, N.J.: Princeton University Press, 1959.

Barton, Anne. "*As You Like It* and *Twelfth Night:* Shakespeare's 'Sense of an Ending.'" In *Essays, Mainly Shakespearean,* 91–112. Cambridge: Cambridge University Press, 1994.

Battenhouse, Roy, ed. *Shakespeare's Christian Dimension.* Bloomington: Indiana University Press, 1994.

Belsey, Catherine. "Disrupting Sexual Difference: Meaning and Gender in the Comedies." In *Alternative Shakespeares,* edited by John Drakakis, 169–193. London: Methuen, 1985.

Brissenden, Alan, ed. *William Shakespeare:* As You Like It. Oxford: Oxford University Press, 1993.

Cody, Richard. *The Landscape of the Mind: Pastoralism and Platonic Theory in Tasso's* Aminta *and Shakespeare's Early Comedies.* London: Oxford University Press, 1969.

Crawford, Julie. "The Homoerotics of Shakespeare's Elizabethan Comedies." In *A Companion to Shakespeare's Works,* vol. 3, edited by Richard Dutton and Jean E. Howard, 137–158. Malden, U.K.: Blackwell, 2003.

Dawson, Anthony B. *"As You Like It."* In *Watching Shakespeare: A Playgoers' Guide.* London: Macmillan, 1988.

Dillon, Janette. "Shakespeare and the Traditions of English Stage Comedy." In *A Companion to Shakespeare's Works,* vol. 3, edited by Richard Dutton and Howard. Malden, U.K.: Blackwell, 2003.

Dusinberre, Juliet. *"As You Like It."* In *A Companion to Shakespeare's Works,* vol. 3, edited by Richard Dutton and Jean E. Howard, Malden, U.K.: Blackwell, 2003.

Dusinberre, Juliet, ed. *William Shakespeare:* As You Like It. London: Thomson Learning [Arden Shakespeare], 2006.

Dutton, Richard, and Jean E. Howard, eds. *A Companion to Shakespeare's Works.* Vol. 3: *The Comedies.* Malden, U.K.: Blackwell, 2003.

Enos, Carol. "Catholic Exiles in Flanders and *As You Like It;* or What If You Don't Like It at All?" In *Theatre and Religion: Lancastrian Shakespeare,* edited by Richard Dutton, Alison Findlay, and Richard Wilson.

Erickson, Peter. "Sexual Politics and Social Structure in *As You Like It.*" In *Patriarchal Structures in Shakespeare's Drama.* Berkeley: University of California Press, 1985.

Fortin, René E. "'Tongues in Trees' in *As You Like It.*" In *Shakespeare's Christian Dimension,* edited by Roy Battenhouse, Bloomington: Indiana University Press, 1994.

Frye, Northrop. "The Argument of Comedy." In *Shakespeare: An Anthology of Criticism, 1945–2000,* edited by Russ McDonald. Oxford, U.K.: Blackwell, 2004.

Garber, Marjorie. "The Education of Orlando." In *Comedy from Shakespeare to Sheridan,* edited by A. R. Braunmuller and James C. Bulman, Newark: University of Delaware Press, 1986.

Gay, Penny. *William Shakespeare:* As You Like It. Plymouth, U.K.: Northcote House, 1999.

Gibbons, Brian. "Amorous Fictions in *As You Like It*." In *Shakespeare and Multiplicity*. Cambridge: Cambridge University Press, 1993.

Hattaway, Michael, ed. *William Shakespeare:* As You Like It. Cambridge: Cambridge University Press, 2000.

Howard, Jean E. "Crossdressing, the Theatre, and Gender Struggle in Early Modern England." In *The Stage and Social Struggle in Early Modern England*. London: Routledge, 1994.

———. "The New Historicism in Renaissance Studies." In *Shakespeare: An Anthology of Criticism, 1945–2000,* edited by Russ McDonald. Oxford, U.K.: Blackwell, 2004.

Hunt, M. *Shakespeare's* As You Like It: *Late Elizabethan Culture and Literary Representation*. Basingstoke, U.K.: Palgrave Macmillan, 2008.

Jackson, Russell, and Robert Smallwood, eds. *Players of Shakespeare 2*. Cambridge: Cambridge University Press, 1988.

Jensen, Ejner. "Performative Comedy in *As You Like It*." In *Shakespeare and the Ends of Comedy*. Bloomington and Indianapolis: Indiana University Press, 1991.

Jernigan, Charles, and Irene Marchegiani Jones, eds. *Torquato Tasso:* Aminta, *a Pastoral Play*. New York: Italica Press, 2000.

Kingsley-Smith, Jane. "'Hereafter, in a better world than this': The End of Exile in *As You Like It* and *King Lear*." In *Shakespeare's Drama of Exile*. Basingstoke, U.K.: Palgrave Macmillan, 2003.

Knowles, Richard, ed. *A New Variorum Edition of* As You Like It. New York: Modern Language Association, 1977.

Kott, Jan. "Shakespeare's Bitter Arcadia." In *Shakespeare Our Contemporary*. 2nd ed. London: Methuen, 1967.

Laroque, François. "Shakespeare's Festive Comedies." In *A Companion to Shakespeare's Works,* vol. 3, edited by Richard Dutton and Jean E. Howard. Malden, U.K.: Blackwell, 2003.

Latham, Agnes, ed. *William Shakespeare:* As You Like It. London: Methuen [Arden Shakespeare], 1975.

Leggatt, Alexander. *Shakespeare's Comedy of Love*. London: Methuen, 1974.

Lodge, Thomas. *Rosalynd,* edited by Brian Nellist. Keele, U.K.: Keele University Press, 1995.

Mangan, Michael. *A Preface to Shakespeare's Comedies*. London: Longman, 1996.

Marshall, Cynthia. *Shakespeare in Production:* As You Like It. Cambridge: Cambridge University Press 2004.

McDonald, Russ, ed. *Shakespeare: An Anthology of Criticism, 1945–2000*. Oxford, U.K.: Blackwell, 2004.

Milward, Peter. "The Golden World of *As You Like It*." *English Literature and Language* 19 (1992): 3–10.

Montrose, Louis A. "'The Place of a Brother' in *As You Like It:* Social Process and Comic Form." In *Materialist Shakespeare,* edited by Ivo Kemps. London: Verso, 1995.

O'Callaghan, Michelle. "Pastoral." In *A Companion to English Renaissance Literature and Culture,* edited by Michael Hattaway. Oxford, U.K.: Blackwell, 2000.

Orgel, Stephen. "'Call me Ganymede.'" In *Impersonations: The Performance of Gender in Shakespeare's England*. Cambridge: Cambridge University Press, 1996.

Rackin, Phyllis. "Shakespeare's Crossdressing Comedies." In *A Companion to Shakespeare's Works,* vol. 3, edited by Richard Dutton and Jean E. Howard. Malden, U.K.: Blackwell, 2003.

Rutter, Carol. "Rosalind: Iconoclast in Arden." In *Clamorous Voices: Shakespeare's Women Today*. London: Women's Press, 1989.

Salingar, Leo. *Shakespeare and the Traditions of Comedy*. Cambridge: Cambridge University Press, 1974.

Scragg, Leah. *"As You Like It."* In *Shakespeare: An Oxford Guide,* edited by Stanley Wells and Lena Cowen Orlin. Oxford: Oxford University Press, 2003.

Shapiro, James. *1599: A Year in the Life of William Shakespeare*. London: Faber & Faber, 2005.

Shapiro, Michael. "Boy Heroines and Female Pages." In *Gender in Play on the Shakespearean Stage*. Ann Arbor: University of Michigan Press, 1996.

Sidney, Philip. *An Apology for Poetry*. Edited by Geoffrey Shepherd. Manchester, U.K.: Manchester University Press, 1973.

Smith, Bruce. "The Passionate Shepherd." In *Homosexual Desire in Shakespeare's England: A Cultural Poetics*. Chicago: University of Chicago Press, 1991.

Thomas-Neely, Carol. "Destabilizing Lovesickness, Gender and Sexuality: *Twelfth Night* and *As You Like It*." In *Distracted Subjects: Madness and Gender in Shakespeare and Early Modern Culture*. Ithaca, N.Y.: Cornell University Press, 2004.

Traub, Valerie. "The Homoerotics of Shakespearean Comedy." In *Desire and Anxiety: Circulations of Sexuality in Shakespearean Drama*. London: Routledge, 1992.

Wade Soule, Lesley. As You Like It: *A Guide to the Text and Its Theatrical Life*. Basingstoke, U.K.: Palgrave Macmillan, 2005.

Watterson, William. "*As You Like It* as Christian Pastoral." In *Shakespeare's Christian Dimension*, edited by Roy Battenhouse. Bloomington: Indiana University Press, 1994.

Wilson, Richard. "'Like the old Robin Hood': *As You Like It* and the Enclosure Riots." In *Will Power: Essays on Shakespearean Authority*. Hemel Hempstead, U.K.: Harvester Wheatsheaf, 1993.

Young, David. "'Earthly Things Made Even': *As You Like* It." In *The Heart's Forest: A Study of Shakespeare's Pastoral Plays*. New Haven, Conn.: Yale University Press, 1972.

FILM AND VIDEO PRODUCTIONS

Branagh, Kenneth, dir. *As You Like It*. With Bryce Dallas Howard, Brian Blessed, and Kevin Kline. BBC, 2006.

Coleman, Basil, dir. *As You Like It*. With Helen Mirren and Brian Stirner. BBC/Time-Life, 1978.

Czinner, Paul, dir. *As You Like It*. With Laurence Olivier, Elisabeth Bergner, and Leon Quartermaine. Inter-Allied, 1935.

Edzard, Christine, dir. *As You Like It*. With Emma Croft, Andrew Tiernan, and James Fox. Sands Films, 1992.

Elliott, Michael, and Ronald Eyre, dirs. *As You Like It*. With Vanessa Redgrave and Patrick Allen. BBC, 1963.

Hirsch, John, dir. *As You Like It*. With Andrew Gillies and Roberta Maxwell. CBC, 1983.

—Chris Butler

The Comedy of Errors

INTRODUCTION

The Comedy of Errors, one of Shakespeare's earliest plays (perhaps the earliest), explores the act of stealing someone else's identity and thereby gaining, in an instant, all his possessions: money, friends, house, even wife. The play examines what it would feel like to have one's identity stolen. It follows with interest one such victim, Antipholus of Ephesus, from whom everything seems to be melting away, and he cannot even guess at the reason. The play is witty and appealing but is often considered an apprentice work, a mere precursor to the greater plays that follow.

The play revolves around a pair of identical twins, the Antipholus brothers, separated at birth. One day, after years of searching, Antipholus of Syracuse blunders into Ephesus, the city where, unknown to him, his brother lives. Immediately, confusion reigns: His servant, Dromio, starts behaving oddly toward him; strangers seem to greet him like an old friend; and a woman claiming to be his wife demands that he come home for his lunch. Meanwhile, we see Antipholus of Ephesus becoming more and more perplexed, locked out of his own house and then chased for a debt that he does not believe he owes. Antipholus of Syracuse fears that he is going mad. Everyone else is convinced that Antipholus of Ephesus is going mad. One brother is arrested, while the other tries in vain to flee a city filled, as he thinks, with witches. Soon, both brothers are on the run.

One of the pleasures of Shakespeare is the way that his work can reflect the concerns of each generation of readers and playgoers. As the critic Jan Kott noted, Shakespeare is truly our contemporary. And so, in a present era obsessed with a brave new world of identities projected online, with social networking, online credit card transactions, and false e-mails, *The Comedy of Errors* gains a new interest. The ordeals of the two Antipholus twins—Antipholus of Ephesus, whose name and face are stolen, and Antipholus of Syracuse, who is mysteriously showered with gifts and greetings in a city he has never visited before—resonate with our modern fears about identity and impersonation and lead us to the deep philosophical question underlying those concerns: What makes someone who they are?

The play is hardly written as a deep philosophical tract. It is rather a helter-skelter farce, which, when well performed, has audiences rocking with laughter. The plot, once set off, spits out a seemingly unstoppable series of incidents: beatings, insults, arrests, escapes, and, above all, chases. In no other Shakespeare play, perhaps, do so many of the characters spend so much of the time running. Underlying all the frenetic activity is a beautifully wrought piece of planning, a masterpiece in juggling times, characters, and situations so as to tell a story of spiraling mayhem.

Even more impressive, the play manages to retain a heart as well. Both the Antipholuses are treated with sympathy: There is warmth in their relationships with their respective servants. There is also a delicate portrait of a marriage in trouble, as we hear, little by little, about the tensions between Adriana, married to a man who she fears no longer

Frontispiece to the 1709 edition of *The Comedy of Errors,* edited by Nicholas Rowe

loves her, and her perpetually exasperated husband. The ending, the almost miraculous reunion of the Antipholuses and all their family after a lifetime apart, can carry, particularly in a theater, a real emotional charge.

The Comedy of Errors, in short, is a play of contradictions. Partly a sharp urban comedy, partly a surreal farce, and partly an almost magical romance, it offers many pleasures to the reader or viewer as the Antipholus twins try to work out what is happening; where they can go to stop it from happening, and, fundamentally, who they really are.

BACKGROUND

The Comedy of Errors was written early in Shakespeare's career, most probably in the period 1590–94. (The play was certainly written by 1594, when, as we will see shortly, there is a record of it having been performed.) By contrast, it was printed late. It survives in a single version, the one included in the 1623 First Folio of Shakespeare's plays, in effect, Shakespeare's "Collected Works," put together by two of his former colleagues. It is the fifth play in that collection, among a group of comedies. By the time it was first printed, then, the play had been in existence, in one form or another, for around 30 years, and its creator had been dead for seven years.

The Comedy of Errors was written in, and for, a society rather different from that of modern-day readers. Its technology, its politics, and its social structures were all different from today in ways that repay attention and that impact on the action of the play. Perhaps the most significant of those ways are two major aspects of the Renaissance experience: the classical and the Christian.

"The classical" refers to the languages of Latin and ancient Greek and the culture of ancient Rome and ancient Greece, the civilizations that had used those languages more than a thousand years before Shakespeare's day. In Shakespeare's lifetime, Latin was not just something to learn in schools but the language spoken in the classroom, and all Renaissance schoolboys studied Latin literature as their principal subject throughout their school careers.

The Comedy of Errors relates to the classical most obviously in that it takes, as an obvious source, one of the best-known texts of Latin drama, Plautus's comedy *Menaechmi* (a debt discussed further in the section "Critical Introduction to the Play." But, one should note here that the importance of the classical to this play runs deeper than just one specific model. In particular, it gives the Renaissance playgoer a rich sense of the Mediterranean Sea, the sea crossed and recrossed by mythical heroes such as Odysseus and Aeneas and by all the politicians and generals of Latin history. The Mediterranean forms the setting for most of the stories that a schoolboy of the period would have studied so that that sea

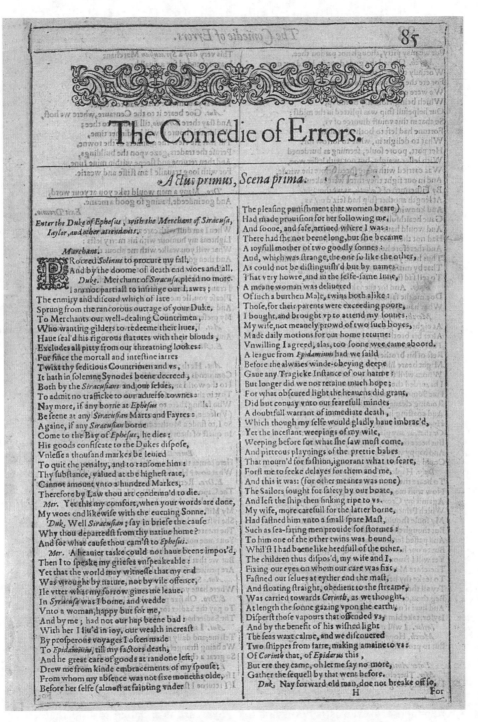

Title page of the First Folio edition of *The Comedy of Errors*, published in 1623

is, in effect, a vast reservoir of classical stories and associations. The average Elizabethan playgoer had never left England, and yet, imaginatively at least, the cities of the ancient Mediterranean—cities such as Syracuse, Ephesus, and Epidamnus of *The Comedy of Errors*—were a home from home.

As for the Christian, Shakespeare's England was a profoundly religious culture in which atheism was exotic and rare. Weekly attendance at church was effectively compulsory, and all Elizabethans were, by 21st-century standards, intimately familiar with both the Old and New Testaments of the Bible. Ephesus, for a modern reader, is a city in Turkey. Renaissance Christian readers would think of it, first and foremost, in the context of Saint Paul's Letter to the Ephesians, part of the New Testament of the Bible, which discusses—among other matters strikingly relevant to *The Comedy of Errors*—the holiness of marriage. The most famous passage in Ephesians is this one:

> Wives, submit yourselves unto your own
>   husbands, as unto the Lord.
> For the husband is the head of the wife, even
>   as Christ is the head of the church: and he is
>   the saviour of the body.
> Therefore as the church is subject unto Christ,
>   so let the wives be to their own husbands in
>   every thing.
> Husbands, love your wives, even as Christ
>   also loved the church, and gave himself for it
>   (5:22–25).

Because the play is set in Ephesus, this whole passage, with its challenge to both husbands and wives to sacrifice themselves for their spouses, could be said to lurk in the background of *The Comedy of Errors*. Other Old and New Testament echoes, of many kinds, can be heard in the play, including the story of Jacob and Esau. Just as *The Comedy of Errors* is perfectly comprehensible to modern audiences who know little about the classical context, equally it is not necessary to be a Christian to enjoy *The Comedy of Errors,* nor even is it necessary to know anything about the Bible. However, one's

sense of the play can be sharpened by an awareness of the classical and Christian contexts and of how Ephesus, for instance, could have been understood by the play's first audience.

SYNOPSIS
Brief Synopsis

The citizens of Ephesus have recently passed a law forbidding, on pain of death, all Syracusans from setting foot in their city. Egeon, a merchant of Syracuse, has fallen foul of this law and is in prison in Ephesus. The Duke of Ephesus sympathizes with his plight but sentences him to die at sunset.

The merchant Antipholus of Syracuse and his servant Dromio of Syracuse, visiting the town, learn of the ban. Nonetheless, Antipholus sets out to see the town, leaving Dromio to look after the money they have brought with them. Unknown to either of them, the city is inhabited by their respective twin brothers, also called Antipholus and Dromio, from whom they were separated shortly after birth. The twins are visually indistinguishable.

In the market-place, the four twins become mixed up, leading to a series of conversations at cross purposes. Antipholus of Syracuse soon finds himself being entertained for lunch by a woman who claims to be his wife (of whom he has no memory). This woman, Adriana, is married to Antipholus of Ephesus, but cannot tell him apart from Antipholus of Syracuse, and she for her part cannot understand why her husband is behaving so erratically.

While they are having lunch, Dromio of Syracuse guards the door of their house, and has a shouted, insulting conversation with intruders trying to get in. The intruders are in fact Antipholus and Dromio of Ephesus, together with some of Antipholus's business contacts.

Enraged by his humiliating exclusion, Antipholus goes to have lunch with a young woman he knows, promising her a gold chain he had intended as a present for his wife. Meanwhile, Antipholus of Syracuse finds that he is in love, not with his supposed wife, but with her sister, Luciana. Dromio of Syracuse is appalled to find that a very fat kitchen servant, Nell, claims that she is his fiancée.

The bewildered Syracusans resolve to leave as soon as possible and split up so that Dromio can find out about ships leaving that night. Again, in the market-place, the wrong servant runs into the wrong master. As the confusions of identity worsen, Antipholus of Ephesus is arrested for a supposed debt relating to the chain and is subsequently declared mad and handed over to the exorcist Dr. Pinch. The Syracusans run for their lives, believing the whole town to be filled with witches, and take sanctuary inside an abbey.

Finally, outside the abbey, the twins come face to face, and the problems of identity are resolved. The Antipholuses are also reunited with their loves; with their father, Egeon; and with their long-lost mother, Emilia the Abbess.

Act I, Scene 1

Syracuse and Ephesus, two cities on the edge of the Mediterranean Sea, are in a trade war with each other. Syracuse has passed a law making it an offense punishable by death for any Ephesian merchant to come to Syracuse, and Ephesus has passed a similar law against Syracusans. Egeon, a merchant from Syracuse, has been caught in the city of Ephesus and appears before the duke of Ephesus, Solinus, to be sentenced.

Solinus explains that under the law, he has no choice but to put Egeon to death today, unless Egeon can raise the money to pay a fine of 1,000 marks. At the moment, though, Egeon's goods are worth scarcely 100 marks, and there seems little prospect of anyone in the city lending him the sum required to be set free. Egeon, for his part, seems resigned to death. Solinus asks Egeon to tell the story of how he came to be in Ephesus, and Egeon reluctantly complies. He explains that some years ago he had a profitable business trading between Syracuse and Epidamium and traveled to Epidamium in connection with urgent business there. His pregnant wife followed him and gave birth to male twins there, in an inn. In the same inn, at the same time, a poor woman gave birth to a second pair of twins, and the wealthy Egeon bought the newborn children

Men of Epidamium rescue Egeon's wife, Antipholus of Ephesus, and Dromio of Ephesus from the storm in Act I, Scene 1 of *The Comedy of Errors*. This is a print from the Boydell Shakespeare Gallery project, which was first conceived in 1786 and lasted until 1805. *(Painting by Francis Wheatley; engraving by James Neagle)*

from her, intending to raise them as servants to his own two baby boys.

Egeon and his wife, with the four babies, boarded a ship heading back to Syracuse. The ship ran into a storm and started to sink, forcing Egeon and his wife to bind the children and themselves to a spare mast and to jump into the sea. As they floated, currents drove them against a rock, and the mast split in two. Egeon, one of his sons, and one of the poor woman's babies were left with one-half of the mast, while the wife and the two other babies, on the other half, drifted away from them.

Each party was rescued, but by a separate ship, and Egeon never managed to find the other ship or hear any more news of his wife and child.

Egeon describes how he returned to Syracuse with the two babies he had managed to save. He gave each of them the names that had belonged to their lost brothers: The son, we later find, is called Antipholus; and the servant, Dromio. For the next 18 years, the three of them lived together in Syracuse. Then Antipholus, accompanied by his servant, decided to set off on a voyage to look for his missing twin and left Syracuse. After some time, dismayed by the lack of news of their progress, Egeon himself set off to look for the search party and has spent five years traveling across Greece and Asia without hearing any news of them. This concludes Egeon's story.

The duke, moved by Egeon's tale but unwilling to set aside the laws of Ephesus, schedules the old man's execution for that evening but rules that Egeon should spend the day attempting to borrow the money that would save his life. Egeon, with no hope of raising the money, regards this as merely an unwelcome stay of execution.

Act I, Scene 2

Unknown to Egeon, and themselves unaware of his presence, Antipholus and Dromio of Syracuse, the boys Egeon raised, are in Ephesus on the day in question. Antipholus talks to an Ephesian merchant, who warns them to conceal the fact that they are from Syracuse. Antipholus gives Dromio 1,000 marks, a considerable sum of money, and instructs him to take it to the inn they are staying in. Dromio leaves. Antipholus explains to the merchant that he intends to walk around the town and see the sights, and the merchant leaves.

Dromio enters again, but this is not Antipholus's servant Dromio of Syracuse but rather Dromio of Ephesus. Mistaking him for his servant, Antipholus asks where his money is and is angered by Dromio's apparent lack of comprehension. Dromio, for his part, mistakes Antipholus of Syracuse for his own master, Antipholus of Ephesus. He explains that he has been sent by Antipholus's wife with the mes-

sage that lunch is ready. Antipholus of Syracuse is so enraged by this apparent nonsense that he beats Dromio, who runs away. Antipholus observes that Ephesus has a reputation as a place of sin and black magic and sets out to return to the inn in the hope of catching up with Dromio.

Act II, Scene 1

Adriana, the wife of Antipholus of Ephesus, and her sister Luciana are waiting for Antipholus. It is two o'clock, and neither her husband nor his servant has returned. Adriana complains about her husband's behavior, and Luciana advises her to bear it patiently, as befits a married woman. Dromio of Ephesus enters and complains that his master has apparently gone mad. He recounts his meeting with him. Adriana beats Dromio and tells him to go and bring his master back at once. Dromio exits.

Adriana complains bitterly to Luciana. She fears she has grown older and unattractive and that her husband is having affairs with younger women. She mentions that Antipholus has promised her a fine gold chain, but she would much rather have a guarantee that he is faithful to her. She exits, weeping. Luciana comments that her behavior is "mad jealousy."

Act II, Scene 2

Antipholus of Syracuse has gone back to the inn and discovered that his money is indeed safely stored there. On the street, he bumps into his own servant, Dromio of Syracuse, and asks why he lied in their previous conversation. Dromio of Syracuse, who knows nothing of that previous meeting, is indignant, and Antipholus, angry at what he takes to be further jesting, inappropriate behavior, beats his servant. Dromio accepts the blows with bewildered resignation; Antipholus calms down and wonders if dinner is ready yet; and master and servant exchange banter on the nature of time.

They are disturbed by the arrival of Luciana and Adriana, who have left the house to look for Adriana's errant husband. Adriana, of course, mistakes the two Syracusans for her husband and his

Antipholus of Syracuse accepts Adriana's invitation to dine in Act II, Scene 2 of *The Comedy of Errors*. The print is from 1752. *(Illustration by Hubert Gravelot; engraving by Gerard Van der Gucht)*

servant. Bitterly, she attacks Antipholus for having, as she sees it, given up on their marriage. She complains that she would be contaminated by his infidelity and begs him not to renege on their love.

Antipholus of Syracuse is amazed and protests he does not know her. Luciana says that they sent Dromio to him, and although Dromio of Syracuse denies any knowledge, Antipholus remembers the conversation he had with Dromio of Ephesus and becomes even more confused. Adriana begs him to

come home for lunch, and Antipholus decides to accept her invitation in the hope thereby of solving the mystery. Dromio fears that they have stumbled into fairyland and are in danger of enchantment.

Adriana, taking heart, invites Antipholus to dine with her in an upper room, instructing Dromio to guard the door and let no one in. Dromio settles down to guard the door.

Act III, Scene 1

The focus shifts back to the street where the audience meets, for the first time, Antipholus of Ephesus. He is talking to Angelo the goldsmith, who is making the gold chain for Adriana. With them is Balthazar, a merchant, and Dromio of Ephesus, who cannot understand why Antipholus is acting so differently from before. For his part, Antipholus assumes that his servant's nonsensical account of the morning meeting is the result of drunkenness.

Antipholus invites Angelo and Balthazar back to his house for lunch. They find the door is locked, since Antipholus of Syracuse has already gained entrance and is eating lunch with Adriana. Dromio of Ephesus shouts through the door, demanding that they be let in. Dromio of Syracuse, on the other side of the door and unable to see whom he is talking to, refuses to let them in. Dromio of Syracuse is joined, on his side of the door, by Luce the servant, who throws insults against the mysterious intruders. Dromio of Ephesus and his master bang on the other side of the door, to no avail.

Adriana joins Luce and Dromio of Ephesus. Antipholus, recognizing her voice, calls her "wife," and she rebuffs him, thinking that since her husband is already in the house, this unseen caller must be a drunk. Antipholus of Ephesus announces an intention to break down the door with a crowbar. His friends dissuade him, arguing that it will cause a public scandal. Instead, Antipholus resolves to go and have lunch at a nearby inn, where the hostess is an attractive young woman whom Antipholus admires (later in the play identified as the Courtesan). He further resolves to present to this woman, and not to Adriana, the chain he has commissioned from Angelo, the goldsmith.

Act III, Scene 2

Antipholus of Syracuse declares to Adriana's sister Luciana that he is in love with her. Luciana is appalled and begs Antipholus to stop. If he must entertain unlawful lust, she pleads, let him do so discreetly, with other women, so as to hurt Adriana as little as possible. Antipholus of Syracuse, still bewildered that Luciana knows his name while he has no idea of hers, says again that he is very much in love with her and has no desire for the weeping Adriana. He asks Luciana to marry him: "give me thy hand." Luciana says she must ask her sister's permission and leaves in a hurry.

Dromio of Syracuse enters at a run. He has discovered that Luce (Nell), a kitchen servant in Adriana's household, claims that she and Dromio are engaged to be married. (In fact, of course, she is engaged to the "other" Dromio.) Luce Nell is very fat and ugly, and Antipholus and Dromio amuse themselves by describing how physically repellent and terrifying she is.

Antipholus and Dromio resolve to make their escape from the bewitched town of Ephesus, though even as he formulates the plan, Antipholus finds himself reluctant to leave the presence of the beautiful Luciana. Antipholus tells Dromio to arrange them passage on any ship leaving the city that night and to meet him again in the marketplace with the details. Dromio leaves.

Angelo, the goldsmith, enters and mistaking Antipholus of Syracuse for his customer Antipholus of Ephesus gives him the gold chain. He refuses to take any payment on the spot and treats Antipholus's puzzled questions as jokes, before departing, leaving Antipholus holding the valuable piece of jewelry. Shaken, Antipholus resolves to go to the marketplace at once to wait for Dromio so that the two of them can make their escape.

Act IV, Scene 1

A merchant of Ephesus asks Angelo, the goldsmith, to repay a long-standing financial debt. Fearful that Angelo may refuse to pay, the merchant has brought along a Sergeant, with the

power to arrest Angelo and take him to a debtor's prison until the debt is paid. Angelo replies that he expects, at this very moment, to be paid by Antipholus for the chain that he gave him earlier in the afternoon. He invites the merchant and the Sergeant to accompany him to Antipholus's house.

On the way, they cross the path of Antipholus (of Ephesus) and Dromio (of Ephesus). Antipholus has just left from his lunch with the Courtesan. He is instructing Dromio to buy a rope with which he will be able to administer beatings to his wife and her confederates who (Antipholus thinks) locked him maliciously out of his house. Dromio exits on this mission.

Antipholus sees Angelo and upbraids him for not turning up with the chain. Angelo cannot understand and requests payment for the chain that (he thinks) he has delivered. Antipholus, himself not understanding, tells Angelo to deliver the chain to Adriana and get her to pay for it. Angelo becomes increasingly agitated, as Antipholus continues to deny having received the chain. In desperation, Angelo himself pays the sergeant to arrest Antipholus for debt, despite Antipholus's angry denials and threats against Angelo.

Dromio of Syracuse enters and again mistakes Antipholus for his twin brother. He tells Antipholus that, as instructed, he has found a ship leaving Ephesus that evening. Antipholus of Ephesus is bewildered, since he sent his Dromio off to buy a length of rope, not to organize passage out of the city. Assuming Dromio is drunk, he threatens that he will punish him later for this misbehavior. In the meantime, though, Antipholus requires Dromio to run an urgent errand, to tell Adriana the news of his arrest. There is a purse of money in the desk at home that will suffice to buy him temporary bail while he works out what has happened, and he gives Dromio the key and tells him also to fetch it. The sergeant then takes Antipholus away, intending to deliver him to the debtors' prison. Dromio of Ephesus, now very confused, resolves to obey his master's strange instructions to the best of his abilities and to take the key to Adriana.

Act IV, Scene 2

Luciana tells her sister Adriana that Antipholus has made a declaration of love to her. Adriana interrogates her about it and is angry at her husband, but confesses that she is still in love with him despite the bitter words she speaks against him. Dromio of Syracuse bursts in, breathless from running, and tells the women the news of the arrest. Adriana asks Luciana to fetch the money in the desk, which she does, and they send Dromio off with the money to free his master.

Act IV, Scene 3

Antipholus of Syracuse muses on the strange world he seems to be living in, where passersby he has never seen before salute him by name. Dromio of Syracuse, hurrying to the prison, enters and is amazed to see his master a free man. Antipholus of Syracuse has no idea what Dromio is talking about and tries to decipher some sense from Dromio's increasingly hysterical jesting about sergeants, debts, and prisons. Antipholus concludes that Dromio is mad; that he, Antipholus, is mad, too; and that both of them are caught in a place of enchantment and illusions.

The Courtesan enters. Seeing Antipholus and mistaking him for his brother with whom she had lunch, she asks about the chain he promised her and also about a ring that Antipholus of Ephesus apparently received from her over the course of lunch. Antipholus of Syracuse and his servant, already very frightened, assume that she is a devil and run away. The Courtesan speaks in soliloquy. Antipholus, she believes, has gone mad. She resolves to go to Adriana and warn her of this fact. She also wants her ring back, and as, for obvious reasons, she cannot tell Adriana the precise circumstances under which Antipholus obtained it, she resolves to lie and to claim that Antipholus burst into her house in a frenzy and seized it from her. This, she hopes, will enable her eventually to get the ring back without awkward questions.

Act IV, Scene 4

Antipholus of Ephesus is being taken to the debtors' prison by the Sergeant. As they go, they come across Dromio of Ephesus, who has now fulfilled the instructions given to him by Antipholus in Act IV, Scene 1 and has obtained a length of rope wherewith to beat Adriana and her servants. Antipholus, of course, expects him to be carrying the money to bail him out, but Dromio of Ephesus knows nothing of all this, and the two talk at cross-purposes until an enraged Antipholus starts to beat him. The Sergeant tries to intervene, and Dromio explains bitterly that he is forever being beaten.

When Antipholus of Ephesus threatens to hit Adriana, a group of men seize him in Act IV, Scene 4 of *The Comedy of Errors*. This print is from the Boydell Shakespeare Gallery project. *(Painting by Francis Wheatley; engraving by James Stow)*

At this point, Adriana, Luciana, and the Courtesan enter, together with a schoolmaster, Doctor Pinch. The three women have concluded that Antipholus may be not merely mad but demonically possessed and have brought along Pinch, an expert in exorcism, to assess the situation. Pinch tries to examine Antipholus, who hits him—sufficient evidence, to Pinch, that Antipholus is possessed. Adriana, Antipholus, and Dromio then cross-examine one another about the events of the day and cannot understand why their accounts differ so wildly. Pinch chips in that not only the master but also the servant are possessed by devils. Antipholus, now furious, threatens to attack Adriana, and a group of helpers arrive. They seize and tie up Antipholus and Dromio. Adriana tells the Sergeant that she herself will pay the debt that Antipholus still owes, and Antipholus and Dromio are both taken away by Doctor Pinch to have the devils cast out of them.

Adriana discovers from the Sergeant that the debt is due to Angelo, the goldsmith, for a chain. The Courtesan says that when she saw Antipholus, he had the chain with him. At this moment, the other pair of twins burst in, Antipholus and Dromio of Syracuse, with their weapons drawn. To Adriana and the others, it appears as if they have somehow magically escaped their captivity from Pinch. All flee, leaving the two Syracusans alone. Antipholus of Syracuse reaffirms his resolution to leave Ephesus as soon as he can.

Act V, Scene 1

Angelo, the goldsmith, and the Second Merchant see Antipholus and Dromio of Syracuse and approach them. The Second Merchant accuses Antipholus of lying to him, and Antipholus is so angry that again he draws his sword. A group of citizens, led by Adriana, Luciana, and the Courtesan, come on the scene, and the Syracusans flee, escaping into a nearby priory. The abbess of the priory comes out, attracted by the noise made by those in the street. Adriana demands her husband back. The abbess interrogates her: How long has he been mad? What sent him mad? Adriana tells the story of Antipholus's growing distance from her over the last week. The abbess, for her part, concludes that Antipholus has gone mad because of Adriana's nagging and pestering. Adriana again demands her husband back: It is her duty to look after him. The abbess again refuses and leaves her in the street.

By chance, the priory stands next to the place in Ephesus where executions are carried out. At this moment Duke Solinus himself enters, with his train, taking Egeon to execution. Adriana appeals to the duke, telling him how her husband and servant have gone mad and are in the priory. The duke resolves to help and summons the abbess.

A messenger bursts in with disturbing news: Antipholus and Dromio (that is, Antipholus and Dromio of Ephesus) have overpowered Doctor Pinch and are amusing themselves by cutting off his hair and burning his beard. At first, no one believes this story, since those on stage have seen Antipholus and Dromio (of Syracuse) making their way into the priory. But, then they hear the sound of Antipholus of Ephesus approaching, and moments later he and Dromio come onto the stage.

Antipholus appeals to the duke, whom he served in the wars, for justice. He alleges that Adriana has abused and dishonored him. As he does so, Egeon recognizes (misrecognizes) him: Egeon thinks he must be Antipholus of Syracuse, the son he raised. Antipholus tells the story of the day from his perspective, relating the indignities he has suffered, while others present—Angelo, the two merchants, the Courtesan—confirm or contradict various of the details depending on what they saw over the course of the day. Egeon greets his son, assuming that he will recognize his father and thinking that he may be able to provide the money to save his life. Antipholus of Ephesus, of course, does not recognize his father at all, and neither does his Dromio, a crushing, inexplicable blow for Egeon, who believes he is now doomed.

At last, the abbess enters, bringing with her Antipholus and Dromio of Syracuse. For the first time in the play, the twins are on stage at once. General amazement ensues, compounded when

Egeon reunites with Emilia, his wife, in Act V, Scene I of *The Comedy of Errors. (Illustration by William Hamilton; engraving by Edward Scriven)*

the abbess declares that she is really Egeon's long-lost wife, Emilia.

With this clue, the brothers start to decipher the story of what has happened to them in the course of the day. Adriana regains her husband, and Luciana realizes she may gain one herself. The abbess, Emilia, invites them all in to discuss events further. Last to leave the stage are the two Dromios. They wonder which of them is the elder brother, with the right to lead the way, but conclude that it does not matter: They leave the stage hand in hand.

CHARACTER LIST

Solinus Duke of Ephesus.

Egeon Syracusan merchant and father of the Antipholus twins. Many years ago, his family suffered a disastrous shipwreck in which he lost his wife and one of his baby twin boys.

Antipholus of Ephesus The "home" Antipholus. Son of Egeon and Emilia and twin brother of Antipholus of Syracuse (although he is not aware of any of these things). Husband of Adriana. A merchant and the owner of the house where much of Act III takes place.

Antipholus of Syracuse The "away" Antipholus. Son of Egeon and Emilia, raised by Egeon in Syracuse. Some years ago, Antipholus left Syracuse to travel the Mediterranean area in search of his lost twin.

Dromio of Ephesus Servant to Antipholus of Ephesus. The Dromio twins, from a poor family, were, in their infancy, bought by Egeon to be brought up as servants to his own twins, and they too were separated in the shipwreck. Like his master, Antipholus of Ephesus, Dromio of Ephesus knows nothing of his lost twin.

Dromio of Syracuse Servant to Antipholus of Syracuse and raised, like his master, in Syracuse by Egeon. He has accompanied his master on his journey to look for the other twins.

Balthazar Merchant of Ephesus and friend of Antipholus of Ephesus.

Angelo A goldsmith of Ephesus, commissioned by Antipholus to make a gold chain that Antipholus originally intended to give to Adriana. He is in debt to the Second Merchant.

First Merchant Of Ephesus. Friend to Antipholus of Syracuse.

Second Merchant Engaged in trade with Persia; he has lent money to Angelo.

Doctor Pinch A schoolmaster and conjurer who is believed to be an expert at dealing with cases of demonic possession.

Emilia Wife to Egeon. After the shipwreck, she was separated from all of her family, and has ended up becoming the abbess in the city of Ephesus, unaware that her son is also growing up in that city.

Adriana Wife of Antipholus of Ephesus.

Luciana The unmarried sister of Adriana. Antipholus of Syracuse falls in love with her.

Luce Kitchen servant to Adriana, also referred to as Nell. Engaged to be married to Dromio of Ephesus.

Courtesan Hostess of the Porpentine and admired by Antipholus of Ephesus.

Sergeant An official licensed to arrest people for debt and take them to a debtors' prison.

CHARACTER STUDIES
The Antipholus Brothers

The Antipholus brothers, considered from the point of view of their characters, are superficially identical: They are, for all those in the play, seemingly the same person. They look the same, dress the same, speak in the same way. They are the same age, of course, and although raised separately, they are of roughly the same social background: wealthy young men of the merchant class. They are indistinguishable to all those around them, and in what does personality consist if not in the way that others read you?

And yet, in spite of these constraints, Shakespeare endows the two of them with individuality—one of the artful pleasures of *The Comedy of Errors*—largely through contrast between them. Their barely sketched personal life stories and contrasting positions in life give them different perspectives. Antipholus of Syracuse, the "away" Antipholus, is like a perpetual backpacker, culturally and emotionally unattached, seemingly with no need to earn a living—money has not been a problem for him in his peregrinations through Europe, and he is far from poor now. He is without family (except for his servant Dromio) and without a permanent residence. His first scene fills in this sense of a restless, rootless character:

> I will go lose myself
> And wander up and down to view the city . . .
> He that commends me to mine own content
> Commends me to the thing I cannot get.
> I to the world am like a drop of water
> That in the ocean seeks another drop,
> Who, falling there to find his fellow forth,
> Unseen, inquisitive, confounds himself:

> So I, to find a mother and a brother,
> In quest of them, unhappy, lose myself
> (1.2.30–40).

Antipholus of Ephesus, by contrast, has a wife, a house, and a routine. He possesses not just one manservant but a whole domestic staff (embodied in the play by Luce/Nell). His extensive network of friends and business contacts is glimpsed, partly in his dealings with Balthazar and Angelo and partly in the misdirected greetings that so surprise Antipholus of Syracuse, perhaps by contrast with his own perpetual vagabondage:

Dromio of Ephesus tells a bewildered Antipholus of Syracuse to return home for lunch in Act I, Scene 2 of *The Comedy of Errors*. This illustration was made for the 1918 edition of Charles and Mary Lamb's *Tales from Shakespeare*. *(Illustration by Louis Rhead)*

There's not a man I meet but doth salute me
As if I were their well-acquainted friend;
And every one doth call me by my name.
Some tender money to me; some invite me;
Some other give me thanks for kindnesses;
Some offer me commodities to buy:
Even now a tailor call'd me in his shop
And show'd me silks that he had bought
 for me,
And therewithal took measure of my body
 (4.3.1–9).

Antipholus of Ephesus is, in this speech, placed in an entire economic system, as a consumer of goods and a member of social networks. Antipholus of Syracuse is, by contrast, suggested to be an outsider to them.

Furthermore—and it is no coincidence that this revelation is held back until the last act of the play, until the point where he has fought his way to freedom and is starting to seem not merely a hapless merchant but a man of action—Antipholus of Ephesus has fought in a war. In his plea to the duke Solinus he alludes to

the service that long since I did thee,
When I bestrid thee in the wars and took
Deep scars to save thy life (5.1.193–195).

The Duke had been wounded and was lying on the ground. Antipholus, he says, actually stood across his body, fighting off enemies that would otherwise have sought to finish him off where he lay. Antipholus of Syracuse, as far as one can tell, has never done anything so violent or serious, or been so hurt. (And why does Adriana not notice the absence of these "deep scars" on Antipholus's body? Is this an elegantly delayed confirmation that she never actually sees the other brother naked?) In return for this war service, it seems, Solinus was instrumental in arranging Antipholus's marriage to Adriana.

As a soldier and a husband, Antipholus of Ephesus is fulfilling more fully a father's expectations for his eldest son (which he, technically, is), whereas

Antipholus of Syracuse, the younger of the twins, is, as might be put today, more in touch with his feminine side. (For further discussion of the question of who is the heir and why it matters, see "Key Passages" below.)

Antipholus of Ephesus's experiences and his responsibilities, then, make him subtly different from his footloose younger brother. One of the jokes of the play is the contrast between the alpha-male attitude of Antipholus of Ephesus, with the mindset of a man used to getting what he wants, and the domestic, financial, and sexual indignities heaped upon him in the course of the play.

The obvious question, and one that the play hardly addresses directly, is how the Antipholus brothers will react to the huge shifts in their world introduced in the play. To some extent, that question is beyond the remit of the play, but readers have often speculated about the likely fate of the twins. Antipholus of Syracuse, one might argue, will have it easier. He has long known that he is incomplete, seeking his missing family, which now he has found, and he has fallen in love as well. Antipholus of Ephesus might well find it harder to adapt to a world in which suddenly he has immediate family close at hand. It will be hard for him to resume his status in Ephesus, where his dignity has taken such a battering, and to pick up again his struggling marriage. It is often said that the happy ending, for him, is a muted one.

There is, though, some room to disagree with this glum assessment, which hardly reflects the uplifting experience one leaves a theater with. There are hints in the play that Antipholus of Ephesus is not merely a middle-aged man whose life has irretrievably fallen apart, but that he is stronger and more adaptable than that. One example is when he and his Dromio escape from their bonds and overpower the hapless Doctor Pinch:

My master and his man are both broke loose,
Beaten the maids a-row and bound the doctor
Whose beard they have singed off with brands
 of fire;
And ever, as it blazed, they threw on him

Great pails of puddled mire to quench the hair:
My master preaches patience to him and the
  while
His man with scissors nicks him like a fool
  (5.1.171–177).

On the one hand, this moment shows what the past war service also suggests: Antipholus of Ephesus is a man of action. His response to the imprisonment, although violent, also shows him able to cooperate, as he and his Dromio for once work harmoniously together. They escape together; they work together in tormenting Doctor Pinch. And, it is also playful, in a rather gruesome way, as the two of them show themselves capable of joining in with the craziness and improvising an appropriately surreal, elaborate, and sarcastic punishment for the would-be exorcist. Antipholus of Ephesus shows, in effect, a flash of anarchist enthusiasm here that will stand him in good stead in the brave new world at the end of the play.

The Dromio Brothers

A trusty villain, sir, that very oft,
When I am dull with care and melancholy,
Lightens my humour with his merry jests
  (1.2.19–21).

This first description of one of the Dromios, by his master Antipholus of Syracuse, sets out the two most important characteristics about them. First, there is the issue of class. Dromio is a "villain," which does not have the modern sense of wickedness but rather indicates that he is lower class, not a gentleman. Strictly speaking, in fact, he is a slave, sold into a life of servitude by his mother, and referred to in the play as a "bondman." It is interesting that while both Dromios complain about their lot, they do not tend to do so in the language of enslavement and emancipation. In fact, slavery being (theoretically at least) unknown in Elizabethan England, Shakespeare tends to present each of them as normal family servants, and unlike their precursors in Plautus, he does not raise the possibility of them being "manumitted," that is, set free

The two Dromios, played by William H. Crane and Stuart Robson, meet for the first time in Act V, Scene I of *The Comedy of Errors*, in this photo by Gebbie & Husson Co., 1888.

from their servitude at the end of the play. Indeed, in his very first moment in the play, Dromio of Syracuse is entrusted by Antipholus with a sum of money that is later revealed to be 1,000 marks. This is an enormous sum—around 600 pounds of Elizabethan money, which had the buying power of very roughly £30,000 or $45,000 at today's prices. Dromio jokes that a man might run away with that amount of money, but it does not occur to him to do so. Slavery, to both of the Dromios, seems to be both inevitable and tolerable.

The second important thing about the Dromios is that they are perceived almost exclusively in terms of their relationship with their masters, providing a contrast, in the initial quotation above, expressed in terms of dark and light. For much of the play, an Antipholus and a Dromio conduct themselves as a double act, each defining the other. As we tend to see the Antipholus brothers in terms of contrasts between each other, it is perhaps equally true to say that, in practical terms, for most of the time they are on stage, we see them through the medium of their respective contrasts with the Dromios. We see the power relationships between and across the two pairs and moments when that relationship is undermined—for example, when Dromio thinks Antipholus is going soft in the head and when a Dromio, even if unknowingly, derides an Antipholus and refuses to let him into his own house. Indeed, one might even say that the relationship between servant and master is one of the things that makes the interlude with Luce/Nell so funny. It is one thing to intrude into another gentleman's personal life, but there is even more of a voyeuristic surprise in intruding into his servant's. (For more on this episode, see "Key Passages" below.)

If the Dromios are so similar, are they effectively differentiated from each other, apart from in the major matter of their feelings toward Luce/Nell? In the text, it is a little less clear than it is with their masters. Dromio of Syracuse, like his master, tends to be seen wondering at the situations he is in, whereas Dromio of Ephesus, like his master, is generally exasperated and reaching for solutions involving violence. Dromio of Syracuse, then, might seem, as a generalization, a little more in touch with wonder than his more grounded brother. But, as with their masters, the answer to the question of the difference between them is obvious in performance, where each has a slightly different physical form and voice, guaranteeing their individuality.

Adriana and Luciana

There is, Laurie Maguire has suggested, a third pair of "twins" in *The Comedy of Errors:* the sisters Adriana and Luciana. In many ways, they too are constructed as a double act, defined in terms of the contrasts between them.

Adriana is the wife of Antipholus of Ephesus. We hear little, directly, about her background. We may guess, from a couple of hints in Act V, that she is from a well-connected family. She tells the duke that she married "Antipholus, my husband, / Whom I made lord of me and all I had, / At your important letters" (5.1.138–140). Evidently, then, the duke Solinus arranged the marriage, and the sense that Adriana was both a trophy wife and someone important enough, in her own right, to deserve the duke's personal attention is reinforced by his own comment on the matter:

Long since thy husband served me in my wars,
And I to thee engaged a prince's word,
When thou didst make him master of thy bed,
To do him all the grace and good I could
 (5.1.163–166).

Indeed, there's a faint implication in these references that her parents are no longer alive, something reinforced by the fact that we meet her unmarried sister, Luciana, who seems to be at home in Adriana's house (rather than, as one would normally expect of an unmarried woman, at her father's). However, the question of whether Adriana's parents are still living is not settled unambiguously. Adriana and Antipholus, one might also add, have been married for some time, long enough for him to get bored (as she fears), but the couple are still childless.

The passage of dialogue that really establishes Adriana in the play is her opening exchange with her sister, Luciana, an exchange of "stichomythia" (single-line speeches) that also sketches in the character of Luciana, defined in opposition to her:

ADRIANA. Why should their liberty than ours be more?

LUCIANA. Because their business still lies out o' door.

ADRIANA. Look, when I serve him so, he takes it ill.

LUCIANA. O, know he is the bridle of your will.

ADRIANA. There's none but asses will be bridled so.

LUCIANA. Why, headstrong liberty is lash'd with woe.
There's nothing situate under heaven's eye
But hath his bound, in earth, in sea, in sky:
The beasts, the fishes, and the winged fowls,
Are their males' subjects and at their controls
(2.1.10–19).

Adriana adopts, in effect, a protofeminist position. She imagines that there ought to be equality between men and women—between "their liberty" and "ours," as she puts it to her sister here—and she is indignant that, in practice, the relationship seems to be unequal. Her husband, she complains, can do what he wants, failing to turn up at the appointed time, whereas he gets angry if she behaves in that sort of way ("When I serve him so, he takes it ill"). With a touch of irony, it is her unmarried sister who preaches what one might call the orthodox doctrine of patriarchy: It is the role of wives to be subservient to their husbands, to be literally their "subjects," and to put up with their husbands' erratic behavior on the grounds that God simply intended husbands to have more "liberty" than their wives. Adriana, on her first appearance, advances what modern readers will recognize as views considerably ahead of their time.

Such views might mark her out as a shrew, in the tradition of Shakespeare's *The Taming of the Shrew*: a woman in need of discipline by a strong man, and Antipholus does threaten violence against her several times in the play. But, later in the scene, one picks up a second layer of complication:

Hath homely age the alluring beauty took
From my poor cheek? then he hath wasted it:
Are my discourses dull? barren my wit?
If voluble and sharp discourse be marr'd,
Unkindness blunts it more than marble hard:

Do their gay vestments his affections bait?
That's not my fault: he's master of my state:
What ruins are in me that can be found,
By him not ruin'd? then is he the ground
Of my defeatures. My decayed fair
A sunny look of his would soon repair
But, too unruly deer, he breaks the pale
And feeds from home . . . (2.1.85–97).

Adriana is here using, not the public language of gender justice, but the private language of love. In this speech, she even concedes the very point that she was arguing with Luciana earlier, accepting as a matter of fact that, as her husband, Antipholus "is master of my state," not so much as a statement of gender politics, as a reflection of the fact that she is still in love with him. As she herself says, all that it would take to make her beautiful again is one smile from him. In fact, in other respects, she is still talking in the language associated with lovers. For instance, she is worried that Antipholus no longer enjoys her "discourses" and her "wit," qualities associated with lovers rather than wives, and qualities that her husband admires in the Courtesan. Adriana compares her beloved to an unruly deer, which is a favorite image in erotic poetry of the time. It was a favorite partly because it is a pun on *deer* and *dear* and partly because it draws an image of a lover as a beautiful but almost untamable animal. (For a good example of it developed at more length, compare Shakespeare's *Venus and Adonis*. For more examples of how Adriana's language resembles what one finds in the love poetry of Shakespeare's contemporaries, see "Key Passages" below.)

Adriana, then, is a wife and a lover and currently satisfied in neither role. Her sister, Luciana, though, is neither a wife nor a lover. One would like to know more of Luciana's story. She hints early on in the play that she would consider getting married and also alludes to a reason for not wanting to:

ADRIANA: This servitude makes you to keep unwed.

LUCIANA: Not this, but troubles of the
  marriage-bed. . . .
Well, I will marry one day, but to try (2.1.26–
  27, 42).

What personal issues lurk in her line about "troubles of the marriage-bed"? Whatever they are, they seem to be swept aside in the course of the play. Appalled at first by Antipholus's advances, we see her flustered and attracted by them, too. In common with many heroines of Shakespeare comedies, she has fewer and fewer lines as the end of the play approaches, and we must presume that she ends the play paired with, and ready to be married to, Antipholus of Syracuse.

If, then, Luciana gains through the play a chance to be a lover and a wife, then perhaps more stress is put on what Adriana gains: a fresh start at both of her roles. Her lunch with her husband's twin, Antipholus of Syracuse, renews her role as a lover—it is as if they have met for the first time. As for her role as wife, she renews that in Act V. In spite of the abbess accusing her of having driven her husband mad and in spite of the fact that her husband is now mad, is patently a danger to those around him and to her in particular, and is safely in the care of an institution where she could decently leave him, she refuses to relinquish him:

I will attend my husband, be his nurse,
Diet his sickness, for it is my office,
And will have no attorney but myself;
And therefore let me have him home with me
  (5.1.100–104).

In making this declaration, she reasserts and reclaims her role as wife, nurse, and homemaker. Ironically, then, although she argued against it early on, it is she who finds a way of accepting and embracing the asymmetry of roles in a marriage relationship. Luciana and she represent, one might say, two complementary models of womanhood, just as the Antipholus twins, with whom they are linked, represent two slightly different flavors of manhood.

DIFFICULTIES OF THE PLAY

For readers the main difficulty of *The Comedy of Errors* is the very thing that makes it pleasurable for an audience: the confusion created by having a pair of identical twins—indeed, two pairs of identical twins—in the same play. In performance, this is a pleasure rather than a problem, because the confusions unfold at speaking pace rather than at reading pace, and because each Antipholus and Dromio is played by a different actor. Typically, although the two Antipholuses are supposed to be indistinguishable, one is slightly taller, one has a rounder face, and they have slightly different regional accents. It is thus easier to follow in performance than on the page. Yet, in reading and in discussion, it is laborious—but important—to keep track of which Antipholus is talking to which Dromio. A reader has to work hard to keep on top of that detail as they read, otherwise the beautifully wrought plot dissolves into nonsense.

Interestingly, discussing this aspect of the play is particularly difficult because Shakespeare seems determined to make the names hard. For instance, in the First Folio, he hesitates over Luciana's name, calling her once—in a stage direction—"Juliana." He gives the kitchen maid two names as well: the dialogue calls her both "Nell" and "Luce," although it is seemingly the same woman being referred to on each occasion. Both of these name problems could be—indeed, probably are—mere oversights, but Shakespeare is certainly deliberate in choosing polysyllabic names both for the twins and for their cities. By and large, Shakespearean characters can be distinguished by names of one, two, or three syllables: Lear, Hamlet, Rosalind. Adriana and Luciana, at four each, are on the upper limit of the normal range. "Antipholus of Ephesus" requires eight syllables, as does his brother, and the Dromios each require seven. In a play already obsessed with names and confusion of names, the deliberately clumsy naming seems to be part of the effect.

Once past the difficulty of names, the next problem one faces in enjoying the play is that it seems unreal: It falls short of the standards of realism one might expect to see in, for instance, modern drama. Could a pair of twins be so alike, not just in facial appearance, but—let us not forget—in dress and accent, after years apart, so as to accidentally deceive not only casual acquaintances but those closest to them? Does not the presence of a second pair of equally identical twins stretch credibility further? The reader may amuse him- or herself picking up further implausible coincidences, unexplained details, and plot holes, such as the lockout scene in Act III, where the whole play would fall apart if any character inside the house thought to look out into the street to see who is causing the commotion.

There are two ways of addressing this bar to enjoying the play. The first is to observe that Shakespeare is working in a tradition that does not share modern attitudes toward realism, as that term is understood today. We have been weaned on novels and drama in which we expect all the characters to have a consistently described appearance, a "backstory" we can work out and measure in years, a recognizable place in society, and a psychologically consistent motivation. Measure any Shakespeare play, or almost any Renaissance work, against such standards, and it will tend to fall short. (Nor, actually, are such standards observed in much modern fiction and drama, but for some reason, incongruity seems to offend us less there.)

In particular, one might add, *The Comedy of Errors* is influenced, not by novels, which did not yet exist, but by the romance, the leading fictional genre of Shakespeare's day. In a typical romance, princes travel endlessly through the lands around the Mediterranean Sea, searching for seemingly unattainable objects, being shipwrecked, separated, and reunited. Mystery and magic are never far away, and plausibility is not at a premium. We can still talk about Shakespeare plays addressing, one might say, an idealized "reality," but Shakespeare is not trying to create the sort of novelistic realism we find lacking in *The Comedy of Errors*.

The other way of addressing the question, though, is to observe that on some counts *The Comedy of Errors* is so realist as to put most modern fictions to shame. The Greek literary theorist Aristotle propounded the idea of the three unities: Good plays should describe events that take place on a single day (the unity of time); they should describe events that take place in a single location (the unity of place); and they should not contain material irrelevant to the main plot (the unity of action). Shakespeare's contemporary Philip Sidney, addressing the faults of Elizabethan popular theater (and offering in the process a vivid picture of plays influenced by romance), commented in particular on how contemporary drama neglects those unities. On the first, Sidney said:

> ordinary it is, that two young princes fall in love, after many traverses she is got with child, delivered of a fair boy: he is lost, groweth a man, falleth in love, and is ready to get another child, and all this is in two hours' space: which how absurd it is in sense, even sense may imagine . . .

Sidney, in other words, was remarking that even "sense" (that is, instinct) should see that there is something absurd about a play whose action occupies 20 years or more. All the action in *The Comedy of Errors,* on the other hand, occurs on a single day, between lunchtime and five o'clock. While the play's "story," one might say, covers many years, from the birth of the Antipholuses to their maturity—just the sort of story, indeed, that Sidney mocks—its plot is all compressed into a single afternoon. Since the action occupies five or six hours, and the play's own running time might be around two hours, the action of the play takes place, not in real time, but at about three times the speed of real time. And yet, this level of fidelity between stage time and real time is much more realist than most fiction attempts. Most fiction is happy to treat time in a much more cavalier fashion, in the interests of telling a story. The long-running television series *24* is a rare exception, one of the few fictional works that does use "real time," but, in general, one may say that *The Comedy of Errors* is unusually rigorous in its treatment of the unity of time.

On the unity of place, Sidney again affectionately condemned contemporary popular drama for its extravagance:

> you shall have Asia of the one side, and Africa of the other, and so many other under-kingdoms, that the player when he comes in, must ever begin with telling where he is, or else the tale will not be conceived . . . we must believe the stage to be a garden. By and by, we hear news of shipwreck in the same place, then we are to blame if we accept it not for a rock. Upon the back of that, comes out a hideous monster with fire and smoke, and then the miserable beholders are bound to take it for a cave . . .

Sidney here imagined a bare stage required to represent, in quick succession, different locations in different places, with the audience struggling to keep up. Again, in contrast, *The Comedy of Errors* is almost austere in the way that it uses location: The action never leaves the city of Ephesus. Not until *The Tempest* would Shakespeare write another play that obeys the unities of time and place as rigorously as this play. *The Comedy of Errors* may be unrealistic in some respects, but in others—perhaps not those we now think of first—it is far more realistic not just than other Shakespeare plays but also than much modern fiction and drama.

Thinking about the play's realism throws up one further surprising observation: This play has no supernatural elements. Romance, as a whole, is forever using enchanted potions or magical spells as plot devices, and one such device would have saved Shakespeare a lot of exposition and special pleading. But, he does not use magical means to set up the situation. Thus, Dromio of Syracuse's assumption that they have blundered into a dangerous enchanted place, a "fairy land," while quite in keeping with the world of romance, is funny to the audience precisely because we know it is not true. In this play, as if in an episode of *Scooby Doo,* all the apparently supernatural occurrences turn out to have a rational, mechanical explanation.

By many measures, in short, this play turns out to be surprisingly realist. It is reality that turns out not be as straightforward as one might think.

KEY PASSAGES
Act II, Scene 2, 112–149

ADRIANA. Ay, ay, Antipholus, look strange and frown:
Some other mistress hath thy sweet aspects;
I am not Adriana nor thy wife.
The time was once when thou unurged wouldst vow
That never words were music to thine ear,
That never object pleasing in thine eye,
That never touch well welcome to thy hand,
That never meat sweet-savor'd in thy taste,
Unless I spake, or look'd, or touch'd, or carved to thee.
How comes it now, my husband, O, how comes it,
That thou art thus estranged from thyself?
Thyself I call it, being strange to me,
That, undividable, incorporate,
Am better than thy dear self's better part.
Ah, do not tear away thyself from me!
For know, my love, as easy mayest thou fall
A drop of water in the breaking gulf,
And take unmingled that same drop again,
Without addition or diminishing,
As take from me thyself and not me too.
How dearly would it touch me to the quick,
Shouldst thou but hear I were licentious
And that this body, consecrate to thee,
By ruffian lust should be contaminate!
Wouldst thou not spit at me and spurn at me
And hurl the name of husband in my face
And tear the stain'd skin off my harlot-brow
And from my false hand cut the wedding-ring
And break it with a deep-divorcing vow?
I know thou canst; and therefore see thou do it.
I am possess'd with an adulterate blot;
My blood is mingled with the crime of lust:
For if we too be one and thou play false,
I do digest the poison of thy flesh,
Being strumpeted by thy contagion.

Keep then far league and truce with thy true
   bed;
I live unstain'd, thou undishonoured.

ANTIPHOLUS OF SYRACUSE. Plead you
   to me, fair dame?

This is the first meeting between Adriana and
Antipholus of Syracuse, the man she wrongly
believes to be her husband. Despite the seriousness
and density of the language—or, rather, because of
it—this can be, in the theater, an extremely funny
moment.

First worth pointing out is the elaborate, formal
patterning in its opening section:

The time was once when thou unurged wouldst
   vow
That never **words** were music to thine **ear,**
That never **object** pleasing in thine **eye,**
That never **touch** well welcome to thy **hand,**
That never **meat** sweet-savor'd in thy **taste,**
Unless I **spake,** or **look'd,** or **touch'd,** or **carved**
   to thee.

Antipholus and Dromio of Syracuse meet Adriana and
Luciana for the first time in Act II, Scene 2 of *The Comedy
of Errors,* in this print published by Longman & Co.
(Illustration by Henry Singleton; engraving by James Neagle)

The boldfaced words draw attention to how the
speech runs through four of the five senses, offering for each an example of how it used to be, and
connecting the four examples together through
the four linking words in the last quoted line. This
type of verse, usefully called "correlative verse,"
is a staple of the love poetry of Shakespeare's
contemporaries, of Edmund Spenser, Sidney, and
others. Its use here marks Adriana as a courtly and
formal speaker and her register as being that of love
poetry. These lines not merely are well-balanced
words but also give one a sense of the language
Adriana is talking: the language of love.

And yet, the amusement lies in the misunderstanding with which this speech is received, as
Antipholus has no idea what she is talking about.
Nor is this merely a matter of the words but of the
performance opportunities that the words throw
up. Thus, Adriana thinks she is pleading to her husband, and the speech contains many cues for her to

come physically close to him, even to touch him.
The most obvious of these "implied stage directions," as they are called, is the line "Ah, do not
tear away thyself from me." For this to make sense,
it requires that the actor playing Adriana get very
close to Antipholus—perhaps even touch him—
while Antipholus backs away in confusion. On the
line about "this body, consecrate to thee," it is
implied that Adriana touches, or at least indicates,
her own body, and there are plenty of other cues in
there for her that are more optional cues for her to
touch parts of Antipholus's body. For Antipholus,
of course, this is a strange and unprovoked sexual
assault. And, there are other details in this speech
that, the audience can see, are likely to strike particular fear into Antipholus of Syracuse, already
wary of Ephesus's reputation for black magic. Lau-

rie Maguire commented, for instance, on the 1977 production: "Judi Dench's Adriana terrified the onstage audience with her eldritch confession 'I am possessed', before continuing, conversationally, 'with an adulterate blot'" (363).

Nor are subsequent lines such as "My blood is mingled with the crime of lust" calculated to put Antipholus's mind at rest, even though we can see that, in context, it is a bold rhetorical paradox (of the sort favored in contemporary love poetry) rather than, as Antipholus might fear, a declaration of nymphomania. All of this impassioned pleading is setting up, of course, the moment at the end of the extract. After a moment's pause—and the pause is critical—Antipholus's reply, a masterly piece of understatement, releases the tension for the audience and generally gets a very strong laugh.

But, the importance of this speech in the play goes beyond being a neatly constructed piece of stagecraft. Adriana is addressing, although she does not know it, the recurring motif of the play: What is it that makes you who you are? If her husband is not the man she thought, then "I am not Adriana." As a woman, in particular, she is defined in terms of her husband, literally "one flesh" with him through the sacrament of marriage. Her personal identity is indivisible from his. If he behaves badly, it poisons not merely his own flesh but hers, too. This concern seems similar to that of the brothers in the play, whose bodily similarity means that benefits gained by one turn into punishments on the head of the other. In particular, in comparing herself to a water drop mixed with her husband, she recalls, unknowingly, Antipholus of Syracuse's use of that very image in Act I, Scene 2:

> I to the world am like a drop of water
> That in the ocean seeks another drop,
> Who, falling there to find his fellow forth,
> Unseen, inquisitive, confounds himself
>   (1.2.35–38).

One of the mysteries of marriage is that it converts a stranger into your own flesh and blood, something also acted out in the main plot of the play.

Act III, Scene 5, 110–151

ANTIPHOLUS OF SYRACUSE. What's her name?

DROMIO OF SYRACUSE. Nell, sir; but her name and three quarters, that's an ell and three quarters, will not measure her from hip to hip.

ANTIPHOLUS OF SYRACUSE. Then she bears some breadth?

DROMIO OF SYRACUSE. No longer from head to foot than from hip to hip: she is spherical, like a globe; I could find out countries in her.

ANTIPHOLUS OF SYRACUSE. In what part of her body stands Ireland?

DROMIO OF SYRACUSE. Marry, in her buttocks: I found it out by the bogs.

ANTIPHOLUS OF SYRACUSE. Where Scotland?

DROMIO OF SYRACUSE. I found it by the barrenness; hard in the palm of the hand.

ANTIPHOLUS OF SYRACUSE. Where France?

DROMIO OF SYRACUSE. In her forehead; armed and reverted, making war against her heir.

ANTIPHOLUS OF SYRACUSE. Where England?

DROMIO OF SYRACUSE. I looked for the chalky cliffs, but I could find no whiteness in them; but I guess it stood in her chin, by the salt rheum that ran between France and it.

ANTIPHOLUS OF SYRACUSE. Where Spain?

DROMIO OF SYRACUSE. Faith, I saw it not; but I felt it hot in her breath.

ANTIPHOLUS OF SYRACUSE. Where America, the Indies?

DROMIO OF SYRACUSE. Oh, sir, upon her nose all o'er embellished with rubies, carbuncles, sapphires, declining their rich aspect to the hot breath of Spain; who sent whole armadoes of caracks to be ballast at her nose.

ANTIPHOLUS OF SYRACUSE. Where stood Belgia, the Netherlands?

DROMIO OF SYRACUSE. Oh, sir, I did not look so low. To conclude, this drudge, or diviner, laid claim to me, call'd me Dromio; swore I was assured to her; told me what privy marks I had about me, as, the mark of my shoulder, the mole in my neck, the great wart on my left arm, that I amazed ran from her as a witch:
And, I think, if my breast had not been made of faith and my heart of steel, She had transform'd me to a curtal dog and made me turn i' the wheel.

In this passage, Dromio of Syracuse tells his master the horrifying news he has just discovered: He appears to be engaged to be married to Luce/ Nell the kitchen wench. As one of the few passages in the play easily detachable from its context, it has been frequently anthologized, but it is also a passage that lends itself very much to close reading.

The form of the exchange is obviously a list of questions and answers: each question from Antipholus referring to a country, each answer from Dromio likening that country to a part of Nell's body. The blazon is a convention of Elizabethan love poetry in which a series of the beloved's features—generally, parts of her body—are described in elaborate similes. Shakespeare's contemporary Spenser writes, for

example, a sonnet, part of which describes how, if one were seeking precious stones, one need go no further than his lover's body:

Lo, my love doth in herself contain
All this world's riches that may far be found,
If Sapphires, lo, her eyes be saphires plain,
If Rubies, lo, her lips be rubies sound:
If Pearls, her teeth be pearls both pure and round:
If Ivory, her forehead ivory ween;
If Gold, her locks are finest gold on ground,
If silver, her fair hands are silver sheen.
But that which fairest is, but few behold,
Her mind adorned with virtues manifold.
(*Amoretti* 15)

The blazon was one of the most common, and most mocked, features of love poetry in Shakespeare's era. This passage from *The Comedy of Errors,* however, could appropriately be called a "contreblazon," a parody of a blazon. The best-known contreblazon in Shakespeare's works is probably Sonnet 130, "My mistress' eyes are nothing like the sun," where, one by one, parts of his mistress are compared to the usual stock comparisons of the blazon and found to be disappointing. This passage offers another example.

Dromio starts by observing that Nell is globular in shape, containing, like Spenser's heroine, a world in herself. For Dromio, this takes the form of a list of countries. The first joke, about Ireland, puns on the idea of "bogs," or latrines, and also reminds an Elizabethan audience of the perenially difficult land on their western flank. Scotland, to the north, is similarly mocked, this time for its barrenness: Whereas one would hope one's lover to have a warm and soft hand, suggesting both potential fruitfulness and also that she has been living a life of privilege, Nell's hand is calloused from the work she has to do. France, England's third close neighbor, this time to the south, is mentioned, making the civil unrest there an excuse for a surreal joke about Nell's forehead making war on her hair. Finally, England itself is mentioned.

Dromio looks for chalky whiteness and does not find it: Basically, like Spenser praising his lover's ivory-white forehead, he would hope that his lover would have perfectly pale and white skin. (This, incidentally, was desirable since it was a sign of a privileged lifestyle: Most of the poor had to work outside for a living and would therefore be more tanned.) Although Dromio's lover may not have chalky skin, like England surrounded by sea, she does have "salt rheum" around her face—a runny nose. She also has bad breath and a nose covered in red spots ("carbuncles") and seemingly also blue ones ("sapphires"). It is customary, of course, to see gemstones in one's lover's face; the Spenser passage cited above offers a textbook example, with ruby lips and sapphire eyes. But, in Dromio's speech, they are subverted and likened to the spots and warts on Nell's nose.

The geography soon grows more exotic. It is, of course, almost mandatory to stop and notice the half-reference here to the Spanish Armada in the phrase about "armadoes of carracks"—this play was written in the years shortly after the attempted Spanish invasion of 1588—and also to notice the reference to America, one of only a handful of times that Shakespeare explicitly refers to the New World. Allusions such as these put the play into a much wider world of international politics. On the other hand, one should also not overlook the hilarious overloading of hideous details. It is not enough that her face be of an unpleasing color; her nose must also be runny, and that nose must be covered in red spots (alarming enough) and also blue ones (almost surreal).

Furthermore, another convention of the blazon, its inevitable tendency to move toward more intimate body parts, comes into play. Blazons, like stripteases, tend to start with reasonably uncontentious parts of the body and proceed toward more erotic ones. Thus, Spenser's blazon, in the example above, teases by claiming to keep the best till last, before revealing that the best, in this case, is not a part of her body at all but rather her virtuous mind. Similarly, having set up the joke, Antipholus offers what is clearly a punch line by inviting Dromio to

describe Nell's "Netherlands." Dromio's mock-shocked response generally gets a round of laughter from the audience and also marks the end of the routine. Instead, he completes the exchange by finishing his story that she claimed she was engaged to him and seemed to know all about the secret marks on his body. He adds that he fears she is magical and might have turned him into a "curtal dog," a small dog whose job was to run around a wheel in the kitchen, like a hamster wheel, thus keeping the spit turning and ensuring that the meat roasted evenly. She is a huge circular world, and he is a tiny dog trapped inside a circle.

The passage is, then, a well-constructed joke, but one might think about its effectiveness in the overall shape of the play. Since Act I, the pace has been increasing, and the confusions, multiplying: Hardly any of the characters has had time to think. This moment is so effective because it offers a release from the accelerating onstage action. In some productions, Antipholus and Dromio actually sit down on the stage for a moment to toss this joke back and forth between them—the first time anyone has had the leisure to sit since, probably, their previous exchange on the nature of time, and perhaps the last rest stop of this sort before the climax of the play. It is also revealing in terms of the easy, friendly relationship between Syracusan master and servant: Like a couple of music-hall comics, they banter easily, the master setting up jokes for the servant to deliver the punch lines.

Finally, many of the themes of the play resurface in the language here. Dromio's fear about transformation into a kitchen animal picks up, both on the animal imagery that runs through the play and on the frequent references to food and cookery studied, for instance, by Joseph Candido. From a gender point of view, Dromio's reaction to Nell's body as so unknown and so scary represents a fear, almost a terror, on the part of the boys from Syracuse of the sexual female that can be traced elsewhere in the play, in particular in the other images in which the women of the play are likened to enchantresses. Like many other passages in the play, here there is play on the paradoxes of individuality and love. Dromio, we learn, shares with his twin not merely his outward appearance but also the secret privy marks of his body—his moles and warts. All the same, his mind seems very different, at least on matters of love and desire. Whereas Dromio of Syracuse is terrified of Nell, Dromio of Ephesus appears quite willing to marry her. The sexual attraction that Dromio of Ephesus presumably feels for her, his twin does not share at all. "She now shall be my sister, not my wife," says Dromio of Syracuse at the end of the play (5.1.916), with an almost audible sigh of relief, just as in the main plot, the Antipholus brothers, Luciana, and Adriana apparently fall out into two tidy married pairs, with no inconvenient attraction between the in-laws. This passage explores the paradox of attraction, that, as Christopher Marlowe put it, "lies not in our power to love or hate," and that we do not all (fortunately) fall in love with the same person.

Nell, of course, is a minor character in the play—in many productions, in fact, she does not appear at all. But, in a play about the paradoxes of geography, in which characters struggle on sea voyages and travel across continents without finding the person they are looking for, it seems fitting that the whole world—its lands, its seas, its countries, their wars, and their ships—should, actually, be condensed into a single person's body.

Act V, Scene 1, 393–425

EMILIA. Renowned duke, vouchsafe to take
  the pains
To go with us into the abbey here
And hear at large discoursed all our fortunes:
And all that are assembled in this place,
That by this sympathized one day's error
Have suffer'd wrong, go keep us company,
And we shall make full satisfaction.
Thirty-three years have I but gone in travail
Of you, my sons; and till this present hour
My heavy burden ne'er delivered.
The duke, my husband and my children both,
And you the calendars of their nativity,
Go to a gossips' feast and go with me;
After so long grief, such nativity.

DUKE SOLINUS. With all my heart, I'll
  gossip at this feast.
*[Exeunt all but Antipholus of Syracuse,
  Antipholus of Ephesus, Dromio of Syracuse and
  Dromio of Ephesus]*

DROMIO OF SYRACUSE. Master, shall I
  fetch your stuff from shipboard?

ANTIPHOLUS OF EPHESUS. Dromio,
  what stuff of mine hast thou embark'd?

DROMIO OF SYRACUSE. Your goods that
  lay at host, sir, in the Centaur.

ANTIPHOLUS OF SYRACUSE. He speaks
  to me. I am your master, Dromio:
Come, go with us; we'll look to that anon:
Embrace thy brother there; rejoice with him.
*[Exeunt Antipholus of Syracuse and Antipholus
  of Ephesus]*

DROMIO OF SYRACUSE. There is a fat
  friend at your master's house,
That kitchen'd me for you to-day at dinner:
She now shall be my sister, not my wife.

DROMIO OF EPHESUS. Methinks you are
  my glass, and not my brother:
I see by you I am a sweet-faced youth.
Will you walk in to see their gossiping?

DROMIO OF SYRACUSE. Not I, sir; you are
  my elder.

DROMIO OF EPHESUS. That's a question:
  how shall we try it?

DROMIO OF SYRACUSE. We'll draw cuts
  for the senior: till then lead thou first.

DROMIO OF EPHESUS. Nay, then, thus:
We came into the world like brother and
  brother;

And now let's go hand in hand, not one before
another.

This passage, the very end of the play, combines
some expected elements with some surprises that
have been kept back until this point. Emilia's
speech, to begin with, does what one might expect
the conclusion of a comedy to do: It announces
that all the characters will enjoy a "feast" and talk
over the excitement of the day. This gives the note
of general celebration that is the keynote of comedy. Similar celebrations end most of the rest of
Shakespeare's comedies (although it is interesting
that they are often somehow made provisional: *As
You Like It,* for instance, ends in dancing and revelry, except for the melancholy Jaques who absents
himself, and seems somehow outside the ending).

Particularly interesting is Emilia's use of the idea
of "nativity": What has happened is like a new birth
for those involved. Her invocation of "thirty-three
years" is significant, too, sending one scurrying
back to earlier references to chronology in the play,
as it seems incompatible with the other references

The abbess brings Antipholus of Syracuse and Dromio
of Syracuse to the duke before revealing herself to be
Egeon's wife, Emilia, in Act V, Scene I of *The Comedy
of Errors.* Print from the Boydell Shakespeare Gallery
project *(Painting by John Francis Rigaud; engraving by
Charles Gauthier Playter)*

to time in the play and indicates that there must
be an error in the continuity somewhere. Interestingly, however, 33 years is a time fixed in the
Renaissance imagination as the life span of Jesus,
from nativity to crucifixion: This timespan brings
an obviously Christian note to the end of the play.
Furthermore, in imagining the celebration as a
"gossip's feast," that is, a godparents' feast, Emilia
likens what is going to happen to a baptism. Baptism was, of course, one of the fundamental elements of Renaissance Christian belief, one of the
few things that even Protestants recognized as
a sacrament, a genuine eruption of the miraculous into the everyday. It was also one of the most
important events in the life of a family. The duke
accedes to her request, following the tendency that
the highest-status character on stage tends to have
the last word in a play, and they all leave to begin
the celebration in the abbey.

However, Shakespeare again slightly subverts
the usual conventions of an ending, because the
duke's word is not the last word. Instead, the four
twins linger behind and begin a new comedy of
errors, instantly mistaking one another again until
Antipholus of Syracuse realizes what is happening
and stops it. For a moment, it seems, one is faced
with the slightly nightmarish prospect of the play
repeating itself again from the start. Even the exit
of the Antipholus brothers, though, turns out to
be a false ending, because the last word in the play
goes not to them but to the humble Dromios.

And here is the surprise mentioned earlier: The
Dromios do not actually know which of them is
older than the other. They do not know which
of them is heir to the family fortune, or which of
them is entitled to the deference of the other. It
is not clear at what point the information is lost—
whether the poor woman even knew which came
out first, or whether Egeon ever knew or cared
which was which, or whether he did not think to
keep track of which was which in the storm. Certainly, Egeon does not consider it an important
element in his telling of the story of the storm in
Act I, Scene 1, whereas he is quite particular about

which of his sons is which (see "Difficult Passages" below). Thus, unlike the Antipholus twins, the Dromios genuinely do not know which of them is the senior, nor is the answer to that question obvious, suggesting the whole idea of seniority conferred by birth might be rather arbitrary. Still, they need to know who is entitled to lead the way off the stage. Their solution is refreshingly, and even movingly, egalitarian: They put aside the whole question of deference and structure—for what little it is worth for themselves—in favor of brotherly love. Many have felt that the end of the play for the two Antipholuses is a little provisional and awkward; the two brothers hardly address each other, and their first conversations are likely to be rather awkward ones. It is the Dromios, though, who are able to demonstrate more eloquently than their masters that they can adapt and build new relationships. Like humanity at the end of John Milton's yet-unwritten *Paradise Lost,* they leave the stage together, hand in hand.

DIFFICULT PASSAGES
Act I, Scene 1, 77–112

EGEON. The sailors sought for safety by our
 boat,
And left the ship, then sinking-ripe, to us:
My wife, more careful for the latter-born,
Had fasten'd him unto a small spare mast,
Such as seafaring men provide for storms;
To him one of the other twins was bound,
Whilst I had been like heedful of the other:
The children thus disposed, my wife and I,
Fixing our eyes on whom our care was fix'd,
Fasten'd ourselves at either end the mast;
And floating straight, obedient to the stream,
Was carried towards Corinth, as we thought.
At length the sun, gazing upon the earth,
Dispersed those vapours that offended us;
And by the benefit of his wished light,
The seas wax'd calm, and we discovered
Two ships from far making amain to us,
Of Corinth that, of Epidaurus this:
But ere they came,—O, let me say no more!
Gather the sequel by that went before.

DUKE SOLINUS. Nay, forward, old man; do
 not break off so;
For we may pity, though not pardon thee.

EGEON. O, had the gods done so, I had not
 now
Worthily term'd them merciless to us!
For, ere the ships could meet by twice five
 leagues,
We were encounterd by a mighty rock;
Which being violently borne upon,
Our helpful ship was splitted in the midst;
So that, in this unjust divorce of us,
Fortune had left to both of us alike
What to delight in, what to sorrow for.
Her part, poor soul! seeming as burdened
With lesser weight but not with lesser woe,
Was carried with more speed before the wind;
And in our sight they three were taken up
By fishermen of Corinth, as we thought.

This passage is difficult on a number of levels. First of all, it seems to make very poor theater. Egeon's long speech is effective exposition—that is, it fills in for the audience the large amount of factual information necessary to make the story understandable—but, while it is being delivered, the two characters involved, himself and the duke, have relatively little to do. Even Duke Solinus's interjection does not, on the page, offer much possibility for drama, and a production must work hard to make the dynamic between the two characters interesting in this important opening scene.

Second, it is actually quite difficult to follow what happens in the moments before the shipwreck. Reading it closely, in conjunction with later events, one can discern:

1. Emilia fastens to the mast the younger son, that is, the future Antipholus of Syracuse. She, we learn, cares about him slightly more than about his elder brother.
2. She fastens to him the future Dromio of Syracuse.
3. A little further along the mast, Egeon ties on the future Antipholus and Dromio of Ephesus.

Since this elder child is, strictly speaking, his son and heir (whereas the other, though only moments younger, is merely a second son), it is appropriate that his father take personal care of his welfare.

4. Egeon and Emilia must change ends, with Egeon tying himself to the end of the mast nearer the children that his wife tied on, while Emilia ties herself to the far end. The reason given for this odd maneuver is so that they can more easily keep an eye on the children they care for more, at the price of being farther away from them ("Fixing our eyes on whom our care was fix'd").

5. Along the mast, then, we have Egeon, younger Antipholus (and servant), older Antipholus (and servant), and Emilia.

6. This party is severed into two equal halves by the rock. (It is interesting that the sea appears, in this account, to flow more like a river. One wonders how much firsthand knowledge Shakespeare actually had of the sea.) Emilia's half, being lighter, which reflects her feminine slightness as opposed to the masculine weight of her husband, floats away more quickly.

An 18th-century critic of the sort who tended to believe that he could offer improvements to the talented but unlettered Shakespeare might well suggest that this is inartistic and clumsy. Why does Shakespeare invent such a specific and improbable method to separate the two parties? Why spend so many words drawing attention to the artifice? In particular, why go to such lengths to make both father and mother end up with the twin they love slightly less?

Some lines of approach to this question would send one into investigating the symbolism of masts. Philip Sidney's *Arcadia,* one of the most famous romances of the period, opens with a shipwreck. In its aftermath, the hero of the *Arcadia* is first seen in the sea clinging, not to a barrel or plank or anything less heroic, but to a mast: Is that part of a wider convention about the representation of shipwrecks in romances? Is a mast a particularly manly thing to be saved by? Come to that, in this era, can

Egeon relates the tale of how a storm separated him from his wife and son in Act I, Scene 1 of *The Comedy of Errors.* This illustration was designed for a 1918 edition of Charles and Mary Lamb's *Tales from Shakespeare.* *(Illustration by Louis Rhead)*

one ever be tied to a mast without recalling, even if only distantly, imagery of the crucifixion? One might also note that the line of the mast forces the characters into a symmetrically patterned group: parent-two children-two children-parent. In a play filled with symmetries, parallels, and balances, perhaps this is more pleasing than merely having three of the six washed off the deck at random.

One is on safer ground, though, in suggesting that this sleight of hand opens up further psychological depths in that each parent ends up with the son who is slightly less dear to them: Egeon has lost not only a son but his heir; conversely, Emilia loves her younger son more but loses him before she loses the other. As discussed in the "Characters" section, one might think that the very masculine Antipholus of Ephesus is slightly more what an Elizabethan would hope for from his elder son and that the more emotionally alive, gentler Antipholus of Syracuse is more of a mother's boy. Each parent, thus, gains at the end of the play not only a son but the son more dear to each—another piece of patterning completed in the dancelike intricacy of *The Comedy of Errors.*

CRITICAL INTRODUCTION
TO THE PLAY

Because of its early date, *The Comedy of Errors* is often thought of primarily as an apprentice piece within Shakespeare's artistic development. Critics group it with the other plays Shakespeare probably wrote in the first half of the 1590s, such as the *Henry VI* plays, *Titus Andronicus,* and *The Taming of the Shrew.* George Saintsbury, for instance, wrote that in the best parts of *The Comedy of Errors,*

> the spirit [of Shakespeare], not quite fullgrown
> as yet, hurries itself through the bonds of
> imperfect training in speech and metre. It is,
> however, on the whole, the crudest and most
> immature of all the plays, and may well have
> been the earliest.

For Saintsbury, as for many other critics, *The Comedy of Errors* is technically adept but emotionally incomplete: the immature work of a talented, but not yet fully great writer. And yet, one might want to disagree with this slightly patronizing frame for the play. One might wonder whether Saintsbury's distaste for "crudity"—by which he means the sexually rude banter between the characters—has prejudiced not just his guess at the date but also his interpretation of the play's merit. Arguably, there is rather more to *The Comedy of Errors* than merely the apprentice piece described by Saintsbury.

By 1594, certainly Shakespeare could no longer be called an apprentice. He had already achieved some sensational theatrical successes, including *Henry VI, Part II,* which, according to the keen Elizabethan playgoer Thomas Nashe, made entire audiences burst into tears. And, he had published the long poems *Venus and Adonis* and *The Rape of Lucrece* that marked him as one of the most talented authors of his generation. He was clearly a rising star. Toward the end of that year, Shakespeare's company was invited to play at a highly prestigious corporate entertainment for London's lawyers. This was the Gray's Inn Revels, organized by and watched by London's leading young law students. In the dining hall at Gray's Inn, on the night of December 28, 1594, the players performed a "*Comedy of Errors* (like to Plautus his *Menechmus*)," which is almost certainly our play. December 28, 1594, is, then, a terminal date for the composition of *The Comedy of Errors*—that is, the play was in existence by then. It is much harder to come up with a cast-iron date marking *after which* it must have been composed. The usual dating of the play is roughly 1590–94, with some recent scholars favoring a date toward the end of this range.

Menaechmi

Critics have been especially prone to disregard *The Comedy of Errors* as an early and immature work because, as it happens, its main source is a text Shakespeare (and many in his audience) would have probably studied at school. The text in question is *Menaechmi* ("The Menaechmus brothers"), one of the surviving comedies of the Roman writer Titus Maccius Plautus, written in Latin in the second century B.C.

In *Menaechmi,* the two brothers are the sons of a Syracusan merchant separated from each other at the age of seven. In the course of the play, the son who remained at home with his father travels to the city of Epidamnus, unaware that the city is the home of his long-lost brother. As the play opens, Menaechmus of Epidamnus, the "home" Menaechmus as we might call him, quarrels with his wife and goes to visit a courtesan with whom he is having an affair. The courtesan and her comic cook come on stage, as well as a character called Peniculus, a hanger-on of Menaechmus. After Menaechmus departs from the courtesan's house, his brother, Menaechmus of Syracuse, happens to wander past. The courtesan greets him warmly, mistaking him for his brother. She gives him, to his surprise, gifts: a mantle and a gold bracelet.

Shortly after Menaechmus of Syracuse goes away, Menaechmus of Epidamnus returns and is dismayed when the courtesan tells him that she has already given him the mantle, which he needs back, as it belongs to his wife. Elsewhere in the city, Menaechmus of Syracuse bumps into his brother's wife, who mistakes him (of course) for her husband. He, on the other hand, has no idea who she is. Since her husband appears to be talking nonsense, she believes he has gone mad and calls for help to tie him up, but he escapes. The brothers finally come face to face; Messenio, the wise-cracking family slave, is granted his freedom; and Menaechmus of Epidamnus resolves to go back to Syracuse with his brother. He simply abandons his irritating wife.

Menaechmi is quite a short play, now easily available in translation. It may also have been available to Shakespeare in English translation, since a version of it, translated by William Warner, appeared in print the year after the Gray's Inn Revels. It is possible that Shakespeare had seen this translation in manuscript. However, most scholars now think that Shakespeare's Latin was sufficiently good that he would not have needed this shortcut. Whether one reads Warner's translation or one of the more modern ones, it is an interesting exercise to examine in detail how Shakespeare reinvents it, changing and expanding his source. The most obvious change is the creation of a second set of twins—the Dromios—to replace the single servant Messenio, allowing for a much more ingenious and complicated plot. In Plautus's play the "home" Menaechmus is explicitly having an adulterous affair. In *The Comedy of Errors,* Shakespeare makes the adultery potential rather than actual and reimagines the

wife, not as a mere hag, but as a much more sympathetic character. A third major change is the introduction of Egeon and Emilia, to create a family reunion rather than a divorce as the play's climax. The hundreds of minor similarities and changes also repay attention.

Furthermore, Shakespeare manages to weave in a scene from another Plautus comedy about mistaken identity. This is the lockout scene (3.1.), which is a knowing imitation of the centerpiece of *Amphitryo,* a play about a man locked out from his own house and whose wife is inside by, it turns out, a lustful and mischievous god who has made himself into an exact replica of him.

In this artistic context, *Menaechmi* and *Amphitryo* would have been plays familiar also to Shakespeare's original audience. As we shall see, one of Shakespeare's audience observed with a touch of smugness that it was "like to Plautus his *Menechmus.*" Part of the delight of *The Comedy of Errors,* for its original audience, was the extent to which it could be considered almost a "cover version" of Plautus's play, weaving new variations on what they knew and might expect.

Themes

Although *The Comedy of Errors* is unique in the Shakespeare canon as an adaptation of a Roman comedy, it has many features that link it to other Shakespeare plays—more, perhaps, than have sometimes been noticed. First of all, it fits in with the other comedies. In its treatment of twins and mistaken identity, it anticipates *Twelfth Night.* In its fascination with the phenomenon of independent-minded married women, it has common ground with *The Taming of the Shrew. The Merchant of Venice,* too, is an obvious point of comparison in depicting a world of merchants and deal making.

It has even more profound affinities with the late plays, or romances, *The Tempest, Cymbeline, Pericles,* and *The Winter's Tale.* As in all of the late plays, the miraculous seems to be never far away. Like *Pericles* and *The Winter's Tale, The Comedy of Errors* features a family fractured and reunited, culminating in the return of a mother long believed dead. Like *The Tempest* and *Pericles,* the plot hinges upon a shipwreck. And like all of the late plays, *The Comedy of Errors* is interested in time: in years-long gaps between the events narrated, in moments that seem to last much longer than the clock-measured time allotted to them, in the properties of the passage of time.

The Comedy of Errors is a play that is obsessed with the paraphernalia of timekeeping and, in particular, with clocks and calendars. Dromio, to Antipholus of Syracuse, is "the almanac of my true date" (1.2.41), the calendar that tells him what day it is, while at the end of the play, those who have observed the reunion of the twins are "the calendars of their nativity" (5.1.407). As discussed earlier, the action of the play depends on a well-defined slice of time between around noon (lunchtime) and around six. The play is, as it were, constantly looking at its watch. Allusions to the time start as early as the first lines of the play, when Egeon forecasts his execution at sunset: "My woes end likewise with the setting sun" (1.1.27). In the following scene, Antipholus of Syracuse uses, not the position of the Sun, but rather his own body clock to tell the time, opining that "Within this hour it will be dinner time" (1.2.11), only to find that he is wrong, at least from the perspective of Dromio of Ephesus: "The capon burns, the pig falls from the spit, / The clock hath strucken twelve upon the bell" (1.2.44–45). Clock chimes recur in Act IV, where a confused Dromio of Syracuse navigates the time by their sound, again with confusing results: "It was two ere I left him, and now the clock strikes one" (4.2.57). In the final scene, the Second Merchant comments that "I think the dial points at five" (5.1.120), but one's sense of how time works has been somewhat thrown into confusion by the multitudes of methods used to try to calculate it.

The importance of time in this play is not merely a matter of the action; it crops up in the imagery of the play and in characters' meditations on the nature of it. Thus Dromio, offering a joking explanation of his remark about time seemingly going backward, comments:

> If any hour meet a sergeant, a turns back for
>   very fear . . .
> Time is a very bankrupt, and owes more than
>   he's worth to season.
> Nay, he's a thief too: have you not heard men
>   say
> That Time comes stealing on by night and day?
>   (4.2.56–60)

Time seems to be something that disobeys the very rules of property and fair exchange that the whole merchant culture of the play depends on. Dromio's lines seem nonsense, but in suggesting that time is rather more elastic and shifting than we usually like to think it, Dromio hits on an important theme of the play. It is surely no coincidence that the banter of the two Syracusans in Act II, Scene 3 also focuses on the mysterious nature of bald Father Time, and whether there is "no time for all things" (2.2.102). When one thinks of Shakespeare's treatment of Father Time, one usually thinks of *The Winter's Tale,* in which Time acts as a choric figure in a play that flaunts its unlikely treatment of time as measured by the clock. Time, in that play, even speaks his own self-description: "I, that please some, try all, / both joy and terror / Of good and bad, that makes and unfolds error" (4.1.1–2). That would also be a good epigraph for the way, or rather ways, in which Time is handled in *The Comedy of Errors.*

As the above references suggest, food is important in *The Comedy of Errors* as a way of telling the time. Its importance goes deeper, too, and this is something it inherits from Plautus's *Menaechmi,* in which the courtesan's cook features quite largely. Throughout *The Comedy of Errors,* eating signifies the good things in life: being linked to a secure home; to hospitality, even to sex, in the form of the suggestive private luncheon upstairs that Adriana offers to the man she believes to be her husband, and his brother's lunchtime rendezvous with the courtesan. Luce/Nell, the fat and greasy kitchen servant who threatens to transform Dromio into a cookery implement, symbolizes, among other things, the extent to which food is important throughout this play. It is no coincidence that the one conspicuously thin character in the play is the joyless Doctor Pinch, "a hungry, lean-faced villain, / A mere anatomy" (5.1.239–240), or that the play ends with a "gossip's feast," an opportunity for feasting and revelry that reaffirms the social bonds of the closing harmony. (The topic of food in *The Comedy of Errors,* indeed, has been explored at length by such critics as Joseph Candido.) And, the play's recurring interest in hospitality and revelry is, of course, given a particular spice by the circumstances of its early performance as part of a corporate event.

The Gray's Inn Revels

The Comedy of Errors was performed at Gray's Inn on December 28, 1594. Few Shakespeare plays have such an important, or informative, context for an early performance. It tells us who the play was thought appropriate for, who was in the audience that night, and how the audience used their imaginations to be creative about what they had seen. It therefore requires our attention.

Gray's Inn was (and is) one of London's Inns of Court, the training schools for British lawyers. Any young and ambitious man wishing to become a lawyer would have to attend an Inn of Court for a while, learn the trade of a lawyer, and make contacts there. In addition, at this date, many wealthy young men would attach themselves to an Inn of Court, not necessarily with a view to becoming lawyers for a career, but because in the litigation-loving world they moved in, it was both desirable and important to have a grasp of the law. As a result, the Inns of Court had an atmosphere something like that of a university. The students were fashion conscious, intellectually active, and deeply competitive.

In 1594, following long-established tradition, the students of Gray's Inn decided to hold an elaborate set of "revels," or entertainments, for themselves. Giving this set of entertainments a unifying theme, they crowned an imaginary king of the inn, the Prince of Purpoole, and embarked on a set of festivities supposedly to celebrate his reign. Throughout the revels, which lasted for some weeks, one of the students took on the role of the king; others took upon themselves the characters of members of his court, making mock speeches and giving mock advice. Throughout the festivities, one of the keynotes was competition and display, especially, display of one's own cleverness. Although these revels appeared to be self-consciously fantastic and frivolous, much building of reputations and careers was also going on behind the scenes.

The revels dominated life at Gray's Inn for weeks. Even the other Inns of Court got in on the act, and on December 28, the Prince of Purpoole was visited by an "ambassador" from the neighboring kingdom of Templaria—in reality, the Inner Temple, another of the major Inns of Court. The Gray's Inn students resolved to entertain him in style and arranged an evening of entertainment in their main dining hall. Among the shows they scheduled, they hired a company of professional actors to perform *The Comedy of Errors.*

There survives an eyewitness account of the night, later printed in a book in called *Gesta Grayorum* (Deeds of the heroes of Gray's Inn). As this title suggests, the book is written in the jokey mock-heroic style that drove much of the Prince of Purpoole festivities. According to *Gesta Grayorum,* the dining hall was crowded for the visit of the ambassador, with students and friends packed in so full that it was impossible to conduct all of the entertainment planned for the evening. In particular, students and gentlewomen visitors sat on the stage itself, making it unusable. The ambassador and his retinue left, apparently rather angrily. In the end, wrote the eyewitness,

> It was thought good not to offer any thing
> of account, saving dancing and revelling with
> gentlewomen; and after such sports, a *Comedy
> of Errors* (like to Plautus his *Menechmus*) was
> played by the players. So that night was begun,
> and continued to the end, in nothing but
> confusion and errors; whereupon it was ever
> afterwards called The Night of Errors.

The following day, the students decided to hold an inquiry, still in character as citizens of the kingdom of Purpoole, into why the night had gone wrong. They did so in the form of a mock trial, in which it was alleged that a magician had got among them, and caused

> A great witchcraft used the night before, whereby there were great disorders and misdemeanours by hurly-burlies, crowds, errors, confusions, vain representations and shows, to the utter discredit of our state and policy. The next night upon this occasion, we preferred judgements thick and threefold, being all against a sorcerer or conjuror that was supposed to be the cause of that confused inconvenience.

The account in *Gesta Grayorum* includes all sorts of fascinating angles on the play. First, it offers a glimpse of Shakespeare's company as entertainers for hire, outside their usual environment of the permanent professional playhouse, and offering instead a one-off performance at what was, in effect, a prestigious corporate event. We know quite a lot about the architecture of Gray's Inn Hall and can reconstruct from the detailed record a good deal about how the play might have been staged in this temporary theatrical venue.

Second, the account gives us a specific constituency that this play appealed to—the lawyers of Gray's Inn. This is a play notably interested in the adventures of young, energetic, and rather louche men. Antipholus of Syracuse acts out, one might say, the fantasy of any young law student. Rich without exertion, generally honored, and sexually attractive to total strangers such as Adriana, he achieves an effect of effortless superiority that many of Gray's Inn's law students would have desired.

The relation to the law might go deeper than that, even. This play has an obsession with legal questions. For instance, how should a head of state, such as Solinus, administer a law he believes to be too harsh? Should he use discretion to offer mercy to individual offenders, or would such special favors make the law toothless and ineffective? This

is, of course, a debate to which Shakespeare returns in *Measure for Measure,* and it is one in which law students could be expected to be particularly interested. The play is interested too in the legal mechanisms around debt (mechanisms in which many of the profligate law students of Gray's Inn had a personal interest): How should debt work? Are verbal contracts legally enforceable (no one asks for a written receipt for anything in the course of the play)? How does one handle a situation in which the alleged debtor simply denies all knowledge of having given his word? Again, these are situations of particular interest to its audience on the Night of Errors.

Furthermore, the play is certainly interested in how the strange, the fantastic, and the downright magical might lurk inside and burst out from an ordinary day, and in that respect, it is like the Gray's Inn Revels as a whole, forever looking to turn the normal into the surreal and mock heroic. It seems in many ways perfect for its intended audience. So perfect, indeed, does it seem, that some recent scholars, including Charles Whitworth, have argued that it might have been written for that venue and that occasion. This idea is still controversial, but regardless of whether one subscribes to it, the Gray's Inn performance is, like the source in Plautus, an important part of the play's world.

EXTRACTS OF CLASSIC CRITICISM
Francis Meres (1565–1647)   [Excerpted from *Palladis Tamia.* Writing in 1598, Meres is our first witness to the play after the 1594 Gesta Grayorum account. Meres's mention of *The Comedy of Errors* looks, at first glance, so brief as to be nonsensical, yet it is interesting in that it gives the play second billing in the list of Shakespeare's comedies. That list lacks, of course, Shakespeare's post-1598 comedies such as *As You Like It, Twelfth Night,* and *Measure for Measure,* all three among his best known: As a result, the list into which Meres puts *Errors* has a rather unfamiliar shape and balance. Secondly, notice how concerned Meres is to see Shakespeare as a worthy competitor with Greek and Latin models, rather than as good in his own right. Here begins

(or continues) the trend in criticism of *The Comedy of Errors* that aligns Shakespeare with Plautus, in particular.]

As *Plautus* and *Seneca* are accounted the best for Comedy and Tragedy among the Latines: so *Shakespeare* among y' English is the most excellent in both kinds for the stage; for Comedy, witnes his *Gentlemen of Verona,* his *Errors,* his *Love labors lost,* his *Love labours wonne,* his *Midsummer night dreame,* & his *Merchant of Venice* : for Tragedy his *Richard the 2. Richard the 3. Henry the 4. King John, Titus Andronicus* and his *Romeo* and *Juliet.*

As *Epius Stolo* said, that the Muses would speake with *Plautus* tongue, if they would speak Latin : so I say that the Muses would speak with *Shakespeares* fine filed phrase, if they would speake English.

Samuel Johnson (1709–1784) [Excerpted from *Preface to Shakespeare* (1765). The great critic Johnson was writing in a climate very different from Meres's, but like him, he is occupied by the question of Shakespeare's relationship to Latin and Greek literature. In particular, Johnson is reacting against what he perceives as a foolish trend to over-read Shakespeare, to see in his work a string of imitations of Latin and Greek literature. Instead, Johnson sees Shakespeare much more in terms of a native wit and brilliance. *The Comedy of Errors* is of particular importance on this battlefield, because it is so obviously, as it seems, an imitation of Plautus and therefore evidence of Shakespeare's knowledge of Latin models. Johnson draws attention, therefore, to the fact that *Menaechmi* was the only Plautus play yet available in English translation and argues that this is the reason that Shakespeare chose to imitate it rather than any of the others: It was the only one for which he did not need to understand Latin. (Incidentally, Johnson has the date of Warner's translation wrong; it did not appear in print until 1595, the year after *The Comedy of Errors* was performed at Gray's Inn).]

Some have imagined, that they have discovered deep learning in many imitations of old writers; but the examples which I have known urged, were drawn from books translated in his time; or were such easy coincidences of thought, as will happen to all who consider the same subjects; or such remarks on life or axioms of morality as float in conversation, and are transmitted through the world in proverbial sentences.

I have found it remarked, that, in this important sentence, *Go before, I'll follow,* we read a translation of, *I prae, sequar* [a Latin phrase used in the comedies of Terence]. I have been told, that when *Caliban,* after a pleasing dream, says, *I cry'd to sleep again,* the authour imitates *Anacreon,* who had, like every other man, the same wish on the same occasion.

There are a few passages which may pass for imitations, but so few, that the exception only confirms the rule; he obtained them from accidental quotations, or by oral communication, and as he used what he had, would have used more if he had obtained it.

The *Comedy of Errors* is confessedly taken from the *Menæchmi* of *Plautus;* from the only play of *Plautus* which was then in *English.* What can be more probable, than that he who copied that, would have copied more; but that those which were not translated were inaccessible?

Thomas Hull (1728–1808) [Excerpted from "Preface" (1793). This is a fascinating document in the history of the play. Like most Shakespeare plays—King Lear being the most famous example, in its happy-ending rewrite by Nahum Tate—*The Comedy of Errors* was, for much of the later 17th and 18th centuries, performed in adapted versions rather than the original. In this preface, one such adapter, Hull, describes his view of the play, what he feels it lacks—a description that might tell us something about the play—and certainly quite a lot about what he feels ought to be in it. The inset quotation from the 1720s Shakespeare critic George Sewell addressed the play's adherence to the classical unities (discussed under "Difficulties of the Play").]

Dr. Sewell, in his remarks on Shakspere's plays, speaks thus of the *Comedy of Errors.*

"This play is exactly regular, as any one may see, who will examine it by the rules. The place is part of one town, the time within the artificial day, and the action, the finding the lost brother, &c. Allowing for the puns, which were the vice of the age he lived in, it is extremely diverting, the incidents are wonderfully pleasant, and the catastrophe very happy, and strongly moving."

Such this comedy always appeared to me; and I was proud to find my slender opinion, (which might, perhaps, be termed little more than conjecture,) confirmed by so solid a judgment as that of our learned commentator. The catastrophe, always peculiarly affected me, though, I must confess, not without some degree of admiration, that in so strange, and unexpected a turn of good fortune as that of Ægeon, Æmilia, and their sons, there should not have been the slightest congratulation, or expression of delight between the parties. To account for this, I have been apt to conjecture some small portion of the original text has been lost; for it appears rather improbable, that so nice and complete a master of the human heart, as Shakspeare, should have restrained his genius, on such an interesting occasion. This reflection first induced me to think of an alteration, and the reader may find, by the liberty I have presumed to take with the fifth act in particular, where I thought such a deficiency lay. For the erasion I have made of some old quibbles, or too frequent jingle,

so unsuitable to our modern taste, I may, perhaps, be easily forgiven by those readers who are acquainted with the original.

In respect to the additional lines and speeches, which are occasionally interspersed through the piece, I throw myself, with great deference, on the candour of the reader. My sole pride has been, an endeavour to restore to the public eye, a neglected, and almost forgotten comedy of our inimitable bard. This the various talents of my brethren of the theatre, have enabled me to do in a very satisfactory manner. The repeated and highly applauded representations of this piece, have sufficiently justified this assertion; and it is with the truest pleasure and gratitude I acknowledge the obligation.

Nathan Drake (1766–1836) [Excerpted from *Shakspeare and His Times* (1817). Drake here also worries about *The Comedy of Errors'* relation to Plautus, but only as part of a broader appreciation of the qualities of the play in the study and on the stage.]

As to the comic action which constitutes the chief bulk of this piece, if it be true that to excite laughter, awaken attention, and fix curiosity, be essential to its dramatic excellence, the "Comedy of Errors" cannot be pronounced an unsuccessful effort; both reader and spectator are hurried on to the close, through a series of thick-coming incidents, and under the pleasurable influence of novelty, expectation, and surprise; and the dialogue . . . is uniformly vivacious, pointed, and even effervescing. Shakspeare is visible, in fact, throughout the entire play, as well in the broad exuberance of its mirth, as in the cast of its more chastised parts, a combination of which may be found in the punishment and character of Pinch the pedagogue and conjurer, who is sketched in the strongest and most marked style of our author. If we consider, therefore, the construction of the fable, the narrowness of its basis, and that its powers of entertainment are almost exclusively confined to a continued deception of the external senses, we must confess that Shakspeare has not only improved on the Plautian model, but, making allowance for a somewhat too coarse vein of humour, has given to his production all the interest and variety that the nature and the limits of his subject would permit.

Samuel Taylor Coleridge (1772–1834)
[Excerpted from *Lectures and Notes on Shakspere* (1818). The great poet and critic Coleridge here places the play precisely in the subgenre of farce, rather than comedy.]

The myriad-minded man, our, and all men's, Shakspere, has in this piece presented us with a legitimate farce in exactest consonance with the philosophical principles and character of farce, as distinguished from comedy and from entertainments.

Charles Armitage Brown (1787–1842)
[Excerpted from *Shakespeare's Autobiographical Poems* (1838). Brown offers a vivid picture of the play's effect in the theater, drawing attention to Doctor Pinch as the crowning comic glory of the work.]

Until I saw it on the stage, (not mangled into an opera,) I had not imagined the extent of the mistakes, the drollery of them, their unabated continuance, till, at the end of the fourth act, they reached their climax with the assistance of Dr. Pinch, when the audience in their laughter rolled about like waves. . . . To the strange contrast of grave astonishment among the actors, with their laughable situations in the eyes of the spectators, who are let into the secret, is to be ascribed the irresistible effect.

Algernon Charles Swinburne (1837–1909)
[Excerpted from *A Study of Shakespeare* (1880). Swinburne was a major poet and critic. Swinburne's criticism can be hard to swallow, with its verbosity, its name dropping, and its addiction to sweeping statements. And yet, there is a keen critical intelligence here. Swinburne, like many of his colleagues, takes a biographical view of this play, reading it as an early stage of Shakespeare's artistic development. Most distinctive from his predecessors is his argument that one can see in the play a lyric beauty (many of his predecessors saw it merely as frenetic farce).]

In the exquisite and delightful comedies of his earliest period we can hardly discern any sign, any promise [of the later masterpieces] at all. One only of these, *The Comedy of Errors,* has in it anything of dramatic composition and movement; and what it has of these, I need hardly remind the most cursory of students, is due by no means to Shakespeare. What is due to him, and to him alone, is the honour of having embroidered on the naked old canvas of comic action those flowers of elegiac beauty which vivify and diversify the scene of Plautus as reproduced by the art of Shakespeare . . . in this light and lovely work of the youth of Shakespeare we find for the first time that strange and sweet admixture of farce with fancy, of lyric charm with comic effect, which recurs so often in his later work, from the date of *As You Like It* to the date of *The Winter's Tale.* The sweetness and simplicity of lyric or elegiac loveliness which fill and inform the scenes where Adriana, her sister, and the Syracusan Antipholus exchange the expression of their errors and their loves, belong to Shakespeare alone; and may help us to understand how the young poet who at the outset of his divine career had struck into this fresh untrodden path of poetic comedy should have been, as we have seen that he was, loth [loath] to learn from another and an alien teacher the hard and necessary lesson that this flowery path would never lead him towards the loftier land of tragic poetry.

George Saintsbury (1845–1933) [Excerpted from "Shakespeare: Life and Plays," in *The Cambridge History of English and American Literature* (1907–21), edited by A. R. Ward et al. Saintsbury's brisk and forthright view of the play is particularly useful because it offers in conveniently concentrated form a number of views of *The Comedy of Errors* that one could argue against. Saintsbury sees the play, for instance, very strongly in biographical terms, as a rather incompetent apprentice piece, and argues that it is its very incompetence that in turn marks it out as early. He is very dismissive about the lack of characterization, he regards the verse as crude, and he disapproves of the punning and the vulgarity, rather than seeing them as doing anything useful toward the themes of the play. All of these claims are open to debate, as is the claim that the play is a "mere adaptation" of Plautus's *Menaechmi*. As we have seen, there is material that one could use to make the argument that the play, in fact, rings changes on its source in ways that take it beyond a mere failure of originality. Saintsbury was a considerable critic, but he found little to praise in *The Comedy of Errors*.]

That *The Comedy of Errors* is, in substance, a mere adaptation of the *Menaechmi* of Plautus would, in itself, have very little to do with probable earliness or lateness; for it is a point so well known as to require no discussion, explanation, apology or even frequent statement, that Shakespeare never gave himself the slightest trouble to be "original." Its earliness is shown by the comparative absence of character, by the mixed and rough-hewn quality of the prosody (a connected view of Shakespeare's versification will be given later) and, last and most of all, by the inordinate allowance of the poorest, the most irrelevant, and, occasionally, the most uncomely

wordplay and "foolery." This last characteristic has, of course, been charged against Shakespeare generally, and the charge will have to be dealt with in general. It need only be said now that in no play or passage from *The Tempest* to *Pericles* is there anything to which, as it seems to the present writer, the words above used can be applied as they can to passage after passage between the Dromios and their masters. He does not therefore think, as would some, that Shakespeare did not write these latter passages; he does think that Shakespeare wrote them before he knew better. But that Shakespeare was certain to know better before long is proved in this very play by the fine, though stiff, tirades of the opening scene, by the extremely beautiful poetry of Adriana and her sister, as well as by touches of nascent power over character in both of them, and by numerous flashes here and there in which the spirit, not quite fullgrown as yet, hurries itself through the bonds of imperfect training in speech and metre. It is, however, on the whole, the crudest and most immature of all the plays, and may well have been the earliest.

MODERN CRITICISM AND CRITICAL CONTROVERSIES

Early criticism of *The Comedy of Errors* tended to see it as a brilliant but superficial adaptation of a previous work. Over the course of the 20th century, this view of the play began to change. The wider context for this change was, of course, the greater sophistication and professionalization of literary studies in general, providing its practitioners with a range of tools and critical languages that freed them from talking only in terms of rhetorical structure or the author's biography. In the case of *The Comedy of Errors,* 20th-century analysis found depths in the play that earlier critics had mostly missed. In an essay written in 1939, for instance, G. R. Elliott drew attention to the "comic horror" implicit in the play. In particular, in this description Elliott was thinking of the identical twins, whose indistinguishable similarity to the other is faintly sinister in that it strikes at ideas of personal identity. In particular, he used the idea of the "uncanny," a keyword from Freudian criticism. To put it very briefly, this is the insight that anything one finds indefinably creepy may be addressing a deep-seated and partially repressed fear of some sort. For Elliott, this repressed fear was about one's very sense of self, and he suggested that there is a dark side to the play that requires further investigation.

Elliott's reading of the play has been taken up by subsequent critics. Harold Brooks, for instance, uses Elliott's frame of reference to draw attention to the play's structured descent into madness:

> Dynamic progress is strongly felt in the mounting violence, from the first mere thwack to the drawing of swords, thrashing with a rope's end, and overpowering of "madmen," and elaborate (narrated) vengeance upon Pinch; in the spreading of error . . . and in the darkening conviction of the imaginative Antipholus that his supernatural experiences are from the devil. (88)

Interestingly, Brooks does not abandon previous critics' obsession with analysis of the structure of *The Comedy of Errors,* but, as the extract above suggests, the reading of the play that results from that analysis is quite different.

This picture of the play suggests that it would be ripe for more fully developed psychoanalytical approaches. Barbara Freedman, taking up this challenge, discusses the play in these terms in her 1991 book, *Staging the Gaze: Postmodernism, Psychoanalysis, and Shakespearean Comedy.* In discussing *The Comedy of Errors,* she brings to bear a terminology based on the work of Jacques Lacan to describe the games that are played with delusion and identity and the ways in which comedy arises from fantasies of aggression and sublimated violence. For instance, in the following passage she uses the medical concept of a "functional" illness, where what appears to be an illness is some-

how useful to its owner. For Freedman, the play's apparent improbability and implausibility actually performs useful work in opening the gateway to repressed fantasies:

> Since farce, like dreams, couples a functional denial of significance with often disturbing content, one can read illogic, contradiction, omission and mistakes as signifiers of a functional dislocation of meaning. (103)

Freedman asks what the crime might be that lies behind the seemingly random punishments of the play displaced on the Antipholuses and Dromios. One possibility, she suggests, is that that source of guilt is Egeon's neglect of his wife during their brief marriage, culminating in and symbolized by his losing her as if she were a misplaced parcel. This, she suggests, is the crime, too distressing to face straightforwardly, that resonates through the play and is variously displaced, replayed, and mispunished until the facing up to that crime at the resolution of the play.

Whereas Elliott, Brooks, and Freedman, then, exemplify one strand in 20th-century criticism of the play—an interest in the play's psychological depths, the things it does not say directly—another, competing strand in 20th-century criticism is to look more seriously at the play in historicist terms—that is, looking at it in terms of the culture and politics from which it comes. One 20th-century landmark in this approach was the work of T. W. Baldwin, who looked to understand the play in terms of the specific events of the late 1580s and early 1590s. His 1931 book about the play was entitled *William Shakspeare Adapts a Hanging.*

In September 1588, notes Baldwin, a man was arrested in London. His name was William Hartley, and he was an Englishman who had gone abroad to train as a Catholic priest, returning secretly to conduct Mass. To do so was illegal, as Hartley well knew, and when the authorities caught him, they sentenced him to death, the usual punishment in such cases. On October 5, 1588, he was executed in Finsbury Fields, in North London, on the site of the old Holywell priory and close to the London theaters at which Shakespeare was probably working at the time.

Baldwin draws a series of parallels between the circumstances of Hartley's execution and Egeon's projected execution next to the priory in *The Comedy of Errors*. He argues that Shakespeare probably watched Hartley's hanging in person and that his play reflects the circumstances of the priest's death.

Subsequent scholars have not entirely accepted Baldwin's ambitious readings of the play in terms of this one specific and biographically tidy event. Nonetheless, they agree, Hartley's execution exemplifies wider fears and tensions of the period that one can legitimately read into the play. For most of us now, for instance, the idea of being in a country where the authorities will kill you simply for being found there is unreal, the stuff, at worst, of a nightmare. But some of the people in Shakespeare's England—Catholic priests such as Hartley, for example—lived, in effect, in just such conditions. Egeon's plight, for them, would have been all too realistic. Conversely, many of the early audience of *The Comedy of Errors* seem to have found the policy of putting to death intruders like Hartley to be reasonable, or at least, not intolerable. Their understanding of Duke Solinus's position might have been quite different from ours.

Baldwin, in short, moves toward historicizing *The Comedy of Errors* rather than reading it as a "transhistorical" text that is somehow exempt from the society that produced it. It is an approach that opens up strange new angles on the play. This approach to the work has also been taken up by later critics, notably Arthur Kinney, who in an important essay explores the play in terms of early modern Christianity, particularly in terms of the play's echoes of Saint Paul. David Bevington, meanwhile, points out the extent to which the play shares concerns with the (now little-read) dramas of the 1580s and 1590s, the works of predecessors such as John Lyly.

In 1997, Laurie Maguire drew attention to the play from a feminist perspective. Adriana and Luciana have often been regarded simply as accessories

to the central four twins, but, Maguire suggests, the two women are, in a metaphorical sense, a pair of twins in their own right, onstage taking opposite sides in a debate about the role of women in marriage and exchanged one for the other when Antipholus, seemingly, switches his love from Adriana to her sister. Maguire's essay also explores the twinning of wives and servants in this play, pointing out that in Elizabethan domestic manuals, the two often had a similar status, as accessories and assistants to the man, the natural head of the household. Maguire further notes that marriage itself is a mystery that revolves around fusing two identities into one, as man and woman become "one flesh." Adriana and Luciana, then, are not mere add-ons to the central interest of the play but fascinating in their own right as characters.

Also in the late 1990s, Shakespeare studies as a whole became newly interested in religion and specifically in the question of whether Shakespeare had been a secretly practicing Catholic, with extensive personal links to men like the unfortunate William Hartley. The problem was, and is, that such an association would have been, by its nature, a closely guarded secret so that much of the possible evidence is necessarily ambiguous. Furthermore, the central documents that do appear to link Shakespeare to England's militant Catholic circles are all factually debatable. Nonetheless, the revival of interest in this idea has had the effect of making people read Shakespeare's plays with new interest, not just against the religion of his England, but against the religions of his England. *The Comedy of Errors* is but one play that has benefited from this approach. One might mention particularly Richard Dutton's piece, "*The Comedy of Errors* and the Calumny of Apelles." Partly, Dutton is concerned about presenting a "new" idea: The play seems to draw on a tradition of representations of calumny that he has traced in numerous classical and 16th-century texts. Dutton, though, develops this further into an elegant meditation on how *The Comedy of Errors* addresses issues of calumny, slander, and the nature of heresy in a way that would have resonated with Elizabethan Catholics. Similar recent work on the play, which like Dutton's is alive to the subtleties of 16th-century religious division, includes Lisa Hopkins's article on "*The Comedy of Errors* and the Date of Easter" and Elizabeth F. Hart's piece, "'Great is Diana' of Shakespeare's Ephesus."

Yet a third current development is to look again, in greater detail, at the idea of the city in the play. Thus, in "Urban Misidentification in *The Comedy of Errors* and the Cony-Catching Pamphlets," Martine van Elk reads the play against the 1590s craze for pamphlets exposing fraud and sharp practice by con men in and around London. These pamphlets, she suggests, address anxieties arising from the growing size and complexity of London. She argues that, like the pamphlets, *The Comedy of Errors* can be seen to be concerned with "urban misrecognition" and with the idea that the old social order is no longer stable and secure.

THE PLAY TODAY

The Comedy of Errors is still very much alive, both as a play in its own right and as the source of a range of creative adaptations. Three of these adaptations demand mention here. The Rodgers and Hart musical *The Boys from Syracuse* premiered on Broadway in 1938, was made into a film in 1940, and has been frequently revived since. In Gulzar's Bollywood film *Angoor* (1982), the confusions play out in an Indian town, dragging in a jeweler, a taxi driver, and a police inspector, among others. *The Bomb-itty of Errors* is an "ad-rap-tation of Shakespeare's comedy" to the music and dance of hip-hop, written by students at New York University and which has enjoyed considerable success in theaters over the last few years.

"Straight" revivals, if such a thing is possible, also continue and tend to highlight interesting angles of the play. Two of the most notable, which between them encompass a number of issues about the play in performance, are the Hunter/Cooke revival at Shakespeare's Globe Theatre in London, in 1999, and Barrie Rutter's Northern Broadsides production, performed in Leeds in 2005 and later transferred to London. The Hunter/Cooke pro-

duction took place in only the third full season of performance at the reconstructed Globe Theatre, at a point when the theater was still trying to define its identity as other than that of academic seriousness. The Globe offered, accordingly, a bold and broad production. For example, one reviewer praised the

> delightfully low comic business. The duel between Antipholus and Balthazar is not fought with swords, but with rubber chickens, and other irresistible cheap laughs dot the action of the play. The outstanding comic set piece is an hilarious tennis match between Antipholus and Dromio that not only underscores and emphasizes the dialogue being delivered by them, but makes an immediate connection for audience members who undoubtedly watched Wimbledon matches on television that very morning (Fisher, n.p.).

It used to be the case that productions, once complete, were hard to document beyond published reviews such as Fisher's. In a sign of the changing times, though, many other sources relating to the production are now accessible. In particular, the Shakespeare's Globe Theatre currently maintains a fascinating and highly recommended online archive, including some photographs and even the rehearsal notes of the principal actors.

But an even bolder decision taken by this production—more so than the rubber chickens—was to have both Antipholuses played by a single actor, and both Dromios by another single actor. The two actors involved were Marcello Magni and Vicenzo Nicoli, both experienced in commedia dell'arte techniques, which they brought to the production to expedite the quick changes between the two characters. This raises, of course, the question of how to stage the ending. *Angoor*, too, had adopted the practice of having one actor play both twins, but being a film, it had the advantage of split-screen technology to stage a denouement in which both twins are apparently face to face, something impossible in the theater. (In fact, the film version of *The Boys from Syracuse* did so, too). Surviving reviews and archives, though, are coy about how exactly the Globe production solved the seemingly insurmountable technical problem of having the two brothers meet at the end—and that is as it should be.

In 2005, Northern Broadsides staged *The Comedy of Errors*. As its own Web site states, the company is best known for "performing Shakespeare and classical texts with an innovative, popular and regional style." For instance, in *The Comedy of Errors* no effort was made to have the characters speak in the plummy, mannered voices that one often fears in connection with Shakespeare. Most of them spoke with distinctively northern accents, with the Dromios' thicker accents compared to the more muted vowels of the Antipholuses "placing" them all with precision in a class structure.

The actors provided their own music, picking up a variety of instruments in the course of the play. Most of the other costumes were 1950s themed, prompting one reviewer to comment:

> men in light suits wield umbrellas instead of
> swords, while Adriana, clad from head to foot
> in canary yellow, and Luciana, pretty in pink,
> look as innocent and pastel as Battenberg
> cake. Only the courtesan, in fur coat and with
> stocking tops, brings a slightly loucher note
> . . . (Hopkins, "Review" n.p.)

Doctor Pinch and his assistants were represented as sinister surgeons with rubber gloves, leading to a hilarious sequence involving them tying up the two Ephesians and loading them onto a trolley, greeted with waves of laughter. The above-mentioned review of the play also includes a photograph of the two Antipholuses, which shows, more effectively than words can, how costume and appearance enabled two actors to look identical, or at least identical enough to allow the necessary suspension of disbelief. Fast, direct, funny, and moving, the Northern Broadsides *Comedy of Errors* demonstrated conclusively to its audience that this play is far from dead.

FIVE TOPICS FOR DISCUSSION AND WRITING

1. **Crime, punishment, and ethics:** This is a play that begins with a death sentence and ends with a near-execution. How many actual crimes are committed or threatened in the course of the play? How are the processes of law and law enforcement treated in the play? Of course, not all of the potential crimes committed in the play are criminal offenses, exactly. Who, in the course of the play, commits actions that should hang heavy on their consciences?

2. **Wealth and goods:** Who has money in the play? In what tangible forms is wealth expressed in it, and when and how do we see that wealth passing from hand to hand? What forms of wealth, if any, do the women have? Why is so much of the play set in a marketplace? Is there a link between the play's fascination with exchange and trading of commodities and the fact that it revolves around an exchange of identities?

3. **Magic:** Can one collect together all the references in the play to magic and the supernatural? In the imagery of the play, who refers to magic, and in what contexts? Is magic, in these references, necessarily a bad thing?

4. **Signs:** Antipholus of Syracuse lodges at an inn identified by a sign showing a picture of a centaur; Antipholus of Ephesus lives at a house with the sign of the phoenix outside it; the Courtesan's house has a sign of the Porpentine, or porcupine. These signs might be quite prominent in the staging of the play, since it is implied that each one hangs over one of the three exits from the stage. What are these creatures? Are they randomly chosen, or might they have some emblematic meanings that connect with the action of the play? To what extent does the whole play revolve around the reading of signs? (Arthur Kinney's essay in the bibliography offers but one example of a "solution" to the question of what they mean.)

5. **Production:** The Hunter/Cooke production of 1999 used one actor to play both Antipholuses. What might be gained by this approach, and

what, if anything, might be lost from the meaning of the play? How big a problem would this pose for staging the climax of the play, and how might this problem be dealt with? More generally, suppose one had an unlimited budget: What actors would one cast in a production of *The Comedy of Errors,* and what settings, costumes, and musical accompaniment might one use?

Bibliography

Baldwin, T. W. *On the Compositional Genetics of* The Comedy of Errors. Urbana: Illinois University Press, 1965.

———. *William Shakspeare Adapts a Hanging.* Princeton, N.J.: Princeton University Press, 1931.

Barton, Anne. *The Names of Comedy.* Toronto, Canada: Toronto University Press, 1990.

Bevington, David. "*The Comedy of Errors* in the Context of the Late 1580s and Early 1590s." In *The Comedy of Errors: Critical Essays,* edited by Robert S. Miola, 335–354. London: Routledge, 1997.

The Bomb-itty of Errors—Home. Available online. URL: http://www.bomb-itty.com/. Accessed January 4, 2010.

Brooks, Harold F. "Themes and Structure in *The Comedy of Errors.*" In *The Comedy of Errors: Critical Essays,* edited by Robert S. Miola, 71–93. London: Routledge, 1997.

Bullough, Geoffrey. *Narrative and Dramatic Sources of Shakespeare.* 8 vols. London: Routledge & Kegan Paul, 1966.

Candido, Joseph. "Dining Out in Ephesus: Food in *The Comedy of Errors.*" In *The Comedy of Errors: Critical Essays,* edited by Robert S. Miola, 199–226. London: Routledge, 1997.

"*The Comedy of Errors* (1999)." Globe Education Online. Available online. URL: http://www.globe-education.org/discovery-space/plays/the-comedy-of-errors-1999. Accessed January 4, 2010.

Dutton, Richard. "*The Comedy of Errors* and the Calumny of Apelles: An Exercise in Source Study." *Religion and the Arts* 7 (2003): 11–30.

Elliott, G. R. "Weirdness in *The Comedy of Errors.*" In *The Comedy of Errors: Critical Essays,* edited by Robert S. Miola, 57–70. London: Routledge, 1997.

Farley-Hills, David. "The Theatrical Provenance of *The Comedy of Errors.*" *Notes and Queries* 49 (2002): 220–222.

Fisher, James. "Inside 'The Wooden O': Shakespeare's *The Comedy of Errors* and *Julius Caesar* at the New Globe." *Early Modern Literary Studies* 5, no. 3 (January 2000): 17.1–19. Available online. URL: http://purl.oclc.org/emls/05-3/globrev.htm. Accessed January 4, 2010.

Freedman, Barbara. "Reading Errantly: Misrecognition and the Uncanny in *The Comedy of Errors.*" In *Staging the Gaze: Postmodernism, Psychoanalysis, and Shakespearean Comedy.* Ithaca, N.Y.: Cornell University Press, 1991. Reprinted in *The Comedy of Errors: Critical Essays,* edited by Robert S. Miola, 261–299. London: Routledge, 1997.

Frye, Northrop. *Anatomy of Criticism: Four Essays.* Princeton, N.J.: Princeton University Press, 1957.

Gay, Penny. *The Cambridge Introduction to Shakespeare's Comedies.* Cambridge: Cambridge University Press, 2008.

Gesta Grayorum, or, The History of the High and Mighty Prince, Henry Prince of Purpoole. London: W. Canning, 1684.

Hart, Elizabeth F. "'Great is Diana' of Shakespeare's Ephesus." *Studies in English Literature* 43 (2003): 347–374.

Hopkins, Lisa. "*The Comedy of Errors* and the Date of Easter." *Ben Jonson Journal* 7 (2000): 55–64.

———. "Review of *The Comedy of Errors.* Presented by Northern Broadsides at the West Yorkshire Playhouse and on Tour, February–June 2005." *Early Modern Literary Studies* 11, no. 1 (May 2005): 17.1–3. Available online. URL: http://purl.oclc.org/emls/11-1/revlherr.html. Accessed January 4, 2010.

Kinney, Arthur F. "Shakespeare's *Comedy of Errors* and the Nature of Kinds." In *The Comedy of Errors: Critical Essays,* edited by Robert S. Miola, 158–182. London: Routledge, 1997.

Leggatt, Alexander. *Shakespeare's Comedy of Love.* London: Methuen, 1974.

————, ed. *The Cambridge Companion to Shakespearean Comedy*. Cambridge: Cambridge University Press, 2002.

Lerner, Laurence, ed. *Shakespeare's Comedies*. Harmondsworth, U.K.: Penguin, 1967.

Maguire, Laurie. "The Girls from Ephesus." In *The Comedy of Errors: Critical Essays*, edited by Robert S. Miola, 355–392. London: Routledge, 1997.

Miola, Robert S. *Shakespeare and Classical Comedy*. Oxford, U.K.: Clarendon Press, 1994.

————, ed. *The Comedy of Errors: Critical Essays*. London: Routledge, 1997.

Molton, Charles Wells, ed. *The Library of Literary Criticism of English and American Authors*. London: Moulton Publishing, 1901.

Nevo, Ruth. *Comic Transformations in Shakespeare*. London: Methuen, 1980.

Parker, Patricia A. *Shakespeare from the Margins: Language, Culture, Context*. Chicago: Chicago University Press, 1996.

Saintsbury, George. "Shakespeare: Life and Plays." In *The Cambridge History of English and American Literature*, edited by A. R. Ward et al. 165–222. New York: G.P. Putnam's Sons, 1907–21.

Salingar, Leo. *Shakespeare and the Traditions of Comedy*. Cambridge: Cambridge University Press, 1974.

Shakespeare, William. *The Comedy of Errors*. Edited by Charles Whitworth. Oxford: Oxford University Press, 2002.

Smith, Emma, ed. *Shakespeare's Comedies*. Oxford: Blackwell, 2004.

Swinburne, Algernon Charles. The Swinburne Project, John Walsh, gen. ed. Available online. URL: http://www.letrs.indiana.edu/swinburne/. Accessed January 4, 2010.

Tillyard, E. M. W. *Shakespeare's Early Comedies*. London: Chatto & Windus, 1966.

van Elk, Martine. "Urban Misidentification in *The Comedy of Errors* and the Cony-Catching Pamphlets." *Studies in English Literature* 43 (2003): 323–346.

Werstine, Paul. "Foul Papers and Prompt Books: Printer's Copy for Shakespeare's *Comedy of Errors*." *Studies in Bibliography* 41 (1988): 232–246.

FILM AND VIDEO PRODUCTIONS

Clark, Cecil, dir. *A Comedy of Errors*. With Michael Williams and Judi Dench. ATV Network, 1974.

Gulzar, dir. *Angoor*. With Sanjeev Kumar. A. R. Movies, 1982.

Sutherland, A. Edward, dir. *The Boys from Syracuse*. With Allan Jones. Universal Pictures, 1940.

—Matthew Steggle

Coriolanus

INTRODUCTION

Commonly described as Shakespeare's most intensely political drama, *Coriolanus* is Shakespeare's second-longest play (after *Hamlet*) and almost certainly the last tragedy he wrote. Most critics regard *Coriolanus* as significantly inferior to the great tragedies that preceded it (*Hamlet, King Lear, Othello, Macbeth,* and *Antony and Cleopatra*), but the play has had important critical champions. Frank Kermode, for example, called it "the last great achievement of English drama" in the tragic genre (*Age of Shakespeare,* 168).

Coriolanus portrays the life and death of one of the legendary heroes of the ancient Roman world. The story of Coriolanus is told in Plutarch's *Lives of the Noble Greeks and Romans,* which was translated into French by Jacques Amyot and then into English by Sir Thomas North in 1579. Shakespeare was well acquainted with this latter source, drawing on it for *Julius Caesar, Antony and Cleopatra,* and *Coriolanus,* as well as, to a lesser extent, several other works. As with all his plays, Shakespeare does not follow his source slavishly. While some sections of the play (Volumnia's intercession for the doomed Rome, for instance) are very close to Plutarch's narrative, other scenes (Act I, Scene 3) or roles (that of Menenius) are entirely Shakespeare's invention or have been augmented considerably.

The play is of a piece with the Renaissance spirit of inquiry into the proper conduct and duties of government. While set ostensibly in the distant past, *Coriolanus* is insistent about the immediacy of such questions as the relationship between the individual and the family and between the individual and the state. At its most fundamental, *Coriolanus* is a play about loyalty and betrayal. Furthermore, in its study of the degree of self-determination the protagonist exercises over his fate, it examines various notions of selfhood and autonomy. It is, therefore, in spite of its relative unpopularity in the repertory, very much a play for today.

BACKGROUND

One could say that the protagonist of *Coriolanus* is Rome itself (the word appears 88 times in the play). The myth of Rome was at the center of the era we now call the early modern period and known at the time as the Renaissance (meaning "rebirth"). The latter term was coined by Giorgio Vasari in *The Lives of the Artists* (1550). During the Tudor and Stuart periods, England adopted the learning and culture of contemporary Italy, which, in turn, considered itself the reincarnation of its Latin forebears. The Renaissance was thus defined as and by the rebirth and dissemination of the classical wisdom of the ancients, including ideas related to mathematics, astronomy, medicine, architecture, literature, music, astrology, philosophy, politics, rhetoric, and the visual arts. This intellectual explosion was known as humanism. Rome's position as the origin of such humanistic thought (along with the equally important Florence) meant that it occupied a central position in the thinking of early modern Europe. The ancient Roman Empire, with Rome itself as its hub of power, provided a model to other European states

Volumnia, wordlessly kneeling before him, asks Coriolanus to look at his son in an 1803 engraving of Act V, Scene 3 of *Coriolanus*. *(Painting by Gavin Hamilton, engraving by James Caldwell, restoration by Adam Cuerden)*

eager to mimic its potency and political influence. But this admiration for Rome was not unalloyed.

Following Henry VIII's failure to obtain a divorce from Catherine of Aragon, the king refuted the authority of the papacy and set himself up as head of both the state and the newly formed Anglican Church. England's shift to Protestantism offered Henry an opportunity to valorize his new marriage to Anne Boleyn as well as the opportunity to condemn the corruption of the Catholic Church, which was being pilloried by such Reformation theologians as Martin Luther. Thus, the emergent English Protestant state defined its own capital, London, against the corruption of Rome. The hitherto most powerful city of Western

Christendom, the seat of the line of popes, which stretched all the way back to Saint Peter, was now vilified as the origin of religious and political corruption, imaged, in the inflammatory rhetoric of the day, as the Whore of Babylon. Italians were demonized as, among other things, sodomites, assassins, and the disciples of Niccolò Machiavelli, an astute and brutally efficient political theorist whose work was known to Shakespeare (Machiavelli himself is referred to in *Henry VI, Part I* and *III* as well as in *The Merry Wives of Windsor*).

Rome's significance was thus deeply ambiguous. On the one hand, the city represented, in the English imagination, the focus of learning, power, and culture. On the other, as the seat of papal authority, it stood for everything that was corrupt and debauched with the old faith from which Henry had divorced his entire kingdom.

Roman history, for Shakespeare and his contemporaries, was just as complex. In a positive light, Roman values included such qualities as selfless service for the state, bravery, honor, and nobility—indeed, all the attributes typified by such Elizabethan courtiers as Sir Philip Sidney, Sir Walter Raleigh, or Robert Devereux, second earl of Essex. The Latin word *vir* translates as "man," and as such *vir*tues were distinctly masculine (the same Latin root gives us the English *virility*, for example). When Ophelia laments Hamlet's decline, she itemizes his virtues, now spoiled by his apparent madness: "O what a noble mind is here o'erthrown! / The courtier's, soldier's, scholar's eye, tongue, sword" (3.1.154–155). The "Renaissance man" was simultaneously a master of courtly behavior, a fearless warrior, and an educated and sophisticated intellectual. This blend of masculine accomplishments had their origins in the warriors and statesmen of classical Rome.

But Rome was also a place of unimaginable barbarity, a culture dependent on and defined by its use of violence, a city with a colosseum purpose-built for the public slaughter of animals and gladiatorial combat in the name of entertainment. According to Roman law, someone convicted of patricide was punishable by being stripped naked, publicly flogged, and then sewn into a sack before being thrown into the river Tiber. Insubordination in the Roman army was punished by a *fustuarium* in which the soldier's closest friends were ordered to surround him and beat him to death. In the present-day world, violence is usually relatively abstract; however, for Shakespeare and his contemporaries, impressment into the army, as well as the spectacle of public execution, not to mention the savagery of such practices as cockfighting and bearbaiting, meant that state-approved violence was much closer to the Roman model.

These ambiguities in relation to the Roman world were exacerbated by the kinds of questions asked by the movement called humanism, ques-

tions which Shakespeare's historical and Roman plays repeatedly raise: What is the nature of political power? Can tyranny be opposed, or must it be passively tolerated? What is the duty of the citizen to the state? What is the duty of the state to the citizen? Is the monarch subject to or above the law? What is the relationship between the ruler and his or her advisers? During the period *Coriolanus* was being staged for the first time, these questions were especially pronounced. Only a few years earlier the Tudor dynasty had come to an end: In 1603, Elizabeth I had died without an heir, and the crown had passed to the Scottish family, the Stuarts. James I derived his claim to the English throne from his great-grandmother, Margaret, daughter of Henry VII. But, that was several generations earlier, and London was not universally impressed with the coronation of a Scottish king. Moreover, although he had been raised as a Protestant, James was the son of Mary, Queen of Scots, Elizabeth's Catholic nemesis, whom she had executed in 1587.

James's relations with his new kingdom were less than cooperative. He chose the title "king of Great Britain" in spite of the insistence of Parliament to keep England as a separate legislature. James was criticized for cronyism as well as the selling of knighthoods. George Villiers, duke of Buckingham and James's alleged homosexual lover, was assassinated in a popular gesture of defiance. James's pacific policies toward the Catholic superpower of Spain were considered to be a feeble resignation of the Protestant independence championed by Elizabeth. Financially, James's court was a burden on the state, and in 1614, Parliament was dissolved as it attempted to avoid bailing out the spendthrift monarch. These questions over the distribution of power—monarch, Parliament, people—are echoed in *Coriolanus* as the patricians, tribunes, and plebeians wrestle over political dominance.

Date and Text of the Play

Most scholars believe the play must have been written between 1605 and 1609, with the majority preferring 1608. The play was first published in the First Folio (1623) edition of Shakespeare's

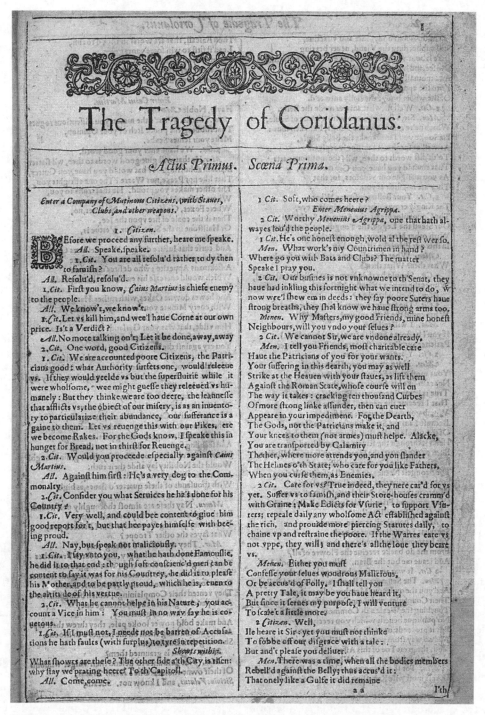

Title page of *Coriolanus* in the First Folio edition published in 1623

works (no previous quarto publications have been discovered), in which it is divided into acts. It also contains a number of detailed stage directions specifying the playing of music. Both features are consistent with its being performed in an indoor playhouse (act divisions allowed the regular trimming of candles, which was not necessary in an open-air theater). As the King's Men (Shakespeare's theater company) had acquired the indoor Blackfriars Theatre in 1608, this is the date often given for the composition of *Coriolanus;* it is also likely that it was Shakespeare's first play written for an indoor playhouse.

SYNOPSIS
Brief Synopsis

Rioting Romans seek the death of Martius, a leading aristocrat and warrior who is known for his pride. Menenius calms them with a humorous fable. Martius arrives and reports that the people have been allowed to elect their own tribunes. News arrives that Rome is threatened by a neighboring tribe, the Volscians, whose general, Aufidius, is a former foe of Coriolanus. Martius agrees to help repel the invaders.

Martius's mother, Volumnia, berates his wife, Virgilia, for not being pleased that Martius has gone to war. Valeria, Virgilia's friend, brings the news that Martius and Cominius have Corioles under siege.

At Corioles, Martius curses the Romans for retreating and charges alone through the city's gates. Soon, he emerges from Corioles, chased by Volscians, and the Romans rally to his defense. After Corioles has been taken, Martius, despite his wounds, joins Cominius, who is forced to withdraw against superior forces. Martius and Aufidius fight. Several Volscians arrive to assist their general, but Martius drives them all away. After the victory, Cominius proposes that in honor of Martius's courage at Corioles, he shall hereafter be known as Coriolanus.

Back in Rome, Menenius berates Sicinius and Brutus, two tribunes, for their animosity toward Martius. Coriolanus is nominated for the consulate, the highest office in Rome, but he asks to be excused from the tradition of exhibiting his wounds to the people. The tribunes refuse to accept the idea and the aristocrats persuade an uneasy Coriolanus to go through with it.

Coriolanus, dressed in the traditional humble garb, asks groups of citizens for their support, though in a surly, begrudging manner. They agree to support him, and Menenius and the tribunes confirm his election. After Coriolanus and Menenius leave, the tribunes convince the citizens to rescind their approval before Coriolanus's formal installation as consul.

Coriolanus hears that Aufidius has expressed a desire to fight him, and he wishes for a war. The tribunes report that a mob has risen against Coriolanus. When Coriolanus angrily declares the commoners unworthy of a voice in the selection of a consul, the tribunes declare him a traitor to the laws of Rome. Following Sicinius's lead, the mob demands that Coriolanus be killed. Menenius convinces the tribunes and the mob to follow legal procedures and try Coriolanus for treason in the tribunes' court.

After a lengthy argument, Volumnia helps the other aristocrats convince Coriolanus to swallow his pride and apologize to the commoners.

Brutus and Sicinius instruct a subordinate to prepare the crowd to support whatever line they take in the trial of Coriolanus. Coriolanus and his friends appear, and at first Coriolanus mildly makes the recantation demanded by the tribunes. When Sicinius calls him a traitor, however, he rejects the authority of the common people in insulting terms. The tribunes convict him and declare him banished from Rome. He departs for exile.

Coriolanus, disguised as a poor man, arrives in Antium and is directed to Aufidius's house, where he reveals himself and offers to fight for the Volscians against Rome. Aufidius agrees enthusiastically. Led by Coriolanus, the Volscians again attack Roman territory outside the city.

The tribunes convince Menenius to beg for mercy for Rome from Coriolanus. When Menenius arrives at the Volscian camp, Coriolanus sends him away. Volumnia arrives with Virgilia, Valeria, and

Coriolanus's son. Their petitions for mercy convince Coriolanus to make peace with Rome.

Coriolanus presents his treaty with Rome to Aufidius, who accuses him of treachery. The crowd turns against Coriolanus and loudly demands that he be killed as an enemy. Aufidius's conspirators attack Coriolanus and kill him. Aufidius stipulates that, as a great warrior, Coriolanus should have a noble funeral.

Act I, Scene 1

Rome is in uproar. The plebeians, convinced that the patricians are hoarding corn, muster with clubs and sticks to riot. They identify Caius Martius as "chief enemy to the people" and determine to kill him. Though some recognize the service he has done Rome, the prevalent mood is one of murderous rage. The conciliatory Menenius attempts to discourage the rebellion and tells an allegory that compares the political workings of the state to the metabolic processes of the human body. In his story, the organs of the body rebel against the belly, accusing it of digesting all the food while they do all the work. The belly responds by pointing out that the sustenance from the food is distributed to the organs, while the belly is left with only the waste. Menenius explains that the senators of Rome are the belly distributing "public benefit" from the center and that, like the riotous organs of the body, the plebeians are ignorant of and ungrateful for the dedication of their betters. At this point, Martius enters. In his very first line, he refers to the plebeians as "dissentious rogues," and there follows a long speech in which he itemizes their cowardice, fickleness, laziness and untrustworthiness. Martius announces that five tribunes, including Sicinius and Brutus, have been appointed to represent the interests of the populace. A messenger brings news that the Volsces (Volsci), under the command of Aufidius, are on the march. Cominius, Lartius, and the tribunes enter, and Martius describes Aufidius's nobility and bravery: "He is a lion / That I am proud to hunt" (1.1.238–239). They exit to the Capitol, leaving the tribunes who curse Martius's pride and disdain.

Act I, Scene 2

Shakespeare moves us from Rome to Corioles and introduces Aufidius of whom we have just heard Martius's glowing description. But, instead of the ideal of a classical warrior, we are presented with a devious and capable politician. Aufidius explains how the Romans are being tipped off as to Volscian military strategy and concludes that this can only be happening through the work of a double agent. The scene raises the theme of spying, which will become important later in the play.

Act I, Scene 3

The focus switches from the masculine world of high politics to the domestic setting of the household. Volumnia talks of the bravery and honor of her son, Martius, while his wife, Virgilia, expresses her concern for his safety. Thus, we have two contrasting female perspectives on battle. Valeria enters and describes how she witnessed Young Martius killing a butterfly in a fit of pique. Volumnia remarks, "One on's father's moods" (1.3.71), perhaps ironically implying that Martius's military achievements amount to little more than the slaughter of harmless creatures. The scene ends with Valeria updating the others on the military campaign: Martius and Lartius are encamped in front of Corioles and are optimistic about a speedy victory.

Act I, Scene 4

The scene moves us to the war with the Volsces, with which the rest of Act I is concerned. The Volsces emerge from the gates of Corioles to fight with the Romans. They push the Romans back.

Instead of cajoling or encouraging his soldiers in the manner of Henry V on the eve of Agincourt, Martius curses their cowardice: "You shames of Rome . . . Boils and plagues / Plaster you o'er" (1.4.31–32). As the gates of Corioles open, Martius enters alone to pursue the Volsces. The gates shut on him, and his soldiers conclude that he is done for. Just as they have given him up, he reenters, and they resolve to follow him into the city.

Act I, Scene 5

Again, we see Martius fulminating at his own troops, this time for looting: "base slaves . . . Down with them!" (1.5.7–8). Martius orders Lartius to secure the conquered city, while he intends to find and dispatch Aufidius. Lartius remarks that Martius should seek medical attention for his wounds but is rebuffed: "Sir, praise me not. / My work hath not yet warmed me" (1.5.17–18). Here we see the embarrassment with which Martius responds to admiration.

Act I, Scene 6

Cominius and his soldiers enter fatigued from battle. He hopes for the success of the other part of the army. A messenger enters with the ominous report that the Volsces have repulsed the Roman push (as in Scene 4 above). This is old news, but the messenger has been forced "to wheel / Three or four miles about" (1.6.19–20) as he was being chased by Volscian spies. Martius enters covered in blood. He embraces Cominius with an intensity that equates battle with sexual activity: "As merry and when our nuptial day was done" (1.6.31). This motif will reappear. Martius updates Cominius on the Romans' success, although he cannot help cursing the cowardice of his troops: "The mouse ne'er shunned the cat as they did budge / From rascals worse than they" (1.6.45–46). Determined to pursue his enemy, Aufidius, Martius selects a few faithful soldiers to follow him.

Act I, Scene 7

In this short scene of just eight lines, Lartius gives commands to a Lieutenant to secure the gates of Corioles while he makes his way to the Roman camp to rejoin Martius and Cominius.

Act I, Scene 8

Finally, we see the head-to-head confrontation of Aufidius and Martius. They agree that the first to surrender will "die the other's slave" (1.8.6). As they fight, several Volsces come to the aid of Aufidius, who is humiliated by their rescue.

Act I, Scene 9

In the Roman camp, Cominius reports the brave deeds of Martius, much to the latter's embarrassment: "Pray now, no more" (1.9.15). Cominius is insistent on Martius being properly rewarded and offers him a tenth of the booty. Martius refuses, so Cominius rewards him with an intangible reward, an honor rather than a prize: "For what he did before Corioles, call him / With all th'applause and clamour of the host, / Martius Caius Coriolanus!" (1.9.63–65). His response is characteristically muted, almost churlish: "I will go wash" (1.9.68). But before he leaves, he requests the freedom of a poor man who accommodated him. Asked to identify the man, Coriolanus cannot recall his name: "my memory is tired" (1.9.91).

Act I, Scene 10

As in Act I, Scene 2, Aufidius is shown as a pragmatic and insidious figure rather than noble or dignified. Enraged at the loss of the city and at the interference of the Volsces who rescued him, he determines to "potch at [Martius] some way, / Or wrath or craft may get him" (1.10.15–16). His victory over Martius will be brutal or underhanded but, one way or another, he resolves to "Wash my fierce hand in's heart" (1.10.27).

Act II, Scene 1

In contrast to the short and active battle scenes of Act I, the opening scene of Act II is long and continuous and set in the city. Menenius clashes with the tribunes and insults them: "a brace of unmeriting, proud, violent, testy magistrates, alias fools" (2.1.46). The three women enter and bring news of Coriolanus's victorious homecoming. Coriolanus enters in triumph and is greeted by Volumnia, Virgilia, Valeria, and Menenius. They exit, and the tribunes are left onstage to mutter darkly about the admiration in which Coriolanus is held, which threatens to undermine their own influence. They determine to remind the populace of Coriolanus's haughtiness.

Act II, Scene 2

At the Senate, a group of officers discuss the character of Coriolanus as well as his standing among the plebeians. The patricians, tribunes, and lictors enter along with Coriolanus, Menenius, and Cominius, the latter of whom is charged with recounting the brave deeds of Coriolanus. As reward, the Senate agrees to appoint him consul. The custom requires Coriolanus to obtain popular support, the people's "voices" (2.2.45). Coriolanus finds this demeaning but reluctantly agrees. The tribunes spot an opportunity to capitalize on his disdain for the plebeians.

Act II, Scene 3

The citizens discuss whether to ratify the appointment of Coriolanus as consul. The majority agree that it would be ungrateful (given his defense of Rome) not to do so. Coriolanus enters in the "gown of humility" discussing, with Menenius, his unwillingness to beg the people's voices. Menenius leaves him, and there follows a brittle and awkward exchange between the citizens and a Coriolanus struggling to conceal his contempt for them. His election is nonetheless approved, and Menenius and the tribunes enter to invite him back to the Senate. They exit, leaving the tribunes to incite the people against Coriolanus. They decide to revoke their election.

Coriolanus shows his wounds to a citizen before his election in Act II, Scene 3 of *Coriolanus,* in this print published by John Bell in 1773. *(Illustration by Edward Edwards; engraving by Matthew Liart)*

Act III, Scene 1

Coriolanus returns to his obsession with Aufidius and discusses with Lartius the current state of Volscian readiness. The tribunes enter and warn Coriolanus that as the "people are incensed against him" (3.1.32), he had better not proceed to the marketplace. Coriolanus accuses the tribunes of manipulating the mob and laments the weakening of patrician rule. It is at this point that Coriolanus explains his opposition to the free distribution of corn: The people are cowards and unworthy of it. The tribunes accuse him of treason, sentence him to death, and attempt to arrest him, but he stands firm, and they exit in a rabble. Menenius determines to defuse the situation, but the mob reenters, led by the tribunes who call for Coriolanus's execution. Menenius agrees to bring Coriolanus to a legal hearing in the marketplace.

Act III, Scene 2

Coriolanus announces his defiance, but Volumnia and Menenius encourage him to swallow his pride and address the people in a conciliatory manner (even if he does not mean it). Coriolanus, under the greatest protest, submits though he can hardly bear the hypocrisy he is put to: "I surcease to honour mine own truth" (3.2.121). He leaves for the marketplace.

Act III, Scene 3

Brutus and Sicinius are seen stage-managing the opposition of the people so that their popular voice will endorse whatever sentence the tribunes decide to pass on Coriolanus, "either / For death, for fine, or banishment" (3.3.13–14). Knowing that he will lose his temper, Sicinius accuses Coriolanus of being tyrannical. Defiant and furious, Coriolanus is "banished / As enemy to the people and his country" (3.3.125–126). Cursing their ignorance and cowardice, he exits.

Act IV, Scene 1

Coriolanus takes his leave of his mother and wife, encouraging them not to lose heart. In spite of Cominius's offer to accompany him, he insists on leaving alone "Like to a lonely dragon" (4.1.30). This scene shows us Coriolanus at his most humane.

Act IV, Scene 2

Volumnia encounters the tribunes and rails at them for engineering the banishment of her son. They dismiss her complaints as madness. Invited to dine by Menenius, she responds with the bitter remark: "Anger's my meat: I sup upon myself / And so shall starve with feeding" (4.2.50–51).

Act IV, Scene 3

Nicanor, a discontented Roman, is bringing military intelligence to Adrian, a Volsce. This picks up the earlier references to spying and switches the focus of the play from the conflict between Coriolanus and the Roman people to the larger tensions between Rome and the Volsces, with which Act I was mainly concerned.

Act IV, Scene 4

In this short scene, Coriolanus, *"disguised and muffled,"* arrives at Antium to seek out his enemy,

Volumnia reproaches Brutus and Sicinus for banishing Coriolanus in Act IV, Scene 2 of *Coriolanus*. Print published by Virtue & Co. in 1877. *(Painting by James Dromgole Linton, etching by James Stephenson)*

Aufidius. Having identified the correct house with the help of a local, Coriolanus pauses to reflect on the nature of friendship and how firm friends can so easily become enemies and enemies friends. He resolves to offer himself to Aufidius: "If he slay me, / He does fair justice; if he give me way, / I'll do his country service" (4.4.24–26).

Act IV, Scene 5

Aufidius's servants are glimpsed organizing a banquet when the disguised Coriolanus enters and refuses to leave. Aufidius enters to quell the disturbance and repeatedly demands the intruder's "name." Coriolanus reveals his identity and offers Aufidius his services. Aufidius accepts and welcomes him. They exit, and the servants are left to discuss the merits of each warrior and their joint mission against Rome.

Act IV, Scene 6

Sicinius and Brutus are relishing the tranquil atmosphere of Rome since the banishment of Coriolanus. No sooner have they finished congratulating each other than the news arrives of the invasion into Roman territories of the Volscian army. The tribunes are incredulous, but then further information is received that not only proves the first dispatch but adds, moreover, that Coriolanus has joined forces with Aufidius. Cominius enters and confirms these reports. The plebeians enter and deny culpability for the banishment of Coriolanus: "though we willingly consented to his banishment, yet it was against our will" (4.6.144).

Act IV, Scene 7

Aufidius hears from his Lieutenant how his soldiers are full of admiration for Coriolanus and that consequently Aufidius is "darkened in this action" (4.7.5). Aufidius reflects upon Coriolanus's inherent nobility and remarks that he will conquer Rome "By sovereignty of nature" (4.7.35). When Coriolanus has taken Rome, Aufidius plans to turn on him. With the brutal pragmatism we have come to expect of Aufidius, he remarks on the temporary nature of political power: "One fire drives out one fire, one nail one nail; / Rights by rights falter, strengths by strengths do fail" (4.7.54–55).

Act V, Scene 1

Cominius reports his failure to negotiate on behalf of Rome a peace with Coriolanus. Sicinius persuades Menenius to assay a similar mission. Menenius exits for the Volscian camp to meet Coriolanus, although Cominius holds out little faith "Unless his noble mother and his wife" (5.1.71) were to undertake to intercede for Rome.

Act V, Scene 2

Menenius's attempt to plead with Coriolanus is met with the latter's icy dismissal. With his tail between his legs, Menenius returns to Rome.

Act V, Scene 3

The play's dramatic climax opens with Coriolanus describing his own resolve to sack Rome, evidenced by his rejection of Menenius. Furthermore, he proclaims that he will not hear any more "embassies and suits" from Rome (5.3.17). Just as he announces this intention, his wife, mother, Valeria, and Young Martius enter. We see Coriolanus steel-

In this 1740 print, Volumnia, Virgilia, and Young Martius kneel before Coriolanus, begging him not to sack Rome. *(Painting by Hubert Gravelot; engraving by Gerard Van der Gucht)*

ing himself to reject their suit: "Let it be virtuous to be obstinate" (5.3.26), but just before Volumnia starts to speak, Coriolanus admits to himself, "I melt, and am not / Of stronger earth than others" (5.3.28–29). Volumnia laments their dejection and deprivation since Coriolanus left Rome, and she goes on to describe how the women's loyalties are divided between their country and their son/husband. Volumnia refuses to wait for the outcome of the war but threatens, unless she can entreat him to cease his campaign and reconcile Rome with the Volsces, to take her own life. Volumnia's repeated invitations for Coriolanus to reply suggest that he is dumbfounded. The women kneel to him and finally Young Martius, silent, kneels, too. Volumnia describes him: "This boy, that cannot tell what he would have, / But kneels and holds up hands for fellowship, / Does reason our petition with more strength / Than thou hast to deny't" (5.3.174–177). In Act III, Scene 2, Volumnia had declaimed "Action is eloquence" (78), and here the kneeling boy, although wordless, seems to offer the most expressive gesture of supplication. It has the desired effect, and Coriolanus relents, though not without pronouncing that in giving up his plans to invade Rome, he faces the wrath of the Volsces: "You have won a happy victory to Rome; / But for your son, believe it, O believe it, / Most dangerously you have with him prevailed" (5.3.187–189). Coriolanus seeks the support of Aufidius in forging a truce. Aufidius, in an aside, reveals that he has no such intention.

Act V, Scene 4
Back in Rome, Menenius is lamenting the intransigence of Coriolanus. A messenger brings news that the "ladies have prevailed" (5.4.44). The mood is quickly transformed into one of celebration.

Act V, Scene 5
In this short scene, really a continuation of the previous one, a procession welcomes back the women, while a Senator calls for the people to "Unshout the noise that banished Martius" (5.5.4). The scene corresponds ironically to Act II, Scene 1, in which Coriolanus entered Rome in triumph. Here, his mother enters in triumph, having defeated her own son.

Act V, Scene 6
Whether Coriolanus really believes he can forge a truce is a moot point, but, perhaps bravely, perhaps foolishly, perhaps even suicidally, he returns to the Volsces. We see Aufidius at the top of the

scene giving orders that a paper accusing Coriolanus of betrayal is to be circulated among the lords of the city. Aufidius will regain his previously powerful position by ridding himself of Coriolanus: "he sold the blood and labour / Of our great action; therefore he shall die, / And I'll renew me in his fall" (5.6.47–49). Coriolanus enters with a document setting out the truce with Rome. Aufidius interrupts, accusing Coriolanus of treason and deliberately insulting him by referring to him as Martius rather than "thy stol'n name / 'Coriolanus'" (5.6.89–90). Worse is to follow, and Aufidius, in a move calculated to provoke Coriolanus's wild temper, addresses him as "thou boy of tears" (5.6.101). Coriolanus falls victim now, not to the Roman populace, but to the Volsces as the people, who until recently considered him their champion, remember the slaughter he has wreaked upon them: "He killed my son!—My daughter!—He killed my cousin Marcus!—He killed my father!" (5.6.122–123). Aufidius capitalizes on this moment of popular support, and he and his conspirators rush in to kill Coriolanus. The Second Lord justifies Aufidius's rage, claiming it was a proportionate response to Coriolanus's own anger. His conclusion is bleakly pragmatic: "Let's make the best of it" (5.6.147). Aufidius, too, announces his own regret and calls for a dignified funeral procession.

CHARACTER LIST
Caius Martius (Coriolanus) A member of the Roman patrician class, Martius is a fierce warrior. Renowned for his bravery and military brilliance, he is respected by but deeply unpopular with the citizens because of his impatience and contempt for those whom he considers to be cowards. After his single-handed victory over the city of Corioles, he is renamed Coriolanus. Unable to control his temper, he alienates both the tribunes and the plebeians and is banished from Rome. He sides with Rome's enemy, Aufidius, and leads a Volscian army to the gates of Rome with the intention of crushing his birthplace.

Menenius Agrippa   Another patrician, Menenius is well liked by the populace and acts as a "go-between" for Martius and the citizens. Older and wiser than Martius, he adopts the role of Martius's foster father and constantly attempts to defuse his angry outbursts.

Titus Lartius   A general in the Roman army and friend of Martius.

Cominius   A general in the Roman army. It is Cominius who awards Martius with the name Coriolanus "For what he did before Corioles" (1.10.63).

Volumnia   Martius's mother. She has raised her son according to the Roman ideals of honor, nobility, and bravery. She even relishes the possibility that he will be wounded in battle. As her son leads an army against Rome, she is forced to beg him to spare the city. In doing this, she knows that the Volsces will consider Martius a traitor and kill him.

Virgilia   Wife of Martius. Unsurprisingly, she is less sanguine than Volumnia about the dangers her husband faces on the battlefield. Volumnia considers Virgilia to be squeamish. As a passive and chaste wife (an early modern as well as a Roman ideal), she says very little, but her presence in the scene in which Volumnia pleads for Rome is essential.

Young Martius   Martius's young son whose chasing after a butterfly and his tearing it to pieces illustrates that he is a chip off the old block. Like Virgilia's, his presence in the intercession scene is critical.

Valeria   Friend of Volumnia and Virgilia and sister of Publicola, one of the first Roman consuls (5.3.64). In Plutarch, it is Valeria who initiates the women's intercession with Martius to spare Rome. She is less prominent in Shakespeare's play, which assigns that role instead to Volumnia and Virgilia (5.2).

Sicinius Velutus   One of the five tribunes elected by the plebeians to protect their interests. In Plutarch, he is described as "the cruellest and stowtest of the Tribunes" (Bullough 523).

Virgilia in Act V, Scene 3 of *Coriolanus*. This is a print from Charles Heath's 1848 edition of *The Heroines of Shakspeare: Comprising the Principal Female Characters in the Plays of the Great Poet*. (Painting by A. Johnston; engraving by H. Austin)

Junius Brutus   Of the five tribunes we hear about (1.1.212), only Brutus and Sicinius are named and appear in Shakespeare's play. Brutus is as anxious as Sicinius to bring down Martius.

Citizens of Rome   Interestingly, Shakespeare identifies a variety of political positions among the Citizens. There are those who hate Martius, those who respect him, and even those who defend him in light of his service to the state.

Tullus Aufidius   Leader of the Volsces and Rome's enemy. He passionately hates Martius, with whom he has fought single-handedly five times. After Volumnia persuades Martius to halt his attack on Rome, Aufidius accuses him of treachery to the Volsces, and he and his conspirators murder Martius in the marketplace.

Servants to Aufidius They are preparing a feast at the house of Aufidius when Martius (in disguise) enters. They are surprised by his strength and nobility. Their bewildered account of the warrior offers one of the few comic episodes in the play: "He had, sir, a kind of face, methought—I cannot tell how to term it" (4.5.157).

Adrian Volscian spy.

Nicanor Roman traitor who feeds information to the Volsces through Adrian. The two of them appear only in Act IV, Scene 3.

Aediles Roman law officers. Unsuccessfully, they try to seize Martius during the attempted arrest (3.1).

CHARACTER STUDIES
Caius Martius/Coriolanus

At the center of Shakespeare's final tragedy is the puzzle of Martius. Haughty, contemptuous, and arrogant, he is also brave, independent, and warm hearted toward his family and friends, as his leave-taking demonstrates: "When I am forth, / Bid me farewell, and smile" (4.1.49–50). Unlike Henry V or Othello, both of whom claim to be rough and ready speakers, but whose oratorical brilliance is masked by a faux practicality, Martius is genuinely not a great public speaker. In fact, all such occasions are acutely embarrassing to him, and he would rather fight than suffer compliments: "Sir, praise me not" (1.5.17); "I have some wounds upon me, and they smart / To hear themselves remembered" (1.9.28–29); "No more of this, it does offend my heart. / Pray now, no more" (2.1.185–186); "When blows have made me stay I fled from words" (2.2.75), and so on. His modesty is accompanied by other virtues. Even one of the Citizens remarks that "You must in no way say he is covetous" (1.1.43) and Cominius echoes this, saying "He covets less / Than misery itself would give" (2.2.131–132). Martius condemns those soldiers who are more interested in carrying off pelf than securing the victory (1.6), and he turns down the 10 percent of the spoils offered him (1.10). The Second Officer concedes that "He hath deserved worthily of his country" (2.2.28), and Roman contempt toward ingratitude ensures that the people are willing to allow him their votes to be consul.

But, on the other hand, his vitriol toward the plebeians is extreme and even shocking. His first line labels them "dissentious rogues" (1.1.167), and his following harangue metamorphoses them into "curs," "hares" and "geese" (1.1.172, 175, 176). He would happily chop them into pieces. There is much attention to the stench of the mob, and the unworthy plebeians become "the mutable, rank-scented meinie" (3.3.66). Humiliated at having to beg for the vox populi "of Hob and Dick" (2.3.123), Martius detests them all but chiefly their

John Kemble as Coriolanus in a production of *Coriolanus*, as depicted in this 1839 print published by M. M. Holloway *(Painting by Sir Thomas Lawrence; engraving by William Oakley Burgess)*

tribunes, whose election he regards as an affront to the natural superiority of the patricians: "I do despise them, / For they do prank them in authority / Against all noble sufferance" (3.1.22–24). Indeed, so appalled is he by the concession to permit the election of such tribunes in the first place that he pays them scant regard, as demonstrated by his failure to remember their names: "Five tribunes . . . / One's Junius Brutus, / Sicinius Velutus, and I know not" (1.1.219–221). Sicinius's political power is mocked as Coriolanus calls him "this Triton of the minnows" (3.1.86). Coriolanus's constant sniping at the plebeians climaxes in his response to the declaration of his banishment: "You common cry of curs, whose breath I hate / As reek o'th'rotten fens, whose loves I prize / As the dead carcasses of unburied men / That do corrupt my air: I banish you!" (3.3.120–123). Is this a heroic inversion of the power of the entire Roman state? Is Coriolanus, single-handedly, the equal and opposite of classical civilization? Or is this the petulant attempt of an outmaneuvered loser, the final lame, playground rejoinder of a "boy of tears" (5.6.101) who can do no more than stick out his tongue?

Aufidius

Shakespeare's pairings of protagonists are rarely symmetrical. The romantic and chivalric Richard II is outflanked by the Machiavellian Bolingbroke, as is the medieval Hotspur by the modern politician Hal. Mercutio's mercurial banter hits a brick wall in the leaden dullness of Tybalt, and Antony's emotional concerns are given short shrift by the pragmatic Octavius. In the first scene of *Coriolanus,* Martius describes his enemy Aufidius as being no less a warrior than himself: "were I anything but what I am, / I would wish me only he" (1.1.232). While the cowardly plebeians are "curs" and "hares" (1.1.172–175), Aufidius is the king of the beasts: "He is a lion / That I am proud to hunt" (1.1.238–239). But Aufidius is far from leonine. In fact, when we see him at the opening of the second scene, he is discussing the cloak-and-dagger exchange of information through a network of secret agents, spies that we later see conferring

in Act IV, Scene 3: "You will be welcome with this intelligence" (30).

For all his heroic rhetoric about confronting Martius single-handedly and washing his "fierce hand in's heart" (1.10.27), Aufidius is rescued at the moment of his apparent defeat—as the stage direction reads at the climax of Act I, Scene 9: *"certain Volsces come in the aid of Aufidius."* How should we interpret this? Is their assistance, as Aufidius declares, unwelcome, "Officious and not valiant" (1.8.14)? Or have they saved him by the skin of his teeth? Just as Aufidius enters to quell the disturbance of his servants' attempted rejection of the disguised Coriolanus, one of them claims, probably disingenuously, "I'd have beaten him like a dog but for disturbing the lords within" (4.5.57). It is all very well to be brave after the event. Does this incident echo that of Aufidius's outrage: "you have shamed me in your condemnèd seconds" (1.8.14–15)? Certainly, the stubborn heroism and nobility of Martius means nothing to Aufidius, for whom might is right: "One fire drives out one fire, one nail one nail; / Rights by rights falter, strengths by strengths do fail" (4.7.54–55).

At the climax of *Troilus and Cressida,* the Trojan champion, Hector, is surrounded by a gang of Achilles' men and hacked to death. Here, as Martius and Aufidius meet single-handedly, Aufidius draws attention to the courage of the Romans' ancestor: "Wert thou the Hector / That was the whip of your bragged progeny, / Thou shouldst not 'scape me here" (1.8.11–13). Yet, with profound irony, Coriolanus's eventual murder, like that of Hector, is the result of a skirmish that pits several against one. Aufidius has organized a group of conspirators to dispatch Coriolanus, whose death will be a new beginning for his own reputation: "I'll renew me in his fall" (5.6.49). Aufidius's ruthless pragmatism seems to have won the day.

Volumnia

Rosalind, Juliet, and Portia are significant female roles in Shakespeare, but they are all young women. Perhaps, along with Paulina and Cleopatra, Volumnia is the most important role Shake-

Ellen Terry as Volumnia in an early 20th-century production of *Coriolanus (Photographed by Window & Grove)*

speare can offer an actress of middle age. This Roman matron idealizes her son's valor, which she claims is inherited from her: "Thy valiantness was mine, thou suck'st it from me" (3.2.128). This assertion is typical in running together images of breastfeeding and valor, and Volumnia's way of speaking about her son skates on very thin incestuous ice: "If my son were my husband . . ." (1.3.2); "I am in this your wife, your son" (3.2.64–65); "Thou art my warrior, / I holp to frame thee" (5.3.63–64). The discourse of maternity is right at the center of Volumnia's plea to spare Rome. Were Coriolanus to invade the city, he would be doing nothing less obscene than trampling on his mother's womb (5.3). Such an argument is unassailable, and for all his resolve to reject intercessions from Rome—"Wife, mother, child, I know not" (5.2.88)—Coriolanus must concede the outrage of rebelling against "the honoured mould / Wherein this trunk was framed" (5.3.22–33). While she has created him independent and exceptional, it is Volumnia's plea that will prove fatal to him, as she knows only too well: "or we must lose / The country . . . or else thy person" (5.3.109–110). In addition, Coriolanus is only too aware of the implications of her defeat of him: "O my mother, mother, O! / You have won a happy victory to Rome; / But for your son, believe it, O believe it, / Most dangerously you have with him prevailed, / If not most mortal to him" (5.3.186–190).

Unlike her son, Volumnia understands the importance of public relations. It is she who advises Coriolanus to humble himself in front of the citizens in order to obtain their political support: "speak / To th'people, not by your own instruction, / Nor by th'matter which your heart prompts you, / But with such words that are but roted in / Your tongue . . . perform a part / Thou hast not done before" (3.2.52–57). Cominius too, using technical vocabulary from the theater, encourages this dissimulation: "Come, come, we'll prompt you" (3.5.105). Yet, in spite of this acting tuition, Coriolanus is unable to dissemble and demonstrates only his incapacity as a performer: "Like a dull actor now / I have forgot my part, and I am out / Even to a full disgrace" (5.3.40–42). In the entrapment of Claudius's guilty conscience, in his staging of *The Mousetrap,* Hamlet illustrates the political efficacy of theater. Here, Coriolanus's incompetence demonstrates his inability to subject his maternally inspired personality to the falsity of performance: "Would you have me / False to my nature? Rather say I play / The man I am" (3.2.15–17). Might it be that the brief fifth scene of Act V, containing Volumnia's triumphant return to Rome to a standing ovation, demonstrates her theatrical brilliance at the expense of her son's leaden incompetence at varieties of impersonation? Shakespeare, himself a professional actor, knew just how important, politically and economically, such thespian proficiency could be.

Menenius

As Plutarch points out, Martius is brought up by Volumnia alone following the death of his father. Menenius is the closest thing Martius has to a surrogate, a fact he makes much of during his attempt to reverse Martius's determination to invade Rome: "my son Coriolanus . . . The glorious gods . . . love thee no worse than thy old father Menenius does! O, my son, my son" (5.2.68–76). But, without the Oedipal forces binding Hamlet to Gertrude or Coriolanus to Volumnia, Menenius is readily rejected: "Mine ears against your suits are stronger than / Your gates against my force" (5.2.94–95). Just as Falstaff is ousted from Hal's affections at the end of *Henry IV, Part 2,* hard politics takes over from previous intimacy. Coriolanus is keen to show Aufidius the extent of his determination to stand by the Volscian cause as evidenced by the abandonment of his previous foster parent: "This last old man, / Whom with a cracked heart I have sent to Rome, / Loved me above the measure of a father, / Nay, godded me indeed" (5.2.8–11).

In spite of the fact that Menenius is a patrician, the people respect him. He is "one that hath always loved the people" (1.1.52), and even though their job is to turn him out following his failed audience with Coriolanus, the watchmen in the Volscian camp readily admit that Menenius is "A noble fellow" (5.2.112). Unlike the lofty Volumnia, Menenius is concerned to act in a conciliatory capacity between Martius and the people and constantly urges, "Let's be calm . . . Not now, not now . . . Well, no more . . . Well, well, no more of that . . . On both sides more respect . . . This is the way to kindle, not to quench" (3.1.57–196).

Although a senior politician in these encounters, Menenius has a Falstaffian mischievousness about him. He readily admits that his reputation is as a "humorous patrician" (2.1.51), meaning frivolous or facetious, and he is unashamed of his partiality to a drink, remarking that he "loves a cup of hot wine with not a drop of allaying Tiber in't" (2.1.52). Frequently drunk—"I will make my very house reel tonight" (2.1.121)—it is to Menenius that Shakespeare often gives words that are dif-

ficult to pronounce, perhaps offering the actor an opportunity to stumble over them for comic effect, as if inebriated: "I cannot call you Lycurguses" (2.1.60); "your bisson conspectuities" (2.1.69); or "I would not have been so 'fidiussed . . ." (2.1.144).

In a parodic allusion to his interest in the allegory of the body politic—his story of the belly in the play's opening scene—he admits that he is "one that converses more with the buttock of the night than with the forehead of the morning" (2.1.56–57), and this comic turn of phrase is developed as Menenius sends up the legal position of the tribunes who, during their hearing of a legal case, are troubled with wind "and in roaring for a chamberpot, dismiss the controversy bleeding" (2.1.76–77). The last word here might mean "unresolved" (that is, the controversy remains without a verdict) or it may refer to the urinating of blood, one of the play's many images of a diseased body politic.

DIFFICULTIES OF THE PLAY

In the opinion of Frank Kermode, *Coriolanus* "is probably the most difficult play in the canon" (244). Much of this difficulty is owing to obscurity of expression (a couple of these passages are examined in the "Difficult Passages" section below), which may originate in textual corruption (there are no quartos of the play, and we only have the text as it appears in the First Folio of 1623). But part of the difficulty experienced by a modern audience is in the play's very specific allusions to the problems of Jacobean England. The more topical a work of literature, the greater is its inseparability from the moment of its composition and the greater the difficulty it presents for an audience distanced from, and therefore unfamiliar with, its historical context.

During the first decade of the 17th century, food shortages caused discontent and rebellion among the rural poor. This reached a high point in 1607, the year of the Midlands Uprising. Janette Dillon explains how exceptionally close the conflict was to Shakespeare's heart: "*Coriolanus* is unusual in engaging so directly with a popular event like a rising, and one that bore more closely on Shakespeare's Stratford connections than on his connections with the court via the King's Men; for the Midlands Rising, as the name indicates, took place across several Midlands counties, including Warwickshire" (140). A number of critics have suggested that the play's surprisingly full and precise stage directions may be because, while his troupe was rehearsing and putting on the play, Shakespeare himself was actually in Stratford. Certainly, the death and funeral of his mother in early September 1608 would have put him in the town at about this time. If so, his acquaintance with the uprising, according to Parker, "whose centre had been very close to Stratford" (Shakespeare 7), would have been even more intimate than Dillon suggests.

Whether he was on the spot, Shakespeare himself had, like the patricians, been accused of stashing grain in order to inflate its price: "he was named in 1598 for having illegally hoarded ten quarters (eighty bushels) of malt or corn during one such shortage" (Dillon 141). In Plutarch, the rebellion is caused by the patricians' tolerance of usury and the hoarding of corn is a secondary grievance, but in Shakespeare's version, hunger is, from the outset, the motivation for the mutiny: "You are all resolved rather to die than to famish?" (1.1.4).

Since the end of the Middle Ages, the feudalistic social structures, with the lord of the manor protecting the serfs in return for their agricultural labor, had started to change as the result of new economic pressures. Strip farming was deemed to be inefficient, and in any case, the burgeoning wool trade with continental Europe required large tracts of land for grazing. Such pasture, hitherto held in common, was fenced in, and the rural poor were evicted to make their way in the world as best they could. Sir Thomas More's *Utopia* captures the impoverished condition of the dispossessed: "your sheep that were wont to be so meek and tame and so small eaters, now, as I hear say, be become so great devourers and so wild, that they eat up and swallow down the very men themselves. They consume, destroy, and devour whole fields, houses, and cities. [The politically powerful] enclose all

into pastures; they throw down houses; they pluck down towns, and leave nothing standing but only the church to be made a sheep-house" (26). The poor, "thrust out of their own," were compelled to make their way to the cities in search of work. This led to an exponential rise in the population of London and a concomitant strengthening of the draconian legislation that attempted to control the new influx.

This panic can be seen in the malevolent figure of the mob that jostles uncontrollably at the edge of Renaissance drama: for example, the illiterate rabble who rebel under Jack Cade in *Henry VI, Part 2,* who kill those who can read simply because they cannot. Again, in *Julius Caesar,* the riotous crowd kill Cinna the poet because he unfortunately happens to share a name with one of the conspirators. In *Coriolanus,* the plebeians are the monster from Greek myth, the "Hydra" (3.1.95), the "many-headed multitude" (2.3.15) and "The beast / With many heads" (4.1.1–2). The Third Citizen is well aware of the suitability of the metaphor given their ungovernable plurality of opinion: "I think if all our wits were to issue out of one skull, they would fly east, west, north, south, and their consent of one direct way should be at once to all points o'th'compass" (2.3.19–22). While the historical background of the play sheds light on treatment of social class, the contempt articulated by the patricians, notably Coriolanus himself, toward the plebeians is sure to sound inimical to modern democratic sensibilities. Again, the imaginative leap required of a modern audience or the reader is to become one of Shakespeare's contemporaries rather than forcing him, as is so often the case, to become one of ours.

KEY PASSAGES
Act I, Scene 1, 99–159

MENENIUS. There was a time when all the
  body's members,
Rebelled against the belly, thus accused it:
That only like a gulf it did remain
I'th'midst o'th'body, idle and unactive,
Still cupboarding the viand, never bearing

Like labour with the rest; where th'other
  instruments
Did see and hear, devise, instruct, walk, feel,
And, mutually participate, did minister
Unto the appetite and affection common
Of the whole body. The belly answered—

[FIRST] CITIZEN. Well, sir, what answer
  made the belly?

MENENIUS. Sir, I shall tell you. With a kind
  of smile,
Which ne'er came from the lungs, but even
  thus—
For, look you, I may make the belly smile
As well as speak—it tauntingly replied
To th'discontented members, the mutinous
  parts
That envied his receipt; even so most fitly
As you malign our senators for that
They are not such as you.

[FIRST] CITIZEN. Your belly's
  answer—what?
The kingly, crownèd head, the vigilant eye,
The counsellor heart, the arm our soldier,
Our steed the leg, the tongue our trumpeter.
With other muniments and petty helps
In this our fabric, if that they—

MENENIUS. What then?
Fore me, this fellow speaks! What then, what
  then?

[FIRST] CITIZEN. Should by the cormorant
  belly be restrained,
Who is the sink o'th'body—

MENENIUS. Well, what then?

[FIRST] CITIZEN. The former agents, if they
  did complain,
What could the belly answer?

MENENIUS. I will tell you,

If you'll bestow a small—of what you have
  little—
Patience a while, you'st hear the belly's
  answer.

[FIRST] CITIZEN. You're long about it.

MENENIUS. Note me this, good friend:
Your most grave belly was deliberate,
Not rash like his accusers, and thus answered:
'True is it, my incorporate friends,' quoth he,
'That I receive the general food at first
Which you do live upon, and fit it is,
Because I am the storehouse and the shop
Of the whole body. But, if you do remember,
I send it through the rivers of your blood,
Even to the court, the heart, to th'seat
  o'th'brain;
And through the cranks and offices of man
The strongest nerves and small inferior veins
From me receive that natural competency
Whereby they live. And though that all at
  once,
You, my good friends'—this says the belly,
  mark me—

[FIRST] CITIZEN. Ay, sir, well, well.

MENENIUS. 'Though all at once cannot
See what I do deliver out to each,
Yet I can make my audit up that all
From me do back receive the flour of all,
And leave me but the bran.' What say you to't?

[FIRST] CITIZEN. It was an answer. How
  apply you this?

MENENIUS. The senators of Rome are this
  good belly,
And you the mutinous members. For examine
Their counsels and their cares, digest things
  rightly
Touching the weal o'th'common, you shall find
No public benefit which you receive
But it proceeds or comes from them to you

And no way from yourselves. What do you
  think,
You, the great toe of this assembly?

In an attempt to defuse the aggression to which
the mob intends to subject Martius, Menenius
tells them an allegory about a human body whose
organs are rebelling against the belly, whom they
consider to be greedy, "idle and unactive, / Still
cupboarding the viand [food]." While the other
organs "Did see and hear, devise, instruct, walk,
feel," the belly remained at the center, apparently
contributing nothing. The citizen agrees with the
rebellious organs itemizing the other parts of the
body in military terms: "The counsellor heart,
the arm our soldier, / Our steed the leg, the
tongue our trumpeter." The body is thus an army
that depends on good counsel, military strength,
transport, and communication, in other words, a
harmonious unity of different elements working
together cooperatively. By contrast, the body of
Menenius's allegory is in disarray as the various
organs fight against the belly for their fair share.
However, Menenius goes on to explain that the
belly is falsely accused, for while it seems not to be
contributing to the body's overall health, in fact,
as the belly itself points out, it has the job of processing the food into nourishment and "send[ing]
it through the rivers of your blood / Even to the
court, the heart, to th'seat o'th'brain." Furthermore, the belly is so generous in sending out supplies, that it is left with "but the bran." The citizens
apparently accept the justice of this story until the
point at which Menenius is required to explain its
relevance to the current situation: "How apply you
this?" one of them asks.

Menenius's response is hardly deferential: "The
senators of Rome are this good belly, / And you
the mutinous members." All "public benefit which
you receive," insists Menenius, originates with the
senators and flows from the Capitol like the nourishment from the belly. Their rebellion not only
is unjust in abusing the senators, who are assidu-
ous in their care of the plebeians, but such sedition
defies the processes of nature itself. Thus, the force

of the metaphor of the body politic lies in characterizing any uprising against the belly / ("senators
of Rome") as fundamentally unnatural. The ideo-
logical effect of the symbol of the body politic is to
naturalize the historically contingent inequalities
of powerful and powerless, patrician and plebeian,
master and servant: Such distinctions are as natural as the difference between the heart and "the
great toe."

Shakespeare probably found the myth of the
belly in various classical sources such as Livy's
Roman History and Plutarch's *Lives,* but he may
also have known such versions as in Philip Sidney's
Apologie for Poetrie (1595) and William Camden's
Remaines of a greater worke concerning Britaine
(1605), published just two or three years before he
wrote *Coriolanus.* The popularity of the tale testifies to the ubiquity of the idea of the human body
as a pattern of the larger schemes of the natural
realm. One of the most common assumptions of
early modern philosophy, theology, and medicine
was the analogical relationship between the human
body and the world surrounding it, a resemblance
sometimes referred to as microcosm-macrocosm.
As exemplified in Leonardo da Vinci's *Vitruvian
Man,* a pen-and-ink drawing (1490) that details
the proportions of the human figure, the harmonious male body was the epitome of the divine plan
of creation itself, at the center of the eternal cir-
cularity of the *"Primum Mobile,"* or "First Mover"
(God). The female body—constantly and immod-
estly leaking and created, to begin with, out of a
crooked rib—was inherently flawed, but the male
body represented the high point of God's creative
capacity. This explains the anatomical drawings of
figures pictured against pastoral landscapes, oblig-
ingly holding open their stomachs or flaying their
own limbs. The mechanics of the body are part of
the natural scheme of things, and there was a connection between the physicality of the body and its
environment. So, for instance, the walnut, consisting of two wrinkled hemispheres housed in a hard
shell, resembled the brain, which was made up of
two wrinkled hemispheres and housed in the skull.
The cure for headaches was therefore walnut, as

there was a "sympathy" between the one and the other (Foucault 17–45).

Similarly, in political discourse, the well-tuned human body symbolized the ordered state. The fact that some organs are more important than others justifies the inequitable distribution of power and money about which the plebeians of *Coriolanus* are so concerned. As Camden put it in 1605, "the stomacke was served, the limbes comforted, and peace re-established. Even so it fareth with the bodies of Common-weale; for albeit the Princes gather much, yet not so much for themselves, as for others: So that if they want, they cannot supply the want of others; therefore do not repine [be discontented] at Princes herein, but respect the common good of the whole publike estate" (Bullough 552). If princes are rich, in other words, it is for the shared benefit of the commonwealth. Such a logic is obviously open to challenge, although in *Coriolanus,* the plebeians barely get the chance to answer back as Martius enters and starts railing at them.

This passage thus serves to illustrate the appeasing personality of Menenius, who attempts to pacify the mob. The tale also introduces a pattern of imagery relating to food and eating, which runs throughout the play and finds its most violent expression in images of cannibalism: Martius talks of the plebeians that "Would feed on one another" (1.1.185); Martius's soldiers, seeing him shut within the gates of Corioles, suspect that he has gone "To th'pot" (1.5.20); Volumnia remarks that "Anger's my meat: I'll sup upon myself" (4.2.53), and Aufidius's servants image the superiority of Coriolanus over their master as though he were devouring him (4.5.193). Finally, the images of the belly, dining, and food are all obviously and immediately relevant to a play that begins in a riot over hunger.

Act I, Scene 3, 32–73

VOLUMNIA. Methinks I hear hither your husband's drum,
See him pluck Aufidius down by th'hair;
As children from a bear, the Volsces shunning him.
Methinks I see him stamp thus, and call thus:

'Come on, you cowards, you were got in fear
Though you were born in Rome!' His bloody brow
With his mailed hand then wiping, forth he goes,
Like to a harvest-man that's tasked to mow
Or all or lose his hire.

VIRGILIA. His bloody brow? O Jupiter, no blood!

VOLUMNIA. Away, you fool! It more becomes a man
Than gilt his trophy. The breasts of Hecuba
When she did suckle Hector looked not lovelier
Than Hector's forehead when it spit forth blood
At Grecian sword, contemning.—
[To the Gentlewoman] Tell Valeria,
We are fit to bid her welcome.
[Exit Gentlewoman]

VIRGILIA. Heavens bless my lord from fell Aufidius!

VOLUMNIA. He'll beat Aufidius' head below his knee And tread upon his neck.
[Enter Valeria, with an usher and the Gentlewoman]
VALERIA. My ladies both, good day to you.

VOLUMNIA. Sweet madam.

VIRGILIA. I am glad to see your ladyship.

VALERIA. How do you both? You are manifest house-keepers.
[To Volumnia] What are you sewing here? A fine spot, in good faith.
[To Virgilia] How does your little son?

VIRGILIA. I thank your ladyship; well, good madam.

VOLUMNIA. He had rather see the swords and hear a drum than look upon his schoolmaster.

VALERIA. O' my word, the father's son! I'll swear 'tis a very pretty boy. O' my troth, I looked upon him o' Wednesday half an hour together: 'has such a confirmed countenance! I saw him run after a gilded butterfly, and when he caught it he let it go again, and after it again, and over and over he comes, and up again, catched it again. Or whether his fall enraged him, or how 'twas, he did so set his teeth and tear it! O, I warrant, how he mammocked it!

VOLUMNIA. One on's father's moods.

VALERIA. Indeed, la, 'tis a noble child.

This scene is part of the play's exposition. Scene 1 introduces us to the mob, Menenius, and Martius; Scene 2, to Aufidius. Now, in this scene, we meet Volumnia, who in the final act, will turn the play 180 degrees with her plea to her son not to sack Rome. Shakespeare's job as a dramatist is to provide us with a portrait of a personality so powerful that at the play's climax, she can stand up to Coriolanus and stop him in his tracks. We have already seen how intractable, headstrong, and intransigent he is. Shakespeare must therefore introduce and, more important, develop a character who is somehow the equal and opposite of Martius. Consequently, this scene is entirely Shakespeare's own invention and not found in any of his sources.

In Plutarch's version, Volumnia is a single parent: "Martius . . . being left an orphan by his father, was brought up under his mother a widowe, who taught us by experience, that orphanage bringeth many discommodities to a childe" (Bullough 505). One such "discommodity," in this case, was a poor schooling to which Plutarch attributes Martius's short temper: "for lacke of education, he was so chollericke and impacient, that he would yeld to no living creature: which made him churlishe, uncivill, and altogether unfit for any mans conversation" (Bullough 506). This thin education is remarked on several times in Shakespeare's play. Menenius notes that Martius "has been bred i'th'wars / . . .

Volumnia and Virgilia discuss Martius in Act I, Scene 3 of *Coriolanus*. This print is from the Boydell Shakespeare Gallery project, which was first conceived in 1786 and lasted until 1805. *(Painting by Robert Ker Porter; engraving by James Stow)*

and is ill-schooled / In bolted [refined] language" (3.1.323–325), and Martius himself admits that he is more competent at fighting than oratory: "oft / When blows have made me stay I fled from words" (2.2.69–70). Yet, far from being maternally embarrassed by her son's weak education, Volumnia prizes violence over learning. Of Young Martius, she remarks glowingly, "He had rather see the swords and hear a drum than look upon his schoolmaster."

The dramatic function of this scene is to demonstrate the household roots of Martius's (and Young Martius's) propensity toward and capacity for brutality. While the scene looks like one of domestic calm, especially since it follows the public violence of the rioting plebeians as well as Aufidius's more sinister plotting, it rapidly moves from the quiet of two women sewing to Volumnia's febrile fantasies on the importance of her son's cutting down his enemies: "Methinks I hear hither your husband's drum, / See him pluck Aufidius down by th'hair; / As children from a bear, the Volsces shunning him." This is a woman who has fully internalized the patriarchal brutality of Roman honor and who imagines, not children cuddling a teddy bear (to be slightly anachronistic), as much as children fleeing from a bear for their lives. In *The Winter's Tale,* Shakespeare juxtaposes, in a single scene, the ferocity of a bear with the vulnerability of a newborn babe. Compressed in Volumnia's image of the Volsces fleeing the growling Martius is the slaughter that would have occurred in *The Winter's Tale* had the bear got his claws on the infant (as it is, he tears out the shoulder of a grown man and dines on the rest of the body). As far as Volumnia is concerned, the more blood the better. "His bloody brow" is his badge of bravery. Virgilia's squeamish reaction— "O Jupiter, no blood!"—is met with Volumnia's scorn: "Away, you fool!"

There then follows one of the most disturbing images in the whole of Shakespeare: "The breasts of Hecuba / When she did suckle Hector looked not lovelier / Than Hector's forehead when it spit forth blood / At Grecian sword, contemning." Images of maternal nurturing and the cloven skull of the Trojan champion are run together in an orgy of the most disturbing kind: breasts, lactation, gushing blood, wounds, weapons. On the one hand, the loveliness of the breastfeeding mother inspires a kind of guilty prurience; on the other, the gushing head wound evokes complete disgust (Who would want Volumnia as a mother?). In an ironic adumbration of the play's final moment, Volumnia prophesies how Martius will "tread upon [Aufidius's] neck." In fact, after he has killed Coriolanus in Act V, Scene 6, the stage direction reads *"Aufidius stands on him."*

In order to prevent Volumnia from getting carried away, Shakespeare has Valeria enter the scene. In Plutarch's version of the story, it is Valeria who initiates the women's embassy to Coriolanus to beg him to spare Rome. Shakespeare's play gives her a less prominent role, and her function here is, at least initially, to change the topic of the conversation from Volumnia's weird blood lust back to domestic and familial matters. Yet, her opening remark, "You are manifest house-keepers," perhaps implies with a hint of mockery that she considers herself to be more a woman of the world than they, and, indeed, later in the scene she provides them with the latest military updates.

In keeping with the homely setting, Valeria inquires about the well-being of Virgilia's little boy. Virgilia responds politely, "I thank your ladyship; well, good madam." But this courteous small talk is ruptured by violence again as Valeria recounts how she watched Young Martius pursue and dismember a harmless butterfly with his teeth. The image of a young boy gratuitously tearing apart the ethereal and delicate butterfly highlights the brutality of Roman "honor." Note how Valeria describes the glinting butterfly wings as "gilded," which ironically echoes Volumnia's excited protestation that blood "more becomes a man / Than gilt his trophy"; the two kinds of gilding—the natural glint of the gossamer wing and the human-made larding of objects with sheet gold—demonstrate the gap between the beauties of nature and the horror of human savagery. In *Coriolanus,* the most domestically peaceful setting is never far from the language and images of violence.

Act IV, Scene 4, 13–26

CORIOLANUS. O world, thy slippery turns!
  Friends now fast sworn,
Whose double bosoms seem to wear one heart,
Whose house, whose bed, whose meal and
  exercise,
Are still together, who twin as 'twere in love
Unseparable, shall within this hour,
On a dissension of a doit, break out
To bitterest enmity. So fellest foes,

Whose passions and whose plots have broke
  their sleep
To take the one the other, by some chance,
Some trick not worth an egg, shall grow dear
  friends
And interjoin their issues. So with me.
My birthplace hate I, and my love's upon
This enemy town. I'll enter. If he slay me,
He does fair justice; if he give me way,
I'll do his country service.
  [*Exit*]

The action-packed world of *Coriolanus* rarely permits the opportunity to listen to characters thinking out loud. The contemplative self-analysis of Hamlet that made him such a sought-after quarry for Sigmund Freud or Ernest Jones in the heady days of the development of psychoanalytic criticism has no place in this broad and rapidly sweeping political drama. On the other hand, the mischievous intimacy that Richard III shares with the audience about his next victim requires him to address us in confidence. Hamlet speaks soliloquies; Richard whispers asides. Martius is unlike both these characters, without the self-consciousness of Hamlet or the ingratiating, if malicious, appeal of Richard. Instead, as he continually insists and as others remark of him, he acts "alone" (1.5.24, 1.8.77, 1.10.8, 4.1.30, 5.6.117). This extract, then, in which Coriolanus ponders the nature of friendship and enmity, is neither soliloquy nor aside, and yet, it shares features with both these kinds of speech. Like the soliloquy, it ponders a human problem that is larger than the predicament in which the tragic hero is currently situated: Questions about the quality and longevity of intimacy (Hamlet asked questions about the morality of suicide, in general, as well as his own, in particular). Like the aside, the speech tells us what this particular speaker intends to do next: To enter Antium and offer his services or his life to Aufidius. It is a rare instance of this play pressing the pause button, as it were, in order to take stock of the reality of lived experience beyond the world of the play. At the same time, it tells us, in narrative terms, what is coming next.

In Plutarch, following his banishment, Coriolanus retires to the country to ponder his options: "he remained a fewe dayes in the countrie at his houses, turmoyled with sundry sortes and kynde of thoughtes, suche as the fyer of his choller dyd sturre up. In the ende, seeing he could resolve no waye, to take a profitable or honorable course, but only was pricked forward still to be revenged of the Romaines: he thought to raise up some great warres against them, by their neerest neighbours" (Bullough 526). This passage of the play corresponds to Coriolanus's rural retreat. Clearly, being faithful to his source would require Shakespeare to devise yet another setting—Coriolanus's country seat, probably peopled with staff (as is the household of Aufidius) and other details. Shakespeare, therefore, found it far more economic to have Coriolanus pause before the house of Aufidius and think through his options out loud.

The speech proceeds logically in two opposing directions. First of all, Coriolanus recognizes the capacity for dissension between friends. Just as apparently unlikely, yet just as possible, is the sudden alliance between enemies. The passage echoes one in which Helena in *A Midsummer Night's Dream* remembers the intimacy she once shared with her childhood friend, Hermia, who now seems to be rejecting her: "We, Hermia, like two artificial gods / Have with our needles created both one flower, / Both on one sampler, sitting on one cushion, / Both warbling of one song, both in one key, / As if our hands, our sides, voices, and minds / Had been incorporate. So we grew together, / Like to a double cherry: seeming parted, / But yet an union in partition, / Two lovely berries moulded on one stem" (3.2.204–212). Note the way the passage repeats and interweaves the words *both* and *one*. The idea is of "union in partition," that the two halves complement each other. The repeated word in Coriolanus's speech is *whose*, while he, too, places pairs of opposites together cramming plurality into singularity and vice-versa: "double . . . one" and "Unseparable . . . dissension." This relates to a commonplace of Renaissance epistemology, that of *discordia concors,* or the belief that the apparent chaos and randomness of the world concealed the harmony of God. At the end of *The Merchant of Venice,* Lorenzo talks about how, since the fall of Adam, we have been unable to hear the music of the spheres: "Such harmony is in immortal souls, / But while this muddy vesture of decay / Doth grossly close it in, we cannot hear it" (5.1.63–65). Under *discordia,* there is *concors.* Under the many, there is the one.

The contention between friends is paradoxically, claims Coriolanus, over something trivial, the "dissension of a doit." A doit was half an English farthing, proverbial for a tiny sum of money as when Menenius remarks that "I'd not have given a doit" (5.4.57). There is then a complete mismatch between the scale of the former friends' reaction—"bitterest enmity"—and the cause of their quarrel. Paradoxically, the smaller the stakes, the more intense the animosity. This paradox is implicit in the description of the two friends who are "fast sworn." "Fast" (like the word *cleave*) contains its own opposite, meaning fixed and still, as in "stuck fast," but also fleeting and rapidly moving, as in "fast runner." It is an instance of the care with which Shakespeare the poet is closely attuned to the idiosyncrasies of the language.

Likewise, though contrariwise, what were two sworn enemies, "fellest foes," may join forces and collaborate against a third party. Again, the determination to destroy the enemy is far in excess of the method of assassination, which may be an opportunistic wile, "Some trick not worth an egg." In *Hamlet,* the Prince remarks on the extravagance of defending a piece of land so small as to be not worth an "eggshell" (4.4.44), while the Fool in *King Lear* goads his master with the thought that he has voided the contents of his kingdom leaving only an empty eggshell behind (1.4.139–142). Significance originates in insignificance: chancy, fickle, or as Coriolanus puts it, "slippery."

Coriolanus concludes with the possibility of forming an alliance with his enemy, Antium, since his former friend, Rome, is now the object of his abhorrence: "My birthplace hate I, and my love's upon / This enemy town." The counterintuitive

logic is conspicuous in the connection between "slay" and "justice": "If he [Aufidius] slay me, / He does fair justice." Poised on the uncertainty of this illogical logic, the scene ends in suspense.

DIFFICULT PASSAGES
Act I, Scene 9, 37–52

MARTIUS. I thank you, general,
But cannot make my heart consent to take
A bribe to pay my sword. I do refuse it,
And stand upon my common part with those
That have upheld the doing.
[A long flourish. They all cry 'Martius!
  Martius!', casting up their caps and lances.
  Cominius and
  Lartius stand bare]
May these same instruments which you
  profane
Never sound more. When drums and trumpets
  shall
I'th'field prove flatterers, let courts and cities be
Made all of false-faced soothing!
When steel grows soft as the parasite's silk,
Let him be made an ovator for th'wars!
No more, I say! For that I have not washed
My nose that bled, or foiled some debile
  wretch,
Which without note here's many else have done,
You shout me forth
In acclamations hyperbolical;
As if I loved my little should be dieted
In praises sauced with lies.

Menenius attributes Martius's rhetorical shortcomings to an education that emphasized martial rather than oratorical skills: "he has been bred i'th'wars / Since a could draw a sword, and is ill-schooled / In bolted language" (3.1.323–325). In this extract, Martius's response to Cominius's offer of reward for his brave fighting typifies his linguistic limitations. The passage is particularly difficult as a result of Martius's embarrassment, which leads him to mangle his speech even more than usual. For all his arrogance, we know that Martius shuns public adulation. Here, his single-handed defeat of

Corioles prompts Cominius to offer him a tenth of all the spoils they have taken. Martius thanks him but "cannot make my heart consent to take / A bribe to pay my sword." So far so good, but when the stage direction calls for elaborate celebration, Martius is intensely ruffled and seeks to justify his self-righteousness by describing the evils of flattery. The instruments used to signal maneuvers on the battlefield, "drums and trumpets," will be "profaned" when used merely as musical accompaniments for empty congratulatory gestures. If soldiers prove flatterers, courts and cities will be even more hypocritical ("false-faced soothing") than they are at present.

There then follows the play's most argued-over couple of lines: "When steel grows soft as the parasite's silk, / Let him be made an ovator for th'wars!" Assuming "him" refers back to "parasite" (a flatterer) and given that "ovator" is, as the *Oxford English Dictionary* defines it, "One who receives an ovation," we might paraphrase the lines as "At that point when armor becomes as yielding as the flatterer's soft clothing, may the flatterer himself be applauded for his contribution to the battlefield." However, other editors have *overture* rather than *ovator* (the First Folio prints *"Ouerture"*), which might, assuming the word means "opening," change the meaning of the lines to something such as, "At that point when armor becomes as yielding as the flatterer's soft clothing, may the flatterer himself lead the attack." Other editors emend *ovator* to *coverture*, meaning that the flatterer should be sent into battle wearing a soft silk costume rather than armor.

Although the passage is textually uncertain and syntactically confusing, in all three cases, flattery is shown to be inimical to the war effort. "No more, I say!"—the simplicity of the imperative contrasts abruptly with the complex language of the previous lines. Just because his nose is still bloody, just because he has defeated "some debile wretch" (*debile* meaning "weak" as in *debilitated*), which many other soldiers have also done, although unnoticed ("without note"), you "shout me forth / In acclamations hyperbolical," you cheer me in

exaggerated approbation as if I desired my small achievements (*"little"* is here a noun, not an adjective) should be nourished in glorifications seasoned with lies. The speech as a whole is typical of Martius's awkward blend of modesty and haughtiness, egocentricity and camaraderie: "I . . . stand upon my common part," meaning he is one with the other soldiers. But for all these protests, he is clearly exceptional.

Act I, Scene 10, 36–53

A SOLDIER. He's the devil.

AUFIDIUS. Bolder, though not so subtle. My
  valour, poisoned
With only suff'ring stain by him, for him
Shall fly out of itself. Nor sleep nor sanctuary,
Being naked, sick, nor fane nor Capitol,
The prayers of priests nor times of sacrifice—
Embargements all of fury—shall lift up
Their rotten privilege and custom 'gainst
My hate to Marcius. Where I find him, were it
At home upon my brother's guard, even there,
Against the hospitable canon, would I
Wash my fierce hand in's heart. Go you to
  th'city.

This is the first time we see Aufidius following his defeat at the hands of Martius (1.9). Clearly still smarting, the tortured syntax and obscurity of diction underline his intense hatred for his lifelong enemy. The soldier offers a straightforward enough comparison: Martius is like "the devil"—furious, vengeful but also to be feared because of his power. Perhaps this is why instead of merely agreeing with or elaborating on his remark, Aufidius is needled by the soldier's fearful respect for Martius and launches into a vehement denunciation of him, likening his hatred of Martius to a kind of religious faith: "The prayers of priests [and] sacrifice" will not be enough to assuage his determination to rip out Martius's heart and "Wash my fierce hand" in his blood. (Shakespeare's audience would have been familiar with the public display of human hearts cut from the chests of publicly executed traitors. In *The*

Merchant of Venice, Shakespeare narrowly avoids staging such a gross butchering.) Aufidius laments that his own bravery is disgraced by that of Martius but determines that wherever he finds Martius, he will murder him, whether that be while Martius is asleep or on his sickbed, even claiming sanctuary in the "fane" (temple) or the "Capitol" itself (one is reminded of the outrageous location of the assassination of Julius Caesar). Even if the priests were to intercede for Martius or the sacred ritual of sacrifice were occurring, neither would stop Aufidius from exercising vengeance for being so humiliated. Supposing Martius were standing as a protective guard over Aufidius's own brother, even that would not be sufficient to save him. Aufidius, in defiance of the laws of noble hospitality, would slaughter him there and then and cut his heart out.

The final perfunctory half-line, "Go you to th'city," suggests that Aufidius has caught himself fantasizing out loud and quickly attempts to revert to his position as cool-headed commander in chief. The speech might be played as a kind of rant out loud. As such, it would both illustrate the intensity of Aufidius's hatred and also imply his own tendency (which he shares with Martius) to allow himself to become unhinged by his temper.

Notice the powerful sense of negation in the extract: "not . . . Nor . . . nor . . . nor . . . nor"—six negatives compressed into the first five lines of Aufidius's response. Note also his nihilistic vocabulary: "poisoned," "suff'ring," "stain," "sick," "fury," "rotten," "hate," "fierce." While Aufidius initiates a new sentence at "Nor sleep nor sanctuary," the verb ("lift up") does not come till three lines later so that the grammar is stumbling as a result of Aufidius's emotional disturbance. Note also the way in which, in a play that insists on the importance of names and voices, Aufidius avoids (except once) the use of Martius's name: "him . . . him . . . him . . . in's." In the final scene, Aufidius refuses to honor Martius with the name of Coriolanus (5.6.90–92). The effect of the passage is to illustrate the emotional intensity of Aufidius's hatred as well as its tendency to destabilize the hater.

CRITICAL INTRODUCTION TO THE PLAY
Theater: Space and Audience

Epic poetry of the classical period very often begins in medias res, in the middle of things, a device Shakespeare borrows for the first scene of *Coriolanus.* Although Shakespeare's main source, Plutarch's *Lives,* describes Martius's family background and upbringing before we get to the story of his dreadful relationship with the populace, Shakespeare dispenses with all the contextual material and begins his play amid a scene of riot—at once more dramatic and arresting than the beginning of his source.

The wrangling between the plebeians opens the play and continues for almost 50 lines until the entry of Menenius Agrippa. Although he is a patrician (the class against whom the mob is revolting), Menenius is held in high regard by the people, and they are prepared to pause their offensive and listen to him. His allegory of the belly is one of those strange protracted speeches in Shakespeare that pauses the frenetic action with which the play has opened. It is not unlike the lengthy and self-indulgent account of the injustices done to him with which Prospero regales his daughter Miranda in Act I, Scene 2 of *The Tempest,* a chronicle so undramatic and potentially tedious that he has to keep checking that she is paying attention: "Thou attend'st not!" (87) or "Dost thou hear?" (106). The soporific effect of his speech is all the more intense following, as it does, the excitement of the storm scene with which *The Tempest* opens. Both in Menenius's fable of the belly and Prospero's account of his usurpation and exile, Shakespeare seems to be testing his audience's capacity to interpret spectacular events—the riot or the storm—and the quieter aptitude for listening to and processing large amounts of information—Menenius's allegory or Prospero's back history. The First Citizen's impatience with Menenius and Miranda's apparent boredom demonstrate that the playwright knows just how big a risk he is taking with his audience.

By 1608, the probable year of the first performance of *Coriolanus,* the professional theater was a comparatively recent invention. Purpose-built auditoriums, in which salaried actors performed fully scripted plays in English (student amateur dramatics were in Latin), had only been around for about three decades: James Burbage's Theatre dated from 1576, and Henry Lanham's Curtain was built the following year. Shakespeare and his contemporary playwrights were thus experimenting with a new art form and pioneering dramatic devices that demanded, for brutal economic reasons, that they be successful. This was a steep learning curve, and one of the most characteristic of Shakespearean devices is the self-consciousness with which such techniques are explored. It is not accidental that the playwright so frequently stages troupes of actors rehearsing or performing for onstage audiences—for example, Bottom and the mechanicals in *A Midsummer Night's Dream,* the masque of the Nine Worthies in *Love's Labour's Lost,* the mumming play in *Henry VIII,* the masque of the goddesses in *The Tempest,* or perhaps the most well known, the traveling players whom Hamlet directs with such determination at Elsinore. Shakespeare seems constantly to be asking questions about the function and practice of theater itself, about the relationship between the player and the audience and among the audience members themselves. The variety of pace with which he opens *Coriolanus* and *The Tempest* is, as we have seen, an instance of the degree to which he is impatiently testing the theater to the point of destruction.

The acquisition by the King's Men of the indoor Blackfriars Theatre in 1608 may have intensified Shakespeare's search for answers to these theatrical questions. Evidence suggests that this was the first play Shakespeare wrote for an indoor playhouse. There were two key differences between outdoor and indoor stagings—the first, technical and to do with the stage; the second, demographic and to do with the audience.

In the first place, the indoor theater provided the King's Men with a number of technical possibilities unavailable in an open-air playhouse. An indoor theater is without natural light and therefore susceptible to variations in artificial lighting levels, depending on the number of candles used as well as their location. As Martin White insists, "A dramatist writing for an indoor playhouse . . . knew he had the facility to adjust the lighting states, if only to a limited degree, and there is substantial evidence in the texts of indoor plays . . . that variations in mood were effected, or at least supported, by appropriate changes in the light levels" (149). In *Coriolanus,* there are several scenes that would benefit atmospherically from being staged in half-light. Act IV, Scenes 4 and 5 appear to take place at "night" (4.4.10), and the crepuscular setting would make the hooded or shrouded figure of the disguised Martius all the more powerful and malevolent. Aufidius's erotic description of his dreams is likely to be intensified and made even more intimate if played by dim candlelight: "I have nightly since / Dreamt of encounters 'twixt thyself and me—/ We have been down together in my sleep . . ." (4.5.124–126). Similarly, the scenes of whispering and spying such as Act I, Scene 2 or the beginning of Act V, Scene 6 might be staged without a bright lighting cover in order to evoke the dark corners and secluded spaces in which political information changes hands. At the top of Act IV, Scene 3, Adrian has difficulty in identifying his old acquaintance, Nicanor, which suggests that their conspiratorial meeting might be taking place in the shadows. There is also the domestic interior of Act I, Scene 3, which may be lit as though taking place in a private chamber. In contrast, there are the obviously public and conspicuous scenes such as the various triumphal entries (for example, 2.1 or 5.5), the battle scenes, or the play's climax, the communal supplication of the women on behalf of Rome (5.3). Throughout, then, there is a constant switching between public spectacle and private intimacy and, were *Coriolanus* staged indoors, these contrasts could be signaled by different lighting states.

The other major technical device promoted by the indoor theater is the use of music. *Coriolanus* is riddled throughout by alarums (as in the stage directions to 1.4.3, 1.8, or 1.9), drums (the stage directions to the opening of 1.4 or 1.9.67), trumpets (the stage directions to 1.8 or 1.9.67) and cornets (the stage direction to 1.9.94). But, as well as these martial instruments, there is also the quieter music for the feast of Aufidius's household; at the top of Act IV, Scene 5 is the stage direction *"Music plays."* Clearly this would be something more mellifluous than the blaring trumpets and loud drums of the battlefield. Again, the triumphal entry of Volumnia in Act V, Scene 5 is met with *"A flourish with drums and trumpets,"* which is likely to be loud and celebratory. In direct contrast to this is the lamentable dirge with which the play ends: *"Exeunt bearing the dead body of Martius. A dead march is sounded."* There is then, throughout *Coriolanus*, a wide variety of different kinds of music from the exultant to the funereal, from the brazenly public to the domestically hushed. The play has more music cues than any other by Shakespeare, and if we are correct in our assumption that *Coriolanus* is his first indoor play, it is more than likely that the play's marked employment of music demonstrates the degree to which the playwright was characteristically experimenting with the very latest technology.

One of the most impressive stage directions in the whole of Shakespeare is the insistence on stillness after much frenzied activity and noise: *"He holds her by the hand, silent"* (5.3.183). In Trevor Nunn's 1973 RSC production, Nicol Williamson's Coriolanus waited for a protracted 60 seconds before taking Margaret Tyzack's Volumnia by the hand. He then paused for a further soundless 90 seconds before the fatalistic, "O mother, mother!" Without the closed interiority of an indoor theater, such an extraordinary effect would be virtually impossible. Both visual (lighting) and aural (music and silence) elements of *Coriolanus* are enhanced by its being staged indoors.

The second important distinction between outdoor and indoor playing spaces has to do with the variation in audience demographic. Andrew Gurr describes the way in which higher prices of admission to the indoor playhouse meant that less affluent Londoners were financially excluded: "Merchants and wealthier citizens could afford the indoor playhouses . . . but distinctly few of the serving men and apprentices could" (89). The implication is that the plays written for indoor audiences may have been influenced by an awareness of their audience's greater erudition and education. Gurr cautions us against dividing indoor (gentlemen) and outdoor (citizen) theaters too firmly especially in the light of the fact that Shakespeare's company was using both kinds of space (Blackfriars and Globe). But it might be worth pondering the suitability of the issues raised by a play like *Coriolanus* to an audience of the educated elite. Questions about governance, high politics, the relationship of the patricians to the plebeians, and the management of power might be particularly well suited to an audience of lawyers or city fathers, those whose daily employment or civic duties compelled them to engage with these very concerns.

Theaters of Power

The consideration of theater both in terms of technical opportunities and audience consistency is central to an understanding of *Coriolanus* because the play is, at one level, all about the theatricality of politics. Politics is not only the art of the possible, but it is the craft of persuading others how probable the possible is. Politics' success is dependent on its plausibility. It is no good wanting to be consul unless the people want you to be consul, too. To reside in authority over the plebeians is to be installed in that position by the plebeians. Without their "voices" (whether they be tricked, cajoled, bribed, or forced into giving them), the consulship is untenable. If, at any point, they decide to rescind a previous approval, as happens when the Third Citizen declaims, "He's not confirmed, we may deny him yet" (2.3.205), the political authority of the appointment evaporates.

As Volumnia, Cominius, and Menenius repeatedly insist, political power resides in keeping the people contented, and should that necessitate currying favor with the many headed Hydra, so be it.

In Act III, Scene 2, Volumnia urges Martius "to speak / To th'people; not by your own instruction, / Nor by the matter which your heart prompts you, / But with such words that are but roted in / Your tongue, though but bastards and syllables / Of no allowance to your bosom's truth" (54–59). The vocabulary here is enough to damn all actor-politicians: In defiance of the integrity of his "heart" or his "bosom's truth," he is to spew forth "bastards and syllables" "that are but roted [learned by rote, like a script]." The successful politician who retains the popular support of the people can never be anything but an insincere performer, ignoring his "bosom's truth" and spouting the party line. It is no accident that the Greek word for "actor," *hupokrites,* gives us the English word *hypocrite.*

In the light of the affectation that she urges on her son, what do we make of Volumnia's speech of intercession? During the play's most political sequence, Volumnia, using nothing but rhetorical tricks and the silent supplication of his kneeling wife and child, not only forces Coriolanus to abandon his intentions to destroy Rome, but to lay down his own life for those very citizens whom he has always hated. She shows here that she is ruthlessly opportunistic and untroubled by anything as awkward as a conscience or an ethical position, a "bosom's truth." Political rhetoric, we have already seen, is independent of sincerity; now it seems completely uninflected by maternal obligation. This is a harsh reading of Volumnia and different performers will evoke different levels of sympathy. Nonetheless, her cynical and pragmatic advice to let the plebeians hear what they want to hear, undermines her own openness: Just how honest is she being at this point? Can someone as manipulative and enthusiastic about lying ever tell the truth?

As we have seen, Martius is not a good dissembler. From his youth, he could have acted but chose not to. In the account of one of Martius's earliest battles, as a 16-year-old, Cominius describes how, even before he was able to grow facial hair, he was still to be found in the thick of the battle: "with his Amazonian chin he drove / The bristled lips before him" (2.2.89–90). Martius slew three enemies and struck Tarquin himself on the knee. Even though his hairless chin suited him to a female impersonation, he was unable to assume the role: "When he might act the woman in the scene, / He proved best man i'th'field" (94–95). Of course, in the theater of Shakespeare's day, in which female roles were taken by boys, this cross-gendered presentation is not as peculiar as it sounds. However, the kind of political facade that Volumnia urges upon him is something Martius detests: "Would you have me / False to my nature? Rather say I play / The man I am" (3.2.14–16). To get on in Roman politics it is necessary to play a part, to simulate a personality, to give a performance. This Volumnia well knows, as do her enemies. Brutus is delighted that he and Sicinius have been so effective in getting Coriolanus banished, but he is quick to recognize that their next roles should be those of humble civil servants rather than powerbrokers: "Now we have shown our power, / Let us seem humbler after it is done / Than when it was a-doing" (4.2.3–5).

While Roman politics demands a proficiency in public relations and the appearance, at least, of plebeian approval, Voscian politics is grounded on brutal force. Aufidius's ulterior philosophy is that might is right and high office lasts only as long as the lull before it is overthrown: "One fire drives out one fire, one nail one nail; / Rights by rights falter, strengths by strengths do fail" (5.1.54–55). Is this any worse than the Roman attitude? Indeed, though profoundly pessimistic about human progress, is it not simply more candid than all the dissembling that Volumnia insists is at the heart of every politician's image? As we have seen, in the case of Martius, his reliance upon nobody but himself, his contempt for political office, which is reliant on popular support, makes him more Volscian than Roman. Of all the people in the play, it is Volumnia who identifies this propensity: Frustrated that her appeal seems not to be sinking in she barks, "This fellow had a Volscian to his mother" (5.3.179).

Perhaps the clearest manifestation of the play's anxieties about performance and the ambiguities of selfhood is its obsession with identity and naming. The play's own name—that is, its title,

Coriolanus—does not exist until Act I, Scene 9, when Cominius, determined to recognize the bravery of Martius's single-handed defeat of Corioles, reconfigures the soldier's identity in the light of his conquest: "For what he did before Corioles, call him, / . . . Martius Caius Coriolanus!" (63–65). This agnomen (additional name) is welded to Martius's selfhood, and so, his very individuality is constituted by his martial capacities. This is, fittingly, no artificial performance, but a veritable metamorphosis; Martius's own identity is modified and redefined by his service to Rome. For Aufidius, at the play's end, it is a name too far. He refuses to call him anything other than Martius: "Dost thou think / I'll grace thee with that robbery, thy stol'n name 'Coriolanus', in Corioles?" (5.6.90–91). The mighty warrior is now nothing more than "Boy," unindividuated, one of the mob from whom Martius has done his utmost to separate himself.

Yet the move toward anonymity is anticipated as Coriolanus himself abnegates his name and, therefore, his fealty to other Roman citizens. Cominius says he "forbade all names, / He was a kind of nothing, titleless, / Till he had forged himself a name o'th'fire / Of burning Rome" (5.1.12–15). Presumably, Coriolanus is intending to swap one agnomen for another, celebrating an even greater victory, and call himself Romanus, although his mother's intercession precludes that rebranding. This uncertainty about identity is unsurprising in a world where fidelities are so easily realigned. Paradoxically, it is at the moment of his being most merciful with a former enemy that Martius's own clumsiness over naming is highlighted. In the very same scene in which he receives his agnomen, he pleads for the life of a prisoner who, though an enemy, had previously sheltered him: "I request you / To give my poor host freedom" (1.9.86–87). Lartius enquires after "his name?" and Coriolanus responds feebly: "By Jupiter, forgot! / I am weary, yea, my memory is tired." Anne Barton suggests that this faulty memory may be just another instance of Coriolanus's disregard for those less important than himself: "a certain aristocratic disdain for the individuality of social inferiors, an individuality bound up with

their proper names, makes itself (not very attractively) felt" (103). It is certainly the case that on previous occasions when he has forgotten names it is because they are too unimportant to remember. As he recounts the election of the tribunes his contempt for their appointment is explicit in his inability to name them: "One's Junius Brutus, / Sicinius Velutus, and I know not" (1.1.213–214).

Perhaps the most overt example of this obsessing with names is the impatience of Aufidius in trying to determine the identity of the shrouded, anonymous, and uninvited guest at his banquet:

AUFIDIUS: Whence com'st thou? What
  wouldst thou? Thy name?
Why speak'st not? Speak, man. What's thy
  name?

CORIOLANUS: [*unmuffling*] If, Tullus,
Not yet thou know'st me, and seeing me dost
  not
Think me for the man I am, necessity
Commands me name myself.

AUFIDIUS. What is thy name?

CORIOLANUS. A name unmusical to the
  Volscians' ears
And harsh in sound to thine.

AUFIDIUS. Say, what's thy name?
Thou hast a grim appearance, and thy face
Bears a command in't. Though thy tackle's torn,
Thou show'st a noble vessel. What's thy name?

CORIOLANUS. Prepare thy brow to frown.
  Know'st thou me yet?

AUFIDIUS. I know thee not. Thy name?

CORIOLANUS. My name is Caius Martius,
  who hath done
To thee particularly, and to all the Volsces,
Great hurt and mischief. Thereto witness may
My surname, Coriolanus. The painful service,

The extreme dangers, and the drops of blood
Shed for my thankless country, are requited
But with that surname—a good memory
And witness of the malice and displeasure
Which thou shouldst bear me. Only that name
remains.

In this short passage, the word *name* (or *surname*) appears no fewer than 12 times as Coriolanus attempts to delay announcing it. Paradoxically what looks like supreme arrogance, holding back his name to create more and more suspense, in fact, turns out to be an act of desperation. As he explains, the name is the only thing he has left: "Only that name remains." It is therefore doubly cruel that Volumnia uses her maternal insight into Coriolanus's proud sense of self to strip him of his name at the very moment she strips him of his autonomy. Without his name, without being who he is, Coriolanus will be rendered powerless. In the most crafty way, Volumnia brings up his name at the point she condemns conceit. But it is the name rather than the man who is so conceited: "To his surname 'Coriolanus' 'longs more pride / Than pity to our prayers" (5.3.171–172). It is her trump card: She knows that the pollution of his identity, the sullying of his name with empty pride is more than he will be able to stand. He immediately concedes.

Aufidius asks for Coriolanus's name in Act IV, Scene 5 of *Coriolanus*, in a print published by F. & C. Rivington in 1804. *(Painting by Henry Fuseli; engraving by Robert Hartley Cromek)*

As far back as the first scene, even the lowly First Citizen was aware of the difficulty of separating Martius's pride and his eagerness to please Volumnia; indeed, the two qualities seem to go together: "he did it [served his country] to please his mother and to be partly proud" (1.1.36). It is Volumnia who will capitalize on this eagerness, and because Martius is ill equipped to affect different roles or subject positions behind his various names, because he has shown her (and us) all the way through that he is unable to hide his identity under a performance, she will crush the name and the warrior at the same time. Her victory over her own son is thus the triumph of the theatrical role, the actor, the theater itself, over the fixed, stable identity. Volumnia stage-manages Coriolanus's fall. It is she who, from the wings, pushes him onto a brightly lit stage with a full house, a hushed and expectant audience. In every thespian's worst nightmare, he cries: "Like a dull actor now / I have forgot my part, and am out / Even to a full disgrace" (5.3.40–42). Previously, Coriolanus's poor memory had cost his host's life; here, it will cost his own.

EXTRACTS OF CLASSIC CRITICISM

Samuel Johnson (1709–1784) [Excerpted from *General Observations on the plays of Shakespeare* (1756). Samuel Johnson was one of the greatest English literary critics, as well as a famous poet, lexicographer, and editor of Shakespeare's works. For Johnson, the importance of Shakespeare's characters was that they embodied general types, as is clear from his description of Coriolanus.]

The tragedy of *Coriolanus* is one of the most amusing of our author's performances. The old man's merriment in Menenius; the lofty lady's dignity in Volumnia; the bridal modesty in Virgilia; the patrician and military haughtiness in Coriolanus; the plebeian malignity, and tribunitian insolence in Brutus and Sicinius, make a very pleasing and interesting variety: and the various revolutions of the hero's fortune fill the mind with anxious curiosity. There is, perhaps, too much bustle in the first act and too little in the last.

William Hazlitt (1778–1830)   [Excerpted from *Characters of Shakespear's Plays* (1817). Hazlitt, a political leftist and one of the best 19th-century critics of Shakespeare, here offers a bracing and perhaps pessimistic reading of the play: "The whole dramatic moral of *Coriolanus* is that those who have little shall have less, and that those who have much shall take all that others have left."]

Shakespear has in this play shewn himself well versed in history and state-affairs. . . . The arguments for and against aristocracy or democracy, on the privileges of the few and the claims of the many, on liberty and slavery, power and the abuse of it, peace and war, are here very ably handled with the spirit of a poet and the acuteness of a philosopher. Shakespear himself seems to have had a leaning to the arbitrary side of the question, perhaps from some feeling of contempt for his own origin; and to have spared no occasion of bating the rabble. What he says of them is very true: what he says of their betters is also very true, though he dwells less upon it. The cause of the people is indeed but little

calculated as a subject for poetry: it admits of rhetoric, which goes into argument and explanation, but it presents no immediate or distinct images to the mind. . . . The language of poetry naturally falls in with the language of power. The imagination is an exaggerating and exclusive faculty: it takes from one thing to add to another: it accumulates circumstances together to give the greatest possible effect to a favourite object. . . . Poetry is right-royal. It puts the individual for the species, the one above the infinite many, might before right. A lion hunting a flock of sheep or a herd of wild asses is a more poetical object than they; and we even take part with the lordly beast, because our vanity or some other feeling makes us disposed to place ourselves in the situation of the strongest party. So we feel some concern for the poor citizens of Rome when they meet together to compare their wants and grievances, till Coriolanus comes in and with blows and big words drives this set of "poor rats," this rascal scum, to their homes and beggary before him. There is nothing heroical in a multitude of miserable rogues not wishing to be starved, or complaining that they are like to be so: but when a single man comes forward to brave their cries and to make them submit to the last indignities, from mere pride and self-will, our admiration of his prowess is immediately converted into contempt for their pusillanimity. The insolence of power is stronger than the plea of necessity. The tame submission to usurped authority or even the natural resistance to it has nothing to excite or flatter the imagination: it is the assumption of a right to insult or oppress others that carries an imposing air of superiority with it. We had rather be the oppressor than the oppressed. The love of power in ourselves and the admiration of it in others are both natural to man: the one makes him a tyrant, the other a slave. Wrong dressed out in pride, pomp, and circumstance has more attraction than abstract right. Coriolanus complains of the fickleness of the people: yet the instant he cannot gratify his pride and obstinacy at their expense, he turns his arms against his country. If his country was not worth defending, why did he build his pride on its defence? He is a conqueror and a hero; he conquers other countries, and makes this a plea for enslaving his own; and when he is prevented from doing so, he leagues with its enemies to destroy his country. He rates the people "as if he were a God to punish, and not a man of their infirmity." He scoffs at one of their tribunes for maintaining their rights and franchises: "Mark you his absolute *shall*?" not marking his own absolute *will* to take every thing from them, his impatience of the slightest opposition to his own pretensions being in proportion to their arrogance and absurdity. If the great and powerful had the beneficence and wisdom of Gods, then all this would have been well: if with a greater knowledge of what is good for the people, they had as great a care for their interest as they have themselves, if they were seated above the world, sympathising with the welfare, but not feeling the passions of men, receiving neither good nor hurt from them, but bestowing their benefits as free gifts on them, they might then rule over them like another Providence. But this is not the case. Coriolanus is unwilling that the senate should shew their "cares" for the people, lest their "cares" should be constructed into "fears," to the subversion of all due authority; and he is no sooner disappointed in his schemes to deprive the people not only of the cares of the state, but of all power to redress themselves, than Volumnia is made madly to exclaim, "Now the red pestilence strike all trades in Rome, / And occupations perish."

This is but natural: it is but natural for a mother to have more regard for her son than for a whole city; but then the city should be left to take some care of itself. The care of the state cannot, we here see, be safely entrusted to maternal affection or to the domestic charities of high life. The great have private feelings of their own, to which the interests of humanity and justice must courtesy. Their interests are so far from being the same as those of the community that they are in direct and necessary opposition to them; their power is at the expense of *our* weakness; their riches of *our* poverty; their pride of *our* degradation; their splendour of *our* wretchedness; their tyranny of *our* servitude. If they had the superior knowledge ascribed to them (which they have not) it would only render them so much more formidable; and from Gods would convert them into Devils. The whole dramatic moral of *Coriolanus* is that those who have little shall have less, and that those who have much shall take all that others have left. The people are poor; therefore they ought to be starved. They are slaves; therefore they ought to be treated like beasts of burden. They are ignorant; therefore they ought not to be allowed to feel that they want food, or clothing, or rest, that they are enslaved, oppressed, and miserable. This is the logic of the imagination and the passions, which seek to aggrandise what excites admiration and to heap contempt on misery, to raise power into tyranny, and to make tyranny absolute; to thrust down that which is low still lower, and to make wretches desperate; to exalt magistrates into kings, kings into gods; to degrade subjects to the rank of slaves, and slaves to the condition of brutes. . . .

Coriolanus himself is a complete character; his love of reputation, his contempt of popular opinion, his pride and modesty are consequences of each other. His pride consists in the inflexible sternness of his will; his love of glory is a determined desire to bear down all opposition, and to extort the admiration both of friends and foes. His contempt for popular favour, his unwillingness to hear his own praises, spring from the same source.

He cannot contradict the praises that are bestowed upon him; therefore he is impatient at hearing them.

Anna Brownell Jameson (1794–1860)

[Excerpted from *Characteristics of Women* (1832). Jameson was an early feminist literary critic. Her readings of Shakespeare's heroines were designed to address and ameliorate the position of women in Victorian society.]

[I]n Volumnia, Shakspeare has given us the portrait of a Roman matron, conceived in the true antique spirit, and finished in every part.

Volumnia, Virgilia, and Young Martius kneel before Coriolanus and beg him not to sack Rome in Act V, Scene 3 of *Coriolanus*, in this print published by Cassell & Company in the 19th century. *(Illustration by Henry Bone; engraving by Tobias Bauer)*

Although Coriolanus is the hero of the play, yet much of the interest of the action and the final catastrophe turn upon the character of his mother, Volumnia, and the power she exercised over his mind, by which, according to the story, "she saved Rome and lost her son." Her lofty patriotism, her patrician haughtiness, her maternal pride, her eloquence, and her towering spirit, are exhibited with the utmost power of effect; yet the truth of female nature is beautifully preserved, and the portrait, with all its vigour, is without harshness.

Edward Dowden (1843–1914)

[Excerpted from *Shakspere: A Critical Study of His Mind and Art* (1875). Dowden was a professor of English at Trinity College, Dublin, and vice president of the New Shakspere Society. His work attempts to trace the development of Shakespeare's own intellect and sensibilities through the plays. Thus, Coriolanus is an embodiment of pride and is a victim of this flaw rather than of a wider political situation.]

The subject of *Coriolanus* is the ruin of a noble life through the sin of pride. If duty be the dominant ideal with Brutus, and pleasure of a magnificent kind be the ideal of Antony and Cleopatra, that which gives tone and colour to Coriolanus is an ideal of self-centred power. The greatness of Brutus is altogether that of the moral conscience; his external figure does not dilate upon the world through a golden haze like that of Antony, nor bulk massively and tower like that of Coriolanus. Brutus venerates his ideals, and venerates himself; but this veneration of self is in a certain sense disinterested. A haughty and passionate personal feeling, a superb egoism are with Coriolanus the sources of weakness and of strength. . . . So suddenly [at the end of the play] has he passed from towering passion to the helplessness of death; the victim of his own violent egoism, and uncontrollable self-will.

Algernon Charles Swinburne (1837–1909)
[Excerpted from *A Study of Shakespeare* (1880). Playwright, novelist, poet, and critic, Swinburne was influenced by classical languages and literature as well as romanticism (he was a champion of William Blake). Here, Swinburne rejects political readings of *Coriolanus* and argues instead that it is a domestic, familial tragedy.]

I cannot but think that enough at least of time has been spent if not wasted by able and even by eminent men on examination of *Coriolanus* with regard to its political aspect or bearing upon social questions. It is from first to last, for all its turmoil of battle and clamour of contentious factions, rather a private and domestic than a public or historical tragedy. As in *Julius Caesar* the family had been so wholly subordinated to the state, and all personal interests so utterly dominated by the preponderance of national duties, that even the sweet and sublime figure of Portia passing in her "awful loveliness" was but as a profile half caught in the background of an episode, so here on the contrary the whole force of the final impression is not that of a conflict between patrician and plebeian, but solely that of a match of passions played out for life and death between a mother and a son. The partisans of oligarchic or democratic systems may wrangle at their will over the supposed evidences of Shakespeare's prejudice against this creed and prepossession in favour of that: a third bystander may rejoice in the proof thus established of his impartial indifference towards either: it is all nothing to the real point in hand. The subject of the whole play is not the exile's revolt, the rebel's repentance, or the traitor's reward, but above all it is the son's tragedy. The inscription on the plinth of this tragic statue is simply to Volumnia Victrix.

A loftier or a more perfect piece of man's work was never done in all the world than this tragedy of *Coriolanus*.

George Bernard Shaw (1856–1950)
[Excerpted from *Man and Superman* (1903). The great playwright Shaw was opposed to what he saw as the sentimentality of those who idolized Shakespeare. His criticism of Shakespeare is often challenging and occasionally caustic. Here, he identifies *Coriolanus* as "the greatest of Shakespear's comedies."]

Neither of them [Shakespeare or Charles Dickens] could do anything with a serious positive character: they could place a human figure before you with perfect verisimilitude; but when the moment came for making it live and move, they found, unless it made them laugh, that they had a puppet on their hands, and had to invent some artificial external stimulus to make it work. This is what is the matter with Hamlet all through: he has no will except in his bursts of temper. Foolish Bardolaters make a virtue of this after their fashion: they declare that the play is the tragedy of irresolution; but all Shakespear's projections of the deepest humanity he knew have the same defect: their characters and manners are lifelike; but their actions are forced on them from without, and the external force is grotesquely inappropriate except when it is quite conventional, as in the case of Henry V. Falstaff is more vivid than any of these serious reflective characters, because he is self-acting: his motives are his own appetites and instincts and humors. Richard III, too, is delightful as the whimsical comedian who stops a funeral to make love to the corpse's son's widow; but when, in the next act, he is replaced by a stage villain who smothers babies and offs with people's heads, we are revolted at the imposture and repudiate the changeling. Faulconbridge, Coriolanus, Leontes are admirable descriptions of instinctive temperaments: indeed the play of *Coriolanus* is the greatest of Shakespear's comedies; but description is not philosophy; and comedy neither compromises the author nor reveals him. He must be judged by those characters into which he puts what he knows of himself, his Hamlets and Macbeths and Lears and Prosperos. If these characters are agonizing in a void about factitious melodramatic murders and revenges and the like, whilst the comic characters walk with their feet on solid ground, vivid and amusing, you know that the author has much to shew and nothing to teach.

A. C. Bradley (1851–1935) [Excerpted from "*Coriolanus*," Second Annual General Shakespeare Lecture (1912). Bradley was a professor of English and history at Liverpool and later professor of poetry at Oxford (1901–06). His *Shakespearean Tragedy* (1904) is one of the most important books of Shakespearean criticism of the 20th century. Bradley tends to treat dramatic characters as real people. Recent approaches have often reacted against this, but Bradley's influence on subsequent criticism remains enormous.]

Coriolanus is beyond doubt among the latest of Shakespeare's tragedies; there is some reason for thinking it the last. Like all those that succeeded *Hamlet,* it is a tragedy of vehement passion; and in none of them are more striking revolutions of fortune displayed. It is full of power, and almost every one feels it to be a noble work. We may say of it, as of its hero, that, if not one of Shakespeare's greatest creations, it is certainly one of his biggest.

Nevertheless, it is scarcely popular. It is seldom acted, and perhaps no reader ever called it his favourite play. Indeed, except for educational purposes, I suppose it is, after *Timon,* the least generally read of the tragedies. Even the critic who feels bound to rank it above *Romeo and Juliet,* and even above *Julius Caesar,* may add that he prefers those dramas all the same; and if he ignores his personal preferences, still we do not find him asking whether it is not the equal of the four great tragedies. He may feel this doubt as to *Antony and Cleopatra,* but not as to *Coriolanus.*

The question why this should be so will at once tell us something about the drama. We cannot say that it shows any decline in Shakespeare's powers, though in parts it may show slackness in their use. It has defects, some of which are due to the historical material; but all the tragedies have defects, and the material of *Antony and Cleopatra* was even more troublesome. There is no love-story; but then there is none in *Macbeth,* and next to none in *King Lear.* Thanks in part to the badness of the Folio text, the reader is impeded by obscurities of language and irritated by the mangling of Shakespeare's metre; yet these annoyances would not much diminish the effect of *Othello.* It may seem a more serious obstacle that the hero's faults are repellent and chill our sympathy; but Macbeth, to say nothing of his murders, is a much less noble being than Coriolanus. All this doubtless goes for something; but there must be some further reason why this drama stands apart from the four great tragedies and *Antony and Cleopatra.* And one main reason seems to be this. Shakespeare could construe the story he found only by conceiving the hero's character in a certain way; and he had to set the whole drama in tune with that conception. In this he was, no doubt, perfectly right; but he closed the door on certain effects, in the absence of which his whole power in tragedy could not be displayed. He had to be content with something less, or rather with something else; and so have we.

T. S. Eliot (1888–1965) [Excerpted from "Hamlet and His Problems" (1919). One of the most famous 20th-century poets, Eliot also wrote many important critical essays. In his essay on *Hamlet,* he finds that tragedy unsatisfactory, identifying a failure of Shakespeare to match internal psychological trauma with the world of the play—the so-called objective correlative. Such problems of structure did not, for him, spoil *Coriolanus*.]

We are surely justified in attributing the play *[Hamlet]*, with that other profoundly interesting play of "intractable" material and astonishing versification, *Measure for Measure,* to a period of crisis, after which follow the tragic successes which culminate in *Coriolanus. Coriolanus* may be not as "interesting" as *Hamlet,* but it is, with *Antony and Cleopatra,* Shakespeare's most assured artistic success.

MODERN CRITICISM AND CRITICAL CONTROVERSIES

Writing in the wake of the modernist movement in poetry, G. Wilson Knight was a pioneer of literary criticism based on analysis of symbolism. His "The Royal Occupation: An Essay on *Coriolanus*" (1931) pays particular attention to the play's metallic imagery: "Coriolanus' wars are terrible in their ringing, iron blows; in the breaking through city walls; in the clamorous concomitant of sounding 'alarums'" (157). He contrasts the play with the rest of the canon and asserts that "here is a swift channeling, an eddying, twisting, and forthward-flowing stream; ice-cold, intellectual, cold as a mountain torrent and holding something of its iron taste" (155). It is the protagonist's metallic hardness and his peerlessness that make him resemble an exceptional machine: "He is rather like a finely-modelled motor-cycle, flashing in bright paint and steel, every line suggesting power and speed, standing among a row of pedal-bicycles" (163). This ruthless and mechanistic quality makes *Coriolanus* "no easy play to enjoy. It has no rich colourings, no luxuriant emotions, no easy melodies of diction" (198).

In the 1960s, Jan Kott echoed this sense of the play's bracing unattractiveness: "[T]here is no enchanting poetry, no music of the spheres, there are no great lovers or superb clowns; no raging elements, or monsters conceived in imagination . . .

There is only an historical chronicle, dry as a bone, though violently dramatized" (141). For Kott, a Polish intellectual who suffered the horrors of Adolf Hitler and Joseph Stalin, history was a bleak unfolding of a grim reality. Shakespeare's genius was in uncovering and dramatizing this nihilism. *Coriolanus* is praised for being "his bitter, most pessimistic and cruel philosophy of history" (146). Central here is Kott's idea of the play as the dramatization of class conflict: "Fate is represented here by class struggle" (143). This is the "reason why *Coriolanus* is a modern play" (147). Kott suggests that though populous, the citizens are without power. Instead, the object lesson of the tribunes is to show us how easily the mob can be manipulated: "To Shakespeare the people are only the object of history, not its actor" (160).

Janet Adelman's approach is psychoanalytic, as suggested by the title of her book, *Suffocating Mothers: Fantasies of Maternal Origin in Shakespeare's Plays,* Hamlet *to* The Tempest (1992). She discusses the play in terms of Coriolanus's family and his doomed Oedipal struggle to assert his independence from Volumnia. For Adelman, Plutarch's mention of the death of Coriolanus's paternal parent is key: "[M]asculinity is constructed in response to maternal power, and in the absence of a father" (146). The tragedy is in the failure of the protagonist to separate himself from the influence of his mother. Adelman considers the play's concern with eating and food (the play begins with a corn riot). She argues that the necessity of eating is symbolic of a kind of vulnerability that Coriolanus desperately tries to eschew. His reluctance to mix with the Roman citizens, his determination to keep himself "alone," is read in terms of a rejection of childish vulnerability: "[I]t has served to reassure him of his potency and his aggressive independence, and therefore to sustain him against fears of collapse into the dependent mode of infancy" (155). Adelman picks up on the play's intensely sexual imagery used in relation to battle, and noting Coriolanus' entry, covered in blood, she speaks of the victory over Corioles as "both a rape and a rebirth" (152). In this sense, his aggression can be read in phallic terms, and so his movement from Rome to Antium represents a flight from the female toward the male. Adelman describes Aufidius as Coriolanus's "alter ego": "Here, far from Rome, Coriolanus at last allows his hunger and his vulnerability to be felt, and he is given food"; food is accepted here because it is not offered by a mother but by "a father-brother-twin" (157). It thus functions to indicate the homosocial bonding between the former enemies. But, in spite of these attempts to break free of his family, "In the end, neither Coriolanus nor *Coriolanus* can sustain the fantasy that he is motherless, the author of himself" (162).

Frank Kermode in *Shakespeare's Language* (2000) proposes that the playwright's discourse changed in style between the Elizabethan and Jacobean periods. Kermode considers *Coriolanus* to have been written in "a harsh, rather cold style suited to its theme of glorious war and civic strife" (244). (Note Knight's similarly frosty description cited above "cold as a mountain torrent.") As Adelman has already pointed out, the most erotic or heated language is reserved for mutual congratulation following scenes of brutality. There is no place in *Coriolanus* for the language of intimacy such as is found in *Twelfth Night* or in the later play *Cymbeline*. As Act I, Scene 3 demonstrates, even childhood is a time when butterflies are dismembered with teeth. The language of ardent desire is reserved here for violence and "cannot be distinguished from emotions relative to love and sex" (252). Without the lyrical songfulness that we associate with Shakespeare's plays about love (notably the poetry of *A Midsummer Night's Dream* or, at about the same time, *Romeo and Juliet*), we are left with a style that, for Kermode, verbalizes the psychological difficulties of the speakers (see "Difficult Passages" above). This results, as he puts it, in a style characterized by "stubborn repetition, free association, violent ellipses; in short, a prevailing ruggedness of tone" (246).

In *"Coriolanus* and the Politics of Theatrical Pleasure"* (2003), Cynthia Marshall focuses on the play's interest in the theater itself and the manner in which display contributes to the narrative—blood, wounds, mouths, and so on: "The relationship between the human body and political or social truth is insistently pondered in the play" (454). Whereas in *Macbeth,* blood is to be avoided or washed away and in *Othello,* Shakespeare changes his source so that Desdemona is not stabbed but bloodlessly suffocated, in *Coriolanus,* blood is liberally spattered over the protagonist who displays it as a badge of his courage and nobility. Cominius asks of the blood-soaked Martius, "Who's yonder / That does appear as he were flayed?" (1.7.22). Marshall points to the prurience of counting Martius's wounds, which are "tallied fetishistically" (454), and she goes on, "the hero's hurt body is the focus of inordinate attention in the play" (458). This sense of display is linked to the idea of the drama itself and the "theatrical dimension of political life" (454). *Coriolanus* offers delight to its audiences through its "simulation of violence" (463); that is, while characters in the play are aware of the importance of seeming and playing a role—"Action is eloquence" (3.2.78)—the play itself is self-consciously raising such theatricality as a device by which to entertain its audiences. This double perspective is typically Shakespearean, but in the case of this play, there is a slightly unnerving and sensational suggestion that, as Marshall puts it, there arises "a gratification derived both from giving and receiving suffering" (463).

Bridget Escolme's "Living Monuments: The Spatial Politics of Shakespeare's Rome on the Contemporary Stage" (2007) is an account of her direction of *Coriolanus* for Flaneur Productions in Minneapolis and Rochester, Minnesota, in April 2006. She reads her own production against Deborah Warner's *Julius Caesar* (Barbican, 2005), finding and condemning in the latter an over-eager search for parallels between the civil strife in Shakespeare's play and the contemporary crisis in Iraq. While such analogies are inevitable, Escolme is impatient with the ways in which the presentation of Warner's production (including photographs in the program) shoehorned audience reaction into a single and specific response. Preferable, she maintains, is the seeking of analogy through the art of

In this 18th-century print, a messenger in Act I, Scene 7 relates to Cominius how the Volsces have pushed back the Romans. *(Illustration by Philippe-Jacques de Loutherbourg)*

others. For instance, she refers to the work of Minnesota photographer Paul Shambroom, who documented a series of council meetings of small towns across the United States. Escolme explains that, for her, they capture "how supremely unglamorous the workings of government are, how hedged about with contingency and tedium" (178). Escolme is refreshingly candid about the coincidental quality of many of her production's best effects. For instance, her actors were assembled in front of a row of TV sets, which suggested the televisual quality of politics, although the presence of these televisions "was entirely fortuitous: they were part of an artist's installation on display at the Art Center at the time" (180). Elsewhere, Coriolanus confronted Menenius in front of the American flag, which the gallery happened to have flying at the time. While in no way rejecting conventional theater seating,

Escolme is keen to foreground "the live encounter between text, space, human figures acting and human figures recalcitrantly being themselves" in order to animate the relationship between the plays and "our own political crises and concerns" (183).

THE PLAY TODAY

As Bradley noted (see "Extracts of Classic Criticism" above), *Coriolanus* "is scarcely popular. It is seldom acted, and perhaps no reader ever called it his favourite play." The stage history of *Coriolanus* is nonexistent until the 1680s, and after that, it appears in a series of rewrites and adaptations such as Nahum Tate's *The Ingratitude of a Commonwealth* (1681) or Thomas Sheridan's *Coriolanus or The Roman Matron* (1754). Players of the role include Edmund Kean (1820), William Charles Macready (1838), Frank Benson (1893–1910), and Henry Irving (1901).

In the 20th century, the period of the rise of the great dictator—Benito Mussolini, Francisco Franco, Stalin, Hitler—the play took on a contemporary urgency. In 1932, Hans Rothe's antimilitaristic translation was banned by the Nazis who, nevertheless, adopted the play as a paean to strong leadership, an inspiration to the Hitler Youth. Martius was seen as a charismatic leader, notes R. B. Parker, "as Adolf Hitler in our days wishes to lead our beloved German father-land" (Shakespeare 124). The play's fascistic credibility led to its being banned by the Allies until 1953. In Paris, fascists used the play to protest against the government of Édouard Deladier; riots broke out, and in 1934, the Comédie Française was closed. At the other end of the political spectrum, Bertolt Brecht regarded *Coriolanus* as prosocialist, and his adaptation, completed after his death, was first staged in 1963. Its stress was on "showing the hero as part of a social pattern and a member of a class rather than as a unique individual surpassing all bounds" (Hortmann 85).

Laurence Olivier assayed the role at the Old Vic in 1938 opposite Sybil Thorndike as Volumnia. When Peter Hall (then only 28) directed the play in 1959 at Stratford, Olivier again played Martius and inspired Laurence Kitchin's brilliant description: "cursing the plebeians, [Olivier] gave the phrases such a charge of emotion that he gathered them into a single rhetorical missile, so that the speech had an impact like jagged stones parcelled together and hurled in somebody's face. There was a bizarre impression of one man lynching a crowd" (148). This was the same production in which Olivier enacted the death of Coriolanus, Tarpeian-like, by falling, head first, from a 12-foot-high platform to the stage below only to be caught by his ankles. This physical daring was not universally admired. Writing in 1966, Glynne Wickham opined, it is "easy to obliterate the tragic stature of Coriolanus in a matter of seconds by allowing him to leap to his death in the manner of a trapeze-artist for the sake of the gasp of surprise in the auditorium" (169). Whether this was populist gimmickry, the images of the dead Mussolini, killed by popular revolt, suspended upside down from a lamp post, illustrate the inseparability of life and art.

Coriolanus can be read as an index of the political engagement, or lack of it, of the major English theater companies. Terry Hands and John Barton's 1989 RSC version was accused of "Keeping politics out of Shakespeare," and Michael Coveney lamented that the central performance, that of Charles Dance, eclipsed the play's wider political concerns: "the Royal Shakespeare Company . . . cannot make *Coriolanus* sound like a play that really matters" (Smith 225). In the same year, at the Young Vic, Jane Howell directed Corin Redgrave as Coriolanus opposite his real-life mother, Rachel Kempson, as Volumnia. Set in the Victorian period, the plebes were Thomas Hardy rustics, while Cominius's martial regalia consisted of a black plumed hat and elaborate collar and sword. The tribunes were burgomasters with winged collars, watch chains, and bowler hats. Volumnia, in black lace cap and full dress, looked like the widowed Queen Victoria herself. The play's interest in empire and invasion was thus appositely rehistoricized, and the extraordinary gloating of Volumnia over her son's wounds transfigured her into a Crimean mother who would, when it arrived,

proudly display her black-edged envelope. But the production took as its main driving force the fierce machismo of its protagonist; the focus of the direction was always toward the center, and Coriolanus's own centripetal presence governed the pace and orientation of the action. Aufidius's final remorseful speech was cut, and instead, Virgilia entered to cover the corpse with a shroud. The play ended with the ending of Coriolanus: The tragedy was his alone.

The Almeida Theatre Company staged, in 1990, *Richard II* and *Coriolanus* in repertory at the Gainsborough Studios. Both productions were directed by Jonathan Kent, and both title roles were played by Ralph Fiennes. The flaw was Fiennes's continuous and unnuanced shouting of his lines. Yet, still, the production seemed readily to take his side. As he emerged from the gates of Corioles (a huge metal sheet, raised and lowered like the blade of a colossal guillotine), he was weilding his sword heroically. The contrast between his staggering belligerence and the plebeians' meek cowardice was emphasized as we saw them, soon after, discussing his actions while on their hands and knees polishing the floor of the Senate. As the triumphant Volumnia entered Rome, the heavens opened with a shower of poppies—an adumbration of the sacrifice of the production's real hero. In 1992, Tim Supple directed 50 local amateurs (as the plebeians) alongside Kenneth Branagh and Judi Dench as Coriolanus and Volumnia. An underpowered Branagh, exacerbated by the ingeniously choreographed and much more watchable crowd scenes, meant that the play's political urgency was buried under an epic grandeur.

In spite of Fran Thompson's politically explicit design, which included blood-spattered banners draped around the Swan Theatre proclaiming "Liberty," "Equality," "Fraternity" as well as a version of Delacroix's *Liberty* upstage, David Thacker's 1994 RSC production was firmly focused on the psychology of Toby Stephens's Coriolanus. The critics were not seduced by the design's overt composition: Michael Billington wrote, "Thacker irons out the political complexities" and Paul Prescott captured the production's prioritization of the hero's pained development at the expense of the play's wider political interests: "Toby Stephens's twenty-four year old was an all-too-plausible boy of tears, a public-school Napoleon for whom the apron-strings were still taut" (Hibbard lxxi). As Ralph Berry concludes, "the essential underlying feature of the modern *Coriolanus* in England is its disengagement from politics. . . . Directors prefer to give the title-role actor his head" (55).

The exception to this tendency was the 1990 English Shakespeare Company production directed by the politically engaged Michael Bogdanov. Read against the disintegration of the Eastern bloc, the play's Rome had become an amalgam of Poland, Rumania, East Germany, and Czechoslovakia. Protesters sang about bread as riot police attempted to control them with searchlights, tear gas, and sirens. Members of the cast sat among the audience so that Michael Pennington's Martius, addressing us in the manner of a press conference, under full houselights, had to deal with hecklers from within our midst. We were positioned on the side of Solidarity, rebelling against the tyranny of Soviet-style communism. Bogdanov unashamedly appropriated the play for this topical reading: "What we have in Europe now, daily, in ten or fifteen places, is in essence the situation we have in *Coriolanus*. People jockeying for power, new regimes taking over, wars starting somewhere else and having to be dealt with, alongside a political situation that changes daily at home" (Background Pack published by ESC, 1990). Bogdanov's production remains a notable exception to the propensity of English stagings of *Coriolanus* toward political quietism.

More recently, Dominic Dromgoole chose *Coriolanus* as his inaugural production as artistic director of London's Globe Theatre, in 2006. In spite of his claim that the Roman Empire "throws up any number of parallels with the world of today" (program note), the production was hamstrung by an inbuilt resistance to modernity in this most conspicuously archaeological of theaters. Why, one wondered, had the production lacked the courage to set its *Coriolanus* in the modern world (as

Bogdanov did)? Iconic of this uncomfortable fudge between ancient and modern were the costumes (designed by Mike Britton): doublets (with ruffs) and hose, over which were draped Roman-esque swags. This issue aside, it was a workmanlike if uninspired production. Interestingly, as the warrior (played by Jonathan Cake) displayed his wounds, he circulated among and was jostled by the audience in the yard. He shook hands in the manner of a politician, "pressing the flesh" though nicely he wiped his hand on his smock as though to rid himself of the plebes'/audience's contaminating sweat. Revealingly, for all their expressed solidarity with the common sort, the tribunes remained on stage to direct the crowd's dissent, never daring to move among them. It was with the playing of the tribunes, notably John Dougall as Brutus, that the production came closest to the play's vicious politics. This was an extremely sotto voce performance without the histrionics that usually accompany outdoor shows. Dougall precisely rendered Brutus's cynical plotting and politic one-upmanship with a quiet determination.

The populism of the Globe's production contrasted with the unfamiliar in Yukio Ninagawa's 2007 epic staged at the Barbican (in Japanese). The main house's huge stage was traversed by an enormous flight of steps potently imaging the strict hierarchies of Roman society. But, typically of Ninagawa, the effective design concept impinged upon the acting—here, literally, as the playing space was reduced to a single level at the top and a shallow band at the bottom. Too much of the action was inhibited by the necessity for actors to climb or descend steps while the sheer scale of the set tended to dwarf the action. Much more compelling was the use of a huge mirror that at moments, served to screen the stage, throwing back onto the audience an image of itself. As the lighting of this mirror shifted, so it became diaphanous and audience members became continuous with the citizens. This was a neat trick but repetitiously used. A bland color coding differentiated the various constituents: plebeians in muddy brown, Volsces in white gowns with samurai swords, and Roman senators in gray. Again, the tyranny of design stifled the performances themselves. As Eleanor Collins concluded, "those aspects that are of interest do not prove sufficiently original or complex in themselves to bear pressure once repeated as many times as they are here. The scale of disappointment nearly matches that of the production, in all of its relentless enormity" (50).

The last production staged in the Royal Shakespeare Theatre (2007) was Gregory Doran's *Coriolanus*. In some ways, it was a fitting valedictory, the production's failures demonstrating why the theater was long overdue for demolition. Richard Hudson had designed a set comprising columns receding into the distance. In a similar way to that of Ninagawa's production (designed by Tsukasa Nakagoshi), the huge space of the stage had been mostly occupied by set, leaving only a clear view of a downstage acting strip. This meant that any action upstage was occluded by the columns and tended to "disappear." Viewed from the theater's too-distant balcony, the stage seemed empty more often than not.

While Bradley may be correct to assert that *Coriolanus* "is scarcely popular," this sample of productions serves to demonstrate how unfixed the play is politically. The range of interpretations occupies the entire spectrum, from fascist to communist. Whenever *Coriolanus* is staged, satisfactorily or not, the play's audiences have no choice but to recognize its anxious attentions to questions about the morality and practice of political organization and social coherence. Whether such questions can ever be adequately answered is, of course, another matter.

FIVE TOPICS FOR DISCUSSION AND WRITING

1. **Rome:** How important do you consider the setting of the action to be? What are the implications for Shakespeare's Jacobean audiences of viewing a play set in ancient Rome? What are the implications for a modern audience? How are they the same? How are they different? (You may wish to consider such fictional representa-

tions of the classical world as Robert Graves's novel *I Claudius* (1934); the film *Gladiator,* directed by Ridley Scott (2000); or the television series, *Rome,* directed by Michael Apted and screened by HBO and BBC in 2005.)

2. **War and heroism:** Is the category of "war hero" historically variable, or is it recognizable in all places and at all times? Might today's hero be tomorrow's tyrant? Martius switches sides following his banishment from Rome. Is this a strategic shift of loyalties or merely retaliation? Martius himself requests his mother not "T'ally my rages and revenges with / Your colder reasons" (5.3.86–87). Can pure "revenge" ever be considered as heroic?

3. **Gender:** As the fates of Lady Macbeth, Cleopatra, and Gertrude demonstrate, the intrusion of women into the masculine world of high politics is always costly. Early modern women, like Roman women, were supposed to behave with modesty and in domestic seclusion as practiced by Virgilia. Yet, Shakespeare devotes most of the climactic scene of this play (5.3) to Volumnia's plea for Rome. What effect does this female prominence have on the final act and/or the play as a whole? What is the function of Act I, Scene 3 in preparing us for Volumnia's intercession? How are the usual gender hierarchies overturned? Might we think of *Coriolanus,* in spite of its macho worldview, as a feminist play?

4. **Politics and class:** Early modern England was so frightened by social mobility that it introduced legislation, known as sumptuary laws, dictating the clothing appropriate to different social and economic classes (see Jardine, 140–168). The intention was to be able to recognize a person's level in the social hierarchy as well as his or her income (gentlemen, barons, knights, earls, and so on). How might we read Martius's fear of and hatred toward the plebeians against such a context? More generally, in what ways might we think of *Coriolanus* as a play about class? Is the mob ever sympathetic? Gloucester in *King Lear* talks about "each man hav[ing] enough" (4.1.65). Might such a sentiment serve

to justify (politically or ethically) the rebellion with which the play begins?

5. **Genre:** When they compiled Shakespeare's First Folio, John Heminges and Henry Condell placed *Coriolanus* first in the group of tragedies. Do you think the play merits such prominence? Is it the equal of *King Lear* or *Hamlet*? Shaw wrote, "*Coriolanus* is the greatest of Shakespear's comedies" (see "Extracts of Classic Criticism" section). Is he being merely mischievous, or does the play contain comic elements? If so, what are they, and what is their dramatic function? Might we also think of the play in other terms: as satire or even debate? Could we describe *Coriolanus* as didactic? If so, what are its lessons?

Bibliography

Adelman, Janet. *Suffocating Mothers: Fantasies of Maternal Origin in Shakespeare's Plays,* Hamlet *to* The Tempest. London: Routledge, 1992.

Barton, Anne. *The Names of Comedy.* Oxford, U.K.: Clarendon Press, 1990.

Berry, Ralph. *Shakespeare in Performance: Castings and Metamorphoses.* Houndmills, U.K.: Macmillan, 1993.

Bullough, Geoffrey, ed. *Narrative and Dramatic Sources of Shakespeare.* Vol. 5: *The Roman Plays.* London: Routledge, 1965.

Burke, Kenneth. "*Coriolanus* and the Delights of Faction." *Hudson Review* 19 (1966): 185–202.

Charney, Maurice. *Wrinkled Deep in Time: Aging in Shakespeare.* New York: Columbia University Press, 2009.

Collins, Eleanor. "*Coriolanus.*" *Cahiers Elisabéthains,* 72 (2007): 48–50.

Dillon, Janette. *The Cambridge Introduction to Shakespeare's Tragedies.* Cambridge: Cambridge University Press, 2007.

Eliot, T. S. *Collected Poems, 1909–1962.* London: Faber, 1974.

Escolme, Bridget. "Living Monuments: The Spatial Politics of Shakespeare's Rome on the Contemporary Stage." *Shakespeare Survey* 60 (2007): 170–183.

Foucault, Michel. *The Order of Things: An Archaeology of the Human Sciences.* London: Tavistock, 1970.

Gurr, Andrew. *Playgoing in Shakespeare's London.* 3d ed. Cambridge: Cambridge University Press, 2004.

Hibbard, G. R., ed. *Coriolanus.* Introduction by Paul Prescott. London: Penguin, 2005.

Hortmann, Wilhelm. *Shakespeare on the German Stage: The Twentieth Century.* Cambridge: Cambridge University Press, 1998.

Jardine, Lisa. *Still Harping on Daughters: Women and Drama in the Age of Shakespeare.* Hemel Hempstead, U.K.: Harvester Press, 1983.

Jones, Ernest. *Hamlet and Oedipus.* London: Victor Gollancz, 1949.

Kermode, Frank. *Shakespeare's Language.* London: Penguin, 2000.

———. *The Age of Shakespeare.* New York: Random House, 2009.

Kitchin, Laurence. *Mid-Century Drama.* London: Faber, 1962.

Knight, G. Wilson. *The Imperial Theme.* London: Routledge, 1931.

Kott, Jan. *Shakespeare Our Contemporary.* Translated by Boleslaw Taborski. London: Routledge, 1967.

Maguire, Laurie E. *Studying Shakespeare: A Guide to the Plays.* Oxford, U.K.: Blackwell, 2004.

Marshall, Cynthia. "*Coriolanus* and the Politics of Theatrical Pleasure." In *A Companion to Shakespeare's Works,* edited by Richard Dutton and Jean E. Howard, 452–472. Oxford, U.K.: Blackwell, 2003.

Miola, Robert S. *Shakespeare's Rome.* Cambridge: Cambridge University Press, 1983.

More, Sir Thomas. *Utopia.* Edited by Richard Marius. London: Everyman, 1988.

Pettit, E. C. "*Coriolanus* and the Midlands Insurrection of 1607." *Shakespeare Survey* 3 (1950): 34–42.

Sawday, Jonathan. *The Body Emblazoned: Dissection and the Human Body in Renaissance Culture.* London: Routledge, 1995.

Shakespeare, William. *Coriolanus.* Edited by R. B. Parker. Oxford: Oxford University Press, 1994.

Smallwood, Robert, ed. *Players of Shakespeare,* vol. 4. Cambridge: Cambridge University Press, 1998.

Smith, Peter J. *Social Shakespeare: Aspects of Renaissance Dramaturgy and Contemporary Society.* Houndmills, U.K.: Macmillan, 1995.

Wells, Stanley, et al., eds. *The Complete Works of William Shakespeare*. Oxford, U.K.: Clarendon Press, 1988.

White, Martin. *Renaissance Drama in Action: An Introduction to Aspects of Theatre Practice and Performance*. London: Routledge, 1998.

Wickham, Glynne. "*Coriolanus:* Shakespeare's Tragedy in Rehearsal and Performance." *Stratford-upon-Avon Studies* 9 (1966): 167–182.

Zeeveld, W. Gordon. "*Coriolanus* and Jacobean Politics." *MLR* 57 (1962): 321–334.

FILM AND VIDEO PRODUCTIONS

Dews, Peter, dir. *The Spread of the Eagle*. With Robert Hardy, Beatrix Lehmann, and Roland Culver. BBC, 1963.

Jenkins, Roger, dir. *Coriolanus*. With John Nightingale, Mary Grimes, and David Stockton. NYT/BBC, 1965.

Leach, Wilford, dir. *Coriolanus*. With Morgan Freeman, Gloria Footer, and Maurice Woods. New York Shakespeare Festival, video, 1979.

Moshinsky, Elijah, dir. *Coriolanus*. With Alan Howard, Irene Worth, and Joss Ackland. BBC, 1984.

Nickell, Paul, dir. *Coriolanus*. With Richard Greene and Judith Evelyn. Worthington Miner, 1951.

—Peter J. Smith

Cymbeline

INTRODUCTION

Cymbeline, one of Shakespeare's last plays, excites both admiration and exasperation from readers and playgoers. It is different from Shakespeare's earlier plays in many respects. In *Cymbeline,* Shakespeare was experimenting with a new form, the tragicomic romance, where he could combine violence and humor, fantasy and realism, fairy tale and history, farce and spirituality, poetry and drama, tragedy and comedy, tears and laughter.

The play is notable for its striking visual elements, including three amazing dramatic moments. First, there is the scene in Imogen's bedroom. Imogen has been reading from Ovid a story of a famous mythological rape. Before her bed is the trunk she has agreed to store for Posthumus's supposed friend Iachimo. She goes to sleep, and after a few moments, the lid of the trunk starts to open from the inside. Out pops Iachimo, a Peeping Tom out of a jack-in-the box! This scene catches an audience or a new reader by surprise, and we watch in horror as, after noting the decorations in the room, Iachimo steals Imogen's bracelet and peeks at her breast (noticing a telltale mole).

The second breathtaking scene comes when Posthumus is in jail, and in a dream, his dead parents and brothers offer a prayer to Jupiter to help Posthumus. But the theatrical surprise comes when, amid thunder and lightning, Jupiter, riding an eagle, actually descends from the heavens. Not all productions have the facilities to stage this descent, but when they do, the result can be a stunning surprise. Shakespeare is here using an extremely old and out-of-date theatrical device: the deus ex machina (literally, "god out of the machine"). In Greek tragedy, the playwright would sometimes introduce a god to resolve the plot, having him descend on a kind of crane (the machine in the phrase). The Latin poet Horace insisted that no playwright should use such a device, and Shakespeare's contemporaries such as Ben Jonson no doubt agreed with Horace. But in the theater, even today, the unexpected appearance of the god Jupiter can both startle an audience and make it smile with awareness of the artificiality of the device.

The third striking visual scene comes when Imogen awakens next to a dead and headless body. At first she thinks she is dreaming, but then she realizes that the dead man is her beloved husband. In this scene, the effect is one of dramatic irony, where the audience knows more than the character. We know the body is the villain's, and when Imogen takes the blood from her dead husband's neck and smears it on her face, we are even more shocked by the scene, for we know the blood is from the man who wanted to rape her and kill her husband.

The play has some other striking dramatic elements as well. Imogen as a character is one of Shakespeare's finest female roles, and many actresses have made great successes with it. And the "pastoral" scenes are also remarkable. After the first half of the play, with the corrupt court, the wickedness of Iachimo, and the sufferings of Imogen, the scene

While Imogen sleeps, Iachimo examines her bedroom and takes Posthumus's bracelet off her wrist in Act II, Scene 2 of *Cymbeline*. This is a print from the Boydell Shakespeare Gallery project, which was first conceived in 1786 and lasted until 1805. *(Painting by Richard Westall; engraving by James Stow)*

with Belarius and Cymbeline's sons (and then with Fidele/Imogen in the Welsh mountains) can seem a breath of fresh air for a reader or especially for an audience.

Many have criticized the final act of the play, but it, too, can be produced beautifully. There is probably more dramatic irony here than anywhere in Shakespeare. As the complicated plot untangles and as the characters figure out what we already know, the effect can be both amusing and exhilarating. This last act seems to suggest that even the most complicated and difficult of situations can work out.

Cymbeline is full of laughter. Cloten can be very funny on the stage, but many of the other scenes can and should be played for laughs even as they are played for emotional effect. The play is also full of some of Shakespeare's finest poetry. It has long been a favorite of poets, especially in the 19th century and on into the 20th. And finally, in addition to its dramatic, poetic, and comic qualities, *Cymbeline* also has a strong spiritual vision. One of the most important themes of the play is forgiveness.

BACKGROUND
Shakespeare and King James

Shakespeare was an actor, playwright, and part owner of the theater company the King's Men. The king in this title was King James I of England (King James VI of Scotland), so Shakespeare worked for the king and was the king's playwright. *Cymbeline* was clearly written to suit King James, perhaps even to provide what one critic has called "royalist propaganda."

Both of King James's parents were descended from a Welshman, Henry Tudor (Richmond in Shakespeare's *Richard III*). In 1485, Henry Tudor landed at Milford Haven to begin the struggle that eventually led him to be King Henry VII and to establish the Tudor dynasty. The Milford Haven scenes in *Cymbeline* would certainly have reminded Shakespeare's audience of King James's own Welsh connections. James also considered himself a great peacemaker (he liked to be called "Jacobus Pacificus"), securing treaties of peace with former European enemies such as the Netherlands. Thus, in *Cymbeline,* it is the villainous Queen and her son Cloten who desire war, while the happy ending of the play depends on a peaceful reconciliation between Rome and Britain.

King James also explicitly identified himself with the Roman emperor Augustus. One of his coronation medals even had the legend (in Latin), "James I, Caesar Augustus of Britain." James was not content with being king of England and king of Scotland; he wanted to be emperor of Great Britain. Thus, when the play was written (probably 1609 or 1610), James was trying to create a legal union between Scotland and England. He was king of each separately, but the countries were not united, as James wanted, in a Great Britain. (The name *Britain,* incidentally came from the legendary Roman founder of the isle, Brutus, son of Aeneas.) So, the union of Britain and Rome at the end of the play would have been welcomed as a version of the political union between Scotland and England that James was trying to achieve. (James never did succeed in this task; England and Scotland were only joined in 1707.)

Shakespeare and Profanity Laws

In 1606, Puritans succeeded in getting legislation passed (the Act to Restraine Abuses of Players) making it a crime to say on stage the name "of God, or of Christ Jesus, or the Holy Ghost or of the Trinity." Shakespeare seems to have responded by writing many plays set in pre-Christian times: *King Lear, Antony and Cleopatra, Coriolanus, Timon of Athens, Pericles, Cymbeline, The Winter's Tale, The Tempest, and The Two Noble Kinsmen.* Unable to have his characters utter the words or make oaths by God or Jesus, Shakespeare was instead able to have his characters utter oaths by Apollo, or Jupiter. And, in *Cymbeline,* he even showed the great god Jupiter as a character on (or more probably above) the stage.

Blackfriars Theatre and Shakespeare's Late Plays

Later critics such as G. E. Bentley have followed Granville Barker's suggestion in 1930 that Shakespeare was influenced in the writing of the late plays, especially of *Cymbeline,* by having a new theater for the company. Richard Burbage, the principal actor in Shakespeare's company, had inherited the Blackfriars Theatre from his father, James Burbage, in 1597. He leased it out for a troupe of boy actors to use, but in 1608, he and the other shareholders in the King's Men took back the playhouse in order to use it for winter (while using the outdoor Globe in the better spring and summer weather). Unfortunately, the plague broke out and closed all the theaters from August 1608

to late 1609 or perhaps 1610. During this time, Shakespeare wrote *Cymbeline* and perhaps also *The Winter's Tale.* In the extended break, it is theorized he had time to construct a new kind of drama, specifically suited for the new indoor theater (which charged more for tickets, got a higher-class audience, and proved to be a monetary success). This new style of drama led to the romances of Shakespeare's late period, written for a smaller, more intimate theater and a more sophisticated audience. The most popular court entertainment of the early 17th century was the masque, which consisted of dancing and pantomime, dialogue and song, together with elaborate special effects, creating something like that of the "production number" in a Broadway musical. In *Cymbeline,* the dream scene culminating with the descent of an eagle was such a masque-like production, a special effect probably more easily engineered in the indoor Blackfriars than in the outdoor Globe (where *Cymbeline* was also performed and seen by Simon Forman in 1611). It has been speculated that the more sophisticated audience at the Blackfriars enjoyed self-consciously arty and artful plays, sophisticated poetry, and theatrical artifice. Thus, the company's purchase of the Blackfriars Theatre probably led Shakespeare in the direction of a new kind of play.

Shakespeare the Man and the Writing of *Cymbeline*

During the extensive closing of the theaters in response to the plague outbreak, it is likely Shakespeare returned to his home in Stratford-upon-Avon. Perhaps this more countrified setting led him in the direction of pastoral plays. In any event, many critics and biographers have speculated that Shakespeare had entered a new phase of his life as well as a new artistic phase. Perhaps Shakespeare looked back on his career and so wrote in *Cymbeline* a "retrospective" or "recapitulatory" play (as it has been called), a play with a great many echoes to earlier plays.

The 19th-century and early 20th-century critic Edward Dowden first suggested that in his late plays, Shakespeare had attained some kind of spiritual serenity. Dowder dubbed this phase of Shakespeare's career "'On the Heights,' signifying thereby that in these exquisite plays Shakespeare had attained an altitude from which he saw human life in a clear and solemn vision, looking down through a pellucid atmosphere upon human joys and sorrows with a certain aloofness or disengagement, yet at the same time with a tender and pathetic interest." Since Dowden, others have also seen in late Shakespeare a more spiritual vision. On the other hand, Lytton Strachey thought the playwright had grown tired and wrote his "romances" while "half bored to death." Some even suggest that Shakespeare was growing senile and had lost his great talent. But the fact that he wrote *The Tempest*, acknowledged as one of his greatest plays, after writing *Cymbeline* suggests otherwise.

Date and Text of the Play

Cymbeline is one of Shakespeare's late romances. Most scholars believe is was written around 1608 or 1609, after *Pericles* but before *The Tempest* and *The Winter's Tale*. Certainly, it was written before 1611, when we have record of a performance. The play was first published in the First Folio collection of Shakespeare's plays in 1623; there are no extant quarto publications prior to this. The text has no major controversies, except for the names, especially Imogen's. The editor of the modern Oxford edition (and others) believe that her name was meant to be *Innogen* but that the Folio scribe misread the two *n*'s for an *m*. In Raphael Holinshed's *Chronicles* (one of Shakespeare's favorite sources), the first British queen was the legendary Innogen. Further, Shakespeare wrote a nonspeaking part for a woman in *Much Ado About Nothing* named *Innogen*. Roger Warren, the Oxford editor, argues that Innogen works better because it echoes the word *innocent* (although *Imogen* has the advantage of echoing the word *imagine*). Additionally, while the text uses the name *Iachimo*, it was likely, according to Elizabethan pronunciation, pronounced with a *j* sound. Thus, some modern editors write *Giacimo* or *Jachimo* (although the

phrase "yellow Iachimo" seems to demand the alliteration of two *y* sounds). Finally, in accordance with Holinshed and other historians who spelled the king's and the play's name *Kymbeline*, it is likely that, in the Celtic manner, *Cymbeline* should be pronounced with a hard *k* sound.

SYNOPSIS
Brief Synopsis

King Cymbeline has several children from a previous marriage (his two sons, Guiderius and Arviragus, have been abducted). His new Queen wants to solidify her family's claim to the throne of Britain through the marriage of her son, Cloten, to Cymbeline's daughter, Imogen. However, against her father's wishes Imogen marries her longtime childhood friend Posthumus. Enraged, Cymbeline imprisons Imogen and banishes Posthumus.

While living in exile in Italy with his friend Philario, Posthumus, who has made great claims for the virtue of his new bride, is challenged by the boastful Iachimo, who predicts that he will seduce Imogen and thus invalidate Posthumus's faith in her fidelity. Posthumus accepts his bet.

Iachimo arrives in Britain and tells Imogen of Posthumus's infidelity. Imogen is only briefly deceived and quickly understands the game Iachimo is playing. Iachimo now has no other recourse but to admit that he was testing her virtue. He praises her husband and takes his leave by asking her to care for a trunk of valuables, which he and some other Romans intend as a present for the Emperor. Imogen agrees.

In the meantime, Britain's Queen seeks the help of a doctor, Cornelius, to bring her a box of poison. The suspicious doctor presents the Queen with a "cordial," or magic potion, that will induce a deathlike sleep but will later cause the "victim" to awaken refreshed.

After Imogen falls asleep, Iachimo emerges from the trunk. While she sleeps, Iachimo makes a thorough inspection of her physical appearance, memorizing details that will convince Posthumus that a seduction did indeed take place. As further proof, Iachimo takes the bracelet Posthumus had

369

THE TRAGEDIE OF
CYMBELINE.

Actus Primus. Scœna Prima.

Enter two Gentlemen.

1. *Gent.*

On do not meet a man but Frownes.
Our bloods no more obey the Heauens
Then our Courtiers:
Still seeme, as do's the Kings.

2 *Gent.* But what's the matter?

1. His daughter, and the heire of's kingdome (whom
He purpos'd to his wiues sole Sonne, a Widdow
That late he married) hath referr'd her selfe
Vnto a poore, but worthy Gentleman. She's wedded,
Her Husband banish'd; she imprison'd, all
Is outward sorrow, though I thinke the King
Be touch'd at very heart.

2 None but the King?

1 He that hath lost her too: so is the Queene,
That most desir'd the Match. But not a Courtier,
Although they weare their faces to the bent
Of the Kings lookes, hath a heart that is not
Glad at the thing they scowle at.

2 And why so?

1 He that hath miss'd the Princesse, is a thing
Too bad, for bad report: and he that hath her,
(I meane, that married her, alacke good man,
And therefore banish'd) is a Creature, such,
As to seeke through the Regions of the Earth
For one, his like; there would be something failing
In him, that should compare. I do not thinke,
So faire an Outward, and such stuffe Within
Endowes a man, but hee.

2 You speake him farre.

1 I do extend him (Sir) within himselfe,
Crush him together, rather then vnfold
His measure duly.

2 What's his name, and Birth?

1 I cannot delue him to the roote: His Father
Was call'd *Sicillius*, who did ioyne his Honor
Against the Romanes, with *Cassibulan*,
But had his Titles by *Tenantius*, whom
He seru'd with Glory, and admir'd Successe:
So gain'd the Sur-addition, *Leonatus*.
And had (besides this Gentleman in question)
Two other Sonnes, who in the Warres o'th'time
Dy'de with their Swords in hand. For which, their Father
Then old, and fond of yssue, tooke such sorrow
That he quit Being; and his gentle Lady

Bigge of this Gentleman (our Theame) deceast
As he was borne. The King he takes the Babe
To his protection, cals him *Posthumus Leonatus*,
Breedes him, and makes him of his Bed-chamber,
Puts to him all the Learnings that his time
Could make him the receiuer of, which he tooke
As we do ayre, fast as 'twas ministred,
And in's Spring, became a Haruest: Liu'd in Court
(Which rare it is to do) most prais'd, most lou'd,
A sample to the yongest: to th'more Mature,
A glasse that feated them: and to the grauer,
A Childe that guided Dotards. To his Mittris,
(For whom he now is banish'd) her owne price
Proclaimes how she esteem'd him; and his Vertue
By her electiō may be truly read, what kind of man he is.

2 I honor him, euen out of your report.
But pray you tell me, is she sole childe to th'King?

1 His onely childe:
He had two Sonnes (if this be worth your hearing,
Marke it) the eldest of them, at three yeares old
I'th'swathing cloathes, the other from their Nursery
Were stolne, and to this houre, no ghesse in knowledge
Which way they went.

2 How long is this ago?

1 Some twenty yeares.

2 That a Kings Children should be so conuey'd,
So slackely guarded, and the search so slow
That could not trace them.

1 Howsoere, 'tis strange,
Or that the negligence may well be laugh'd at:
Yet is it true Sir.

2 I do well beleeue you.

1 We must forbeare. Heere comes the Gentleman,
The Queene, and Princesse. *Exeunt*

Scena Secunda.

Enter the Queene, Posthumus, and Imogen.

Qu. No, be assur'd you shall not finde me (Daughter)
After the slander of most Step-Mothers,
Euill-ey'd vnto you. You're my Prisoner, but
Your Gaoler shall deliuer you the keyes

z z 3   That

given Imogen and sets off for Italy. There, he convinces Posthumus that he has seduced Imogen.

Back at the British court, Caius Lucius, the ambassador sent by Augustus Caesar, arrives to demand the tribute that Cymbeline's uncle had promised to Julius Caesar. Before the King can reply, the Queen and Cloten absolutely and rudely refuse to comply. Cymbeline realizes that the Queen's belligerence will provoke war with Caesar.

Meanwhile, Pisanio, Posthumus's servant, who has remained in Britain, receives a letter commanding him to take Imogen to Milford Haven in Wales and kill her for her act of betrayal. Incapable of believing Imogen guilty, Pisanio reveals his orders to her. He suggests that Imogen flee the court, disguised in male clothing, with the aid of a magic potion that will cure everything.

Belarius, another exiled lord, has been rearing Cymbeline's two long-lost son in a rural retreat in Wales. Imogen meets up with the two sons at the cave home of Belarius, and they take her in. Later, a sick Imogen takes the magic "cordial" Pisanio had previously given her and falls into a deep sleep.

Cloten, who has disguised himself as Posthumus, finds Imogen asleep in the cave and insults Guiderius, who decapitates him. Believing she is dead, Belarius and his two "sons" perform the rituals of mourning, only to have her awaken next to the decapitated body of Cloten. She mistakes him for Posthumus, because he wearing Posthumus's clothes. Imogen is grief-stricken and outraged against both Pisanio and Cloten, holding them responsible for the bloody deed.

Posthumus, who believes Imogen is dead, now regrets his rage. He decides to don the clothes of a peasant and join the war against the Romans. Meanwhile, Cymbeline is captured by the Romans and then rescued by Belarius and his two sons, with Posthumus's help. The Romans are defeated. After the battle, Posthumus, now dressed again as a Roman, offers himself to the British as a prisoner.

In the end, all the diverse plots are brought together. Imogen is reunited with Posthumus, and she exacts an admission of guilt from Iachimo. The identity of Cymbeline's lost sons is also revealed. Finally, the young lovers are reinstated into the royal court, Cymbeline promises to pay the tribute he owes, and complete harmony is restored to the state.

Act I, Scene 1

A conversation between two gentlemen explains the story. King Cymbeline is unhappy that his daughter Imogen has married Posthumus Leonatus, "a poor but worthy gentleman" (1.1.6). The King wanted his daughter to marry Cloten, son of the woman the king has recently married and thus made queen. This son, Cloten, the gentlemen agree, is "a thing/ Too bad for bad report" (1.1.16–17). They extensively praise Posthumus, whose brothers died in war, which caused his father to die of grief; the mother then died giving birth to the aptly named Posthumus. Posthumus was then adopted by the king, but after marrying Imogen, he has been banished. Finally, they say that the king's two sons were kidnapped 20 years before and are still missing.

Act I, Scene 2

The Queen tells Posthumus and Imogen that she will be their supporter and friend. When she leaves, Imogen exclaims that the Queen was lying. Posthumus tells Imogen he will remain her loyal husband while living in Rome. The Queen reenters, telling them to be brief in their leavetaking as they do not want the king to see them, then leaves after saying in an aside that she will bring the king to find them. Imogen gives Posthumus a diamond ring, and Posthumus gives Imogen a bracelet. King Cymbeline enters and forces Posthumus to leave immediately, then he and Imogen argue. Posthumus's servant Pisanio enters and recounts a fight between Posthumus and Cloten, where Posthumus refrained from hurting Cloten.

Act I, Scene 3

Cloten boasts to a lord how he won the fight with Posthumus, while a second lord mocks him in asides to the audience.

Act I, Scene 4

Pisanio describes Posthumus's departure to Imogen.

Act I, Scene 5

At Philario's house in Rome, Philario, Iachimo, a Frenchman, a Dutchman, and a Spaniard discuss Posthumus. Then Posthumus enters and is welcomed by his friend Philario. The Frenchman recounts a quarrel Posthumus had in France about his claim that his mistress (Imogen) was the most virtuous ("least attemptable") in the world. Iachimo challenges Posthumus to a wager: his estate against Posthumus's diamond ring that he can seduce Imogen. The angry Posthumus accepts the bet.

Act I, Scene 6

Back in England, Cornelius the doctor has given the Queen what she believes to be a slow-acting poison, but Cornelius, not trusting her, has only given her a powerful sleep inducer. She then gives the box of drugs to Pisanio, telling him they are a powerful restorative.

Act I, Scene 7

Iachimo, now at the British court, meets Imogen. He describes Posthumus's life in Italy as one of partying and infidelity and says that Posthumus mocks the idea of a woman actually being faithful. He tells Imogen she should be revenged, and when she asks how, he says by sleeping with him. When Imogen rejects this offer and calls for help, Iachimo claims to have only been testing Imogen's virtue to see if Posthumus's great praise was accurate. He goes on to praise Posthumus as a kind of a saint, and Imogen is mollified. He then asks Imogen if she will store overnight a chest containing presents for the emperor (partially bought by Posthumus, Iachimo claims). Imogen agrees to keep the chest in her bedchamber.

Act II, Scene 1

Cloten complains to Two Lords of his gambling losses at lawn bowling, with the second lord fre-

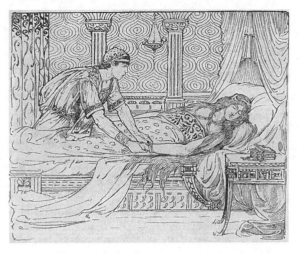

Iachimo removes Posthumus's bracelet from Imogen's wrist while she sleeps in Act II, Scene 2 of *Cymbeline*. This illustration was designed for a 1918 edition of Charles and Mary Lamb's *Tales from Shakespeare.* *(Illustration by Louis Rhead)*

quently criticizing Cloten in asides. When Cloten and the first lord leave, the second lord offers a soliloquy in sympathy for Imogen, who must endure the attentions of the stupid Cloten and the plots of Cloten's crafty mother.

Act II, Scene 2

Imogen is reading in bed then goes to sleep. Iachimo emerges from the trunk, writes down what the room looks like, takes Posthumus's bracelet from Imogen's wrist, and examines Imogen's sleeping body, noticing a five-spotted mole on her left breast. Confident he will be able to convince Posthumus he has seduced Imogen, he climbs back in the trunk and closes the lid.

Act II, Scene 3

Cloten, who has been up all night, complains about losing at cards and, in a vulgar way, asks musicians to play and awaken Imogen. They play and sing a lovely song. Cymbeline and the Queen enter, and Cymbeline asks Cloten to join him in speaking to the Roman ambassador once he has awakened Imogen. Having failed to awaken her with music, he knocks loudly. Imogen enters and tries politely to reject Cloten's advances. Finally losing her temper, she tells Cloten that she values Posthumus's "meanest garment" (2.3.157) more than all of Cloten. Pisanio enters, and Imogen asks him to get her women servants to search for her bracelet, which Imogen realizes is missing. Imogen and Pisanio depart, leaving Cloten, who is completely enraged at the "meanest garment" remark and vows revenge.

Act II, Scene 4

Having returned to Rome, Iachimo claims to have won the bet. First, he describes Imogen's bedchamber in detail, but this fails to convince Posthumus. He then produces the bracelet, and Posthumus is immediately convinced. Others suggest the bracelet may have been stolen, so Posthumus asks for more proof but is convinced of Imogen's guilt again when Iachimo swears "by Jupiter" that he has enjoyed Imogen (2.4.121). Others demand more proof, while Posthumus seems convinced, so Iachimo describes the mole under Imogen's breast. Everyone leaves except Posthumus, who, convinced of Imogen's guilt, rants a misogynistic soliloquy about the evil in women.

Act III, Scene 1

Caius Lucius, a Roman general, comes as ambassador to Britain and tells King Cymbeline that he owes tribute to the Roman emperor. The Queen and Cloten make jingoistic speeches about not paying the tribute, and Cymbeline agrees with them. Lucius responds by "in Caesar's name" declaring war on Britain (3.1.66).

Act III, Scene 2

Pisanio reads a letter from Posthumus that orders him to kill Imogen as punishment for her supposed adultery. Pisanio decides Posthumus has been deceived and resolves not to follow his master's order. Imogen enters, and he gives her another letter from Posthumus, which tells her to go to Milford-Haven (in Wales) to meet him. She resolves to go immediately, disguised as a "franklin's housewife" (3.2.78).

Act III, Scene 3

Belarius, Guiderius, and Arviragus stand in front of their cave in Wales. Belarius praises their life in the wild, but his "sons" Guiderius and Arviragus lament that they miss the opportunities for education and valor that court life offers. Belarius, to convince them of the evils of court life, tells them how he was unjustly exiled from the court. His sons go off to begin the hunt, and Belarius reveals that his sons are actually the king's sons, whom he kidnapped when he was exiled. In this wilderness exile, Belarius has taken the name *Morgan* and given the princes the names *Polydore* and *Cadwal*.

Act III, Scene 4

Arriving in Milford-Haven, Imogen is distressed not to find Posthumus. By way of explanation, Pisanio gives her the letter proclaiming her an adulteress and ordering her execution. The disconsolate Imogen asks Pisanio to kill her, but Pisanio proposes that he only claim to have killed her and that Imogen should disguise herself as a page boy and seek employment with Lucius. Perhaps this way she will be able to go to Italy and see Posthumus. Before he leaves, Pisanio gives Imogen the medicine he got from the Queen, in case she feels ill.

Act III, Scene 5

Lucius bids good-bye to Cymbeline and makes his way to Milford-Haven. Cymbeline and the Queen realize Imogen is missing. The Queen hopes Pisanio has given her the drug, and she is dead. Cloten then interrogates and threatens Pisanio, until Pisanio surrenders the letter Posthumus wrote to Imogen telling her to go to Milford-Haven. Cloten sends Pisanio to retrieve some of Posthumus's clothes. In revenge for Imogen's insult, Cloten plans to dress in Posthumus's garments, kill Posthumus in front of Imogen, and then rape Imogen.

Act III, Scene 6

Imogen, in boy's clothes, soliloquizes about her difficult life, how tired and hungry she is. She discovers Belarius's cave, which she enters, sword drawn, looking for food.

Imogen, disguised as Fidele, asks Belarius, Guiderius, and Arviragus not to harm her in Act III, Scene 7 of *Cymbeline*. This illustration was designed for a 1918 edition of Charles and Mary Lamb's *Tales from Shakespeare*. (Drawing by Louis Rhead)

Act III, Scene 7

Belarius, Guiderius, and Arviragus return from their hunting to discover a strange boy in their cave eating their food. Imogen claims to be "Fidele" in search of a kinsman bound for Italy from Milford-Haven. Guiderius and Arviragus declare they will love this boy as a brother, and Fidele accepts their hospitality.

Act III, Scene 8

In Rome, a senator announces the impending war against Britain, with Lucius as general.

Act IV, Scene 1

Cloten, alone in Wales, soliloquizes about his superiority to Posthumus and his plans to kill him and rape Imogen.

Act IV, Scene 2

Imogen is ill but tells Belarius, Guiderius, and Arviragus to follow their usual routine and go hunting. She takes the drug Pisanio gave her and retreats inside the cave. Cloten enters, and Belarius thinks Cloten has come to apprehend him. Guiderius asks to be left alone to deal with Cloten, and Belarius and Arviragus go off to search for others in Cloten's party. Cloten and Guiderius insult each other, then exit the stage fighting. Belarius and Arviragus return, then Guiderius enters carrying Cloten's head. Belarius worries that they are "all undone" for having killed the son, but the brothers exult in the deed (4.2.124). Their mood changes when Arviragus, checking on Fidele's health, returns with the seemingly dead Fidele in his arms. The brothers lay Fidele down (head to the east) and chant a ceremonial song for him. Belarius returns with Cloten's headless body, lays it next to Fidele, and they depart. Imogen awakes, sees the body next to her, and wonders if she has been dreaming. Then she notices that the headless body is wearing Posthumus's clothes, and she thinks she recognizes his wonderful body. She smears her face with the body's blood (to scare those who might find her) and falls upon the body. Lucius, his captains, and his soothsayer enter. Imogen identifies herself as the boy Fidele, page of Richard du Champ, the headless man beside her. Lucius takes her as his page, orders his men to bury the body, and they all depart.

Act IV, Scene 3

Cymbeline is upset that his wife is feverish and mad (because of the absence of her son) and that his daughter is missing. He is told that the Roman army has landed on the coast, and he withdraws to prepare for the war. Pisanio, in soliloquy, admits to being totally confused and says he will have to trust to fortune.

Act IV, Scene 4

At Belarius's cave, the brothers convince Belarius to join the battle and fight for the British army.

Act V, Scene 1

Posthumus, alone in the Roman camp, looks at the bloody cloth Pisanio has sent him as evidence that Imogen has been killed. Filled with remorse, Posthumus forgives Imogen (while still thinking her guilty), criticizes Pisanio for following his unjust order, and resolves to fight on the British side, even though he has been brought to fight with the "Italian gentry" (5.1.18).

Act V, Scene 2

This is a battle scene, with the British and Roman armies fighting. In the battle, Posthumus, dressed as a poor soldier, defeats and disarms Iachimo. Iachimo assumes he has been defeated by such a "drudge" because he has lied about the country's princess and so the country's air enfeebles him (5.2.5). The battle continues, and Cymbeline is taken. Belarius, Guiderius, and Arvirargus come to Cymbeline's rescue and are joined by Posthumus. They rescue Cymbeline, and the Roman army (including Lucius, Imogen/Fidele, and Iachimo) flees.

Act V, Scene 3

Posthumus converses with a British lord who fled the battle, describing how an old man and two young ones saved the day. When the lord leaves because Posthumus has grown angry, Posthumus decides to seek death by pretending to have fought on the Roman side. A British captain and his soldiers are discussing the fourth man who helped the old man and his two sons in the battle, when they discover Posthumus (who says he fought on the Roman side) and take him prisoner.

Act V, Scene 4

In jail, Posthumus looks forward to death, so he can offer up his life in exchange for having taken Imogen's. He falls asleep, and music brings forth an "apparition" (his dream). His dead fam-

ily—father Sicilius Leonatus, mother, and two brothers—circle the sleeping Posthumus as music plays. In rhyme, they ask the great god Jupiter to help Posthumus. In response, there is thunder and lightning, and Jupiter descends on an eagle, while the "ghosts" of Posthumus's family fall on their knees. Jupiter somewhat petulantly explains that Posthumus will have a happy end, will marry Imogen, and end up the happier because of his various afflictions. He gives them a tablet to put on Posthumus's chest. Posthumus wakes, reads the tablet (which makes no sense to him), greets the jailer who is to take him to be executed, and is surprised to be called to the king.

Act V, Scene 5

Cymbeline honors the "preservers" of his throne (5.5.2), Belarius, Guiderius, and Arvirargus, and they all lament that they cannot locate the heroic poor soldier who fought with them. Cornelius the doctor comes in to report that the Queen has died, confessing that she never loved Cymbeline and had planned to poison him and make Cloten king. But, with Cloten gone, her plot was pointless, so she died in despair. The Roman prisoners are brought in (including Lucius, Iachimo, the soothsayer, Posthumus, and Imogen/Fidele). Lucius is prepared to be executed but asks that Cymbeline spare his innocent page, Fidele. Fidele not unreasonably looks familiar to Cymbeline and so is spared and allowed to ask any favor of Cymbeline. Lucius expects his page to beg for Lucius's life, but instead, Imogen/Fidele asks Iachimo to explain how he obtained the diamond he is wearing. Iachimo tells a more or less true version of the events, and Posthumus steps forward calling Iachimo a villain and also blaming himself. When he invokes Imogen as "My queen, my life, my wife, O Imogen, / Imogen, Imogen!" (5.5.226), Imogen/Fidele herself steps forward, and Posthumus, upset at being interrupted by a "Scornful page" (5.5.227), strikes her. Pisanio suggests that now indeed Posthumus really has killed Imogen, but fortunately, Imogen awakes. She blames Pisanio for poisoning her, but Pisanio and the doctor Cornelius soon straighten this story out. Posthumus and Imogen embrace lovingly as Belarius and the brothers figure out what has happened. Pisanio explains how he sent Cloten to Milford-Haven, and Guiderius completes the story by telling how he slew Cloten there. Since Guiderius killed a prince, King Cymbeline has no choice according to law but to sentence him to death. Belarius then reveals that the two brothers are not his sons Polydore and Cadwal but are actually King Cymbeline's sons Guiderius and Arvirargus. The final proof comes when Guiderius shows the mole upon his neck, which Cymbeline of course remembers. In guilt, Iachimo volunteers for execution, but Posthumus forgives him and asks him to behave better in the future. Inspired by his son-in-law, Posthumus, Cymbeline frees all the Romans. The soothsayer, Philarmonus comes forth to explain the prophecy, and Cymbeline decides to submit to the Romans and pay the usual tribute, which the wicked queen had dissuaded him from. So Cymbeline is reunited with his two sons and his daughter, Imogen is reunited with Posthumus, and the world is at peace.

CHARACTER LIST

Cymbeline   King of Britain during Roman times and at the time of Christ's birth. His two sons were abducted in childhood, so his only remaining child is his daughter, Imogen. His wife has recently died, and he has remarried a woman who controls him.

Queen   Cymbeline's second wife. She is Cloten's mother by an earlier marriage and Imogen's stepmother. She is a fairy-tale wicked stepmother, like the queen in "Snow White." She is beautiful but evil. Set on making her stupid son king, she is interested in poisons.

Imogen   Daughter of Cymbeline by a former queen, she is a paragon of virtue and beauty. She is also smart, brave, and resourceful. She disguises as a page boy, Fidele, in order to flee the court and seek her husband, the relatively lowborn Posthumus. People tend to fall in love with her, for example, Guiderius, Arviragus (her lost brothers), and Caius Lucius.

Cloten   Son to the Queen by a former husband, so stepson to King Cymbeline. Cloten is remarkably stupid and vain, inclined to gambling and violence.

Posthumus Leonatus   A gentleman, husband of Imogen. As an orphan, he was taken into the king's family and raised with Imogen. He marries Imogen against the king's wishes, loves her madly, but shows little faith or trust in her.

Belarius   A banished lord, disguised under the name of Morgan. Falsely accused of treason by Cymbeline, he stole the king's two sons and has lived with them for 20 years in the wilds of Wales.

Guiderius   Cymbeline's older son and heir. Guiderius has been raised as Belarius's son under the name Polydore.

Arviragus   Cymbeline's younger son. Arviragus has been raised as Belarius's son under the name Cadwal.

Philario   Italian friend of Posthumus. He hosts Posthumus when Posthumus is banished.

Iachimo   A friend of Philario. Iachimo is a stereotypical Italian Renaissance villain, the Machiavelle. He cynically doubts all women's virtue, and when he fails to seduce Imogen as he has wagered Posthumus he can, he cleverly convinces Posthumus that he has.

Caius Lucius   Roman ambassador to Britain and subsequent general of the Roman forces.

Pisanio   Servant of Posthumus, then, when Posthumus is banished, servant of Imogen. He is typical of the "loyal servant" character.

Cornelius   A physician. He shows his virtue and goodness in not giving the Queen the poison she asks for but instead giving her a sleeping potion.

Philarmonus   A Roman soothsayer. He predicts the future and interprets the tablet Jupiter gave Posthumus.

Frenchman   Friend of Philario. He recounts the argument Posthumus had in France about Imogen's superlative virtue, which leads to the unfortunate wager with Iachimo.

Two Lords of Cymbeline's court   They accompany Cloten, with the first lord treating him respectfully and the second mocking him in asides to the audience.

Two Gentlemen of Cymbeline's court   They describe the opening situation for the audience.

Two Gaolers   They guard Posthumus and provide some comic relief.

Helen   A Lady who attends Imogen.

Jupiter   Thunder god and king of the gods in Roman mythology.

CHARACTER STUDIES

Like *Pericles* (written just before *Cymbeline*), *Cymbeline* is one of Shakespeare's least character-driven plays, with some of the characters seemingly "stock": the faithful servant, the wicked stepmother, the Italian villain, the persecuted maiden. Still, even within the constraints of these theatrical conventions, Shakespeare creates memorable characters.

Cloten

If Cloten is not Shakespeare's stupidest character, he is certainly Shakespeare's stupidest prince. His very name evokes stupidity, for while *clot* means a mass or a lump in general parlance, in informal British English (in Shakespeare's time and ours), a clot is a blockhead, a dolt, or, to use a related word, a clod. And as a stupid fool, he is a character who can get laughs from an audience.

Cloten's character is established not just by what he says and does but also by what is said about him. Thus, in his first scene, the first words of the First Lord are about how Cloten should change his shirt, how he literally reeks (from an offstage confrontation with Posthumus). Cloten brags about his valor to two lords, but one of them, in eight asides, makes sure we the audience know he is actually a coward and a fool. Thus, we see Cloten not only as stupid but also as self-deluded. Typically, he cannot understand why Imogen would prefer Posthumus to himself and says, "And that she should love this fellow, and refuse me!" to which the Second Lord replies in an aside, "If it be a sin to make a true election, she is damned." (1.2.24–26)

Cloten's second appearance is again with the two lords, and again the Second Lord makes sure we know the truth by denigrating Cloten in six asides. In this scene, we learn that Cloten has been gambling and losing at bowls (lawn bowling, which seems to have been Shakespeare's favorite sport). In frustration at losing 100 pounds (a lot of money in Shakespeare's time), he took to swearing but, told not to swear by his opponent, in response broke his opponent's skull with a bowl. As in Cloten's first scene, we see that he is violent and cowardly and that he does not have the respect of those who serve him.

In Cloten's third appearance, he has again lost at gambling (this time at cards). Apparently, he has been up all night gambling, as it is now morning. Following someone's advice he is wooing Imogen with music. "I am advised to give her music a mornings, they say it will penetrate," he says. Lest we are not sure he is being vulgar in his choice of language, his next words to the entering musicians are "Come on, tune: if you can penetrate her with your fingering, so: we'll try with tongue too . . ." (2.3.11–14). Eventually, Imogen does appear and tries to be polite, but Cloten's stubborn pursuit of her drives her to say she hates him and finally drives the insulted Cloten to pursue revenge against her. Since Imogen is by all accounts the paragon of virtue, after this encounter, Cloten has sunk even lower.

In the scene with the Roman ambassadors, Cloten seems a patriot (counseling was again Rome), but in the context of the play, he is a war-mongering chauvinist. Cloten's final scenes show him not just as stupid and violent but also as crazy and evil. He goes to Milford-Haven to kill Posthumus and to rape Imogen madly wearing Posthumus's clothes. The king's son Guiderius ends up beheading him, an almost allegorical action where good triumphs over evil.

The Queen

Many of Shakespeare's late plays, of which *Cymbeline* is one, have fairy-tale elements. Probably more than any other character in these plays, the Queen in *Cymbeline* is a fairy-tale character. Indeed, many critics think Shakespeare had a version of a tale like "Snow White" in mind when he created this nameless queen (and indeed her lacking a name is itself typical of fairy tales). The Queen in *Cymbeline* is a wicked but beautiful stepmother. She plots to poison her stepdaughter, the young princess (in *Cymbeline,* with the doctor's drugs; in "Snow White," with a poisoned apple), and she ends up forcing the girl to run away to the wilderness (in "Snow White," to a "wild forest"; in *Cymbeline,* to the wilds of Wales) where she is protected by a group of men (three in *Cymbeline,* seven in "Snow White"). And so, the Queen is purely evil, plotting death to an innocent princess and even to her husband, the king.

Iachimo

Iachimo's character owes much to the Italian villain in *Othello,* Iago. Indeed, *Iachimo* means "little Iago." Like Iago, he tricks a loving husband into such a mad jealousy as to want to kill his wife. But Iago's reason famously is a "motiveless malignity" as Coleridge wrote, while Iachimo's has clearer sources.

Iachimo's character is much indebted to Shakespeare's typically Renaissance English stereotypes about Italians. He is Machiavellian, valuing victory more than morality, willing to use deception and trickery without concern for morality. Thus, in his confession in the fifth act, he explains his trick to Posthumus, how once Imogen rejected him his "Italian brain / Gan in your duller Britain operate / Most vilely" (5.5.196–198). Whatever else you say about him, Iachimo is extremely clever, a successful trickster.

But, unlike that other clever, successful trickster Iago, Iachimo has clear motivations. In a group of males, when Posthumus brags about his wife as the most virtuous, the most "unattemptable" in the world, Iachimo, as a stereotypical Italian, thinks of himself as an irresistible lover and is willing to say he can seduce any woman in the world, including Imogen. This is a man confident in his attractiveness to women. And he is further motivated by

material concerns, winning a priceless diamond from Posthumus in the wager.

At the end of *Othello,* Iago vows never to speak again, never to explain his actions. Iachimo, on the other hand, both explains and repents his "villainy," showing a surprising moral dimension, willingly offering his life, which he believes he owes. But Posthumus forgives him, saying, "Live / And deal with others better" (5.5.420–421). And, in the fairy-tale world of the play, the audience or the readers will try to believe that indeed the evil Iachimo can indeed live and learn to deal with others better. Cloten is an unredeemable villain, but Iachimo is redeemable and finally redeemed.

Posthumus Leonatus

Posthumus Leonatus goes through major character transformations in the course of the play. The play opens with Two Gentlemen discussing his marriage to the king's daughter. While they praise Posthumus and denigrate Cloten (who had been the planned husband for Imogen), they admit that Posthumus's value has been increased by his marrying the king's daughter: "By her election may be truly read / What kind of man he is" (1.1.53–54). Similarly, Philario and Iachimo in Italy talk about how marriage "makes him both without and within" (1.4.9). That his character (within) has been improved by the marriage proves highly doubtful, but certainly his status is improved by marrying a princess. Iachimo explicitly points to the problem in evaluating Posthumus's character: "The matter of marrying his king's daughter, wherein he must be weighed rather by her value than his own" (1.5.12–14). At the beginning of the play, then, he is basically a lucky guy in that he has married the king's daughter but unlucky in that this has resulted in the king banishing him. He does seem sincerely in love, exchanging vows and tokens with Imogen, and like many a literary lover, he is finding that the course of love does not run smooth. The fact the he and Imogen are truly in love and their love is being thwarted makes him a sympathetic figure, a typical hero in a love story.

Philario welcomes Posthumus into his home in Act I, Scene 5 of *Cymbeline*. This drawing was designed for the Chiswick edition of Shakespeare, published in 1900. *(Illustration by John Byam Lister Shaw)*

Posthumus shows himself lacking "within" when he is in Italy. An unnamed Frenchman reminds Posthumus about a duel Posthumus was ready to fight (which the Frenchman averted), to prove that his mistress was "more fair, virtuous, wise, chaste, constant, qualified, and less attemptable than any the rarest of our ladies in France" (1.4.66–67). Posthumus insists the "quarrel was not altogether slight" (1.4.51) and then gets into the same quarrel with Iachimo, ending up with the wager and Iachimo going to England (with a letter of introduction from Posthumus) to try to seduce

Imogen. Posthumus shows himself to be violent and shallow, too ready to fight, and too in need of proving to the world the value of his mistress (and thus of his own value, perhaps). Only an immature man would make such a wager about his own wife and would be ready to engage in mortal combat about such an issue.

Posthumus acquits himself even worse when Iachimo returns with supposed evidence of his conquest of Imogen. Posthumus is too easily convinced with the sight of the bracelet and Iachimo's swearing "by Jupiter" (2.4.121). He believes Imogen's guilt even before Iachimo mentions the mole on her breast. Anyone who is deceived so easily is too credulous, too naive. It never dawns on Posthumus that Iachimo might be capable of tricking him. And then, at the very end of Act II, Posthumus delivers one of the most misogynistic speeches in literature: "Is there no way for men to be, but women / Must behalf workers?" (2.4.153–154). Suddenly, our hero has shown himself to be violent, immature, credulous, and misogynistic. And soon we learn from Pisanio that Posthumus has sunk even lower, commissioning his servant to kill Imogen. Now our hero is a would-be murderer!

Imogen unintentionally suggests Posthumus's villainy when she mistakes the body of the headless Cloten (wearing Posthumus's clothes) for Posthumus. Surely, the audience, too, cannot help but think of the similarity between Cloten the villain and Posthumus the hero: Both are immature, stupid, violent, and misogynistic. (The similarity of Posthumus to Cloten might have been tellingly suggested on Shakespeare's stage, where it is likely the same actor played both roles; Shakespeare's company routinely doubled roles, and Posthumus and Cloten are never on stage at the same time and must wear about the same size in clothes.

Posthumus is tellingly absent from the stage until the beginning of Act V, and when he appears, he has been transformed. Carrying the bloody cloth that Pisanio has sent as evidence of Imogen's death, Posthumus makes a remarkable statement:

You married ones,
If each of you should take this course, how
  many
Must murder wives much better than
  themselves
For wrying but a little?

                                    (5.1.2–5)

The wager story is an old one, existing in fiction
and folktales that Shakespeare no doubt knew. But,
in all other Renaissance versions of this story, the
husband only forgives the wife after he discovers
she is innocent. The remarkable thing about Posthumus's words, as a modern critic has pointed out,
is that Posthumus forgives Imogen while he still
believes she is guilty, describing her supposed adultery as "wrying but a little." His is a remarkable
attitude, even more remarkable in the Renaissance.
This soliloquy shows that Posthumus has indeed
been transformed, somewhat different "within."

Soon Posthumus shows himself true to the
surname *Leonatus,* with the courage and skill he
shows in battle, helping save the king and defeat
the Romans. But, conscious of his sins, he pretends to be a Roman so he will be put to death.
In jail, he has a dream that promises him a comic
ending. Jupiter appears (at the bequest of Posthumus's dead family) and promises happiness for
Posthumus. Jupiter tells us the reason for Posthumus's good fortune: "Our Jovial star reign'd at his
birth" (5.4.105). This is telling. Posthumus is not
rewarded for his virtue (we and he know he is lacking in that department) but because he has been
blessed by Jupiter at birth. Similarly, Shakespeare,
in the godlike role of author, has chosen Posthumus as the hero of this story, even while making
it clear that he does not necessarily deserve to be
the hero. Shakespeare chooses his heroes much as
Jupiter does, not on the basis of their moral qualities. (Similarly, Bertram in *All's Well That Ends
Well* and Claudio In *Much Ado About Nothing* are
heroes with some clear moral deficiencies.) What
makes Posthumus more admirable, though, is that
he has become clearly aware of his moral failings.
Acknowledging his own sinfulness, a traditional

part of Christian conversion experience, is a precursor to his redemption.

But in the last scene of the play, Shakespeare
makes us doubt Posthumus's recovery, at least a little bit. Posthumus is proclaiming his own villainy
and crying out for Imogen, when Imogen, dressed
as Fidele, approaches him, saying "Peace my lord,
here, hear—." Astoundingly, Posthumus strikes
the page, she falls, and Pisanio says, "You ne'er
killed Imogen till now" (5.5.225–226). Depending on the production, someone seeing the play for
the first time might think that Imogen is indeed
now dead, that *Cymbeline* really is the tragedy it
is labeled as in the First Folio. But, instead, Imogen recovers, she and Posthumus embrace lovingly,
and Posthumus shows his moral transformation in
his treatment of Iachimo. Iachimo returns Posthumus's ring and offers his own life, but Posthumus
forgives him. This forgiveness inspires the king to
spare all the Romans and to pay the tribute and
seek peace. Posthumus, knowing his own sinfulness, chooses mercy and forgiveness, displaying
Christian virtues.

Imogen

Since the 19th century, Imogen has probably
excited more adoration than any other Shakespeare heroine. She is beautiful, virtuous, and
feminine, but she is also spirited, smart, and brave.
She refuses to play the passive heroine, suffering
patiently and waiting to be rescued by a man.

In her first scene, the Queen pretends to be on
her and Posthumus's side, but when the Queen
leaves, Imogen makes it clear she is not fooled
by the Queen's "dissembling courtesy" (1.1.84).
And, when the king enters, banishes Posthumus,
and upbraids Imogen for her love of Posthumus,
Imogen talks back to her father firmly: "Harm
not yourself with vexation / I am senseless of your
wrath" (1.1.136–137). She is far less deferential to
her father than similarly love-oppressed women
such as Juliet *(Romeo and Juliet)* and Hermia (in
A Midsummer Night's Dream). And, when she
realizes Iachimo is attempting to seduce her, she
three times calls for help ("What ho, Pisanio!"),

tells Iachimo to go away, and threatens him with the power of her father, the king. (Admittedly, she does seem a little quick to accept Iachimo's explanation, but perhaps, she is just so pleased to hear Iachimo praise Posthumus, the man she loves so fully). She is similarly forceful in her rejection of Cloten's advances, moving from the attempted politeness of "I am sorry, sir, / You put me to forget a lady's manners" (2.3.103–104) to the more forceful truth of "I hate you" (5.5.109). And, when Pisanio informs her that Posthumus has commissioned her murder for supposed adultery, her sarcastic rage and her willingness to die show her strength of character. She is willing to venture off to Milford-Haven in disguise, then transform herself into a boy, going out into the wilderness alone. This brave transformation echoes those of Viola in *Twelfth Night* and Rosalind in *As You Like It* and similarly shows the courage and ability to function in a masculine world. She draws a sword on entering Belarius's cave, and when she awakens next to a headless man, she smears blood on her own face so as to seem "horrider" to those who might chance to find her. Imogen is no pushover:

> All of her that is out of doors most rich!
> If she be furnished with a mind so rare,
> She is alone th' Arabian bird, and I
> Have lost the wager
>
> (1.7.15–18).

(The "Arabian bird" refers to the phoenix, the mythological bird that when it dies in flames is reborn in its own ashes.) When Iachimo peeks at Imogen's sleeping body, he is even more extensive in his praise for her beauty. Posthumus, of course, has won her love, but Cloten also pursues her. Even disguised as a boy, she excites spontaneous love from her brothers (who at the time do not know they are her brothers) and the Roman Caius Lucius, who upon meeting her disguised as Fidele, with a bloody face, promises that if she enters his service, she will be "beloved" (4.2.383). Imogen's beauty and character repeatedly excite love and respect in men.

Imogen in Act I, Scene 7 of *Cymbeline*, as depicted in a print from Charles Heath's 1848 edition of *The Heroines of Shakspeare: Comprising the Principal Female Characters in the Plays of the Great Poet (Painting by J. W. Wright; engraving by W. H. Mote)*

While she shows courage and is willing to adopt male dress, Imogen reveals her feminine side in occasional flashes of delicate poetic language. Thus, she describes her longing to see her beloved Posthumus as "beyond beyond" (3.2.57), beautifully suggesting the almost infinite depths of her longing. She often uses images of diminution, of littleness, evoking a female point of view. Thus, when Pisanio tells her of watching Posthumus leaving on ship, Imogen says:

> I would have broke mine eye-strings, crack'd
>   them, but
> To look upon him, till the diminution
> Of space had pointed him sharp as my needle:

Nay, followed him, till he had melted from
The smallness of a gnat, to air: and then
Have turn's mine eye, and wept.

(1.4.17–22)

When Imogen wakes up from the sleeping drug, before noticing the headless body, she uses the charming exclamation "'Ods pitikins" (4.2.293), a diminutive of "God's Pity," that is, "May God have pity." Then, when she notices the body, she is filled with fear and utters prayerful words that again move to the diminutive: "but if there be / Yet left in heaven as small a drop of pity / As a wren's eye, fear'd gods, a part of it" (4.2.303–305).

Imogen's outstanding character trait is no doubt her capacity to love Posthumus and have faith in him. (Her faithfulness is suggested by her taking the name *Fidele* when she disguises as a boy). She never wavers in her love for Posthumus, despite his bad behavior. No wonder so many 19th-century men idolized her. She epitomizes the wonder of having the love of a good woman.

DIFFICULTIES OF THE PLAY
Genre

The genre of the play has been confused from the start. The First Folio labels the play a tragedy, perhaps because nobles die (the evil Queen and her evil son, Prince Cloten), whereas it labels *The Winter's Tale* a comedy, even though the innocent Prince Mamillius dies. Most criticism calls it a romance or a tragicomedy (which for Shakespeare tends to be much the same thing). It has also been labeled a pastoral play, because the journey to the natural world of Wales brings renewal to the corrupt court. It is also in some ways a history play, since Cymbeline was a historic king of Britain at the time of Augustus. And, of course, it can in large part also be seen as a comedy, as all (except the two dead villains) come to a happy ending. Perhaps, Polonius, in describing the actors to Hamlet, best labeled the genre of *Cymbeline:* "The best actors in the world, either for tragedy, comedy, history, pastoral, pastoral-comical, historical-pastoral, tragical-historical, tragical-comical-historical-pastoral, scene

individable, or poem unlimited" (2.2.415–419). "Tragical-comical-historical-pastoral poem unlimited" describes the play well.

Patriotic Speeches

When Caius Lucius asks Cymbeline to pay his usual tribute to Caesar, the Queen and Cloten give extensive patriotic speeches refusing, speeches likely to have gained applause, at least from the groundlings at the Globe Theatre. These fiery patriotic speeches have puzzled many critics. About Cloten's call to arms, G. Wilson Knight suggested that, as often happens in real life, a national crisis can "render violent instincts respectable." Cloten has shown himself to be inclined to violence, so perhaps it is reasonable that rather than seeking peace he embraces war. Harold Bloom gives a more unusual response, characterizing these speeches as "Shakespearean self-chastisement for his earlier indulgences in patriotic bombast" (622). In other words, after writing jingoistic speeches for *Henry V, Richard II,* and other plays, here at the end of his career, Shakespeare wants to criticize such "patriotic bombast" by putting it in the mouths of the evil characters. Recently, critics such as Ros King and Leah S. Marcus have suggested that having villains articulate chauvinistic readiness for war was a reflection of King James's foreign policy. He thought of himself as a new Augustus, ready to unite England and Scotland into Britain (a British Empire), and he thought of himself as the leader who would bring peace to Europe (like the *Pax Romana* Augustus brought).

Imogen's Innocence

Iachimo tells Imogen that Posthumus is unfaithful to her while in Italy, then asks Imogen to revenge this infidelity by sleeping with him. Imogen figures out that Iachimo is villainous. How, then, can the clever Imogen be so naive as to accept Iachimo's explanation for his lies?

The best defense of her naïveté in terms of realistic human psychology is to say that Imogen is so in love with Posthumus and has been missing him so much that when Iachimo starts praising

Posthumus, he is saying what Imogen believes and wants to hear. And so, Imogen believes the explanation Iachimo slips in before his extensive praise of Posthumus, that he was just testing Imogen to see if she really was so deserving of Posthumus's trust. Another explanation (which can be used to explain a lot in *Cymbeline*) is to point to the genre and nature of this play. Shakespeare uses a tremendously complicated romance plot (which generates its own kind of pleasure), but the cost of using such a romance–fairy-tale structure for the plot is the difficulty in maintaining psychological realism. In any event, this scene is a challenge for the actress playing Imogen.

Imogen and the Headless Body

At the end of a long soliloquy upon awakening next to the headless body, Imogen says, puzzlingly, "Give color to my pale cheek" (4.2.330). Not all editors agree, but J. M. Nosworthy, in *The Arden Edition of* Cymbeline, states the likely truth: "There seems no escape from the gruesome conclusion that she smears her face with his blood, or is about to do so" (136). Imogen is alone in the wilderness next to what she thinks is the headless body of her husband. She says she smears the blood on her face so she might frighten away any would-be attackers, and so, she does here show remarkable courage. But, the dreadful irony is that this is the blood of the man she hates, Cloten; perhaps then, this gruesome moment has a hint of comedy (the way some gruesome moments in horror movies can elicit laughter). Again, this is a difficult moment for the actress, and not all actresses and directors choose to have Imogen smear her face with blood.

Imogen Today

Students often wonder how contemporary women can admire Imogen. Part of the problem is that so many male literary critics have idealized her, for her beauty, her purity, and especially her fidelity (which is why she takes the name *Fidele*). But, certainly up until the last act of the play, she does display qualities women as well as men can admire. Judi Dench, who played Imogen for the Royal

Shakespeare Company in 1979, explained how she saw Imogen:

> She's a lady of great and rare spirit. I had a long letter from someone who saw the play when I was in it who said she found it extraordinary that Shakespeare should write this girl who is never brow-beaten, never gives in and who, whatever happens to her, springs back to life every time. She accepts every kind of challenge. I used to feel downbeat by the interval but the director, David Jones, said you mustn't feel that at all. She's defied everyone, including her father who is little better than a tyrant. She's a rebel and you must play her as such. (Cook, 82)

But, the problem for contemporary feminist critics is in the last scene when she forgives Posthumus for

Viola Allen as Imogen in a 1908 production of *Cymbeline*

trying to have her murdered, embracing him with seemingly true love. While most modern women would reasonably enough be looking for a divorce lawyer or at least a counselor at this time, Imogen is not a modern woman. Indeed, she is something of a fairy tale heroine, so thinking she should not forgive Posthumus and bring us the happy ending is like thinking Hansel and Gretel should not forgive their father (who under the influence of the wicked stepmother did abandon them in the forest). Some critics of the fairy tale and of *Cymbeline* apply contemporary realistic standards to these stories, which makes for very interesting literary criticism but perhaps for less enjoyment of the literature. *Cymbeline* is not "realistic," so to enjoy the play, perhaps you need to accept the unrealistic fairy-tale elements, as even actress Ellen Terry, apparently struggled to do but did achieve:

> When I came to know her well—it was in 1896 at the Lyceum—I was able to understand how, after all the crimes her husband has committed against her—and the worst I think is his writing that lying love letter to bring her to Milford Haven within reach of his revenge— she can throw her arms round him and say in an ecstasy of tenderness "why did you throw your wedded lady from you?"

KEY PASSAGES
Act II, Scene 4, 1–34

POSTHUMUS. Is there no way for men to be but women
Must be half-workers? We are all bastards,
And that most venerable man, which I
Did call my father, was I know not where
When I was stamp'd; some coiner with his tools
Made me a counterfeit: yet my mother seem'd
The Dian of that time: so doth my wife
The nonpareil of this. O, vengeance, vengeance!
Me of my lawful pleasure she restrain'd
And pray'd me oft forbearance; did it with
A pudency so rosy the sweet view on't

Might well have warm'd old Saturn; that I thought her
As chaste as unsunn'd snow. O, all the devils!
This yellow Iachimo, in an hour, was't not?
Or less; at first? Perchance he spoke not, but
Like a full-acorn'd boar, a German one,
Cried 'O!' and mounted; found no opposition
But what he look'd for should oppose and she
Should from encounter guard. Could I find out
The woman's part in me—for there's no motion
That tends to vice in man, but I affirm
It is the woman's part: be it lying, note it,
The woman's: flattering, hers; deceiving, hers:
Lust and rank thoughts, hers, hers: revenges, hers:
Ambitions, covetings, change of prides, disdain,
Nice longing, slanders, mutability;
All faults that may be named, nay, that hell knows, why hers
In part or all; but rather, all. For even to vice
They are not constant, but are changing still;
One vice, but of a minute old, for one
Not half so old as that. I'll write against them,
Detest them, curse them: yet 'tis greater skill
In a true hate, to pray they have their will:
The very devils cannot plague them better.

Posthumus, convinced by Iachimo of Imogen's infidelity, gives a misogynistic soliloquy. The opening thought, a wish that men might be conceived without women, goes back to medieval traditions. "We are all bastards," Posthumus proclaims in an unmetrical but powerful piece of hyperbole. He is claiming that Imogen's supposed action reflects a universal truth about all women. And so, Posthumus's own father would not have been there when Posthumus was actually "stamped," that is, conceived. Posthumus's metaphor here is of a coin maker, so a bastard is like a counterfeit coin. But, the metaphor is grossly extended by the use of "tools": "some coiner with his tools/ Made me a counterfeit." On the one hand, the tools are the tools of the counterfeit coin maker, but on the other hand, tools are clearly the male genitalia of Posthumus's supposed real father.

Yet, Posthumus admits, both his mother and his wife seemed like the goddess Diana, one of whose chief attributes was chastity. Interestingly, there are four other references to Diana in *Cymbeline,* three of them by Iachimo, invoking Diana's chastity. Iachimo tries to convince Imogen that she should not allow Posthumus to make her "live like Diana's priest" (1.6.134), he describes a picture of "chaste Dian bathing" in Imogen's bedchamber (2.4.82), and he recounts how Posthumus bragged about Imogen's chastity, speaking of her "as Dian had hot dreams" (5.5.180). While Jupiter is the featured god in the play (even making an appearance), chaste Diana is the featured goddess.

Posthumus then curiously talks about his sex life with Imogen, a woman he does call his wife, saying that she often restrained him from his "lawful pleasure." Some commentators have suggested that perhaps this admission suggests their marriage was never consummated (so Cloten might have some hope in pursing Imogen). There is no way of knowing, of course, but certainly we have a reinforced image of chaste, modest Imogen. And Imogen's restraining Posthumus from sex had the effect of turning on Posthumus even more. She rejected him with a "pudency" (a word seemingly coined by Shakespeare, meaning modesty and related to the Latin *pudendum,* a word for female genitalia). Her pudency might well have warmed the god Saturn, known for his age, his melancholy, and his coldness.

Posthumus imagines the scene where Iachimo had intercourse with his wife, suggesting that like animals they found no need even to speak. Iachimo, in this vision, was like a "full acorned boar" (Germany was supposedly known for the fierceness of its boars, and therefore, perhaps, Posthumus's imaginary boar is German). "Full acorned" means full from eating acorns, but perhaps there is a testicular allusion here as well. In any event, the image is of animals having sex, with Iachimo the boar (punning on *boor*) simply grunting and mounting.

"Could I find out the woman's part in me," Posthumus begins, but he never grammatically completes the thought (though his intended meaning is clear, that he would like to eliminate the "woman's part" from himself). He does not complete the thought because he is so insanely worked up, so a victim of his own paranoid fantasy. He goes on to list various kinds of vice—lying, flattering, deceiving, lust and dirty thoughts, revenge, ambition, covetousness, "changes of pride" (whatever these are, but presumably related to the sin of pride), disdain, "nice longing" (like lust and dirty thoughts, making it twice that Posthumus mentions these in his list, though in different words), slander, changeability, and all the faults there are—as being the woman's part. Near the end of the list, the sense of the verse all but breaks down, with "All faults that name" not quite making grammatical sense (but implying "all faults that could be named"). And the metrical sense of the blank verse also breaks down, with "In part, or all: but rather all. For even to vice" containing a line-busting 13 syllables (some editors do not follow the First Folio here and break this too long line into two, at "For even to vice"). The effect is that Posthumus's language shows him breaking down as he speaks.

He seems to conclude with a perfect couplet, the way many Shakespeare speeches and most of his plays end: "Detest them, curse them; yet 'tis greater skill / In a true hate, to pray they have their will." But, Posthumus is incapable of ending on a note of order and, instead, adds a line, to end with the 11-syllable, unrhyming "The very devils cannot plague them better."

This speech shows Posthumus as, in effect, mad (thus explaining why he commissions Imogen's murder). And, ironically, the speech does not seem to contain a hint that Posthumus has any woman's part at all in his mind or soul.

Act IV, Scene 2, 258–281

GUIDERIUS. Fear no more the heat o' the
  sun,
Nor the furious winter's rages,
Thou thy worldly task hast done,

Home art gone, and ta'en thy wages.
Golden lads and girls all must,
As chimney-sweepers, come to dust.

ARVIRAGUS. Fear no more the frown o' the
 great,
Thou art past the tyrant's stroke,
Care no more to clothe and eat,
To thee the reed is as the oak:
The sceptre, learning, physic, must
All follow this, and come to dust.

GUIDERIUS. Fear no more the lightning-flash,

ARVIRAGUS. Nor the all-dreaded
 thunder-stone.

GUIDERIUS. Fear not slander, censure rash.

ARVIRAGUS. Thou hast finish'd joy and
 moan.

GUIDERIUS/ARVIRAGUS. All lovers
 young, all lovers must
Consign to thee, and come to dust.

GUIDERIUS. No exorciser harm thee!

ARVIRAGUS. Nor no witchcraft charm thee!

GUIDERIUS. Ghost unlaid forbear thee!

ARVIRAGUS. Nothing ill come near thee!

GUIDERIUS/ARVIRAGUS Quiet
 consummation have;
And renowned be thy grave!

This is the funeral song Guiderius and Arviragus chant (rather than sing) over the supposedly dead body of Imogen/Fidele. Perhaps they do not sing it because Guiderius explains that he "cannot sing" (4.2.240), or perhaps Shakespeare thought the formality of a chant was more suitable than a song for this somber scene.

There is a similar scene—the young woman being mourned as dead when she has really taken a sleeping potion—in *Romeo and Juliet,* when Juliet is found supposedly dead in her bed. And, while there is no funeral scene in *Romeo and Juliet,* subsequent theatrical history shows many productions that staged elaborate funerals. There is a similar theatrical pleasure in this scene in *Cymbeline,* where although the audience knows the girl is not dead, they still enjoy the pleasure of a beautiful ceremony mourning her death, perhaps especially enjoying it because she is not really dead. (There is something similar in the pleasure Tom Sawyer takes in seeing his own funeral in Mark Twain's *Tom Sawyer.*)

Guiderius and Arviragus lay Fidele where they buried their (supposed) mother, Euriphile, and offer the same words they offered to their late "mother." They emphasize the consolation of death, the relief from suffering, in the first line of the chant offering probably the most famous lines from the play: "Fear no more the heat o' th' sun . . ." (These lines appear in Virginia Woolf's *Mrs. Dalloway,* and other writers, such as T. S. Eliot and W. H. Auden, have adapted them in their own work as well.)

"Fear no more," they say again and again to the dead Fidele and to the general dead. (Interestingly, Posthumus's jailer in prison offers Posthumus similar consolation about the prospect of being executed, telling him that after death he will then "fear no more tavern-bills" [5.4.158].) Along with the lack of fear, death brings the consolation of finally going "home," presumably to God. In the couplet at the end of their first stanza, they say, "Golden lads and girls all must, / As chimney-sweepers come to dust." Shakespeare frequently uses *golden* as a superlative adjective, and the adjective perhaps especially fits "lads and girls" here because northern European children frequently have blond hair, which darkens as they grow older. That all our bodies come to dust is a biblical theme that Shakespeare returned to throughout his plays (repeatedly, for example, in *Hamlet*). But this couplet has a secondary meaning that most of Shakespeare's original audience would have responded to. *Golden lads* (and Girls) was a nickname for a dandelion-like plant (the plantain ribwort), which first produces golden flowers but then when dying produces wispy or spiky heads that were called "chimney-sweepers." That life was like a flower was one of Shakespeare's favorite ideas. The song "It was a lover and lass," in *As You Like It,* emphasizes, "How that life was but a flower" (5.3.29). The golden lad–chimney sweep image of living and dying flowers breathes new life into this popular flower = life metaphor. And after the song, when Belarius brings in Cloten's body, he echoes the metaphor, saying to the bodies, "You were as flowers, now withered" (4.2.286).

Through the first three stanzas, Guiderius and Arviragus emphasize the relief death brings (no more fear of the powerful, of having food and clothing, of lightning and thunder, slander or blame) and the inevitability of death (power, learning, medicine, like every lover, must "come to dust"). In the last stanza, they change approach and invoke protection for the buried body, asking for quiet and renown for Fidele's grave.

While exciting sympathy for Fidele, this ritual also creates respect for Belarius and his sons. They had earlier showed their natural religiosity, contradicting the uncivilized wildness we might expect from men living in the Welsh mountains. When they first emerge on stage from their cave, Belarius says, "Stoop, boys: this gate / Instructs you how t' adore the heavens" and then, in what is obviously a daily ritual, they each say, "Hail, heaven!" (3.3.2–3, 8–9). As opposed to the corrupt world of the court, the mountain world of Wales is both natural and spiritual. And, this spirituality is nowhere better shown than in their beautiful funeral song, "Fear no more."

Act V, Scene 4, 22–29

POSTHUMUS. For Imogen's dear life take mine; and though
'Tis not so dear, yet 'tis a life; you coin'd it:
'Tween man and man they weigh not every stamp;
Though light, take pieces for the figure's sake:

You rather mine, being yours: and so, great powers,
If you will take this audit, take this life,
And cancel these cold bonds. O Imogen!
I'll speak to thee in silence.

These are the last lines Posthumus speaks before he has his important dream. The main metaphor here interestingly echoes his misogynistic soliloquy in Act II, where he assumes his father was not actually there when he was "stamp'd," but rather "some coiner with his tools" made him a "counterfeit" (2.5.5–6). But, here, the stamper is not some adulterous lover but rather God, who stamps us with our images (just as the realm's coins were stamped with the image of the sovereign). Posthumus is again like the counterfeit coin, but only because of his own moral "light"ness. In offering his life to "cancel these cold bonds," there is probably a pun, with "bonds" meaning both the manacles he is wearing and "financial obligations." This last meaning is echoed elsewhere in Shakespeare by characters who refer to owing God a death (and the possible pun on "debt" brings to mind the money metaphors Posthumus uses here). Posthumus is ready to pay his debt with his death.

DIFFICULT PASSAGES
Act IV, Scene 2, 291–312

IMOGEN. *[Awakes]* Yes sir, to Milford-Haven, which is the way?
I thank you: by yond bush? Pray, how far thither?
'Ods pitikins: can it be six mile yet?
I have gone all night: faith I'll lie down and sleep.
But, soft! No bedfellow! O gods and goddesses!
[Seeing the body of Cloten]
These flowers are like the pleasures of the world;
This bloody man, the care on't. I hope I dream:
For so I thought I was a cave-keeper,
And cook to honest creatures: but 'tis not so:
'Twas but a bolt of nothing, shot at nothing,

Which the brain makes of fumes. Our very
  eyes
Are sometimes like our judgments, blind.
  Good faith,
I tremble stiff with fear: but if there be
Yet left in heaven as small a drop of pity
As a wren's eye, fear'd gods, a part of it!
The dream's here still: even when I wake, it is
Without me, as within me: not imagined, felt.
A headless man? The garments of Posthumus?
I know the shape of's leg: this is his hand;
His foot Mercurial: his Martial thigh:
The brawns of Hercules: but his Jovial face—
Murder in heaven!—How—'? 'Tis gone.

In an 1896 letter to the actress Ellen Terry (who was preparing to play Imogen), George Bernard Shaw offered some useful advice on how an actress might act the beginning of this soliloquy:

> . . . you wake up, you sit up, half awake, and you think you are asking the way to Milford Haven—*the blessed Milford,* since for the moment you have forgotten your unhappiness. You lie down to sleep again, and in doing so touch the body of Cloten, whose head (or no head) is presumably muffled in a cloak. In your dim, half asleep funny state of consciousness, you still have the idea that you musnt go to bed with anybody else but Posthumus, and you say "But soft, no bedfellow." Then in rousing yourself sufficiently to get away from this vaguely apprehended person, you awaken a little more at this very odd, dreamlike thing, that the bedfellow is covered with flowers. You take up a flower, still puzzly-dreamy, and look curiously at it. It is *bloody,* and then in an instant you are broad awake—"Oh gods and goddesses! etc. . . . When you utter the prayer "If there be yet left in heaven as small a drop of pity as a wren's eye, feared gods, give me a part of it," I suppose you kneel and cover your eyes with your hands in the hope that when you remove them your prayer will be answered and the nightmare gone. You take down you

hands and dare to look again. "The dream's here still. Even when I wake it is without me and within me, not imagined—felt" [Shaw's punctuation is retained here; the full letter can be read in *Ellen Terry and Bernard Shaw: A Correspondence.*]

One useful thing Shaw points out here is that the speech proceeds in stages, with Imogen's consciousness going through a series of changes. At the beginning she is still half asleep, imagining she is still talking to the two beggars who gave her directions to Milford-Haven. (In front of the cave of Belarius in Act III, she had said, "Two beggars told me / I could not miss my way" [3.6.9–10]). Perhaps she has been walking to Milford-Haven in her dream, and she dreams she needs to lie down and rest, and then she sees the body beside her, reacting with a ladylike exclamation, "O gods and goddesses."

Her next lines in some ways sum up this whole speech and perhaps the whole play: "These flowers are like the pleasures of the world; / This bloody man, the care on't." These lines embody the tragicomic vision, where we have both the pleasurable flowers of comedy and the distressing blood of tragedy. The whole speech has this double-edged quality. Imogen gradually discovers she is in a horrible situation, with a headless corpse beside her that she concludes is her husband, Posthumus. This is the stuff of tragedy, and in a tragedy, one could imagine her acting like Juliet and taking her own life. But the dramatic irony is spectacular here, and the audience knows she's wrong, that it is Cloten's body (and that she is also wrong, later in the speech, when she blames the actually trustworthy Pisanio). So, while this scene does have tragic horror, there is also something comic about it. The audience is glad Cloten is dead, and while we feel for Imogen's pain, we might also smile at the absurd wrongness of her conclusions.

She is not sure what is the dream and what the reality. "I hope I dream," she says, referring to her present situation, but she concludes that her acting as cook and cave keeper to the three men was indeed the dream. (Her difficulty distinguishing dream from reality will shortly be mirrored by Posthumus when he wakes from his jailhouse dream.) She describes the dream state well, using dreamy language: "a bolt of nothing shot at nothing." She asks for just a drop of pity, even just the size of the eye of the smallest bird (a wren). Then, as Shaw says, she becomes fully awake when she realizes her situation is "not imagined" but actually "felt." Then she goes on to mistake the body for Posthumus's (now Posthumus thinks Imogen is dead, just as Imogen thinks Posthumus is dead), praises Cloten's body in extravagant terms, and ends by discovering that the body is headless. This is an odd, almost embarrassing situation. "No, that's the villain's body, not the hero's!" we may want to cry out. Perhaps, as has been suggested, in this scene the Cloten-like qualities of Posthumus are buried in preparation for the transformation of Posthumus's character—his becoming a real hero and finally being reunited with his loving wife, Imogen.

Act V, Scene 4, 123–151

POSTHUMUS. [*Waking*] Sleep, thou hast
  been a grandsire, and begot
A father to me: and thou hast created
A mother, and two brothers: but, O scorn!
Gone! they went hence so soon as they were
  born:
And so I am awake. Poor wretches that depend
On greatness' favour, dream as I have done,
Wake and find nothing. But, alas, I swerve:
Many dream not to find, neither deserve,
And yet are steep'd in favours: so am I,
That have this golden chance, and know not
  why.
What fairies haunt this ground? A book? O
  rare one!
Be not, as is our fangled world, a garment
Nobler than that it covers. Let thy effects
So follow, to be most unlike our courtiers,
As good as promise.
[*Reads*] When as a lion's whelp shall, to
himself unknown, without seeking find, and

be embraced by a piece of tender air; and when from a stately cedar shall be lopped branches, which, being dead many years, shall after revive, be jointed to the old stock and freshly grow; then shall Posthumus end his miseries, Britain be fortunate and flourish in peace and plenty.

'Tis still a dream: or else such stuff as madmen
Tongue and brain not: either both or nothing,
Or senseless speaking, or a speaking such
As sense cannot untie. Be what it is,
The action of my life is like it, which
I'll keep, if but for sympathy.

Posthumus awakes from the kind of dream that many people with dead family have had, excited about having just seen his dead father, mother, and brothers. But then, he realizes that it was "just a dream," and he falls into self-pity about having woken to find nothing, about his fate being that typical of a "poor wretch." Then he reconsiders and thinks that the dream may predict a favorable outcome for him, that indeed the dream might be a "golden chance." As often in Shakespeare (as in "golden lads and girls"), *golden* is the superlative adjective.

Then he sees the tablet Jupiter left for him, which he calls a "book," and he speculates that it has been brought by "fairies." He knows that only something supernatural could drop off a book for him when he is locked up in prison. He offers a wish to the effect that the book not be "as is our fangled world, a garment / Nobler than that it covers." (*Fangled* here means the same as newfangled.) Posthumus is saying, "You can't judge a book by its cover." His use of the word *garment* calls to mind many of the play's themes, especially Cloten's ranting about Imogen, saying she valued Posthumus's "meanest garment" more than innumerable Clotens. And, since Cloten has just been slain in Posthumus's garments, we can appreciate here an example of a major theme of the play. The inside is truly as valuable as the outside. Indeed, Posthumus himself seems, for much of the play, not as valuable or worthy within as he seems to be without.

Then Posthumus reads the baffling words, which he does not understand at all and which the soothsayer interprets at the end of the play. Clearly, though, since his surname is *Leonatus,* the attentive reader should see that he is the lion's whelp, the one who can never triumph through heroic action, but rather, in the words of the prophecy, must "without seeking find, and be embraced by a piece of tender air"—this "piece of tender air," the soothsayer explains via a tortuous Latin etymology, means a woman. As to the curious use of the word *piece,* the commentator Edward Dowden points out that Shakespeare often used the word in reference to "persons and often as indicating supreme excellence." Thus, Prospero, for example, in *The Tempest* describes his wife (Miranda's mother) as a "piece of virtue" (1.2.54).

Posthumus will not succeed through his own action but must trust fate or divine guidance. While Posthumus is unable to unravel the mystery of his dream, there is nonetheless a piece of it left behind, the tablet, as evidence of the reality of the dream experience, which, in this case, is also a religious experience. His dream vision cannot therefore be dismissed just because it does not make sense. The presence of this tablet is evidence of the reality of the dream, of the power of psychic reality.

Thus, both the dream and the tablet reinforce his lack of power and of the necessity to submit to forces beyond himself. His comments on the writing describe it as "still a dream," the kind of things madmen say and do not understand, or speech that makes no sense or cannot be understood. And then, amazingly, Posthumus says that the action of his own life is like a dream, mad speech, or senseless talk, so he will keep the tablet for "sympathy," because its meaninglessness is like his own seemingly meaningless life. Posthumus's final words here are much like Macbeth's conclusion that life "is a tale / Told by an idiot, full of sound and fury, / Signifying nothing" (5.5.26–28). On a happier note, it echoes Prospero's statement in *The Tempest:* "We are such stuff / As dreams are made on"

(4.1.156–157). Shakespeare was obviously attracted to this image of life as something that does not make easy sense, that cannot really be understood or given a clear meaning. Thus, also, in *All's Well That Ends Well,* Lafew says, "They say miracles are past; and we have our philosophical persons, to make modern and familiar, things supernatural and causeless. Hence it is that we make trifles of terrors, ensconcing ourselves into seeming knowledge, when we should submit ourselves to an unknown fear" (2.3.1–6). Posthumus in this speech suggests he has learned this essential Shakespearean lesson, that the worldly knowledge of witty courtiers and reductionist philosophers must finally be renounced in our submission to an unknown fear, to the senseless mystery, dream, or madness that is life. This attitude is what John Keats, in a letter to his brother, described as the essential Shakespeare attitude, calling it "negative capability"—"that is when a man is capable of being in uncertainties, mysteries, doubts, without any irritable reaching after fact and reason."

CRITICAL INTRODUCTION
TO THE PLAY
Transformation

In *Cymbeline,* characters change clothes and names, transform themselves, lose their identities, seem to die and are reborn. Posthumus is at first a British gentleman with the seemingly good luck of marrying the king's daughter, then he is a banished gentleman in Italy, then part of the Roman army with the Italian gentry, then a supposed British peasant who fights for King Cymbeline, then a supposed Italian soldier who is imprisoned, and finally himself again, reunited with the wife he thought he had had killed. In the process of these outer changes and changes in garments (clothes imagery is very frequent in the play), he also changes within, becoming conscious of his own guilt and of the need for forgiveness (for himself and even for Iachimo).

Imogen begins as a princess but dresses down as a franklin's housewife (the wife of a non-noble property holder) in an effort to reunite with Post-

Imogen, dressed as a boy, enters Belarius's cave with her sword drawn in Act III, Scene 6 of *Cymbeline*. Print from the Boydell Shakespeare Gallery project *(Painting by Richard Westall; engraving by James Parker)*

humus. Then she becomes the male page Fidele and lives briefly like a brother with her real brothers and Belarius. She seemingly dies, then awakes from this death and becomes a page for the Roman Caius, and then, at the end, she becomes herself, reuniting with Posthumus.

Morgan and his sons Cadwal and Polydore live in the wilderness of the Welsh mountains. But the sons discover at the end of the play who they really are: They are princes—Cymbeline's sons, Arviragus and Guiderius—and Morgan is really Belarius, who stole them. Iachimo, too, changes at the end, admitting his guilt and seeking punishment in death. And, while Cloten is too dull

to be able to change, he does at least change his clothes, dressing in Posthumus's clothes. Perhaps the most important change is in British foreign policy, where King Cymbeline, following Posthumus's lead, forgives the Romans for their attack, promises to resume paying tribute, and so makes peace. (Perhaps it was because of the national level of this transformation that Shakespeare named the play *Cymbeline,* even though the king is far from the most important character.) Cymbeline's transformation of British policy toward Rome is a historic, not a personal, change.

Pastoral Renewal

The pastoral genre began as poetry about shepherds (who were of a lower class than the authors and readers of pastoral poems) and eventually came to refer to any literary work that took place in the countryside. The great critic William Empson further broadened the term, using it to refer to stories about lower-class people. The dramatic action in pastoral stories is retreat from city/court to the rejuvenating world of the country and, frequently, a return to the city/court. The pastoral journey brings some sort of renewal or new life, as is the case in *As You Like It* and *The Winter's Tale,* as well as *Cymbeline.*

The rejuvenating pastoral world in *Cymbeline* is the mountains of Wales, where Cymbeline's lost sons live and where Imogen/Fidele takes refuge. In *Cymbeline,* the corrupt court defines the first half of the play, with the wicked Queen, the evil Iachimo, and clueless King Cymbeline ascendant. The country, on the other hand, is a place of simple life, of natural religion, and of love. Out of these hills come the forces that are largely responsible for the defeat of the Romans.

Imogen's brothers, skilled hunters and warriors as well as tender mourners, blend the natural and the spiritual. When, with Belarius, they first appear on stage (coming out of their cave), they all three demonstrate their spirituality:

BELARIUS. A goodly day not to keep house
  with such

Whose roof's as low as ours! Stoop, boys; this
  gate
Instructs you how t'adore the heavens; and
  bows you
To a morning's holy office. The gates of
  monarchs
Are arch'd so high that giants may jet through
And keep their impious turbans on, without
Good morrow to the sun. Hail, thou fair
  heaven!
We house I' th' rock, yet use thee not so hardly
As prouder livers do.

GUIDERIUS. Hail, heaven!

ARVIRAGUS. Hail heaven!

BELARIUS. Now for our mountain sport, up
  to yond hill!

                              (3.3.1–12)

Their life contains a daily natural religious
ritual ("Hail heaven!"), followed by the natural
sport of hunting (the contrast with Cloten's early
morning gaming is obvious). The two young men
also show their natural spirituality in their funeral
for Fidele. In their grief, they exhibit tenderness
of feeling (like that exhibited in their original love
for Fidele). The word *nature* is consistently associated with two brothers, who are in tune with
nature. When Cymbeline hears how they and Imogen loved at first sight, he says, "O rare instinct!"
(5.5.382). They are in touch with their natural
instincts

In Act III, Scene 3, the appearance of Belarius,
Guiderius, and Arvirargus before Belarius's cave in
Wales can seem to an audience like the proverbial
breath of fresh air. Not only the pastoral sentiments they express but also their relatively simple
language and clothes and their evocation of a
natural outdoor life make the audience relax. The
simple language they use contrasts sharply with
the convoluted diction Iachimo uses at court. In
Belarius's cave, we are in a world where people (and
audiences) can finally relax.

When eventually Cymbeline's daughter has
entered the cave world, Belarius has clearly become
a surrogate (and superior) father to Cymbeline's
three children. The family love and the spiritual life
that are lacking in the court still exist in the cave
and country world. Belarius as Morgan embodies
the spiritual wisdom the egotistical king lacks, that
an ideal king (or father) should have. When Belarius and the princes come from the natural world to
court, they bring renewal: Cymbeline and Belarius
are reconciled, and the three missing children are
reunited with their father.

But there is another pastoral journey as well,
when Posthumus throws off his upper-class clothes,
dresses as a British peasant, and joins Belarius and
the brothers in defeating the Romans. Here, he is
getting in touch with his natural self (and his natural British self), in a parallel way to how Arviragus and Guiderius have gotten in touch with their
natural selves. In dressing down, he renounces the
pretence and prestige of court.

Clothes
Cymbeline has three characters who change
clothes: Imogen (twice), Posthumus, and Cloten.
It also frequently uses clothing imagery, along with
related discussion of the difference between the
inner and the outer.

In the first scene of the play, the First Gentleman describes Posthumus: "I do not think / So
fair an outward, and such stuff within / Endows a
man, but he" (1.1.22–24). And, at first, Posthumus
seems a worthy protagonist. But how is an outside
observer, a courtier like the First Gentleman, really
able to evaluate Posthumus's inner self? Similarly,
at Philario's house, Philario responds to Iachimo's
lack of admiration for Posthumus (based on a previous acquaintance) by saying, "You speak of him
when he was less furnish'd than now he is with
that which makes him both without and within"
(1.5.8–10). The "that which" is Imogen. That she
might make him "without" is indisputable—she is
the king's daughter. But, to Philario's assumption
that an inner transformation had necessarily com-
plemented the outer marriage, Iachimo brings the

hard-headed truth: "This matter of marrying the king's daughter, wherein he must be weighed rather by her value than his own, words him (I doubt not) a great deal from the matter" (1.5.14–17).

When Posthumus arrives on the scene and we see him for the first time without Imogen, he shows himself to be puffed up with pride in his persona as the accomplished courtier. Having gained the king's daughter, he thinks himself complete within and without. Thus, Posthumus falls to bragging about his mistress in a group of men, makes a stupid wager, and loses his stone (and his soul). He will learn about the difference between within and without.

When Imogen wakes up beside the headless Cloten, she thinks, because of his clothes, that she is next to her dead husband. She thus equates the villain Cloten (a would-be rapist) with Posthumus (a would-be murderer). And Posthumus has shown himself to be like the vulgar Cloten, an egotistical and adolescent gamester. Imogen's judgment is based on the "without," and the audience or reader is forced to recognize that so far Posthumus has not shown any true virtues, that his qualities have all been superficial, without rather than within.

Posthumus's changing his clothes from those of a gentleman to those of a peasant (a pastoral transformation, like a prince dressing up as a shepherd) is emblematic of an inner transformation. Posthumus declares after adopting his new clothes: "To shame the guise o' th' world, I will begin, / To fashion less without, and more within" (5.1.32–33). Posthumus is now conscious of his own failings and shows concern with his inner life rather than his outer appearance.

After his jailhouse dream, when Posthumus awakes and sees the tablet Jupiter has left, he asks:

> What fairies haunt this ground? A book? O
>   rare one,
> Be not, as is our fangled world, a garment
> Nobler than that it covers:
>
> (5.4.133–135)

This clothes image once again emphasizes the distinction between within and without. Posthumus,

no longer superficial, has discovered the difference between the false self of the without (represented by the courtier's clothes) and the true self of the within.

Nature

In April 1611, Dr. Simon Forman saw *Cymbeline* at the Globe Theatre. He recounted in a notebook how Imogen's two brothers lived in a "cave in the woods" and how, when they thought Imogen was dead, they "laid her in the woods". Forman's two references to woods perhaps suggest actual trees were used in the Globe performances. And still today, productions sometimes use trees to create the atmosphere of the Milford-Haven natural world. Such stage trees not only give an image of natural health to contrast with the sickness of the court, they also reinforce a tree symbolism that is woven through the whole play.

Indeed, the prophecy that structures the play's action (on the stone tablet Jupiter gives the sleeping Posthumus) is about a tree:

> When as a lion's whelp shall, to himself
> unknown, without seeking find, and be
> embraced by a piece of tender air: and when
> from a stately cedar shall be lopp'd branches,
> which, being dead many years, shall after
> revive, be jointed to the old stock, and freshly
> grow, then shall Posthumus end his miseries,
> Britain be fortunate, and flourish in peace and
> plenty. (5.4.138–145)

At the end of the play the soothsayer explains:

> The lofty cedar, royal Cymbeline
> Personates thee: and thy lopp'd branches point
> Thy two sons forth: who, by Belarius stol'n,
> For many years thought dead, are now reviv'd,
> To the majestic cedar join'd; whose issue
> Promises Britain peace and plenty.
>
> (5.5. 453–458)

The cedar, sometimes called the king of trees, has lost vital branches. Once these cut-off branches (the dead sons) are rejoined with the old tree (the king), the king and the country are healed. Stories of sick kings in need of cure abound in mythology and fairy tales, for example, the Grimm brothers's "The Water of Life" and Wolfram von Eschnebach's *Parzival*. In *Parzival,* the maimed king can only be healed by a pure and natural youth. King Cymbeline's children, mysteriously kept alive in a cave in the woods, are similarly natural youths, personifications of the king's lost natural instinct. As in *The Winter's Tale,* the sick king's child flourishes in a natural world and represents a more natural and non-neurotic attitude toward life. Shakespeare's pastoral uses the movement from city to country to represent a movement from the sick world of the court to the healing world of nature; he further represents this healing in terms of a tree being brought back to life.

Cymbeline's lack of contact with nature manifests itself in his own lack of understanding of human nature (including his own). Thus, in the prehistory of the play, he trusted the false villains and banished the true Belarius, precipitating the abduction of his sons. Cymbeline is duped by surfaces; he trusted the Queen "For she was beautiful" (5.5.63), and he "thought her like her seeming" (5.5.65). Cymbeline's sons, on the contrary, exhibit a natural instinctive feeling, correctly loving their sister at first sight when they believe her to be the boy Fidele.

King Cymbeline, "the lofty cedar," is earlier in the play imaged as a wind destructive of new growth. Imogen tells how, at Posthumus's departure,

> ere I could
> Give him the parting kiss, which I had set
> Betwixt two charming words, comes in my
> father,
> And like the tyrannous breathing of the north,
> Shakes all our buds from growing.
>
> (1.2.33–37)

Cymbeline lacks the natural love manifested by his children, who embody the goddess nature. Belarius says of the boys,

> O thou goddess,
> Thou divine Nature; thou thyself thou blazon'st
> In these two princely boys: they are as gentle
> As zephyrs blowing below the violet,
> Not wagging his sweet head; and yet as rough,
> (Their royal blood enchafed) as the rudest
> wind,
> That by the top doth take the mountain pine,
> And make him stoop to th' vale. 'Tis wonder
> That an invisible instinct should frame them
> To royalty unlearn'd, honour untaught,
> Civility not seen from other, valour
> That wildly grows in them, but yields a crop
> As if it had been sow'd.
>
> (4.2.169–181)

Whereas his sons' rough wind bends but does not destroy the mountain pine, Cymbeline (unlike his "tender air" daughter and his "gentle zephyrs" sons) is only destructive. The image of Cymbeline as the north wind that destroys the buds parallels the image of Cymbeline as the dying cedar tree with the lopped-off branches. As the cedar tree will be renewed, so will the buds of love be reborn.

Belarius images his own history in similar terms:

> And when a soldier was the theme, my name
> Was not far off: then was I as a tree
> Whose boughs did bend with fruit. But in one
> night,
> A storm, or robbery (call it what you will)
> Shook down my mellow hangings, nay, my
> leaves,
> And left me bare to weather.
>
> (3.3.58–63)

Cymbeline's mistrust for Belarius shook the fruit from the tree, exposing it to injurious weather. Belarius explains:

> two villains, whose false oaths prevail'd
> Before my perfect honour, swore to Cymbeline
> I was confederate with the Romans: so
> Follow'd banishment. . . .
>
> (3.3.66–69)

Lacking any natural intuitive feeling, Cymbeline trusted two villains instead of Belarius. And, fooled by her surface beauty, he trusted the evil Queen (just as Posthumus too easily trusted the false Iachimo).

In *Cymbeline,* Shakespeare again and again makes us think in tree images. A person being like a tree is an old metaphor, appearing in lots of world mythology thus, sometimes a tree is planted at the birth of a child, or two trees at a wedding). Shakespeare uses the motifs of the tree and the renewed king to suggest a natural process of renewal in human life: People grow like trees, and like trees, they can seem dead and come back to life, even have cut-off branches reattached.

While her father is seen as the tree, Imogen is imaged in relation to the air, to the fairy and the angel (spiritual winged creatures), and to the bird (specifically the phoenix). Iachimo says in an aside, after first seeing her:

> All of her that is out of door most rich!
> If she be furnish'd with a mind so rare,
> She is alone th' Arabian bird; and I
> Have lost the wager.
>
> (1.7.15–18)

Beautiful within and without, spiritually and physically, she is the sole Arabian bird, the divine phoenix that dies in its own flames and is reborn. Thus, Arviragus says, as he carries in the dead Fidele: "the bird is dead / That we have made so much on" (4.2.118–119). And Guiderius says, seeing Fidele alive at Cymbeline's court, "The same dead thing alive" (5.5.123). Imogen, therefore, does undergo a "death" (complete with funeral) and a rebirth/awakening.

In mythology, the phoenix is sometimes seen as a bird that dies in the setting Sun. A similar image is evoked in the soothsayer's dream, which he tells to Caius Lucius just before they encounter Imogen upon the headless body:

> Last night the very gods showed me a vision
> (I fast, and pray'd for their intelligence) thus:

> I saw Jove's bird, the Roman eagle, wing'd
> From the spongy south to this part of the west,
> There vanish'd in the sunbeams. . . .
>
> (4.2.346–350)

The soothsayer incorrectly interprets his vision to mean success to the Roman host. Rather, it seems to point to some sort of death, albeit a death that can be followed by a rebirth, as the Sun dying in the west is reborn in the morning in the east. Caius Lucius then notices the headless body and asks, "Soft ho, what trunk is here? / Without his top?" (4.2.352–353). This image of the trunk without its top parallels the image of the old cedar tree seemingly dead from having its branches lopped off. And, as the tree (symbolically Cymbeline) revives, so will the seemingly dead Posthumus (this trunk without a head) be granted new life.

Imogen tells Lucius who she is: "I am nothing or if not, / Nothing to be were better" (4.2.367–368). (*Cymbeline* abounds in uses of the word *nothing:* Imogen's words here echo her summary of her pastoral life as "a bolt of nothing shot at nothing" (4.2.300) and anticipate Posthumus's appraisal of his dream message as "nothing" (5.4.129).) Just as the eagle "Lessen'd herself and in the beams o' the sun / So vanished" (5.5.72–73), so has Imogen in her pastoral journey vanished and become nothing. She suffers a kind of death, losing her identity as Imogen to become Fidele. Then, she seemingly dies, is reborn, and eventually becomes herself (Imogen) again.

Renewal images abound in *Cymbeline.* Nosworthy, editor of the Arden edition, points out how we can connect the phoenix imagery to the tree imagery: the Phoenix's throne, "the sole Arabian tree," was a dry tree that was mysteriously renewed. The union of Imogen and Cymbeline is therefore symbolically "the union of the Phoenix and 'the sole Arabian tree,' and further the union of bird and sun. The restoration of Cymbeline's lost sons, too, is in exact accord with the Phoenix myth since the tree is a dry tree which is mysteriously restored" (lxxxii).

The myth of the phoenix is about transformation achieved through death and rebirth. This

After reading Posthumus's letter, Imogen asks Pisanio to kill her in Act III, Scene 4 of *Cymbeline.* Print from the Boydell Shakespeare Gallery project *(Painting by John Hoppner; engraving by Robert Thew)*

transformation can be a psychological and moral one. For example, both King Cymbeline and Posthumus abandon their faulty old selves and become better. And, it is Imogen who makes Posthumus's rebirth possible. She is the "piece of tender air" who embraces the lion's whelp (Posthumus Leonatus), fulfilling Jupiter's prophecy. As the soothsayer ingeniously interprets this phrase from Posthumus's dream, the piece of tender air is the woman. "Piece of tender" evokes a certain fleshliness, but "air" emphasizes equally the spiritual aspect. This image of woman, like love itself, encompasses both the physical (the natural) and the spiritual. When, at the end of the play, Posthumus is embraced by his piece of tender air (Imogen), he employs a final tree metaphor: "Hang there like fruit, my soul, / Till the tree die" (5.5.264–265). Just as the cedar tree (Cymbeline) has been reborn, so have Posthumus and Imogen been reborn as a couple. Like a tree that shows its life with fruit, Posthumus shows he has a new life with Imogen, his soul.

Religion

Shakespeare and at least some of his audience would have known that Cymbeline was king of England at the time of Christ's birth, which they would have associated with a time of peace on Earth, or what the Romans called the Pax Romana. The play ends with the word *peace,* and Cymbeline's peace with Rome suggests that now Christ has been or will be born. The play seems to emphasize Christian themes, notably forgiveness. As Posthumus forgives Iachimo, so Cymbeline pardons all the Romans and seeks peace. (And, of course, Imogen forgives Posthumus.)

Posthumus, critics have suggested, undergoes something like "Christian regeneration" or a "conversion experience." But, while the conversion experience in Cymbeline is explicitly pagan—it is Jupiter who appears, not Christ—the language of the play (with words such as *elect* and *grace*) frequently echoes the language of a Christian, specifically a Protestant, conversion experience. The classic conversion experience involves the penitent reaching a state of "holy desperation." Aware of his own sinfulness (especially in comparison to God's goodness), the penitent gives himself wholly up to God's mercy. Posthumus's transformation comes from transcendental intervention—God (Jupiter) comes to him. This pattern is tragicomic. Posthumus, plagued with suffering and guilt, is near death. But despair leads to grace, and tragedy turns to comedy. Posthumus, a potentially tragic hero, seems unable to surmount his fate—death—but free pardon, God's grace, brings comic consummation.

Such religious ideas illuminate the comic justice at work in *Cymbeline.* In the first act, Posthumus is like one of the "elect" (a key term in Protestant theology). Thus, the First Gentleman and the Second Lord evaluate Posthumus in terms of Imogen's loving him: "and his virtue / By her election may be truly read / What kind of man he is" (1.2.52–54), and "If it be sin to make a true election, she is damn'd" (3.3.26–27). Iachimo commends Imogen on her "great judgment / In the election of a sir so rare, / Which you know cannot err" (1.7.174–176). These comments, urge us not to evaluate Posthumus in terms of his own actions because one of the elect can attempt murder (as Posthumus does) and not forfeit his salvation; he does not earn

God's grace by good works. While early on we see Posthumus as elect of the virtuous Imogen, later on we see that he is also one of God's (Jupiter's) elect. In Posthumus's dream vision, his dead family asks Jupiter to give Posthumus "The graces for his merits due" (5.4.79). Jupiter, after descending in thunder and lightning, makes no mention of Posthumus's merits but rather emphasizes his own love: "whom best I love, I cross; to make my gift, the more delayed, delighted" (5.4.101–102). One is "elected" independent of virtue. Thus, Jupiter tells his family to have faith: Posthumus is destined to a happy ending because "Our Jovial star reign'd at his birth" (5.4.105).

Shakespeare is not writing an allegory of a Christian religious experience; he is using symbols to describe a process of psychological transformation that has a parallel in religious conversion. Posthumus is explicitly described as elect, and he does seem to have been elected by Jupiter, but he has also been elected by Imogen; it is her love for him, as well as Jupiter's, that secures his heaven on earth.

Comedy

Cymbeline is a spiritual play, but it can also be a very funny play, especially in performance. The reason for this is that much of the humor in Cymbeline comes from dramatic irony—the audience knows things the characters do not. As one director pointed out, there are 27 pieces of dramatic irony in the final scene, and there are many elsewhere in the play, such as when we know the headless body next to Imogen is Cloten's but she thinks it is Posthumus's. And, because of the dramatic irony, this gruesome scene often elicits laughter when played on the stage. When there is a lot of dramatic irony, the audience can have a godlike perspective: Posthumus thinks Imogen is dead but we know she is not; Imogen thinks Posthumus is dead, but we know he is not; King Cymbeline thinks his sons are dead, but we know they are not; and so on.

The writer Garrison Keillor once said, "God is a humorist, but He is working to a slow audience." The characters in *Cymbeline* are such a slow audi-

ence, suffering and suffering, but we have God's perspective and can see the humor in the situation. Shakespeare does a similar trick in *A Midsummer Night's Dream,* where, for example, the audience can see the fairies and the characters (except for Bottom) cannot. The characters suffer, but we have a detached perspective that lets us laugh at their suffering even as we sympathize. "Lord what fools these mortals be," Puck says (3.2.115), and this is a lesson of *Cymbeline,* too. Human beings do not understand their lives; they are God's slow audience. But, we in the audience have a clearer view of God's plan, which is also Shakespeare's plan ("whom best I love I cross" [5.4.101]), so we can laugh as well as cry. This is the spiritual and comic power of the tragicomedy *Cymbeline.*

EXTRACTS OF CLASSIC CRITICISM
Samuel Johnson (1709–1784) [Excerpted from *General Observations on the Plays of Shakespeare* (1756). Here, the great critic explains his negative evaluation of Cymbeline.]

> This play has many just sentiments, some natural dialogues, and some pleasing scenes, but they are obtained at the expense of much incongruity. To remark, the folly of the fiction, the absurdity of the conduct, the confusion of the names and manners of different times, and the impossibility of the events in any system of life, were to waste criticism upon unresisting imbecility, upon faults too evident for detection, and too gross for aggravation.

William Hazlitt (1778–1830) [Excerpted from Character of Shakespeare's Plays (1817). *Cymbeline,* a favorite of Hazlitt's, is the first play he discusses in this important book.]

> *CYMBELINE* is one of the most delightful of Shakespeare's historical plays. It may be considered as a dramatic romance, in which the most striking parts of the story

are thrown into the form of a dialogue, and the intermediate circumstances are explained by the different speakers, as occasion renders it necessary. The action is less concentrated in consequence; but the interest becomes more aerial and refined from the principle of perspective introduced into the subject by the imaginary changes of scene as well as by the length of time it occupies. The reading of this play is like going [on] a journey with some uncertain object at the end of it, and in which the suspense is kept up and heightened by the long intervals between each action. Though the events are scattered over such an extent of surface, and relate to such a variety of characters, yet the links which bind the different interests of the story together are never entirely broken. The most straggling and seemingly casual incidents are contrived in such a manner as to lead at last to the most complete development of the catastrophe. The ease and conscious unconcern with which this is effected only makes the skill more wonderful. The business of the plot evidently thickens in the last act; the story moves forward with increasing rapidity at every step; its various ramifications are drawn from the most distant points to the same centre; the principal characters are brought together, and placed in very critical situations; and the fate of almost every person in the drama is made to depend on the solution of a single circumstance—the answer of Iachimo to the question of Imogen respecting the obtaining of the ring from Posthumus. . . .

The pathos in *Cymbeline* is not violent or tragical, but of the most pleasing and amiable kind. A certain tender gloom o'erspreads the whole. Posthumus is the ostensible hero of the piece, but its greatest charm is the character of Imogen. Posthumus is only interesting from the interest she takes in him, and she is only interesting herself from her tenderness and constancy to her husband. It is the peculiar characteristic of Shakespeare's heroines,

that they seem to exist only in their attachment to others. They are pure abstractions of the affections. We think as little of their persons as they do themselves, because we are let into the secrets of their hearts, which are more important. We are too much interested in their affairs to stop to look at their faces, except by stealth and at intervals. No one ever hit the true perfection of the female character, the sense of weakness leaning on the strength of its affections for support, so well as Shakespeare—no one ever so well painted natural tenderness free from affectation and disguise—no one else ever so well showed how delicacy and timidity, when driven to extremity, grow romantic and extravagant; for the romance of his heroines (in which they abound) is only an excess of the habitual prejudices of their sex, scrupulous of being false to their vows, truant to their affections, and taught by the force of feeling when to forgo the forms of propriety for the essence of it. His women were in this respect exquisite logicians; for there is nothing so logical as passion. They knew their own minds exactly; and only followed up a favourite idea, which

Posthumus places a bracelet on Imogen's arm as King Cymbeline enters in Act I, Scene 2 of *Cymbeline*. This is a print from the Boydell Shakespeare Gallery project. *(Painting by William Hamilton; engraving by Thomas Burke)*

they had sworn to with their tongues, and which was engraven on their hearts, into its untoward consequences. . . .

We have almost as great an affection for Imogen as she had for Posthumus; and she deserves it better. Of all Shakespeare's women she is perhaps the most tender and the most artless. Her incredulity in the opening scene with Iachimo, as to her husband's infidelity, is much the same as Desdemona's backwardness to believe Othello's jealousy. Her answer to the most distressing part of the picture is only, 'My lord, I fear, has forgot Britain.' Her readiness to pardon Iachimo's false imputations and his designs against herself, is a good lesson to prudes; and may show that where there is a real attachment to virtue, it has no need to bolster itself up with an outrageous or affected antipathy to vice. The scene in which Pisanio gives Imogen his master's letter, accusing her of incontinency on the treacherous suggestions of Iachimo, is as touching as it is possible for any thing to be. . . .

The characters of Bellarius, Guiderius, and Arviragus, and the romantic scenes in which they appear, are a fine relief to the intrigues and artificial refinements of the court from which they are banished. Nothing can surpass the wildness and simplicity of the descriptions of the mountain life they lead. They follow the business of huntsmen, not of shepherds; and this is in keeping with the spirit of adventure and uncertainty in the rest of the story, and with the scenes in which they are afterwards called on to act. How admirably the youthful fire and impatience to emerge from their obscurity in the young princes is opposed to the cooler calculations and prudent resignation of their more experienced counsellor! How well the disadvantages of knowledge and of ignorance, of solitude and society, are placed against each other! . . .

The forest of Arden in *As You Like It* can alone compare with the mountain scenes in *Cymbeline:* yet how different the contemplative quiet of the one from the enterprising boldness and precarious mode of subsistence in the other! Shakespeare not only lets us into the minds of his characters, but gives a tone and colour to the scenes he describes from the feelings of their imaginary inhabitants. He at the same time preserves the utmost propriety of action and passion, and gives all their local accompaniments. If he was equal to the greatest things, he was not above an attention to the smallest. Thus the gallant sportsmen in *Cymbeline* have to encounter the abrupt declivities of hill and valley: Touchstone and Audrey jog along a level path. The deer in *Cymbeline* are only regarded as objects of prey, 'The game's a-foot', &c.—with Jaques they are fine subjects to moralize upon at leisure, 'under the shade of melancholy boughs'.

We cannot take leave of this play, which is a favourite with us, without noticing some occasional touches of natural piety and morality. We may allude here to the opening of the scene in which Bellarius instructs the young princes to pay their orisons to heaven:

—Stoop, Boys! this gate
Instructs you how t' adore the Heav'ns;
  and bows you
To morning's holy office.
GUIDERIUS. Hail, Heav'n!
ARVIRAGUS. Hail, Heav'n!
BELLARIUS. Now for our mountain-
  sport, up to yon hill.

What a grace and unaffected spirit of piety breathes in this passage! In like manner, one of the brothers says to the other, when about to perform the funeral rites to Fidele:

Nay, Cadwall, we must lay his head to
  the east;
My Father hath a reason for't.

Shakespeare's morality is introduced in the same simple, unobtrusive manner. Imogen will not let her companions stay away from the chase to attend her when sick, and gives her reason for it:

> Stick to your journal course; THE
>   BREACH OF CUSTOM
> IS BREACH OF ALL!

When the Queen attempts to disguise her motives for procuring the poison from Cornelius, by saying she means to try its effects on 'creatures not worth the hanging', his answer conveys at once a tacit reproof of her hypocrisy, and a useful lesson of humanity:

> —Your Highness
> Shall from this practice but make hard
>   your heart.

John Keats (1795–1821) [Excerpted from a review for *The Champion* (1817). Here, the famous romantic poet discusses Shakespeare's work, including *Cymbeline*.]

The poetry of "Romeo and Juliet," of "Hamlet," of "Macbeth," is the poetry Shakespeare's soul—full of love and divine romance. It knows no stop in its delight, but "goeth where it listeth"—remaining, however, in all men's hearts a perpetual and golden drea. The poetry of "Lear," "Othello," "Cymbeline," etc., is the poetry of human passions and affections, made almost ethereal by the power of the poet.

Edward Dowden (1843–1913) [Excerpted from *Shakespeare* (1877). Dowden was a professor of English at Trinity College, Dublin, and vice president of the New Shakspere Society. Here, he discusses *Cymbeline* in the context of Shakespeare's other late plays.]

From the tragic passion which completed its climax in *Timon of Athens,* we suddenly pass to beauty and serenity; from the plays concerned with the violent breaking of human bonds, to a group of plays which are all concerned with the knitting together of human bonds, the reunion of parted kindred, the forgiveness of enemies, the atonement for wrong—not by death, but by repentance— the reconciliation of husband with wife, of child with father, of friend with friend. *Pericles* is a sketch in which only a part of the subject of these last plays is clearly conceived; it is in some respects like a slighter and earlier *Tempest,* in which Lord Cerimon is the Prospero. It also contains hints afterwards worked out in *The Winter's Tale;* the reunion of the Prince of Tyre and his lost Thaisa is a kind of anticipation of the rediscovery by Leontes of the wife whom he had so long believed to be dead. Posthumus's jealousy, his perception of his error, his sorrow, and his pardon, may be contrasted with the similar series of incidents in *The Winter's Tale,* and the exquisitely impulsive and generous Imogen may be set over against the grave, statue-like Hermione, whose forgiveness of her husband follows the long years of suffering, endured with noble fortitude. Prospero is also wronged; his enemies are in his power; but he has employed his supernatural ministers to lead them to penitence rather than to bring them to punishment. He has learned that 'the rarer action is in virtue than in vengeance.' In these plays there are two sets of dramatis personæ: the sufferers, aged and experienced—Pericles, Prospero, Belarius, Hermione, afterwards (in King Henry VIII.) Queen Katherine; and the young and beautiful children in the brightness of the morning of life—Marina, Miranda, Perdita, Arviragus, and Guiderius; and Shakespeare seems to render homage to both: to the aged sufferers for their virtue and patience and sorrow; to the young men and maidens for their beauty and their joy. There is a romantic element about these plays. In all there is the same romantic incident of lost children recovered by those to whom they are dear—the daughters of Pericles and Leontes, the sons of Cymbeline and Alonzo. In all there is a beautiful romantic background of sea and mountain. The dramas have a grave beauty, a sweet serenity, which seem to render the name 'comedies' inappropriate; we may smile tenderly, but we never laugh loudly, as we read them.

Algernon Charles Swinburne (1837–1909) [Excerpted from *A Study of Shakespeare* (1880). The poet Swinburne discusses his favorite play, *Cymbeline,* and his favorite heroine, Imogen.]

The play of plays, which is *Cymbeline,* remains alone to receive the last salute of all my love. I think, as far as I can tell, I may say I have always loved this one beyond all other children of Shakespeare. The too literal egoism of this profession will not be attributed by any candid or even commonly honest reader to the violence of vanity so much more than comical as to make me suppose that such a record or assurance could in itself be matter of interest to any man: but simply to the real and simple reason, that I wish to show cause for my choice of this work to wind up with, beyond the mere chance of its position at the close of the chaotically inconsequent catalogue of contents affixed to the first edition. In this casualty—for no good thing can reasonably be ascribed to design on the part of the first editors—there would seem to be something more than usual of what we may call, if it so please us, a happy providence. It is certain that no studious arrangement could possibly have brought the book to a happier end. Here is depth enough with height enough of tragic beauty and passion, terror and love and pity, to approve the presence of the most tragic Master's hand; subtlety

enough of sweet and bitter truth to attest the passage of the mightiest and wisest scholar or teacher in the school of the human spirit; beauty with delight enough and glory of life and grace of nature to proclaim the advent of the one omnipotent Maker among all who bear that name. Here above all is the most heavenly triad of human figures that ever even Shakespeare brought together; a diviner three, as it were a living god-garland of the noblest earth-born brothers and love worthiest heaven-born sister, than the very givers of all grace and happiness to their Grecian worshippers of old time over long before. The passion of Posthumus is noble, and potent the poison of Iachimo; Cymbeline has enough for Shakespeare's present purpose of "the king-becoming graces"; but we think first and last of her who was "truest speaker" and those who "called her brother, when she was but their sister; she them brothers, when they were so indeed." The very crown and flower of all her father's daughters,—I do not speak here of her human father, but her divine—the woman above all Shakespeare's women is Imogen. As in Cleopatra we found the incarnate sex, the woman everlasting, so in Imogen we find half glorified already the immortal godhead of womanhood. I would fain have some honey in my words at parting—with Shakespeare never, but for ever with these notes on Shakespeare; and I am therefore something more than fain to close my book upon the name of the woman best beloved in all the world of song and all the tide of time; upon the name of Shakespeare's Imogen.

Edward Dowden (1843–1913) [Excerpted from Dowden's introduction to *Cymbeline* 1899. Here, he discusses the character Cloten.]

I do not feel that there is a want of consistency in the character of Cloten, at least to the degree imagined by Mr. Fleay. Cloten is a fool, but not a fool absolute. Wherever his personal vanity is concerned, he shows his dulness and grossness. Where for a moment he escapes from his heavy egoism, he shows that he is not quite brainless. And in this there is no greater inconsistency than may be found in human nature. Miss Seward declared that she knew in real life an exact replica of Cloten.

Lytton Strachey (1880–1932) [Excerpted from Strachey's discussion of *Cymbeline* and Shakespeare's other late plays in *Books and Characters* (1906). Strachey suggests that in writing the late plays, Shakespeare was bored.]

Measure for Measure is, like nearly every play of Shakespeare's before *Coriolanus,* essentially realistic. The characters are real men and women; and what happens to them upon the stage has all the effect of what happens to real men and women in actual life. Their goodness appears to be real goodness, their wickedness real wickedness; and, if their sufferings are terrible enough, we regret the fact, even though in the end they triumph, just as we regret the real sufferings of our friends. But, in the plays of the final period, all this has changed; we are no longer in the real world, but in a world of enchantment, of mystery, of wonder, a world of shifting visions, a world of hopeless anachronisms, a world in which anything may happen next. The pretences of reality are indeed usually preserved, but only the pretences. Cymbeline is supposed to be the king of a real Britain, and the real Augustus is supposed to demand tribute of him. . . .

Thus strangely remote is the world of Shakespeare's latest period; and it is peopled, this universe of his invention, with beings equally unreal, with creatures either more or less than human, with fortunate princes and wicked step-mothers, with goblins and spirits, with lost princesses and insufferable

Margaret Mather as Imogen (disguised as Fidele) in an 1890 production of *Cymbeline (Photographed by Joseph Byron)*

kings. And of course, in this sort of fairy-land, it is an essential condition that everything shall end well; the prince and princess are bound to marry and live happily ever afterwards, or the whole story is unnecessary and absurd; and the villains and the goblins must naturally repent and be forgiven. But it is clear that such happy endings, such conventional closes to fantastic tales, cannot be taken as evidences of serene tranquility on the part of their maker; they merely show that he knew, as well as anyone else, how such stories ought to end. . . .

It is difficult to resist the conclusion that he was getting bored himself. Bored with people, bored with real life, bored with drama, bored, in fact, with everything except poetry and poetical dreams. He is no longer interested, one often feels, in what happens, or who says what, so long as he can find place for a faultless lyric, or a new, unimagined rhythmical effect, or a grand and mystic speech.

Arthur Quiller-Couch (1863–1944) [Excerpted from *Notes on Shakespeare's Workmanship* (1917).

The critic Quiller-Couch follows the 19th-century tradition of praising Imogen.]

> For Imogen is the be-all and end-all of the play. She has all the wrongs of Desdemona, plus the serene courage to conquer them and forgive. She has all the fond trust of Desdemona, with all the steel and wit which Desdemona fatally lacks. Range out the great gallery of good women—Silvia, Portia, Beatrice, Rosalind, Viola, Helena, Isabella, Marina, Perdita, Miranda—Heavens what a list!—and over all of them Imogen bears the bell.

MODERN CRITICISM AND CRITICAL CONTROVERSIES

Cymbeline has always been controversial, with both detractors and supporters. In his *Prefaces to Shakespeare* (1930), Harley Granville Barker sees *Cymbeline* as full of imperfections, with the play's "inept lapses" either the result of Shakespeare writing the play while "at odds with himself," or, more likely, the result of a lesser collaborator, "a strange finger in the pie". He thinks the play's soliloquies show an unusual "artlessness," but still he admits the play is a dramatic achievement. He has special praise for Act V (which some other critics find the weakest part of the play), asserting that the audience along with the characters are in this final act "reconciled in their happiness". He finds Imogen the most successful character in the play, the most lifelike, and he argues persuasively that the theme of the play is chastity, particularly "married chastity" (85).

Caroline Spurgeon in *Shakespeare's Imagery* (1935) is typically empirical and nonjudgmental in discussing *Cymbeline*. She points out that there are two main clusters of images in the play. The first, accounting for about 40 percent of all the images in the play, are "country images," suitable for a play with a pastoral structure. These nature images are most frequently of trees, birds, flowers, and the wind. But there is a second type of image in the play, images related to "the theme of buying and selling, value and exchange, every kind of payment, debts, bills and wagers."

E. M. W. Tillyard in *Shakespeare's Last Plays* (1936) emphasizes the religious nature of *Cymbeline* and the other late plays. These plays make explicit the regeneration that is implied in Shakespeare's tragedies. He says the pastoral scenes in Shakespeare's late plays, for *Cymbeline* in the Welsh mountains, are integral to this regenerative pattern, helping create the sense of what Tillyard calls "planes of reality". This phrase, Tillyard explains, "implies a state of mind akin to the religious; for simply to present different planes of reality without imposing a pattern on them is an act of homage to the unknown, of humility, the very reverse of self-assertion" (67). Still, Tillyard sees *Cymbeline* as less successful than *The Tempest* or *The Winter's Tale*.

The great playwright George Bernard Shaw thought *Cymbeline* was "one of the finer" of Shakespeare's late plays, but he thought that in the last act the play "goes to pieces," in large part because Shakespeare got tangled up in resolving an overly complicated plot. So, Shaw rewrote Act V for a production in Stratford-upon-Avon and published this revision with a foreword in 1936 (*Cymbeline Revisited*). He explains in the foreword that he thought the jail scene (the masque with Jupiter descending) was excellent but that in the last act the only character "really left alive" was Posthumus (who retains many of his original lines in Shaw's version). He could not stand the old device of the lost prince being recognized by a mole on his neck and tells an amusing story of how this device was killed by the famous farce *Box and Cox:* "Box asks Cox whether he has a strawberry mark on his left arm. 'No says Cox. 'Then you are my long lost brother' says Box as they fall into one another's arms and end the farce happily." Shaw adds, "One could wish that Guiderius had anticipated Cox." With his feminist sympathy, Shaw also could not stand "that Imogen is so dutiful that she accepts her husbands attempt to have her murdered with affectionate docility." In the revision, Guiderius and Arviragus are reluctant to return to court and stand in succession to be king, with Arvirargus telling the king, "I am tired of being preached at." And Imogen harps on Posthumus's bad behavior, saying "My husband thinks all is settled now / And this a happy ending!" and reminding him repeatedly, "You bade your servant kill me." And so, their happy reconciliation is tempered by a modern perspective, with Imogen's final words being, "I will not laugh. I must go home and make the best of it / As other women must." Even though almost all productions use Shakespeare's final act, not Shaw's, many of Shaw's problems with the last act are reflected in subsequent literary criticism, particularly feminist criticism.

G. Wilson Knight in *The Crown of Life* (1947) sees *Cymbeline* primarily as a historical play about the origins of Shakespeare's nation. It is primarily a national play, therefore, with the addition of a typical Shakespearean jealousy story—like Othello's, Claudio's (in *Much Ado About Nothing*), Ford's (in *The Merry Wives of Windsor*), and Leontes' (in *The Winter's Tale*). Posthumus Leonatus has a Roman-sounding name, suggesting that he and the play unite British and Roman virtues. But, for Knight, the play is not an allegory but rather a parable that marries Shakespeare's two national faiths: faith in ancient Rome and faith in England.

In a lecture on *Cymbeline* and *Pericles* given in 1947 (published in *Lectures on Shakespeare*, 2000), the poet W. H. Auden begins by generalizing about the nature of artists' last works. Late works, he says, show an indifference to what both critics and audience might think, and the artist "is sometimes shocking out of his indifference to whether he shocks or not" (Kirsch 271). Late works like *Cymbeline* (with its "conscious exploitation of tricks: asides, etc.") appeal to lowbrows and sophisticated highbrows, but not so much to middlebrows. And often, the best parts of late works are not the big climaxes but the little things, the bridges between the big speeches; Auden suggests that "anyone who practices verse writing returns again and again to such things, rather than to spectacular things" (222). Auden points to several such passages in *Cymbeline,* and so continues the 19th-century tradition of poets (Alfred, Lord Tennyson, Swinburne, Keats) showing special appreciation of

the poetry of *Cymbeline*. In praising the language of the play, Auden also astutely points out how Iachimo's language changes when he finally asks forgiveness; because his diction has changed, we feel that he has indeed changed. And at the end of his lecture, he articulates why some people love this play so much: "The characters are not separate individuals in their own right, you are not fond of them as you are of Beatrice and Rosalind. . . . But like a fairy-tale story, this the world as you want it to be, and nothing makes one more inclined to cry" (283).

Harold Goddard in *The Meaning of Shakespeare* (1951) emphasizes the many contrasts between England and Italy in the play, seeing it as a moral and political allegory, with an England returned to its roots (Posthumus as an English peasant, Belarius and the princes in Wales), purged of corruption, defeating the malicious influence of Italy (and the Italian Renaissance). Goddard sees Shakespeare here as more sympathetic to the spirit of the Reformation than of the Renaissance, even of being on the side of the Puritans. In the allegory, Imogen represents true England; Posthumus, English manhood and valor; King Cymbeline and the Queen, corrupt English throne; Cloten, false nobility; Guiderius and Arvirargus, genuine nobility.

John Wain in *The Living World of Shakespeare* (1964) offers a spirited defense of Cymbeline's greatness and an ingenious explanation for why so many critics have undervalued the play. *Cymbeline,* according to Wain, is Shakespeare's most avant-garde, experimental, and "modern" work. The play's visual elements are remarkably sophisticated and strange, with so many vivid moments. The strongest mark of Shakespeare's "experimental imagination" in *Cymbeline* is the verse, which has "strange haunting rhythms" (213). (It was because of this remarkable verse, Wain claims, that it was Tennyson's favorite play, "and his beloved copy was buried with him in the grave" (213). This sophisticated verse was aimed at highly sophisticated playgoers (presumably at the Blackfriars rather than the Globe), with Shakespeare here showing off his "literary virtuosity" (213). The work has serious themes (like nature versus nurture), but because the work is so avant-garde, it sometimes tends to parody and abandons realism, much as, in Wain's fine example, Pablo Picasso's *Guernica* does. Frank Kermode in *Shakespeare: The Final Plays* (1963) makes much the same argument as Wain, saying that in *Cymbeline* Shakespeare was experimenting with a new kind of play and that it is "superb."

Janet Adelman, in *Suffocating Mothers: Fantasies of Maternal Origen in Shakespeare's Plays,* Hamlet *to* The Tempest (1991) offers an ingenious psychoanalytical feminist reading of *Cymbeline.* She points to Posthumus's speech wishing men could be born without mothers and to the recently widowed Cymbeline's welcome of his lost sons with the words "O, What am I?/ A mother to the birth of three?" as suggestive of the play's central fantasy: male parthenogenesis, asexual procreation without mothers that robs women of their power. (Belarius's raising the princes by himself is a sign of an all-male pastoral wish fulfillment.) This theme of masculine authority is clearest in King Cymbeline's case, where once he is freed from the evil Queen (and her mother-bound son, Cloten), he can establish a male realm, reunited with his sons (who replace Imogen as heirs and successors) and reunited with the patriarchal all-male world of realm. Adelman is able to explain many details of the play according to this central idea, for example, that the bloody handkerchief Posthumus keeps "through its allusion to menstrual blood . . . assures him the she—not he—is the bearer of the woman's part. Imogen, the play's 'primary defining figure,' has by the last act, then, learned her place" (214). The play elevates male power, and the price of making Posthumus one of the male heroes who saves the king is a weakened Imogen: "robbed of her own powerful selfhood, put entirely under male command, she becomes imaginatively the victim not only of Posthumus's revenge and Cloten's rape fantasy but also of her author's cruelty" (211).

Harold Bloom in *Shakespeare: The Invention of the Human* (1998) sees *Cymbeline* as an experimental play that mostly fails, calling it "more a dramatic poem than it is a play" and "more a mixed travesty than a romance" (638). The play is "overloaded with plot," full of "authorial self-parody," and shows Shakespeare's fatigue and disgust (621). Some of the scenes (like the Jupiter dream scene) Bloom sees as deliberately bad, which he can only explain as Shakespeare's "compulsive self-parody" (635). He calls Posthumus Shakespeare's "most tiresome hero" and says that the play's characters lack real personalities, except for Imogen, whose voice, for Bloom, is the only distinctive one in the play. Only Imogen redeems the play, and Bloom, like various 19th-century critics, admits to loving her. In Imogen, Shakespeare created a personality

Imogen, disguised as Fidele, eats Belarius's food in Act III, Scene 7 of *Cymbeline*. This illustration was designed for a 1918 edition of Charles and Mary Lamb's *Tales from Shakespeare. (Illustration by Louis Rhead)*

(an important character, such as Falstaff, Hamlet, or Rosalind), showing he still had the power to bring a human being with a real personality to life.

Kermode in *Shakespeare's Language* (2000) sees *Cymbeline* as a fundamentally unserious play, perhaps written to amuse the more sophisticated audience at the new Blackfriars Theatre with a "sophisticated parody of older, simpler, romance plays". Thus, the play tends toward farce, especially the Act V recognition scene (which can draw laughs from an audience). Kermode points to the garments repetition, which he sees more as a trick meant to amuse than as an emphasis meant to imply a deeper meaning. Kermode considers the verse of the play to be "overworked," as difficult as the language in *The Winter's Tale* but without the same need for difficulty. While the play has many fine speeches, some are too confused and some oddly inappropriate, as when Cloten speaks with good sense.

THE PLAY TODAY

Cymbeline has not been frequently staged in recent history, perhaps because it is a difficult play to do well and has a very mixed critical reputation. At the new Globe Theatre in London, Mike Alfred directed *Cymbeline* (2001). His Director's Notes called the play "very modern," and he staged it in a modern, indeed experimental way. To balance the complexity of the plot, the production was extremely simple. There were only six actors (all in identical white satin pajamas) and two musicians, on an empty stage, against a black wall. One reviewer said this production "invented a rather beautiful new genre: Ikea Shakespeare." (Actually there is some history to doing the play with bare stages and extremely simple costumes: productions by William Gaskill at Stratford-upon-Avon in 1962 and Jean Gacon at the Stratford Canadian Shakespeare Festival in 1970, for example.) With only six actors in the Globe production, there had to be extensive doubling, with Mark Rylance particularly effective as a muscular, loud Cloten and a shy, less sure Posthumus. Since the actors wore identical costumes, the comic effect was striking when the actors disguised themselves, for example,

when Rylance as Cloten dressed as Posthumus. The actors announced their dramatis personae at the beginning of the production and occasionally gave stage directions, as when Imogen (Jane Arneild) came on stage with a cartwheel and announced, "Enter Imogen, dressed as a boy." In his Director's Notes, Alfred described *Cymbeline*'s final scene as one of "exceptional technical virtuosity in which 27 pieces of information, already known to the audience, are revealed to the characters." This production built upon each one of those 27 moments of dramatic irony, with King Cymbeline obviously befuddled by the revelations. There was much audience laughter as the tangles in the plot were unraveled.

There are striking visual scenes in *Cymbeline* that different productions are more or less successful in bringing out. (Roger Warren suggests, for example, that the scene of Iachimo emerging from the trunk is more easily staged in a smaller theater.) Peter Hall in his National Theatre production at the Olivier Theatre in London had a striking success with the heavens above opening to reveal Jupiter in the night sky upon a three-dimensional eagle. And, in Patrick Tucker's *Cymbeline* at the California Shakespeare Theatre in 1981, the audience was similarly shocked and awed by the descent of Jupiter upon an eagle. *Cymbeline*'s deus ex machina can be a magical theatrical moment.

One of the most original recent versions of *Cymbeline* (directed by Will Pelligrini, adapted by Angela Berliner) was presented by The Actor's Gang in Culver City, California, in August 2009. *Cymbeline the Puppet King*—with the wicked Queen as the puppet master—showed that this play can work for children as well as adults, albeit once you add puppets, eliminate Iachimo and Posthumus, and have Imogen call Cloten "Cloten the Rotten." They played up the fairy-tale elements and the humor; Imogen's waking up next to the headless body was one of the funniest moments.

Interestingly, there have been two silent films made of *Cymbeline*, perhaps because the play has so many striking visual elements: a 1913 American film directed by Lucius Henderson and a

1925 German film directed by Ludwig Berger. Yet, no talking films have been made of *Cymbeline,* although there was a made-for-TV video. With Renaissance settings and costumes (lots of ruffs worn around the necks), this production was part of the BBC Shakespeare project in the late 1970s and early 1980s to make videos of all of Shakespeare's plays. *Cymbeline,* directed by Elijah Moshinsky, was released in 1982. Constraints of time and budget meant that there was little spectacle in any of these productions, and so, in *Cymbeline,* for example, Jupiter's descent in thunder and lightning sitting upon an eagle is missing both eagle and lightning. Nonetheless, this is a successful and entertaining production.

The actors are excellent, with Michael Pennington as Posthumus and Robert Lindsay as Iachimo, although Paul Jesson's Cloten may seem too over-the-top stupid even for a character like Cloten. But the stars of this production are the women. Claire Bloom makes the Queen every bit as wicked as Snow White's stepmother but nonetheless a believable human (unlike the way Paul Jesson's Cloten seems more parody than person). And Helen Mirren is a total delight as Imogen, making *Cymbeline,* at least in this production, Imogen's play. Mirren's Imogen is not the Victorian stereotype: Moshinsky said he cast her because, "I wanted an actress of great sexual voltage" (*Shakespeare in Performance,* 70). Mirren was especially striking in her soliloquy on waking up next to headless Cloten (a shocking but entertaining bloody scene). And when, at the end of the play, Posthumus strikes her (thinking she is the page Fidele), she falls down in a way that might convince one who had not read the play that now Posthumus has really killed his mistress. The magic of the play, and this production, is not in the characters, however, but in the plot. Despite being cut (especially in the second half of the play), this production runs almost three hours. All of the complications of the plot are strongly developed, and the last scene, with revelations and plot twists one after another, is sure to make any sympathetic watcher smile if not laugh.

FIVE TOPICS FOR DISCUSSION AND WRITING

1. **The character of Imogen:** Imogen has been praised as a model for the ideal woman and criticized for being too willing to accept and forgive Posthumus's bad behavior. How is she or is she not a role model for women?

2. **The character of Posthumus:** Write a character study of Posthumus, describing how he changes throughout the course of the play. Show how his actions, dress, and speech reflect these changes.

3. **Spirituality and religion in *Cymbeline*:** Analyze the play's spiritual elements. These can include but need not be limited to the Christian.

4. **The last act:** Act V has been attacked as a failure and praised as a masterwork. Discuss how you would evaluate it, describing how it achieves its success or failure.

5. **Directing *Cymbeline*:** Imagine that you have been asked to direct *Cymbeline.* Write a letter to your cast members describing your ideas as to how to put the play on stage.

Bibliography

Adelman, Janet. *Suffocating Mothers: Fantasies of Maternal Origin in Shakespeare's Plays,* Hamlet *to* The Tempest. New York: Routledge, 1991.

Barker, Harley Granville. *Prefaces to Shakespeare.* London: B. T. Batsford, 1930.

Blake, N. F. *Shakespeare's Language: An Introduction.* London: Macmillan, 1983.

Bloom, Harold. *Shakespeare: The Invention of the Human.* New York: Riverhead Books, 1998.

Boyce, Charles. *Shakespeare A to Z: The Essential Reference to His Plays, His Poems, His Life and Times, and More.* New York: Facts On File, 1990, 1997.

Brown, Richard Danson, and David Johnson, eds. *Shakespeare 1609:* Cymbeline *and the Sonnets.* New York: St. Martin's Press, 2000.

Cook, Judith. *Women in Shakespeare.* London: Harrap, 1980.

Dowden, Edward. *Introduction to Shakespeare.* London: Blackie & Son, 1893.

———. *Shakespeare.* London: Macmillan & Co., 1918.

Goddard, Harold. *The Meaning of Shakespeare.* Chicago: Phoenix Books, 1951.

Halliday, F. E. *Shakespeare and His Critics.* New York: Schocken Books, 1963.

Hazlitt, William. *Lectures on the Literature of the Age of Elizabeth and Characters of Shakespear's Plays.* London: George Bell, 1878.

Hunter, Robert Grams. *Shakespeare and the Comedy of Forgiveness.* New York: Columbia University Press, 1965.

Kermode, Frank. *Shakespeare's Language.* New York: Farrar, Straus & Giroux, 2000.

King, Ros. Cymbeline: *Constructions of Britain.* Aldershot, U.K.: Ashgate Publishing, 2003.

Kirsch, Arthur, ed. *W. H. Auden: Lectures on Shakespeare.* Princeton, N.J.: Princeton University Press, 2000.

Knight, G. Wilson. *The Crown of Life.* London: Methuen, 1952.

Mowat, Barbara. *The Dramaturgy of Shakespeare's Romances.* Athens: University of Georgia Press, 1976.

Nosworthy, J. M. Introduction and Notes to *The Arden Edition of Cymbeline.* Cambridge, Mass.: Harvard University Press, 1955.

Ryan, Kiernan, ed. *Shakespeare: The Last Plays.* London and New York: Longman, 1999.

Spurgeon, Caroline. *Shakespeare's Imagery.* London: Cambridge University Press, 1939.

St. John, Christopher, ed. *Ellen Terry and Bernard Shaw: A Correspondence.* New York: Putnam, 1932.

Thorne, Allison, ed. *Shakespeare's Romances.* New York: Palgrave Macmillan, 2003.

Tillyard, E. M. W. *Shakespeare's Last Plays.* London: Athlone Press, 1991.

Wain, John. *The Living World of Shakespeare.* London: Macmillan, 1964.

Warren, Roger. *Shakespeare in Performance: Cymbeline.* Manchester and New York: Manchester University Press, 1989.

Warren, Roger, ed. *The Oxford Shakespeare: Cymbeline.* Oxford: Clarendon Press, 1998.

FILM AND VIDEO PRODUCTIONS

Moshinsky, Elijah, dir. *Cymbeline.* With Claire Bloom, Robert Lindsay, Helen Mirren, and Michael Pennington. BBC Video, 1982.

—John Boe

Edward III

INTRODUCTION

Edward III is the most recent addition to the Shakespearean canon. This does not mean that Shakespeare wrote it last among his plays—if Shakespeare wrote it at all, it is an early composition, from 1595 or before—but that it has been most recently added to the body of work known as Shakespeare's. The play was not included in the landmark First Folio publication of Shakespeare's plays in 1623. In the 1990s, scholars, using digital or computer-based techniques, reached a new consensus that the play, if not totally by Shakespeare, was at least significantly by Shakespeare. This new attribution of the play has allowed scholars to consider its concerns in light of larger questions in the Shakespearean oeuvre: For example, *Edward III* represents an early period in the ongoing saga of English kings and wars that Shakespeare examined in seven other plays. Prominent themes in this play, as elsewhere in Shakespeare, include the relation between private and public life and the different types of character in leadership, empire, and national identity. Nonetheless, the majority of scholars believe that the play was a collaborative effort and that Shakespeare himself probably only wrote the first two acts.

Edward III, who reigned from 1327 to 1377, had perhaps the most successful tenure of any English king. Under his rule, England recovered from the court intrigue and uncertain leadership that had characterized the reign of his father, Edward II—a reign captured in a memorable play (ca. 1592) by Christopher Marlowe—and launched an aggressive and ambitious foreign policy, warring unfruitfully against Scotland, and, far more successfully, against France. Edward III epitomized an era when the ideals of chivalry were at their height and the prestige of the monarchy—buttressed not only by his own leadership but also by the martial valor of his son, Edward, the Black Prince—was unrivaled. One might not think there would be much potential for drama here, as there was no overt crisis, no tragedy during this period. True, Edward's son died before him, the Black Death ravaged England during the middle of his reign, and his considerable gains in France were partially erased by the time he died. But, these events could not be attributed to defects in Edward's own character or choices.

What, then, was the dramatist to do? He chose to focus on the gap between the private and public Edward, between the firm and commanding exterior Edward showed to his courtiers and subordinates and the often uncertain, bumbling, and compromised self he exhibited to his intimates. The occasion for the discovery of Edward's self is the depraved proposal of the Countess of Salisbury to Edward that both should jointly murder their spouses in order to realize their love. This grisly scenario and the emotional responses it generates turn the tone of the play in a visibly darker direction. Used to both the authority that comes with his being king and the moral absolutism of the chivalric code by which he and his court have affected to live, Edward is pushed suddenly to an ethical precipice, and the audience watches to see whether he will fall.

EDWARDVS · III ·

Portrait of Edward III by an unknown artist from the 16th century

Once the vista of the play shifts to the fighting in France, Edward regains more secure ground and displays himself to his subjects and to the audience as a charismatic martial leader. In France, the chief character of the play becomes Edward's son, the Black Prince. When the prince is erroneously reported by the Count of Salisbury to be dead, Queen Philippa, the king's wife and the mother of the Black Prince, breaks out into an outraged lament. This is proven to be only rhetorical some lines later, when the prince returns, scarred but alive to fight a new day. Yet, this near death casts a shadow over the otherwise triumphant last half of the play. This shadow is in turn compounded by Queen Philippa having been morally wronged by the king through his infidelity, at a time when she is pregnant. (From this pregnancy she will bear

a son, John, who will be John of Gaunt and, in Shakespeare's *Richard II,* will pronounce the play-wright's great statement of English patriotism.) Furthermore, he who delivers the false news about the Black Prince is the husband of the woman with whom the king had been committing adultery, once again pointing out the inextricability of public and private in the play.

No matter one's perspective on the play's authorship question, *Edward III* presents a fascinating perspective on the questions of power and conscience that preoccupy Shakespeare throughout his work and, in his history plays, are embedded in concrete relation to questions of national identity and polity. Edward refrains from going too far in private circumstances, but the humiliating capitulation he forces on King John of France, compelling him to renounce the throne for himself and his son, raises the question of whether Edward III has gone too far in his public life and has sought empire at the expense of balance and what Ulysses in *Troilus and Cressida* would call "degree." The play features two of England's great royal and martial heroes. It by no means is an unequivocal paean to heroism, or patriotism. The ambivalence *Edward III* evinces, even while affirming a sense of national pride and confidence, is a visible link to other plays in the Shakespearean oeuvre, among which it is finding an increasingly firmer place in the early 21st century.

BACKGROUND

The headline to Helen Castor's review of Ian Mortimer's biography of King Edward III in the March 5, 2006, edition of the (London) *Daily Telegraph* may sum up the paradoxes of Edward III's reign: "He lived too long to be great." Many critics, noting the exclusion of a play about Edward III from the Shakespearean canon of histories, as formerly assessed, might have speculated that Edward III's reign was too stable and successful to be the stuff of Shakespeare. The first critic to seriously consider ascribing the play to Shakespeare was Edward Capell (1713–81), but even Capell based his claim on intuitive rather than more empirical grounds, saying "there was no known equal to such a play." In other words, since none of Shakespeare's contemporaries could have written it, he believed it must be by Shakespeare. This reasoning did not sway critics, and it was not until the 1990s that scholars such as Eric Sams (wholeheartedly) and Giorgio Melchiori (more guardedly) argued for the play's full or partial admission into the Shakespearean canon. This convinced enough mainstream scholars for the play to be included in some, though not all, of the major published collections of Shakespeare's work. The semi-admission of *Edward III* into the Shakespearean canon changed the way the histories as a group are considered. With the inclusion of *Edward III,* the histories now range over a longer stretch of time that incorporates one of England's most successful reigns and are characterized even more prominently by a troubling gap between public reputation and private virtue.

The main source for the play is Raphael Holinshed's *Chronicles of England, Scotland, and Ireland,* nearly contemporaneous with Shakespeare, supplemented by the *Chronicles* of the 14th-century French historian Jean Froissart, a younger contemporary of Edward III himself. The 46th story of the first volume of William Painter's *The Palace of Pleasure* (1566, 1575), a collection of semi-historical tales from antiquity to the high Middle Ages adapted from the works of Bandello and containing accounts of such Shakespearean figures as Lucrece, Romeo and Juliet, Coriolanus, and Timon of Athens, contains an account of Edward III focused on the countess of Salisbury episode and is a palpable source for the play. Being an Englishman, Painter was well aware that Bandello's conception of the story—for instance, having Edward not be married at the time of his dalliance with the countess—was ahistorical and proffered it to his English readers with this apology. The playwright's sources were thus a mix of the historical and the fictive—in a way mirroring the same split between the public and the private that preoccupies *Edward III.*

Date and Text of the Play

Most scholars believe that the play was a collaboration initiated by someone else and that Shakespeare was most likely invited to participate in recognition of his previous achievements. It is less likely, though still conceivably possible, that the play was a fledgling solo or joint effort by a young and inexperienced Shakespeare just arrived in the metropolis from Stratford.

Edward III was published in 1596 by Cuthbert Burby, the same bookseller who later printed quartos of *Love's Labour's Lost* and *Romeo and Juliet.* Burby was not himself a printer but an impresario, an entrepreneur, who employed printers; in consequence, there are a significant amount of errors in the text of *Edward III* as well as in most of the works he printed. (The second edition, printed for Burby by Simon Stafford, contains somewhat fewer errors.) Burby entered the play on the Stationers' Register on December 1, 1595. Presumably, the performance date of the play would be earlier, most likely from 1592 to 1594, putting it, if it is indeed Shakespeare's, among his early works. The play must have been written after 1588, however, as a reference to the methods of naval warfare used in the English repulsion of the Spanish Armada of 1588 occurs within the play, and Edward's naval expedition is also described as a "proud Armado" (3.1.64). Some have proposed 1590 as the earliest date the play could be written, based on the standard prose accounts of the Armada only being available from that year. But, if we assume substantive oral or anecdotal accounts circulated earlier, or that there are anterior printed sources that did not attain the same currency as the later ones but circulated effectively in their day, the earliest date could be extended back to 1589. Basically, the earlier the play is, the less likely it is to have been by Shakespeare.

Burby states that the play had been performed "sundry times" in London before its publication. This might lead to the conclusion that the play was tremendously popular, yet a caveat must be issued; as Giorgio Melchiori points out, Burby used this characterization of many plays he had printed, and it seems almost a stock phrase. All we can conclude from the "sundry times" is that the play had been performed and that a performance record was manifested that was substantive enough for Burby to obtain a fair text.

The list of Shakespeare's plays compiled during his lifetime—such as Francis Meres's list in 1598—do not contain the play, and John Heminges and Henry Condell did not include it in the First Folio. In Thomas Goffe's posthumously published catalog of all printed plays known to him, issued in 1656, *Edward III* is ascribed to Shakespeare, but its omission from the Heminges and Condell First Folio led most critics to consider it by another hand until Capell, in 1760, contended, on mainly aesthetic grounds, that it was part of the Shakespearean canon. Most scholars, though, were unconvinced until a wave of computer-generated studies in the 1990s prompted reconsideration. Before this wave, which prompted several new editions, the most-used texts of the play were, in the 19th century, edited by Nicolaus Delius and John Payne Collier and, in the 20th, by James Winny and Kenneth Muir. Many of the later textual scholars had to disentangle Capell's own emendations, which often were taken for original aspect of the texts, from the variant offered by the original printed edition, while retaining Capell's corrections of many of the initial printing errors. The recent debate about the attribution of the play has meant that *Edward III* received arguably as much textual consideration in the years from 1990 to 2010 as any play in the Shakespearean canon.

SYNOPSIS
Brief Synopsis
John has claimed the kingship of France invoking the archaic and quasi-mythical precedent of the Salic law, that only male heirs generated through the male line can inherit. If one allows inheritance through the female line, Edward III of England, through his French mother, would be king of France. Defying a demand for homage from the French king, Edward claims his legacy and vows to reclaim the kingship he feels is rightfully his. While

Edward's son begins to organize the expedition against France, the king heads to Scotland to deal with that state's insubordination.

In the north, King David of Scotland has forsworn his former allegiance. Edward is particularly determined to rescue Alice, Countess of Salisbury, who is confined to a castle besieged by Scots soldiers. Indeed, he is more preoccupied by his romantic infatuation with her than with repelling the Scots led by the complacent and self-regarding King David. Employing his secretary, Lodowick, to write a love letter to the Countess, Edward seeks to woo her despite the fact that both are married. The Countess, while seeming to reciprocate Edward's ardor, responds with an idea that staggers Edward: She suggests that they mutually plot to murder their respective spouses, Queen Philippa and the Earl of Salisbury, so that they will be maritally unencumbered and thus free to be with each other. Edward, nearly crazed by love, agrees, but then the Countess contends that her idea was not a serious one but merely a test to see what level of outrage Edward would commit in order to fulfill his desire. Chastened by this indication of his moral shortcomings, Edward speeds out of Scotland and heads south to pursue the expedition against France.

An initial English naval win at Sluys—the first of the great naval victories of the English realm—is followed by spectacular campaigns led by Prince Edward and, finally, by a crushing triumph at Crécy, which gives King Edward and the English troops a glorious victory over France. The king is informed that the prince is under threat but withholds help so that his son will be able to prove himself a warrior in his own right. The prince not only emerges alive from this test but arrives with the head of King John of Bohemia, the chief French ally in the war. The son begins to seem a braver and more accomplished warrior than the father. King John of France flees in humiliation, but instead of pursuing him, the king and prince go to the seaboard town of Calais, where the king shows his mercy in his treatment of the local inhabitants.

Meanwhile, French resistance has been stiffened by the counsel of the French king's heir, the dauphin, Prince Charles, who is as determined and resourceful as his father is not. But miscommunication among the French gives the English victory once again, and the battlefield talent of Prince Edward is once again affirmed. This vindication appears, though, to be at heavy cost, as the Earl of Salisbury brings King Edward a report of his son's death in battle. As Queen Philippa mourns her loss, Prince Edward miraculously reappears, with the French king and prince in tow. England has won the day, and the uncertainties and moral confusion that had characterized much of the play yield to a sense of patriotic affirmation and a celebration of the honor of the chivalric code, despite the king's earlier ethical breaches.

Act I, Scene 1

In colloquy with the Count of Artois, a former French noble whom King Edward has granted an equivalent position in his own realm, King Edward ascertains the nature and provision of the French royal succession. Noting that all three sons of Philip le Bel (Philip IV of France, called Philip the Fair) had died without issue, he asks Artois why is it that Edward himself, as the son of King Philip's daughter, is not eligible for the French throne. Artois points out that the French claim inheritance can pass only through the male, and that descending through the female is a disqualifier for any claimant. Artois indicates that he thinks this feeling is fallacious and, in essence, has been devised or articulated for the express purpose of keeping Edward off the throne. No sooner is Edward convinced of his claim than an emissary from the French king, the Duke of Lorraine, arrives to demand fealty from Edward. (Given that the English crown holds hereditary territories in Guienne, in the southwest of France under the terms of feudalism, the French king is, technically, the English king's overlord in this respect). King Edward rejects this demand, noting his right to the entire kingdom. Lorraine pronounces defiance to the king and is met by a belligerent threat from the king's son, Prince Edward. Lorraine insults the king as a "degenerate traitor" (1.1.105) and

is warned by Artois to go before his own life is threatened. Lorraine leaves, claiming that what he sees as the false logic of the English claim is more insulting than any physical threats. Sir William Montague then enters and says that David, the king of Scotland, has reneged on the treaty he had earlier signed, is attacking English towns along the Anglo-Scottish border, and is besieging a castle where dwells the Countess of Salisbury. The king recalls the Countess is the daughter of one of his chief advisers and vows to hasten north to liberate her and repel the Scots threat. Meanwhile, he directs Audley and his other subordinates to begin preparations against France, and exhorts Prince Edward to leave aside his schoolbooks and begin seriously training as a warrior.

Act I, Scene 2

The Countess of Salisbury stands pensively, wondering whether Montague, her cousin, will be able to exhort King Edward with enough strength to prompt the sovereign to come to her rescue. King David, the Countess's "everlasting foe," comes to the entrance and reveals that he has been in conference with Lorraine about a Franco-Scottish alliance against England. David vows to Lorraine to continue to fight England on its northern border while France girds for an invasion from the sea. Meanwhile, David, and his liegeman, the Earl of Douglas, quarrel over which one will sexually possess the Countess after the castle has been taken. Douglas reveals his ardor as more generally possessive than erotic when he says that he will be satisfied with the Countess's jewels if he cannot have her person. A messenger brings news of the king of England's imminent arrival; meanwhile, the Countess, having overheard the conversation of the two Scotsmen, taunts them over their debate over which shall have her and which her jewels. Montague arrives, bearing word that the king will shortly come. The Countess greets her cousin gratefully, asking in what vein she should receive the king. At this moment, King Edward, with a sizable retinue, enters, along with the Countess's father, the Earl of Warwick. While the Countess kneels before the king in gratitude for his saving her from the Scots, Edward begins to have more than merely politics on his mind, as he notes the "strange enchantment" of the Countess's face (1.2.102). The king desires to hurry on to Scotland to pursue the retreating enemy, but through flattery and guile, the Countess insists that the king honor her by accepting her hospitality overnight at the castle.

Act II, Scene 1

In the gardens of the castle, Lodowick, Edward's secretary, notes that Edward has been completely distracted from his duties by his infatuation with the Countess. Lodowick fears that "peevish love" (2.1.23) will keep the King and the nation he leads from the cause of punishing the Scots. Edward enters, besotted with the Countess, savoring the wit of her recounting of the Scots siege and her sardonic imitation of the besieger's Scottish accents. Edward hyperbolically states that he cannot blame the Scots who assaulted her castle, as he means to pursue a similar plan in amorous terms. Edward asks Lodowick for ink and paper so he can press his suit, and recognizing Lodowick's skill as a rhetorician and man of learning, Edward asks him to compose a love letter for him. Lodowick knows just to whom the letter is being addressed but, playing coy, extracts from the king the information that the recipient is a woman, she is of high estate, and Edward esteems her in the hyperbolic language of Petrarchan praise. Edward bids Lodowick strike references to chastity and to the biblical example of Judith because they would not accord with his seductive intent. As Lodowick is struggling with these two dueling imperatives, the Countess enters, and the king bids Lodowick go. King Edward speaks to the Countess of his love for her, which at first the Countess affects to understand in terms of feudal praise and loyalty. When the king's erotic intent becomes clear, the Countess says she would rather give up her life than her chastity. The Countess points out that the king gains his authority only from God, in whose image he reigns, and that Adam, as a mar-

ried man, preceded the advent of kings on earth. She leaves, pledging continued allegiance to her husband. The king remains obsessed with her and intent on his seductive goals; the Countess's father, Warwick, enters. Warwick sees the king is sad and offers to help his sovereign in any way that he can. The king warns Warwick this will mean violating Warwick's honor. The king finally confesses his love for the Countess and then exits. Warwick is riven with doubt but decides to follow his oath to the king and bid the Countess unlearn all the moral precepts he had preached to her and bid her to follow. Warwick admits to his daughter that his mission is dishonorable but suggests that the station of being the love of a king is so great that this will compensate for her sin. When the Countess resolutely refuses this suggestion, Warwick praises her idealism and fidelity and says that he will fully support her and that moral standards cannot be jettisoned simply because the sheer might of a king bids them so. Prince Edward enters, his martial skills honed, schooled for war. The prince's valor not only shames his father's lust and self-interest, but the prince's facial resemblance to his mother reminds the king of his incipient infidelity.

Act II, Scene 2

The Earl of Derby comes in with the latest news from France. Audley greets him and is pleased by Derby's news that the Holy Roman (German) Emperor has endorsed Edward's cause in France. Derby gives Audley the news that the king seems unhappy and distracted: For example, when he receives news of the key endorsement from the emperor, Europe's highest-ranking ruler, all the king does is sigh and aver he wishes it had been the Countess who endorsed him. Lodowick enters with the news that the Countess will have a definitive answer to the king that night. While Edward muses on the difference between the struggles of love and war, Lodowick reenters and says the drums the king earlier heard denote the troops led by Prince Edward, who has heeded his injunction to be more martial and has mobilized a goodly mass of soldiers. Lodowick reenters yet again, saying the Countess wishes to see him, and Edward reverses his state of mind, denouncing his wife, and indicates that he is prepared to abandon the war if the Countess wishes. Killing men at war, he muses, is more sinful than unauthorized love. When he sees the Countess, she makes him an unusual proposal: to eliminate those who stand between them, his wife and her husband. The king protests this would be impossible, but the Countess dares him to do it to prove his love. The king succumbs and pledges to kill Salisbury and the Queen. The Countess reveals two knives and says she will kill her husband with one, bidding Edward to take the other and kill the queen. Stunned by her apparent cooperation, or perhaps realizing that she is making grisly mock of his entire plan, the king is roused to his senses and pledges never to violate her honor again. Calling in his liegeman, he announces he is recovered and that the war against France is shortly to begin.

Act III, Scene 1

King John of France, his son Charles, and other of his liegemen stand on the French shore, anticipating the English attack. Charles skeptically recounts reports that the English have put aside their customary dissension and are now unified in war, though the Scots vow to continue fighting against the English. The French note that the Dutch as well as the Holy Roman Emperor are on the English side, though the French in turn have the loyalty of Denmark, Poland, Bohemia, and Sicily. The French are caught up in chivalric rhetoric and expectations and are overconfident. They also are insulated by their taking comfort in the belief that as long as the king is king, he is likely to win, possession being most of the game. The king and his retinue are stunned when the English force the French fleet to beat a hasty retreat. A mariner arrives and gives a detailed, graphic description of the naval battle, demonstrating that England has won all.

Act III, Scene 2

In the fields of Picardy, near Crécy, an ordinary Frenchman conveys to two others the news of the decisive English naval victory. A woman utters a prophecy that a lion wearing a fleur-de-lis (the national symbol of France) shall destroy France. A fourth Frenchman comes in bringing new details of English victories and the devastation in their wake. Utterly demoralized, the common people of the area flee for their lives.

Act III, Scene 3

The Battle of Crécy begins. Gobin de Grace, a Frenchman, has given the English army information on how to ford the Somme River, and Edward thanks him for this service. The prince arrives bringing the news of great land victories he has led. The king is regretful that so many French can oppose the idea of his rule of France. King John enters the battlefield and insults Edward, condemning him as a usurper and a wretch. Edward firmly defends himself and avows his determination to win the crown he claims. The prince backs him up, saying the English do not need to resort to insults in order to win their point. Audley urges the French soldiers to switch sides, whereas Charles upbraids Audley for his age. Prince Edward defends Audley, stating that age can bring wisdom. Derby follows up on this point by noting the Valois house's recent arrival to kingship, further bringing together the themes of age and legitimacy. John pleads for support on the grounds of French patriotism, and Edward and his men assume the shields and swords of battle.

Act III, Scene 4

In the midst of the battle, King John wonders why, since the French army so outnumbers its English counterpart, his forces are yet flying from the English. He is told that several of his regiments are tired and irresolute and that their initial flight demoralized much of the army and caused it to fade.

Act III, Scene 5

Edward takes a pause in the battle while his son fights on. Artois comes to warn the king that the prince is in danger, but the king bids his subordi-

David Mendolsohn as Edward, the Black Prince, in the 2001 Pacific Repertory Theatre production of *Edward III* (Photograph by Pacific Repertory Theater)

by extracting her own blood. So does the prince thrive upon the carnage of warfare.

Act IV, Scene 1

In Brittany, in the English camp, Lord Mountford, having reestablished himself in the dukedom from which he earlier had been ousted by the French, bids the Earl of Salisbury to convey his allegiance to King Edward. Salisbury asks Villiers, a French prisoner, to request of Prince Charles a safe-conduct letter for Salisbury to go to Calais, the seaport where the English plan to attack the French, in return for Salisbury's release of Villiers. Villiers pledges to do so; Salisbury makes him swear and says he will count on this to be the one time where a Frenchman will keep his honor

Act IV, Scene 2

In the English camp before Calais, Edward vows to besiege the city, as the citizens will not open the gate. Approached by a group of poor inhabitants from Calais, the king offers them food and shelter instead of, as they ask, killing them, despite the town's holdout against the English, partially out of pity, partially because he scorns to kill a weak opponent. Lord Percy comes with the news that Queen Philippa is arriving from England and also that King David of Scotland has capitulated; moreover, the queen is pregnant. There is a problem, though; the man who has taken King David prisoner, John Copland, refuses to surrender his prize to anyone but the king himself, much to the annoyance of the queen. The king determines to dispatch a herald to summon Copland and awaits the queen's arrival. Meanwhile, the wealthy class of Calais offers to surrender the town in return for Edward's mercy. The king, affronted by their resistance, spurns this offer and will permit only six of the town's wealthiest men to beg and humble themselves before him.

Act IV, Scene 3

Villiers reaches Prince Charles and asks him to grant Salisbury safe conduct through Calais. Charles resists this, saying that Villiers is already

nate to let the prince fight. Derby comes and says Prince Edward is in immediate peril, but the king is still unmoved. Audley then bids the king for permission to fight himself in relief of the prince, but the king says the prince's fate should be in his own hands, he should make his own destiny. If he dies, the king has other sons, and the prince's reputation will be swelled by honor and praise. Audley condemns the king as a cruel father, but the trumpet of retreat then sounds. The French army has been bested and the prince returns in triumph, saying he has killed the king of Bohemia and that the king of France has fled. Knighted by his father, he takes as his heraldic image a pelican, who feeds her young free and does not need to have him do Villiers a favor to secure his freedom. Villiers points out that he has given his honor in the promise to Salisbury and that the king must abide by this pledge. Moved by Villiers's principles, the prince agree to the safe conduct, Villiers leaves, and King John enters, with the news that the French army has surrounded the prince. Charles urges his father to fight, declaring a prophecy that one day the French king will be as far in England as the English king now is in France. The prophecy also predicts that when certain unlikely portents occur, all should be lost; but Charles dismisses the possibility of those events ever occurring and urges the French army to capture the son as a stepping stone to capturing the father.

Act IV, Scene 4
Prince Edward notes the strength of the French army and realizes that the battle outside Calais will not be a repeat of Crécy, that the French army is on the verge of surrounding him. Audley describes in detail the French military formation and begins to despair of the fate of the English army. The prince, though, notes that what is seemingly large is composed of small constituents and that a mighty agglomeration of millions of drops of water is only "rain." For him, it is ultimately one army, of whatever size and strength, against another, and he remains confident he can hold his own. The French king as well as one of his sons offer Prince Edward surrender terms, but the prince adamantly refuses them. The prince sends Audley forth to declare his intentions to resist and takes succor from the old man's fierceness and determination.

Act IV, Scene 5
The French king and his son note an eerie silence, which is broken by the entrance of the Duke of Normandy saying the battlefield is contested and the English are strong, Salisbury is captured but shows Prince Charles his safe conduct procured via Villiers, and the prince lets him through. King John reproaches him for the improvidence of this,

but the prince, as Villiers had earlier argued to him, stands upon honor.

Act IV, Scene 6
Artois fears Prince Edward has been shot, but he is only impeded by dust and smoke. Artois complains the English do not have enough arrows; the prince exhorts him to have courage.

Act IV, Scene 7
King John notes that, despite their numbers, the French army is confused and demoralized. His sons tell him there is no hope, and the royal retinue flees the scene.

Act IV, Scene 8
Audley is wounded. A soldier warns him the wound might be fatal, and Audley says if this is so, he will go out of life with honor.

Act IV, Scene 9
Prince Edward has captured both King John and Prince Charles. King John says it was luck, not superior skill, that gave the English the victory, a statement that Prince Edward interprets to mean that heaven is on England's side. The wounded Audley is brought in, speaking of his own death. Prince Edward bids him to be carried out on a litter with honor.

Act V, Scene 1
King Edward assures Queen Philippa that Copland, the captor of King David of Scotland who had refused to surrender him to the queen, shall be duly punished for his insubordination. Six formerly rich men of Calais enter the king's presence, attired in humble clothes and abase themselves before him. The king agrees to spare the town but insists on punishing the men whom he sees as servile and ignoble. Queen Philippa, though, pleads for mercy toward them, which the king eventually grants. Derby brings in Copland and King David. When questioned by the king as to why he had not surrendered the Scotsman, Copland protests that he wanted acknowledgment of the honor of doing the

deed and could not have achieved this except in the presence of the king. Pleased by Copland's reasoning, and his distinction between Edward's "name," which Philippa can rule in, and his "person," which only the king can possess, King Edward grants Copland clemency and grants him a knighthood and a pension. Lord Salisbury comes in, bearing news of Prince Edward's death, heroically and against overwhelming odds. Queen Philippa, desolated by the loss of her son, bewails the paradox of this loss amid victory. As Edward attempts to console his wife, a herald announces that the prince in fact has survived and is about to enter. The prince comes in, presents his father with King John's crown and is embraced by his rejoicing parents. Edward informs John that John is to be taken to England as a hostage, at which point John realizes the prophecy of his going as far into England as Edward is now in France has quite a different connotation than he had imagined. Prince Edward gives a final declaration of England's strength as the king prepares to take his spoils back to England in a mood of general triumph and congratulation.

CHARACTER LIST

Edward III   King of England, husband of Queen Philippa, and father of Prince Edward. Edward is presented as a valiant king, determined to take up his claim to the French throne, when, in rescuing the Countess of Salisbury from her Scottish assailants, he falls violently in love with her and seeks to seduce her. Brought to his senses by her intricate wiles, he awakes to his old self and leads the English army in successful naval and land engagements in France. Willing to sacrifice the life of his son so that the prince may earn glory on his own, the king acclaims his son when he proves victorious.

Prince Edward   Son of King Edward and Queen Philippa. A young, untried man at the beginning of the play, the prince is challenged by his father to learn the arts of war. He does this so well that he proves far more steadfast to the cause than his father and proves his mettle again and again, finally attaining a knighthood through his valor on the battlefield. Thought dead in the Battle of Poitiers, he reappears to the delight and acclaim of all.

Alice, Countess of Salisbury   Daughter of the Earl of Warwick and wife of the Earl of Salisbury, the Countess is besieged by David, king of the Scots, and is rescued by King Edward. Their relationship turns suddenly from one of feudal loyalty to amorous intrigue when the king abruptly falls in love with her and attempts to seduce her. The Countess proposes that both she and the king kill their spouses. After initially considering going along with the plan, King Edward sees the error of his ways and pledges to treat her honorably from now on.

King John of France   Head of the Valois line, he has claimed the throne despite being further away in degree of kinship from King Philip IV than is King Edward. John uses as justification the Salic law in France, which mandates that succession only occur through the male line. Vain and indecisive, the king is no match for Edward and his son.

Prince Charles of France   Sharper and more responsible than his father, Charles is yet led astray by his punctiliousness—he grants Villiers his plea for Salisbury's safe conduct, which helps cost the French the Battle of Calais—and also his intellectual self-satisfaction, as occurs when he misinterprets a prophecy.

Earl of Warwick   Father of the Countess of Salisbury; despite being a loyal servant of the king, he is appalled when Edward discloses his plan with respect to his daughter and is pleased when the Countess demonstrates her intention to resist the king's advances.

Earl of Salisbury   Husband of the Countess in the play, he is unaware of what has happened between his wife and King Edward. Guaranteed safe conduct from Brittany to Calais through Villiers' intervention, he plays a decisive role at the final battle.

William Montague   Salisbury's nephew.

Villiers   Prisoner of the English-allied Duke of Brittany. He is released by Salisbury so he can go to Prince Charles and ask his permission for Salisbury's safe conduct from Brittany to Calais.

Queen Philippa Wife of King Edward and mother of Prince Edward. She arrives in France, pregnant, to bring news of the capitulation of the Scottish king and to complain of Copland's refusal to surrender him; the son she will bear is to become John of Gaunt (featured in Shakespeare's *Richard II*).

King David of Scotland King of England's northern neighbor who challenges Edward's authority by besieging the Countess of Salisbury's castle. He is repulsed by Edward's forces and eventually defeated and taken prisoner by the English.

Earl of Douglas Subordinate of King David who at first avers his romantic desire for the Countess, then steps back to settling for her jewels.

Earl of Audley Knight in the English army, Audley is an older experienced veteran called upon by King Edward and the prince for his wise counsel. He is seriously wounded, but not killed, in the battle.

Earl of Derby Nobleman who provides news from France.

Duke of Lorraine Emissary of the king of France to England and later Scotland.

Count of Artois French nobleman who has defected to Edward's side.

John Copland Man who captures King David of Scotland but refuses to surrender his prize to anyone but King Edward himself.

Gobin de Grace Frenchman who helps the English army ford the Somme.

Lord Mountford Duke of Brittany.

Lord Percy Second baron Percy.

CHARACTER STUDIES
Edward III

Edward III can be seen either as an admirable man seized by a fit of madness and lust or an ambiguous figure who mingles courage and charisma with selfishness and a reluctance to do good for others. When he chooses to lead, he is decisive and commanding, able to be both resolute and merciful as the occasion calls for it, as shown by

his stern but not unyielding treatment of both the poor and the burghers of Calais. His soldiers and liegeman respect him, even such originally French vassals as Artois and the Duke of Brittany. There is never any articulated tension between him and Queen Philippa, and when they are together in France, he is both supportive of her in her resentment about the Copland matter and comforting of her in the brief interval during which they both suppose their son is lost. In addition, in contrast to his father, who was suspected of homoerotic sexual relations with his favorite, Piers Gaveston, Edward III was unimpeachably, even rampantly, heterosexual. As opposed to his grandson Richard II, later written about by Shakespeare, Edward III was of robust physique and sired several children. Indeed, Edward III is still busy siring children at the end of this play, as even with a grown son, the queen becomes pregnant again.

But, the king's role as father, both literally (to his son) and figuratively (to his people), alternates in the play with his role as adulterous lover, and in both these roles, his performance is mixed. The king's error in courting the Countess of Salisbury is threefold. First, he is a married man asking her to violate her marriage as well as his own. Though adultery was frequent in both Shakespeare's own society and the one he depicts, it was manifestly declared a sin by the church and was not thought honorable: A knight, for example, was allowed to yearn for an unattainable lady, but sexual relations in violation of marriage was disapproved of. Second, he is violating his own bond with the Countess; she is his liege and has held out against the Scots not only on her own behalf but also on his as a subordinate of the king. In effect, she is almost like a soldier under his command. Under the feudal system, questions of loyalty and mutual responsibility were taken seriously; indeed, when King Edward invades France, it is less notable that he is infringing upon another country's sovereignty, as modern rules of statecraft would have it, than that he is violating the feudal oath he swore to the French throne in his capacity as duke of Guienne. In other words, the king already had a meaningful relationship with the Countess—as lord to vassal—and his attempt to insert another meaningful relationship—as romantic love interests—trivializes and scants. Third, the king, by courting the Countess, is neglecting his duty. He has boldly, and, arguably rashly, refused to submit to the rule of the French king and asserted his own rights to the French throne. To almost immediately forget about all this, to jettison the crowning political ambition of his career for an impetuous passion, lets down not only the king himself but all who have pledged to fight for him.

King Edward recovers himself in time, but he cannot regain an unambiguously benign status. Questions also arise about his relationship with his son. He plays the role of an exhortatory father, urging his son at the beginning to prove himself in the arts of war. But, the king is caught short when, in the middle of the imbroglio with the Countess, the prince shows up, mobilized and prepared for battle. Perhaps the king had not expected the prince to prepare himself so quickly and adeptly in a way that showed up his own irresponsibility. Similarly, the prince's achievement once the war in France begins has the potential to stir up jealousy on the part of the king, much as in the biblical story of David and Saul, where the people's cry of "Saul has slain his thousands and David his ten thousands" inevitably rankles the older man as the younger man is more acclaimed (1 Samuel 18:7). In forbidding his men from aiding the prince at the height of battle, the king enables the prince to show his mettle and prove himself without having the security of his father's protection every time he gets into trouble. But there is also something deliberately cruel, sadistic, and begrudging about the king's action; it is a stance more congruent with Roman stoicism and would be less jarring in one of Shakespeare's Roman plays than a play set in a Christian society. Although the king and the prince never have any overt conflict, and the prince shows nothing but loyalty and reverence for the king, the father's behavior is unnatural enough to be noted by his courtiers. Although the king appears morally cleansed by the time he leaves for France, this tacit

sparring with his son may be a legacy of his own guilt and feelings of moral inadequacy stemming from the Countess episode.

Another way to look at the Countess episode is to see it as a product of Edward's own tension about going to war. That he would commence a dalliance with a woman not his wife in the midst of two wars—against Scotland, which he has not totally repelled, and against France—is almost a signal that he does not really wish to fights the wars, or that he doubts his own martial prowess. This can, of course, be a sign of conscience as much as of cowardice, as when the king declares: "The sin is more to hack and hew poor men / Than to embrace in an unlawful bed" (2.2.115–116). Interpretations that wish to emphasize the king as a great warrior and the play as a history chronicle of his victories in France can see the Countess episode as underscoring the doubts and divisions that even such a strong leader as Edward has about war.

Alice, Countess of Salisbury

The Countess herself is a fairly straightforward psychological figure; she is grateful to King Edward for his rescue of her and appalled at his lust for her and at the reckless abandon with which he pursues it. But, several questions can be asked of her as well. Her pleading that the king stay the night at her castle rather than pursue the Scottish armies, as would usually happen, is unexpected. She has just been in grave danger from the Scots, and only a hot pursuit, while the English army has the upper hand, will totally anneal any danger from them. Therefore, a ceremonial offer of hospitality is one thing, but to insist that the king remain in the castle suggests an eagerness to be in proximity to him, far more even than, say, Hermione's extension of a similar hospitable offer to Polixenes in *The Winter's Tale,* which moved her husband Leontes to a fit of jealousy. Thus, even if King Edward is misinterpreting her warmth, he is not totally without grounds for doing so, and if the Countess wanted her rescue to pass without incident, she should not have been quite so exuberant.

The Countess's proposal to the king that they mutually kill their spouses is also perplexing. It is reasonably clear that she makes it in order to bring home to the king the force of the moral violation that he is proposing To have an adulterous affair would, symbolically, be to assault both their marriages; hence, all the Countess is doing is literalizing the metaphor. Indeed, the proposal has, after some delay, the effect on the king that she must have originally desired: to wake him out of his lust-filled torpor and remind him of his obligations as king and sovereign. However, to even conceive this plot, however little she actually intended to go through with it, speaks to her possessing at the very least a dark imagination. Just as we cannot see the king in the same way after his behavior, we cannot see the Countess in an entirely virtuous light after her proposal, and in tacit recognition of this, she disappears from the play. As a woman capable of protecting herself and of launching vigorous arguments on behalf of her moral positions, the Countess stands with those female characters in Shakespeare's histories who are not content to be mere baubles exchanged for men's convenience in games of diplomacy or social capital. The Countess, in her manipulation of the king and her willingness to use indecent possibilities to achieve her end, also has something Machiavellian about her, something ingenious and even underhanded. It is perhaps this quality in her that makes her father, the Earl of Warwick, surprised when she articulates such an eloquent and moral rationale in response to his reluctant urging of her to succumb to the king's unwholesome desires.

Prince Edward

The prince has no such moral complications as King Edward and the Countess of Salisbury. Regarding Prince Edward the play is a simple bildungsroman, or chronicle of education and maturation. He starts out an untried boy and becomes at the end an acclaimed warrior and leader of men, the equal of his regal father. He is concentrated on his own duties and his own development as man and leader; he seems oblivious to the charged

An illustration of Edward the Black Prince, from Cassell's *History of England,* published in 1902

emotional currents surrounding his father's private life. This could stem from a combination of factors. He could simply be too young and naive to sense them. He could sense them but not register his apprehension of them on any conscious level because of a sense of deference to the king, who is not just his father but also his feudal lord. Or, he could have decided that the best way to remain virtuous is not to worry about other people's lack of virtue—especially his father's. The prince is the ideal of knighthood that his father is not. Yet, the play is about his father, and for all the prince's military merit, the play does not suggest that the ultimate credit for the victories over France were not due to King Edward. For the audience, the prince's character might have been less one-dimensional than it would seem in later days, simply because it was still commonly known that the prince did not live to succeed his father, dying a year before Edward III's death in 1377.

DIFFICULTIES OF THE PLAY

Since *Edward III* has only recently been considered a truly Shakespearean play and lacks the critical tradition of most of the others, it can be hard to take it seriously as part of the Shakespearean canon. Many past critics, notably A. C. Swinburne, have deemed it unworthy of Shakespeare. Moreover, the inclusion of *Edward III* in the canon posits an altered image of Shakespeare's relationship to history, which can be difficult to accept. Shakespeare often introduces ahistorical characters in his plays (such as Falstaff, only loosely based on Sir John Oldcastle) and telescopes times, as in *Richard III,* where Richard's courtship of Lady Anne and his ascension to the throne occurred much further apart in real life than they do in the play. But, he seldom invents characters intended to play a historical role; when he mentions history, it is largely accurate. Thus, it is striking that *Edward III* skips a generation in its depiction of the French monarchy, utterly eliminating Philip VI—who in fact was the king who claimed descent from the male inheritance and established the Valois dynasty—and, in effect, moving his son John and grandson Charles forward a generation. This action, without equivalent in any of Shakespeare's plays based on English history, is a major difficulty for those who wish to prove the play Shakespearean. This stumbling block has been sidelined by modern critics for whom the succession of French kings is little known and unimportant, but for the historical sources of the play—Holinshed and, before him, Froissart—it most assuredly was important. The ahistoricity of the depiction of the French monarchy cannot simply be explained by the playwright not wanting to reproduce the name Philip too much—after all, the play's two most prominent male characters are both named Edward and are father and son—or by any other dramatic convenience. Nor can, they be explained by Francophobia, as the moving a generation forward brings the canny and determined Dauphin Charles into the picture, whereas conventional understandings of history would have kept this most worthy of 14th-century French monarchs offstage. The entire scenario is suggestive, not of Shakespeare, but of a contemporary playwright such as George Peele, who, in plays such as his depiction of Edward III's grandfather *The Famous Chronicle of King Edward the First* (1593), combined historical settings with ahistorical renditions of them. It also suggests a rather heavy dependence on Painter, even though Painter's scenario is even more ahistorical, as he represents King Edward and the countess of Salisbury as eventually getting married.

If Shakespeare did not definitely write *Edward III,* though, it is incontestable that he knew of it and that it influenced him. The most apparent signs of this influence are where they should be—in *Henry V* the other play about an English king who successfully campaigns in France during the Hundred Years' War. In actually conquering Paris and getting, for a time, the French monarchy to acknowledge him as the proper claimant to the throne, Henry V finished Edward III's mission.

KEY PASSAGES
Act II, Scene 1

KING EDWARD. Then in the summer arbour
  sit by me,
Make it our council-house, or cabinet;
Since green our thoughts, green be the
  conventicle
Where we will ease us by disburd'ning them.
Now, Lodwick, invocate some golden muse
To bring thee hither an enchanted pen
That may, for sighs, set down true sighs indeed;
Talking of grief, to make thee ready groan;
And, when thou writ'st of tears, encouch the
  word,
Before and after, with such sweet laments,
That it may raise drops in a Tartar's eye,
And make a flint-heart Scythian pitiful:
For so much moving hath a poet's pen;
Then, if thou be a poet, move thou so.
And be enriched by thy sovereign's love.
For, if the touch of sweet concordant strings
Could force attendance in the ears of hell;
How much more shall the strains of poet's wit
Beguile and ravish soft and human minds.

This speech by King Edward to his secretary, Lodowick, in Act II, Scene 1 is virtually an exercise in literary criticism or, indeed, comparative criticism of the arts: He exalts poetry over music, stating that poetry can be even more persuasive, implicitly because it is done with more conscious craft and has all the wit of formulated language behind it. To some degree, the playwright, by putting these sentiments in the mouth of the lascivious Edward, is mocking the high-flown rhetoric of Petrarchan love poetry, especially because Edward hopes that the "enchanted pen" will be used to work the dark magic of seduction rather than the benign hex of loving courtship. This provides another link to the sonnets, as one of the major rhetorical tools of the sonnets is a simultaneous use and deflation of the standard repertory of amorous phrases and sentiments associated with the mode of Petrarch. But the praise of poetry as a mode can also be likened to contemporary Elizabethan writings on poetry, particularly Philip Sidney's *Defence of Poetry,* which makes much of the independence of poetry from fact and its suppleness as a mode of cognitive insight. The use of the Scythian and Tartar similes are reminiscent of Latin poets such as Horace and bespeak a writer who has had at least the grammar school–level classical education that we know Shakespeare received. The range, density, and internal play of the language here seem like Shakespeare, are reminiscent of him, as is the very Shakespearean motif of the internal letter within the play, explored in the early 2000s by the scholar Alan Stewart. But, as any reader of *Hamlet* knows, there is a big difference between *seems* and *is* and, therefore, between seeming Shakespearean and being Shakespearean.

Act II, Scene 1

WARWICK. How shall I enter in this graceless
  errand?
I must not call her child, for where's the father
That will in such a suit seduce his child?
Then, 'wife of Salisbury'; shall I so begin?
No, he's my friend, and where is found the
  friend

That will do friendship such indammagement?
[To the Countess.]
Neither my daughter nor my dear friend's wife,
I am not Warwick, as thou thinkst I am,
But an attorney from the Court of hell,
That thus have housed my spirit in his form,
To do a message to thee from the king.
The mighty king of England dotes on thee:
He that hath power to take away thy life,
Hath power to take thy honor; then consent
To pawn thine honor rather than thy life:
Honor is often lost and got again,
But life, once gone, hath no recovery.
The Sun, that withers hay, doth nourish grass;
The king, that would disdain thee, will
  advance thee.
The Poets write that great Achilles' spear
Could heal the wound it made: the moral is,
What mighty men misdo, they can amend.
The Lyon doth become his bloody jaws,
And grace his forragement by being mild,
When vassel fear lies trembling at his feet.
The king will in his glory hide thy shame;
And those that gaze on him to find out thee,
Will lose their eye-sight, looking in the Sun.
What can one drop of poison harm the Sea,
Whose huge vastures can digest the ill
And make it loose his operation?
The king's great name will temper thy
  misdeeds,
And give the bitter potion of reproach,
A sugared, sweet and most delicious taste.
Besides, it is no harm to do the thing
Which without shame could not be left
  undone.
Thus have I in his majesty's behalf
Appareled sin in virtuous sentences,
And dwell upon thy answer in his suit.

Warwick is torn between several loyalties: to his monarch, to his daughter, to his son-in-law, and to his own conscience. In medieval times, unlike those of today, loyalty to his king would have been, at least nominally, the highest, a feudal obligation to his sovereign prevailing over the intimate and

The Countess of Salisbury (Julie Hughett) holds the Earl of Warwick (Alex Peckman) in the Pacific Repertory Theatre 2001 production of *Edward III*. (*Photograph by Pacific Repertory Theater*)

affective ties that would be more highly valued in later ages. It is not the conflict between king and daughter that makes Warwick feel unvirtuous but the vileness of what the king contemplates. Warwick comforts himself by saying that the king's iniquity will not be held against him because of the king's importance—"What can one drop of poison harm the Sea?"—and also that any misdeed by the king can be quickly healed, much like the lion's bloody jaws can be effaced merely by a mild gaze. This use of natural and animal imagery, not just in comparison to human motives, but to intensify their meaning and complexity, presents one of the strongest intuitive arguments for Shakespearean authorship.

Act IV, Scene 1

SALISBURY. Villiers, thou knowest, thou art
  my prisoner,
And that I might for ransom, if I would,
Require of thee a hundred thousand Francs,
Or else retain and keep thee captive still:
But so it is, that for a smaller charge
Thou maist be quit, and if thou wilt thy self.

And this it is:
Procure me but a passport
Of Charles, the Duke of Normandy, that
I Without restraint may have recourse to Calais
Through all the Countries where he hath to do;
Which thou maist easily obtain, I think,
By reason I have often heard thee say,
He and thou were students once together:
And then thou shalt be set at liberty.
How saiest thou? wilt thou undertake to do it?

In this speech by the captor, Salisbury, to his hostage, Villiers, he at once acknowledges his sway over his prisoner but also indicates that Villiers has some latent power, as, by his release, he can petition his master's son, the dauphin, to give Salisbury safe passage so he can intervene at Calais. Even as Salisbury seemingly holds all the cards in the situation, both the codes of honor between gentleman and the "rules" attendant upon the role of hostage give Villiers enough power to be able to negotiate the terms of that contract. What Salisbury offers Villiers is a deal, a settlement, something to be gained by persuasion and agreement, mandated by dictate. Salisbury calls upon the personal in the midst of the political, not just in the frankness of his man-to-man request to Villiers but in his acknowledgment of Villiers's childhood bond with the dauphin, his sense that the two Frenchmen do not just have a political master-liege relationship but are personal friends. Once again, the play's reigning dichotomy, that between the private and public, comes into play, although here, unlike in the situation between King Edward and the Countess of Salisbury, it is a public, indeed a military objective that Salisbury seeks to gain by his acknowledgment of a private bond and hope of prevailing over it.

DIFFICULT PASSAGES
Act I, Scene 2

COUNTESS. Let not thy presence, like the
  April sun,
Flatter our earth, and suddenly be done:
More happy do not make our outward wall

Than thou wilt grace our inward house withal.
Our house, my liege, is like a country swain,
Presageth naught; yet inly beautified
With bounty's riches, and fair hidden pride;
For where the golden ore doth buried lie,
The ground, undecked with nature's tapestry,
Seems barren, sere, unfertile, fruitless, dry;
And where the upper turf of earth doth boast
His pride, perfumes, and particoloured cost,
Delve there, and find this issue and their pride
To spring from ordure and corruption's side.
But, to make up my all too long compare,
These ragged walls no testimony are
What is within; but, like a cloak, doth hide
From weather's waste the under garnished
   pride.
More gracious than my terms can let thee be,
Entreat thyself to stay awhile with me.

This speech by the Countess of Salisbury to King Edward in Act I, Scene 2 is difficult not only linguistically but in terms of psychology and motive. The elaborate simile comparing the king to the Sun ramifies into a plea for an extension of the outward to the inward, for the king's military liberation of the castle to extend into a domestic residence there. The Countess uses the same imagery of outside and inside, appearance and reality that could well represent the opposition between the king's outward valor and his inward lust. Though there is nothing in the Countess's words to suggest a sexual invitation or to plausibly give the king any indication that she would encourage his suit, the fervor of the entreaty is perhaps a bit more than the circumstances would call for and sets a verbal, if not necessarily a moral, basis for the king's ensuing misbehavior. The Countess also takes advantage of one of the few powers allotted to women in this society—to offer hospitality—but she soon finds that the hospitality she has offered is her potential undoing.

Act II, Scene 1

COUNTESS. As easy may my intellectual soul
Be lent away, and yet my body live,

As lend my body, palace to my soul,
Away from her, and yet retain my soul.
My body is her bower, her Court, her abbey,
And she an Angel, pure, divine, unspotted:
If I should leave her house, my Lord, to thee,
I kill my poor soul and my poor soul me.

The Countess's speech beginning at line 246 of Act II, Scene 1 asserts a complicated mutual independence between body and soul and is impossible to understand without some understanding of both the Platonic doctrine of the immortality of the soul—the very word *intellectual* here alludes to the Platonic view of the mind—and the Christian insistence that the body is as much a part of an individual's personal integrity as is his or her soul, as no body can live—can have human, sentient, as opposed to merely biological life—without a soul. Equally, says the Countess, there is no hope of maintaining the soul's integrity while polluting the body. What the Countess is arguing against is the idea that she may yield her body to the king under duress of his power and sovereignty and still maintain the purity of her soul; impurity of one will corrupt the other. As occurs many times during this scene if the passage is read as Shakespeare, there are what can be seen as anticipations of Isabella's similar posture in *Measure for Measure*.

CRITICAL INTRODUCTION TO THE PLAY

The play is often seen as one great era of English valor paying homage to another. In the wake of victory in fending off the Spanish Armada, Elizabethan England swelled with pride at defeating the leading continental power. Memories inevitably gravitated to the last struggle England waged with a continental power, the Hundred Years' War (1337–1453) with France. Though this conflict was very different from the recent war with Spain—it was a generations-long struggle in which England was originally the aggressor and which was waged over the possibility of England's permanent suzerainty in France—the heroes and situations of the earlier conflict were readily adaptable in light of

England's current situation. This was aided by the rich historical record provided by the chronicles of Froissart and, later, Holinshed, supplemented by colorful fictional accounts such as Painter's.

Yet, despite this obvious political relevance and the repute in which Edward III was held as a king who expanded England's territory during a long and fruitful reign, the play itself, as it stands, is difficult to reconcile with an overtly patriotic mission. If the entire play were in the style of the last two acts—the chronicle-like, staccato sequence of annalistic battle accounts—the play could be seen as a simple endorsement of post–Spanish Armada pride. But, the domestic entanglements of the first three acts and Edward III's less-than-noble conduct present a contradiction. The reader, thus, has two options. One is to see the play as a collaborative venture, rigged up under tremendous pressure of time and composed by diverse hands, possibly including Shakespeare. The necessary contradictions would be an inevitable result of the need for speed to realize a crowd-pleasing play on a popular and timely subject. Alternatively, one could see the contradiction as a result of trying to reach two different audiences, as might be done in a popular contemporary movie that has both an action-adventure plot and a love plot. It might have been this genre need, complicated by the fact that the only aspect of either Edward III's or the Black Prince's love life was the slightly indigestible Countess of Salisbury plot, that led to the play being the way it is—this scenario could assume either joint or individual authorship and either Shakespearean, part-Shakespearean, or non-Shakespearean composition.

But another solution would be to hypothesize an underlying unity between the private and public parts of the play. This has indeed been attempted, and the most fruitful direction these inquiries have taken is to center the play on the Order of the Garter, a rank of knighthood established in the mid-14th century, in the early years of the Hundred Years' War. Indeed, it is the very knighthood Edward III bestows on his son near the end of the play. The Order of the Garter today is still England's most prestigious order, entirely separate from the ordinary knighthoods conferred on, say, actors or civil servants. The garter is extended only to members of the royal family and prominent politicians or other notable individuals; it is a select fraternity even within the circle of the prominent and the aristocratic. Part of the prestige of this order was cemented in the Elizabethan era, the time of Shakespeare, when the Order of the Garter was revitalized and held in particular regard as representing the most admirable values of chivalry.

What of the association of the garter with the events of the play? First of all, a garter is a device of clothing used to keep stockings up; it is a humble and everyday appurtenance, not normally associated with the derring-do and inevitable hyperbole of knightly achievement. Part of the resonance of the order being named after the garter is the stress on the knight displaying small courtesies, of behaving well in a minute matrix as well as an immense one. But, another valence is that the garter had a connotation of sexual seduction; taking off a garter meant unfastening someone's clothes, taking off their garments. In the context of men seducing women, taking off a woman's garter was seen as a stage in a man's persuasion of a woman to have sex with him. A stray garter might be seen as a token that a woman had capitulated to a man's seductive suit.

A clue here is an anonymous 14th-century work produced perhaps some decades after the events of *Edward III:* the poem *Sir Gawain and the Green Knight.* In this alliterative poem, a young knight resists the seductive advances of Lady Bertilak, the wife of his host; it is revealed at the end to have been an elaborate game designed to test his loyalty and his capacity to be a true man of chivalry. The slogan of the Order of the Garter, "Honi soit qui mal y pense," is medieval Norman-French for "shame on him who thinks ill of it." The "it" is supposed to refer to a lady dropping her garter; not necessarily with seductive intent, but as an accident. People might think ill of it because the lady was slovenly or did not groom herself properly as much as that she was loose or wanton with her chastity. The phrase thus signifies a willingness to overlook small errors, a chivalrous generosity and magnanimity to accept the reality of minor mistakes in life and to transcend them in a spirit of inclusiveness and generosity.

Some have traced the origin of the phrase to an incident between Edward and the countess of Salisbury, where the countess dropped a garter, and the king is said to have uttered the phrase. This was simply a gentlemanly gesture of the king to a lady of the court. No sexual innuendo at all was intended. But the play and its inherited tradition of stories from the two chroniclers and Painter may well have tacitly associated the fictional seduction of the countess with this ascribed, iconic real-life incident. In terms of the interplay of fiction and history, it is crucial for the viability of the garter theme in the Elizabethan age to recall that the early 16th-century historian Polydore Vergil, an Italian writer working at the court of Henry VII whose research invalidated the legend of the Trojan origin of western European peoples, nonetheless accepted the historicity of the garter story. This could, in empirical terms, be laid to Polydore's relative ignorance of English matters and his consequent credulity with respect to the lore of the locals. But, the fact that a Renaissance humanist who had discredited so many legends nonetheless affirmed the garter story was an important index of veracity and authority in the Elizabethan age. (Even in the 21st century, the Order of the Garter is Britain's most prestigious ceremonial honor and one whose diversity—including prominent members of the royal family, distinguished British politicians, and figures from the commonwealth and elsewhere—represents both the tenacity and flexibility of the English vision of aristocracy.)

A "garter" reading of *Edward III* would see the scene at the Countess's castle as a kind of testing ground for the king, one in which he must prove his moral mettle. If compared to *Sir Gawain*, the best-known "garter text," Edward III's conduct in this play is far from perfect: Edward continues to avow not only importunate and authorized lust but, when pressed, even considers the murder of his queen, the mother of his child. But, the Salis-

bury story could, with only moderate difficulty, be adapted to a "garter purpose" by the dramatic adjacency of Edward's coming to his senses and renouncing his desire for the Countess in admiration of her virtue and his energetic pursuit of the English cause in France. Edward could, in a sense, have purified himself through his renunciation of the Countess and segued from his admittedly belated moral refreshment into victory in France. That the final scene at Poitiers is in a domestic as well as military context, with the king and queen as proud parents greeting their miraculously saved son and the queen in turn about to bear another child, point to a potential garter harmony, a resolution of the double plot under the aegis of the ideal of the garter. The garter, in other words, provides not only a redemptive sanctification of the king's moral peril and repentance but a satisfactory way to connect the public and private strands of the play. Recognition of the garter theme increases the possibility of the play having a unified conception and being written by a single hand. From kings and countesses to an ordinary Frenchman to the poor man of Calais who seek King Edward's succor, the wealthy, the middle class, and the poor are all proportionately represented. This testifies to the chronicle scenes' ability to indicate broad social panoply as well as their interest in dimensions of life beyond the regal and military.

The play's structure is unusually foreshortened by the brevity of the fifth act, which consists of one medium-length scene, almost entirely taken up with the playing out of the Battle of Poitiers and the successful return of the prince. Depending on interpretive taste, this can be seen either as symmetrical—the first act is not long either, acting as a sort of bookend or as an indication of hasty composition and a rushed effort by a collaborative authorship to get the play to the public as soon as possible. If the play is Shakespeare's, the garter theme strongly reinforces the plausibility of Shakespeare coming at the piece with a sustained artistic and moral intention.

Against all this is the fact that the garter theme is hardly obvious in the play (certainly compared to *Sir Gawain*); there is no moment at which the order itself is born (as opposed to the individual knighting of the prince). Neither the word *garter* nor the phrase "honi soit qui mal y pense," or any approximation of it, occurs in the play. The garter theme in the play is dependent on inference and our assumption that the garter relevance would have been obvious to the original audience. Failing those leaps, the most one can say is that the play has garter values.

Another of the play's preoccupations, indeed an even more manifest one, is national identity and patriotism. If we grant Shakespearean authorship, this play would stand in a line stemming from *King John,* which ends with the hope of joy if "England to itself do rest but true" (5.7.118), to the praise by John of Gaunt—the unborn baby with which Queen Philippa is pregnant at Poitiers—of "this scepter'd isle" in *Richard II* (2.1.40) to the glorious speech (most likely not written by Shakespeare) in *Henry VIII* in which the reign of Elizabeth I is seen as a future paradise. In terms of the self-awareness of English nationalism, though, this play is closer to that of *King John* than the narratively subsequent ones. *Edward III* can be seen as finally undoing the subservience to the Continent imposed on and resisted by his great-great-grandfather in the earlier-set play. Although in political terms, *Edward III* is a chronicle of English aggression against France, in cultural terms, it represents the distinct manifestation of an English national identity. For centuries, in the wake of the Norman Conquest of 1066, the monarchy and aristocracy of England had been of Norman-French descent. Edward III is often seen as the first king of the Plantagenet dynasty (itself a French name) to be totally "English" in orientation. So, in a sense the patriotic mood is one of cultural resurgence in the wake of an alien cultural force. It is no accident that poems like *Sir Gawain,* written in the century of Edward III, reverted to the alliterative meter of Anglo-Saxon times. The 14th century can be seen as the time Norman and Saxon strands in English identity finally met and fused.

Other aspects of nationalism were more contemporary to the play's own time. In the play, England and France were neither friends nor enemies. Most theatergoers would have seen France as a metaphor or stand-in for Spain. But, the play's antagonism toward Scotland is discernible and deeply felt. Many have used this to explain why the play could conceivably be by Shakespeare yet unacknowledged as such in his lifetime. As Elizabeth I aged, it became clear that her heir would be her first cousin once removed, King James VI of Scotland. This distant relative from a traditionally hostile country was a most unusual heir, and this circumstance informs many of the uncertainties over succession and lineage in Shakespeare's work. Once James was the obvious heir, and even more when he was king, such an anti-Scottish theme would hardly be politic, not just because of James's Scottish descent and title but because under his rule Scotland and England were on their way to becoming one united kingdom. Thus, the play, though Shakespeare's, had to be suppressed as long as James and his heirs were king, and by the time the need to be pro-Scottish was less urgent, his authorship had been forgotten. This is an ingenious rationale for explaining how the play could be by Shakespeare and yet not be fully attested as his. Yet, there are problems here, as well. Although at the play's time of composition (presumably in the early 1590s) James was not the only or inevitable heir to Elizabeth, he was certainly one of the leading candidates. Moreover, the anti-Scottish aspect of the play is neither simplistic nor polemical; it is while he is fighting the Scots, not the French, that Edward's personal liabilities emerge. Edward treats King John of France graciously while a prisoner, even as the hardly morally unambiguous John Copland drags around King David. Scotland and France are in a sense two sides of Edward's psyche, with Scotland being the introverted, conflicted one and France being the confident, extroverted one. Thus, the negativity about Scotland also has to do with the negative feelings and trouble Edward had felt in proximity to the countess in the Scottish border country.

Though it is true that the spectacle of a Scottish king dragged as booty across England and France (in reality, King David was never brought as a prisoner to France) would hardly appeal to a Scottish king of a latter day, nor to his allies, the Scottish topic can also be seen in a broader perspective. Edward is not vengeful against King David and clearly sees France, the continental enemy, as more urgent an opponent than Scotland, the insular enemy. The entire mooting of Scottishness in the play can be seen as part of a working out of emotions between England and Scotland that was part of the transition to the dual sovereignty of James, especially since the execution of James's mother, Mary, Queen of Scots, in 1587 had removed the possibility of actual subversion emanating or alleged to be emanating from Scottish sources. It may be that the need to link the Scottish theme to the authorship question and to use it as evidence for a Shakespearean authorship has actually led to simplification of the dynamics of Englishness, Scottishness, and even a nascent Britishness at work on the ground level of the play. The play is an early event in the gradual warming up to Scotland that much later culminated with the accession of James I. This is a very different tenor than *Henry V,* in which Scots are portrayed as part of an incipiently united Britain, with Jamy being called by Fluellen "a marvelous valorous gentleman" (3.2.81).

As always in Elizabethan historical drama, there are anachronisms, references to events or phenomena that could not have been known at the time of the play's setting. Some are intentional, like the Armada reference. The valence in some is unclear, such as King John's reference to Edward in Act III, Scene 1 as "Bayardlike, blind, overweaning Ned" (58). This compares Edward III, in his alleged chivalric overconfidence, to Pierre, chevalier de Bayard, a French knight who flourished in the early 16th century—over a century and a half after the play's setting. Whether the playwright deliberately introduced this comparison to bring home the force of John's mockery to the audience, or whether there was just a confusion of historical periods, the anachronism is notable.

Some references in the play seem pitched to a contemporary audience: not just the Armada reference, but, for example, the role of Calais in the play, which was the last English possession on the European continent, surrendered only in 1558, within living memory of the play's audience. At times, knowledge of the future landscape seeps in almost as a condition of the play's premise. Prince Edward's final speech is not just prophetic but clairvoyant, as it looks forward to an era not only when England shall have armies fighting Spain and Turkey but when Spain and Turkey would exist as unified entities; in Edward III's day, Spain was still divided among Castile, Aragon, and Navarre, as well as the remaining Islamic state of Granada, while what was later Turkey was only beginning to be organized under the rule of the Ottoman sultanate, with the remnants of the Byzantine Empire still holding on. But the play's premise was to represent England as a strong, confident world power, and for that, Spain—England's great Christian enemy—and the Ottoman Empire—the principal non-Christian power in Europe—must be present as opponents over whom England's might could potentially tower.

Themes

The play's preeminent theme is the divide between statecraft and personal life, figured most apparently in the contrast between Edward's ignoble private behavior and his noble championship of the English cause against the French. Yet, what makes this a theme rather than simply an issue in character development is that this dichotomy applies to other individuals besides the king. The marriage of the Earl and Countess of Salisbury presents this opposition: The Earl is a warrior and a magistrate, yet achieves his triumph through his interpersonal negotiation with Villiers for safe passage. The Countess is preyed upon by the king as a private individual, yet she has earlier defended her castle, as its lord in absentia, until the king's army arrives in relief, after she has already fended off the Scottish invasion for a good while. Prince Edward does not have the amorous travails of his

Nineteenth-century painting of Queen Victoria and Prince Albert dressed as Queen Philippa of Hainault and King Edward III *(Painting by Edwin Landseer)*

father, even though he is far more of an age to sow wild oats. Yet, there is a private-public dichotomy here, too, in that the younger Edward must grow into a public man, must undergo risk and maturation before he is honored, by his father, with the ultimate public accolade—the knighthood of the Order of the Garter. Even Queen Philippa, the very woman the king had not only scorned but momentarily plotted to murder in Act II, has a public moment, as she attempts to compel the surrender of the body of King David by Copland. Copland refuses the queen the public role, but the queen not only claims it for herself but goes to France, to the battlefront, in order to pursue it.

The Order of the Garter itself is the other unifying theme of the play. The mythology surrounding the order's origin is the only possible strand that can reconcile the Countess of Salisbury incident with the play's chronicle of the early battle of the Hundred Years' War. The garter legend, in its association of private shame with public virtue and in its structuration of the rescue of the former by the latter, sutures the fractured nature of the play. It also helps explain some of the play's subsidiary characters, as the garter suggests both high moral standards and a willingness to allow some room for negotiation, to admit that human behavior cannot always be perfect. People act from mixed motives: Copland wishes to serve his sovereign but also gain credit for himself, Salisbury wishes to give Villiers his freedom but also to find a scheme by which he can participate in the English cause, the king may feel some jealousy of the prince even as he plays the role of stern paternal pedagogue. But the metaphorical role of the garter in turning self-interested dross into public-spirited gold can operate as a prevailing image here.

A major issue here, however, is that this play was largely unread and not considered Shakespeare's during an era when thematic, and for that matter, formalistic, readings flourished. That the play has emerged only in our day, when literary study is dominated by complicated interdisciplinary readings, means it has been deprived of the basic, elementary critical framework that exists for all of the other Shakespeare plays whose readings have now been so usefully complicated. This may be a reason why there has been surprisingly little criticism of the play in the 21st century.

Structure
In terms of place, the structure of the play can be divided into two parts: the English and the French, the private and the public. The English part, consisting of the first two acts, operates in a way not uncharacteristic of early Shakespeare in general. The scenes are long and sustained, only two to an act; they involve public proclamation and private asides, speeches made to a general audience and those (as seen in Edward's wooing of the Countess) to one particular person. Starting with Act III not only does the play turn to a historical military focus, but also there are many more scenes to an act, and the scenes all chronicle a specific

historic occurrence or anecdote. Whereas in the first two acts the play intensifies and complicates itself in order to capture the disordered turmoil of inchoate private emotions, in the latter three acts it extends itself to unfurl a panoramic overview of two great nations at war and the myriad individuals who stand on either side or who, like the four ordinary Frenchmen and the poor people and then the burghers of Calais, are caught between both. Just as the first part of the play relies on the contrast between Edward's public vow to claim his rights in France and to retaliate sharply against the Scottish infringement and his private obsession with the Countess, so does the second part of the play rest on much symmetry. There is the symmetry between England and France—indeed, as far as Edward is concerned, it is in one way not so much a contest between England and France as between France and France, as he, Edward, claims to be king of France and, therefore, can be personified as "France." We see both claimants, John and Edward, each with at least one son. Moreover, Artois, the Frenchman who has come to Edward's side, is parallelled by Salisbury, an Englishman in the activity of the French. Moreover, Shakespeare takes care to represent the entire breadth of the French population, from the wealthy burghers of Calais to the middle-class Frenchman encountered in the countryside of Crécy to the poor man of Calais.

Similarly, the presence or absence of characters in the play can be seen as presenting principles of structural apposition. As soon as the Countess has vanished, her alternative as Edward's mate, Queen Philippa, enters. Salisbury and Copland, both hostage holders, alternate scenes in Act IV, and in this same act, we see Villiers and the dauphin joined as both oath breakers. This sense of symmetry is an underlying thread helping establish some ties of concordance between the seemingly drastically split public and private halves of the play. The latter half of the play may seem chronicle, whereas the first seems psychological minuet. But, if we see the chronicle portion not just as a dramatic staging of the annalistic approach of Holinshed but as a deliberately panoramic, overall approach—like that used in their treatments of war by such early 20th-century dramatists as Thomas Hardy and Karl Kraus—the opposition seems to be between two deliberate structural choices rather than between a well-organized portion and one simply given over to historical names and events.

Style

As Swinburne (see "Extracts from Classic Criticism" below) pointed out in 1880, the language in the play is not always typical of Shakespeare. The sense of verbal plenty, of action going on in every clause, even every word, is less present than is a kind of straightforward, propulsive trajectory, occasionally accompanied by Marlovian rhetoric that is bejeweled and resplendent but lacks Shakespeare's flexibility. Nonetheless, there are many "Shakespearean" passages in the play. Even Swinburne, the play's chief aesthetic detractor, concedes that the scene with the Countess has the internal flourishes and sense of paradox and involution, or double business, characteristic of Shakespearean language. More directly, there are individual phrases in the play strongly associated with Shakespeare. Of these, none has attracted more notice than a famous Shakespeare line spoken by the Countess as she reacts to her father's seeming demand that she succumb to Edward's wanton lusts: "lilies that fester smell far worse than weeds" (2.1.451). This, of course, is the famous last line of Shakespeare's Sonnet 94. In both the sonnet and the play, the line signifies that it is more distressing to see the decay of an ideal than of something that has always been corrupt: It is when the sweet becomes sour, the pure becomes rancid, that despair truly ensues. Yet, in their immediate contexts, the lines are deployed very differently. The sonnet is discussing a beloved who will not return the love of her suitor, portraying her as a lily that festers by immuring itself in its stonehearted purity. The Countess in the play is commenting on a man who had once seemed the flower of chivalry, Edward III, acting like a lust-crazed old goat. In other words, the line is used more straightforwardly in the play. If we see the play as Shakespeare's, this supports a hypothesized time line of composition that places the sonnet later than the play; perhaps Shakespeare, having come up with the line in the dramatic context, later felt free to reposition it more subtly in the more emotionally suggestive context of the lyric love poem. But it is also possible that Shakespeare saw this line in a play by another hand that he admired, or that "lilies that fester smell far worse than weeds" was a common proverb or an apothegm coined by some Elizabethan wit that independently found its way into both texts. There are, though, echoes of other sonnets in the play: For example, "bootless cries" (5.1.10), when Edward coldly entertains the suit of the rich men of Calais, also occurs in Sonnet 29; "scarlet ornaments" (2.1.10) occurs both in Sonnet 142 and in the play just before Edward begins his seduction of the Countess. Suggestively, both instances of "scarlet ornaments" provide a combination of regality and the danger of its profanation or besmirching. This thematic conjunction strengthens the congruity of two deployments of a phrase otherwise probably too commonplace to be seen as an indicator of authorial continuity. Other instances of similar word use, such as *bruit* or *orison,* can support the contention that, as Shakespeare used these words more than Christopher Marlowe and George Peele, the play must be Shakespeare's. Ultimately, however, the argument serves more to disqualify Marlovian or Peelean authorship more than to fortify Shakespearean authorship.

Many have argued that the meter of the play resembles that of *Richard III.* Again, this could attest to various things. It could be that both plays truly were entirely Shakespeare's or that one influenced the other (certainly there is also a slight affinity between each play's respective seductive scenes, although Richard's courtship of Lady Anne is not only successful but more anchored in historical fact than was Edward's of the Countess). It could also mean that both plays were patterned after the same predecessor. The Shakespearean solution is the most convenient and, in many ways, the most appealing. Yet, it is not necessarily the most authoritative. Moreover, some of the verbal patterns here are very different from *Richard III.* In the Countess's speech beginning at Act II, Scene 1, line 250, the off-rhyme "love/give" is employed in the second and third lines of the speech, and "give" is repeated two lines later as well. This is very different from the generally consistent blank verse of *Richard III,* where meter, not repetition for assonance, carried the rhythmic capability. These sorts of rhyming patterns are much more reminiscent of Peele, in fact, whose 1593 play about Edward I has frequent rhyme. *Edward III* does not rhyme or assonate nearly as much as Peele's play, and one could say that the playwright, Shakespeare or otherwise, was influenced by Peele's work, here or in earlier plays. But, the critic who made this argument would then have to wrangle with the relative lack of such discernible Peelean influences in *Richard III* or the *Henry VI* trilogy.

Language and Imagery

Although the play does not consistently rhyme like the plays of Peele, to which it is in some way indebted, it is in verse throughout; there are no interruptions by prose that, in other works in the Shakespearean canon, provide shifts in mood and tone. For instance, in other plays by Shakespeare, the seduction of the Countess scene might well have been accompanied by "low talk" among the castle's servants, or in the battlefield scenes (as occur in *Henry V*), the high palaver of kings and courtiers might be offset by the earthy gripes of the common soldier. As it stands, the ceremony of, say, the dialogue between the King and the Prince in Act V, Scene 1 from line 191 onward—with the King saying, "As things long lost when they're found again / So doth my son rejoice his father's heart," and the Prince replying, "My gracious father, here receive the gift / This wreath of conquest and reward of war"—does not stand out the way such discourse elsewhere would. The repetition of the *war* sound in the prince's phrase "rewards of war" seems slightly jarring, or at least utilitarian; perhaps this is a more colloquial register trying to break through the studied elevation that is the norm.

In the Countess's section, the imagery is more involved, more wound in on itself: For instance, when the Countess first enters and the king asks Warwick to identify his daughter, Warwick says "even, she, my liege, whose beauty tyrants fear. As a may blossom with pernicious winds, / have sullied, withered, overcast, and done" (1.2.95–96), Warwick is stating that resistance to tyrants (in the past, to the king of Scotland and perhaps, in the future to the king of England himself) has sullied and worn out her beauty, but also more literally that the Countess is capable of withstanding the fear of tyrants even if emerging physically the worse for it. The tautness of the construction has some reversibility in it, indicating that perhaps it is not totally her fear of tyrants but tyrants' fear of her.

The play is replete with imagery, not just in the Countess section but even in the war section, where the sighs of the English army at the apparent loss of the prince are "as black as water turning into smoke" (5.1.154). Of particular note are the animal images: Edward's comparing himself to a lion scorning to touch the yielding prey when the men of Calais surrender to him, or the prince's castigation of the French warriors as "creeping serpent" (3.3.99) compared to the forthrightness of the English troops, or Edward's comparison of the Scottish army to "stealing foxes" (1.2.90) who leave before they can be properly hunted. All these images cited above occur in the military passage of the play, but they underscore the issues also raised in the Countess episode: of the thin line between civilized and animal nature, between human wisdom and creaturely appetite, which the stresses of love and war can, equally, break down. If one discerns a garter theme in the play, it is the threat raised by this recurrent animal imagery that the values represented by this renowned order of knighthood are meant to counter.

EXTRACTS OF CLASSIC CRITICISM
Algernon Charles Swinburne (1837–1909)
[Excerpted from *A Study of Shakespeare* (1879). A perceptive and original critic, Swinburne's stud-

ies were key in reviving interest in early modern drama.]

"The Raigne of King Edward the third: As it hath bin sundrie times plaied about the Citie of London," was published in 1596, and ran through two or three anonymous editions before the date of the generation was out which first produced it. Having thus run to the end of its natural tether, it fell as naturally into the oblivion which has devoured, and has not again disgorged, so many a more precious production of its period. In 1760 it was reprinted in the "Prolusions" of Edward Capell, whose text is now before me. This editor was the first mortal to suggest that his newly unearthed treasure might possibly be a windfall from the topless tree of Shakespeare. Being, as I have said, a duly modest and an evidently honest man, he admits "with candour" that there is no jot or title of "external evidence" whatsoever to be alleged in support of this gratuitous attribution: but he submits, with some fair show of reason, that there is a certain "resemblance between the style of" Shakespeare's "earlier performances and of the work in question"; and without the slightest show of any reason whatever he appends to this humble and plausible plea the unspeakably unhappy assertion that at the time of its appearance "there was no known writer equal to such a play"; whereas at a moderate computation there were, I should say, on the authority of Henslowe's Diary, at least a dozen—and not improbably a score. In any case there was one then newly dead, too long before his time, whose memory stands even higher above the possible ascription of such a work than that of the adolescent Shakespeare's very self. Of one point we may be sure . . . The author of *King Edward III.* was a devout student and a humble follower of Christopher Marlowe, not yet wholly disengaged by that august and beneficent influence from all attraction towards the "jigging veins of rhyming mother-wits"; an fitter on the whole to follow this easier and earlier vein of writing, half lyrical in manner and half elegiac, than to brace upon his punier limbs the young giant's newly fashioned buskin of blank verse. The signs of this growing struggle, the traces of this incomplete emancipation, are perceptible throughout in the alternate prevalence of two conflicting and irreconcilable styles; which yet affords no evidence or suggestion of a double authorship. For the intelligence which moulds and informs the whole work, the spirit which pervades and imbues the general design, is of a piece, so to speak, throughout; a point imperceptible to the eye, a touchstone intangible by the finger, alike of a scholiast and a dunce.

Another test, no less unmistakable by the student and no less indiscernible to the sciolist, is this: that whatever may be the demerits of this play, they are due to no voluntary or involuntary carelessness or haste. Here is not the swift impatient journeywork of a rough and ready hand; here is no sign of such compulsory hurry in the discharge of a task something less than welcome, if not of an imposition something less than tolerable, as we may rationally believe ourselves able to trace in great part of Marlowe's work: in the latter half of *The Jew of Malta,* in the burlesque interludes of *Doctor Faustus,* and wellnigh throughout the whole scheme and course of *The Massacre at Paris.* Whatever in *King Edward III* is mediocre or worse is evidently such as it is through no passionate or slovenly precipitation of handiwork, but through pure incompetence to do better. The blame of the failure, the shame of the shortcoming, cannot be laid to the account of any momentary excess or default in emotion, of passing exhaustion or excitement, of intermittent impulse and reaction; it is an indication of lifelong and irremediable impotence. And it is further to be noted that by far the

least unsuccessful parts of the play are also by far the most unimportant. The capacity of the author seems to shrink and swell alternately, to erect its plumes and deject them, to contract and to dilate the range and orbit of its flight in a steadily inverse degree to the proportionate interest of the subject or worth of the topic in hand. There could be no surer proof that it is neither the early nor the hasty work of a great or even a remarkable poet. It is the best that could be done at any time by a conscientious and studious workman of technically insufficient culture and of naturally limited means. I would not, however, be supposed to undervalue the genuine and graceful ability of execution displayed by the author at his best. He could write at times very much after the earliest fashion of the adolescent Shakespeare; in other words, after the fashion of the day or hour, to which in some degree the greatest writer of that hour or that day cannot choose but conform at starting, and the smallest writer must needs conform for ever. By the rule which would attribute to Shakespeare every line written in his first manner which appeared during the first years of his poetic progress, it is hard to say what amount of bad verse or better, current during the rise and the reign of their several influences,—for this kind of echo or of copy work, consciously or unconsciously repercussive and reflective, begins with the very first audible sound of a man's voice in song, with the very first noticeable stroke of his hand in painting—it is hard to say what amount of tolerable or intolerable work might not or may not be assignable by scholiasts of the future to Byron or to Shelley, to Mr. Tennyson or to Mr. Browning. A time by this rule might come—but I am fain to think better of the Fates—when by comparison of detached words and collation of dismembered phrases the memory of Mr. Tennyson would be weighted and degraded by the ascription of whole volumes of pilfered and diluted verse now current—if not yet submerged—under the name or the pseudonym of the present Viceroy—or Vice-empress is it?—of India. But the obvious truth is this: the voice of Shakespeare's adolescence had as usual an echo in it of other men's notes: I can remember the name of but one poet whose voice from the beginning had none; who started with a style of his own, though he may have chosen to annex—"annex the wise it call"; *convey* is obsolete—to annex whole phrases or whole verses at need, for the use or the ease of an idle minute; and this name of course is Marlowe's. So starting, Shakespeare had yet (like all other and lesser poets born) some perceptible notes in his yet half boyish voice that were not borrowed; and these were at once caught up and re-echoed by such fellow-pupils with Shakespeare of the young Master of them all—such humbler and feebler disciples, or simpler sheep (shall we call them?) of the great "dead shepherd"— as the now indistinguishable author of *King Edward III.*

In the first scene of the first act the impotent imitation of Marlowe is pitifully patent. Possibly there may also be an imitation of the still imitative style of Shakespeare, and the style may be more accurately definable as a copy of a copy—a study after the manner of Marlowe, not at second hand, but at third. In any case, being obviously too flat and feeble once to make way for the second.

For this also must be noted; that the resemblance here is but of stray words, of single lines, of separable passages. The whole tone of the text, the whole build of the play, the whole scheme of the poem, is far enough from any such resemblance. The structure, the composition, is feeble, incongruous, inadequate, effete. Any student will remark at a first glance what a short-breathed runner, what a broken-winded athlete in the lists of tragic verse, is the indiscoverable author of this play.

Charles Wordsworth (1806–1892) [From *Shakespeare's Historical Plays: Roman and English* (1883). Charles Wordsworth, the nephew of the poet William Wordsworth, was a bishop, schoolmaster, and scholar.]

There is also a play called King Edward III, first known and printed in 1596, and popular for some years, which in 1760 Capell reprinted and published "as thought to be by Shakespeare" though it had never appeared, previously in any edition of his works Mr. Furnivall pronounces it to be clearly not Shakespeare's, both from external and intrinsic evidence. Nonetheless it now takes its place in the Leopold edition, at the end of the volume.

Georg Brandes (1842–1927) [Excerpted from *William Shakespeare: A Critical Study* (1895; translated by W. Archer et al., 1898). Brandes, an important Danish scholar, wrote extensively on Shakespeare's plays.]

There is extant a historical play dating from 1596, entitled *The Raigne of King Edward third. As it had bin sundrie times plaied about the Citie of London,* which several English students and critics, among them Halliwell-Phillips, have attributed at least in part to Shakespeare, arguing that the better scenes, at least, must have been carefully retouched by him. Although the drama as a whole, is not much more Shakespearean in style than many other Elizabethan plays and although Swinburne, the highest of all English authorities, has declared the play to be the work of an imitator of Marlowe, yet there is a good deal to be said in favor of the hypothesis that Shakespeare had some hand in *Edward III.*

F. W. Moorman (1872–1919) [From *The Cambridge History of English Literature* (1912). Moorman was a professor at Leeds University.]

Of the historical plays attributed to Shakespeare, but not included in the first folio, the most important is *Edward III*. The conjecture that he had a hand in this play was not put forward during his lifetime, and rests entirely on internal evidence. *Edward III* was first published, anonymously, in 1596, and a second edition followed in 1599; but it was not until Capell re-edited the play in his *Prolusions* (1760) that the claim for Shakespearean authorship was seriously put forward.

Written in verse throughout, the play opens with a scene which is similar to the first scene of *Henry V;* but no sooner are the preparations for king Edward's foreign campaign begun than the main action is impeded by the introduction of the romantic love story of the king and the countess of Salisbury, which occupies the rest of the first, and the whole of the second, act. Then, when the monarch has at last conquered his adulterous passion, the narrative of military conquest, with the prince of Wales as its hero, is resumed, and proceeds, without further break, along the path prescribed to the dramatist by Froissart and Holinshed. But, although the countess episode impairs the little unity of action which this desultory chronicle play would otherwise have, it must be remembered that that episode is no extraneous matter foisted into the play for the sake of dramatic effect; the author goes to Bandello, or, rather, to Bandello's English translator, William Painter, for the details of the story, but the main outlines of it are faithfully recorded by Froissart and subsequent chroniclers of English history. If, however, the double plot of the play furnishes, in itself, no reason for assuming double authorship, that assumption must, nevertheless, be made on other and more substantial grounds. In diction and verse, in the portrayal of character and in the attainment of dramatic effect, the author of the love scenes stands apart from the author of the battle scenes. The number of riming verses and verses with double endings in the love scenes, is considerably greater than in all the remainder of the play. Soliloquy is unknown in the battle scenes, whereas, in the countess episode, one sixth of the total number of verses are spoken in monologue. The love scenes are also distinguished from the rest of the play by the strain of lyricism in which the author indulges; it would, indeed, be difficult to find in the whole range of Elizabethan drama a passage more completely imbued with lyric feeling than that in which Edward converses with Lodowick, his secretary. It is not the tempestuous lyricism of Marlowe which we meet with here, but the elegiac lyricism of the sonneteers, the unfeigned delight in the play of amorous fancy and the fond lingering over airy sentiment. Characteristics such as these isolate the countess episode from the rest of the play, and, at the same time, associate it with much of the early work of Shakespeare, above all with *Romeo and Juliet.*

But, in the absence of all external authority, it would be unsafe to claim the episode for Shakespeare upon such evidence as this alone; and the same may be said for the resemblances of idea, imagery and cadence which many passages in these love scenes bear to passages in his canonical works. If the claim for Shakespearean authorship is to be put forward at all, it must be based upon those elements of Shakespeare's genius which ever elude the grasp of the most skilful plagiarist—the creation of character, the reaching after dramatic effect and the impalpable spirit of dramatic art. It is in the person of the countess of Salisbury that the genius of Shakespeare first seems to reveal itself, and it has been well said that, without her, his gallery of female characters would be incomplete.

> Here by my side do hang my wedding knives:
> Take thou the one, and with it kill thy
>   queen,

And learn by me to find her where she
lies;
And with this other I'll despatch my
love,
Which now lies fast asleep within my
heart:
When they are gone, then I'll consent
to love.

The king's soliloquies, too, as he beholds
first his son all afire with military ardour, and
then his secretary returning with a message
from the countess, produce a feeling of true
dramatic tension; and, as we see the monarch
borne this way and that by the impulse of
contending passions, we realise once again
the hand of the master.

If we ascribe the countess episode to
Shakespeare, there still remains for consideration the difficult problem of determin-
ing the nature of his task. The choice lies
between collaboration of Shakespeare with
another dramatist and revision by Shakespeare of a play already in existence. The latter theory seems the more reasonable. The
battle scenes, by virtue of their loose, episodic character, point to a date previous to
that reform of the chronicle play which was
effected by Marlowe's *Edward II* (ca. 1590).

MODERN CRITICISM AND CRITICAL CONTROVERSIES

The question of authorship has dominated discussion of the play ever since Capell's suggestion of
it in 1760. The arguments against Shakespearean
authorship were powerful but subjective and aesthetic in nature. Swinburne eloquently asserted in
1880 that the play was simply not good enough to
be Shakespeare's. These powerful but highly opin-
ionated and methodologically ungrounded assertions dominated the reception of the play, until new,
computer-aided quantitative techniques established
that statistical patterns of word usage in the play
strongly resembled Shakespeare's. These statistical
conjectures were given ballast by the play's two

powerful advocates, Eric Sams and Giorgio Melchiori, both of whom published editions of the play
that presented it to its full advantage and strongly
lobbied for its admission into the canon. Their
goal was largely met by the 2000s, by which time
most major anthologies of Shakespeare and series
of Shakespearean texts include the play. The eviden-
tiary and quantitative hypotheses of Sams and Melchiori are convincing. Yet, it must be remembered
that their era was at the very beginning of digital
and computer-assisted study of the humanities. Certain questions of procedure that no doubt will be
clarified in the course of the 21st century remained
salient. Could not the statistical patterns have been
indicative of a strong influence of Shakespeare on
the writer, or perhaps the strong influence of the
author of *Edward III* on Shakespeare? When one
reads an author, steeps oneself in a text, or goes to a
performance played sundry times about London, do
not some of the verbal or semantic patterns sink into
the marrow of one's own linguistic expression? Are
some of these phrasings stock formulations, men-
talities of thought, idioms specific to the age that,
lacking sound recordings or much of a sense of how
Elizabethan language was formed excepting textual
remains, we will never quite intuit?

There is an additional split between people who
think that Shakespeare had some hand in the play
but did not write it entirely, such as Melchiori, and
those who see the play as the unified product of a
single hand, such as Eliot Slater and Sams. Jonathan Hope has staked out an intermediate position, hypothesizing that the play's two obvious
parts were written by the same hand but at disparate positions in time. All three—Slater, Hope, and
most emphatically, Sams—believe that the single
hand who wrote the play was Shakespeare's. As
convincing as their arguments are, and as much
as they operate in a world of empirical scholarship
and historical reconstruction, one has to ask: Why
the 1990s? Why did the play resurface then? Two
different, perhaps equally compelling, answers suggest themselves.

Swinburne's objections to the play basically
depend on a core assumption: There was a certain

aesthetic standard that Shakespeare not only met but defined; nothing that was not distinctively accomplished or dazzlingly proficient, at the very least, could be Shakespeare's. In the late 20th century, however, what Deborah T. Curren-Aquino called "bad Shakespeare" began to be the object of scholarly interest. The discovery by Gary Taylor of the "Shall I die?" lyric in 1985 and his convincing argument for its being Shakespeare's further complicated matters, as this slight lyric had none of the density of Shakespeare's sonnets. The dissociation of Shakespearean authorship from ideas of aesthetic excellence led to a greater acceptance of material that could be plausibly conjectured as Shakespearean in historical terms even though it did not meet a prima facie standard of aesthetic excellence.

This aspect of the climate that welcomed *Edward III* reflected postmodern skepticism and relativism, but another, converse aspect of the postmodern climate also helped the play: its renewed fascination with power, prosperity, and the glamour of sovereignty. These were all qualities that the modernist period (roughly 1900–75) had been skeptical of both because of modernism's dissent from Victorian ideas of bourgeois progress and because of the menacing incarnations of political power posed by totalitarian regimes of Nazi Germany and the Soviet Union. That the play was not in the canon in the modernist period signified not only a skepticism toward royal authority and the very idea of prosperous reigns but a caution as to historical sweep, a sense that history was, in the words of James Joyce's character Stephen Dedalus, a nightmare from which one was trying to awake. For Shakespeare to write about Edward's grandson, Richard II, a failed king who had to be overthrown, and for Marlowe to write about Edward III's father, Edward II, another failed king who had to be overthrown and killed, not only fit the requirements of tragic form as the more farcical *Edward III* does not, but also, in the 1900–75 era, were seen as appropriate images of power curtailed, of a sense that the less power was exercised, the less threat would transpire of power running amok.

Though the postmodern era brought increased skepticism on many fronts, it also brought a less inhibited stance toward the idea of grand historical narratives. There was a great desire for a more optimistic idea of history and for a reversion to or resuscitation of great men and figures who were substantial historical actors. Even though Shakespeare, or whoever wrote the play, substantively represents the middle and lower classes in this play, not only as individuals but (as in the case of both the burghers of Calais and the poor men of that city) as collectivities, it is the idea of the great king that is most likely to beguile initial readers of the play.

In addition, once the Swinburnean aesthetic objection was removed, there was a pressure to enlarge the idea of Shakespeare as much as possible, because the name *Shakespeare,* as a kind of brand, meant as much or even more after a strict aesthetic measurement was abandoned. The temptation is to make as much as possible Shakespeare's, simply because that is a way to get it talked about and taken more seriously, not just in the parochial sense of assisting one's own academic career but in the broader sense of enhancing Shakespeare, making him even more multidimensional. Similarly, if the middle-class tragedy *Arden of Feversham,* long thought in the past to be at least possibly by Shakespeare, though few think that today, was seen as Shakespeare's, that would also expand our belief in Shakespeare's ability to write not just about the high and mighty.

THE PLAY TODAY

The entry of this "new" Shakespeare play in the 1990s meant that it experienced an inevitable conjunction with the critical and performance trends of the era. As noted above in the "Difficulties of the Play" section, the postmodern willingness to accept a more purposive sense of historical action, its willingness to see Shakespeare as ideologically invested in the power and majesty of a king such as Edward III, helped make the play more acceptable than would have occurred in a more stringent and cautious high-modern era. But the postmodern fascination with sovereignty and power also had its more skeptical side, as represented in the work of the thinkers Michel Foucault and Giorgio Agamben. Foucault's idea of a power that may be transferable between individuals but is fundamentally alterable in substance, even if the individual wielding it should wish to change it, is potentially heuristic with respect to the characters in the play: Edward is pulled back from the brink of personal self-destruction perhaps not by a sudden awakening of conscience, but, in a Foucauldian reading, by the constraints of the power he was bound to exercise, which make him renounce the Countess and go to France, despite his personal desire. Agamben's focus on individuals outside state boundaries, on the "bare life" that is often an object of state aggrandizement, and of the "state of exception" that promotes an emergency situation outside normative legal constraints are all applicable to this play. Hostage situations come up at least three times in *Edward III*—with the two kings, David of Scotland and John of France, and with Salisbury. The two kings, once captured by Edward, are no longer kings in effect—they cannot efficaciously exercise office as a king, as they are in the power of another head of state. Yet, their ceremonial status as kings still matters; Edward boasts of carrying "three kings, two princes, and a queen" back to England, even though he himself is the only king that matters, and his son, the only prince. For the other kings and princes, it is not their sovereign power but, in fact, their dispossession of it that is celebrated.

Villiers is another potential Agambenian exemplar: as a stateless individual, a hostage of the English, who, in securing his own personal liberty, helps enable the success of the English in war. Salisbury himself acknowledges the sovereignty of the French dauphin in pleading with his subordinate Villiers for free passage to Calais; he thus underscores the sinuousness of state mechanisms. Salisbury's independence of definition—reminiscent of 21st-century categories such as the detainee, the refugee, the asylum seeker, the terrorist—represents a very different kind of medieval relationship to the state than the hierarchy of liege, lord,

Edward III as depicted in the 1902 edition of *Cassell's History of England—Century Edition*

and vassal emphasized in so many other areas of the play. That he is the husband of the threatened Countess, herself resident on the border between England and Scotland, intensifies the presentation of individuals who find little solid ground within state apparatuses, as does the fact that Villiers, his prisoner, is a Norman lord—of a region once part of the English domains, one that had conquered England in 1066—and bears a surname most associated with the English, not the French, nobility.

Similarly, a gender critique of the play would upend the dichotomy we have sustained in the majority of this treatment, of the depraved private Edward and the virtuous public Edward. If a darker view of state power than was typically the Elizabethan norm is adopted, one that sees the state as an agent of coercion and of external control over what Foucault and Agamben label "biopower"—suzerainty over people's bodies—there is not much difference between his role as conqueror of France and putative conqueror of the Countess's body. In both cases, his rank and station are used to compel people's bodies into states of subservience and disruption. Also, the Countess's role as *host* is not that far from her husband's role as keeper of a *host*age. These are only two of many configurations *Edward III* could yield if analyzed in light of the ideas and methodologies prevalent in literary and cultural criticism in the early 21st century. As time goes on, the play becomes more analyzed, and critical fashions change, the play will also be rendered readable by those future practices.

The play's contemporary performances have also been influenced by a variety of techniques and practices. In a time when theatrical troupes are going beyond the crowd-pleasing set of 12 to 15 Shakespeare plays generally performed in the late 20th century to look at neglected corners of the Shakespearean canon as well as, increasingly, of his Elizabethan and Jacobean contemporaries, *Edward III* has become a natural object of theatrical discovery. Anthony Clark's production of the play, staged in summer 2002 by the Royal Shakespeare Company at the Swan Theatre in Stratford-upon-Avon, stressed the incipient nationalism in the play by having the three kings, of England, Scotland, and France, dress in obvious national costume. Clark rendered Lodowick, as performed by Wayne Cater, a comic figure, a capering clown who subverted rather than advanced his master's vile suit. David Rintoul, who played King Edward, was praised for his deft handling of the rapid shifts in emotion undergone by his character.

As opposed to the very demonstrative staging of the Royal Shakespeare production, the more austere, bare-bones approach of the National America Shakespeare Company in Pasadena, California, in 2003 foregrounded the language, forsaking the effort to make the play dramatically full bodied, as in other Shakespeare works. Generally, in performance, the gap between this play and Shakespeare's other plays seemed greater than in reading. The play's intellectual and historical interest and the puzzles it presents to scholars helped suture it to the other plays in the canon, whereas a theatrical audience's expectation of Shakespeare were often disconcerted by the disjunctive, bipartite nature of the play and its only intermittent interest in the psychology of its characters. The Pasadena production took advantage of the then-contemporary war in Iraq to foreground the themes of sovereignty and invasion of the play, striking the same chord as the possible Agambenian interpretations mentioned above. The play will continue to find troupes eager to perform it and, thus, eventually bestow on the play the performance tradition that has enriched and ramified the dramas printed beside it in the standard collection of Shakespeare's work.

The play's setting has also proved itself of interest to 21st-century audiences; witness the success of Brian Helgeland's 2001 film *A Knight's Tale,* starring the late Heath Ledger and Rufus Sewell and set in the 1770s, even featuring the Black Prince as a character, though its literary connections are Chaucerian rather than Shakespearean. A play such as *Edward III* might well be popular among similar audiences if played the right way. Yet, though productions have occurred at a steady pace (the 1999 German production staged in Cologne was another landmark in the performance history of *Edward III*), there has not been an avalanche of performances, nor has criticism of the play in literary journals been as robust as one would think a restored play with much to explore within its bounds would warrant. As of 2010, the major names in criticism of the play remain the two scholars most responsible for its revival, Sams and the late Melchiori. Statistics may "prove" authorship in the minds of quantitatively inclined critics, but for the play to fully enter the effectual Shakespearean canon in the 21st century, it will have to attain a consistent performance tradition and be a locus for large-scale, interpretive critical argument, treatments that discuss the play's theme, language, and significance and move beyond exploring the intricacies of the authorship question.

FIVE TOPICS FOR DISCUSSION AND WRITING

1. **The authorship question:** From this play and from your readings of established work by

Shakespeare, does this play seem "Shakespearean"? Does it seem of the quality and tone of Shakespeare's other works? If it were proved irrefutably that it was or was not by Shakespeare, would this change your response to the play? Bearing in mind that such an assessment is invariably subjective, is it "as good as the rest of Shakespeare"?

2. **Relationship to other histories:** How does this play compare to the extant history plays ascribed to Shakespeare, particularly *Henry V,* which is also about a powerful English king invading France, and *Richard II,* which is about Edward's grandson, who cuts far less of a figure than his great forebear? How does it flesh out the Shakespearean history cycle? What does it matter to have this major period in history covered by a Shakespeare play?

3. **Private and public:** What is the difference between Edward as private man and public figure? Do these different roles reveal contrasting sides of his personality? Or are they continuities to be found in his personal and political behavior? Does the play imply that private vices and public virtues coincide or conflict?

4. **Moral lesson or grisly tale:** Is Edward's dalliance with the Countess meant as a parable, or is it meant to shock and horrify? Are you, as a reader, intrigued or repelled by the episode? How did you think it would be resolved? Did you recover from the episode?

5. **A great king:** Looking at the play alone—without turning to history books or reference articles—would you say Edward III was a great king? Would his son, the prince, have been a better one if fate had ever allowed him to ascend the throne? Does Edward III stand with the ideal of Shakespearean kingship? Or is he more an ambivalent figure?

Bibliography

Conlan, J. P. "Shakespeare's *Edward III:* A Consolation for English Recusants," *Comparative Drama* 35, no. 2 (Summer 2001): 177–207.

Forker, Charles R. "Royal Carnality and Illicit Desire in the English History Plays of the 1590s," *Medieval and Renaissance Drama in England,* volume 15 (January 2005): 99–131.

Hope, Jonathan. *The Authorship of Shakespeare's Plays.* Cambridge: Cambridge University Press, 1994.

Melchiori, Giorgio. *Shakespeare's Garter Plays:* Edward III *to* The Merry Wives of Windsor. Cranbury, N.J.: Associated University Presses, 1994.

Merriam, Thomas. "Influence Alone? Reflections on the Newly Canonized *Edward III.*" *Notes and Queries* 46, no. 2 (June 1999): 200–206.

Munkell, Marga, and Beatrix Bussy. "Aspects of Governance in Shakespeare's *Edward the Third:* The Quest for Personal and Political Identity." In *Literature as History/History as Literature: Fact and Fiction in Medieval to Eighteenth-Century British Literature,* edited by Sonia Fielitz and Wolfram R. Keller. Frankfurt, Germany: Peter Lang, 2007.

Sams, Eric. *Shakespeare's* Edward III. New Haven, Conn.: Yale University Press, 1996.

Slater, Eliot. *The Problem of* The Reign of King Edward III: *A Statistical Approach.* Cambridge: Cambridge University Press, 1986.

—Nicholas Birns

Hamlet

INTRODUCTION

Hamlet is one of the central texts of Western civilization, and Hamlet is the most self-conscious literary figure ever created. A. C. Bradley commented that Hamlet is the only Shakespearean character who could have written Shakespeare's plays. His most famous soliloquy explores the power of the mind to overcome mortality, juxtaposing human unbounded imagination—"how infinite in faculties" (2.2.304)—with the physical limitations of the flesh. That contrast informs the entire play. Gertrude speaks of Ophelia's floating "mermaid-like" until she sinks "to muddy death" (4.7.176, 183). The Player King observes, "Our thoughts are ours, their ends none of our own" (3.2.208). Therein lies the human triumph and tragedy: Infinite mind trapped in finite being.

The play's own infinitude has prompted more discussion than any other piece of secular literature. In 1992 alone, 479 books and articles were written about it. It is a work that inspires superlatives. In *Shakespeare: The Invention of the Human,* Harold Bloom calls Hamlet "the most intelligent character in all of literature" and "the most aware and knowing figure ever conceived" (388, 404). According to Roland Mushat Frye, Hamlet displays "the finest mind of any literary character in our tradition"; the prince is "Shakespeare's most interesting [and] his most admirable protagonist" (177, 280). For Harry Levin, the work is "the most problematic play ever written by Shakespeare or any other playwright" (105).

William Wordsworth wrote that Shakespeare unlocked his heart in his sonnets, but the playwright may have been even more autobiographical in this play. Great artists, however, do not express only themselves; they express us, as well. Hamlet is not just Shakespeare but everyone. C. S. Lewis observed:

> I believe that we read Hamlet's speeches with interest chiefly because they describe so well a certain spiritual region through which most of us have passed and anyone in his circumstances might be expected to pass, rather than because of our concern to understand how and why this particular man entered it (15).

Hamlet says that acting should "hold as 'twere the mirror up to nature" (3.2.22), and his play reflects the image of each observer. Emily Dickinson wryly maintained: "Hamlet wavered for all of us". Samuel Taylor Coleridge noted: "I have a smack of Hamlet myself if I may say so" (volume 6, 285). William Hazlitt wrote: "It is we who are Hamlet" (260).

Harold C. Goddard wrote that the various spectators of *The Murder of Gonzago,* the play within the play, see the piece differently depending on their perspectives (331). Perspective informs much of Renaissance art, as famously exemplified in Hans Holbein's *Ambassadors,* in which the skull in the painting is discernible only from a particular, eccentric angle. *Hamlet,* too, serves as a study in perspective and hence inspires so much critical

Sarah Bernhardt as Hamlet in a 19th-century production of the play

debate. The title character embodies all that Shakespeare had created up to 1600: the poetic sensibility and introspection of Richard II, the skeptical wit of Falstaff, Brutus's idealism, Jaques's melancholy, Prince Hal's charm, and Hotspur's devotion to honor. Hamlet also anticipates Shakespeare's future protagonists, such as Othello, with his nobility, love, and jealousy, and Prospero, with his desire for revenge and love of stagecraft. Hamlet epitomizes the complexities, the vices and virtues of Shakespeare's characters, Shakespeare's audiences, and, perhaps, Shakespeare himself.

BACKGROUND

The story of Hamlet dates from at least the 1100s. At the end of the 12th century, Archbishop Absa-lon of Lund asked Saxo Grammaticus to write the history of the Danes. The result was his *Historiae Danicae,* first printed in 1514. Hamlet—here called Amleth—appears in Books 3 and 4.

According to this account, the brothers Horwendil and Feng are joint governors of Jutland, serving under the Danish king Rorik. Horwendil is married to Rorik's daughter, Gerutha, and they have a son, Amleth. Feng privately kills Horwendil, claiming that he acted to protect Gerutha, whom he then marries.

Amleth feigns madness to survive until he can avenge his father's death; in fact, the name *Amleth* means "foolish" or "stupid." This story of Amleth may owe something to the Roman historian Livy, who wrote that Lucius Junius Brutus, nephew of King Tarquin, feigned stupidity (*Brutus,* like *Amleth,* means "stupid") until he could expel the ruler and establish the Roman Republic.

Amleth's uncle suspects that his nephew may have merely assumed an antic disposition, so he tests him with a woman. If Amleth has sex with her, as any sane Danish man would, then Feng will know that the young man is only pretending to be mad. The woman Feng chooses turns out to have known Amleth when they were children. Amleth has sex with her but asks her to deny that he did so. Hence, when Amleth claims that he has slept with her, no one believes him. One of Feng's courtiers spies on a conversation between Amleth and Gerutha. Amleth discovers him, kills him, chops him up, and feeds him to the pigs.

Feng does not know what has become of his spy, but he still sends his nephew to England, a Danish tributary, in the company of two men bearing an order to the English king to kill Amleth. During the journey, Amleth changes the commission to order the immediate death of his two companions. Also, according to this altered document, the English king is to give his daughter to Amleth as his wife.

At the end of a year, Amleth returns to Denmark, burns down Feng's palace, kills Feng with Feng's own sword, and becomes ruler. Subsequently, Amleth marries the queen of Scotland, in addition to the English princess. Before Amleth leaves for his last battle, his second wife pledges eternal fidelity to his memory, but she quickly marries Amleth's killer.

François de Belleforest, in volume five of his *Histoires tragiques* (1570), alters this account in some ways. Here Fengon kills his brother openly, though with the same pretext. In Belleforest's account, Fengon and Geruth were lovers while Horwendil still lived. Geruth, however, denies any involvement with Horwendil's death, promises not to reveal Amleth's sanity, and wishes him success in avenging Horwendil's murder.

Sometime in the late 1580s, this story came to the English stage. In the preface to Robert Greene's romance *Menaphon* (1589), "To the Gentlemen Students of Both Universities," Thomas Nashe described the play in this passage: "yet English Seneca [*Seneca His Tenne Tragedies* was published in 1581, edited by Thomas Newton] read by Candlelight yields many good sentences, as *Blood is a begger,* and so forth; and if you intreate him faire in a frostie morning, he will afford you whole Hamlets, I should say handfuls of tragicall speeches" (315). This play, known as the *Ur-Hamlet,* held the stage for some years. In June 1594 it was performed at Newington Butts outside London; both troupes, the Lord Admiral's Men and Shakespeare's Lord Chamberlain's Men, shared this venue. Thomas Lodge referred to this work in his 1596 *Wit's Miserie,* in which he writes of a devil who looks "as pale as the visard of the ghost which cried so miserably at the Theatre, like an oister-wife, Hamlet, revenge." The Theatre was where the Lord Chamberlain's Men regularly performed in the mid-1590s.

The text of the *Ur-Hamlet* does not survive, nor is its authorship known. Bloom argues in *Shakespeare: The Invention of the Human* that Shakespeare himself wrote the piece. Nashe's comments imply that it was written by Thomas Kyd, author of one of the most famous and popular revenge tragedies of the period, *The Spanish Tragedy* (ca. 1589). Geoffrey Bullough found 20 parallels between Kyd's play and Shakespeare's *Hamlet.*

Among these are a ghost calling for revenge, a secret crime that must be confirmed, an avenger who feigns madness and a woman who in fact goes mad, revenge delayed and an avenger who berates himself for procrastination, the avenger's comments on the theater, the use of a play within a play, and a character named Horatio (16–17). It seems likely that Shakespeare inherited these elements from the *Ur-Hamlet,* though he could have borrowed them from *The Spanish Tragedy* or Seneca's works themselves.

Hamlet draws on classical as well as Scandinavian literature. The Roman emperor Claudius was the second husband of Agrippina, who was Claudius's niece. Nero thus became Claudius's great-nephew and stepson. Agrippina poisoned Claudius to ensure the succession of Nero to the throne; Nero later killed his mother. On his way to visit his mother after *The Murder of Gonzago,* Hamlet declares: "let not ever / The soul of Nero enter this firm bosom, / . . . / I will speak daggers to her, but use none" (3.2.393–396). Virgil influenced the play. The speech that the First Player delivers in Act II, Scene 2 is based on Aeneas's account of the fall of Troy in Book 2 of the *Aeneid.* Pyrrhus, son of Achilles, killed Priam to avenge the death of his father. The concluding lines of the player's speech are a fair rendition of the *Aeneid*'s "sunt lacrimae rerum et mentem mortalia tangunt" (1.462). Hamlet's promise to remember the ghost "whiles memory holds a seat / In this distracted globe" (1.5.96–97) is a translation of Aeneas's promise to Dido to remember her "dum memor ipse mei" (*Aeneid,* 4.336). The First Player's speech also recalls Christopher Marlowe and Nashe's *Dido, Queen of Carthage* (1594). In both, Priam is knocked down by the wind from the sword of Pyrrhus. Hamlet's "To be or not to be" (3.1.55) translates Aristotle's "on kai me on," probably by way of the first scene of Marlowe's *Doctor Faustus* (performed ca. 1593; printed in 1604), though both Abraham Fraunce's *The Lawyer's Logic* (1588) and William Perkins's *A Discourse of Conscience* (1596) also contain this phrase. Elizabeth, while contemplating the execution of her cousin Mary, Queen of Scots, supposedly repeated, "aut fer, aut feri" (to act or to be acted upon).

Hamlet's speech "What a piece of work is a man" (2.2.303–307) echoes Pico della Mirandola's *Oration on the Dignity of Man* (1486). When Hamlet urges Lucianus to "leave thy damnable faces and begin / Come, the croaking raven doth bellow for revenge" (3.2.253–254), he is repeating (or parodying) a line from *The True History of Richard the Third,* a source for Shakespeare's play about that king: "The screeking Raven sits croaking for revenge." Hamlet's observation that "There is special providence in the fall of a sparrow" (5.2.219–220) recalls Matthew 10:29: "Are not two sparrows sold for a farthing? And one of them shall not fall on the ground without your Father." In the same speech, Hamlet declares, "the readiness is all" (5.2.222), perhaps referring to Matthew 24:44, "Therefore be ye readie: for in the houre that ye thinke not, wil the sonne of man come." More generally, revenge tragedy was popular on the Elizabethan stage. In addition to Kyd's *Spanish Tragedy,* examples include Marlowe's *The Jew of Malta* (1589–90), *Alphonsus, Emperor of Germany* (ca. 1594–97), John Marston's *Antonio's Revenge* (ca. 1600), George Chapman's *Bussy D'Ambois* (ca. 1604), and Cyril Touneur's *The Revenger's Tragedy* (1606–07).

Historical events would have heightened interest in such works and particularly in the story of Hamlet. In 1538, the duke of Urbino was killed by a barber-surgeon, bribed by two of the duke's relatives, who poured poisoned lotion in his ears. Titian painted a portrait of the duke, frequently reproduced in engravings, showing him in full armor with his visor up, his hair curled, and his beard grizzled, resembling the description of the ghost that Bernardo, Marcellus, and Horatio give to Hamlet in Act I, Scene 2. The court of Urbino would have been familiar to Elizabethans through Baldassare Castiglione's *Il Cortegiano* (translated to English in 1561); Hamlet is modeled on Castiglione's ideal courtier. Closer in time and space to Shakespeare's London, in 1567, James Hepburn, earl of Bothwell, lover of Mary, Queen of Scots,

killed her second husband, Henry Darnley, and then married the queen three months later. Darnley's parents commissioned Livinus de Vogelaare to paint a memorial urging Darnley's son, James VI of Scotland, to avenge his father's death. James married Anne of Denmark, and Bullough notes correlations between revivals of the *Ur-Hamlet* and notable events in the Scottish court. James's first son was born in February 1594; *Ur-Hamlet* was staged in June. A daughter, Elizabeth, was born to him in 1596, the year of Lodge's reference to the play, perhaps prompted by another performance of the work. The first quarto of Shakespeare's play was first printed in 1603 shortly after James succeeded to the English throne.

Polonius may have been modeled on William Cecil, first baron Burghley, Elizabeth's chief adviser, noted for prolixity, and Hamlet might be drawn at least in part from Cecil's chief rival, Robert Devereux, second earl of Essex. Essex and the third earl of Southampton, to whom Shakespeare dedicated *Venus and Adonis* (1593) and *The Rape of Lucrece* (1594), were allies; Shakespeare's only direct reference to contemporary events praises Essex in the Chorus before Act V of *Henry V* (1599). On the eve of Essex's uprising against Elizabeth, the earl arranged for Shakespeare's company to perform *Richard II,* showing the deposition of a king. Ophelia calls Hamlet "Th' expectation and the rose of the fair state" (3.1.152). John Hayward dedicated *The First Part of the Life and Reign of King Henry IV* (1599) to Essex. The dedication, in Latin, reads "You are great in hope, greater in the expectation of future time." Upon his unauthorized return from Ireland in September 1599, Essex broke into Elizabeth's closet, as Hamlet visits Ophelia's. In a possible example of life's imitating art, when Essex was executed in February 1601, he wore all black.

The War of the Theatres, in which children's acting companies threatened their adult counterparts in the summer of 1601, is discussed in the First Folio version of the play. This contemporary issue is referenced in a scene with Rosencrantz and Guildenstern, in an obvious effort to lampoon the controversy. Shakespeare also drew on his own experiences in creating this work. In December 1579, a Katherine Hamlet drowned in the Avon near Stratford, and in 1596, Shakespeare's 11-year-old son, Hamnet (a variant of *Hamlet*) died. This play could be seen as living monument to him.

Date and Text of the Play

In his copy of the 1598 edition of Geoffrey Chaucer's works, Gabriel Harvey wrote, "The younger sort takes much delight in Shakespeares Venus, & Adonis: but his Lucrece, & his tragedie of Hamlet, Prince of Denmarke, have it in them, to please the wiser sort." This statement is part of a longer note that includes a reference to the earl of Essex, who apparently is still alive. Essex was executed in February 1601, so the play appears to have been produced before early 1601. Francis Meres's 1598 *Palladis Tamia* does not mention the work in his list of Shakespeare's plays. In *Hamlet,* Polonius says that in college he played Julius Caesar and was killed by Brutus in the Capitol (3.2.102–103), an allusion to Shakespeare's play on this subject, which appeared in 1599. The reference is an in-joke: John Heminge played both Caesar and Polonius, while Richard Burbage played both Brutus and Hamlet. Burbage, in these roles, therefore, stabbed Heminge in both plays. *Hamlet* likely was first staged about 1600, with the reference to the War of the Theatres added in 1601.

On July 26, 1602, John Roberts entered in the Stationers' Register "A booke called the Revenge of Hamlett Prince Denmarke as yt was latelie Acted by the Lo: Chamberleyne his servants." The first version of the play appeared in print the next year. Since its title page states the work was "acted by his Highnesse seruants," it must have been printed after May 19, 1603, the day the Lord Chamberlain's Men became the King's Men (with James VI's ascension to the English throne as James I). Roberts had nothing to do with this edition. It was printed by the shady Valentine Simmes for Nicholas Ling and John Trundle. This version, which contains some 2,200 lines, is known in only two copies, the first of which was found by Sir Henry Bunbury in 1823 and the other acquired (or perhaps stolen from his father-in-law, the bibliomaniac Sir Thomas Phillipps) by James Orchard Halliwell-Phillipps in 1856. One copy now resides in the British Library, the other at the Huntington Library.

The text of this version is carelessly printed, and it is evidently a memorial reconstruction by the actor who played Marcellus and perhaps Lucianus and Voltemand. The first act, the only one in which Marcellus appears, is less garbled than the remainder of the play. Despite its flaws, though, this particular text, known as Q1, has been staged successfully in modern times, first by William Poel at St. George's Hall in 1881 and more recently in 1982 at University College, Swansea, and in 1985 at the Orange Tree Theatre, Richmond. The text is clearly based on a performed work, and some of its stage directions are unique. It names Polonius Corambis and Reynaldo Montano. The nunnery scene, now in Act III, Scene 1, is brought forward (perhaps more logically) to Act II, Scene 2. A German version of the play, *Der Bestrafte Brudermord* (Fratricide revenged), acted in the early 1600s, shares these elements.

In 1604, Roberts printed a second quarto, nearly twice as long as Q1, at some 3,800 lines. The title page describes Q2 as "Newly imprinted and enlarged to almost as much againe as it was, according to the true and perfect Coppie." This edition was apparently printed from Shakespeare's foul papers, his first draft, with some reliance on Q1 for the first act. The title page does not claim that this version was ever acted, and many scholars believe that it would have been too long to stage, requiring some five hours. It contains some 220 lines that do not appear elsewhere.

The third important text of the play, printed in the First Folio (1623), is known as F. It is shorter than Q2 by about 130 lines, since 220 lines from Q2 are absent, but 70 new lines appear only here. F's stage directions suggest that it also was an acting version, though it is hardly shorter than Q2. All the cuts that F makes from Q2 are also made in Q1, supporting the view that Q1 derives from actual performance.

THE
Tragicall Hiſtorie of
HAMLET,
Prince of Denmarke.

By William Shakeſpeare.

Newly imprinted and enlarged to almoſt as much
againe as it was, according to the true and perfect
Coppie.

AT LONDON,
Printed by I. R. for N. L. and are to be ſold at his
ſhoppe vnder Saint Dunſtons Church in
Fleeſtſtreet. 1605.

Title page of the second quarto of *Hamlet,* published in
1604

Neither quarto marks act and scene divisions; F
notes only Act I, Scenes 1–3 and Act II, Scene 2.
Most modern editions conflate Q2 and F, making
Shakespeare's longest play even longer and introducing some added difficulties to an already complicated work. For example, in Act V, Scene 2, Q2
introduces a lord who tells Hamlet that Gertrude
suggests the prince "use some gentle entertainment to Laertes" to patch up their quarrel in the
graveyard (5.2.206–207). In F, this lord does not
appear, but Hamlet regrets his behavior to Laertes
and promises to "court his favors" (5.2.78). This
pledge is absent in Q2. The Riverside edition, a

conflated text, includes both speeches and, so,
offers two differing motivations for Hamlet's apology to Laertes before the duel.

SYNOPSIS
Brief Synopsis
Thirty years before the play opens, on the very day
that young Hamlet was born, Old Hamlet, king of
Denmark, killed Old Fortinbras, king of Norway,
in single combat and thereby won from him all the
lands that the vanquished ruler had conquered.
Old Hamlet has died recently, supposedly of a
snake bite, and young Fortinbras has taken advantage of the occasion to assemble an army to recapture the lands his father lost.

Denmark therefore is on a war footing. As the
play begins, Bernardo and Marcellus relieve Francisco, who has been guarding the battlements of
the castle of Elsinore. They have brought with
them the scholar Horatio because they have seen
a ghost who resembles Old Hamlet. They want
Horatio to confirm their sighting and speak to the
spirit. Horatio expresses skepticism, but his doubts
fade when the ghost appears. It will not, however,
speak to him. The men resolve to inform young
Hamlet of what they have seen. They believe that
the ghost will speak to him.

The next day, King Claudius, who has succeeded to his brother's throne and married his
brother's wife, Gertrude, holds court. He dispatches
Voltemand and Cornelius to Norway to negotiate a peaceful settlement to the dispute between
that country and his, and he grants permission to
Laertes, son of the Lord Chamberlain, Polonius, to
return to his studies in Paris. Claudius and Gertrude
urge Hamlet to abandon his mourning for his father
and his plans to return to Wittenberg University.

Hamlet's caustic comments reveal his hatred for
Claudius, but he agrees to obey his mother. After
the court departs, Marcellus, Bernardo, and Horatio tell Hamlet about the ghost. Hamlet agrees to
join them on the battlements that night.

In another part of the castle, Laertes, preparing
to return to Paris, warns his sister, Ophelia, not to
believe Hamlet's professions of love for her. Their

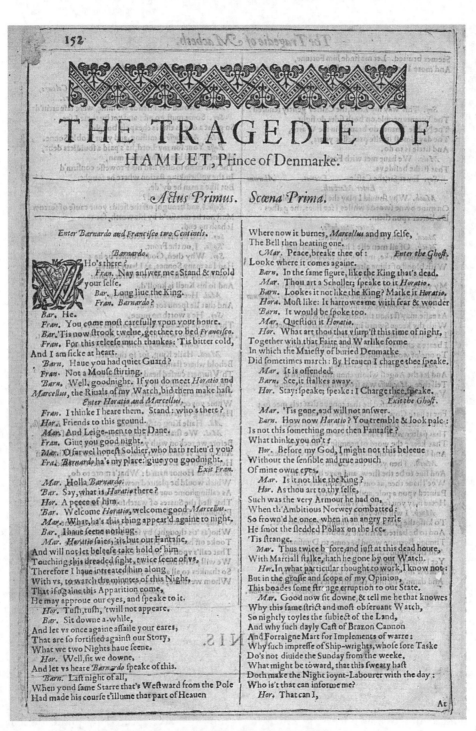

THE TRAGEDIE OF

HAMLET, Prince of Denmarke.

Actus Primus. Scœna Prima.

Enter Barnardo and Francisco two Centinels.

Barnardo.

Ho's there?

Fran. Nay answer me: Stand & vnfold
your selfe.

Bar. Long liue the King.

Fran. Barnardo?

Bar. He.

Fran. You come most carefully vpon your houre.

Bar. 'Tis now strook twelue, get thee to bed Francisco.

Fran. For this releefe much thankes: 'Tis bitter cold,
And I am sicke at heart.

Barn. Haue you had quiet Guard?

Fran. Not a Mouse stirring.

Barn. Well, goodnight. If you do meet Horatio and
Marcellus, the Riuals of my Watch, bid them make hast.

Enter Horatio and Marcellus.

Fran. I thinke I heare them. Stand: who's there?

Hor. Friends to this ground.

Mar. And Liege-men to the Dane.

Fran. Giue you good night.

Mar. O farwel honest Soldier, who hath relieu'd you?

Fra. Barnardo ha's my place: giue you goodnight.

Exit Fran.

Mar. Holla Barnardo.

Bar. Say, what is Horatio there?

Hor. A peece of him.

Bar. Welcome Horatio, welcome good Marcellus.

Mar. What, ha's this thing appear'd againe to night.

Bar. I haue seene nothing.

Mar. Horatio saies, 'tis but our Fantasie,
And will not let beleefe take hold of him
Touching this dreaded sight, twice seene of vs,
Therefore I haue intreated him along
With vs, to watch the minutes of this Night,
That if againe this Apparition come,
He may approue our eyes, and speake to it.

Hor. Tush, tush, 'twill not appeare.

Bar. Sit downe a-while,
And let vs once againe assaile your eares,
That are so fortified against our Story,
What we two Nights haue seene.

Hor. Well, sit we downe,
And let vs heare Barnardo speake of this.

Barn. Last night of all,
When yond same Starre that's Westward from the Pole
Had made his course t'illume that part of Heauen

Where now it burnes, Marcellus and my selfe,
The Bell then beating one.

Mar. Peace, breake thee of: *Enter the Ghost.*
Looke where it comes againe.

Barn. In the same figure, like the King that's dead.

Mar. Thou art a Scholler; speake to it Horatio.

Barn. Lookes it not like the King? Marke it Horatio.

Hora. Most like: It harrowes me with feare & wonder

Barn. It would be spoke too.

Mar. Question it Horatio.

Hor. What art thou that vsurp'st this time of night,
Together with that Faire and Warlike forme
In which the Maiesty of buried Denmarke
Did sometimes march: By Heauen I charge thee speake.

Mar. It is offended.

Barn. See, it stalkes away.

Hor. Stay: speake; speake: I Charge thee, speake.

Exit the Ghost.

Mar. 'Tis gone, and will not answer.

Barn. How now Horatio? You tremble & look pale:
Is not this something more then Fantasie?
What thinke you on't?

Hor. Before my God, I might not this beleeue
Without the sensible and true auouch
Of mine owne eyes.

Mar. Is it not like the King?

Hor. As thou art to thy selfe,
Such was the very Armour he had on,
When th'Ambitious Norwey combatted:
So frown'd he once, when in an angry parle
He smot the sledded Pollax on the Ice.
'Tis strange.

Mar. Thus twice before, and iust at this dead houre,
With Martiall stalke, hath he gone by our Watch.

Hor. In what particular thought to work, I know not:
But in the grosse and scope of my Opinion,
This boades some strange erruption to our State.

Mar. Good now sit downe, & tell me he that knowes
Why this same strict and most obseruant Watch,
So nightly toyles the subiect of the Land,
And why such dayly Cast of Brazon Cannon
And Forraigne Mart for Implements of warre:
Why such impresse of Ship-wrights, whose sore Taske
Do's not diuide the Sunday from the weeke,
What might be toward, that this sweaty hast
Doth make the Night ioynt-Labourer with the day:
Who is't that can informe me?

Hor. That can I,

At

A painting of John Philip Kemble as Hamlet in an 1802 production of the play *(Painting by Sir Thomas Lawrence)*

father echoes this advice and forbids her to see the prince.

That night, the ghost of Old Hamlet appears again. Leading Hamlet away, he reveals that Claudius killed him. The ghost demands revenge but insists that Hamlet leave Gertrude to her conscience.

Two months elapse between the first and second acts. Hamlet has been acting strangely but has not avenged his father's death. When Ophelia tells Polonius that a disheveled Hamlet has visited her in her bedroom and frightened her with his odd manner, Polonius believes that the young man has gone mad for Ophelia's love and hastens to tell the king.

After Voltemand and Cornelius report the successful conclusion of their mission, Polonius tells Claudius about Hamlet's love madness, which he and the king will test further. Meanwhile, Claudius

has summoned to court two of Hamlet's former friends, Rosencrantz and Guildenstern, in the hope that they will learn the cause of the prince's curious behavior. Hamlet easily discovers their intent and deflects their inquiries, but he is delighted with their news that a troupe of players has arrived. Hamlet will use the actors to determine whether the ghost spoke the truth.

The next day, Polonius and Claudius stage a meeting between Ophelia and Hamlet to test Polonius's theory. Hamlet's harsh treatment of Ophelia explodes the notion. That night, the visiting actors perform *The Murder of Gonzago,* which depicts the murder of a king in the manner Old Hamlet claims he was killed. When Claudius sees the staged murder, he rushes from the performance.

Gertrude summons Hamlet to her room. On his way there, Hamlet encounters Claudius at prayer. Hamlet could kill the king but refrains, claiming that he wants to be certain that Claudius's soul will be damned.

In his interview with Gertrude, Hamlet condemns her remarriage. Fearing violence, she calls for help. Polonius, who has been spying on the conversation from behind a curtain, joins her cries, thus exposing himself. Hamlet, thinking that the voice is that of Claudius, runs his sword through the tapestry and kills the Lord Chamberlain.

Claudius had already resolved to send Hamlet to England with Rosencrantz and Guildenstern. He puts this plan into effect immediately. Guildenstern and Rosencrantz bear letters ordering the English king to kill Hamlet.

Her father's death drives Ophelia to madness and her brother, Laertes, to rage. Intent on revenge, he bursts into the castle. Claudius convinces him that Hamlet alone is responsible, and Laertes resolves to kill the prince, a resolution strengthened by the news that Ophelia has drowned herself.

Hamlet returns to Denmark. In a graveyard, he tells Horatio of substituting Claudius's commission with his own, which orders the instant execution of Rosencrantz and Guildenstern. He also explains how he was captured by pirates and returned to Denmark. Ophelia's funeral procession enters. As she is laid in the grave, Laertes leaps in after her. Hamlet does so as well, and the two scuffle before separating.

That afternoon, Claudius stages a fencing match between Hamlet and Laertes. The latter plans to kill Hamlet with an unbated, poisoned foil, and Claudius, who has approved the scheme, will provide a poisoned cup of wine for Hamlet to drink. In the duel, Hamlet and Laertes mortally wound each other. The queen drinks from the poisoned cup and dies, and Hamlet kills Claudius before expiring himself. At the end of the play, Fortinbras arrives with his army to claim the Danish throne.

Act I, Scene 1

The play opens on a cold winter's night. A lone sentinel, Francisco, stands guard on the battlements of the castle at Elsinore, Denmark. As the clock strikes 12, Bernardo enters to relieve him. Francisco reports that he has had a quiet watch. He departs as Marcellus and Horatio enter.

Twice before, Bernardo and Marcellus have seen a ghost. Horatio asks whether the Ghost has appeared again. Bernardo says it has not but that it appeared before just at this hour. As Bernardo is speaking, the apparition materializes in the shape of Old Hamlet, the recently deceased Danish king. Horatio speaks to it, but it departs silently.

After the men discuss the Ghost, Marcellus asks why the country is preparing for war. Horatio replies that years ago, Old Hamlet defeated Old Fortinbras, king of Norway, in single combat, thereby winning all the lands that the latter had conquered. Now young Fortinbras, the dead Norwegian king's son, has assembled an army to retake those lost territories.

The Ghost reappears, and Horatio again addresses it. It seems about to respond when a cock crows; it then vanishes. The men agree to inform young Hamlet of what they have seen. The Ghost, Horatio says, surely will speak to his own son.

Act I, Scene 2

In the morning, inside the castle, the court assembles, led by King Claudius and Queen Gertrude,

with young Hamlet and sundry others bringing up the rear. Claudius thanks his courtiers for supporting his decision to marry his dead brother's wife. He then addresses the Norwegian threat, announcing that he has written to that country's aged, ailing king to restrain his nephew, Fortinbras. Cornelius and Voltemand are dispatched to deliver this letter.

Claudius grants permission to Laertes, son of Polonius, the Lord Chamberlain, to return to his studies in Paris. Finally, the king turns to Hamlet. Claudius and Gertrude urge him to cease mourning for Old Hamlet and to abandon his plan to return to the university at Wittenberg. Hamlet replies that he will obey his mother. Ignoring Hamlet's slight to him, Claudius expresses satisfaction with this answer.

The court departs, leaving Hamlet alone to deliver his first soliloquy, a lament for his mother's hasty remarriage. Horatio, Marcellus, and Bernardo enter to report their sighting of the Ghost. Hamlet agrees to accompany them that night to watch on the battlements and asks them to keep their sighting secret.

Act I, Scene 3

In Polonius's apartment in the castle, Laertes prepares to return to France. He warns his sister, Ophelia, not to trust Hamlet's professions of love because even if they are sincere, he is not free to choose his bride: He will have to marry for reasons of state. Polonius arrives. He urges Laertes to make haste to the ship and then delays him with a series of wise saws and modern instances. At last effecting his departure, Laertes urges Ophelia to remember his advice.

What advice is that, Polonius asks. Something about Hamlet, she replies. Polonius tells her that he, too, distrusts Hamlet's claim that he loves Ophelia and, despite Ophelia's protestations, orders her not to see the prince again. She submits to his command.

Act I, Scene 4

On the battlements of Elsinore that night, Hamlet, Horatio, and Marcellus hear a flourish of trumpets and the report of cannon. To Horatio's

Horatio tries to hold Hamlet back from following the ghost of Old Hamlet in a 1789 depiction of Act I, Scene 4 of *Hamlet*. This is a print from the Boydell Shakespeare Gallery project, which was first conceived in 1786 and lasted until 1805. *(Painting by Henry Fuseli; engraving by Robert Thew)*

query about the meaning of these noises, Hamlet replies that they customarily accompany the king's drinking. Just as Hamlet concludes his explanation, the Ghost appears. It responds to Hamlet's address by silently summoning him to follow him to a secluded spot. Despite his friends' opposition, Hamlet goes with him.

Act I, Scene 5

Alone with Hamlet, the Ghost reveals himself to be the dead king's spirit, condemned to wander the nights and spend his days in Purgatory. He declares that while napping in his orchard, he was poisoned by Claudius, and he urges young Hamlet to avenge his murder. At the same time, Hamlet is not to corrupt his thoughts or harm Gertrude, despite her adultery. As dawn breaks, the Ghost fades while enjoining his son to remember him.

Hamlet promises that he will heed his dead father's words. Horatio and Marcellus join him and ask what the Ghost said. Hamlet evades their questioning but insists they swear not to tell anyone what has happened. The Ghost echoes this request. Hamlet also makes them promise not to expose him should he choose to feign madness. They agree and go off together.

Act II, Scene 1

Two months after the events shown in the first act, Polonius gives Reynaldo letters and money for Laertes, along with instructions to spy on the young man to discover how he is behaving in Paris. Reynaldo is not, however, to interfere with Laertes' activities.

Reynaldo leaves as Ophelia enters. She reports that as she was sewing in her room, Hamlet, disheveled, pale, and trembling, entered. He took her by the wrist, held her, and stared at her for a long time. Then, shaking her arm, he nodded thrice, sighed, released her, and, with his eyes fixed on her, departed. Polonius ascribes Hamlet's plight to Ophelia's rejection and resolves to inform the king of this occurrence.

Act II, Scene 2

In another part of the castle, Claudius and Gertrude welcome Guildenstern and Rosencrantz, two of Hamlet's former friends, whom the king has summoned to Elsinore to discover the cause of Hamlet's odd behavior. When they go off, Polonius enters to report the return of Cornelius and Voltemand. He adds that he knows the cause of Hamlet's distraction, which he will reveal after the king's ambassadors report their news.

He ushers in the two men. Voltemand announces their success: Old Norway has rebuked Fortinbras, who now intends to direct his army against Poland. The young warrior seeks permission to march peacefully through Denmark.

Promising to consider this request, Claudius dismisses the ambassadors. Polonius now launches into a long disquisition, the burden of which is that Hamlet's madness stems from his thwarted love for Ophelia. To test this theory, Polonius will arrange a meeting between his daughter and the prince, which he and Claudius will secretly observe.

Hamlet enters reading a book. Polonius strikes up a conversation in which Hamlet's speeches are at once rambling and astute. Polonius departs, to be replaced by Rosencrantz and Guildenstern. Their meeting begins pleasantly, but Hamlet quickly recognizes that Claudius has engaged them to spy on him to discover the cause of his discontent. They conclude that it derives from his ambition to be king.

They inform Hamlet that a troupe of actors has just reached the castle. Polonius enters to repeat this information, followed by the actors themselves. Hamlet welcomes them and asks for a sample of their wares, a speech about Pyrrhus's killing of Priam. The actor becomes so emotionally wrought as he delivers the lines that Polonius stops him. As the actors retire, Hamlet takes the speaker aside to ask whether the next night the company can perform *The Murder of Gonzago,* with certain additions Hamlet will provide. The actor assures him they can undertake it.

Alone, Hamlet again soliloquizes, chastising himself for delaying his revenge. Yet, he states that the Ghost might be a demon seeking to damn him. Hamlet will use *The Murder of Gonzago* to determine Claudius's guilt and the Ghost's veracity.

Act III, Scene 1

The next day, Claudius, Gertrude, Rosencrantz, and Guildenstern gather to discuss Hamlet. The spies report that they have learned nothing but inform the royal couple that Hamlet has arranged a play for their amusement that evening.

Rosencrantz, Guildenstern, and Gertrude leave. Claudius and Polonius now put their plan into practice to test the latter's theory that Hamlet's madness stems from "the pangs of despis'd love" (71). Polonius stations Ophelia where Hamlet, having been summoned, will meet her, while her father and the king spy on them from behind a curtain.

Hamlet enters and delivers his "To be or not to be" soliloquy. As he concludes his speech, he notices Ophelia. She attempts to return the love tokens Hamlet had given her. He refuses them and verbally assaults her, shouting that she should withdraw to a nunnery. As he departs, he makes a thinly veiled threat against Claudius.

Lamenting Hamlet's madness, Ophelia withdraws. Claudius and Polonius emerge from hiding. The king is convinced that whatever the cause of Hamlet's mad behavior, love is not it. He resolves to

Hamlet (Edmund Russell) tells Ophelia (Jane Schenck) to "get thee to a nunnery" in Act III, Scene 1 of *Hamlet*. This photograph was published by the Byron Company in 1903.

send Hamlet to England to get him out of the kingdom. Polonius still thinks that thwarted love began Hamlet's transformation. The Lord Chamberlain suggests that after the play, Gertrude should try to ferret out the source of Hamlet's discontent, while he, again in hiding, spies on their conversation.

Act III, Scene 2

As the players prepare to present *The Murder of Gonzago,* Hamlet instructs them in the art of acting. They then go off to get ready, and Horatio enters. Hamlet tells his friend how much he admires the man's stoicism. He then enjoins Horatio to mark Claudius's reaction to the evening's entertainment, one scene of which will reproduce the assassination of Old Hamlet as the Ghost described it. If Claudius does not blench, then Hamlet will know that the Ghost is demonic.

The court enters. Hamlet converses caustically with Claudius and Polonius. When Gertrude asks Hamlet to sit by her, he replies that he prefers the company of Ophelia, whom he then taunts with sexual innuendoes.

The play begins. Following a dumb show, the Player King and Player Queen enter. He observes that he is aging and soon will die, after which his queen perhaps will remarry. She professes her eternal love for him and pledges never to take another husband. When the Player King reflects that people change their minds, she vows that she will not. The Player King then lies down for a nap.

Claudius, growing uneasy, asks Hamlet whether the play contains anything offensive. Hamlet replies that since he and the king have clear consciences, they have no reason to worry. The play resumes with the entrance of Lucianus, whom Hamlet identifies as the Player King's nephew. As Lucianus pours poison into the king's ear, Hamlet says that the murderer will soon gain the love of the dead man's wife.

Furious, Claudius rises and leaves, followed by the rest of the court, leaving Hamlet and Horatio behind. Hamlet rejoices at the success of his plot. Rosencrantz and Guildenstern enter to report that the king is enraged and that Gertrude wants to see him in her room. Hamlet condemns the king's agents for spying on him. Polonius joins the group to summon Hamlet to Gertrude. After teasing the old man, Hamlet replies that he will go to her. On his way to her room, Hamlet promises himself that he will speak harshly to her but will eschew violence.

Act III, Scene 3

Claudius tells Guildenstern and Rosencrantz that Hamlet is to be sent to England in their company forthwith. When they depart, Polonius passes through to say that he is on his way to Gertrude's chamber.

Alone, Claudius confesses his guilt. He considers praying but acknowledges that he cannot expect to be forgiven as long as he retains the fruits of his sin: his crown and queen. Still, he will try what prayer can do.

As he kneels in devotion, Hamlet enters. The prince recognizes that here is the perfect opportunity to dispatch Claudius. Then he considers that if Claudius dies while praying, his soul will go straight to heaven, whereas Hamlet's father, having died without extreme unction, is suffering in Purgatory. Hamlet sheathes his sword, determined to wait until he can kill the king while engaged in an activity that will assure Claudius's damnation. After Hamlet departs, Claudius rises, admitting that his supplications are futile.

Act III, Scene 4

In Gertrude's apartment, Polonius urges the queen to reprimand Hamlet; he then hides behind a tapestry. Hamlet enters and begins arguing with his mother. She tries to leave, but he prevents her. She calls for help, and Polonius joins in her cries, thereby exposing his presence. Hamlet, thinking that Claudius is concealed in the room, thrusts his sword through the tapestry, killing the eavesdropper.

Undaunted by this murder, Hamlet rebukes Gertrude for marrying Claudius. As he is railing against the couple, the Ghost materializes to remind Hamlet of his mission and to urge him to

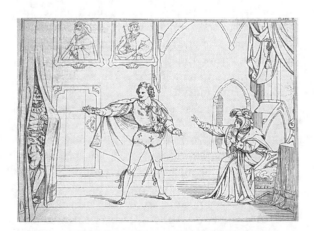

Hamlet stabs Polonius through the curtain while Gertrude protests in Act III, Scene 4 of *Hamlet*. This is a plate from *Retzsch's Outlines to Shakespeare:* Hamlet, published in 1828. *(Illustration by Moritz Retzsch)*

comfort Gertrude. The Ghost then vanishes. Gertrude, who cannot see or hear the Ghost, believes that Hamlet is truly mad. Hamlet assures her that he is as sane as she. He implores her to stop sleeping with Claudius and to conceal from the king that Hamlet is only pretending to be mad.

Gertrude promises to keep her son's secret safe. He reminds her that he must leave for England, accompanied by Guildenstern and Rosencrantz, whom he does not trust and whose plot he will undermine. He then leaves, dragging Polonius.

Act IV, Scene 1

Claudius asks Gertrude about Hamlet. She replies that her son is mad, and in his madness, he has killed Polonius. Claudius recognize himself as the intended victim and announces that Hamlet will be sent to England at sunrise. He dispatches Rosencrantz and Guildenstern to find Hamlet and Polonius. Claudius leaves with Gertrude to consider how he can escape blame for the old man's death.

Act IV, Scene 2

Rosencrantz and Guildenstern find Hamlet and inquire as to the whereabouts of Polonius's body. Hamlet responds by warning them that Claudius will use and then discard them. They again ask about the corpse. Hamlet offers a riddling answer and runs off, pursued by Rosencrantz and Guildenstern.

Act IV, Scene 3

Rosencrantz tells Claudius that Hamlet has been apprehended, but the prince has not revealed the location of the body. Hamlet enters in the custody of Guildenstern. After taunting Claudius, Hamlet tells him where to find Polonius. Claudius dispatches Hamlet to England with Guildenstern and Rosencrantz. Alone, the king reveals that his agents bear letters to the king of England ordering the immediate execution of Hamlet.

Act IV, Scene 4

As Hamlet goes to his ship, Fortinbras passes by and sends a captain to Claudius to request peaceful passage through Denmark for the Norwegian army. Hamlet meets the captain and asks about the soldiers. The two discuss Fortinbras's impending attack on a worthless piece of Polish territory. Alone, Hamlet delivers his final soliloquy, in which he again condemns himself for delaying his revenge and resolves that henceforth his thoughts will be bloody.

Act IV, Scene 5
Gertrude, distraught, initially refuses to see the mad Ophelia, but Horatio counsels her to do so. The girl enters and sings about her dead father and then her lost lover, Hamlet. As she leaves, she vows to inform Laertes about recent events.

Laertes already knows about his father's death. With a band of supporters he breaks into the royal chambers. Dismissing his followers, Laertes demands his father of Claudius. Gertrude tries to hold Laertes back, but Claudius insists that the young man be allowed to ask whatever he wants.

Ophelia reenters, carrying various herbs and again singing about her father. She aptly distributes her plants and then, with another song, departs. Claudius invites Laertes to go with him to discuss his (Laertes') grievances.

Laertes reaches out to a mad Ophelia, while Claudius and Gertrude look on in Act IV, Scene 5 of *Hamlet*. This print is from Malcolm C. Salaman's 1916 edition of *Shakespeare in Pictorial Art*. *(Painting by Stephen Reid)*

Act IV, Scene 6
A sailor gives Horatio a letter from Hamlet announcing the prince's return to Denmark.

Act IV, Scene 7
Claudius has convinced Laertes that Hamlet alone is to blame for Polonius's death. When a messenger gives Claudius letters reporting Hamlet's return, the king and Laertes plot the prince's death. Claudius will arrange a fencing match between Hamlet and Laertes. The latter will use an unblunted foil, and with it he will kill his opponent. Laertes declares that he will poison the tip, and Claudius adds that he will poison a cup of wine for Hamlet to drink during the bout. Just as the plotters complete their plans, Gertrude enters to announce the drowning of Ophelia.

Act V, Scene 1
Two gravediggers, who are preparing for Ophelia's interment, debate whether she deserves burial in sanctified ground. They express their discontent that the gentry enjoy greater freedom to kill themselves than ordinary folk are allowed. After the First Gravedigger sends his partner to fetch some liquor, Hamlet and Horatio enter and watch as the First Gravedigger shovels skulls out of the ground (graves were reused in Renaissance England). Hamlet asks him whose grave he is digging. The gravedigger replies equivocally and then shows the prince the skull of Yorick, Old Hamlet's jester. Holding the skull, Hamlet reflects on mortality.

A funeral possession enters the cemetery. Hamlet and Horatio hide. Laertes protests the abridged burial rites accorded his sister, thereby informing Hamlet whose grave was being dug. As Ophelia is being laid in the ground, Laertes leaps into the grave and asks to be buried with her. Hamlet, emerging from concealment, joins him, and the two scuffle. Gertrude seeks to part them, and Hamlet departs. Claudius assures Laertes that he will immediately put their plot into practice.

Laertes and Hamlet fight during Ophelia's funeral in Act V, Scene 1 of *Hamlet*. This is a plate from *Retzsch's Outlines to Shakespeare:* Hamlet, published in 1828. *(Illustration by Moritz Retzsch)*

Act V, Scene 2

Hamlet tells Horatio how on his voyage to England he learned of Claudius's plot to have him beheaded and how he changed the commission to order the immediate execution of Rosencrantz and Guildenstern, instead.

Osric, a court fop, enters and in his own overblown idiom, states that Claudius has laid a wager on a fencing match between Hamlet and Laertes and would like for the match to occur at once. Hamlet accepts the challenge, though he tells Horatio of his misgivings. Horatio urges the prince to refuse to fence, but Hamlet replies that providence directs all events.

The final court scene ensues. Hamlet asks Laertes' forgiveness, and Laertes pretends to accept his apology. Claudius sets out a stoop of wine, and the bout begins. After Hamlet scores the first point of the match, Claudius drinks to him and then poisons the cup while seeming to drop a pearl into it. When Hamlet scores the next point as well, the queen drinks to Hamlet and thus poisons herself. Laertes then wounds Hamlet with the envenomed foil. Hamlet, incensed at this treachery, gets Laertes' sword and wounds him with it.

Gertrude collapses. Claudius tries to allay suspicion by saying that she swoons at the sight of blood, but the dying Gertrude declares that the wine has been poisoned. Laertes confesses that the unbated foil is poisoned, too, and blames the king for the plot. Hamlet stabs Claudius and pours some of the poisoned wine down his throat. The king dies. Laertes pardons Hamlet and asks his forgiveness, then dies. Sensing his end, Hamlet asks Horatio to clear his name. Horatio initially refuses; he tries to kill himself by drinking what remains of the poisoned wine, but Hamlet stops him.

Osric announces the return of Fortinbras from Poland and the arrival of ambassadors from England. Before he dies, Hamlet casts his vote for Fortinbras to succeed to the Danish throne. Fortinbras enters with the ambassadors, who report that Rosencrantz and Guildenstern are dead. Horatio asks that the dead bodies be displayed and he be allowed to relate the events that led to this tragedy. Fortinbras agrees and orders a salute of cannon, which sounds as the play ends.

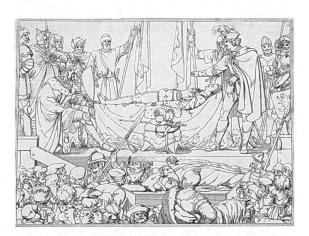

Horatio asks Fortinbras to place the bodies of Hamlet, Gertude, Claudius, and Laertes on a stage so that all may know of Denmark's tragedy in Act V, Scene 2 of *Hamlet*. This is a plate from *Retzsch's Outlines to Shakespeare:* Hamlet, published in 1828. *(Illustration by Moritz Retzsch)*

CHARACTER LIST

Hamlet Prince of Denmark, grieving for his dead father.

Old Hamlet/Ghost Recently deceased warrior king of Denmark, who returns as a ghost to the castle of Elsinore to demand that his son avenge his murder.

Claudius King of Denmark and brother of Old Hamlet. Claudius killed his brother to get the throne and his brother's wife.

Gertrude Queen of Denmark; now wife of Claudius, she had been married to Old Hamlet. She is young Hamlet's mother.

Polonius Denmark's garrulous, spying Lord Chamberlain, loyal to Claudius.

Laertes Son of Polonius. He is a student at the University of Paris.

Ophelia Daughter of Polonius. She loves Hamlet.

Horatio Hamlet's fellow student and one true friend.

Voltemand Danish ambassador to Norway.

Cornelius Another Danish ambassador to Norway.

Rosencrantz Hamlet's former friend, he has been suborned by Claudius to spy on the prince.

Guildenstern Hamlet's former friend, now in league with Claudius.

Osric A rich fop who hangs about the court of Claudius.

Marcellus A guard at Elsinore.

Bernardo A guard at Elsinore.

Francisco A guard at Elsinore.

Reynaldo Servant of Polonius sent to spy on Laertes in Paris.

Fortinbras Norwegian prince. His uncle is king of Norway. His father was killed by Old Hamlet. Fortinbras has assembled an army to conquer the lands that his father lost to Old Hamlet.

First Gravedigger The wittiest character in the play except for Hamlet.

Second Gravedigger First Gravedigger's assistant.

Player King Leading member of a troupe of players who visit Elsinore; he takes the role of the king in *The Murder of Gonzago.*

Player Queen A male actor of the visiting acting troupe; he assumes the role of the Player King's wife.

Lucianus A member of the troupe. He is supposed to be the Player King's nephew and poisons his uncle in the piece they perform.

CHARACTER STUDIES
Hamlet

In this work, title character and play are essentially one, hence the common expression "*Hamlet* without the prince," which connotes a serious if not fatal omission. Hamlet speaks some 1,400 lines, or about three-eighths of the tragedy, 300 more than any other character created by Shakespeare. Yet, Shakespeare so constructs this work that, except for the final duel, the audience knows no more than the prince. Whereas it is clear that Othello should not trust Iago, that Macbeth should not kill Duncan, that Lear errs in dividing his kingdom, in rejecting Cordelia, and in trusting his fate to Goneril and Regan, with Hamlet, it is different. Whereas one empathizes with the protagonists of Shakespeare's other major tragedies but at the same time cannot wholly identify with them, Shakespeare has designed *Hamlet* so that reader and viewer must solve the same problems as the prince. For example, is the Ghost telling the truth? Both Catholic and Protestant doctrine recognized that apparitions might be either demonic or angelic. Critics continue to debate the question of Old Hamlet's ghost; even though he tells the truth about his murder, he may still be a "goblin damned" rather than "a spirit of health" (1.5.40). As Banquo observes in *Macbeth,* "oftentimes, to win us to our harm, / The instruments of darkness tell us truths, / Win us with honest trifles, to betray 's / In deepest consequence" (1.3.123–126).

Because *Hamlet* is familiar even to those who have never read or seen the play, modern audiences and critics know that Claudius is guilty. Hamlet does not, although he has his suspicions, until Act III, Scene 3. Claudius's aside, "The harlot's cheek, beautified with plast'ring art, / Is not more ugly to the thing that helps it / Than is my deed to my

Johnston Forbes-Robertson as Hamlet in an 1897 production

acting, but even in the popular genre of revenge tragedy of the period, characters much less conscious and conscientious than Hamlet debated the legitimacy of private retribution. Killing a monarch would be still more questionable. Claudius, who has himself killed a king, tells Gertrude, "There's such divinity doth hedge a king / that treason can but peep to what it would, / Acts little of his will" (4.5.124–126). Shakespeare must have intended the irony, but Claudius expresses a widely held view of a king's inviolability.

Audience and character confront the same questions of what Hamlet should do. They also face the problem of whether Hamlet is mad or sane. Hamlet says that he may "put an antic disposition on" (1.5.172). In the sources from which Shakespeare drew, Amleth (the early version of Hamlet) has to play the fool-madman to survive until he can effect his revenge. In Shakespeare's play, Hamlet's unconventional behavior arouses and at length confirms the suspicion of Claudius that Hamlet intends to kill him. Charles Kemble in the early 19th century was the first to play Hamlet as truly mad, but the play clearly admits this interpretation. Perhaps Hamlet himself does not know when he is acting and when he crosses the line into actual madness. In the nunnery scene (3.1), for example, how does he speak the line "it hath made me mad" (3.1.147): "it hath made me *mad*"? Or, "it *hath* made me mad"?

Hamlet's "inky cloak [and] customary suits of solemn black" (1.2.77–78) proclaim him not only in a state of mourning but also in melancholy, a state much in vogue among Elizabethan intellectuals but considered a disease nonetheless, caused, they believed, by an imbalance of the four humors of yellow bile (choler), phlegm, blood, and black bile (melancholy). Timothy Bright's *A Treatise on Melancholy* (1586) describes the melancholic thus:

Sometimes furious, and sometimes merry in
appearance, through a kinde of sardonian,
and false laughter, . . . exact and curious in
pondering the very moments of things; . . .
given to fearefull and terrible dreames. . . .
Of memory reasonable good, if fancies deface

most painted word" (3.1.50–52), does not clearly refer to the murder. Even Claudius's reaction at *The Murder of Gonzago* might be prompted by Hamlet's thinly veiled threat to kill the king, since he identifies the murderer Lucianus as the nephew, not the brother, of the victim. That is the interpretation everyone on stage except Hamlet and Horatio place on Claudius's abrupt departure. Even Gertrude understands Claudius's reaction so.

Even more problematic for Hamlet, and for audiences since 1600, is the question of what to do even if the Ghost is telling the truth. The Ghost himself poses a paradox, demanding vengeance while enjoining Hamlet, "Taint not thy mind" (1.5.85). Hamlet's delay in obeying his dead father's cry for revenge has prompted much critical speculation. Perhaps his scruples are merely excuses for not it not, firme in opinion, and hardly remoued [difficult to dissuade] when it is resolued: doubtfull before, and long in deliberation: suspicious, painefull in studies and circumspect; (102)

Significantly, they were also capable of provoking rash and sudden actions. The above serves as an accurate summation of Hamlet's character. Bright also maintains, "Sometimes it falleth out that melancholie men are found verie wittie, and quickly discerne" (130). Or, as Polonius phrases the matter, "How pregnant sometimes his replies are! a happi-

ness that often madness hits on" (2.2.210–212). To what extent, then, is "Hamlet from himself . . . ta'en away" (5.2.234)? Does he himself know?

Hamlet's relationship with the two women in the play provides yet another puzzle. Hamlet's first soliloquy shows the prince more distressed by his mother's remarriage than by his father's death. Laurence Olivier's 1948 movie version of the play was much influenced by Ernest Jones's Oedipal reading of the prince. For the closet scene, Olivier produced a large bed, on which he (Hamlet) and Gertrude undertake much rolling around. Hamlet's speeches suggest a sense of disappointment

Publicity photo for the 1948 film version of *Hamlet,* with Laurence Olivier as Hamlet and Eileen Herlie as Gertrude

and betrayal rather than thwarted love: "Frailty, thy name is woman!" (1.2.146). Yet, he entrusts his secret to her that "I essentially am not in madness, / But mad in craft" (3.4.187–188), that he knows that Claudius has killed Old Hamlet, and that he intends to subvert Claudius's plot involving Rosencrantz and Guildenstern. Even his final words to Gertrude admit of multiple meanings. What does he intend by "Wretched queen, adieu" (5.2.333)? Even in 1600, the word might mean unhappy, contemptible, or weak. Perhaps he intends all three.

His treatment of Ophelia proves at least as perplexing. He tells her, "I loved you once" and, several lines later, "I lov'd you not" (3.1.114, 118). Though he is not mad for her love, he includes "the pangs of despis'd love" among "the whips and scorns of time" (3.1.71, 69). When he visits her in her room and behaves so oddly there, as she reports to her father in Act II, Scene 1, is he using her, as Claudius uses so many others, knowing that she will report the encounter to her father and so, for at least a time, suggest that his madness stems from disappointed love? In dismissing her, as he does "with a sigh so piteous and profound / as it did seem to shatter all his bulk / And end his being" (2.1.91–93), is he recognizing that she is too weak to help him in his quest for revenge, that despite her love for him, she would betray him to her father? Is he trying to protect her, reluctantly abandoning the woman he loves so as to spare her the consequences of the revenge he must exact? Does he pity her for the sorrow he knows she will experience as he sets about his ghost-imposed task?

The same questions arise in the nunnery scene. Hamlet's harsh treatment of Ophelia has received varying interpretations. Coleridge argued that Hamlet knows that Claudius and Polonius are spying on him, "and his after-speeches are not so much directed to her as to the listeners and spies" (Volume 4, 159). For Charles Lamb, Hamlet's words and actions here reveal not anger but grief and "love awkwardly counterfeiting hate" (200). Hazlitt argues that Hamlet's behavior springs from "disappointed hope, of bitter regrets," that his revenge bars him from wooing Ophelia as he would

Hamlet (Sir Henry Irving) orders Ophelia (Lily Brayton) to a nunnery in Act III, Scene 1. Depiction of a 1905 production of *Hamlet (Illustration by Max Cowper)*

like to do (264). Even his consigning her to a nunnery is ambiguous. Does he think her too pure to expose herself to a corrupt world? Does he think her frailty requires cloistering? By nunnery does he mean a brothel, "for virtue cannot so inoculate our old stock but we shall relish of it" (3.1.116–118)?

He mocks Ophelia with sexual innuendoes in the following scene, but when he sees her dead, he cries out: "I lov'd Ophelia. Forty thousand brothers / Could not with all their quantity of love / Make up my sum" (5.1.269–271). Her burial seems to unhinge him momentarily, as he acknowledges in conversing with Horatio soon afterward: "But I am very sorry, good Horatio, / That to Laertes I forgot myself" (5.2.75–76). This is the only action for which he apologizes in the entire play. Even in the Q2 version, though Hamlet does not speak of his remorse, when his mother suggests that he "use some gentle entertainment to Laertes" (5.2.206–207), the prince acknowledges that she is correct. Ophelia's death unnerves him as nothing else can.

However one understands Hamlet's mental state, there can be no denying his intelligence. Shakespeare gives him the most profound expressions of the human dilemma. Hamlet has no answers, but that is because there are none. He understands that to be human is to live in doubt. He recognizes, as he tells Horatio, "There are more things in heaven and earth . . . / Than are dreamt of in your [our, in the F version] philosophy" (1.5.166–167). Because the other characters lack Hamlet's perception, they are certain. Fortinbras does not question going to war for a piece of land. Laertes has no scruples about vengeance. Guildenstern and Rosencrantz collude with Claudius, even though Hamlet warns them of their fate. Hamlet easily outwits everyone in the play but the First Gravedigger.

Hamlet is not just an intellectual; he is the ideal prince, able to strike home with his wit or his sword. He can engross a royal commission and grapple with pirates, instruct actors how to perform and write dialogue for them, wrestle with Laertes in the same graveyard where he perspicaciously ponders mortality. Ophelia summarizes his qualities:

> The courtier's, soldier's, scholar's eye, tongue,
>   sword,
> Th' expectation and rose of the fair state,
> The glass of fortune and the mold of form,
> The observ'd of all observers
>
> (3.1.151–154).

Throughout the first four acts, as he vacillates between action and delay, he tries to control fate. If Hamlet has a tragic flaw, it is this. In seeking revenge, he becomes too much like his opponents. He spies on Claudius even as Claudius spies on him and plots to entrap the king just as Claudius seeks to ensnare him. He refuses to heed the Ghost's injunction to leave Gertrude to heaven and her

conscience. In Acts 1–4, he seems very much the adolescent Wittenberg undergraduate.

By Act V, however, he has matured and aged. According to the First Gravedigger (5.1), Hamlet is 30 years old, making him a rather ancient student. Yet, in this act, Hamlet reveals a new understanding of the world. He no longer defies fate but accepts it. He reflects: "There is special providence in the fall of a sparrow" (5.2.231). He recognizes: "If it be now, 'tis not to come; if it be not to come, it will be now; if it be not now, yet it will come—the readiness is all" (5.2.232–233). He has at last found the answer, or at least his answer, to the question he famously poses in Act III, Scene 1, to be or not to be, telling Horatio, "let be" (5.2.224). Working with fate rather than against it, he achieves his goal, though at the cost of his life.

Claudius

Were it not for Hamlet, Claudius would be the tragic hero of the play. He is a forerunner of Macbeth, a man undone by ambition and love. Neither old nor young Hamlet likes him. Old Hamlet, his brother, calls him "wretch" and "garbage" (1.5.51, 57). To young Hamlet, he is a "satyr," "a mildewed ear," "the bloat king" (1.2.140; 3.4.64, 181). His relationship with Gertrude probably is adulterous and certainly is incestuous. He has been played as a drunken, lascivious, cruel ruler. He has a Swiss guard that would suggest tyranny to Shakespeare's audience, and he carouses late into the night while Hamlet and his friends wait on the battlements for the Ghost to appear. He engages in espionage to try to uncover the reason for Hamlet's odd behavior, suborning his nephew's friends to help in this effort, and when he recognizes the danger Hamlet poses, Claudius arranges for Hamlet's death. When his first attempt to have Hamlet killed by Denmark's tributary English king fails, he seduces Laertes to become his instrument and succeeds, though at a far higher price than he had imagined.

Yet, Claudius can also be presented as a good ruler and loving husband whose flaws undo him, in other words, as the paradigm of the Aristotelian tragic hero. Hamlet suggests this interpretation

Claudius sits behind Polonius in this print, published by Selwyn and Blount in 1922. *(Illustration by John Austen)*

of Claudius. Listening to the sounds of the king's revelry in the castle while Hamlet stands on the battlements, the prince observes:

> So, oft it chances in particular men,
> That for some vicious mole of nature in them,
> As in their birth, wherein they may not be
>   guilty
> (Since nature cannot choose his origin),
> By their o'ergrowth of some complexion
> Oft breaking down the pales and forts of
>   reason,
> Or by some habit, that too much o'erleavens
> The form of plausible manners—that these
>   men,
> Carrying, I say, the stamp of one defect,
> Being nature's livery, or fortune's star,
> His virtues else, be they as pure as grace,
> As infinite as man may undergo,
> Shall in the general censure take corruption

> From that particular fault: the dram of eale
>   [evil?]
> Doth all the noble substance of a doubt
> To his own scandal.
>
> (1.4.23–38)

Claudius proves a competent king in dealing with the crisis created by young Fortinbras, settling the dispute peacefully. He tells Laertes of his love for Gertrude, and the play offers no evidence to contradict that claim. His protests of affection for Hamlet, whom he names as his heir to the throne, may also be sincere, at least initially. His pricks of conscience certainly are. These manifest themselves in his aside in Act III, Scene 1 (48–53) and again in Act III, Scene 3, in which he tries unsuccessfully to pray for forgiveness. This he recognizes he cannot obtain because he will not surrender the fruits of his fratricide: his crown and his queen. Like Macbeth, he had hoped that after one murder, he could reign and love peacefully; like Macbeth, he discovers that one crime begets another. As Rosencrantz observes,

> The cess of majesty
> Dies not alone, but like a gulf doth draw
> What's near it with it. Or it is a massy wheel
> Fix'd on the summit of the highest mount,
> To whose huge spokes ten thousand lesser
>   things
> Are mortis'd and adjoined, which when it falls,
> Each small annexment, petty consequence,
> Attends the boist'rous ruin.
>
> (3.3.15–22)

His killing of Old Hamlet requires him to try to kill young Hamlet as well, and those attempts lead to the deaths of Rosencrantz, Guildenstern, Laertes, Gertrude, himself, and the heir to the throne. Polonius dies spying for him, and that death causes Ophelia's. As Laertes says, "the King, the King's to blame" (5.2.320).

Gertrude

In Belleforest's (and John Updike's) retelling of the Danish story, Gertrude and Claudius were lovers before Old Hamlet's death. Old Hamlet calls Claudius "that adulterate beast" (1.5.41), and if Claudius was committing adultery, Gertrude must have been as well. She does not appear to be complicit in the death of her first husband: She is shocked when Hamlet accuses her in Act III, Scene 4. Her ascribing Hamlet's melancholy to her hasty marriage and his father's death also suggests that she knew nothing of Claudius's murder.

Although she recognizes that her remarriage was hasty, she wants her son to forget his father as quickly as she did. Perhaps she regards Hamlet's continued mourning as a rebuke to her lack of grief. When Hamlet in the closet scene contrasts the pictures of Old Hamlet and Claudius, often productions have him wear a portrait of his father around his neck while Gertrude has Claudius's around hers. She shrinks from unpleasantness: In a play that repeatedly speaks of conscience, Gertrude never uses the word, and when the mad Ophelia wishes to see her in Act IV, Scene 5, Gertrude refuses to admit the young woman until Horatio advises the queen to let Ophelia speak with her.

She will, however, defend those whom she loves. When Laertes, incensed, bursts into the castle demanding an accounting from Claudius for Polonius's death, Gertrude physically restrains him and proclaims the king's innocence in this matter. Similarly, when Laertes and Hamlet grapple in Ophelia's grave, she again tries to pacify Laertes. As Shakespeare originally drafted the play (Q2), Gertrude, in Act V, Scene 2, sends a message to Hamlet to make up with Laertes, though this part of the scene vanishes in the Folio.

In Q1, at the end of the closet scene, Gertrude agrees to help Hamlet gain his revenge, declaring,

> *Hamlet,* I vow by that maiesty,
> That knows our thoughts, and lookes into our
>   hearts,
> I will conceale, consent, and doe my best,
> What stratagem soe'er thou shalt deuise.
>
> (3.4.103–106)

Claudius (Nikolai Osipovich Massalitinov) and Gertrude (Olga Knipper) in Edward Gordon Craig and Constantin Stanislavski's 1911 production of *Hamlet*

Did Shakespeare ever write these lines into his play? Or, did the actor transcribing the play from memory incorporate lines from *The Spanish Tragedy* in which Bel-Imperia tells Hieronimo, "I will consent, conceal / And ought that may effect for thine avail, / Join with thee to revenge Horatio's death" (4.1.46–48). Perhaps the lines in Q1 appeared in the *Ur-Hamlet,* Kyd repeating himself in the two revenge tragedies.

Her attitude toward her son after the closet scene remains more ambiguous in Q2 and F. In some stagings, she remains physically distant from Claudius in the play's final two acts. Hamlet has asked her not to reveal that his madness is a mask, and when Claudius asks about her interview, she tells her husband that Hamlet is "Mad as the sea and wind when both contend / Which is the mightier" (4.1.7–8). She may thus be obeying Hamlet's request, but she may be saying what she believes. In the previous scene, Hamlet claimed to see his father's ghost, which Gertrude did not observe, and Hamlet has just stabbed Polonius. In relating this event, she tries to mitigate Hamlet's guilt by saying that Hamlet acted in madness and now "weeps for what is done" (4.1.27), when in fact Hamlet shows no remorse. Her drinking the poisoned chalice is sometimes presented as her final effort to help her son; in these performances, she recognizes that Claudius has poisoned the wine.

Polonius

In Q1, this character is named *Corambis,* the name he assumes in *Der bestrafte Brudermord* as well and that likely derives from the *Ur-Hamlet.* Sir Israel Gollancz suggested that the name comes from *corambe,* "reheated cabbage," reflecting the character's habit of repeating platitudes and himself. More likely, the word derives from the Latin *cor,* or "heart," and *ambo,* "both," hence, "two-hearted"—a man who is not what he seems.

An actor in college, he displays a passion for disguise and intrigue, seeking "By indirections [to] find directions out" (2.1.63). He dispatches Reynaldo to Paris to spy on Laertes. He devises a meeting between Ophelia and Hamlet to determine whether Hamlet is mad for Ophelia's love. Giving her a book, probably a prayer book, to hold while she waits, he comments, "with devotion's visage / And pious action we do sugar o'er / The devil himself" (3.1.46–48). He hides behind a tapestry to watch this encounter, as later he conceals himself behind another in Gertrude's room to overhear her conversation with her son. This last attempt costs him his life. As Hamlet remarks, "Thou find'st to be too busy is some danger" (3.4.33).

The advice that Polonius gives Laertes in Act I, Scene 3 perhaps supports Hamlet's judgment of the Lord Chamberlain as a "wretched, rash, intruding fool" (3.4.31). These precepts lack origi-

nality and may be drawn from John Lyly's *Euphues* (1578–80). In that novel, Euphues advises Philautus, "Be not lavish of thy tongue," and "It shall be there better to hear what they say, than to speak what thou thinkest" (226). He also counsels, "Be not quarrellous for every light occasion: they never fight without provoking, and once provoked they never cease" (226). They may also parody the precepts that William Cecil, Lord Burghley, offered his son Robert. They certainly seem ill timed: Polonius has just urged his son to hurry to his ship and then detains him with a long speech. Polonius is fond of the sound of his own voice, making lengthy addresses (though he dislikes the First Player's long speech), one of which provokes Gertrude to tell him, "More matter with less art" (2.2.95), but even this royal request cannot make him come to the point. Samuel Johnson summed him up well: "Polonius is a man bred in courts, exercised in business, stored with observation, confident in his knowledge, proud of his eloquence, and declining into dotage. . . . Such a man is positive and confident, because he knows that his mind was once strong, and knows not that it is become weak" (190).

Hamlet drags Polonius's body from the queen's chambers in Act III, Scene 4. Illustration published by Selwyn and Blount in 1922 *(Illustration by John Austen)*

Laertes

When Laertes and Hamlet are selecting their weapons for their duel, Hamlet remarks, "I'll be your foil, Laertes" (5.2.255). Throughout the work, Laertes serves as Hamlet's opposite, beginning with Shakespeare's choice of university for each. Laertes attends the University of Paris, Europe's leading Catholic institution, whereas Hamlet studies at the University at Wittenberg, Martin Luther's alma mater. Whereas Hamlet never trusts his uncle, Claudius easily pacifies Laertes, turning him into one of his agents. When the king asks what Laertes would do to gain his revenge for his dead father, Laertes replies: "To cut his throat i' th' church" (4.7.126). So, earlier, he had declared: "Conscience and grace, to the profoundest pit! / I dare damnation" (4.5.134). Hamlet and Laertes want vengeance for a dead father, but in Act III, Scene 3, Hamlet precisely does not cut Claudius's throat while the king prays. Hamlet claims that he spares Claudius to damn Claudius's soul later, but that statement seems more rationale than reason for inaction. Hamlet hesitates because he fears his own dam-

Claudius offers Hamlet poisoned wine during his swordfight against Laertes in Act V, Scene 2 of *Hamlet*. This is a plate from *Retzsch's Outlines to Shakespeare: Hamlet*, published in 1828. *(Illustration by Moritz Retzsch)*

nation, a point he makes repeatedly in his soliloquies. Laertes lacks Hamlet's scruples.

In Q1, as Laertes and Claudius devise their plan for killing Hamlet in a fencing match, Claudius suggests not only Laertes' use of an unbated foil but also poisoning the tip. In Q2 and F, the idea of the poisoned sword comes from Laertes, thus darkening his character. Just before the duel, after Hamlet asks forgiveness for offending Laertes, the latter pretends to accept his apology but still proceeds with his plan for revenge. Hamlet recognizes that both he and Laertes have lost a father and desire revenge. Laertes, however, lacks the conscience and consciousness of Hamlet and, through his deficiency, makes Hamlet shine the brighter.

Fortinbras

Like Laertes, Fortinbras serves as a foil to Hamlet. His father, too, has been killed, and to avenge that murder, he has gathered an army to attack Denmark so that he may at least regain his father's lost lands. Like Hamlet, too, he has been passed over for the throne, and the kingship has been awarded to his uncle. He is even less scrupulous than Laertes, though. Laertes will not "swoop-stake, . . . draw both friend and foe" (4.5.143). Fortinbras, whose name means "strong armed," acts without reflection; he values deeds for their own sake. Hence, when he is diverted from attacking Denmark, he marches his army against Poland. When he becomes ruler of Denmark at the end of the play, the country receives a warrior king in the mold of Old Hamlet, but in Hamlet's death, it has lost a philosopher king.

Old Hamlet

Young Hamlet idolizes his father, likening him to Hyperion, Jupiter, Mars, and Mercury (1.2.140, 3.4.56–58). But Old Hamlet is not a soul in bliss. He returns from Purgatory, where he must burn off "the foul crimes done in my days of nature" (1.5.12).

He belongs to an older world; perhaps Hamlet's classical references indicate the elder's antique

Hamlet describes him as "so loving to [Gertrude] / That he might not beteem the winds of heaven / Visit her face to roughly" (1.2.140–142). The Ghost instructs Hamlet not to "contrive / Against thy mother aught" (1.5.85–86), and in the closet scene, he urges Hamlet to "step between [Gertrude] and her fighting soul" (3.4.113). Yet, the gravedigger says that young Hamlet was born the very day that Old Hamlet killed Old Norway, so Gertrude's husband was not near her when she gave birth to their only son. Gertrude never expresses any love for her first husband and quickly ceases grieving for him. He demands love from Hamlet—"If thou didst ever thy dear father love" (1.5.23)—but never expresses love for his son in return.

Ophelia

Like so many other characters in the play, Ophelia provides a contrast to Hamlet. She manifests true madness in contrast to Hamlet's assumed antic disposition. She loves Hamlet and, despite the suspicions of Polonius and Laertes, might well have become his wife. Gertrude sought no better match for her son. She lacks, however, the strength of the character of Juliet, for example, to defy her father's wishes and so refuses to see Hamlet and then participates in the test that Polonius and Claudius devise, a chastened version of the one Feng used. In some productions, she reveals divided loyalty when Hamlet asks her, "Where's your father?" Though she lies, "At home, my lord," she may gesture to indicate that Polonius is hiding behind a tapestry (3.1.129–130).

Her relationship with Hamlet is ambiguous. Does her bawdy song in Act IV, Scene 5 result from her insanity? Or is she recalling a sexual encounter with the prince? Her mad scene and drowning have attracted many artists, especially among the pre-Raphaelites. Of the eight deaths that occur in the play, hers is the saddest because only she is wholly innocent. Shakespeare's plays repeatedly show that when evil is unleashed, it destroys not only the guilty but also the blameless.

Horatio and Marcellus try to hold Hamlet back from following the ghost of Old Hamlet in Act I, Scene 4. This illustration was designed for a 1918 edition of Charles and Mary Lamb's *Tales from Shakespeare.* (*Illustration by Louis Rhead*)

values. Only Old Hamlet appears in full armor, a medieval figure in a Renaissance court. Young Hamlet's classical references also relate to his father's demand for revenge. Belleforest places the Amleth story in pre-Christian Denmark; Christianity frowns on vengeance, at least in theory. Old Hamlet's armor relates to his military career, the only aspect of his kingship that the play mentions. He killed the king of Norway, and Horatio speaks of Old Hamlet's smiting "the sledded Polacks / poleaxe" during "an angry parle" (1.1.62–63).

A mad Ophelia sings about Polonius and Hamlet in Act IV, Scene 5 of *Hamlet.* This print is from Charles Heath's 1848 edition of *The Heroines of Shakspeare: Comprising the Principal Female Characters in the Plays of the Great Poet. (Painting by J. Hayter; engraving by W. H. Mote)*

Horatio

Hamlet praises his one true friend as

> . . . one in suff'ring all that suffers nothing,
> A man that Fortune's buffets and rewards
> Has ta'en with equal thanks;
>
> (3.2.66–68)

Horatio is the true stoic, an example of the Renaissance neo-Stoic revival. When Hamlet is dying at the end of the play, Horatio tries to kill himself in the manner of ancient Romans such as Cato. He is also a skeptic, one who takes nothing on faith. His name contains the Latin *ratio,* or "reason." He doubts the existence of the Ghost when Bernardo and Marcellus report seeing it. When Marcellus relates the legend about cocks crowing all night at the Christmas season and so banishing ghosts, Horatio replies: "So have I heard and do in part believe it" (1.1.165). In explaining the cause of Denmark's preparations for war, he says: "At least the whisper goes so" (1.1.80).

Hamlet prevents him from killing himself in Act V, Scene 2 because the prince wants Horatio to tell the world his story. Horatio thus becomes for Hamlet what Hamlet was for his father, the voice of memory. Hamlet has chosen an apt spokesman, as Horatio's name contains the Latin *oratio,* the "act of speaking." Horatio appears in the play's first scene as the person the guards have chosen to speak to the Ghost, and in that scene, he relates the cause of Denmark's warlike preparations. His Latinate name corresponds to his scholarship. Like Hamlet, he is a student at Wittenberg, and his education fits him to address a ghost in the proper manner. Hamlet trusts his powers of observation, charging him to watch Claudius's reaction to *The Murder of Gonzago.* Indeed, Hamlet trusts him with his deepest secrets.

Horatio's age is indeterminate. He is supposedly Hamlet's schoolfellow, but he says that he saw Old Hamlet killing Old Fortinbras, an event 30 years in the past. He supposedly is Danish, but he does not know about the practice of accompanying the king's drinking with fanfare, nor does he know Laertes, whom Hamlet identifies for him in Act V, Scene 1. While Hamlet trusts and consults him, no one else in the court pays attention to him.

DIFFICULTIES OF THE PLAY

Regarding *Hamlet,* the first challenge facing any student, actor, or director is to determine what Shakespeare wrote. Every one of Shakespeare's plays presents textual problems, but no text is more vexed than *Hamlet,* because the play exists in two authoritative versions and a third that comes in questionable shape but derives from performance rather than the author's manuscript. These different texts present varying visions of the work. For example, the stage direction at the beginning of Act I, Scene 2 in F reads: *"Enter Claudius King of*

Denmarke, Gertrude the Queene, Hamlet, Polonius, Laertes and his Sister Ophelia, Lords Attendant." In this procession, order and degree are observed; Hamlet is treated like a prince and heir apparent. Q1 also places Hamlet right after the king and queen. According to Q2, however, Hamlet enters at the end of the line, indicating that in the new court of Claudius, he is treated as one of the king's lesser attendants (or places himself among them). Here, what Elizabethans would have understood as the natural order is perverted, showing that something is rotten in the state of Denmark.

The confusion is apparent even to casual readers, as different modern editions print different versions of very famous lines. Does Hamlet in his first soliloquy wish that his "too too sallied flesh would melt" (1.2.129), the Q2 reading, or is his flesh "too too solid," as the Folio would have it? In Q1, his flesh is "too much grieved and sallied," and some editors have regarded "sallied" (assaulted) as a misreading for *sullied* (tainted by sin). *Sallied* links this soliloquy to that in Act III, Scene 1, in which Hamlet again reflects on the various assaults life makes on each person. *Sullied* implies that Hamlet regards the body as sinful, a view he expresses to Ophelia, also in Act III, Scene 1, while *solid* indicates his regret that the body so clings to life.

To cite but another instance, the opening of the play is completely different in the three texts. In Q1, the first sentinel (called in later printings Francisco) challenges the second, Bernardo, who is coming to relieve him. This is the proper procedure: The person on guard demands the password of the one coming to take his place. In Q2 and F, Bernardo challenges Francisco. Such a breach of protocol indicates that the time is indeed out of joint and that Bernardo is so nervous that he challenges the guard on duty. Like the court's procession in Act I, Scene 2 of Q2, the opening scene in Q2 and F depicts a maimed rite, a world turned upside down.

Even without textual confusion, Shakespeare's language always poses a challenge to modern audiences, and the language of *Hamlet* is especially complicated. Shakespeare, born in 1564, was closer in time to Chaucer, who died in 1400, than modern readers and viewers are to Shakespeare. Even though Shakespeare wrote (and spoke) what linguists call early modern English, his texts require glossing. Some of his vocabulary is long obsolete. Laertes speaks of "nature crescent" (1.3.10). In that same passage he uses the words *"cautel"* (deceit), *"credent"* (trusting), and *"blastments"* (blights), and he calls flower buds *"buttons"* (1.3.15, 30, 40, 42). Old Hamlet laments that he was killed "Unhous'led, disappointed, unanel'd" (1.5.77), that is, without benefit of the Eucharist, spiritual preparation for death, and the last rites. The visiting players' lines reflect speech patterns outdated by 1600 so that they use what even Shakespeare's first audiences would gave regarded as archaic terms, such as *"bison rheum"* (blinding tears, 2.2.506) and *"milch"* (moist, 2.2.517). Happily, modern editions gloss such terms. Students may also wish to consult the *Oxford English Dictionary* to trace the etymology and transformation of words' meanings.

No glossary, however, can eliminate all ambiguities in this play's extraordinarily dense language. Thus, in Act III, Scene 2, Hamlet toys with Ophelia:

HAMLET. Lady, shall I lie in your lap?

OPHELIA. No, my lord.

HAMLET. I mean, my head upon your lap.

OPHELIA. Ay, my lord.

HAMLET. Do you think I meant country matters?

OPHELIA. I think nothing, my lord.

HAMLET. That's a fair thought to lie between maids' legs.

OPHELIA. What is, my lord?

HAMLET. Nothing.

(112–121)

Hamlet's "country matters" means things rustic, but it is also a sexual pun. When Ophelia says that she thinks nothing, does she mean that she has no thoughts? That she, like Hamlet in his soliloquy (3.1), contemplates nothingness? That she thinks about *nothing,* a Renaissance term for female genitalia? And when Hamlet replies, "That's a fair thought to lie between maid's legs," does he mean that nothing should lie between a maid's legs, as opposed to something, that is, a penis? Or, that the thought of lying between a maid's legs is a fair, in other words, pleasant, thought? Hamlet's reply, "Nothing," might mean that thinking about female genitalia is pleasant, or it may refer back to reflecting on nothingness. Most likely, Hamlet and Shakespeare intend all these meanings at once. Similarly, when Hamlet says, "there is nothing either good or bad, but thinking makes it so" (2.2.249–250), he may be speaking as a relativist, identifying "good" and "bad" as subjective terms, or he may instead mean that nothing at all exists and we only think things are real. Or, he may intend both of these interpretations.

Beyond the language, a question that haunts the play is that of Hamlet's delay in acting against Claudius. On a practical level, if Hamlet were to learn of his father's murder in Act I, Scene 5 and kill Claudius in Act II, Scene 1, the play would be over, so some delay is necessary. But if Hamlet's hesitation had no other motivation or purpose than to sustain the length of the play, the play would indeed be what T. S. Eliot called it in his 1919 essay "Hamlet and His Problems," an artistic failure. Explaining Hamlet's procrastination, if procrastination it is, nonetheless has challenged audiences for as long as anyone has written about the work. As he does so often, Shakespeare complicates his source: In the original story, Amleth has no opportunity to avenge his father's death until he returns from England. Shakespeare (or the *Ur-Hamlet*), on the contrary, provides a perfect opportunity in Act III, Scene 3, and still Hamlet lets Claudius live.

In that scene, Hamlet says that he spares Claudius because the king is praying. Whereas Old Hamlet was killed without the opportunity of

Hamlet comes upon King Claudius praying in Act III, Scene 3. This depiction was printed in 1843. *(Illustration by Eugène Delacroix)*

repentance, leaving his soul to suffer in Purgatory, Claudius's would go straight to heaven, which to Hamlet is intolerable. He says he wants to damn his father's murderer, not just take his life. Even for those who would not hesitate at revenge, such a desire is shocking. If Hamlet means what he says, he is guilty of trying to play God, and he is to blame for all the deaths that follow in the play. A more palatable reading, for those who want to find in Hamlet the ideal Renaissance prince, would treat his words merely as another rationalization for delay. Moreover, killing someone at prayer, no matter how guilty that person may be, seems itself impious.

Other challenging aspects of the play include Hamlet's relationship with the two women characters, Ophelia and Gertrude. The character of Fortinbras, though far less complex than Hamlet's, also poses a challenge, one that again hinges in large part on textual matters. In Q1 and Q2, Fortinbras is reported to have gathered an army of "lawlesse Resolutes" (1.1.98). In F, they are "Landlesse" and hence perhaps more deserving of sympathy because Fortinbras in the Folio can be regarded as trying to recover his father's lost lands to provide living space for the homeless. The Folio also greatly condenses Act IV, Scene 4, omitting Hamlet's final soliloquy and also his exchange with a Norwegian captain, who reports that Fortinbras is fighting for a worthless piece of land.

Yet another curiosity in the work is Claudius's failure to respond to the dumb show in the play within the play, which shows the killing of a king exactly as Old Hamlet reports his murder. Yet, when the scene is played with words, Claudius becomes instantly enraged and storms away. Is Claudius able to brazen out the first representation but cannot bear to see his crime enacted twice? Perhaps what angers Claudius is not the reproduction of his crime but rather Hamlet's identifying the murderous Lucianus as the king's nephew. Hamlet thus threatens Claudius, and the prince goes on to say that Lucianus will get the love of the dead king's wife, thereby criticizing Gertrude. Is Claudius's reaction prompted by his love for her? In allowing the dumb show (which he could have omitted, and which is often cut in productions) to proceed without Claudius's reaction, does Shakespeare imply that the aural is more powerful than the visual? Shakespeare's contemporary dramatist Ben Jonson made a distinction between spectators and audiences. Spectators watch what actors do; audiences listen to the playwright's words. Perhaps Shakespeare, too, privileges the latter over the former. One way directors of the play have resolved this problem on stage is to have Claudius not see the dumb show because he is talking to Gertrude or Polonius, or to have someone blocking his view. Another interpretation, not much favored, is that

Claudius does not react to the dumb show because he did not kill Old Hamlet in that manner—in other words, the Ghost is lying to Hamlet about his death.

KEY PASSAGES
Act I, Scene 2, 129–159

HAMLET. O that this too too sallied flesh
  would melt,
Thaw, and resolve itself into a dew!
Or that the Everlasting had not fix'd
His canon 'gainst self-slaughter! O God, God,
How weary, stale, flat, and unprofitable
Seem to me all the uses of this world!
Fie on't, ah, fie! 'tis an unweeded garden
That grows to seed, things rank and gross in
  nature
Possess it merely. That it should come to this!
But two months dead, nay, not so much, not
  two.
So excellent a king, that was to this
Hyperion to a satyr, so loving to my mother
That he might not beteem the winds of heaven
Visit her face too roughly. Heaven and earth,
Must I remember? Why, she would hang on
  him
As if increase of appetite had grown
By what it fed on, and yet within a month—
Let me not think on't! Frailty, thy name is
  woman!—
A little month, or ere those shoes were old
With which she followed my poor father's
  body,
Like Niobe, all tears—why she, even she—
O God, a beast that wants discourse of reason
Would have mourned longer—married with
  my uncle,
My father's brother, but no more like my father
Than I to Hercules. Within a month,
Ere yet the salt of most unrighteous tears
Had left the flushing in her galled eyes,
She married—O most wicked speed: to post
With such dexterity to incestuous sheets,
It is not, nor it cannot come to good,
But break my heart, for I must hold my tongue.

Even though he has not yet seen his father's ghost or learned of Claudius's foul deed, Hamlet already is distraught. This first of his soliloquies reflects his disordered mind through its tortured syntax. It contains few complete sentences, and it lurches from topic to topic. Hamlet's sense of time is equally unsettled, as the interval between Old Hamlet's death and Gertrude's remarriage shrinks from two months to one month to less than a month to less than the time it takes for tears to dry.

Gertrude's marriage is indeed hasty: In 16th-century England a woman was expected to mourn her husband for at least a year. Anne of Bohemia, daughter of James I, would mourn hers for more than a decade. Hamlet is also correct in calling the marriage incestuous. Leviticus 18:16 and 20:21 forbade the marrying of a brother's wife, though Deuteronomy 25:5–10 made an exception if the brother died without issue. Shakespeare's audience would have recalled that Henry VIII had required a papal dispensation to marry Catherine of Aragon, who had been the wife of Henry's older brother, Arthur. After Arthur died, Henry and Catherine wed. Twenty years later, Henry claimed that their failure to produce a male heir was God's punishment for incest, and he asked the pope to annul their union. When the pope refused, Henry broke with the Catholic Church to marry Anne Boleyn, mother of the sitting queen in 1600.

In this speech, Hamlet mourns his mother's remarriage more than his father's death. Throughout the play, he will lament the former more than the latter. His sense of betrayal is reflected in his reference to Niobe, who wept so much for her dead children that she turned to stone. Gertrude would have been weeping for her deceased husband, but Hamlet's classical reference, drawn from Shakespeare's favorite Roman writer, Ovid, rhetorically makes Hamlet the object of her false tears and, hence, betrayal. He extrapolates what he regards as her treachery to the entire female sex, thus poisoning his relationship with Ophelia. For Hamlet, no woman can be trusted; all are sexually voracious. Therefore, in Act III, Scene 1, he will consign Ophelia to a nunnery as the only location where she might remain chaste, or to a brothel as a fitting place for female sexual depravity.

This soliloquy employs the doubling of words that characterizes Hamlet's speech throughout the play. It also reveals Hamlet's hatred for his uncle, whom he compares to a satyr, probably Pan, who was brother to Hyperion/Apollo. And it expresses the *tedium vitae* (weariness for life) that afflicts Hamlet even before the Ghost has imposed upon him the task of revenge or revealed how out of joint the times are.

A key image of the speech is the Garden of Eden. Hamlet implies that when his father lived and was married to Gertrude, his world existed in a state of innocence. In Act I, Scene 5, Old Hamlet will develop this reference to paradise lost when he says that he was killed in his garden, supposedly by a serpent. That serpent, Old Hamlet says, now wears the Danish crown. Here, in Act I, Scene 2, Hamlet seems to regard Gertrude as the snake who has destroyed his innocence through her lust that has led to her hasty remarriage. The sibilants in "post / with such dexterity to incestuous sheets" conjure up the very hissing of the sexual serpent Hamlet imagines his mother to be. She is not the virginal *hortus conclusus* (an enclosed garden related with the Virgin Mary in the Renaissance) but rather a postlapsarian garden that has gone to seed, representing her sexualized body. The references to Hyperion and satyr reinforce this theme of sexuality. As sun god, Hyperion impregnates chastely with his beams, unlike the lascivious satyr. The reading of "sallied flesh," here, as *sullied* flesh, as offered in other versions, would be consistent with the sexual nausea Hamlet expresses throughout this speech.

Act II, Scene 2, 576–633

HAMLET. O, what a rogue and peasant slave
  am I!
Is it not monstrous that this player here,
But in a fiction, in a dream of passion,
Could force his soul so to his own conceit
That from her working all the visage wann'd,
Tears in his eyes, distraction in his aspect,

A broken voice, an' his whole function suiting
With forms to his conceit? And all for nothing,
For Hecuba!
What's Hecuba to him, or he to Hecuba,
That he should weep for her? What would
 he do
Had he the motive and the cue for passion
That I have? He would drown the stage with
 tears,
And cleave the general ear with horrid speech,
Make mad the guilty, and appall the free,
Confound the ignorant, and amaze indeed
The very faculties of eyes and ears. Yet I,
A dull and muddy-mettled rascal, peak
Like John-a-dreams, unpregnant of my cause,
And can say nothing; no, not for a king,
Upon whose property and most dear life
A damn'd defeat was made. Am I a coward?
Who calls me villain, breaks my pate across,
Plucks off my beard and blows it in my face,
Tweaks me by the nose, gives me the lie i' th'
 throat
As deep as to the lungs? Who does me this?
Hah, 'swounds, I should take it; for it
 cannot be
But I am pigeon-liver'd, and lack gall
To make oppression bitter, or ere this
I should 'a' fatted all the region kites
With this slave's offal. Bloody, bawdy villain!
Remorseless, treacherous, lecherous, kindless
 villain!
Why, what an ass am I! This is most brave,
That I, the son of a dear father murthered,
Prompted to my revenge by heaven and hell,
Must like a whore unpack my heart with
 words,
And fall a-cursing like a very drab,
A stallion. Fie upon't, foh!
About, my brains! Hum—I have heard
That guilty creatures sitting at a play
Have by the very cunning of the scene
Been strook so to the soul, that presently
They have proclaim'd their malefactions.
For murther, though it have no tongue, will
 speak

With most miraculous organ. I'll have these
 players
Play something like the murder of my father
Before mine uncle, I'll observe his looks,
I'll tent him to the quick. If 'a do blench,
I know my course. The spirit that I have seen
May be a dev'l, and the dev'l hath power
T' assume a pleasing shape, yea, and perhaps,
Out of my weakness and my melancholy,
As he is very potent with such spirits,
Abuses me to damn me. I'll have grounds
More relative than this—the play's the thing
Wherein I'll catch the conscience of the King.

Hamlet in many ways is a play about acting. In this second of his soliloquies, Hamlet begins by reflecting on the artificiality of the stage, and he concludes by noting the real influence of the theater on its spectators. Shakespeare challenges his audience by pointing out the unreality of the situation that the player has just created in his speech: Priam killed by Pyrrhus and Hecuba mourning for him. So, too, Hamlet, Polonius, Ophelia, and the rest of the cast of the play being staged at the Globe are but shadows creating an insubstantial pageant. Yet, the actor who delivered those lines about Hecuba was himself moved, and those watching *Hamlet* are emotionally involved. F. Scott Fitzgerald said that a first-class intelligence can maintain two opposing ideas at once. Hamlet possesses that quality.

Recognizing the theater's power, Hamlet intends to use *The Murder of Gonzago* to test Claudius's guilt. Hamlet recognizes what his audience understood about spirits: They might be demonic. Whereas Laertes and Fortinbras act without thinking, Hamlet refuses to behave rashly. Unlike Laertes, he will not "dare damnation" (4.5.134).

This speech is infected with the rhetoric of the First Player, as by railing against Claudius, the prince tries to arouse in himself the emotional state that he has just witnessed. He is too honest to persevere in this effort, though. He understands that in speaking so, he acts like a prostitute (or an actor), who pretends to feel what she (or he) does not. Ophelia observes that Hamlet is "as good as a chorus" (3.2.245). Here, he illustrates that quality by commenting on his own speech, demonstrating the extent of his consciousness and self-awareness.

Act III, Scene 1, 56–88

HAMLET. To be, or not to be, that is the
  question:
Whether 'tis nobler in the mind to suffer
The slings and arrows of outrageous fortune,
Or to take arms against a sea of troubles,
And by opposing, end them. To die, to sleep—
No more, and by a sleep to say we end
The heart-ache and the thousand natural
  shocks
That flesh is heir to; 'tis a consummation
Devoutly to be wish'd. To die, to sleep—
To sleep, perchance to dream—ay, there's the
  rub,
For in that sleep of death what dreams may
  come,
When we have shuffled off this mortal coil,
Must give us pause; there's the respect
That makes calamity of so long life:
For who would bear the whips and scorns of
  time,
Th' oppressor's wrong, the proud man's
  contumely,
The pangs of despis'd love, the law's delay,
The insolence of office, and the spurns
That patient merit of th' unworthy takes,
When he himself might his quietus make
With a bare bodkin; who would fardels bear,
To grunt and sweat under a weary life,
But that the dread of something after death,
The undiscover'd country, from whose bourn
No traveler returns, puzzles the will,
And makes us rather bear those ills we have,
Than fly to others that we know not of?
Thus conscience does make cowards of us all,
And thus the native hue of resolution
Is sicklied o'er with the pale cast of thought,
And enterprises of great pitch and moment
With this regard their currents turn awry,
And lose the name of action.

Hamlet's third (and in the Folio version, final) soliloquy is so well known that its brilliance can be lost in familiarity. Charles Lamb commented, "I confess myself utterly unable to appreciate that celebrated soliloquy in *Hamlet,* beginning, 'To be, or not to be,' or to tell whether it be good, bad, or indifferent; it has been so handled and pawed about by declamatory boys and men, and torn so inhumanly from its living place and principle of continuity in the play, till it has become to me a perfect dead member" (192). In Q1, the speech's "living place" is in Act II, Scene 2, before Hamlet has devised his plot involving *The Murder of Gonzago.* In that location, his soliloquy seems a continuation of his contemplation of suicide that he broached in Act I, Scene 2. Just before Hamlet delivers these lines in Q1, Claudius remarks: "see where hee comes poring vppon a booke." Thus, this speech responds to something he is reading, perhaps Aristotle, perhaps Christopher Marlowe's *Doctor Faustus.* Both contain the soliloquy's opening words. Given this context, the version in Q1 does not seem as garbled as it might otherwise appear. In Q1, the speech begins:

> To be, or not to be, I there's the point,
> To Die, to sleepe, is that all? I all:
> No, to sleepe, to dreame, I mary there it goes.

In moving this speech to the third act, Shakespeare—presumably it was he who relocated it—turns the lines from a melancholic's reflection on suicide to a profound though enigmatic meditation on the human condition. Though often understood as a speech about suicide, Hamlet's lines do not express a wish to die but rather ponder how to live. Having devised a test of Claudius's guilt, Hamlet has moved beyond his state of despair.

The opening words raise a much deeper question: What is the nature of being? For Augustine and Plato, contemplation is the highest state of existence. Dante represented this view in his *Paradiso,* where the three highest spheres contain the contemplatives. Renaissance humanism, however, valued action: "A man of words but not of deeds /

Herbert Beerbohm Tree as Hamlet in an 1892 production of *Hamlet*.

to determine how to behave in it. Francis Bacon wrote, "In this theatre of man's life it is reserved only for God and Angels to be lookers on" (380). Sir Richard Barckley, in his *Discourse of the Felicitie of Man* (1598), maintained: "For he deserveth not the name of a good man, that forbeareth to do evil, as though good were a privation, & a defect only from evil. . . . For good is not a defect, but an effect: not placed in idlenesse, but in doing." Polonius's discussion of Hamlet's supposed madness, in which he speaks of "the cause of this effect, / Or rather say, the cause of this defect" (2.2.101–102), indicates that Shakespeare had read Barckley.

Hamlet recognizes, though, that "there is nothing either good or bad, but thinking makes it so" (2.2.249–250). He is restrained by conscience in the sense of that inner monitor of what is right and wrong, but also by his consciousness, by his acute awareness. Fyodor Dostoyevsky's Grand Inquisitor remarks in *The Brothers Karamazov* (1879–80), "Nothing is more beguiling to man than freedom of conscience, but nothing is more tormenting either." Small wonder, then, that at the end of his meditation on how to live in a fallen world without falling himself, Hamlet asks for Ophelia's prayers: "Nymph, in thy orisons / Be all my sins rememb'red" (3.1.88–89). Only in Act V will Hamlet find the answer to life's persistent questions he poses here. He will discover the proper solution to the riddle of to be or not to be as he tells Horatio, "let be" (5.2.224).

DIFFICULT PASSAGES
Act II, Scene 2, 490–519

FIRST PLAYER. Anon he finds him
Striking too short at Greeks. His antique
  sword,
Rebellious to his arm, lies where it falls,
Repugnant to command. Unequal match'd,
Pyrrhus at Priam drives, in rage strikes wide,
But with the whiff and wind of his fell sword
Th' unnerved father falls. Then senseless
  Ilium,
Seeming to feel this blow, with flaming top
Stoops to his base, and with a hideous crash

Is like a garden full of weeds," Hamlet's unweeded garden. Should one submit to suffering in Christian humility? Or, should one act to remove the cause(s) of that suffering, not by killing oneself but rather, in Hamlet's case, by avenging his father's death? Such action will, however, carry with it consequences not only in this world but also in the next. Unlike Macbeth, Hamlet will not, cannot, "jump the life to come" (*Macbeth* 1.7.7).

Though a prince, Hamlet faces the same trials any other person confronts. The woman he loves refuses to see him. A man who has wronged him and his family has gone unpunished for his crime. Hamlet also must answer the universal question of how the good person should act. He is not concerned in this speech with metaphysics but with ethics, not with leaving the world but in trying

Takes prisoner Pyrrhus' ear; for lo his sword,
Which was declining on the milky head
Of reverent Priam, seem'd i' th' air to stick.
So as a painted tyrant Pyrrhus stood
And, like a neutral to his will and matter,
Did nothing.
But as we often see, against some storm,
A silence in the heavens, the rack stand still,
The bold winds speechless, and the orb below
As hush as death, anon the dreadful thunder
Doth rend the region; so after Pyrrhus' pause,
A roused vengeance sets him new a-work,
And never did the Cyclops' hammers fall
On Mars's armor forg'd for proof eterne
With less remorse than Pyrrhus' bleeding sword
Now falls on Priam.
Out, out, thou strumpet Fortune! All you gods,
In general synod take away her power!
Break all the spokes and fellies from her wheel,
And bowl the round nave down the hill of
    heaven
As low as to the fiends!

Hamlet has asked for a taste of the actors' quality, that is, a sample of their skills, and he recalls a play that was either never acted or staged but once, because it did not please the multitude. A particular speech in this work pleased him: part of Aeneas's account to Dido of the fall of Troy. Hamlet begins the monologue and then yields to the First Player, who relates the death of Priam. Shakespeare often pays homage to his great predecessor Marlowe, that marvelous youth who perished in his prime. Marlowe and Nashe had written *Dido, Queen of Carthage*, which includes the story of Priam's death. The inflated, archaic language reflects a less naturalistic approach to theater than that adopted by Shakespeare's company. Edward Alleyn, who was the star of the Lord Admiral's Men and who played Marlowe's leading men, chose a more stylized manner, which may be represented here.

The subject is relevant to *Hamlet* because Pyrrhus acts to avenge his father's death. Paris, Priam's son, had killed Pyrrhus's father, Achilles, in the temple of Diana. Pyrrhus therefore has the same cause as Hamlet and, later, Laertes, but the Greek avenger resembles the latter more than the former. Here, all sympathy is for the victim, who is himself not the offender. Those in Shakespeare's audience who knew their classics would have recalled that Achilles pitied Priam and refrained from harming the old man when Priam came to reclaim Hector's body. This passage thus problematizes the Ghost's desire for revenge, and it shows why Hamlet hesitates to act as his father's spirit instructed him.

Pyrrhus's sword suspended over Priam's head anticipates Hamlet's sword poised to kill Claudius in Act III, Scene 3. Whereas Hamlet sheathes his sword, Pyrrhus does not. More generally, Pyrrhus's momentary pause resembles Hamlet's long delay. The speech links the death of Priam and fall of Troy. So the death of Old Hamlet has disordered Denmark, as shown in the play's various maimed rites, from the opening scene to Ophelia's funeral and the final fencing match.

Act III, Scene 2, 196–224

PLAYER KING. I do believe you think what
    now you speak,
But what we do determine, oft we break.
Purpose is but the slave of memory,
Of violent birth, but poor validity,
Which now, the fruit unripe, sticks on the tree,
But fall unshaken when they mellow be.
Most necessary 'tis that we forget
To pay ourselves what to ourselves is debt.
What to ourselves in passion we propose,
The passion ending, doth the purpose lose.
The violence of either grief or joy
Their own enactures with themselves destroy.
Where joy most revels, grief doth most lament;
Grief joys, joy grieves, on slender accident.
This world is not for aye, nor 'tis not strange
That even our loves should with our fortunes
    change:
For 'tis a question left us yet to prove,
Whether love lead fortune, or fortune love.
The great man down, you mark his favorite
    flies,
The poor advanc'd makes friends of enemies.

And hitherto doth love on fortune tend,
For who in want a hollow friend doth try,
Directly seasons him his enemy.
But orderly to end where I begun,
Our wills and fates do so contrary run
That our devices still are overthrown,
Our thoughts are ours, their ends none of our
 own:
So think thou wilt no second husband wed,
But die thy thoughts when thy first lord is dead.

The Player Queen has just pledged eternal loyalty to her husband's memory and never to remarry. The Player King is not convinced that she will keep her word. Though Hamlet chose the imaginary *Murder of Gonzago* to play before Claudius to test his guilt, the work equally addresses female frailty, since the Player Queen will remarry, and her second husband will be her first husband's killer. Gertrude is therefore as much the target of the play as Claudius is.

The Player King sounds like Claudius. The comment "Grief joys, joy grieves" (3.2.199) recalls Claudius's oxymoronic statement that he married Gertrude shortly after burying his brother "With an auspicious, and a drooping eye, / With mirth in funeral, and with dirge in marriage" (1.2.11–12).

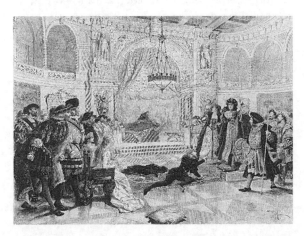

Claudius rises to leave during *The Murder of Gonzago*, in a 19th-century production of Act III, Scene 2 of *Hamlet*. *(Illustration by Adrien-Emmanuel Marie)*

In that same scene, Claudius observes to Hamlet that every father eventually dies. The echoing speeches show that Claudius, too, is a player king, someone pretending to be the monarch but not legitimately so. He has usurped the throne from his brother and stolen it from Hamlet, who should have succeeded to the crown. The shift in fortune that the Player King notes also reflects on Claudius. Commenting on changes in fortune, Hamlet had observed to Rosencrantz and Guildenstern, "those that would make mouths at [Claudius] while my father liv'd, give twenty, forty, fifty, a hundred ducats for his picture in little" (2.2.364–366). Or, as King Lear puts it, "A dog's obey'd in office" (*King Lear,* 4.6.158–159).

The actor's speech excuses Hamlet's delay. He had promised to avenge his father quickly, but in the succeeding two months, he has not acted. Perhaps he really distrusts the Ghost and wishes to test him. Perhaps, though, his passion has cooled. The Player King further warns that plots can go awry. Hamlet's plan for revenge has so far miscarried. So, too, have the schemes of Polonius and Claudius, and both plotters will be hoist with their own petards: "Our thoughts are ours, their ends none of our own." Hamlet will come to accept this truth, acknowledging, "There's a divinity that shapes our ends, / Rough-hew them how we will" (5.2.10–11).

CRITICAL INTRODUCTION
TO THE PLAY
Themes

Ophelia describes Hamlet as "The courtier's, soldier's, scholar's eye, tongue, sword / Th' expectation and rose of the fair state, / The glass of fashion and the mould of form" (3.1.151–153). Shakespeare seems to have fashioned Hamlet after Castiglione's ideal courtier, one who unites Mars (action) and Mercury (reason). He presents the antithesis of the Machiavellian prince. In his first conversation with his mother, Hamlet declares: "I know not 'seems'" (1.2.76). Machiavelli had urged rulers to pretend to possess good qualities they actually lacked. Hamlet rejects such pretense, thereby distinguishing himself from Claudius and his court.

Claudius, on the other hand, is the ultimate pretender, a fratricide-regicide who has usurped the Danish throne, which rightly belongs to Hamlet as son of the deceased monarch. In his first speech, Claudius feigns sadness for his brother's death, but he has hastily married Old Hamlet's widow. Later, he will make a show of praying. He pretends to send Hamlet to England for the prince's safety but in fact to have him executed. He stages a fencing match that in reality is an attempt to assassinate his nephew. Gertrude seemed to love her first husband but soon forgets him. Rosencrantz and Guildenstern act as if they are Hamlet's friends but serve as Claudius's agents.

Hamlet's challenge in such a world is to penetrate the Machiavellian masks that surround him, to distinguish reality from appearance. Is the ghost his father's spirit or a devil that has assumed his father's shape? How guilty is his mother? Whom can he trust? He rejects Horatio's radical skepticism and rationality as inadequate tools for discovering truth, but what can he substitute for these?

The answer may lie in the very essence of the drama itself. Acting can be pure feigning, but it can also expose, even create, a higher truth. Hence Hamlet, who shuns seeming, will assume an antic disposition. In the privileged guise of the court fool, he can, like other of Shakespeare's jesters, speak and discover truths barred to those who supposedly possess more of their wits, though less wit. Hence, too, he uses the visiting players to expose Claudius's guilt and determine the Ghost's veracity.

Even Hamlet's intelligence, though, cannot always distinguish reality from illusion. He easily determines that Rosencrantz and Guildenstern are spying on him and not to be trusted. He exposes Claudius's murder. He cannot, however, know that Claudius's prayers are ineffectual in Act III, Scene 3; he does not suspect Laertes and Claudius of plotting his death in the climactic duel. He kills Polonius, thinking that the king is hiding behind the tapestry in Gertrude's room.

In this work, as in all his others, Shakespeare challenges his audiences to recognize the indeterminacy of reality. The play within the play is the perfect vehicle for making this point. The audience at the Globe watches Claudius and his court watch a production of *The Murder of Gonzago,* which is a version of the story of *Hamlet.* When Horatio asks Fortinbras and the English ambassadors, "What is it you would see? / If aught of woe or wonder, cease your search" (5.2.362–363), he is speaking to the audience as well as to those on stage. Similarly, when the dying Hamlet addresses "you that look pale, and tremble at this chance, / That are but mutes or audience to this act," he refers not just to his fellow actors but to everyone in the theater (5.2.334–335). Hamlet's letter to Ophelia similarly challenges scientific certainty:

Doubt thou the stars are fire,
Doubt that the sun doth move,
Doubt truth to be a liar . . .

(2.2.116–118)

This letter's final line offers the only palliative to all this doubting: "But never doubt I love" (2.2.119).

Hamlet's undoubted love for his father places him in a dilemma posed by the Ghost's injunctions. As the embodiment of an older, chivalric order, he requires his son to avenge his murder. At the same time, he tells Hamlet, "Taint not thy mind," and his last words are "remember me" (1.5.85, 91). The Ghost thus lays upon Hamlet three distinct and incompatible commands. In *Hamlet,* Shakespeare writes not only a revenge tragedy but also a commentary upon the genre and its underlying morality.

As Eleanor Prosser demonstrates in *Hamlet and Revenge* (1971), the subject of revenge was hot in question when Shakespeare wrote this play. In church, Elizabethans would have heard in the reading from *Certaine Sermons or Homilies,* "In so going about to revenge evil, we shew our selves to be evil, and, while we will punish, and revenge another mans folly, we double, and augment our own folly." Innocent Gentillet's *A*

Discourse . . . Against Nicholas Machiavelli the Florentine, translated by Simon Patericke (1602), declares vengeance to be "not onely farre from all Christian pietie, but also from all humanitie and common sense". *The Catechism of Thomas Becon* (1560) maintains, "After this manner ought all Christians to be affected, not to revenge, but ready to forgive, . . . not to render evil for evil, but to overcome evil with goodness, leaving all vengeance to God, which saith: 'Vengeance is mine: I will reward.'"

Other voices challenged this position. Barckley's *A Discourse of the Felicitie of Man* observed, "All praise patience, and yet who resisteth the sweet passion of revenge?" Geoffrey Fenton's *Golden Epistles* (1577) similarly recognized the appeal of vengeance: "to the nature of man, nothing is more Sweete then the passion of revenge." Sir William Segar argued in favor of revenge in his *Book of Honour and Armes* (1590). In his 1600 essay "Of Patience," William Cornwallis debates with himself whether he would avenge a wrong done to him. He knows he should not but concludes he would not "refuse the first good quarrel and . . . performe it as well as I can."

The theater also presented opposing views. John Pykerying's *Horestes* (1567) put Aeschylus's *Oresteia* on the Elizabethan stage. Orestes kills his mother, Clytemnestra, in revenge for her killing his father. He becomes king and marries the daughter of Menelaus. Hieronomo avenges his son's death in Kyd's *The Spanish Tragedy.* He, like Hamlet, dies in achieving his revenge but is promised happiness in Elysium. The Senate approves the vengeance of the eponymous character in John Marston's *Antonio's Revenge* (ca. 1600). Cordelia invades England to avenge the wrongs done to Lear; Macduff kills Macbeth for his executing Macduff's wife and children. Both avengers appear admirable.

Cyril Tourneur's plays offer a different take on the subject. The aptly named avenger Vindici in *The Revenger's Tragedy* (ca. 1606) is a nasty piece of business. In *The Atheist's Tragedy* (ca. 1607), the ghost of Charlemont's father tells his son not to avenge his death. Frankford in *A Woman Killed*

with Kindness (1602) and Malevole in Marston's *The Malcontent* (1604) eschew revenge. The avenging Aaron and Tamora are the villains of *Titus Andronicus.*

Even the Scriptures provide a mixed message. The Hebrew Bible repeatedly describes situations in which God orders vengeance. David on his deathbed tells his son Solomon to reward certain people for their kindnesses but to punish others. *The Catechism of Thomas Becon* quotes from Romans 12:19. The next chapter in Romans reads, however, "The prince is the minister of God to take vengeance on him that doeth evil" (13:4). In his second soliloquy, Hamlet declares that he is "Prompted to my revenge by heaven and hell" (2.2.584), highlighting the problem that the play refuses to answer and that goes far in explaining Hamlet's hesitancy to act: Is the Ghost's urging him to vengeance demonic or divine, actual justice or what Bacon called "wild justice" ("Of Justice," 1625)? Pyrrhus and Laertes are unattractive avengers in the play. How can Hamlet avoid resembling them?

Hamlet's problem is compounded by Claudius's kingship. Claudius has himself killed and usurped a legitimate ruler. Elizabeth's grandfather had taken the throne from a sitting king, Richard III, and she had, however reluctantly, ordered the execution of Mary, Queen of Scots. Shakespeare's history plays had shown the repeated depositions that punctuated the Wars of the Roses. Fear of a recurrence of the chaos of that prolonged civil war as well as a philosophical view of the king as God's agent on earth prompted many works warning against regicide. Just as Elizabethans heard in church a homily against revenge, so they would have been told that "a rebel is worse than the worst prince, and rebellion worse than the worst government of the worst prince that hitherto hath been" ("The Homily against Disobedience and Willful Rebellion"). The Protestant bishop John Hooper refused to support Lady Jane Grey's claim to the throne, siding with Mary Tudor even though she was Catholic, because he believed the latter had a better claim to the throne. Even though Pope Pius V's bull *Regnans in Excelsis* (1570) exempted Catholics from obedience to Elizabeth, the Catholic Sir Thomas Tresham remained loyal to the queen.

Some Protestants and Catholics took the opposite position. In 1580, the Catholic Humphrey Ely sought to kill the queen. Pope Gregory XIII endorsed his plan. In 1589, a Catholic theology student assassinated the French king, Henry III, in revenge for his killing the leaders of the Catholic League, which in the 1580s had sought to deny the Protestant Henry de Bourbon, Henry III's son, the throne and supported Cardinal Charles de Bourbon, Henry III's brother, instead. Juan de Mariana's *De Rege et Regis Institutione* (1599) justified regicide. So did John Knox, chaplain to the very Protestant Edward VI: "For it is no less blasphemy to say that God hath commanded Kings to be obeyed when they command iniquity, than to say that God by his precept is author and maintainer of all iniquity" (389). John Calvin defended the deposition of unjust rulers, as did George Buchanan's *De Jure Regni apud Scotos* (1578).

Thomas Bilson tried to distinguish between justifiable and wrongful tyrannicide in *The True Difference between Christian Subjection and Unchristian Rebellion* (1585), a work dedicated to Queen Elizabeth. He argued the Anglican position of passive obedience to Elizabeth, but he also supported toppling Catholic monarchs abroad. In addition, he differentiated between hereditary and elective rulers, maintaining that the latter lacked the legitimacy of the former. Only in the last scene of *Hamlet* does the audience learn that Denmark is an elective monarchy. Elizabethans would have expected young Hamlet to succeed his father and so, throughout the play, would have viewed Claudius as a usurper. Making him elected does not remove from him the air of illegitimacy, but it does make his assassination less problematic. Still, the play recognizes even as it questions the divinity that doth hedge a king and makes Hamlet's task even more difficult than if he had been asked to kill a commoner.

"Revenge," "Taint not thy mind," "remember me": Is the second command compatible with the third any more than with the first? *Hamlet* is an act of remembrance. It is impossible not to link the tragedy's title with Shakespeare's only son, Hamnet, who died in 1596. There are the Marlovian echoes in the first words of Hamlet's best-known soliloquy and the First Player's speech in Act II, Scene 2. There is the tribute to Marlowe's roommate, Kyd, probable author of the *Ur-Hamlet*. Like Pan's pipes and Apollo's laurel, grief is transmuted into art.

But memory can be debilitating as well as creative. Ophelia's grief maddens her; Laertes' and Pyrrhus's grief turn them into conscienceless killers. For four acts, Hamlet is trapped in memory. Only in the play's final act is he able to triumph over the past. Accepting death's universality in a cemetery, Hamlet can, however briefly, become again the prince that Ophelia described in Act III, Scene 1. In this final act, he no longer communes with himself in soliloquies; he is no longer ghost haunted. He can assert his identity, proclaiming himself "Hamlet the Dane" (5.1.257). He kills Claudius, not for his father, but for himself (and perhaps his mother). In Act I, Scene 5 he had dedicated himself to his father's command, but in Act V, Scene 2 the orders he gives are his own. And his final injunction to Horatio erases even as it repeats that of the Ghost's "Remember me," for it is his own life, not his father's death, that he wants recalled.

Structure

Hamlet observes a classical five-act structure. The first act provides the necessary background information and introduces the major characters. In the second act, these characters plan their various stratagems. Hamlet uses *The Murder of Gonzago* to determine Claudius's guilt. Polonius stages a meeting between Hamlet and Ophelia to test his theory that the prince is mad for love. Claudius employs Rosencrantz and Guildenstern to learn why Hamlet is acting strangely. Together, these first two acts form what Aristotle called the play's protasis. These plots begin to work out in Act III (Aristotle's epitasis, or development stage). Hamlet's encounter with Ophelia explodes Polonius's explanation for

Hamlet's antic disposition; the play within the play exposes Claudius's guilt.

The climax comes in Act III, Scene 3. Hamlet has the perfect opportunity to kill Claudius but does not. His restraint will lead to the deaths of Polonius, Ophelia, Rosencrantz, Guildenstern, Laertes, and Gertrude, as well as his own demise. The first of these deaths follows at once in Act III, Scene 4. Once Polonius dies, the subsequent catastrophes become inevitable. Ophelia's death follows in Act IV, which concludes with the plot of the duel that will enmesh the remainder of the victims. Hamlet's return in Act V prepares the way for the tragic conclusion that unfolds in the final scene (5.2).

The play may also be viewed as built around three court scenes equidistantly spaced. In the first of these (1.2), set in daylight, Hamlet's inky cloak is the only dark spot among the bright attire and pomp. Claudius controls the action, dispatching ambassadors to Norway, allowing Laertes to return to school, and preventing Hamlet from doing so. The second court scene (3.2) occurs at night, indicative of darkness growing to engulf the characters and representative of the poison that Claudius has loosed and that is spreading in Elsinore. Lucianus, who is Hamlet's double (nephew to the king) as well as Claudius's (regicide) in the play within the play, probably mirrors Hamlet's dark attire. His speech certainly invokes the same gloomy imagery as the prince's mourning garb: "Thoughts black, hands apt, drugs fit, and time agreeing, / Confederate season, else no creature seeing, / Thou mixture rank, of midnight weeds collected (3.2.255–257). Claudius imagines himself still in control, unaware that for Hamlet *The Murder of Gonzago* serves as "The Mousetrap." By scene's end, Hamlet has seized the initiative. Claudius's guilt is clear to him (though not yet to the court) as Claudius flees, leaving the stage to the prince.

The final court scene (5.2), which ends the play, again occurs in daylight. Yet, at the Globe in late fall and winter, the shadows would be long, as evening would be closing in; it would be about 4:00 P.M. or even a bit later when this scene opens. The poison manifested by blackness in the first two

In this photograph published by the Byron Company in 1903, Hamlet (Edmund Russell) utters his last words to Horatio, while around him lie Claudius (William Hazeltine), Gertude (Louise Morewin), and Laertes.

court scenes is invisible on stage except through those shadows; even Hamlet no longer wears black. Yet, the audience is aware that Laertes' foil and the stoup of wine are tainted, and by the end of this scene, four bodies will lie dead on stage as a result. The scene works out Claudius's plot to kill Hamlet. As such, the king directs the action initially. But his plan goes horribly awry, making these events a synopsis of all his frustrated efforts. Hamlet orders that the doors be locked (5.2.311), and Claudius's appeal for help goes unheeded, just as his request that Gertrude not drink the poisoned wine is ignored (5.2.290–291). Hamlet has achieved his revenge, and for a few moments, he is officially ruler of Denmark. Hamlet has triumphed over Claudius, though at the expense of his own life.

Shakespeare alternates moments of tension with calm or comic relief. Hamlet's encounter with his father's ghost (1.5) precedes Polonius's instructions to Reynaldo to spy on Laertes (2.1). Hamlet's confrontation with Ophelia at the end of Act III, Scene 1 is succeeded by his address to the players at the beginning of Act III, Scene 2. Even within scenes, this alternation occurs. When Hamlet confronts Gertrude at the beginning of Act III, Scene

4, he is filled with passionate intensity, but after the Ghost appears following line 101, the prince becomes less agitated.

Such mood shifts reflect the skilled playwright's recognition that audiences need opportunities to relax. The juxtaposition of scenes also serves as commentary. In Act II, Scene 1, Ophelia reports Hamlet's visit to her closet. Even though this event occurs two months after Act I, Scene 5, it results from the prince's encounter there with the Ghost. Hamlet's rationality in addressing the players immediately after railing at Ophelia suggests that he was assuming an antic disposition in Act III, Scene 1 and not truly mad.

The play's structure moreover conveys the sense of delay. At the end of Act I, Scene 1, Marcellus, Bernardo, and Horatio resolve to inform Hamlet of their sighting of the ghost. They do not fulfill that intention for 200 lines. At the end of Act I, Scene 2, the men resolve to watch on the battlements that night, but they must wait until Act I, Scene 4; Polonius's dismissal of Laertes and warning to Ophelia intervene in Act I, Scene 3. Having learned of Ophelia's encounter with Hamlet in her closet, Polonius resolves to inform the king (end of 2.1), but first the ambassadors to Norway report on the success of their mission (beginning of 2.2). Also in Act II, Scene 2, Polonius and Claudius plan an encounter between Ophelia and Hamlet, but in Q2 and F, this meeting is delayed until Act III, Scene 1. Perhaps Shakespeare initially placed it in Act II, Scene 2, as Q1 indicates, but pushed it back to provide another instance of action delayed. Yet another example of the play's procrastination appears in the drowning and burial of Ophelia. Gertrude reports her death at the end of Act IV, Scene 7; her funeral begins some 215 lines later in Act V, Scene 1.

Other actions remain uncompleted. Bernardo's account in Act I, Scene 1 is interrupted by the Ghost's entry. The Ghost is ready to speak when the cock crows, so his message remains undelivered. Marcellus, Bernardo, and Horatio then break up their watch. Polonius interrupts the First Player's speech ("Prithee no more," 2.2.520). The performance of *The Murder of Gonzago* is never finished. Hamlet never completes his education or reaches England. Claudius's repentance fails; Ophelia's funeral is truncated, as is Polonius's. The marriage between Hamlet and Ophelia that Gertrude had expected cannot take place. Hamlet would "have prov'd most royal" (5.2.398), but his reign must remain speculative since his life is cut short. Such "maimed rites" (5.1.219) ensue from Claudius's regicide, which has destroyed order in the realm. The interruption of Old Hamlet's life causes all these other lapses. As Ulysses comments in *Troilus and Cressida,* "Take but degree away, / untune that string, / And hark what discord follows" (1.3.109–110).

Style and Imagery

In "The World of Hamlet," Maynard Mack observes: "Hamlet's world is preeminently in the interrogative mood. It reverberates with questions, anguished, meditative, alarmed" (504). The opening line of Shakespeare's plays often introduces the work's central concern. *Richard II* begins, "Old John of Gaunt, time-honored Lancaster"; the play shows the demise of the old medieval order represented by Gaunt, supplanted by a new world view exemplified by Bolingbroke. In *King Lear*'s first speech, Kent observes: "I thought the King had more affected the Duke of Albany than Cornwall." Again, the clash of values these two men represent will work itself out in the ensuing five acts. Philo remarks at the start of *Antony and Cleopatra:* "Nay, but this dotage of our general's / O'erflows the measure." The play will trace Antony's decline (dotage) and subsequent recovery of greatness. So *Hamlet* opens with Bernardo's "Who's there?" It is the question that pervades the play. Is Hamlet mad? How guilty is Gertrude? Who is to be trusted? So many characters pretend to be what they are not. Shakespeare knew that the Greek word for actor is *hupocritos* (hypocrite).

The word *question,* in fact, appears 17 times in the tragedy, more than in any other of Shakespeare's plays, and questions fill the work. Why is Denmark preparing for war? Is the Ghost honest? Did Ophelia drown herself? Many questions transcend the

Hamlet holds the skull of Yorick while the gravedigger continues his work and Horatio stands by Hamlet's side in this print published by Amies in 1888. *(Illustration by Felix Octavius Darley)*

play's context to interrogate the human condition. "To be, or not to be" (3.1.55). "What is man, / If his chief good and market of his time / Be but to sleep and feed?" (4.4.33–35). Are humans "the beauty of the world; the paragon of animals" or a "quintessence of dust" (2.2.307–308). Are honesty and beauty compatible?

Supporting this questioning are the play's many riddles. Hamlet is himself a riddle, as he tells Rosencrantz and Guildenstern in Act III, Scene 2. "What is he that builds stronger than either the mason, the shipwright, or the carpenter?" (5.2.41–42). Laertes declares of Ophelia's ramblings, "This nothing's more than matter" (4.5.174). Why does Hamlet call Polonius a fishmonger (2.2.174)?

Shakespeare loved the use of syllepsis (puns). Johnson remarked that the pun was Shakespeare's Cleopatra for which he would gladly lose the world, introducing wordplay even when it was inappropriate. Whatever the merits of Johnson's censure in some instances, in *Hamlet,* punning reinforces the play's emphasis on ambiguity. What does Hamlet mean when he says of Claudius, "A little more than kin, and less than kind" (1.2.65). *Kind* here means "like Hamlet," as well as "considerate." When Claudius asks, "How fares our cousin Hamlet?" meaning how matters are going with him, Hamlet construes the question as referring to his dining (3.2.92–95).

Punning reveals, moreover, the debasement of language along with everything else in Claudius's Denmark. Signifiers and signified no longer correspond. As Hamlet remarks, "The Body is with the King, but the King is not with the body" (4.2.27–28). In this riddle, Hamlet alludes to the belief in the king's two bodies, one mortal, the other, associated with his office, unending. Because Claudius is a player king, he does not embody true kingship. When the king is a thing of nothing (4.2.28–30), meaning vanishes. Paradox replaces sense.

Claudius's first speech reveals how far language has sunk. He calls Gertrude his sister and his queen, Hamlet his cousin and his son. He speaks of "a defeated joy," of "mirth in funeral, and . . . dirge in marriage" (1.2.10, 12). Highlighting the fact that Claudius but plays the king, Shakespeare gives a similar line to the Player King in *The Murder of Gonzago:* "Grief joys, joy grieves" (3.2.199). As Hamlet comments, "This was sometime a paradox, but now the time gives it proof" (3.2.113–114).

Hamlet's quest is not only to avenge his father's death but also to restore unity to a duplicitous world. Just as in Book 1 of Edmund Spenser's *Faerie Queene* (1590), in which the false Duessa opposes the true Una and for a time supplants her, so in *Hamlet,* duality has supplanted the singleness of truth. *Hamlet* is filled with doubles, often without any reason: Voltemand and Cornelius, Rosencrantz and Guildenstern, Old and young Hamlet (in the play's sources father and son have different names), Old and young Fortinbras (Shakespeare or the *Ur-Hamlet* invented them). The Ghost appears twice in Act I, Scene 1, as it had appeared two nights before. Two months have elapsed between Old Hamlet's death and the beginning of the play; another two months pass between Acts 1 and 2. Hamlet is captured by pirates on his second day at sea. *The Murder of Gonzago* is acted twice, once in dumb show, then in words. Lamord spoke of Laertes' fencing skills "Two months since" (4.7.81). When Laertes asks Claudius why he did not restrain Hamlet, Claudius replies, "O, for two special reasons" (4.7.9). Hamlet scores two hits against Laertes before Laertes wounds him. Hamlet kills Claudius twice, with poisoned rapier and poisoned wine.

The play's language mirrors this doubling. As George T. Wright observes, a prominent rhetorical device here is hendiadys, the use of two words of the same part of speech (usually nouns, but sometimes adjectives) joined by "and" in which one of the words actually modifies the other. Horatio speaks of "the gross and scope of mine opinion" (1.1.68), meaning the full range of his opinion. A bit further on he uses "law and heraldry" (1.1.87) for heraldic law and refers to "this post-haste and romage in the land" (1.1.107), that is, hasty, bustling activity. Other examples include "fashion and a toy in blood" (1.3.6) for fashionable toy, "voice and yielding" (1.3.23) for permitting voice, "shot and danger" (1.3.35) for dangerous shot, and "youth and observation" (1.5.101) for youthful observation. Altogether the play contains 66 instances of this rhetorical device, more than twice as many as in any other of Shakespeare's plays. *Othello* comes in second with 28 examples.

Linguistic doubling takes two other forms in the play as well. Shakespeare repeatedly uses two words or phrases where one would suffice: "food and diet" (1.1.99), "disjoint and out of frame" (1.2.20), "sweet and commendable" (1.2.87), "simple and unschool'd" (1.2.97), "rank and gross in nature" (1.2.136), and "foul and pestilent contagion of vapors" (2.2.302–303). This list could be greatly extended. The other stylistic peculiarity is

repetition. Hamlet's first soliloquy begins, "O that this too too sallied flesh would melt" (1.2.129). A few lines later Hamlet exclaims: "O God, God" and "Fie on't, ah fie!" (1.2.132, 135). Told of his father's ghost's appearance, Hamlet remarks: "Indeed, indeed sirs" (1.2.227) and "very like, very like" (1.2.236). Horatio says that the Ghost remained as long as one might count to 100, but Marcellus and Bernardo protest, "Longer, longer" (1.2.238). Laertes warns: "Fear it, Ophelia, fear it" (1.3.33). Polonius urges his son, "Aboard, aboard, for shame!" (1.3.55). Hamlet tells the Ghost, "Rest, rest perturbed spirit" (1.5.182). These are but a small sampling of the duplications in characters' speeches.

While almost every character employs these doublings, only Hamlet and his dead father cling to the unity of truth. The Ghost appears when the clock strikes one (1.1.39). In the closet scene, Gertrude declares that Hamlet's chiding has "cleft [her] heart in twain"; Hamlet urges her to "throw away the worser part of it, / And live the purer with the other half" (3.4.157–158), in other words, to exchange her double (false) heart for a single (true) one. Hamlet reflects that "a man's life's no more than to say 'one'" (5.2.74). Scoring the first point in his fencing match with Laertes, Hamlet announces, "One" (5.2.280). In a work in which duplicity rules, references to oneness are uncommon, their very rarity a comment on the world of the play.

The play's imagery emphasizes the theme of corruption and decay. Marcellus observes: "Something is rotten in the state of Denmark" (1.4.90). Laertes cautions Ophelia,

> The canker galls the infants of the spring
> Too oft before their buttons be disclos'd,
> And in the morn and liquid dew of youth
> Contagious blastments are most imminent.
>
> (1.3.39–42)

Claudius confesses that his "offense is rank, it smells to heaven" (3.3.36). The royal marriage bed is "Stew'd in corruption" (3.4.93). Hamlet tells the king that if Polonius's body is not found, "You shall nose him as you go up the stairs into the lobby" (4.3.36–37). To Hamlet's question of how long a person will "lie i' th' earth ere he rot," the gravedigger replies that a body will last eight or nine years "if 'a be not rotten before 'a die—as we have many pocky corses, that will scarce hold the laying in" (5.1.163–168).

The source of Denmark's pervasive rottenness is Claudius's killing of the rightful king. Shakespeare chose to have Claudius poison Old Hamlet rather than kill in some other way, and this poison, an apt image of corruption, spreads throughout the world of the play. Lucianus poisons the Player King; Laertes anoints his foil with poison, and Claudius poisons a cup of wine. Five of the nine characters who die in *Hamlet* (including Old Hamlet) are killed by poison. The discussion of the play's structure notes how the image of poison spreads visually. It also infects the play's language. Rosencrantz and Guildenstern are like "adders fang'd" (3.4.203). Hamlet speaks of "the dram of eale" (the Q2 reading of 1.4.36) that destroys the entire "noble substance" (1.4.37). Claudius ascribes Ophelia's madness to "the poison of deep grief" (4.5.75).

Both nature and humanity are blasted by that dram of eale that Claudius pores into Old Hamlet's ear. The Edenic world of Old Hamlet's reign has become "an unweeded garden / That grows to seed, things rank and gross in nature / Possess it merely" (1.2.135–137). Hamlet, who had been "the expectation and rose of the fair state," is destroyed (3.1.152), as is Ophelia, that "rose of May" (4.5.158). Claudius is "like a mildewed ear / Blasting his wholesome brother" (3.4.64–65). Ophelia can find no violets to give to Gertrude because those symbols of faithfulness have "wither'd" (4.5.185).

Caroline Spurgeon, in *Shakespeare's Imagery and What It Tells Us,* observes that "the idea of an ulcer or tumour, as descriptive of the unwholesome condition of Denmark morally, is, on the whole, the dominating one" in the play (316). She notes that Hamlet describes his mother's sin as a blister on the "fair forehead of an innocent love" (3.4.43).

Hamlet reaches to the sky while images of Yorick's skull and Ophelia's face float above him, in this illustration of Act V, Scene 1 of *Hamlet* published by Selwyn and Blount in 1922. *(Illustration by John Austen)*

To marry Claudius, her sense must be not merely "sickly" but "apoplex'd" (3.4.80, 73). He warns her that to ascribe his behavior and words to madness "will but skin and film the ulcerous place, / Whiles rank corruption, mining all within, / Infects unseen" (3.4.147–149). When the mad Ophelia comes to see Gertrude, the queen declares, "To my sick soul, as sin's true nature is, / Each toy seems prologue to some great amiss" (4.5.17–18).

Guildenstern reports that Claudius is "much distemper'd" with an excess of choler (3.2.301–303), one of the four humors of Renaissance medical theory, which held that an imbalance of any of these produced disease. When Hamlet spares Claudius in Act III, Scene 3 because the king is praying, the prince observes: "This physic but prolongs thy sickly days" (3.43.96). Claudius states that Hamlet rages "like a hectic [fever] in my blood" (4.3.68); the poison he has unleashed affects even him, who will die by a double dose of his own toxins. He likens himself to "the owner of a foul disease, / To keep it from divulging, let it feed / Even on the pith of life" (4.1.21–23). He is referring to Hamlet, but the words more aptly apply to his own guilt. Claudius declares that the people of Denmark have become "Thick and unwholesome in their thoughts and whispers" (4.5.82), poisoned by his regicide. Hamlet calls young Fortinbras's senseless attack on Poland "th' imposthume [abscess] of much wealth and peace, / That inward breaks, and shows no cause without / Why the man dies" (4.4.27–29). So the play moves to the universal graveyard that might hold all the dead from Cain (5.1.77)—the first fratricide—to Caesar and Alexander, to Yorick, the king's jester, and it will serve, by play's end, as the repository of Polonius, Ophelia, Gertrude, Laertes, Hamlet, and Claudius, whose primal murder before the play begins sets the table for proud death's feast served up in the final scene.

EXTRACTS OF CLASSIC CRITICISM

Samuel Johnson (1709–1784) [Excerpted from *The Plays of William Shakespeare* (1765). Unlike the romantic critics who came after him, Johnson focuses on plot more than character. Nor is he a bardolator; his objections to the work anticipate T. S. Eliot's judgment that *Hamlet* is an artistic failure because Hamlet's emotions, especially regarding Gertrude, lack sufficient motivation. Feminist critics would rebel against Johnson's portrait of an anodyne Ophelia.]

If the dramas of Shakespeare were to be characterized, each by the particular excellence which distinguishes it from the rest, we must allow to the tragedy of *Hamlet* the

praise of variety. The incidents are so numerous, that the argument of the play would make a long tale. The scenes are interchangeably diversified with merriment and solemnity; with merriment that includes judicious and instructive observations, and solemnity, not strained by poetical violence above the natural sentiments of man. New characters appear from time to time in continual succession, exhibiting various forms of life and particular modes of conversation. The pretended madness of Hamlet causes much mirth, the mournful distraction of Ophelia fills the heart with tenderness, and every personage produces the effect intended, from the apparition that in the first act chills the blood with horror, to the fop in the last, that exposes affectation to just contempt.

The conduct is perhaps not wholly secure against objections. The action is indeed for the most part in continual progression, but there are some scenes which neither forward nor retard it. Of the feigned madness of Hamlet there appears no adequate cause, for he does nothing which he might not have done with the reputation of sanity. He plays the madman most, when he treats Ophelia with so much rudeness, which seems to be useless and wanton cruelty.

Hamlet is, through the whole play, rather an instrument than an agent. After he has, by the stratagem of the play, convicted the king, he makes no attempt to punish him, and his death is at last effected by an incident which Hamlet has no part in producing.

The catastrophe is not very happily produced; the exchange of weapons is rather an expedient of necessity, than a stroke of art. A scheme might easily have been formed, to kill Hamlet with the dagger, and Laertes with the bowl.

The poet is accused of having shewn little regard to poetical justice, and may be charged with equal neglect of poetical probability. The apparition left the regions of the dead to little purpose; the revenge which he demands is not obtained but by the death of him that was required to take it; and the gratification which would arise from the destruction of an usurper and a murderer, is abated by the untimely death of Ophelia, the young, the beautiful, the harmless, and the pious.

Johann Wolfgang von Goethe (1749–1832) [Excerpted from *Wilhelm Meister's Apprenticeship* (1795; translated by Thomas Carlyle, 1824). Wilhelm here offers his explanation as to why Hamlet procrastinates, a question that has occasioned much throwing about of brains.]

Conceive a prince such as I have painted him, and that his father suddenly dies. Ambition and the love of rule are not the passions that inspire him. As a king's son, he would not have been contented; but now he is first constrained to consider the difference which separates a sovereign from a subject. The crown was not hereditary; yet his father's longer possession of it would have strengthened the pretensions of an only son, and secured his hopes of succession. In place of this, he now beholds himself excluded by his uncle, in spite of specious promises, most probably forever. He is now poor in goods and favor, and a stranger in the scene which from youth he had looked upon as his inheritance. His temper here assumes its first mournful tinge. He feels that now he is not more, that he is less, than a private nobleman; he offers himself as the servant of every one; he is not courteous and condescending, he is needy and degraded.

His past condition he remembers as a vanished dream. It is in vain that his uncle strives to cheer him, to present his situation in another point of view. The feeling of his nothingness will not leave him.

The second stroke that came upon him wounded deeper, bowed still more. It was the marriage of his mother. The faithful, tender son had yet a mother, when his father passed away. He hoped, in the company of his surviving noble-minded parent, to reverence the heroic form of the departed: but his mother, too, he loses; and it is something worse than death that robs him of her. The trustful image, which a good child loves to form of its parents, is gone. With the dead there is no help, on the living no hold. Moreover, she is a woman; and her name is Frailty, like that of all her sex.

Now only does he feel completely bowed down, now only orphaned; and no happiness of life can repay what he has lost. Not reflective or sorrowful by nature, reflection and sorrow have become for him a heavy obligation. It is thus that we see him first enter on the scene. I do not think that I have mixed aught foreign with the play, or overcharged a single feature of it. . . .

Figure to yourselves this youth, . . . this son of princes; conceive him vividly, bring his state before your eyes, and then observe him when he learns that his father's spirit walks; stand by him in the terrors of the night, when even the venerable ghost appears before him. He is seized with boundless horror; he speaks to the mysterious form; he sees it beckon him; he follows and hears. The fearful accusation of his uncle rings in his ears, the summons to revenge, and the piercing, oft-repeated prayer, Remember me!

And, when the ghost has vanished, who is it that stands before us? A young hero panting for vengeance? A prince by birth, rejoicing to be called to punish the usurper of his crown? No! trouble and astonishment take hold of the solitary young man: he grows bitter against smiling villains, swears that he will not forget the spirit, and concludes with the significant ejaculation,—

The time is out of joint: O cursed spite,
That ever I was born to set it right!

Claudius and Polonius listen to Hamlet and Ophelia's conversation in Act III, Scene I. This is a plate from *Retzsch's Outlines to Shakespeare:* Hamlet, published in 1828. *(Illustration by Moritz Retzsch)*

In these words, I imagine, will be found the key to Hamlet's whole procedure. To me it is clear that Shakespeare meant, in the present case, to represent the effects of a great action laid upon a soul unfit for the performance of it. In this view the whole play seems to me to be composed. There is an oak tree planted in a costly jar, which should have borne only pleasant flowers in its bosom: the roots expand, the jar is shivered.

A lovely, pure, noble, and most moral nature, without the strength of nerve which forms a hero, sinks beneath a burden it cannot bear and must not cast away. All duties are holy for him: the present is too hard. Impossibilities have been required of him,—not in themselves impossibilities, but such for him. He winds and turns, and torments himself; he advances and recoils; is ever put in mind, ever puts himself in mind; at last does all but lose his purpose from his thoughts, yet still without recovering his peace of mind.

Sigmund Freud (1856–1939) [Excerpted from *The Interpretation of Dreams* (1900). Freud's Oedi-pal reading of *Hamlet* influenced subsequent psychological criticism of the play. This view of the prince informs Laurence Olivier's 1948 film and Ernest Jones's 1949 *Hamlet and Oedipus.* Freud's attempt to pluck out the heart of Hamlet's creator mirrors other 19th- and 20th-century efforts to discover through the plays the mind that conceived them.]

Another of the great poetic tragedies, Shakespeare's *Hamlet,* is rooted in the same soil as *Oedipus Rex.* But the whole difference in the psychic life of the two widely separated periods of civilisation, and the progress, during the course of time, of repression in the emotional life of humanity, is manifested in the differing treatment of the same material. In *Oedipus Rex* the basic wish-fantasy of the child is brought to light and realized as it is in dreams; in *Hamlet* it remains repressed, and we learn of its existence—as we discover the relevant facts in a neurosis—only through the inhibitory effects which proceed from it. In the more modern drama, the curious fact that it is possible to remain in complete uncertainty as to the character of the hero has proved to be quite consistent with the overpowering effect of the tragedy. The play is based upon Hamlet's hesitation in accomplishing the task of revenge assigned to him; the text does not give the cause or the motive of this hesitation, nor have the manifold attempts at interpretation succeeded in doing so. According to the still prevailing conception, a conception for which Goethe was first responsible, Hamlet represents the type of man whose active energy is paralysed by excessive intellectual activity: "Sicklied o'er with the pale cast of thought." According to another conception, the poet has endeavoured to portray a morbid, irresolute character, on the verge of neurasthenia. The plot of the drama, however, shows us that Hamlet is by no means intended to appear as a character wholly incapable of action. On two separate occasions we see him assert himself: once in a sudden outburst of rage, when he stabs the eavesdropper behind the arras, and on the other occasion when he deliberately, and even craftily, with the complete unscrupulousness of a prince of the Renaissance, sends the two courtiers to the death which was intended for himself. What is it, then, that inhibits him in accomplishing the task which his father's ghost has laid upon him? Here the explanation offers itself that it is the peculiar nature of this task. Hamlet is able to do anything but take vengeance upon the man who did away with his father and has taken his father's place with his mother—the man who shows him in realisation the repressed desires of his own childhood. The loathing which should have driven him to revenge is thus replaced by self-reproach, by conscientious scruples, which tell him that he himself is no better than the murderer whom he is required to punish. I have here translated into consciousness what had to remain unconscious in the mind of the hero; if anyone wishes to call Hamlet an hysterical subject I cannot but admit that this is the deduction to be drawn from my interpretation. The sexual aversion which Hamlet expresses in conversation with Ophelia is perfectly consistent with this deduction—the same sexual aversion which during the next few years was increasingly to take possession of the poet's soul, until it found its supreme utterance in *Timon of Athens*. It can, of course, be only the poet's own psychology with which we are confronted in *Hamlet;* and in a work on Shakespeare by Georg Brandes (1896) I find the statement that the drama was composed immediately after the death of Shakespeare's father (1601)—that is to say, when he was still mourning his loss, and during a revival, as we may fairly assume, of his own childish feelings in respect of his father. It is known, too, that Shakespeare's son, who died in childhood, bore the name of Hamnet (identical with Hamlet). Just as *Hamlet* treats of the relation of the son to his parents, so *Macbeth,* which was written about the same period, is based upon the theme of childlessness. Just as all neurotic symptoms, like dreams themselves, are capable of hyper-interpretation, and even require hyper-interpretation before they become perfectly intelligible, so every genuine poetical creation must have proceeded from more than one motive, more than one impulse in the mind of the poet, and must admit of more than one interpretation. I have here attempted to interpret only the deepest stratum of impulses in the mind of the creative poet.

MODERN CRITICISM AND CRITICAL CONTROVERSIES
New Criticism

Formalism, or New Criticism, a movement that began in the 1930s, emphasized close textual readings as opposed to focus on the historical and the biographical elements. New Critics treated a piece literature as a self-contained artifact, with a single discoverable meaning that could be determined through a study of its images, structure, and other formal (relating to form) aspects. They avoided treating characters as if they were real people, with lives outside the fictional works in which they appeared.

An early example of this approach is Spurgeon's *Shakespeare's Imagery and What It Tells Us* (1935). Her close study of *Hamlet*'s language revealed a preponderance of references to sickness, disease, and medicine—more than in any other of Shakespeare's plays. Indeed, in Table 7 of that work, she observes: "in *Hamlet* we are almost startled at the constant conception of a corrupt and hidden tumour or cancer which is the central imaginative symbol of the tragedy." Spurgeon's aim was not image tracking for its own sake but rather using images to pluck out the heart of the play's mystery. From her investigation she concluded:

> The problem in *Hamlet* is not predominantly that of will and reason, of a mind too

philosophic or a nature temperamentally unfitted to act quickly; [Shakespeare] sees it pictorially *not as the problem of an individual at all,* but as something greater and even more mysterious, as a *condition* for which the individual himself is apparently not responsible, any more than the sick man is to blame for the infection which strikes and devours him, but which, nevertheless, in its course and development, impartially and relentlessly annihilates him and others, innocent and guilty alike. (318–319)

Maynard Mack's "The World of *Hamlet*" (1952) provides another example of the New Critical approach. Mack also looks at the play's language, focusing on its use of questions and riddles. He finds many uses of the words *apparition, seems, assume, shape* (in the sense of disguise), and *put on,* which emphasize the problem of distinguishing reality from appearance. Other image patterns relating to this theme concern clothes and painting. Gertrude wears widow's weeds but then exchanges them for a wedding dress. Claudius contrasts his actions to his "most painted word" (3.1.52). Hamlet criticizes women's use of cosmetics to disguise themselves: "God hath given you one face, and you make yourselves another" (3.1.143–144).

Whereas for Spurgeon, the play's central image is disease, for Mack, it is "show" (512). He argues that everyone pretends to be something other than what he or she is. *Hamlet,* for Mack, is thus a play about playing: "The court plays, Hamlet plays, the players play, Rosencrantz and Guildenstern try to play on Hamlet. . . . And the final duel, by a further extension, becomes itself a play, in which everyone but Claudius and Laertes plays his role in ignorance" (514).

Deconstruction

Jacques Derrida coined the term *deconstruction,* the premise of which he set forth in *L'Écriture et la différence* (1967), *De la grammatologie* (1967), and *Dissemination* (1972). Like New Criticism, deconstruction does not look outside a work for mean-

ing. Derrida famously observed, *"il n'ya pas hors de texte"* (there is nothing outside the text). Formalists and deconstructionists recognize that irony and ambiguity pervade literature. But, whereas formalists believe that close reading can expose the work's meaning, deconstructionists emphasize contradiction and ambiguity.

Marjorie Garber's "*Hamlet:* Giving Up the Ghost" illustrates the deconstructionist approach. Like the critic George T. Wright, she explores the play's use of hendiadys and doubling. She notes that Hamlet's father and Laertes' father are both killed, that the play within the play is acted twice, once without speech and once with, that Hamlet visits Ophelia's closet and then Gertrude's, that Hamlet sees his father's ghost twice.

She also examines the play's references to remembering, which she regards as antithetical to acting. She cites a passage in Friedrich Nietzsche's "The Use and Abuse of History," in which he argues that if the past is not forgotten it becomes "the gravedigger of the present." Garber argues that Shakespeare anticipates Nietzsche's insight by introducing the gravediggers in Act V, Scene 1. Hamlet's true task, according to Garber, is not to remember but to forget.

Psychological Criticism

Whereas New Criticism and deconstruction rejected older approaches to literature, modern psychological criticism builds on insights dating from the beginnings of psychoanalysis. One of the best and best-known examples of this approach is Jones's *Hamlet and Oedipus* (1949). A concern that pervades the excerpts cited above and the New Critical and deconstructionist interpretations is the question of Hamlet's procrastination. At the end of Act I, Hamlet's father's ghost orders the prince to take revenge, but Hamlet does not act until Act V, Scene 2.

Jones reviews the various explanations offered up to 1949. Those taking what Jones calls the objective view maintain that Hamlet requires evidence so that he will not himself be viewed as a killer. Also in this reading, Hamlet lacks opportunity to carry out the Ghost's command. In Act III, Scene 3 he refrains from killing Claudius because Claudius is praying. Hamlet's second chance comes in Act V, Scene 2, and he seizes that one. Advocates of this explanation include Hartley Coleridge, James Orchard Halliwell-Phillips, W. H. Widgery, and Alice Brotherton. Jones rejects this argument, noting that Hamlet never speaks of external barriers to acting, only internal ones.

Those who favor what Jones terms the subjective view maintain that the task of revenge was too great for Hamlet. The selection from Goethe above illustrates one facet of this argument. F. S. Boas, in *Shakespeare and His Predecessors* (1896), writes that Hamlet is "a man of genius, with a will atrophied through an abnormal development, not only of the reflective, but of the emotional faculties" (407). According to Sir Edmund Chambers, *Hamlet* is "the tragedy of the *intellectual,* of the impotence of the over-cultivated imagination and the over-subtilized reasoning powers to meet the call of everyday life for practical efficiency" (182). Yet, Hamlet acts impulsively to kill Polonius. He writes incriminating lines for *The Murder of Gonzago* and boards a pirate ship to fend off an attack.

A third group of critics, including John Dover Wilson, claim that Hamlet's delay defies explanation. In *What Happens in* Hamlet (1935), Wilson states: "We were never intended to reach the heart of the mystery" (229). W. F. Trench's *Shakespeare's* Hamlet: *A New Commentary* (1913) declares: "We find it hard, with Shakespeare's help, to understand Hamlet: even Shakespeare, perhaps, found it hard to understand him" (115).

Jones first broached his explanation in "The Oedipus Complex as an Explanation of Hamlet's Mystery," published in the *American Journal of Psychology* in 1910. He repeated his view in "A Psycho-Analytic Study of Hamlet" that appeared in Jones's *Essays in Applied Psycho-Analysis* (1923), and then, most fully, in his 1949 book. Hamlet cannot kill Claudius, Jones claims, because "his uncle incorporates the deepest and most buried part of his own personality, so that he cannot kill him without also killing himself" (100). Jones builds on Freud's view

of Hamlet's Oedipal desire for Gertrude (see the excerpt from *The Interpretation of Dreams* above). Hamlet does not kill Claudius because he wants the incestuous relationship between his uncle and Gertrude to continue, thus vicariously fulfilling his desire. Also, if he kills Gertrude's husband, he will manifest his Oedipal impulses, so he does nothing. For Jones, *Hamlet* is finally a play about a person struggling with his own soul. Jones's view influenced Olivier's 1948 film version of *Hamlet,* in which Act III, Scene 4 is played out between Hamlet and Gertrude on an oversized bed.

Janet Adelman's "'Man and Wife Is One Flesh': *Hamlet* and the Confrontation with the Maternal Body," in *Suffocating Mothers: Fantasies of Maternal Origin in Shakespeare's Plays,* Hamlet *to* The Tempest (1992) offers a different psychological view of the play. Adelman notes that in Shakespeare's plays before *Hamlet,* the protagonist seeks to supplant

Gertrude (Olga Knipper) holds Hamlet (Vasili Kachalov) in Edward Gordon Craig and Constantin Stanislavski's 1911 production of *Hamlet.*

and hence become his father (Brutus and Caesar, Henry V and Henry IV). Claudius's killing of Old Hamlet makes Claudius the new father figure. Hamlet needs to differentiate between the true and false father, heroic Old Hamlet and unheroic Claudius. To make that distinction, he requires Gertrude to acknowledge a difference. For Adelman, the key scene in the play is Act III, Scene 4, Hamlet's confrontation with his mother.

Adelman argues that Hamlet seeks not to avenge his father's death but to remake his mother. Hamlet believes that he succeeds, which is why when he returns from his sea voyage he can call himself "Hamlet the Dane" (5.1.57) and act. Even on shipboard, he becomes his father when he uses Old Hamlet's signet ring to seal the order to execute Rosencrantz and Guildenstern.

The sexuality that troubles Hamlet, Adelman writes, is not his incestuous desire for Gertrude but rather Gertrude's sexual nature, which Hamlet links to death. Hamlet's first soliloquy opens with a wish to eliminate the flesh. He links Gertrude's sexuality with the Fall, which concerns him more than Claudius's recapitulating the crime of Cain. Hamlet rejects Ophelia because he regards all women as betrayers. The play within the play treats the queen as the murderer: "None wed the second but who kill'd the first"; "A second time I kill my husband dead, / When second husband kisses me in bed" (3.2.180, 184–185). Adelman concludes: "In creating for Hamlet a plot in which his mother's sexuality is literally the sign of his betrayal and of her husband's death, Shakespeare recapitulates the material of infantile fantasy, playing it out with a compelling logic that allows its expression in a perfectly rationalized, hence justified, way" (35).

Feminist Criticism

In shifting the focus of Hamlet's concern from father to mother, Adelman reflects the influence of feminist critics. Even before this school achieved official recognition, Carolyn Heilbrun defended Gertrude in "The Character of Hamlet's Mother" (1957). Bradley in *Shakespearean Tragedy* (1904) had written of the queen that she

was not a bad-hearted woman, not at all the woman to think little of murder. But she had a soft and animal nature, and was very dull and very shallow. She loved to be happy, like a sheep in the sun. . . . The belief at the bottom of her heart was that the world is a place constructed simply that people may be happy in it in a good-humoured sensual fashion. (137)

Wilson's *What Happens in* Hamlet grants her courage but regards Gertrude as always hoping for the best. Wilson also sees her as an adulterous wife and comments: "Had the body or flesh of Gertrude been weaker, and her conceit or imagination stronger, King Hamlet might still have been alive and the 'bed of Denmark' undefiled" (251).

Heilbrun concedes Gertrude's lust but denies her adultery. Gertrude for her is "strong-minded, intelligent, succinct, and . . . sensible" (11). The queen has a passionate nature, but she acknowledges her fault in Act III, Scene 4. More important for Heilbrun is Gertrude's intelligence and the concern she exhibits for others. She wants to protect Claudius from Laertes, to inform Laertes of Ophelia's death in the least painful way possible, and to have Hamlet restored to happiness.

In "Feminist Modes of Shakespearean Criticism" (1981), Carol Neely argues that feminist critics should tell Ophelia's story. Elaine Showalter's "Representing Ophelia: Women, Madness, and the Responsibilities of Feminist Criticism" (1985) takes up that challenge, examining how Ophelia has been portrayed on stage and in criticism over the centuries. Showalter notes that for most critics of *Hamlet,* Ophelia is a minor character, interesting only for what she reveals about the prince. Showalter maintains, however, that Ophelia holds up as it were a mirror to society's vision of all women in any given period. In 1600, Showalter argues, Ophelia's madness would have been seen as proceeding from thwarted love (eratomania). Whereas Hamlet's madness is intellectual in origin, Ophelia's derives from female sexuality. In the 18th century, she was portrayed more decorously, less sexually. Johnson

Ophelia drowns in a 19th-century depiction of Act IV, Scene 7 of *Hamlet. (Painting by John Everett Millais)*

described her as "young, . . . beautiful, . . ., harmless, . . . and pious," the model female of the period (196). On stage, her lines were cut to excise all sexual references. For the romantics, she represented emotional excess. They embraced her madness, presenting her as one who feels too much. She thus contrasts with Hamlet, who is given to excessive thinking.

For the Victorians, she exemplified female madness and hysteria, but they recognized her sexuality. John Everett Millais's 1852 pre-Raphaelite painting of her stresses her sensuality. Eugène Delacroix's 1843 *La Mort d'Ophélie* shows her in an erotic trance. Mary Cowden Clarke's *The Girlhood of Shakespeare's Heroines* (1852) claimed that Ophelia witnessed and barely escaped sexual abuse. Ellen Terry, who began playing the role in 1878, portrayed Ophelia as afraid of her father, her lover, and life.

The anonymous *The True Ophelia* (1914) maintained that she was an intelligent woman destroyed by men. Jones's *Hamlet and Oedipus* viewed her as sensual. Mid-20th-century productions treated her as schizophrenic; in later 20th-century performances her madness serves as a rebellion against patriarchy. Helen Mirren, Marianne Faithfull, and Yvonne Nicholson have shown her as sexually attracted to her brother. For R. D. Laing, Ophelia exemplifies the plight of neglected daughters. In Melissa Murray's *Ophelia* (1979), she becomes

a lesbian, runs off with a servant-lover, and joins a guerrilla commune. Ophelia, then, is a seismograph measuring shifts in social perceptions of the female.

New Historicism

Drawing on the social sciences as well as literary theory, new historicism seeks to situate a work of art in its larger context, not to regard it, as New Critics and deconstructionists tend to do, as a self-contained artifact. As Stephen Greenblatt, one of the founders of the new historicist critical school, states in *Renaissance Self-Fashioning* (1980), literary criticism should avoid "permanently sealing off one type of discourse from another or decisively separating works of art from the minds and lives of their creators and their audiences" (5).

Karín S. Coddon uses this approach to explore the political implications Hamlet's madness held for Renaissance audiences. In "Suche Strange Desygns": Madness, Subjectivity, and Treason in *Hamlet* and Elizabethan Culture" (1989), Coddon, drawing on work by Michael Foucault, links madness to rebellion, particularly that of Robert Devereux, earl of Essex, who led an unsuccessful uprising against Elizabeth on February 8, 1601, shortly after *Hamlet* was first staged. Shakespeare's company had performed *Richard II,* with its deposition scene, on the eve of his rebellion. Essex was beheaded later that month, and the earl of Southampton, Shakespeare's early patron, was imprisoned in the Tower of London. Shakespeare thus was close to the leading conspirators and may have drawn Hamlet in part from Essex.

Coddon quotes from the diary of John Harington, who commented, "It resteth wythe me in opinion, that ambition thwarted in its career, dothe speedily leade on to madnesse". Harington cited Essex as an illustration of this principle: "the mans soule seemeth tossede to and fro, like the waves of a troubled sea." William Camden, another contemporary, reflected on Essex's discourtesy to Elizabeth. "Nor was he excusable in his deportment to the Queen herself, whom he treated with a sort of insolence, that seemed to proceed rather from a mind that wanted ballast, than any real pride in him." "An Exhortation Concerning Good Order and Obedience, to Rulers and Magistrates," one of the homilies regularly read in Elizabethan churches, describes resistance to monarchs as "an intolerable ignorance, madness, and wickedness," not just sinful, then, but psychologically aberrant (176).

Rosencrantz and Guildenstern assume that Hamlet's madness stems from thwarted political ambition (2.2.252–253). Even before Claudius learns of Hamlet's knowledge of the murder of his father, Claudius recognizes that the prince's madness threatens him: "Madness in great ones must not unwatch'd go" (3.1.189). Authority depends on subjects' controlling their disobedient impulses. Madness rejects such restraint and hence has political implications.

On the scaffold, Essex performed the ars moriendi, the art of dying well, apologizing to the queen and the world. Coddon likens Hamlet's apology to Laertes in Act V, Scene 2 as a scaffold speech, in which the speaker affirms the order he violated and denies any intentional wrongdoing. While Hamlet in Act V, Scene 2 embraces the orthodox Elizabethan view of a providential universe that he has heretofore rebelled against, Horatio's précis of what he will relate to the "yet unknowing world" suggests that madness rather than order has triumphed:

> So shall you hear
> Of carnal, bloody, and unnatural acts,
> Of accidental judgments, casual slaughters,
> Of deaths put on by cunning and forc'd cause,
> And in this upshot, purposes mistook
> Fall'n on th' inventors' heads:
>
> (5.2.379–385)

Another fascinating new historicist reading of *Hamlet* is Francis Barker's "Hamlet's Unfulfilled Interiority," in *The Tremulous Private Body: Essays in Subjection* (1984). Barker, to some extent, anticipates Bloom's claim that Shakespeare invented the modern understanding of what it means to be human. According to Barker, Shakespeare broke with the Renaissance view that the external is all. Barker maintains that Hamlet is the first literary character who has interiority: "I have that within that passes show" (1.2.85). Hamlet's mystery derives from Shakespeare's inability to articulate the nature of that interiority because his culture lacked terms to express it. Later critics have sought to read back into Hamlet the concepts of subjectivity developed in the 17th century by René Descartes and other philosophers. In Act V, Hamlet reverts to being a conventional Elizabethan hero who does not challenge societal values and the belief in a providential universe, although in the first four acts he had done so.

Greenblatt's *Hamlet in Purgatory* (2001) regards the stage less as a political arena than as a substitute for the banned Catholic faith. In the 12th century, the Catholic Church adopted a belief in purgatory, an intermediary place between heaven and hell. Purgatory linked the living and the dead not just by cords of memory but also by practical actions that the former could perform for the latter. Prayers and charity could shorten the penitential suffering of souls and speed them on their way to heaven. Once these souls reached heaven, they in turn could intercede for the living.

In 1563, the Anglican Church rejected the idea of purgatory (Article 22). Thomas Wilcox described purgatory as "vain and idle imaginations" (*The Vnfouldyng of Sundry Vntruths and Absurde Propositions,* 1581). John Frith, in *A Disputation of Purgatory,* dismissed it as "but a vain imagination" and its fires as "poetry". In a 1626 sermon, John Donne called purgatory the invention of poets. Banished from the church, the spirits of the dead resurface in poets' works on the Renaissance stage, which becomes its own middle ground, a new site for linking living and dead. *Hamlet* enacts "an ontological argument about spectrality and remembrance" that the church no longer accommodated (249).

THE PLAY TODAY

Hamlet is the tragedy of critics who cannot make up their minds. No analysis of the work can be complete; there is always something left over. Jacqueline Rose called it the *Mona Lisa* of literature. Jones, in *Hamlet and Oedipus,* described it as "the Sphinx of modern literature" (25–26). The play begins with a question and ends without an answer. Wilson observed: "*Hamlet* is a dramatic essay in mystery; that is to say: it is so constructed that the more it is examined the more there is to discover" (*What Happens in Hamlet* 19). Bloom concurs, writing in Hamlet: *Poem Unlimited,* "There is always something else in Hamlet" (142), a statement equally true of the character and of his play.

John Keats maintained that artists required a quality he called "negative capability," which he defined as the ability to remain "in uncertainties, mysteries, doubts, without any irritable reaching after facts and reason . . . remaining content with half-knowledge" (57). According to Keats, Shakespeare possessed this quality more fully than any other writer. He might have added that *Hamlet* exhibits this characteristic more than any other play. *Hamlet* continues to appeal to readers, viewers, and critics because it refuses to admit to closure. As Ralph Waldo Emerson observed, "A beauty not explicable is dearer than a beauty we can see the end of" (85).

In her essay "Against Interpretation," Susan Sontag called interpretation "the revenge of the intellect upon art" (98). *Hamlet* may be viewed as the revenge of art against intellect, since no critical study can denote it truly. It is its own argument against analysis, teasing us out of thought. When is a suicide not a suicide? When is madness not madness? When is a funeral not a funeral? When is prayer not prayer? When is an action not an action? When is a mother or father not a parent? How can the body be with the king but the king not be with the body? To be or not to be? Who's there?

Like the *Mona Lisa, Hamlet* always looks back at us, always wears that enigmatic smile that questions us at least as much as we question the work. It is a perfect artifact, in which the spectator continually finds something new while recognizing that the heart of its mystery remains unplucked. What

Hamlet says of Laertes is true of the play: "his semblable is his mirror, and who else would trace him, his umbrage, nothing more" (5.2.118–120). The only epitome of *Hamlet* is the work itself. At the end of the play, Horatio prepares to tell Hamlet's story. His first words will have to be "'Who's there?' / 'Nay, answer me.'"

Hamlet is very much in the public consciousness, with frequent performances on stage and screen and many references in literary and popular culture. Important critics continue to be fascinated by the play. Both Bloom (in Hamlet: *Poem Unlimited*) and Greenblatt *(Hamlet in Purgatory)* have written whole books more or less solely on the subject of the play. In addition, it is one of the most often assigned works of literature in both high school and college classrooms.

The play has been adapted for the screen more than 25 times. Influential film versions have included Olivier's 1948 adaptation (which used voiceovers for the soliloquies); the 1964 Russian version by Grigori Kozintsev, based on a translation by Boris Pasternak; Franco Zefferelli's 1990 version, with Mel Gibson as Hamlet and Glenn Close as Gertrude; Kenneth Brannagh's 1996 version,

Hamlet (Edmund Russell) leans over Ophelia's (Jane Schenck) body during her funeral in Act V, Scene I of *Hamlet.* Photograph published by the Byron Company in 1903

starring himself as Hamlet; and Michael Almereyda's unusual 2000 version, set in modern Manhattan and starring Ethan Hawke. In addition, many important actors have played Hamlet on stage since 1950, including John Gielgud, Richard Burton, and Derek Jacobi, as well as, more recently, Kevin Kline, Simon Russell Beale, and many others. In 2009, Jude Law played Hamlet to sold-out theaters in the West End of London and on Broadway in New York. Even today, it seems that no other Shakespearean play captures the public imagination quite as much as *Hamlet*.

FIVE TOPICS FOR DISCUSSION AND WRITING

1. **Nature of the tragedy:** Is *Hamlet* a traditional Aristotelian tragedy, in which the protagonist falls through a tragic flaw? If so, what is that flaw? Is Hamlet overwhelmed by forces over which he has no control?
2. **Hamlet's madness:** Is Hamlet mad? When he appears irrational, is he merely acting? Are there times in the play when he is at least temporarily insane?
3. **Gertrude:** The section above on feminist criticism notes some varying views about this character. Is she a weak, lustful, adulterous woman? Is she an innocent, intelligent one?
4. **Revenge:** Does the play endorse the doctrine of revenge? Should Hamlet obey the Ghost's injunction? Does the Ghost's command cause the tragic events that unfold in the work?
5. **Delay:** Hamlet repeatedly chides himself for failing to act. Does he procrastinate? Does he proceed as quickly as he can? If he does delay, why? If not, why does he repeatedly accuse himself of postponing his revenge?

Bibliography

Adelman, Jane. "'Man and Wife Is One Flesh': *Hamlet* and the Confrontation with the Maternal Body." In *Suffocating Mothers: Fantasies of Maternal Origin in Shakespeare's Plays,* Hamlet *to* The Tempest, 11–37. New York: Routledge, 1992.

Aldus, P. G. *Mousetrap: Structure and Meaning in* Hamlet. Toronto, Canada: University of Toronto Press, 1977.

Alexander, Nigel. *Poison, Play, and Duel: A Study in* Hamlet. Lincoln: University of Nebraska Press, 1971.

Alexander, Peter. Hamlet: *Father and Son*. Oxford: Clarendon Press, 1955.

Bacon, Francis. *Essays or Counsels, Civil & Moral with Other Writings of Francis Bacon*. London: George Neunes Limited, 1902.

Bevington, David, ed. *Twentieth-Century Interpretations of* Hamlet. Englewood Cliffs, N.J.: Prentice Hall, 1968.

Bloom, Harold. Hamlet: *Poem Unlimited*. New York: Riverhead Books, 2003.

———. *Shakespeare: The Invention of the Human*. New York: Riverhead Books, 1998.

Boas, F. S. *Shakespeare and His Predecessors*.

Bradley, A. C. *Shakespearean Tragedy: Lectures on* Hamlet, Othello, King Lear, *and* Macbeth. London: Macmillan, 1904.

Bright, Timothy. *A Treatise of Melancholie*. London: Thomas Vautrollier, 1586.

Brown, J. R., and Bernard Harris, eds. *Hamlet*. Stratford-upon-Avon Studies 5 (1963).

Bullough, Geoffrey. *Narrative and Dramatic Sources of Shakespeare*. Vol. 7: *Major Tragedies:* Hamlet, Othello, King Lear, Macbeth. New York: Columbia University Press, 1973.

Calderwood, James L. *To Be and Not to Be: Negation and Metadrama in* Hamlet. New York: Columbia University Press, 1983.

Cantor, Paul A. *Shakespeare:* Hamlet. Cambridge: Cambridge University Press, 1989.

Chambers, Edward. *Shakespeare: A Survey*. London: Sedgwick and Jackson, 1925.

Charney, Maurice. *Style in* Hamlet. Princeton, N.J.: Princeton University Press, 1969.

Coddon, Karin S. "Suche Strange Desygns: Madness, Subjectivity, and Treason in *Hamlet* and Elizabethan Culture." *Renaissance Drama* 20 (1989): 51–75.

Coleridge, Samuel Taylor. *The Complete Works of Samuel Taylor Coleridge*. 6 Vols. New York: Harper & brothers, 1853.

Dawson, Anthony B. Hamlet: *Shakespeare in Performance*. Manchester. U.K.: Manchester University Press, 1995.

De Grazia, Margreta. Hamlet *without Hamlet*. Cambridge: Cambridge University Press, 2007.

Dodsworth, Martin. Hamlet *Closely Observed*. Dover, N.H.: Athlone Press, 1985.

Elliott, G. R. *Scourge and Minister: A Study of* Hamlet *as a Tragedy of Revengefulness and Justice*. Durham, N.C.: Duke University Press, 1951.

Emerson, Ralph Waldo. *Works of Ralph Waldo Emerson*. London: George Routledge and Sons, 1883.

Frye, Roland Mushat. *The Renaissance Hamlet: Issues and Responses in 1600*. Princeton, N.J.: Princeton University Press, 1984.

Garber, Marjorie. "*Hamlet:* Giving Up the Ghost." In *Shakespeare's Ghost Writers: Literature as Uncanny Causality,* 124–176. New York: Methuen, 1987.

———. *Shakespeare after All*. New York: Pantheon, 2004.

Goddard, Harold C. *The Meaning of Shakespeare*. Chicago: University of Chicago Press, 1951.

Gottschalk, Paul. *The Meanings of* Hamlet: *Modes of Literary Interpretation since Bradley*. Albuquerque: University of New Mexico Press, 1972.

Greenblatt, Stephen. *Hamlet in Purgatory*. Princeton, N.J.: Princeton University Press, 2001.

———. *Renaissance Self-Fashioning*. Chicago: University of Chicago Press, 1980.

Gurr, Andrew. *Hamlet and the Distracted Globe*. Edinburgh, Scotland: Sussex University Press by Scottish Academic Press, 1978.

Hazlitt, William. *Twenty-two Essays of William Hazlitt*. Boston: D.C. Heath & Co., 1918.

Heilbrun, Carolyn. "The Character of Hamlet's Mother." *Shakespeare Quarterly* 8 (1957): 201–206.

Johnson, Samuel, and Walter Raleigh. *Johnson on Shakespeare*. London: Henry Frowde, 1908.

Jones, Ernest. *Hamlet and Oedipus*. New York: W. W. Norton, 1949.

Kastan, David Scott, ed. *Critical Essays on Shakespeare's* Hamlet. New York: G. K. Hall, 1995.

Keats, John. *The Letters of John Keats*. Edited by H. Burton Forman. London: Reeves & Turner, 1895.

Kerrigan, William. Hamlet's *Perfection*. Baltimore, Md.: Johns Hopkins University Press, 1994.

Kinney, Arthur F., ed. Hamlet: *New Critical Essays*. New York: Routledge, 2002.

Knights, L. C. *An Approach to* Hamlet London: Chatto & Windus, 1960.

Knox, John. *The History of the Reformation of Religion in Scotland*. Glasgow: Blackie, Fullarton & Co., 1831.

Lamb, Charles. *The Life, Letters, and Writings of Charles Lamb*. London: E. Moxon and Co., 1876.

Leavenworth, Russell E., ed. *Interpreting* Hamlet: *Materials for Analysis*. San Francisco, Calif.: Chandler, 1960.

Levin, Harry. *The Question of* Hamlet. New York: Oxford University Press, 1959.

Lewis, C. S. *Hamlet: The Prince or the Poem?* London: Milford, 1942.

Lyly, John. *Euphues: The Anatomy of Wit*. London: George Routledge & Sons Ltd., 1916.

Maek, Maynard. "The World of *Hamlet*." *Yale Review* 41 (Summer 1952): 502–523.

McGee, Arthur. *The Elizabethan Hamlet*. New Haven, Conn.: Yale University Press, 1987.

Nashe, Thomas. *The Works of Thomas Nashe*. London: A. H. Bollen, 1905.

Prosser, Eleanor. *Hamlet and Revenge*. 2d ed. Stanford, Calif.: Stanford University Press, 1971.

Rose, Jacqueline. "*Hamlet*—The *Mona Lisa* of Literature." *Critical Quarterly* 28 (1986): 35–49.

Rosenberg, Marvin. *The Masks of Hamlet*. Newark: University of Delaware Press, 1992.

Sontag, Susan. *A Susan Sontag Reader*. Introduction by Elizabeth Hardwick. New York: Vintage, 1983.

Spurgeon, Caroline F. E. *Shakespeare's Imagery and What It Tells Us*. Cambridge: Cambridge University Press, 1935.

Trench, W. F. *Shakespeare's* Hamlet: *A New Commentary*. London: John Murray, 1913.

Williamson, Claude. C. H., comp. *Readings on the Character of Hamlet, 1661–1947*. London: George Allen & Unwin, 1951.

Wilson, John Dover. *What Happens in* Hamlet. Cambridge: Cambridge University Press, 1935.

Wofford, Susanne L., ed. *William Shakespeare:* Hamlet. *Case Studies in Contemporary Criticism.* New York: St. Martin's Press, 1993.

Wright, George T. "Hendiadys and *Hamlet*." *PMLA* 96 (1981): 168–193.

FILM AND VIDEO PRODUCTIONS

Bennett, Rodney, dir. *Hamlet.* With Derek Jacobi, Patrick Stewart, Claire Bloom, and Eric Porter. BBC, 1980.

Branagh, Kenneth, dir. *Hamlet.* With Kenneth Branagh, Derek Jacobi, Julie Christie, Kate Winslet, Richard Briers, and Michael Maloney. Castle Rock Entertainment, 1996.

Kline, Kevin, dir. *Hamlet.* With Kevin Klein, Brian Murray, Dana Ivey, and Diane Venora. Great Performances, 1990.

Olivier, Laurence, dir. *Hamlet.* With Laurence Olivier, Basil Sydney, Jean Simmons, Felix Aylmer, and Eileen Herlie. Rank/Two Cities, 1948.

Zeffirelli, Franco, dir. *Hamlet.* With Mel Gibson, Alan Bates, Glenn Close, Helena Bonham Carter, and Ian Holm. Warner/Nelson Entertainment, 1990.

—Joseph Rosenblum

Henry IV, Part 1

INTRODUCTION

Henry IV, Part 1 is one of Shakespeare's finest history plays. Shakespeare's histories were written in response to popular demand, but his achievement lies in the creation of characters rather than in presenting a unified story. In *Henry IV, Part 1,* the main action of Henry IV's victory at Shrewsbury provides a climax to the action while not overshadowing the portrayal of the characters. In Shakespeare's hands, the play becomes a drama of human emotions.

While Shakespeare's other histories revolve around princes and nobles and in general lack comedy, the two parts of the *Henry IV* contain a pronounced comic element as expressed in the character of Sir John Falstaff and the depiction of common characters and tavern life. Indeed, the comic subplot running throughout the play makes it unique among the histories, as the others are laden with a heavy, serious atmosphere. *Henry IV, Part 1* also has the distinction of introducing Falstaff, who has become one of the theater's most celebrated comic figures. But beyond the unscrupulous, happy-go-lucky Falstaff, the play's diversity of characters is a remarkable feature: the elegant King Henry IV; the haughty, short-sighted, but brave warrior Hotspur; and a gallery of truly brilliant minor characters such as Worcester, Glendower, and Mortimer. The plot unravels through the political conflict between the king and Hotspur and the personal vendetta between Prince Hal, the king's eldest son, and Hotspur. The grim fabric of that vendetta is intermittently checkered by the ribald fun that Falstaff introduces, making *Henry IV Part 1* one of the most enjoyable of Shakespeare's history plays.

In a sense, *Henry IV, Part 1* is an extension of the story Shakespeare began in *Richard II,* and the story continues in *Henry IV, Part 2,* with the civil war in England looming. Finally, the saga concludes with the play that depicts Prince Hal's actions as king in *Henry V.* Critics often consider these four plays a tetralogy, which they sometimes call "The Henriad."

BACKGROUND

In total, Shakespeare's eight histories of England span almost 100 years, from the 1377–99 reign of Richard II, who was deposed by Henry IV and killed in 1400; to the battle of Bosworth Field, where Richard III was defeated and killed; to the establishment of the Tudor dynasty by Henry VII. Shakespeare first wrote the four plays that cover the latter part of this history: the three Henry VI plays and *Richard III. Henry IV, Part 1* belongs to tetralogy, or a group of four plays, covering the periods between 1399 and 1413. The other plays of this category are *Richard II, Henry IV, Part 2,* and *Henry V.*

This tetralogy begins with the tale of the deterioration of the highly promising King Richard II and closely (but imperfectly) follows the history as Shakespeare knew it. Richard II's pro-French policies and ungovernable temper led to his alienation

Prince Henry and Ned rob Falstaff and his companions in Act II, Scene 2 of *Henry IV, Part 1*. This is a print from the Boydell Shakespeare Gallery project, which was first conceived in 1786 and lasted until 1805. *(Painting by Robert Smirke and Joseph Farington; engraving by Samuel Middiman)*

from the courtiers. Richard's uncle, John of Gaunt, had protected him for some time, but the latter's death in February 1399 left Richard exposed to the anger of commoners as well as nobles. Richard exiled his uncle's son, Henry Bolingbroke, and after Gaunt's death, Richard confiscated the estate of Lancaster, extending Henry's exile for life. But Henry was not easily daunted. Returning from exile, he landed at Ravenspur in Yorkshire and gathered support by proclaiming that he simply wanted his rights as a landlord and a nobleman—he was not eyeing the throne. Thus, he garnered support from the Percys: Northumberland, his brother Thomas Worcester, and his son Henry, nicknamed Hotspur. When Richard returned from Ireland, he found that he had little support. Realizing danger to his life, Richard offered to pass the crown to Henry, who killed him in an uprising in 1400.

Henry IV's usurpation met with much hostility, as Richard had already nominated the earl of March as his heir in 1398. This hostility seethed until finally Hotspur defied the king's orders to hand over prisoners of the war of Holmedon, which the former had fought against the earl of Douglas.

With an empty treasury, Henry IV could not pay his nobles for their military services. Further angering the nobles, Henry refused to ransom an important prisoner. The agitation of the nobles, who joined forces with the Percys, came to a head in 1403.

With dissidents joining forces against Henry IV, the rebel troops were stronger than expected. Henry acted promptly, preventing all the rebel troops from coming together. In the Battle of Shrewsbury, which is the climax of *Henry IV, Part 1*, the king, with the help of his brave son, killed Hotspur and held Worcester and Douglas captive before Glendower and Northumberland could come to their rescue. However, the year 1405 proved more dangerous for Henry IV than 1403 ever did. In 1405, Glendower, Mortimer, and Northumberland agreed to divide England and Wales into three parts, and the Archbishop of York revolted against the king. His allies included his nephew William Plumpton and the marshal of England, Lord Bardolph; they captured and executed the king's general Westmoreland. Northumberland and Bardolph fled to Scotland, and in 1408, they were killed at Brahmam Moor by the sheriff of Yorkshire. Thus, Henry firmly established his authority, crushing the second rebellion successfully.

However, Henry's reign was never free from rebellion and oppositions. His son, with whom he could never reconcile, became a strong opponent. Moreover, his foreign policies caused strife. At the time, France was split in two factions, Burgundy and Armagnac. In July 1411, the duke of Burgundy approached Henry IV with the offer of marrying his daughter to Prince Henry (whom Shakespeare calls "Hal") in return for a military alliance. The prince consented to the marriage, and it had the support of many nobles. But the king was against it. Henry IV again acted promptly and dismissed his son from the council of ministers. Also, the next year, the king signed an agreement with the Armagnacs, who were Burgundy's enemies. Prince Henry, who loved the lavish life, wanted to assume power from his father prematurely. Dissidents gathered around the prince, making him stronger. However, the king's death in March 1413 prevented the need of any rebellion, and the prince became the king unopposed.

Shakespeare, as he often did, took liberties with this history and twisted the facts. He drew his material first and foremost from Raphael Holinshed's *Chronicles of England, Scotland and Ireland,* which was published in 1577 and 1587. He also collected material from *Famous Victories of Henry V,* which was published in 1588 and 1598. Samuel Daniel's narrative poem of 1595, *The First Fowre Bookes of the Civile Wars Between the Two Houses of Lancaster and Yorke,* was another source. Daniel's poem follows the historical events of this period, and Shakespeare followed the poet when he decided, for example, that Glendower would be absent from Shrewsbury (the Welsh were there according to Holinshed). While Daniel confused the two Edmund Mortimers, Shakespeare took Holinshed for authority.

Drawing from several sources, Shakespeare dwelled on the idea that a parallel could be made between Hal and Hotspur. He borrowed from John Stow's *Annales of England* for the incident in which Prince Hal returns robbed money to the merchants. He based the incident of the prince's saving his father from Douglas on the battlefield on Daniel's *Civile Wars.* The prince's challenge to Hotspur is reminiscent of Percy's in *The Ballad of the Chevy Chase* by Daniel, an epic poem about the Wars of the Roses. The basis of the confrontation scene (3.2) between Henry and Hal comes from Holinshed, who writes that the tales Henry had heard about his son "brought no small suspicion into the kings head, least his son would presume to vsurpe the crowne . . ." (154). Also, the prince's mourning over Hotspur's body parallels Percy's lament over Douglas's dead body in Daniel's *Ballad* and two anonymous, humorous plays: *Woodstock* and *The Famous Victories of Henry the Fifth.*

Shakespeare found inspiration for other characters in various additional sources. Sir John Falstaff, one of the play's most memorable characters, is based on John Oldcastle, a prominent minister. Shakespeare went so far as to use Oldcastle's name (Hal's pun on it remains in the first scene) in the first performances of the play. However, William Brooke, Lord Cobham, Elizabeth I's Lord

Chamberlain and John Oldcastle's descendant, apparently forced Shakespeare to change it, and Oldcastle has been Falstaff ever since (except in Oxford University's 1986 *Complete Works*).

Shakespeare's most notable deviations from accepted history are the following:

1. Prince Hal has been represented as the same age as Hotspur, while actually Hal was 14 years younger. This parallelism of age accentuates the dramatic effect of their combat on the battlefield.
2. Shakespeare hurries the reconciliation between Henry IV and Prince Hal. In real life, Prince Henry and his father were reconciled in 1412; in the play, the event occurs just before the Battle of Shrewsbury, which was fought in 1403. The critic James B. Collins explains: "Since the reconciliation is the turning point of the play, it was necessary to precede it with some action to preserve the dramatic balance of the whole."
3. Richard J. Beck mentions Shakespeare's glorification of the prince, who is shown to save his father from death by rescuing him during the Battle of Shrewsbury. In reality, the prince was only 16 at the time, and the king was saved due to his cunning use of impersonations on the battlefield (a ruse which is used in the play). In Holinshed, the king is a valiant soldier, and there is no mention of his son's intervention to save him.
4. Shakespeare paints Henry IV as a kind king who was merciful to the defeated rebels. History tells us that Hotspur's body was crushed between millstones and then chopped into pieces.
5. Shakespeare, as well as Holinshed, takes the earl of March for Henry's uncle Mortimer. In reality, it was the earl of March whose ransom was so important for Henry, as a main objective of the rebellion was to place the earl of March on the throne.
6. In 1402, when the play opens, King Henry IV was around 35. Hotspur was three years older than the king, while Prince Hal was 15. Shakespeare's Hotspur is the prince's age, and Henry IV is portrayed as an old man.
7. As a 15-year-old, the real prince was probably not as wild as Shakespeare paints him. Also, in 1398, the prince was in Ireland with Richard, and between 1400 and 1403, he was in Wales against Glendower.
8. Lady Percy's name has been changed from Elizabeth to Kate.
9. The triple division of England happened in 1406, long after the Battle of Shrewsbury.

Date and Text of the Play

Henry IV, Part 1 appeared in two separate quartos in 1598, the second of which serves as the standard text for most modern editions. There were five more quartos printed in 1599, 1604, 1608, 1613, and 1622, testifying to the play's popularity. In 1623, the First Folio appeared; it adopted the 1613 version, with the alteration of a few swear words following passage of the Profanity Act in 1606.

In the Stationer's Register, the play is entered on February 25, 1598, with the title *The History of Henrie the Fourth*. Francis Meres's *Palladis Tamia* (1598) mentions this play, so it was clearly written before 1598. Stylistic indications, such as the absence of puns, rarity of rhymed lines, and use of prose, lead scholars to believe that it was written between 1596 and 1597.

SYNOPSIS
Brief Synopsis

Henry Bolingbroke kills Richard II and, after usurping his throne, becomes King Henry IV of England. His reign is disturbed by his nobles' revolt, and he must drop his plans for a crusade to Palestine because of these interventions. Harry Percy, who successfully quashed a Scottish uprising, refuses to hand over prisoners of war to the king. When the king refuses to ransom Mortimer, who was held captive in the Scottish trouble, Percy (known by his nickname *Hotspur*) plans a rebellion against him. He is joined by Worcester, Owen Glendower, and Northumberland, all of whom earlier had helped Henry dethrone Richard II.

The serious main plot of the play revolves around the rebellion against Henry's authority; the comic

46

The First Part of Henry the Fourth,
with the Life and Death of HENRY
Sirnamed HOT-SPVRRE.

Actus Primus. Scœna Prima.

Enter the King, Lord Iohn of Lancaster, Earle of Westmerland, with others.

King.

SO shaken as we are, so wan with care,
Finde we a time for frighted Peace to pant,
And breath shortwinded accents of new broils
To be commenc'd in Stronds a-farre remote:
No more the thirsty entrance of this Soile,
Shall daube her lippes with her owne childrens blood:
No more shall trenching Warre channell her fields,
Nor bruise her Flowrets with the Armed hoofes
Of hostile paces. Those opposed eyes,
Which like the Meteors of a troubled Heauen,
All of one Nature, of one Substance bred,
Did lately meete in the intestine shocke,
And furious cloze of ciuill Butchery,
Shall now in mutuall well-beseeming rankes
March all one way, and be no more oppos'd
Against Acquaintance, Kindred, and Allies.
The edge of Warre, like an ill-sheathed knife,
No more shall cut his Master. Therefore Friends,
As farre as to the Sepulcher of Christ,
Whose Souldier now vnder whose blessed Crosse
We are impressed and ingag'd to fight,
Forthwith a power of English shall we leuie,
Whose armes were moulded in their Mothers wombe,
To chace these Pagans in those holy Fields,
Ouer whose Acres walk'd those blessed feete
Which fourteene hundred yeares ago were nail'd
For our aduantage on the bitter Crosse.
But this our purpose is a twelue month old,
And bootlesse 'tis to tell you we will go:
Therefore we meete not now. Then let me heare
Of you my gentle Cousin Westmerland,
What yesternight our Councell did decree,
In forwarding this deere expedience.

West. My Liege: This haste was hot in question,
And many limits of the Charge set downe
But yesternight: when all athwart there came
A Post from Wales, loaden with heauy Newes;
Whose worst was, That the Noble *Mortimer*,
Leading the men of Herefordshire to fight
Against the irregular and wilde *Glendower*,
Was by the rude hands of that Welshman taken,
And a thousand of his people butchered:

Vpon whose dead corpes there was such misuse,
Such beastly, shamelesse transformation,
By those Welshwomen done, as may not be
(Without much shame) re-told or spoken of.

King. It seemes then, that the tidings of this broile,
Brake off our businesse for the Holy land.

West. This matcht with other like, my gracious Lord,
Farre more vneuen and vnwelcome Newes
Came from the North, and thus it did report:
On Holy-roode day, the gallant *Hotspurre* there,
Young *Harry Percy*, and braue *Archibald*,
That euer-valiant and approoued Scot,
At *Holmedon* met, where they did spend
A sad and bloody houre:
As by discharge of their Artillerie,
And shape of likely-hood the newes was told:
For he that brought them, in the very heate
And pride of their contention, did take horse,
Vncertaine of the issue any way.

King. Heere is a deere and true industrious friend,
Sir *Walter Blunt*, new lighted from his Horse,
Strain'd with the variation of each soyle,
Betwixt that *Holmedon*, and this Seat of ours:
And he hath brought vs smooth and welcome newes.
The Earle of *Dowglas* is discomfited,
Ten thousand bold Scots, two and twenty Knights
Balk'd in their owne blood did Sir *Walter* see
On *Holmedons* Plaines. Of Prisoners, *Hotspurre* tooke
Mordake Earle of Fife, and eldest sonne
To beaten *Dowglas*, and the Earle of *Atholl*,
Of *Murry*, *Angus*, and *Menteith*.
And is not this an honourable spoyle?
A gallant prize? Ha Cosin, is it not? Infaith it is.

West. A Conquest for a Prince to boast of.

King. Yea, there thou mak'st me sad, & mak'st me sin,
In enuy, that my Lord Northumberland
Should be the Father of so blest a Sonne:
A Sonne, who is the Theame of Honors tongue;
Among'st a Groue, the very straightest Plant,
Who is sweet Fortunes Minion, and her Pride:
Whil'st I by looking on the praise of him,
See Ryot and Dishonor staine the brow
Of my yong *Harry*. O that it could be prou'd,
That some Night-tripping-Faiery, had exchang'd
In Cradle-clothes, our Children where they lay,
And call'd mine *Percy*, his *Plantagenet*:

Then

Title page of the First Folio edition of *Henry IV, Part I*, published in 1623

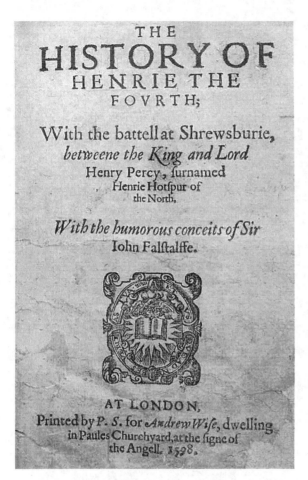

THE
HISTORY OF
HENRIE THE
FOVRTH;

With the battell at Shrewsburie,
betweene the King and Lord
Henry Percy, furnamed
Henrie Hotspur of
the North,

With the humorous conceits of Sir
Iohn Falſtalffe.

AT LONDON,
Printed by *P. S.* for *Andrew Wiſe,* dwelling
in Paules Churchyard, at the ſigne of
the Angell. 1598.

Title page of the 1598 quarto edition of *Henry IV, Part 1*

land of Palestine. He discloses his plan to bring all the scattered sections of the English nation under one banner and shares how he has been working toward fulfilling his dream of ending the civil wars that have infested England for the past year. Westmoreland informs him how the defeat of the English forces at Welsh's hand has led to Mortimer's arrest, and the matter of the crusade suddenly takes a backseat. Mortimer has not only been captured by Glandower, but he has also married the latter's daughter.

The king and Westmoreland also discuss Hotspur's victory in the Battle of Holmedon. Hotspur has been daring enough not to hand over the prisoners of war to the king, who wistfully compares Hotspur's valor to his own son's worthlessness. Westmoreland adds to Henry's anger by telling him about Hotspur's humiliating attitude toward his uncle, the Earl of Worcester.

The scene ends with the king informing his friend that he has asked Hotspur to explain his arrogance and to answer the charges brought against him. He has decided to shelf the pilgrimage project in view of the impending political troubles. Henry here appears as a visionary having a utopian dream of a peaceful, unified England. However, this dream proves short lived in light of news of rising rebellion against him.

The king's sadness at heart and disappointment with his son highlight this scene. Comparing Prince Hal to Hotspur, Henry finds his son nowhere a match. His resentment knows no boundaries, and he even shares his desire to switch his son with Hotspur, as Hotspur has all the qualities of a king's son.

Act I, Scene 2

After the political and personal intrigue of the previous scene, this scene is designed to bring comic relief. Prince Hal and his friend Falstaff are engaged in a battle of wits. They talk of the poor plight of highwaymen, and it becomes clear not only that their sympathies lie with the robbers, but they themselves are involved in such schemes. Ned Poins, a companion in these misdeeds, enters

subplot reveals the flippant dallying of Henry's son, Prince Hal, and his friends, the most prominent of whom is Falstaff. With his rabble-rousing ways, Prince Hal creates constant trouble for his father.

The rebellion is fought at Shrewsbury. During the battle, the prince not only saves his father but also kills Hotspur, Worcester and Glendower are captured, and the rebellion is crushed, paving way for Henry's smooth reign.

Act I, Scene 1

King Henry IV is in conversation with his brother-in-law, the Earl of Westmoreland. The king expresses his will to join the crusade in the holy to divulge plans for another robbery. The prince does not seem excited about the plan so Ned asks Falstaff to leave the job to him. Falstaff leaves; Ned suggests robbing Falstaff, once he has executed the highway robbery project. The prince readily agrees to join Ned. This scene ends with Hal's soliloquy in which he shows his true nature is not as frivolous as he projects.

The scene has several functions, not the least of which is to reveal Prince Hal's seriousness at heart. The scene also includes foreshadowing, as when Falstaff tells Hal, "by the lord, I'll be a traitor then, when thou art king" (130). This indeed proves true in *Part 2*. Also, Hal's statement, "so, when this loose behavior I throw off, / And pay the debt I never promised, / By how much better than my word I am" (190–193) comes true in Act V.

Act I, Scene 3

At the palace in London, the king gives audience to Hotspur; his father, the Earl of Northumberland; and his uncle, the Earl of Worcester, who annoys the king and is asked to leave. Northumberland defends his son, who blames Hotspur's haughtiness on the king's messenger, who had irritated Hotspur by his rudeness. The king is not satisfied with Hotspur's explanation and orders Hotspur to hand over the prisoners of war to him.

After the king leaves, Hotspur complains to his father that he is furious at Henry's charges against Mortimer and vows not to return the prisoners. Worcester reveals that Richard II had nominated Mortimer as his heir, meaning that Henry IV is a usurper who should fear Mortimer. Hotspur turns his anger against his father and uncle, both of whom had helped Henry IV when he returned from exile.

After a heated discussion among the three, Hotspur is placated by Northumberland's disclosure of a plan to revolt against Henry. It is decided that Hotspur will make the son of Douglas his ally in Scotland and foster support from nobles; Northumberland will befriend the Archbishop of York. Hotspur makes it clear that nothing is more precious to him than his honor, and he hates honor

Gadshill attempts to engage two carriers in conversation in Act II, Scene 1 of *Henry IV, Part 1*. This print is from the Boydell Shakespeare Gallery project. *(Painting by Robert Smirke; engraving by James Fittler)*

going to undeserving people. Honor is an important theme in the play, and this theme is introduced here. They exit, excited about their plans.

Act II, Scene 1

This scene takes place in Rochester, in the yard of an inn. It is early morning, and two carriers on their way out complain about the inn's poor condition. Gadshill enters and tries to start a conversation with them. The carriers rightly presume that he is a robber and do not respond to his overtures. When the carriers leave, Gadshill calls the chamberlain, who informs Gadshill about a couple of wealthy gentlemen carrying a lot of money. As they are preparing to leave, it would be a convenient time for Gadshill to rob them. Gadshill leaves, promising to share the loot with the chamberlain. The scene functions to offer a glimpse of the dangerous highway conditions for travelers at that time. *Henry IV, Part 1* has many common characters, unlike Shakespeare's other histories. The whole scene is written in prose; Shakespeare makes sure that the dialogue here echoes language spoken by the commoner.

Act II, Scene 2

On the highway, the stage is set for Hal, Ned, and Falstaff to execute their robbery. But Ned and Hal have stolen Falstaff's horse as a joke, much to Falstaff's consternation.

Gadshill enters to inform them about the impending arrival of their targets. Hal and Ned hide down the hill; Falstaff and his other comrades rob the travelers. As the robbers share the booty, the prince and Ned appear in disguise and rob the robbers. Falstaff tries to run away, his heavy body becoming the butt of the prince's joke. The scene is devised to show the prince's playful nature. Because he loves having fun and is not a serious robber, the transformation to a brave, loyal son becomes somewhat more convincing.

Act II, Scene 3

At Warkworth Castle, Hotspur is furious upon reading a letter from a man he asked to be an ally in the rebellion against Henry IV. This letter warns Hotspur against the consequences of such rebellion. Hotspur's wife, Lady Percy, enters. She has noticed Hotspur's recent unrest and accuses her husband of indifference. She also asks him why, in his sleep, he has been muttering words connected with warfare. Instead of responding to his wife, Hotspur calls out to a servant inquiring about a horse. Angry that her husband has not told her about any attempts to secure the release of her brother, Edmund Mortimer, Lady Percy threatens to leave him. Hotspur finally responds, saying that times are grim and he does not have time to dally. He refuses to divulge any of his real

This print, published by Cassell & Company in the 19th century, shows Hotspur and Lady Percy arguing in Act II, Scene 3 of *Henry IV, Part 1*. (Painting by Alfred Edward Chalon; engraving by W. Ridgway)

intentions to his wife, saying that women cannot keep secrets.

Women often are insignificant characters in Shakespeare's history plays, but in this play, the rebels' wives play a role. Still, in this scene, Hotspur does not attach any importance to his wife's presence and refuses to share any secrets with her because, though loyal to him, she is, after all, a woman. Shakespeare's depiction of women in this play has come in for a great deal of criticism.

Act II, Scene 4

A long scene at Boar's-Head Tavern begins with Prince Hal and Ned joking at the expense of a waiter, Francis, who seems only to be able to say

"Anon! Sir, Anon!" Falstaff and his companions enter. Falstaff complains to Hal about his desertion on the highway, and he informs the prince that he had plundered 1,000 pounds that day. But he cannot produce the booty, which he says was robbed from him by a band of about 100 robbers. He then gives an exaggerated account of his valor against the robbers. According to his story, he captured the miscreants only to come against another band that set the captives free. The prince, then, reveals his and Ned's joke on Falstaff, who takes a turn, saying he did not resist the "robbers" because he had recognized the prince immediately.

The inn's hostess appears with information about the arrival of Sir John Bracy, who has news of Percy's revolt against the king. But Hal and Falstaff continue their games, with Falstaff impersonating the king and the prince playing Falstaff. Soon, they switch roles. This role-play between Hal and Falstaff highlights the scene. Hal's command of language and his skill to play any role shine through here. Hal also imitates Hotspur and his wife, making Hotspur the butt of his humor and foregrounding Hal's performance on the battlefield, where he appears as brave and deft in warfare as Hotspur.

The sheriff arrives, along with constables. Hal hides Falstaff behind the tapestry and assures the sheriff that he will hand over the "fat man" if he happens to find him. Falstaff falls asleep behind the curtains.

Act III, Scene 1

In the house of the archdeacon at Bangor, Hotspur, Worcester, Mortimer, and Glendower are meeting. Glendower boasts of his magical powers with which he claims he can win the rebellion. Hotspur dismisses Glendower's bragging. Mortimer draws their attention to the proposed division of the kingdom among himself, Hotspur, and Glendower after their victory. Hotspur has some objections, which Glendower responds to with sarcasm. Somehow, Hotspur gives in, and they plan to take leave of their wives before going to the battlefield. There are humorous moments between Mortimer and

his wife: She speaks only Welsh, while Mortimer speaks only English.

This scene illustrates differences in the three rebels' characters. Hotspur stands apart in his vision and daring. He is not easy to convince, and also, he is too immature to understand the importance of keeping the rebels unified.

Act III, Scene 2

In the royal palace, Henry IV chides his son for his wayward life. The prince is apologetic, but he defends himself by saying that he is not as bad as has been rumored. The king compares the prince with Richard II and reminds him that Richard was ruined because of his low company. Then, he contrasts his son's character with that of Hotspur and wonders if Hal could be bribed by Hotspur. Hal assures his father of his loyalty. Blunt enters to inform the king that the rebel forces have assembled at Shrewsbury.

In this reconciliation scene, Prince Hal makes his serious intentions clear before the king, who derives much solace from it. As is usual in Shakespeare, this turning point marks the middle of the play. The high-water mark of this scene is when the prince vows to mend his vagabond ways. In this

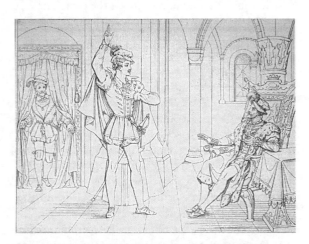

Prince Hal assures King Henry of his loyalty as Blunt enters, in Act III, Scene 2 of *Henry IV, Part 1*. This is a plate from *Retzsch's Outlines to Shakespeare: Henry IV, Part 1*, published in 1846. *(Illustration by Moritz Retzsch)*

sense, the scene foregrounds Act V, Scene 3, in which Hal follows through on his promise.

Act III, Scene 3

Another humorous scene set in the Boar's-Head Tavern has Falstaff talking to Bardolph, the former repentant, but also making fun of Bardolph. The hostess, Mistress Quickly, enters to demand payment of bills. Falstaff complains, telling her that it was in her inn that somebody picked his pocket and stole his gold ring. The hostess responds that the prince told her the ring is made of copper. Hal and Ned enter; the hostess tells the prince that Falstaff has been telling her that the prince owes him 1,000 pounds. Falstaff tries to correct the hostess, saying he had said that the prince owes him his love worth 1,000 pounds.

The prince reveals to Falstaff that it was he who emptied his pocket, which contained nothing of value. The prince also informs Falstaff that his father is pleased with him; Falstaff suggests the prince take advantage of his favorable position by robbing the exchequer. Hal tells Falstaff about his plans to fight against the rebels, and Falstaff is to be the commander of the foot soldiers.

Besides showing Falstaff's wit, this scene does not do much by way of advancing the plot. The fact that Hal returned the stolen money to the sheriff brings some hope that he will prove true to what he promised in his soliloquy in Act I, Scene 2 and to his father in the previous scene.

Act IV, Scene 1

The rebel camp at Shrewsbury provides the setting. Hotspur, Worcester, and Douglas are in conversation. A messenger delivers a letter from Northumberland, informing the rebels that his illness prevents him from mobilizing allies and taking part in the battle. Still optimistic, Hotspur feels it is good that all their troops will not be involved at once. Douglas agrees, but Worcester worries that Northumberland's absence may demoralize his forces. Vernon enters and informs them of his march toward Shrewsbury. When Hotspur asks about the prince, Vernon draws a picture of the

prince's bravery, which makes Hotspur jealous. Hotspur waits eagerly for the break of the day, when he will get the opportunity to fight Hal. Vernon informs them that the king has an army of 30,000 soldiers. Hotspur becomes a little nervous, but Douglas maintains his courage. This scene foregrounds the fate of the rebellion; Hotspur's impatient nature shines through, making it clear that the rebels will meet a sad fate. Vernon's description of Hal as "feathered mercury" (106) is especially remarkable for its aptness and brilliance.

Act IV, Scene 2

Falstaff and Bardolph are on a public road near Coventry. Falstaff sends Bardolph to bring him some wine, and then he starts a soliloquy that reveals his vileness to the core. He built up his troop by strong-arming people who did not want to join. The reluctant would-be soldiers bribed him for their release, putting 300 pounds in Falstaff's pocket. Then, he filled the vacant places with rogues and tricksters, creating an ill-equipped army. Prince Hal and Westmoreland enter; Hall remarks that Falstaff's soldiers look poor and wretched. He wonders how such weaklings will face the enemy.

This brief scene illustrates Falstaff's wretched nature. As the commander of the prince's army, he is not inspired to fight for his country. His materialistic temperament understands only monetary gains, and he makes money by accepting bribes. His speech "If I be not ashamed of my soldiers, I am a soused gurnet. I have misused the king's press damnably . . ." (11–49) is a prologue to his legendary speech on honor in Act V, Scene 2.

Act IV, Scene 3

At the rebel camp at Shrewsbury, Hotspur and Douglas argue for fighting immediately while Vernon and Worcester advise against such hasty action. Blunt enters with a message of reconciliation from the king, who will forgive Hotspur and redress his grievances. Hotspur reminds Blunt of how Henry used the Percys to oust Richard II, only to betray them once he became the king. Blunt expresses his earnest desire to see Hotspur united with the king; Hotspur defers the reply till next morning.

Hotspur's haughty temperament becomes clear in his speeches with Blunt. His anger is uncontrolled and does not hesitate to humiliate the king at every opportunity.

Act IV, Scene 4
At the palace of the Archbishop of York, the Archbishop is worried about Hotspur's weak position. Since he knows that he will be the next target if Hotspur is defeated, he gives letters to Sir Michael for the Lord Marshal and Scroop, the Archbishop of York, to support Hotspur. This is the only appearance of the Archbishop of York and serves to establish sequential connection with *Part 2,* where he has a more important role.

Act V, Scene 1
The king is in his camp near Shrewsbury with Hal, Lancaster, Westmoreland, Blunt, and Falstaff. When Worcester and Vernon arrive, the king expresses his disappointment at Worcester for joining the rebels. Worcester pleads the case of the rebels, saying that the king wronged the Percys, hence, their anger is justified. The king denies the charges. The prince says that he has high regards for Hotspur's valor, but he would go to any extent to defend his father. He also offers to fight Hotspur in a single combat to decide the matter; that way, they would save lives that might otherwise be lost in battle. The encounter reminds the audience of the heated exchange between Hotspur and Blunt in Act IV, Scene 3. And, after his vow of redemption in Act III, Scene 2, Hal appears true to his royal lineage.

Worcester and Vernon leave, and the prince remarks that Hotspur is so confident of defeating any army that they will not accept the offer of friendship. The king leaves after issuing orders to his commanders to be ready to fight at any moment.

Most remarkable in this scene is Falstaff's speech on honor, which presents his pragmatic approach to such idealistic notions. He makes fun of royalty who sacrifice men for the sake of false honor.

Act V, Scene 2
In the rebel camp, Worcester discloses to Vernon his plans of giving a mutilated version of the king's message to Hotspur. Vernon disagrees with the idea, but Worcester convinces him by telling that it is in Hotspur's best interest not to join the king. The king might forgive him for the moment, Worcester says, but resentment and distrust against Hotspur will remain—even after joining hands with the king, Hotspur will never get the respect due to a friend.

Hotspur and Douglas appear and order the release of Westmoreland, who was held hostage to ensure Worcester's and Vernon's safe return from their mission to the king. Worcester informs them that the king is adamant about fighting the rebels and that the prince has challenged Hotspur to a single combat. However, Vernon adds that this challenge was given in an honorable manner by the prince, who has great respect for Hotspur. A messenger enters with some letters, but Hotspur is too agitated to read them. Instead, he harangues his friends about the war. Worcester's treacherous, selfish nature is brought to the fore.

Act V, Scene 3
On the battlefield, Douglas confronts Blunt, taking him for the king. He tells him that Lord Strafford has been killed at his hands because Strafford was disguised as the king. In the fight that ensues, Douglas kills Blunt. When Hotspur enters, Douglas says that he has killed the king, but Hotspur tells him it was Blunt disguised as the king. Douglas vows he will kill all those who are in king's guise until he happens to kill the king himself.

They leave; Falstaff enters and looks at Blunt's body. In a sarcastic eulogy, he prays to God to protect the dead man from bullets. He says that only three of his soldiers are alive. The prince enters, rebukes Falstaff for evading the battleground, and demands Falstaff's sword. Falstaff boasts of his bravery and claims to have killed Percy. He offers the prince a bottle of wine instead of the sword. The prince takes him to task, throws the bottle, and leaves the stage. Falstaff, in a soliloquy, says that he will never face Hotspur because he prefers life to such an honorable death as Blunt's.

Act V, Scene 4

The prince is wounded in battle. The king wants him to retire with Lancaster, but he refuses. Douglas appears and, taking the king for an impersonator, says the king is growing Hydra's heads. The king not only declares his identity but also challenges Douglas to a fight. When the king gets in danger in the fight, his son rescues him. Douglas flees, and Henry praises his son's bravery and loyalty.

Hotspur appears; Hal praises him but also challenges him to a fight. Falstaff appears and starts commenting on this fight. Douglas reappears and wounds Falstaff, who falls down, pretending to be dead. Douglas leaves, and immediately after that, Hotspur succumbs to the prince's attack. While dying, Hotspur says that he has been robbed not only of his life but also his reputation. The prince pays tribute to the brave rebel. When the prince leaves, Falstaff jumps up, and to ensure Hotspur's death, he stabs his body. Hal reenters, and Falstaff gives him a false account of his bravery. He reports

Falstaff tells Prince Henry that he killed Hotspur in Act V, Scene 4 of *Henry IV, Part 1*. Plate from *Retzsch's Outlines to Shakespeare:* Henry IV *(Illustration by Moritz Retzsch)*

that Hotspur was alive when the prince left and that he bravely finished him. Retreat sounds, and the prince understands it as a sign of royal victory.

Hotspur's passion; Hal's sincerity, quick wit, and valor; Douglas's bravery and elegance; and Falstaff's meanness and cowardice all shine through the battle scene.

Act V, Scene 5

Worcester and Vernon are presented as prisoners of war before the king, who chides Worcester for having misrepresented his message to Hotspur. He orders that the prisoners be beheaded and then announces the outcome of the battle. Hal requests that his father set Douglas free because he is a brave man; the king agrees. The king appoints Lancaster to deliver this message of mercy to Douglas and to fight against Northumberland and the Archbishop of York. He and his son, meanwhile, will march against Glendower and Mortimer. Thus, he is confident they will crush the rebels completely.

CHARACTER LIST

King Henry IV   The ruling king of England, also known as Henry Bolingbroke, is an uncertain, guilty person at the outset of the play. His reign is marked with internal strife in England, which has erupted into an even larger, more violent civil war. There is another thorn in his side: his son, whose wild ways are a major concern.

Henry, Prince of Wales   King Henry IV's son, who will eventually become King Henry V, is sometimes called Harry Monmouth, after the town he was born in, and he is known as Hal to his friends in Eastcheap. Complex and shrewd, the prince becomes the central figure in the play.

Hotspur   The son and heir of the Earl of Northumberland and the nephew of the Earl of Worcester, Hotspur's real name is Henry Percy, but he is usually referred to by his nickname, which he earned due to his impetuous and rash temperament. He is a member of the powerful Percy family that helped bring King Henry IV to power after pushing aside Richard II. Quick tempered and impatient, Hotspur is preoccupied with the idea of honor and glory, to the exclusion of all other qualities.

Sir John Falstaff A fat, lascivious, dishonorable old knight, Falstaff spends most of his time in the taverns of Eastcheap, a grubby area of London, and appears to make his living as a thief and a highwayman. He acts as a kind of mentor to Prince Henry, and he is the only character in the play who can match Henry's sharp wit.

Earl of Westmoreland A nobleman, military leader, and close companion and valuable ally to King Henry IV.

Lord John of Lancaster The king's younger son; Prince Hal's sibling. Lancaster proves wise and valiant in battle, despite his youth.

Sir Walter Blunt A loyal and trusted ally of King Henry IV and a valuable warrior.

Thomas Percy, Earl of Worcester Hotspur's uncle. Shrewd and manipulative, Worcester is the mastermind behind the Percy rebellion.

Henry Percy, Earl of Northumberland Hotspur's father. Northumberland conspires and raises troops on the Percy side, but he claims that he is sick before the Battle of Shrewsbury and does not actually bring his troops into the fray.

Edmund Mortimer A brave warrior, called the Earl of March, and the brother of Hotspur's wife, Lady Percy. Mortimer has a strong claim to the English throne because before Richard II was deposed by Henry, Richard had nominated him as his successor.

Owen Glendower The leader of the Welsh rebels and father of Lady Mortimer. Glendower joins with the Percys in their insurrection against King Henry. Well read, English educated, and highly capable in battle, Glendower claims to command black magic. Some editions refer to Glendower by his Welsh name, Owain Glyndwr.

Lady Percy Hotspur's wife is a lively match to her irascible husband. She disapproves of Hotspur's military plans.

Lady Mortimer The daughter of Owen Glendower and the new wife of Edmund Mortimer, she speaks only Welsh, so she cannot fully communicate with her beloved husband.

Hotspur's wife, Lady Percy, in Act II, Scene 3 of *Henry IV, Part 1*, as depicted in this print from Charles Heath's 1848 edition of *The Heroines of Shakspeare: Comprising the Principal Female Characters in the Plays of the Great Poet.* (Painting by J. W. Wright; engraving by W. H. Egleton)

Archibald, Earl of Douglas The leader of the large Scottish faction rebelling against King Henry. Usually called simply "the Douglas" (a traditional way of referring to a Scottish clan chief), the deadly and fearless Douglas fights on the side of the Percys.

Lord Marshal Thomas Mowbray; first duke of Norfolk.

Sir Richard Vernon A relative and ally of the Earl of Worcester.

Archbishop of York The Archbishop, whose given name is Richard Scroop, conspires on the side of the Percys, lending the rebellion his authority as a religious leader.

Ned Poins, Bardolph, Peto Drinking friends of Falstaff and the prince who assist them in highway robbery and accompany them in war.

Gadshill Another highwayman and friend of the prince, Falstaff, and company. Gadshill seems to be nicknamed after the place on the London road—Gad's Hill—where he has set up many robberies.

Mistress Quickly Hostess of the Boar's-Head Tavern, a squalid dive in Eastcheap, London, where Falstaff and friends drink.

Francis An assistant drawer, or tavern servant, at the Boar's-Head.

Sir Michael A member of the Archbishop's household.

CHARACTER STUDIES
Henry IV

As Henry Bolingbroke in *Richard II,* he was a handsome young rebel who won the hearts of people; in this play, he is portrayed as an aged, care-worn monarch. Though ambitious and brave, Henry IV is exhausted with rebellions surrounding him while his son whiles away his time in trivialities, unmindful of the troubles that await England. Remorseful for his young haughty days, Henry wants to compensate for the bloodshed that he has brought upon England. He now wants to work to bring harmony and peace, saying "No more the thirsty entrance of this soil / Shall daub her lips with her own children's blood" (1.1.5–6). Yet, even his desire to participate in the crusade to Palestine is later revealed to be cunning strategy: His real intention is to send his nobles away from England and thereby squash any rebellion.

Henry is the archetypal Machiavellian ruler, and his attempt to wage a crusade is sheer brilliance, according to Machiavellian doctrine. Critics believe that Henry's plan of crusade is not as reflective of his religiosity as it is an act of policy. A crafty politician, Henry is dictated by policy in all his actions. He knows how to exploit people to further his interests. Earlier, he garnered the support of the powerful Percy family by promising that he wanted only his duchy of Lancaster when he returned to

England from exile. Then, he betrayed the family by usurping the throne from Richard II. This treachery is the reason for Worcester's distrust, as he indicates in Act V, Scene 2: "For treason is but trusted like the fox, / Who, ne'er so tame, so cherished and locked up, / Will have a wild trick of his ancestors" (10–12). Worcester correctly sees into Henry's real intentions when he sends the message of truce to Hotspur.

At the outset of the play, Henry talks about ending civil strife. As soon as the news of rebellion is brought to him, he drops the ambitious plan to indulge in what may correctly be called more bloodshed. He does not consult his councillors. At the end of the Battle of Shrewsbury, when he has successfully crushed the rebellion, he does not stop before ordering the execution of Worcester and Vernon.

Henry is proud of his kingly bearings and maintains a distance from all his nobles and lords. He believes that "familiarity breeds contempt," and says, "By being seldom seen, I could not stir / but like a comet I was wondered at" (3.2.46–47).

On the one hand, the king speaks about his intentions to establish harmony, and on the other, he challenges Hotspur to war if he does not hand over the prisoners of war. In fact, he is afraid of Hotspur's growing power and knows that if the latter keeps the prisoners of war, his powers will enhance, so he makes a big issue of the return of the prisoners. Hotspur offers an insightful analysis of the king's character in Act IV, Scene 3, when he describes Henry's rise from poverty to power in these words: "Broke oath on oath, committed wrong on wrong, / And in conclusion drove us to seek out / This head of safety, and withal to pry / Into his title, the which we find / Too indirect for long continuance" (108–111).

In the hands of Shakespeare, Henry IV becomes a crafty, arrogant, but steady man who has complete control over his temper. Unlike Hotspur, Henry is firm and subtle. His political foresight is the object of envy for the rebels, and his skill in the art of dissembling proves his biggest strength. In his heart, he nurtures his grudge against the rebels but sends them a message of forgiveness and friendship. A strong man, Henry shows his softer side only as a father when he wistfully compares Hotspur and the prince: "O that it could be proved / That some night-tripping fairy had exchanged / In cradle-clothes our children where they lay, / And call'd mine Percy, . . ." (1.1.87–90).

The proud king comes across as a sad, unfortunate father in the opening scene. He learns about Hotspur's rebellion and cannot help compare his son Hal to Hotspur, who is brave and passionate about his cause. Henry feels helpless at this time of crisis, for he doubts that his son would join hands with him in the war. In due course, however, he finds his son to be wiser and braver than Hotspur when he truly needs him. It is the prince who not only saves Henry from Hotspur but also kills Hotspur in battle.

Prince Hal

The first quarto publication of *Henry IV, Part 1* mentioned Hotspur and Falstaff on the title page, while the character of Prince Hal went unmentioned. It was in the 20th century that directors and actors started taking more interest in this character. A controversial figure, Hal is praised by critics such as A. C. Bradley and Walter Raleigh but disliked by George Bernard Shaw. The character of Hal appears in various histories, beginning in *Richard II*, where he is a minor character; to here, where he starts out an immature youth and grows into a mature, clever, and firm warrior; and ending in *Henry V*, where he is an efficient, revered monarch.

Hal is a central figure in both the comic subplot and the serious main plot. The action of both the plots is unified through him. Portrayed by Shakespeare as a strong man of convictions, Hal has two opposing sides to his character: the frivolous, playful friend of Falstaff in Act I, Scene 2, and the brave, loyal Hal of Act V, Scene 4, where he saves his father from Douglas. In fact, though the professed hero of the play is Henry IV, the play revolves around the rivalry and parallels between Hotspur and Hal. While the first half of the play portrays Hotspur as a brave, sincere, passionate

person to whom Hal can never match up, the second half proves Hal superior to Hotspur in wisdom, cunning, and valor. Examining the duality of this character, Lewis J. Owen has written: "Hal understands his father's troubles and faces the terrible burden of the fact of his ensuing duties. Also that he knows what his father expects of him. You could further say that because the burden seems so great, he escapes it by evasion and revolt. That he is only postponing responsibility and the solemnity of the court, that they are things which he fundamentally knows he must eventually accept" (28).

The audience is introduced to Hal in Act I, Scene 1, when his father presents him in an unfavorable light; this makes his emergence later on, as a brave and loyal son, all the more intriguing. In Act I, Scene 2, he plots a highway robbery with Falstaff, asking "Where shall we take a purse tomorrow, Jack?" (1.2.111). Later, he shows much enthusiasm at the prospect of committing a double robbery by robbing Falstaff of his booty. But, as soon as the plan is hatched and the ruffians leave, Hal presents his completely different personality before the audience in his famous soliloquy: "My reformation, glittering o'er my fault, / Shall show more goodly and attract more eyes / Than that which hath no foil to set it off. / I'll so offend, to make offence a skill; / Redeeming time when men think least I will" (195–199).

It is the artificiality of court life that makes Hal turn to earthy characters like Falstaff; however, his royal blood restrains him from becoming one of them. He accepts Falstaff and Ned as they are; at the same time, he has highest regard for people like Hotspur. He robs for fun, not money. In fact, he returns the money he stole from Falstaff.

Hal is a loyal and generous person who not only laughs at Falstaff's expense in happy days but, in time of rebellion, appoints Falstaff as troop commander to give him a chance to mend his ways. Indeed, Hal gives Falstaff not one but many chances to prove himself. Hal kills Hotspur, and when Falstaff claims credit, the prince magnanimously allows it. Not only is he brave, but he also has highest respect for bravery, as is seen when he asks

Prince Henry fights Hotspur in Act V, Scene 4 of *Henry IV, Part I*. Print from the Boydell Shakespeare Gallery project *(Painting by John Francis; engraving by Thomas Ryder)*

his father to forgive Douglas, whom Hal believes is brave. He then gives the honor of announcing Douglas's pardon to his younger brother, John.

Some critics regard Falstaff as superior in intellect to the prince. In his poem "Up, Jack," American poet Richard Wilbur makes Falstaff's resurrection at the end of the play a symbol of well-being for Hal and all the audience: "Great Falstaff *(rising)* clears his thirsty throat / And I'm content, and Hal is hale again."

Hal becomes as interesting a character as his father. In his first soliloquy, Hal gives the audience a glimpse into his real self. History remembers the real Hal as a man devoid of his father's royal nature, but Shakespeare makes it clear that his Hal has inherited his father's greatness. Bored by the company of solemn people like Westmoreland and Blunt, Hal takes to the company of the jovial Falstaff. However, inside the prince's disorganized, undisciplined facade, there is a meticulous, loyal, and brave man. On the battlefield, he is seen fighting with as much ease as he displays while drinking wine at the tavern. While the prince initially is compared unfavorably to Hotspur, he is the one who brings the hot-headed rebel to doom.

Hotspur

Set in a knightly contrast to Prince Hal, Hotspur (Harry Percy) is a serious, sincere, passionate rebel against the king. Highly idolized by the other rebels and their troops, Hotspur is engrossed in the cause of rebellion. Completely unmindful of his wife and his earldom, he is passionate about war.

A bold man, Hotspur refuses to succumb to any pressures or temptations from the king. Most firmly, he tells the king that he will not hand over the prisoners of war to him. Hotspur is zealous about honor, and for its sake, he will go to any lengths. Dangers attract him, and he dares to challenge dangers at every step. Hotspur is about the only character whose heart does not like any intrigue or policy. Rather, he wears his heart on his sleeves. Even his father, who loves him, does not like his passionate flights of temper. He gets easily provoked by outside stimuli and loses his patience, as when the king's messenger behaves rudely: "To be so pester'd with a popinjay, / Out of my grief and my impatience, / Answer'd neglectingly I know not what, / He should or he should not; for he made me mad" (1.3.51–54).

In contrast to Hal, Hotspur is tactful. In fact, he is as brave as the prince, but his lack of foresight and self-control makes him a victim to Hal's wisdom in war. In conversation with Glendower and Worcester, he often shows a haughty temperament. He refuses to trust his wife with secrets.

On the one hand, Hotspur is an appealing character because of his lack of cunning; on the other, he fails to reap benefits of his intelligence because of the lack of craft. Hal's tribute to Hotspur as "the most stout man" is fitting because Hotspur is more a strong body than a clever soul. He has animal courage but no judgment. Hotspur rebukes and humiliates his father for supporting Henry IV against Richard II, blaming him for the present menace in the most unpleasant manner: "But shall it be that you, that set the crown / Upon the head of this forgetful man / And for his sake wear the detested blot / Of murderous subornation, shall it be, / That you a world of curses undergo, / Being the agents, or base second means, / The cords, the ladder, or the hangman rather?" (1.3.164–170).

Harry Percy's nickname, *Hotspur,* is proof enough of his hot and impulsive nature. It is his impulsiveness that makes him blind to the virtues of Prince Hal, while Hal holds him in high esteem. Beck also notices the selfish pursuits of personal glory as a hallmark of his character. His rebellion is a way of revenge against a personal wrong. It is this that marks Hotspur as different from Hal, who does all he can for his country and lets others take credit for his deeds.

Hotspur also shows lack of policy and wisdom with the rebels; he does not realize the importance of keeping them in good humor so that they form a stronger bond than the king's soldiers. This is evident when he challenges Glendower's claims of magical powers. When Glendower claims that the earth shook at the time of his birth, Hotspur sneers: "And I say the earth was not of my mind, / If you suppose as fearing you it shook" (3.1.22–23).

Hotspur is unparalleled as a friend, and in this, he commands the audience's respect: "Yea, on his part I'll empty all these veins, / And shed my dear blood drop by drop in the dust, / But I will lift the down-trod Mortimer / As high in the air as this unthankful king / As this ingrate and canker'd Bolingbroke" (1.3.133–137). One has to consider that his selfish pursuit is not so selfish after all in view of his fighting the battle to avenge Mortimer's honor and the honor of the Percy family. Because Henry deceived his nobles by using them against Richard II and then furthered his ambitions to the throne, Hotspur could be seen as justified in plotting the rebellion. In a Machavellian world, Hotspur is a traditional politician holding onto virtue and personal prowess only to realize that such political naïveté meets deceit in this world.

His character can be summed up in his father's comment: "Before the game's afoot thou still let'st slip" (1.3.283). Critics like Owen are enamored by what they observe as Hotspur's charm:

> Although he does not think of himself as childish, he has a kind of innocence which sets him apart from the more calculating of his fellow conspirators. He is impulsive when they are scheming; he is boyish in his love of adventure for its own sake (or for his personal honor), while they are coldly playing for higher stakes. Every piece of bad news he receives only spurs him on in his resolution to fight the King. He thinks there will be greater glory in defeating the King against greater odds. He is, therefore, obviously seeking honor and not power. He has little or no interest in the political aspects of the revolution. (23)

Sir John Falstaff

The fat knight, apparently based on a famous Protestant martyr named John Oldcastle, is a rogue, a knave, a liar, a coward, a robber, and yet, he commands more love than any other Shakespearean character and is one of the most discussed comic characters in English literature. The early critic Sir Maurice Morgann devoted an essay to his vindication. Other critics have compared him to Hamlet. Anthony Quayle, one of the 20th century's most famous Falstaffs, describes him as a "monster" and "desperate" yet "infinitely lovable" (Cook 73). The critic William Richardson writes: "Having no sense of character, he [Falstaff] is never troubled with shame" (Vickers 207).

Falstaff is an old man with a youthful zeal who will go to any extent to make merry. Completely careless, he can transform even a grim battlefield into a stage for comedy. An intelligent man, he knows how to convert even a boring, dangerous, and profitless position such as that of a commander of troops into a profitable venture. He makes money by forcing reluctant soldiers to join

James H. Hackett as Falstaff in Act IV, Scene 2 of a 19th- century production of *Henry IV, Part 1*. *(Photogravure of an engraving by Gebbie and Company)*

his troop, then accepting their bribes for release from duty. His fat mass accentuates the effect of humor, as when Hal and Ned steal his horse. He is also witty, and it is his wit that allows him to adapt to any and every situation. His verbal agility, such as his sharp use of puns, bails him out of some difficult situations. Harold Bloom says of Falstaff: "no other literary character . . seems to me so infinite in provoking thought and in arousing emotion" (313).

Falstaff has a phenomenal capacity for telling lies, but critics rightly defend him. He seems to lie not because he is a liar but because he likes to keep the prince amused. On the grim battlefield of Shrewsbury, Falstaff comes like a breath of fresh air. His apparent cowardice is actually his wisdom. He never claims to be a warrior; it is his love for the prince that stops him from refusing the position as troop commander. Falstaff's character deteriorates

in *Part 2*, but judging by *Part 1*, Falstaff is a brilliantly etched Renaissance character.

Malice free, Falstaff creates mirth at the cost of everyone around him. A glutton, a habitual drunkard, he is loved by all his companions despite all his follies. In fact, it is because of his follies that he lost his position as the page to John of Gaunt, who was Henry IV's father. Whatever his defects, he is about the most intelligent character in this play. It has been said that Queen Elizabeth so loved the character of Falstaff that she requested an entire play based around the character. This may or may not be true, but in *The Merry Wives of Windsor*, Falstaff moves from the 15th-century setting of *Henry IV, Part 1* to what seems to be a contemporary Elizabethan setting.

Earl of Northumberland

A faithless betrayer, the Earl of Northumberland is Hotspur's father. Northumberland had earlier supported Henry IV against Richard II but then turned against Henry IV. After instigating his partners against the king, Northumberland absents himself from the battlefield, feigning illness. Northumberland's character is not developed at length; in the rebel group, it is Hotspur who emerges as the central character.

Even as a father, Northumberland fails to impress. In Act I, Scene 3, he pleads for his son to the king, but his plea comes across as mild: "Either envy, therefore, or misprision / Is guilty of this fault and not my son" (1.3.28–29). Then, he leaves Hotspur to speak for himself, though he knows full well that Hotspur's passionate nature may defeat his cause. Northumberland does nothing to check his son's temper, knowing that temper can incite his enemies. Only once, when Worcester is annoyed at Hotspur's show of fury, does Northumberland rebuke his son. In so doing, he exposes his male chauvinism, too: "Why, what a wasp-stung and impatient fool / Art thou to break into this woman's mood, / Tying thine ear to no tongue but thine own!" (240–242). He does not join his son on the battlefield, and when Hotspur's death is announced, he grieves only for a while before preparing to run away to Scotland to save his own skin. His weakness will makes him lie to the Archbishop of York, falsely reporting that since he could not foster a big army for the rebellion, he has retired to Scotland.

Earl of Worcester

The Earl of Worcester comes across as an intelligent person; among all the rebels, he has the greatest control over his temper and is as polished a person as he is a brave warrior. He is Hotspur's uncle and is a strong, positive influence on him. During a quarrel among the rebels, Worcester mediates and placates Hotspur and humors Glendower.

Worcester is a better judge of situations, and unlike Hotspur, he foresees the true impact of Northumberland's absence from the battlefield. Worcester rightly advises the rebels to wait until all the troops are ready for battle, but Hotspur and Douglas ignore his advice, resulting in the failure of their rebellion.

The fact that he misrepresents the king's message of clemency to Hotspur, however, blights his character. One does not forgive the fact that, but for Worcester, so much of bloodshed could have been avoided. Worcester is a master diplomat, and whatever wise decisions Hotspur takes, he does according to Worcester's advice. It is only in misrepresenting the king's message that he acts selfishly. Knowing that the king might forgive Hotspur but not himself, he does not convey the message of friendship to Hotspur.

Owen Glendower

The fiery Welsh chieftain Owen Glendower is one of the rebels. Glendower proclaims to have magical powers and maintains a respectable distance from his friends, as he thinks he is too superior to them: "at my nativity / The front of heaven was full of fiery shapes, / Of burning cressets; and at my birth / The frame and huge foundation of the earth / Shaked like a coward" (3.1.13–17). Hotspur does not believe in his magical powers, but the king is in awe of Glendower because of his connections with the superhuman world.

Mortimer

Glendower's son-in-law, Edmund Mortimer is held in high esteem by Hotspur. He is depicted in the play more as a loving husband than a brave warrior. There is a huge language problem between his wife and him, as he speaks only English while his wife speaks only Welsh. However, there is no gap in terms of communication between them because love knows no language.

Vernon

Vernon has a sane mind and timid spirit in a brave body. Though a minor character, he appears as a brave, intelligent, and chivalrous person. He gives good advice to Hotspur about the division of land and also agrees with Worcester that Northumberland's absence in the battlefield might have a discouraging effect on the troops. While brave, he is not as impulsive as Hotspur. Although an ally of the rebel group, he is full of praise for the prince, which shows the magnanimity of his character.

There is only one drawback in Vernon's character, and that is his meek obedience to Worcester. Had he objected to Worcester's misrepresentation of the king's message to Hotspur, he could have helped avert the war of Shrewsbury. Although a good man, he does not remain true to his character and meets a sad fate.

DIFFICULTIES OF THE PLAY

One obvious difficulty students have regarding *Henry IV Part 1* is that to fully understand it, the audience should be acquainted with the incidents in *Richard II* and perhaps with English history of the time. But, even beyond the sequential nature of the plot, some students have trouble tracking the development of the characters, especially Prince Hal and his father, the king. Prince Hal, for instance, transforms himself from a flippant, reckless companion of highwaymen to a serious, valiant, loyal warrior. He seems to undergo three clear stages of progression: realization, motivation, and transformation. He gives the audience a glimpse into his innate seriousness in his soliloquy at the close of Act I, Scene 2 ("I know you all, and will awhile uphold" [177–199]). Some could argue that Shakespeare does not successfully answer the question of why the prince would befriend people, like the highwaymen, who are contrary to his own nature. But Hal's nature is very complicated. In the subsequent play, of course, Hal abandons Falstaff and these friends.

Understanding the character of King Henry IV offers another challenge. In *Richard II,* the younger Henry was able to defeat Richard II by cleverly garnering support from other nobles and lords; to do so requires political will and acumen that should have matured with the passing of time. Yet, King Henry IV shows little of his younger capabilities. The simple issue of the handing over of prisoners becomes overwhelming because of his lack of political maturity and farsightedness. Some readers find it difficult to understand how the same person who allied with the powerful Percy family to oust Richard would now infuriate his allies, knowing that their wrath could disturb his reign. An example of the seeming erosion of Henry's political savvy occurs in Act I, Scene 3. Hotspur is in a humble, rather apologetic mood, and it seems that the strife (whatever it be) will end, paving way for ties between Henry and nobles to be strengthened. The king has all reason to overlook minor issues because Hotspur has crushed a major uprising in Scotland. However, behaving in an illogical manner, the king humiliates Hotspur, using expressions such as "foolish Mortimer," "willfully betrayed," "a traitor" (1.3.80–81, 86). He goes so far as to use "sirrah" for Hotspur (1.3.118). But, aging kings do not always behave rationally, and clearly, Henry's personality has changed as he has matured during his difficult reign.

Shakespeare's political vision is another difficulty in some readers' understanding of the play. Does Shakespeare himself support Hotspur's rebellion against Henry IV? Does he justify the theory of the king's divine right to rule? Does Henry IV face rebellion because he dared to oust Richard II, who had legitimately inherited the crown, or for other reasons? These questions have interested scholars for many years.

KEY PASSAGES
Act I, Scene 2, 219–241

PRINCE HAL. I know you all, and will
  awhile uphold
The unyoked humour of your idleness:
Yet herein will I imitate the sun,
Who doth permit the base contagious clouds
To smother up his beauty from the world,
That, when he please again to be himself,
Being wanted, he may be more wonder'd at,
By breaking through the foul and ugly mists
Of vapours that did seem to strangle him.
If all the year were playing holidays,
To sport would be as tedious as to work;
But when they seldom come, they wish'd for
  come,
And nothing pleaseth but rare accidents.
So, when this loose behavior I throw off
And pay the debt I never promised,
By how much better than my word I am,
By so much shall I falsify men's hopes;
And like bright metal on a sullen ground,
My reformation, glittering o'er my fault,
Shall show more goodly and attract more eyes
Than that which hath no foil to set it off.
I'll so offend, to make offence a skill;
Redeeming time when men think least I will.

This is an interesting passage in that it establishes Prince Hal's character as a serious, imaginative person, able to rise above Falstaff and his clownish companions. A prince whose "brow was stained by riot and dishonor" at the beginning of Act I, Scene 1 (1.1.85) emerges as a calm, controlled man of royalty who would "falsify men's hopes." This passage makes the first step into the process of Hal's transformation.

Prince Hal is the central character in the play, and his poetic soliloquy, his use of rhetoric, reveals an intriguing side of his personality. This soliloquy is replete with metaphors, including the metaphor of the Sun that becomes a recurring image in the play. The soliloquy also lays the groundwork for Act V, Scene 4 when the prince proclaims that his arms are strengthened by "the spirits of valiant Shirley, Stafford and Blunt" (42). Ultimately, Hal saves the king from Douglas, forcing the king to "redeem his lost opinion" (5.4.49).

Hal's philosophy of life comes forth in this passage. His agenda is similar to his father's; unlike the popular opinion of him, the prince has as much royalty in his blood as his father could require. However, this passage is a creation of Shakespeare's imagination. Historical records show that the real prince had a turbulent relationship with his father all his life. In fact, toward the end of Henry IV's life, his son was gathering forces to oust him. It was the king's death in 1413 that saved him from this ordeal.

Act V, Scene 1, 127–143

FALSTAFF. 'Tis not due yet; I would be loath to pay him before his day. What need I be so forward with him that calls not on me? Well, 'tis no matter; honour pricks me on. Yea, but how if honour prick me off when I come on? how then? Can honour set to a leg? no: or an arm? no: or take away the grief of a wound? no. Honour hath no skill in surgery, then? no. What is honour? a word. What is in that word honour? What is that honour? air. A trim reckoning! Who hath it? he that died o' Wednesday. Doth he feel it? no. Doth he hear it? no. 'Tis insensible, then. Yea, to the dead. But will it not live with the living? No. Why? detraction will not suffer it. Therefore I'll none of it. Honour is a mere scutcheon: and so ends my catechism.

This is one of Falstaff's great speeches. Honor is an important theme in the play. Hal has his own view of honor, and Hotspur has yet another. Falstaff here presents a completely different, matter-of-fact view of honor. Falstaff declares that he has no use of honor because it befits only the dead. He values life and its pleasures more than death and its glories. In complete contrast to Hotspur's opinion, Falstaff emerges as the only worldly-wise character in the play. This catechism undermines excessive devotion to honor, often so blindly pursued that its real glory becomes unattainable.

Act V, Scene 2, 4–25

EARL OF WORCESTER. Then are we all
  undone.
It is not possible, it cannot be,
The king should keep his word in loving us;
He will suspect us still and find a time
To punish this offence in other faults:
Suspicion all our lives shall be stuck full of eyes;
For treason is but trusted like the fox,
Who, ne'er so tame, so cherish'd and lock'd up,
Will have a wild trick of his ancestors.
Look how we can, or sad or merrily,
Interpretation will misquote our looks,
And we shall feed like oxen at a stall,
The better cherish'd, still the nearer death.
My nephew's trespass may be well forgot;
it hath the excuse of youth and heat of blood,
And an adopted name of privilege,
A hair-brain'd Hotspur, govern'd by a spleen:
All his offences live upon my head
And on his father's; we did train him on,
And, his corruption being ta'en from us,
We, as the spring of all, shall pay for all.
Therefore, good cousin, let not Harry know,
In any case, the offer of the king.

Worcester, afraid for his life, forbids Vernon to disclose the king's message of clemency to Hotspur. Knowing that Hotspur's "trespass may be well forgot," Worcester wants Hotspur to fight the king, lest the king nurture a grudge against himself. This passage marks a turning point in the play. Had Worcester not played this trick on Hotspur, there would not have been any bloodshed. The Battle of Shrewsbury is fought because of Worcester's insecurity. He is worried that the king might forgive Hotspur—but not him.

Act V, Scene 4, 77–101

HOTSPUR. O, Harry, thou hast robb'd me of
  my youth!
I better brook the loss of brittle life
Than those proud titles thou hast won of me;
They wound my thoughts worse than sword
  my flesh:
But thought's the slave of life, and life time's
  fool;
And time, that takes survey of all the world,
Must have a stop. O, I could prophesy,
But that the earthy and cold hand of death
Lies on my tongue: no, Percy, thou art dust
And food for—[*Dies.*]

PRINCE HAL. For worms, brave Percy: fare
  thee well, great heart!
Ill-weaved ambition, how much art thou
  shrunk!
When that this body did contain a spirit,
A kingdom for it was too small a bound;
But now two paces of the vilest earth
Is room enough: this earth that bears thee
  dead
Bears not alive so stout a gentleman.
If thou wert sensible of courtesy,
I should not make so dear a show of zeal:
But let my favours hide thy mangled face;
And, even in thy behalf, I'll thank myself
For doing these fair rites of tenderness.
Adieu, and take thy praise with thee to heaven!
Thy ignominy sleep with thee in the grave,
But not remember'd in thy epitaph!

Prince Hal has wounded Hotspur (Harry Percy).
Throughout the play, Hotspur has been depicted
in contrast to the prince. The prince makes this
distinction clear: "I am the prince of Wales, and
think not, Percy, / To share with me in glory any
more" (5.4.65–66). Hal's defeat of Hotspur is
chance to prove his mettle not only to the king
but to the people over whom he aspires to rule
in the future. The contrast between the two is
seen in terms of Hal's magnanimity. Hal praises
Hotspur, even though Hotspur is his enemy, while

This depiction of Prince Henry battling Hotspur in the
field in Act V, Scene 4 of *Henry IV, Part I* appeared
in *Retzsch's Outlines to Shakespeare:* Henry IV, 1846.
(Illustration by Moritz Retzsch)

Hotspur fails to match the prince's grandeur. The
"the ignominy . . . epitaph" passage is particularly
generous.

DIFFICULT PASSAGES
Act I, Scene 3, 29–69

HOTSPUR. My liege, I did deny no prisoners.
  But I remember, when the fight was done,
  When I was dry with rage and extreme toil,
  Breathless and faint, leaning upon my sword,
  Came there a certain lord, neat, and trimly
    dress'd,
  Fresh as a bridegroom; and his chin new reap'd
  Show'd like a stubble-land at harvest-home;
  He was perfumed like a milliner;
  And 'twixt his finger and his thumb he held
  A pouncet-box, which ever and anon
  He gave his nose and took't away again;
  Who therewith angry, when it next came there,
  Took it in snuff; and still he smiled and talk'd,
  And as the soldiers bore dead bodies by,
  He call'd them untaught knaves, unmannerly,
  To bring a slovenly unhandsome corse
  Betwixt the wind and his nobility.
  With many holiday and lady terms

He question'd me; amongst the rest, demanded
My prisoners in your majesty's behalf.
I then, all smarting with my wounds being
  cold,
To be so pester'd with a popinjay,
Out of my grief and my impatience,
Answer'd neglectingly I know not what,
He should or he should not; for he made me
  mad
To see him shine so brisk and smell so sweet
And talk so like a waiting-gentlewoman
Of guns and drums and wounds,—God save
  the mark!—
And telling me the sovereign'st thing on earth
Was parmaceti for an inward bruise;
And that it was great pity, so it was,
This villanous salt-petre should be digg'd
Out of the bowels of the harmless earth,
Which many a good tall fellow had destroy'd
So cowardly; and but for these vile guns,
He would himself have been a soldier.
This bald unjointed chat of his, my lord,
I answer'd indirectly, as I said;
And I beseech you, let not his report
Come current for an accusation
Betwixt my love and your high majesty.

This speech sounds like an apology to the king for having refused to hand over the prisoners of war to him; in fact, in many ways, it does not seem to suit Hotspur's character to speak like this. Why would a man whose "blood more stirs / to rouse a lion than to start a hare" and who roars "but I will find him when he lies asleep, / And in his ear I'll holla 'Mortimer'!" (1.3.27–28) indulge in such glib talk? Hotspur here talks about "my love," but this professed love gives way to wrath at the mention of Mortimer. Hotspur's highly changeable character can be difficult for readers to grasp.

CRITICAL INTRODUCTION
TO THE PLAY

Henry IV, Part 1 is a play about rebellions and intrigues. Shakespeare's political philosophy is typical of his time. He holds the king as God's deputy on Earth. Henry IV's usurpation of the kingdom, thus, violated the natural order. Bishop Carlisle's prophecy in *Richard II*—that Henry's insurrection against King Richard would result in the suffering of generations to come—comes true in *Henry IV, Parts 1* and *2*. Usurpations and assassinations bring divine retribution. Just as Henry IV suffers because he has not rightfully inherited the crown, Hotspur is, at least for a time, painted in positive light because he is out to mend a wrong done to his family, the Percys. Such a portrayal of history would naturally resonate with Elizabethan theatergoers. Queen Elizabeth was in her 60s when the play was written, and there was no heir to the throne. The English audience at that time was anxious about the issue of inheritance of the crown.

Shakespeare's Henry faces rebellion from a handful of nobles, and it is his political sophistication that helps him nip the rebellion in the bud. The historical Henry is vastly different from Shakespeare's Henry, who is an ineffectual ruler. But, the rebels, too, are very flawed. In Act III, Scene 1, Hotspur shouts: "a plague upon it! / I have forgot the map" (3.1.1.) Hotspur shows himself as incapable of leading the rebellion intended to oust the king; a warrior who forgets a map is certainly not a capable ruler. But more than that, the very idea of rebellion is a threat to the nation itself. Jean E. Howard and Phyllis Rackin write in *Engendering a Nation* that "the rebel cause is discredited, not only or even chiefly because it defies the authority of the monarch, but because it threatens to dismember the body of the land, a threat that is graphically illustrated when the rebel leaders haggle over the map of Briton and agree finally to have the river Trent turned from its natural cause in the interest of their bargain" (162–163).

The king is a calculating manipulator, and in true Machiavellian tradition, he does not hesitate to touch the extremes of cruelty, such as executing Glendower at the same time that he offers clemency to Douglas at the play's end. Another Machiavellian character is Prince Hal, who befriends Falstaff seemingly to learn the reality of the common people and in the end remains detached from his sur-

Hotspur, Worcester, Mortimer, and Glendower discuss the future division of the kingdom in Act III, Scene 1 of *Henry IV, Part 1*. Print from the Boydell Shakespeare Gallery project *(Painting by Richard Westall; engraving by Jean Pierre Simon)*

roundings, single-mindedly targeting the crown. His mastery of language has another Machiavellian quality.

The play is not only an examination of high politics. The diversity of locations enables Shakespeare to explore a wide range of humanity. The play's two worlds are civil strife and tavern life, with the world of civil strife encompassing the king, Hotspur, and the nobles and lords, and tavern life populated by Falstaff, Ned, and other rogues. Hal, interestingly, serves as the bridge between these two cultures. The play moves in space from the king's palace in London to the Rochester inn, from the highway infested with

robbers to Warkworth Castle and on to the Boar's-Head Tavern at Eastcheap. Not only settings but characters, too, provide notable contrasts: Henry IV and his son, Hal and Falstaff, Hal and Hotspur. High and low, good and evil are contrasted even within characters. Hotspur's treachery is deemed bravery. Falstaff's expounding on counterfeiting and honor highlight that contrast. The king, supposedly brave and religious, hides behind impersonators to save his life. The comic subplot allows Shakespeare to deal with serious themes such as virtue, honor, inheritance, rebellion, and humanity without the play becoming dismal and staid.

Themes

The play explores notions of what is true and false, right and wrong, real and counterfeit. Henry IV himself is counterfeit, as he has usurped the throne. He also plants counterfeits in the battlefield to save his life. Hotspur wants to defeat Henry, but Hotspur's own right to the throne is challengeable. Falstaff observes: "Counterfeit? I lie, I am no counterfeit: to die, / is to be a counterfeit; for he is but the counterfeit of a man who hath not the life of a man: / but to counterfeit dying, when a man thereby / liveth, is to be no counterfeit, but the true and perfect image of life indeed" (5.4.115–118).

Hotspur, Hal, and Falstaff present three distinct concepts of honor. On one extreme is Hotspur, who devotes his talents and energies to his simplistic view of honor: "By heaven, methinks it were an easy leap, / To pluck bright honour from the pale-faced moon, / Or dive into the bottom of the deep, / Where fathom-line could never touch the ground, / And pluck up drowned honour by the locks" (1.3.203–207). He is obsessed with honor, as shown by his rushing to war against his allies' counsel. His wife, Lady Percy, argues that this fixation has robbed Hotspur of his peace of mind. In his famous speech on honor, Hotspur declares that he is greedy for it and would not share it with a partner. To a close reader, it becomes clear that Hotspur's honor is selfish, which makes him a menace not only to himself but also to his family and friends. Prince

Hal, meanwhile, is as aware of his honor as Hotspur, but unlike him, Hal has a preset plan to attain honor. He knows how to win honor by "glittering o'er his fault" (1.3.237). He is also aware that Hotspur's glory is proportionate to his shame, so he has to redeem his honor at Hotspur's cost.

Finally, Falstaff's view of honor is contrary to both Hotspur's and Hal's. He prefers a life of shame to an honorable death. He counterfeits death to save his life in the battlefield. For him, honor is a hollow word, "a mere scutcheon" (5.2.142). He does not believe in the popular meaning of the word: "Give me life! / which if I can save, so; if not, honour comes unlook'd / for" (5.3.159–161). He is practical and governed by self-preservation. He will bask in the glory of honor as long as he does not have to sacrifice a single hair on his head. "Can honour set a leg?" is his clownish but relevant question (5.1.132). He believes in things that he can see, hold, or enjoy; honor belongs to those who would die for it.

The play also constantly explores the conflict between virtue and vice. Morality is disturbed from the start because Henry has usurped the throne by betraying the faith of the Percy family. The prince is torn between morality as expressed by his noble father and immorality as illustrated by his rapscallion friends. Hal robs people for the thrill of the game until he realizes the hollowness of vice and turns to virtue, starting with his soliloquy in Act I, Scene 2. The vice of vanity brings about Hotspur's doom, while the virtue of modesty ensures Hal's success.

Style and Imagery

Henry IV, Part 1 contains a range of styles and symbols. The Sun is a recurrent image; both Henry IV and his son imply it several times. In his famous revelation soliloquy, the prince vows "Yet herein will I imitate the sun" (1.2.179). Comparing his low-class companions to dark, ill-looking clouds, Hal says that he has allowed them to cover his brilliance but plans to break through them and shine like the Sun. This also parallels his shining in the affection of his father, Henry. In Act III, Scene 2,

the king advises Hal to maintain the prince-like dignity that he sees in the Sun: "Such as is bent on sun-like majesty, / When it shines seldom in admiring eyes" (2.2.79–80).

Other characters use the same image. In Act II, Scene 4, Falstaff says "Shall / the blessed sun of heaven prove a micher and eat / blackberries? a question not to be asked. Shall / the sun of England prove a thief and take purses? a / question to be asked" (2.4.372). He seems to refer to the prince's earlier soliloquy; although Falstaff was not present when Hal made that speech, the audience can presume that it was a habit of Hal's to compare himself to the Sun or that Falstaff is making a pun on *son* and *Sun*.

The Language of the Play

Critics have noticed the important difference between prose and verse in the play. Falstaff and his followers all speak prose; the higher-born characters speak poetry, in both the comic and the serious scenes. Shakespeare's poetry here is much improved from the more rigid and conventional blank verse of his early period. The style changes with the speaker. The king, who is cold, calculating, and level-headed, speaks in a controlled, terse style: "So shaken as we are, so wan with care, / Find we a time for frighted peace to pant, / And breathe short-winded accents of new broils/To be commenced in strands afar remote" (1.1.1–4). When he forgives Douglas, he says only "With all my heart" (5.5.25). On the other hand, Hotspur's speeches are marked with both masculine vigor and fanciful sentimentality. He bursts into what may be called poetic speeches because he is an impulsive, passionate man: "Send danger from the east unto the west, / So honour cross it from the north to south, / And let them grapple: O, the blood more stirs / To rouse a lion than to start a hare!" (1.3.197–200). In fits of rage, such as when he is reading a letter in Act II, Scene 3, his speech is full of angry words like "What a lack brain is this?" (2.3.17) or "What a frosty spirited rogue is this?" (2.3.21).

The prince himself switches smoothly between the styles, speaking prose to the rogues and poetry to everyone else. In Act I, Scene 4, lines 1 through 455 are in prose; when the sheriff enters, lines 456 to 476 are in verse. The style changes again to prose in line 477 until the close of the scene. The prince's two styles of speaking illustrate his facade of comic foolery that he has built over his inherently serious nature. His poetry can indeed be sublime: "I do not think a braver gentleman, / More active-valiant or more valiant-young, / More daring or more bold, is now alive / To grace this latter age with noble deeds" (5.1.90–93).

Some critics think Shakespeare's prose in this play is even more brilliant than the poetry. Joseph Porter makes a special mention of Shakespeare's "naming" in the play. In the witty dialogues between Hal and Falstaff, "abusive appellations" become an important vehicle for an exchange of wits: "fatguts," "sweet wag," "All; hall own summer," "starveling," "eel-skin," "dried neat's tongue," "stock-fish," "fat-kidneyed rascal," "bull's puzzle," and "mad wag" are some of the names bantered about. Indeed, Shakespeare explores the complete range of the English language in this play.

The prose dialogues between the prince and Falstaff contain many classical allusions and alliterations: "Marry, then, sweet wag, when thou art king, let not / us that are squires of the night's body be called / thieves of the day's beauty: let us be Diana's / foresters, gentlemen of the shade, minions of the / moon; and let men say we be men of good government, / being governed, as the sea is, by our noble and / chaste mistress the moon, under whose countenance we steal" (1.2.21–27).

Brian Vickers notes an interesting use of prose in Act II, Scene 3 between Hotspur and his wife. Hotspur reads a letter in prose; his angry comments are also in prose. Just then, his wife enters, and when the audience might, as Vickers says, "expect him to grant her the respect of verse", he uses flat prose: "How now, Kate? I must leave you within two hours." Vickers observes that "Hotspur's refusal of verse is less a deliberate snub . . . than a sign how the illegality of rebellion can destroy family and loving relationships."

EXTRACTS OF CLASSIC CRITICISM
William Hazlitt (1778–1830) [From *Lectures on the Literature of the Age of Elizabeth and Characters of Shakespeare's Plays* (1817). The famous romantic essayist Hazlitt was one of the most important Shakespearean critics of the 19th century.]

Falstaff's wit is an emanation of a fine constitution; an exuberance of good-humour and good-nature; an overflowing of his love of laughter and good-fellowship; a giving vent to his heart's ease, and over-contentment with himself and others. He would not be in character, if he were not so fat as he is; for there is the greatest keeping in the boundless luxury of his imagination and the pampered self-indulgence of his physical appetites. He manures and nourishes his mind with jests, as he does his body with sack and sugar. He carves out his jokes, as he would a capon or a haunch of venison, where there is cut *and come again;* and pours out upon them the oil of gladness. His tongue drops fatness, and in the chambers of his brain "it snows of meat and drink." He keeps up perpetual holiday and open house, and we live with him in a round of invitations to a rump and dozen.— Yet we are not to suppose that he was a mere sensualist. All this is as much in imagination as in reality. His sensuality does not engross and stupify his other faculties but "ascends me into the brain, clears away all the dull, crude vapours that environ it, and makes it full of nimble, fiery, and delectable shapes." His imagination keeps up the ball after his senses have done with it. He seems to have even a greater enjoyment of the freedom from restraint, of good cheer, of his ease, of his vanity, in the ideal exaggerated description which he gives of them, than in fact. He never fails to enrich his discourse with allusions to eating and drinking, but we never see him at table. He carries his own larder about with him, and he is himself "a tun of man." His pulling out the bottle in the field of battle is a joke to shew his contempt for glory accompanied with danger, his systematic adherence to his Epicurean philosophy in the most trying circumstances. Again, such is his deliberate exaggeration of his own vices, that it does not seem quite certain whether the account of his hostess's bill, found in his pocket, with such an out-of-the-way charge for capons and sack with only one halfpenny-worth of bread, was not put there by himself as a trick to humour the jest upon his favourite propensities, and as a conscious caricature of himself. He is represented as a liar, a braggart, a coward, a glutton, &c., and yet we are not offended but delighted with him; for he is all these as much to amuse others as to gratify himself. He openly assumes all these characters to shew the humorous part of them. The unrestrained indulgence of his own ease, appetites, and convenience, has neither malice nor hypocrisy in it. In a word, he is an actor in himself almost as much as upon the stage, and we no more object to the character of Falstaff in a moral point of view than we should think of bringing an excellent comedian, who should represent him to the life, before one of the police offices. We only consider the number of pleasant lights in which he puts certain foibles (the more pleasant as they are opposed to the

Falstaff pretends to be the king while he jokes with Prince Henry in Act II, Scene 4 of *Henry IV, Part 1*. Print from the Boydell Shakespeare Gallery project *(Painting by Robert Smirke; engraving by Robert Thew)*

received rules and necessary restraints of society) and do not trouble ourselves about the consequences resulting from them, for no mischievous consequences do result. Sir John is old as well as fat, which gives a melancholy retrospective tinge to the character; and by the disparity between his inclinations and his capacity for enjoyment, makes it still more ludicrous and fantastical.

The secret of Falstaff's wit is for the most part a masterly presence of mind, an absolute self-possession, which nothing can disturb. His repartees are involuntary suggestions of his self-love; instinctive evasions of every thing that threatens to interrupt the career of his triumphant jollity and self-complacency. His very size floats him out of all his difficulties in a sea of rich conceits; and he turns round on the pivot of his convenience, with every occasion and at a moment's warning. His natural repugnance to every unpleasant thought or circumstance, of itself makes light of objections, and provokes the most extravagant and licentious answers in his own justification. His indifference to truth puts no check upon his invention, and the more improbable and unexpected his contrivances are, the more happily does he seem to be delivered of them, the anticipation of their effect acting as a stimulus to the gaiety of his fancy. The success of one adventurous sally gives him spirits to undertake another: he deals always in round numbers, and his exaggerations and excuses are "open, palpable, monstrous as the father that begets them." His dissolute carelessness of what he says discovers itself in the first dialogue with the Prince.

> *Falstaff.* By the lord, thou say'st true, lad; and is not mine hostess of the tavern a most sweet wench ?
>
> *P. Henry.* As the honey of Hibla, my old lad of the castle; and is not a buff-jerkin a most sweet robe of durance?

> *Falstaff.* How now, how now, mad wag, what in thy quips and thy quiddities ? what a plague have I to do with a buff-jerkin?
>
> *P. Henry.* Why, what a pox have I to do with mine hostess of the tavern?

In the same scene, he afterwards affects melancholy, from pure satisfaction of heart, and professes reform, because it is the farthest thing in the world from his thoughts. He has no qualms of conscience, and therefore would as soon talk of them as of anything else when the humour takes him.

MODERN CRITICISM AND CRITICAL CONTROVERSIES

Like all Shakespearean plays, *Henry IV, Part 1* has invited diverse opinions and generated controversies. Mark Van Doren declares it to be one of Shakespeare's greatest: "No play of Shakespeare is better than *Henry IV*. Certain subsequent ones may show him more settled in the maturity which he here attains almost at a single bound, but nothing that he wrote is more crowded with life or happier in its imitation of human talk. The pen that moves across these pages is perfectly free of itself. The host of persons assembled for our pleasure can say anything for their author he wants to say" (97). But the great playwright (and contrarian critic) George Bernard Shaw disagrees completely: "Everything that charm of style, rich humor, and vivid natural characterization can do for a play are badly wanted by *Henry IV*, which has neither the romantic beauty of Shakespeare's earlier plays nor the tragic greatness of the later ones . . . The combination of conventional propriety and brute masterfulness in his [Prince Hal's] public capacity with a low-lived blackguardsman in his private tastes is not a pleasant one" (426). Shaw has particular objections to the character of Prince Hal, who, he argues, would be quite the same had he been a farmer.

Critics are divided on the character of Falstaff. Many call him a rogue and coward, as, for instance, when he stabs Hotspur's dead body. Yet, the great poet Samuel Taylor Coleridge says his intellect overshadows many of his follies: "Even his sensuality was subservient to his intellect, for he appeared to drink sack that he might have occasion to show his wit" (Volume 4, 67). And the early 20th-century critic A. C. Bradley has a high opinion of Falstaff: "He makes truth appear absurd by solemn statements, which he utters with perfect gravity and which he expects nobody to believe" (263). Other critics have noted the wealth of comic material in the play. One writes, "Had Falstaff been omitted, there is enough in Mrs. Quickly, Shallow and Silence to have furnished out the reputation of any other comic dramatist."

Another critical point of contention is the play's hero. Henry IV gives the title of the play, but many believe that Prince Hal is the central character, and a few others consider Falstaff the true center. J. Dover Wilson points out that Hal is really at the heart of the play, linking the low life with the high life.

David Bevington in his 1997 Oxford edition of the play, describes his "battle" with the series' general editors over whether to use the name *Falstaff*—his choice—or *Oldcastle*—as is found in Oxford University's 1986 *Complete Works.* To use *Oldcastle,* he argues, is to thrust the work of editors upon the "fictional space" of the play "where a character's name must exist primarily as a contract between dramatist and audience on the identity of the character in question" (Velz 28).

Herbert and Judith Weil's 1997 New Cambridge Shakespeare edition of the play emphasizes the centrality of Falstaff, declaring that he "brings us to the heart of the play's key relationships and draws attention to its problematic themes" (28). The reviewer Barbara Hodgdon called their edition "the first truly Falstaff-friendly *1 Henry IV*" (374). Hodgdon also notes the Weils' examination of Shakespeare's use of historical sources, particularly the ways he adapted Holinshed: "Calling attention to the differing treatments of the Northern rebellion—for Shakespeare an exclusively English event, for Holinshed one set within a wider cultural and national framework—the Weils show how much more parochial Shakespeare's England was than Holinshed's" (373).

In the 2002 Arden edition of the play, editor David Scott Kastan discusses the very notion of the play as a "history." In Kastan's view, Shakespeare's histories do not simply tell the tale of a country punished and redeemed by divine providence. In fact, Shakespeare transforms history into historical drama by "manipulating sources such as Holinshed and interweaving them with fictional comic material" (Highley 76). Kastan also comments on the ongoing debate over Falstaff as a parody of his original namesake, Oldcastle, a Reformation Protestant hero whose supporters apparently pressured Shakespeare to rename the character. Shakespeare, Kastan argues, adopts a moderate Protestant position by satirizing Oldcastle on stage, as Oldcastle was embraced by the radical or Puritan wing of the community (Highley).

THE PLAY TODAY

In contemporary times, the play is typically portrayed as a coming-of-age story. Hotspur, once considered an important character, has receded, while Hal—ignored in the play's earliest advertisements—has evolved in significance. Falstaff is one character whose stature has not suffered any major change. He has always been considered supremely important and unique.

Adaptations of the *Henry IV* plays have always been popular in performance, and some of the most intriguing new ideas regarding the play have come forth in recent adaptations. A notable modern cinematic interpretation is Gus Van Sant's *My Own Private Idaho* (1991), which stars River Phoenix and Keanu Reeves as two male street hustlers in Portland, Oregon, and takes elements from both *Henry IV* plays, much like Orson Welles's 1965 film *Chimes at Midnight.* The *Idaho* script—credited to Van Sant with "additional dialogue by William Shakespeare"—blends elements of modern street slang with the bard's language. It also includes internal jokes and references to Shakespeare: In one scene, the Falstaff character, Bob, says, "We have heard the chimes at midnight," a line that Falstaff speaks in *Henry IV, Part 2*. The next scene shows Reeves drinking a Falstaff beer ("Trivia"). Reeves plays Scott, the Prince Hal character who troubles his father, the city's mayor, by hanging out with hustlers and street addicts (Davis). Bob Pigeon (played by William Richert) is the Falstaff character: Scott's mentor, former lover, and "true father." Finding an analogue for Phoenix's character, Mike, who becomes Scott's lover in the film, is more complicated. Some say he represents the Ned Poins character; the critic Hugh Davis argues that he is a "second avatar of Falstaff in this restructured *Henriad . . .* He is the younger Falstaff who, before events of the plays, cavorted with Hal as a brother" (117).

The story has also been interpreted on the small screen. In 1979, the BBC and Time-Life Television Productions produced *Henry IV, Part 1*, directed by David Giles and notable for Anthony Quayle's performance as Falstaff.

Quayle presents a link between the screen and the British stage, for the 1979 production followed, by many years, his work as codirector of the Henriad for the Royal Shakespeare Company (RSC) in 1951. Also playing Falstaff in that production, Quayle joined a young Richard Burton as Hal. "Since then, *1 Henry IV* has never played alone at the RSC," notes Derek Peat (381), who also argues that Quayle's Falstaff represented the last time the character was the major "star" of the show, at least on the RSC's Stratford stage.

In 2007, both parts of *Henry IV*, along with *Richard II*, returned to Stratford as part of the RSC's ambitious Complete Works festival. The nine-hour production of *Henry 1* and *2* and *Richard* drew mixed reviews: The *Daily Mail* complained that *Henry* needed "more fizz" (Marmion), while the *Daily Telegraph* praised the production's innovative staging and the director and cast for being "alertly responsive to the shifting rhythms and moods of [all three] plays" (Spencer).

More recently, the London Globe's 2010 production of *Henry IV, Part 1* and *Part 2* earned rave reviews, dubbed by the (London) *Independent* as one of the five best productions of the season. "There are some wonderfully rumbustious goings on in Dominic Dromgoole's hearty productions of these two Shakespearean histories," says reviewer Julie Carpenter for the (Scotland) *Express*. "They start from the moment Prince Hal appears on stage—with his trousers round his ankles and his female conquest fleeing—and it continues through the celebrated tavern scenes involving the convivial, self-serving, larger than life, Falstaff." With Roger Allam as Falstaff and Jamie Parker as Hal, the Globe interpretation "emerges as a play about brothers, too; the roistering, apparently carefree Hal is in sharp contrast to Hotspur, a boy who already knows how to play the hero too well and who will pay the price for it. It's also a drama about an old England that, like Falstaff himself, is riddled with ills, in decline and in urgent need of rebirth" (Gardner).

In the United States, the 2003–04 theater season, in particular, provided a curious upswing in productions of the play nationwide, noted Celia Wren for the *Washington Post*. Companies staging versions of the play that season included the Shakespeare Theatre in Washington, D.C. (its first staging of both parts), a star-studded production at the Lincoln Center Theater in New York (a combination of both parts, with Kevin Kline as Falstaff and Ethan Hawke as Hotspur), the Los Angeles Women's Shakespeare Company, and the Shakespeare Tavern in Atlanta. In New York, the *New York Times* celebrated Kline's performance as a "watershed": "He delivers a finely measured performance that matches the actor's infinite resourcefulness with that of the character he plays" (Brantley). While Hawke may have seemed too "contemporary" an actor for the role, "he's great fun to watch as he fumes and fulminates" (Brantley).

The Folger Theater's 2008 production was celebrated for its sophisticated presentation not just of Falstaff's and Hal's relationship "but of how personal grievances drive public turmoil in Henry IV's England. The rift between king and son mirrors the strife dividing the kingdom. It's as if the realm were a gigantic feuding family, torn apart by doubts over the usurping Henry's legitimacy and by former allies' simmering resentments at the king's broken commitments and military missteps" (Marks).

FIVE TOPICS FOR DISCUSSION AND WRITING

1. **Low life vs. high life:** *Henry IV, Part 1* is Shakespeare's only history that portrays commoners alongside royalty. How does this unique perspective affect our understanding of the play?
2. **Honor:** Hal, Falstaff, and Hotspur have different opinions on honor. Which is the most persuasive? Some say that Falstaff is the sanest of the three. Do you agree?
3. **Domestic vs. political life:** Why does Shakespeare include a scene in which Douglas and Hotspur take leave of their wives before battle? Is Hotspur dismissive of his wife? Do we respect her as a character?
4. **Morality:** The critic Arthur Quiller-Couch, citing the play's "morality structure," argues that its main subjects are Prince Hal's education and the salvation of his soul. Do you agree?
5. **Hero:** The play is named after Henry IV. In what sense (besides the title of the play) is he actually the hero, instead of Prince Hal?

Bibliography

Amirthanayagam, David P. "'I Know Thee Not, Old Man': The Renunciation of Falstaff, Literary Imagination." In *Ancient and Modern: Essays in Honor of David Grene,* edited and introduced by Tod Breyfogler, 209–227. Chicago: University of Chicago Press, 1999.

Barber, C. L. "From Ritual to Comedy: An Examination of *Henry IV.*" In *Shakespeare: Modern Essays in Criticism,* edited by Leonard F. Dean, 144–166. New York: Oxford University Press, 1972.

———. "Rule and Misrule." In *Twentieth Century Interpretations of Henry IV, Part One: A Collection of Critical Essays,* edited by R. J. Dorius, 51–70. Englewood Cliffs, N.J.: Prentice Hall, 1970.

Barish, Jonas A. "The Turning Away of Prince Hal." In *Twentieth Century Interpretations of Henry IV, Part One,* edited by R. J. Dorius, 83–88. Englewood Cliffs, N.J.: Prentice Hall, 1970.

Barker, Roberta. "Tragical-Comical-Historical Hotspur." *Shakespeare Quarterly* 54, no. 3 (2003): 288–307.

Bevington, David, ed. *The Complete Works of Shakespeare.* Updated 4th ed. Chicago: University of Chicago Press, 1997.

Bloom, Harold. *Falstaff.* New York: Chelsea House, 1992.

Bradley, A. C. "The Rejection of Falstaff." In *Oxford Lectures on Poetry,* 247–273. New York: Macmillan, 1909.

Brantley, Ben. "Theater Review: Falstaff and Hal, With War Afoot," *New York Times,* November 21, 2003, p. 85.

Bullough, Geoffrey. "Introduction to *Henry V.*" In *Twentieth Century Interpretations of Henry V,* edited by Ronald Berman, 20–28. Englewood Cliffs, N.J.: Prentice Hall, 1968.

Campbell, Lily B. "English History in the Sixteenth Century." In *Shakespeare: The Histories,* edited by Eugene M. Waith, 13–31. Englewood Cliffs, N.J.: Prentice Hall, 1965.

Carpenter, Julie. "Bed & Bard Delivers a Fun Fest at the Double," *Express* (Scotland), July 23, 2010. p. 49.

Coleridge, Samuel Taylor. *The Complete Works of Samuel Taylor Coleridge Volume 4.* New York: Harper & Brothers, 1853.

Cook, Judith. *Shakespeare's Players: A Look at Some of the Major Roles in Shakespeare and Those Who Have Played Them.* London: Harrap, 1983.

Council, Norman. *When Honour's at the Stake.* New York: Barnes & Noble, 1973.

Davis, Hugh H. "'Shakespeare, He's in the Alley': *My Own Private Idaho* and Shakespeare in the Streets." *Literature Film Quarterly:* 29, no. 2 (2001): 116–121.

Desai, R. W. *Falstaff: A Study of His Role in Shakespeare's History Plays.* Delhi, India: Doaba House, 1976.

Duthie, George Ian. *Shakespeare.* London: Routledge, 1954.

Eastman, A. M., and G. B. Harrison, eds. *Shakespeare's Critics: From Jonson to Auden.* Ann Arbor: University of Michigan Press, 1964.

Gabrieli, Vittorio. "Falstaff and Mr. Badman: Libertine and Purita." *Notes & Queries* 35, no. 2 (June 1988): 165–167.

Gardner, Lyn. "Review: Theatre: A Steely Prince Hal Sets England Marching towards History: *Henry IV* parts one and two Shakespeare's Globe." *Guardian* (London), July 16, 2010, p. 38.

Girard, Rene. *To Double Business Bound.* Baltimore, Md.: Johns Hopkins University Press, 1988.

Goldberg, Jonathan. "The Commodity of Names: 'Falstaff' and 'Oldcastle' in *1 Henry IV.*" *Bucknell Review: A Scholarly Journal of Letters, Arts & Sciences* 35, no. 2 (1992): 76–88.

Grady, Hugh. "Falstaff: Subjectivity between the Carnival and the Aesthetic." *Modern Language Review* 96, no. 3 (July 2001): 609–623.

Greenblatt, Stephen Jay. *Shakespearean Negotiations: The Circulation of Social Energy in Renaissance England.* Berkeley: University of California Press, 1988.

Griffin, Alice. "Shakespeare through the Camera's Eye: IV." *Shakespeare Quarterly* 17, no. 4 (Autumn 1966): 383–387.

Grimley, Terry. "Culture: Bard Still Busting the Box Office; The Royal Shakespeare Company, Currently on a Roll with Its Successful Complete Works Festival, Has Announced Plans for Next Year, Writes Terry Grimley." *Birmingham Post,* November 22, 2006, p. 11.

Halliday, F. E. *A Shakespeare Companion, 1564–1964.* Baltimore, Md.: Penguin, 1964.

Hartwig, Joan. "Falstaff's Parodic Nexus for the Second Tetralogy." *The Shakespeare Yearbook* 1 (Spring 1990): 28–36.

Hazlitt, William. *Characters of Shakespeare's plays.* London: Oxford University Press, 1966.

Highley, Christopher. Review of The Arden Shakespeare *King Henry IV, Part I. Shakespeare Quarterly* 55, no. 1 (Spring 2004): 75–77.

Hodgdon, Barbara. "Falstaff: History and His Story." *Iowa State Journal of Research* 53 (1979): 185–190.

———. Review of The New Cambridge Shakespeare *The First Part of King Henry IV. Shakespeare Quarterly* 50, no. 3 (Autumn 1999): 372–375.

———. *William Shakespeare: First Part of Henry the Fourth.* New York: Bedford, 1997.

Howard, Jean E., and Phyllis Rackin. *Engendering a Nation: A Feminist account of Shakespeare's English histories.* London: Routledge, 1997.

Hunter, Robert G. "Shakespeare's Comic Sense as It Strikes Us Today: Falstaff and the Protestant Ethic." In *Shakespeare: Pattern of Excelling Nature,* edited by David Bevington and Jay L. Halio, 125–132. Newark: University of Delaware Press, 1978.

Jenkins, Harold. "The Structural Problems in Shakespeare's *Henry the Fourth.*" In *Structural Problems in Shakespeare,* 96–98. London: Arden, 2002.

Kantor, Andrea, and Michael Spring, eds. *William Shakespeare's Henry IV Part I.* Barron's Book Notes. New York: Barron's Educational Series, 1984.

Kastan, David Scott, ed. "King Henry IV Part 1." *The Arden Shakespeare: Third Series.* London: Arden, 2002.

Kaul, Mythili. "Falstaff and Dr. Faustus." *American Notes & Queries* 20, nos. 3–4 (November–December 1981): 36–37.

Kermode, Frank. *Shakespeare's Language.* New York: Penguin, 2000.

Kernan, Alvin B. "The Henriad: Shakespeare's Major History Plays." In *Modern Shakespearean Criticism,* 245–278. San Francisco: Harcourt Brace, 1970.

Knowles, Ronald. *Shakespeare's Arguments with History.* New York: Palgrave Macmillan, 2002.

Krims. Marvin B. "Hotspur's Antifeminine Prejudice in Shakespeares *1 Henry IV.*" *Literature and Psychology* 40, nos. 1–2 (1994): 118–131.

———. "Prince Hal's Play as Prelude to His Invasion of France." *Psychoanal Review* 88: 495–510.

Kris, Ernst. "Prince Hal's Conflict." In *Approaches to Shakespeare,* edited by Norman Rabkin, 183–202. New York: McGraw-Hill, 1964.

Levin, Lawrence L. "Hotspur, Falstaff, and the Emblem of Wrath in *1 Henry IV.*" *Shakespeare Studies* 10 (1977): 43–65.

London, Todd. "Shakespeare in a Strange Land" *American Theatre* 15, no. 6 (July–August 1998): 22–28.

Machiavelli, Niccolò. "The Prince." In *The Bedford Companion to Shakespeare,* edited by Russ McDonald, 334–336. New York: Bedford/St. Martin's, 2001.

Marks, Peter. "Folger's Powerful Cast Reigns in Nuanced 'Henry IV,'" *Washington Post,* October 18, 2008, p. C1.

Marmion, Patrick. "By Harry, Shakespeare's Marathon Is Nine Hours Well Spent," *Daily Mail,* August 24, 2007, p. 73.

McEachern, Claire Elizabeth. *Henry IV Part I.* London: Penguin Classics, 2000.

McLaverty, J. "No Abuse: The Prince and Falstaff in the Tavern Scenes of Henry IV." *Shakespeare Survey: An Annual Survey of Shakespeare Studies and Production* 34 (1981): 105–110.

Morgann, Maurice. *An Essay on the Dramatic Character of Sir John Falstaff.* London: Wheatley & Adlard, 1825.

Owen, Lewis J., et al. *Lectures on Four of Shakespeare's History Plays.* Pittsburgh, Pa.: Carnegie Institute of Technology, 1953.

Paris, Bernard J. *Character as a Subversive Force in Shakespeare.* Rutherford, N.J.: Fairleigh Dickinson University Press, 1991.

Peat, Derek. "Falstaff Gets the Sack." *Shakespeare Quarterly* 53, no. 3 (2002): 379–385.

Pilkington, Ace G. *1 Henry IV.* (Originally published in *Insights* [Summer 1996]). Available online. URL: http://dsc.dixie.edu/shakespeare/henry4ess.htm. Accessed September 20, 2010.

Prior, Moody E. *The Drama of Power: Studies in Shakespeare's History Plays.* Evanston, Ill.: Northwestern University Press, 1973.

Quiller-Couch, Arthur Thomas. *Notes on Shakespeare's Workmanship.* New York: Henry Holt, 1917.

Reese, M. M. *The Cease of Majesty: A Study of Shakespeare's History Plays.* London: Edward Arnold, 1961.

Ribner, Irving. *The History Play in the Age of Shakespeare.* Princeton, N.J.: Princeton University Press, 1957.

Richmond, H. M. *Shakespeare's Political Plays.* New York: Random House, 1967.

Riggs, David. *Shakespeare's Heroical Histories:* Henry IV *and Its Literary Tradition.* Cambridge, Mass.: Harvard University Press, 1971.

Rose, Alexander: *Kings in the North—The House of Percy in British History.* Phoenix, Ariz.: Orion Books Ltd., 2002.

Saccio, Peter, *Shakespeare's English Kings.* Oxford: Oxford University Press, 2000.

Sanders, Norman. "The True Prince and the False Thief." *Shakespeare Survey* 30 (1977): 29–34.

Schelling, Felix E. *The English Chronicle Play: A Study in the Popular Historical Literature Environing Shakespeare.* New York: Macmillan, 1902.

Shakespeare, William. *Henry the Fourth, Part 1.* Edited by James L. Sanderson. 2d ed. New York: W. W. Norton, 1969.

Shakespeare, William. *The Norton Shakespeare.* Edited by Stephen Greenblatt, et al. New York: W. W. Norton, 1997.

Shalvi, Alice. *The Relationship of Renaissance Concepts of Honour to Shakespeare's Problem Plays.* Salzburg, Austria: University of Salzburg, 1972.

Shaw, George Bernard. *Dramatic Opinions and Essays by G. Bernard Shaw Volume One.* New York: Brentano's, 1906.

Sisk, J. P. "Prince Hal and the Specialists." *Shakespeare Quarterly* 28 (1977): 520–524.

Smith, Emma. *Shakespeare's Histories: A Guide to Criticism.* London: Wiley-Blackwell, 2003.

Spencer, Charles. "A Richly Rewarding Theatrical Marathon," *Daily Telegraph,* August 18, 2007, 14.

Steadman, John M. "Falstaff as Actaeon: A Dramatic Emblem." *Shakespeare Quarterly* 14 (1963): 231–244.

Stewart, Douglas J. "Falstaff the Centaur." *Shakespeare Quarterly* 28 (1977): 5–21.

Stewart, J. I. M. "The Birth and Death of Falstaff." In *Henry the Fourth, Part 1,* edited by James L. Sanderson, 404–407. New York: Norton, 1969.

Stroud, T. A. "Shake-Speare, Fal-Staff, and Hotspur." *Iowa State Journal of Research* 58, no. 3 (February 1984): 329–334.

Taylor, Mark. "Falstaff and the Origins of Private Life." *Shakespeare Yearbook* 3 (1992): 63–85.

Tillyard, E. M. W. *Shakespeare's History Plays.* New York: Chatto and Windus, 1946.

Toliver, Harold E. "Falstaff, the Prince, and the History Play." *Shakespeare Quarterly* 16 (1965): 63–80.

Traversi, Derek. *Shakespeare: From* Richard II *to* Henry V. Stanford, Calif.: Stanford University Press, 1957.

"Trivia for *My Own Private Idaho*." Internet Movie Database. Available online. URL: http://www.imdb.com/title/tt0102494/trivia. Accessed 2010.

Van Doren, Mark. *Shakespeare.* Garden City, N.Y.: Doubleday, 1939.

Velz, John W. Review of The Oxford Shakespeare *Henry IV, Part 1. Shakespeare Quarterly* 43, no. 1 (Spring 1992): 107–109.

Vickers, Brian. *William Shakespeare: The Critical Heritage, 1774–1801.* London: Routledge, 1981.

Waith, Eugene M., ed. *Shakespeare: The Histories.* Englewood Cliffs, N.J.: Prentice-Hall, 1965.

Weil, Herbert, and Judith Weil, eds. *The First Part of King Henry IV* (New Cambridge Shakespeare). New York: Cambridge University Press, 1997.

Wilbur, Richard. *New and Collected Poems.* New York: Harcourt Brace Jovanovich, 1988.

Wilson, J. Dover. *The Fortunes of Falstaff.* Cambridge: Cambridge University Press, 1944.

Winny, James. *The Player King: The Theme of Shakespeare's Histories.* London: Chatto & Windus, 1968.

Wren, Celia. "Prince Hal, Suddenly the Rogue in Vogue," *Washington Post,* January 4, 2004, p. N1.

Woolf, D. R. *The Idea of History in Early Stuart England.* Toronto: University of Toronto Press, 1990.

Yamada, Akihir. "An Eighteenth-Century Stage Adaptation of the Falstaff Part in The First Part of *Henry IV.*" *Shakespeare Quarterly* 21 (1970): 103–104.

FILM AND VIDEO PRODUCTIONS

Van Sant, Gus, dir. *My Own Private Idaho.* With River Phoenix and Keanu Reeves. New Line Cinema, 1991.

Welles, Orson, dir. *Chimes at Midnight* With Orson Welles, John Gielgud, Keith Baxter, Margaret Rutherford, and Norman Rodway. Alpine Films, 1965.

—Asha Choubey

Henry IV, Part 2

INTRODUCTION

Henry, IV Part 2, thought to have been written about 1597, is the third in a sequence of eight historical plays stretching from the reign of Richard II (1377–99) to the beginning of the reign of Henry VII (1485–1509), who was the grandfather of Queen Elizabeth I, Shakespeare's sovereign. Many critics regard *Richard II* (1595); *Henry IV, Part 1* (1596–97) and *Henry IV Part 2;* and *Henry V* (1599) as one unit, commonly referred to as "the Henriad," as they all feature Henry IV and/or Henry V among their principal characters and were written at an earlier time in Shakespeare's career than the other four historical plays about English monarchs.

Henry IV, Part 2 suffers from being regarded as a sequel or a middle play of a sequence, but this is not necessarily just. Although many modern movies have sequels, the retreading of familiar ground does not necessarily lead to trite repetition. It can instead offer imaginative reinterpretations that sometimes surpass the original, as is often seen in the genre of the modern science fiction movie. Nonetheless, some disapproving critics have suggested that *Henry IV, Part 2* is a weak copy of *Part 1* created to cash in on the popularity of Falstaff; others that the darker tone of *Part 2* is incompatible with both the more optimistic feel of *Part 1* and the patriotic triumphant air of *Henry V.* However, the more world-weary, embittered social dealings portrayed in *Part 2* provide the audience a more realistic worldview. In particular, the idea of kingship has lost all its appeal. It is shown to be an illusion, for the wealth and power of the king are weighed down by responsibility, doubt, guilt, and fear: No king can sleep as well as his lowliest subject. In this play, we see the essential contrast between Falstaff's self-image and the realities that show through the cracks, his vanities, meanness, and dishonesty. In *Part 1,* we could never understand how Prince Hal could cast off his mirthful companion; in *Part 2,* we see how very necessary it is.

Henry IV, Part 2 is essential reading. It shows the transformation of Prince Hal from unthinking, callow, if courageous, youthfulness to thoughtful maturity, from boy to man, from prince to king. Without this maturing process, including his true acceptance of the nature of kingship and his casting aside of childish things, Hal could never become the national hero who led England to glory at Agincourt.

BACKGROUND
The Rise of a National Identity

The late 1500s was an exciting time in English history. At this time, there was no United Kingdom of Great Britain as such. Instead, England ruled Wales and part of Ireland. Although the Irish were rebellious, the last great Welsh uprisings had taken place during the reign of Henry IV, almost 200 years earlier. Scotland remained a separate country until the reign of Elizabeth's successor, James I, who was already James VI of Scotland when he inherited the English Crown. In 1585, Sir Richard Grenville established the first English colony in the New World on Roanoke Island, just off the North

Carolina coast. Unfortunately, the colony failed, and a second attempt in 1587 by Sir Walter Raleigh ended in mystery, as, when it was visited four years later, all the colonists had vanished and were never seen again. In 1588, the English defeated the Spanish Armada, a huge fleet of ships sent by Philip of Spain to invade England in revenge for the execution of the Catholic captive Mary, Queen of Scots (James's mother). A number of factors led to the defeat of the Armada, but one of the most important was the huge storms that wrecked many of the ships—a victory assigned by the English to God in true Lancastrian style.

Under these circumstances, the queen was very keen to keep unwelcome images from public view. Shakespeare's *Richard II* was censored, removing the abdication scene. By contrast, *Henry IV, Part 1* and *Part 2* must have been very pleasing, as they show a usurper suffering physical and mental anguish for his crime, unable to sleep, and constantly at war with the nation.

England was becoming aware of itself as an entity in competition with other states for colonies and commodities in the New World. It was the beginning of an empire, even before there was a united Britain. This situation forced the question "What qualities make us English?" The strong interest in the story of Henry V relates to this question. In the various accounts of his life, he is shown to be, as Brian Vickers notes, the embodiment of "maturity, decency, chivalry, courage, wit, authority" and filled with "a sense of future responsibilities which he must and can assume with dignity and justice" (259). His is the story of a man who unites his country against external enemies and is successful at expanding his kingdom through overseas conquest. He becomes an inspirational figure filled with the characteristics that make a good Englishman. By contrast, the English create a series of "others" to contain the personality traits they would prefer to believe are not English. Plays and prose fictions offer a whole range of these racial stereotypes: frivolous and untrustworthy Frenchmen, wicked scheming poisoning Italians, Turkish eunuchs, avaricious Jews, and lusty, bestial Moors.

In 1590, Edmund Spenser (1552–99) produced the first three books of his *Faerie Queene,* following up with three more in 1596. This epic poem (intended to be 24 books long) created an allegorical representation of England as a pastoral fairyland, through which knights travel learning lessons as they are tested by various evils along the way, including villains clearly identifiable as Catholics and Irishmen. The pastoral theme is present in a number of prose fictions and plays, and Shakespeare adopted it (although not in idealized form) in *Henry IV, Part 2* as one of his visions of England.

Death

For the Elizabethans, living in a world where there was little health care, a high infant mortality rate, no antibiotics, and no health and safety laws, death was commonplace, happening in the home or on the streets without the romance, mystery, and taboos we assign to it today. In Act IV, Scenes 4 and 5 of *Henry IV, Part 2,* Clarence comments that the king's skin is "So thin that life looks through and will break out" and that "His eye is hollow, and he changes much". His observations are accurate, for the skin of the dying can take on an almost translucent appearance while the flesh seems to fall away leaving the face seeming almost skeletal. These symptoms would have been familiar to the audience and signified that the king was very close to death, his life hanging by a thread. In Scene 4, Gloucester and Clarence also talk about signs and portents foretelling the king's death: unnatural births, unseasonal weather, and unusual behavior of the Thames, a tidal river.

Rhetoric

An important element in the construction of speeches in Renaissance drama was the use of rhetorical devices. Rhetoric is the art of using language as a means to persuade and was taught at schools and universities. Students would learn Latin and Greek and then be taught to argue persuasively on any angle on any topic regardless of their personal feelings about the subject. This art is continued (usually in one's native tongue) by debating societies today, and many of these techniques are used by political speech writers.

There are at least 60 different forms of rhetorical device, and playwrights, poets, and prose authors through the centuries have used them all. The devices we are probably most familiar with today are alliteration (repeating the consonant sound at the beginning of words, for example, "snakes and serpents slithered through the ceiling"), similes (where something is compared to something else using the words *like* or *as,* for example, "her face shone like a full moon," or "he was as talkative as a parrot"), metaphors (comparing one thing to something else by saying they are the same thing, for example "the crowd was a field of wheat waiting to be harvested by the guns"), and rhetorical questions (the posing of a question without wanting or expecting a response, often because the response is obvious, for example, "How could anyone think that we would enjoy a holiday on a building site?").

During Shakespeare's time, the English language was going through amazing changes and was far more flexible than it is today; spelling and grammar had not yet settled down into their modern accepted forms, and the first dictionary was still some years away. (Robert Cawdry produced the first English dictionary with definitions of the words in 1604, although it was very limited, arbitrary in its choice of words to define, and often gave only a one-word definition.) Shakespeare was particularly good at creating interesting and imaginative metaphors, and many of them have since entered the English language (for example, "the milk of human kindness") and can be found in the dictionary.

Sources of the Play

Much of the play's story is taken from *The Chronicles of England, Scotland, and Ireland,* Raphael Holinshed's history, a second edition of which was published in 1587. However, the events of this play described by Holinshed as taking place over a number of years (ca. 1405–13) are shrunk by Shakespeare into a period of a few months, conflating three separate rebellions—that of the archbishop of York and the Earl Marshal Thomas Mowbray with that of Lord Hastings, Lord Fau-conbridge, Sir John Coleville of the Dale, and Sir John Griffith with that of the Earl of Northumberland and Lord Bardolph. King Henry IV, who enters at Act III, Scene 1, laments his loss of sleep due to cares the common man cannot know; Holinshed's king discovers murderous spikes in his bed placed by traitors at the very start of his reign. Shakespeare also combines the king's reconciliation with his son, the incident of the prince taking the crown before his father is dead, and the actual death of the king—events separated by several months in Holinshed. Holinshed's king begins major preparations for his crusade during the year before he dies with the intention of diverting the nobles from internal squabbling by presenting them with an external foe, while for Shakespeare's king, this is a pipe dream to be passed on to his son as advice. Holinshed explains the division between the king and Prince Henry as being largely caused by self-serving courtiers spreading lies, rumors, and gossip to create fear and jealousy in the king. Shakespeare's calculating prince feigns friendship to study the workings of the lower classes in order to be a better king. However, Shakespeare does use Holinshed's incident of the Lord Chief Justice justifiably locking up one of the prince's acquaintances, being struck by the prince for it, and then locking up the prince. Likewise, as reported in the *Chronicle,* Shakespeare has the newly crowned Henry V surrounding himself with wise and just advisers and banning his wilder companions from coming within 10 miles of him (but providing them means to support themselves), although he makes this much more personal by the use of Falstaff.

These last two incidents are also reported in John Stow's *The Annales of England,* published in 1592. Stow details the events of the challenge to the Lord Chief Justice's position, expanding the story: The prince is furious and demands his servant back; the justice considers his position but stands firm. His reply causes the prince to snatch up his sword and charge the judge, perhaps even intending to kill him. The justice remains motionless, making a speech pointing out that he is a representative of the king and that any attack on him is an attack on the king's justice. The prince is so impressed by the speech and demeanor of the Lord Chief Justice that he allows himself to be arrested. The king is delighted to find that he has a truly honest judge and a son who is prepared to submit himself to the law. This story is repeated in the anonymous 1598 play *The Famous Victories of Henry the Fifth: Containing the Honourable battell of Agin-court,* in which the servant is described throughout as "thief" and the prince is portrayed more humorously. He suggests his thief only robs people for a joke and does not draw his sword but instead boxes the Lord Chief Justice on the ear.

Another source Shakespeare may have used is *The First Fowre Bookes of the Civile Wars Between the Two Houses of Lancaster and Yorke* by Samuel Daniel, published in 1595. The following is Daniel's description of the changeability of the will of the people:

> Thus muttred lo the malecontented sort
> That loue kings best before they haue them still,
> And neuer can the present statecomport,
> But would as oft change as they change their
> will:
> For this good Duke had wonne them in this sort
> By suckring themand pittying of their ill,
> That they supposed straight it was one thing,
> To be both a good man, and a good king.
> (Book 1, Verse 71)

This short passage is reminiscent of Rumour's "still-discordant wav'ring multitude" (Induction.19) in *Henry IV, Part 2,* as well as the Archbishop's speech at the end of Act I:

> They that, when Richard liv'd, would have him
> die
> Are now become enamour'd on his grave.
> Thou that threw'st dust upon his goodly head,
> When through proud London he came
> sighing on
> After th'admired heels of Bolingbroke,
> Cry'st now, 'O earth, yield us that King again,

> And take thou this!' O thoughts of men
> accurs'd!
> Past and to come seems best; things present
> worst.
> (1.3.101–108)

Daniel's king fears that the sins he committed in gaining the crown—that is, usurping the throne from Richard II and his involvement in Richard's death—may curse his son's reign, too. The Prince's response in Daniel's work follows as such:

> Nay father since your fortune did attaine
> So hye a stand: I meane not to descend,
> Replyes the Prince; as if what you did gaine
> I were the spirit vnable to defend:
> Time will appease them well that now
> complaine,
> And ratefie our interest in the end;
> What wrong hath not continuance quite
> outworne?
> Yeares makes that right which neuer was so
> borne.
> (Book 3, Verse 125)

This passage is echoed by Shakespeare's Prince Henry:

> My gracious liege,
> You won it, wore it, kept it, gave it me;
> Then plain and right must my possession be,
> Which I with more than a common pain
> 'Gainst all the world will rightfully maintain.
> (4.5.220–224)

However, while Daniel's King Henry still expresses uncertainty about the future of a monarchy based on his sins of usurpation, Shakespeare's King Henry is certain that the kingship will descend to his son "with better quiet, / Better opinion, better confirmation." King Henry believes that "the soil of the achievement" will die with him (4.5.187–189).

Stow's *Annales,* published in 1592, provides a more in-depth version of the archbishop of York's rebellion, but the trickery practiced on the rebels is very clearly orchestrated by the earl of Westmoreland; Shakespeare transfers it to John of Lancaster, Prince Henry's younger brother, who would have been only 16 at the time, stressing the political expediency within the nature of the Lancaster family. This provides an echo of how Henry Bolingbroke gained the crown in the first place and perhaps a foreshadowing of Henry V's achievement at the siege of Harfleur some years later, where he defeats the defenders by offering them the chance to surrender and paints a terrifying word picture of the consequences to the town and its citizens if they make him fight to the finish:

> If I begin the battery once again,
> I will not leave the half-achieved Harfleur
> Till in her ashes she lie buried.
> The gates of mercy shall be all shut up,
> And the fleshed soldier, rough and hard of
>   heart,
> In liberty of bloody hand shall range
> With conscience wide as hell, mowing like grass
> Your fresh-fair virgins, and your flowering
>   infants.
>
> (*Henry V*, 3.3.7–14)

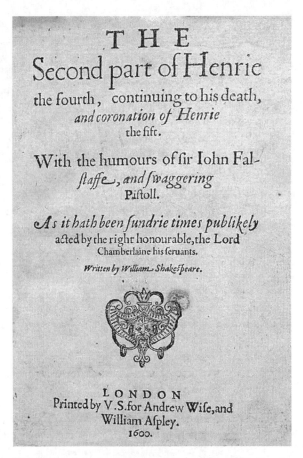

Title page of the first quarto edition of *Henry IV, Part 2,* published in 1600.

Date and Text of the Play

This play was probably written in 1597 or 1598. A early quarto edition (known as Qa) was published in 1600, leaving out Act III, Scene 1; a slightly later quarto (Qb) includes that scene. Together, the quartos form the basis for most modern editions of the play. The version of the text that appears in the 1623 First Folio publication of Shakespeare's plays is not as complete as the quartos, although it does contain some important minor differences and seeming improvements.

SYNOPSIS
Brief Synopsis

Having defeated the rebels in the Battle of Shrewsbury, as depicted in *Henry IV, Part 1,* King Henry IV and his son, Prince Henry (or Hal), watch their triumph fade; the country is decaying due to years of civil war and unrest. A new group of rebels take the field against the king, including the Archbishop of York, whose presence inspires men to believe that their cause is just and holy. While Sir John Falstaff plots to make money out of war and prepares to reap the rewards of his friendship with the crown prince, Prince Henry comes to terms with what it means to be a king and with the consequences of assuming the throne. The rebels are ultimately defeated by trickery. King Henry IV, already very ill, dies shortly after hearing the news of his victory. Before his death, he and Prince Henry are reconciled. Falstaff, hearing

74

The Second Part of Henry the Fourth,
Containing his Death : and the Coronation
of King Henry the Fift.

Actus Primus. Scœna Prima.

INDVCTION.

Enter Rumour.

Pen your Eares : For which of you will ftop
The vent of Hearing, when loud *Rumor* fpeakes?
I, from the Orient, to the drooping Weft
(Making the winde my Poft-horfe) ftill vnfold
The Acts commenced on this Ball of Earth,
Vpon my Tongue, continuall Slanders ride,
The which, in euery Language, I pronounce,
Stuffing the Eares of them with falfe Reports :
I fpeake of Peace, while couert Enmitie
(Vnder the fmile of Safety) wounds the World :
And who but *Rumour*, who but onely I
Make fearfull Mufters, and prepar'd Defence,
Whilft the bigge yeare, fwolne with fome other griefes,
Is thought with childe, by the fterne Tyrant, Warre,
And no fuch matter? *Rumour*, is a Pipe
Blowne by Surmifes, Ieloufies, Coniectures;
And of fo eafie, and fo plaine a ftop,
That the blunt Monfter, with vncounted heads,
The ftill difcordant, wauering Multitude,
Can play vpon it. But what neede I thus
My well-knowne Body to Anathomize
Among my houfhold? Why is *Rumour* heere?
I run before King *Harries* victory,
Who in a bloodie field by Shrewsburie
Hath beaten downe yong *Hotfpurre*, and his Troopes,
Quenching the flame of bold Rebellion,
Euen with the Rebels blood. But what meane I
To fpeake fo true at firft? My Office is
To noyfe abroad, that *Harry Monmouth* fell
Vnder the Wrath of Noble *Hotfpurres* Sword :
And that the King, before the *Dowglas* Rage
Stoop'd his Annointed head, as low as death.
This haue I rumour'd through the peafaut-Townes,
Betweene the Royall Field of Shrewsburie,
And this Worme-eaten-Hole of ragged Stone,
Where *Hotfpurres* Father, old Northumberland,
Lyes crafty ficke. The Poftes come tyring on,
And not a man of them brings other newes
Then they haue learn'd of Me. From *Rumours* Tongues,
They bring fmooth-Comforts-falfe, worfe then True-
wrongs.   *Exit.*

Scena Secunda.

Enter Lord Bardolfe, and the Porter.

L.Bar. Who keepes the Gate heere hoa?
Where is the Earle?
Por. What fhall I fay you are?
Bar. Tell thou the Earle
That the Lord *Bardolfe* doth attend him heere.
Por. His Lordfhip is walk'd forth into the Orchard,
Pleafe it your Honor, knocke but at the Gate,
And he himfelfe will anfwer.
Enter Northumberland.
L.Bar. Heere comes the Earle.
Nor. What newes Lord *Bardolfe*? Eu'ry minute now
Should be the Father of fome Stratagem;
The Times are wilde : Contention (like a Horfe
Full of high Feeding) madly hath broke loofe,
And beates downe all before him.
L.Bar. Noble Earle,
I bring you certaine newes from Shrewsbury.
Nor. Good, and heauen will.
L.Bar. As good as heart can wifh :
The King is almoft wounded to the death :
And in the Fortune of my Lord your Sonne,
Prince *Harrie* flaine out-right ; and both the *Blunts*
Kill'd by the hand of *Dowglas*, Yong Prince *Iohn*,
And Weftmerland, and Stafford, fled the Field.
And *Harrie Monmouth's* Brawne (the Hulke Sir *Iohn*)
Is prifoner to your Sonne, O, fuch a Day,
(So fought, fo follow'd, and fo fairely wonne)
Came not, till now, to dignifie the Times
Since *Cæfars* Fortunes.
Nor. How is this deriu'd?
Saw you the Field? Came you from Shrewsbury?
L.Bar. I fpake with one (my L.) that came frō thence,
A Gentleman well bred, and of good name,
That freely render'd me thefe newes for true.
Nor. Heere comes my Seruant *Trauers*, whom I fent
On Tuefday laft, to liften after Newes.
Enter Trauers.
L.Bar. My Lord, I ouer-rod him on the way,
And he is furnifh'd with no certainties,
More then he (haply) may retaile from me.
Nor. Now *Trauers*, what good tidings comes frō you?
                                        Tra.

Title page of the First Folio edition of *Henry IV, Part 2*, published in 1623 news of the coronation races to London to meet his prince and gain his reward. Prince Henry rejects him publicly as virtually his first act on becoming king.

Induction

The play opens in front of the Earl of Northumberland's castle at Warkworth. Rumour enters the stage and boastfully introduces itself to the audience. It describes the speed at which rumors travel and the inaccuracy of the information carried. It then explains the current situation to the audience, relating the events at the end of *Henry IV, Part 1*. At the Battle of Shrewsbury, Henry IV's forces have been victorious, and Prince Henry has killed Harry Percy, known as Hotspur. However, Rumour has spread news that the rebels have been victorious and that the prince is dead and the king is captive. Rumour gloats as these tales are just about to reach the Earl of Northumberland, the father of Hotspur, raising his hopes only to make their destruction even more devastating.

Act I, Scene 1

Lord Bardolph enters the castle. His brief conversation with the Porter allows him to tell the audience who he is, and he, in turn, names the Earl of Northumberland as he enters the stage. Northumberland is agitated and desperate for news. Lord Bardolph says his news is certain but instead delivers the news Rumour has already told the audience is false. Lord Bardolph's information was supplied by a stranger he had met who was traveling away from the battle. Northumberland's servant Travers, who had been sent for news, enters. Originally, he had received the same joyful news as Lord Bardolph but had later been overtaken by a gentleman riding his horse into the ground and, from him, received the news of the rebellion's downfall at Shrewsbury. Lord Bardolph defends his version of the news, but at this point, Morton arrives. Northumberland notes his unhappy face and asks if he has come from Shrewsbury. Morton replies he ran from Shrewsbury. On further ques-

Lord Bardolph delivers news of the failure of the rebellion to the Earl of Northumberland in Act I, Scene I of *Henry IV, Part 2*. This drawing was designed for the Chiswick edition of Shakespeare, published in 1900. *(Illustration by John Byam Lister Shaw)*

tioning by the earl, he breaks the tragic news that although Northumberland's brother and their Scottish ally, Douglas, have survived, his son is dead. Morton personally witnessed Hotspur fall to Prince Henry's sword, swiftly followed by the rebel soldiers running away and reports that the king is sending a force against Northumberland. The earl, in despair, determines to throw off his sickness and hazard everything he has against the king. Lord Bardolph and Morton counsel against futile gestures. Morton has heard that the Archbishop of York is now preaching rebellion and suggests that they form an alliance with him, dividing the king's forces. They leave the stage to continue planning.

Act I, Scene 2

Sir John Falstaff and his page are conversing as they walk along a London street. Falstaff speaks wittily at considerable length, making clear that the Page was put in his employ by Prince Henry, showing little respect for the prince, and intimating that he is old, in ill health, and a poor credit risk. The Lord Chief Justice enters, wanting to speak to Falstaff with regard to a robbery. Falstaff tries to avoid him, feigning deafness and then frequently changing the subject. Due to Falstaff's actions at Shrewsbury, the Lord Chief Justice is prepared to overlook his past misdeeds and notes that King Henry is sending Falstaff with Prince John of Lancaster, separating him from Prince Henry (Falstaff thinks that the Lord Chief Justice may have arranged this). Falstaff tries to hit on him for money to outfit his troop, but the Lord Chief Justice is not foolish enough to give him anything. Falstaff sends his page off with begging letters to the prince, Lancaster, Westmoreland, and an old mistress and believes that the war will provide him with something to turn to profit.

Act I, Scene 3

In York, the Archbishop, Mowbray, Hastings, and Lord Bardolph consult with one another over their chances in the coming conflict. While the others seem fairly optimistic, Lord Bardolph expresses caution, suggesting that if they cannot prevail without Northumberland—who let down his own son in the previous rebellion—they should not extend themselves. The Archbishop, Mowbray, and Hastings believe that King Henry cannot put his full force against them as he also has to fight the Welsh and the French, and will only send Lancaster and Westmoreland against them. They leave the stage determined to continue their plans at speed.

Act II, Scene 1

Mistress Quickly prepares to arrest Falstaff with two officers of the law, Sergeant Fang and Yeoman Snare. She has taken out a suit against Falstaff for not repaying 100 marks that he has borrowed from

her. Falstaff, his Page, and his friend Bardolph appear and respond with violence. The Lord Chief Justice enters with his men and attempts to get to the bottom of the situation. Mistress Quickly explains that Falstaff has literally eaten her out of house and home; she then conjures up a scene of domestic tranquillity in which Falstaff proposed marriage to her and then borrowed more money. Falstaff protests that she is a mad woman and then cites his need to be off to the wars as reason he should be excused. The Lord Chief Justice, however, insists that Falstaff must settle his accounts with Mistress Quickly immediately. While the Lord Chief Justice reads a letter containing the latest news presented to him by Gower, Falstaff converses with Mistress Quickly, coaxing her into lending him more money on top of the original debt he owes her, which she can only supply by pawning her treasured belongings. She is persuaded on a shaky promise of future payment, and Bardolph accompanies her to ensure that the money is procured. Before leaving the stage with Bardolph, Fang, Snare, and the Page, she coaxes Sir John into dining with her that night. Falstaff unsuccessfully attempts to join the conversation between Gower and the Lord Chief Justice, who ignore him. They are discussing the king's return from Shrewsbury and Prince John's mission to fight the new rebellion fostered by Northumberland and the Archbishop of York. Falstaff tries to persuade Gower to take dinner with him, but Gower refuses. The Lord Chief Justice chastises Falstaff for still being in London when he should be levying troops and traveling to join Prince John.

Act II, Scene 2

Prince Henry exclaims that he is exhausted. Poins suggests that royalty is beyond such things. Prince Henry rallies his wits and discourses upon the small things he knows about Poins, of which a prince should be ignorant. Poins takes him to task for joking when his father is so ill. Prince Henry speaks of his sorrow and his inability to express it in public for fear of being thought a hypocrite; he has shown himself to be a bad son in the eyes of the world by his close association with Falstaff and the other low-bred characters (including Poins who does not see himself in this light), and his earlier wild behavior. Bardolph and the Page bring a letter from Falstaff, which Prince Henry reads aloud. It contains a blatant attempt to damage Poins's relationship with the prince while Falstaff is absent from London. Prince Henry plots with Poins to attend Falstaff's meal that night and pays Bardolph and the Page to keep quiet about his return to London.

Act II, Scene 3

The Earl of Northumberland, Lady Northumberland, and Lady Percy discuss whether he should join the new rebellion. Northumberland believes he must go or lose his honor. Lady Percy points out that his honor was lost when he failed to reinforce her husband, his own son Hotspur, at Shrewsbury. Why should he waste honor on strangers that he could not summon up for his own son? Northumberland is despondent but still protests he needs to go and face his fate, for fear that it will find him later in worse circumstances. The women, sensing his hesitation, counsel fleeing to Scotland, letting the rebels try their luck, and reinforcing them if they look to be winning. Northumberland still protesting his desire to join the rebels is persuaded to flee to Scotland and wait for the right moment.

Act II, Scene 4

In the Boar's-Head Tavern, Eastcheap, the waiting staff discuss old jests between Falstaff and Prince Henry and remind the audience that the prince and Poins will be disguised as fellow servers to play a trick on Falstaff. One server is sent off to find Sneak's band for some music, as the diners move unexpectedly early from the overly warm dining room to relax after the meal. Mistress Quickly and Doll Tearsheet enter first, the former concerned that the latter has drunk too much. Falstaff enters singing, inquires after Doll's health, and then jokes about her profession as a courtesan passing venereal diseases to her clients. The banter between the three is interrupted by the arrival of

Pistol who wishes to speak with Falstaff. Mistress Quickly has recently been warned to be careful of her house's reputation; the women are against Pistol being let in, for his quarrelsome nature may call unwelcome official attention to the tavern, but Falstaff overrides their voices and Pistol is admitted. He enters with Bardolph and the Page. The women, particularly Doll, are hostile toward him, and there is much sexual innuendo regarding his name. The row between Doll and Pistol escalates while Mistress Quickly, Bardolph, and the Page try to calm him. He draws his sword. He is calmed down and lays down his sword. Falstaff, having kept clear of the quarrel, now expresses a desire for quiet. Attempts to send Pistol downstairs result in a revival of the brawl, and Falstaff orders Bardolph to push him downstairs. Pistol picks up his sword again, and Falstaff also draws. Bardolph successfully forces Pistol down the stairs and returns to say that Pistol has been wounded in the shoulder by Falstaff. Doll is impressed by his heroic stance. The musicians arrive, as do Prince Henry and Poins in disguise. Doll questions Falstaff about the prince and Poins, as they flirt and flatter. His answers are insulting to both men, who listen with growing exasperation in the background. When Falstaff calls for more wine, they both step forward and he recognizes them. Prince Henry interrogates him while Falstaff wriggles his way out of his accusations, saying he was saving them from the attentions of the wicked. The conversation ends abruptly with the arrival of Peto who brings news that King Henry is at Westminster and that many Captains are searching for Falstaff. The prince parts abruptly from the gathering to go to his father accompanied by Poins. Further knocking produces a summons to the court for Falstaff. He bids the women farewell, and they express their sorrow that they may not see him again. Before he has gone very far, he summons Doll to his side.

Act III, Scene 1

King Henry, in his nightgown, summons the Earls of Surrey and Warwick. He then muses on the sleeplessness of kings whose subjects, despite poverty, hunger, and discomfort are able to sleep soundly. Warwick and Surrey wish him a good morning as it is past one o'clock. The king is disturbed by the news of his kingdom, but Warwick compares the situation to the final stages of a disease from which the body will recover and grow strong once more. The king is depressed, viewing the actions of man as pointless in the face of time. He talks of the failings of friendship and appears disturbed that Richard II's prophecy that Northumberland would turn on him has come true. Warwick points out that this was a fair guess on Richard's part. Henry expresses his fear that Northumberland and the Archbishop of York have too huge a number for his forces to prevail against. Again, Warwick reassures the king that the numbers are mere rumor and encourages the king to bed. Henry expresses his desire to go to the Holy Land once his kingdom is in order.

Act III, Scene 2

Falstaff stops in Gloucestershire to pick up recruits for his army at the house of Justice Robert Shallow, who is accompanied by his cousin, Silence. While they wait, the cousins exchange family news and reminisce about their long-lost (and, allegedly, wild) youth, working in the Inns of Court, where Shallow associated with a young Falstaff, and bemoaning that so many friends of these days have now died. Bardolph and Falstaff arrive and quickly get down to the task of recruiting. The recruits are Mouldy, Shadow, Wart, Feeble, and Bullcalf. Wart is rejected out of hand. Falstaff, Shallow, and Silence head off for dinner, discussing a whore, Jane Nightwork, they knew 55 years before. Bullcalf and Mouldy bribe Bardolph to release them from service, while Feeble makes a noble speech expressing his willingness to serve his prince. When Falstaff and the justices return, Bardolph informs Falstaff of the bribes. Although he is supposed to take the four best men he can get, Falstaff takes Shadow, Wart, and Feeble. The justices leave, and the new recruits are marched away by Bardolph. Falstaff alone remains on stage, mocking Justice Shallow's exaggerations and lies about his youth.

He shares his plan to return after the war and leach away Shallow's wealth.

Act IV, Scene 1

The rebels are gathered in the forest of Gaultree, in Yorkshire. The Archbishop has just received word from Northumberland that he has abandoned their cause and gone to Scotland. A messenger arrives with news that the enemy numbers about 30,000 troops, which is what the rebels had calculated. The Earl of Westmoreland arrives with messages from Prince John as general of the king's forces. Westmoreland points out that the Archbishop owes his life and livelihood to peace and that the Archbishop is fighting a cause not his own. Likewise, he points out that Mowbray's claim of ill treatment by the Crown is invalid, as he only has his lands because King Henry restored them to him. Westmoreland then moves on to the real reason for his visit. Prince John is willing to hear their demands, and if they are just, he will set them right. The Archbishop hands over a list of their grievances for the prince to examine and says if these are met and also if all those involved in the rebellion are forgiven, then they will agree to peace. Westmoreland leaves with their schedule but does not make any comment or agreement on their condition of forgiveness.

The rebels discuss their future. Mowbray expresses some fears, but they are mostly confident that King Henry is exhausted by rebellions and has learned the lesson that violence breeds only more violence. Westmoreland returns with the news that Prince John is ready to meet them.

Act IV, Scene 2

Prince John greets the rebels graciously and then upbraids the Archbishop for misusing his power as the speaker and interpreter of God's words to lead others into battle against their king, God's representative on Earth. They move on to the articles, which Prince John says he agrees are just and fair and shall all be swiftly put right. He asks the rebels to disband their army, saying he will do likewise, and asks them to share a drink and depart in peace.

The rebel army disbands almost immediately, while apparently Prince John's troops have said they will wait for him to speak to them personally. As soon as they are sure the rebel army has disbanded, Westmoreland arrests all three of the rebel leaders for treason. When they protest, Prince John explains that he only promised them that their demands would be met; he made no such promises regarding their personal safety or that of their army. Prince John assigns this bloodless victory to God and sets his army to chase the remainder of the rebel army from the field.

Act IV, Scene 3

Falstaff and Sir John Coleville of the Dale run into each other in the aftermath of the battle. Coleville is one of the rebels and recognizes Falstaff from his reputation. His reputation is strong enough that he is able to persuade Coleville to yield to him without having to strike a blow. Prince John, Westmoreland, Blunt, and others enter. Prince John commands Westmoreland to stop the army from chasing the rebels. Westmoreland exits the stage to carry out his order. Prince John then asks Falstaff where he has been hiding during the action. Falstaff after protesting his valor presents Coleville as proof of it. Prince John shows his awareness of Falstaff's untrustworthiness and verbally fences with him. Falstaff surrenders his prisoner to Prince John, who checks his identity. Blunt is assigned to take Coleville to be executed with the other rebel leaders in York. Falstaff seeks permission to travel back through Gloucestershire and asks Prince John to speak well of him. Prince John says he will speak better of him than he deserves. Alone on stage, Falstaff muses on the fact that Prince John will not be entertained or swayed by his jokes and counsel and puts it down to lack of wine (sherris-sack) in his blood. He then expounds on the two ways in which sherris is good for a man: It sharpens his wit and provides him with courage. He states that sherris is the reason for Prince Hal's valiant behavior, unlike his lean and sterile father. Falstaff sets off for Gloucestershire, where he intends to squeeze Justice Shallow for whatever he can get.

Act IV, Scene 4

King Henry (carried in a chair), Warwick, Thomas of Clarence, Humphrey of Gloucester, and an entourage enter the Jerusalem Chamber at Westminster. The king expresses hope for a swift successful conclusion to the rebellion, followed by a long peace, in which the only need to draw weapons will be in God's name on a crusade. He then inquires the whereabouts of the crown prince, who has gone hunting in Windsor, unaccompanied by any of his brothers. He lectures Thomas, as Prince Henry's favorite brother, to stick by the prince and hopefully temper his wilder behavior when he comes to power. In turn, by keeping in his brother's good graces, Thomas will be able to protect and enhance the status of the rest of the family and make them a strong unit, enabling them to hold onto the throne of England. The king, however, is disturbed to find that Prince Henry is dining once more with his less salubrious companions and worries about what will become of the country if these people influence the prince's future rule. Warwick interjects that, like a true potential king, Prince Henry is merely learning the ways of the common man to inform his future.

Westmoreland arrives with the news that the rebels have been defeated by Prince John without bloodshed. Harcourt brings the news that the Earl of Northumberland and Lord Bardolph have also been defeated. Despite the good news, the king's already failing health takes a turn for the worse. Although Warwick tries to reassure those present that King Henry will rally, the king's sons Gloucester and Clarence can see that he is very close to death. Warwick hushes them as the king rallies and asks to be taken somewhere quiet. They lay him on a bed and carry him across the stage.

Act IV, Scene 5

The king continues speaking from the previous scene, asking for quiet and soft music. His followers attempt to make him comfortable. Prince Henry arrives and decides to stay by the sleeping king as the rest withdraw. Alone, Prince Henry muses on the crown, comparing it to armor that should protect but instead, in the heat of the day, burns the wearer. The crown has separated his father from sleep, and now Henry observes that the final sleep of death appears to have separated his father from the crown. Unable to discern any signs that the king is breathing or get any response from him, Henry takes the crown and tries it on. Distraught, he leaves the room.

Instantly, the king awakes, calling out in alarm. Warwick, Gloucester, and Clarence rush into the room. The king demands to know why they left him alone, and they tell him that Prince Henry was with him. With his absence comes the discovery of the missing crown. The king sends Warwick to find the prince and bitterly muses on the thankless task of raising sons and providing for them, only to have them wishing you dead before your time. Warwick returns; he has found Prince Henry, who was weeping piteously in the next room. As Prince Henry enters, the king dismisses everyone else. The king berates his son, accusing him of being greedy for the crown and wishing for his father's death. The king despairs for the kingdom's future on the basis of the prince's riotous youth. Kneeling at his father's feet, Prince Henry makes an impassioned speech explaining that he had thought his father dead and, in grief, took the crown and remonstrated with it as an enemy that had killed his father and was now his to fight. The king responds with relief and joy. In private, the king is able to express some regret over the death of Richard II and the harm his usurpation has done the country. Reunited with his son, he gives him his last piece of advice: maintain peace at home by making war abroad. Prince Henry assures his father that he will do this.

Prince John arrives. The king greets John and praises him for the victory he has brought. However, his health is failing. He asks Warwick the name of the room he first fainted in; it was the Jerusalem Chamber. He muses on the irony that it was prophesied he would die in Jerusalem; he had thought this would be on a crusade to the Holy Land but accepts his fate and bids them carry him there to die.

Shallow welcomes Falstaff's page into his home in Act V, Scene 1 of *Henry IV, Part 2*. Drawing designed for the Chiswick edition *(Illustration by John Byam Lister Shaw)*

Act V, Scene 1

Falstaff is persuaded by Shallow to stay overnight for dinner in Gloucestershire. Shallow's servant Davy undertakes arrangements while continuing to sort out the day-to-day running of the estate and also influencing his master's decisions in a friend's favor with regard to a future law case. Shallow is cultivating Falstaff as a useful influence in the court, while Falstaff plans to use Shallow as a figure of fun to make the prince laugh.

Act V, Scene 2

At Westminster Palace, Warwick informs the Lord Chief Justice of the king's death. They are both concerned that the new king will mistreat him due to their past encounters, and they express fears for the realm. Lancaster, Clarence, and Gloucester join the conversation. King Henry V enters and speaks kindly to his brothers. He then turns to the Lord Chief Justice and asks him how he, the king, can be expected to forget the way the Lord Chief Justice treated him. The Chief Justice defends his actions as those of the king's representative and counters by asking Henry, now that he is king, whether he would welcome his laws being disregarded and disdained by his son and whether he would prefer to have them upheld for him by his servant. Henry responds by confirming the Lord Chief Justice in his original position and stating that he will be as a spiritual father to him, to give wise counsel now that Henry's own father is gone. They leave the stage to undertake the coronation.

Act V, Scene 3

Falstaff, Shallow, Silence, Davy, Bardolph, and the Page are in Shallow's orchard after dinner. They are all rather merry; Silence keeps bursting into song. Pistol arrives from London with the news that King Henry IV is dead. Falstaff instantly offers Shallow any position he wants and sends Bardolph to saddle the horses. He prepares to race to the new king's side and believes that the laws of England will no longer apply to him.

Act V, Scene 4

Doll Tearsheet and Mistress Quickly are dragged off to prison by Beadles, possibly to be whipped or hanged, as a man they and Pistol beat up has died.

Act V, Scene 5

Near Westminster Abbey, the new king and his train pass over freshly strewn rushes to the coronation. Falstaff, Shallow, Pistol, Bardolph, and the Page wait outside the abbey for the newly crowned king to return. Falstaff's confidence is high: He has borrowed 1,000 pounds from Shallow, the king will see him and bestow favorable looks on his companions, he will attract the king's goodwill by his hasty journey, and he will use his influence to free Doll and Mistress Quickly. The king and his retinue, including the Lord Chief Justice, return, but Henry ignores Falstaff's overtures. When Fal-

staff persists, the king snubs him, saying he does not know him, and that, old as he is, he should look to his soul. He will provide Falstaff with a basic living allowance and advance his career in accordance with his behavior, but Falstaff is not allowed to come within 10 miles of him. The final insult is that the Lord Chief Justice, Falstaff's long-term adversary, is to oversee his case. Shallow wants his money back, but Falstaff clings to the hope that the king will send to him in private. However, the Lord Chief Justice and Prince John appear with some soldiers, and Falstaff and all his company are taken off to the Fleet Prison. Alone on the stage, Prince John confides to the Lord Chief Justice his pleasure at the king's treatment of his old companions and the fact that they shall probably soon be at war with France.

Epilogue

The author states that he is paying the audience for their patience with an earlier, poor play with this (hopefully) better one. He kneels before them, apparently in supplication for their goodwill, but then, instead, says it is to pray for the queen. After some banter, he promises that Falstaff will turn up in another play (implying it will be *Henry V*) and stresses that Sir John Falstaff is not Sir John Oldcastle.

CHARACTER LIST

Rumour, the Presenter The characterization of rumor opens the play, bringing the audience up to speed on the events of *Henry IV, Part 1* and setting the tone as both urgent and full of misdirection.

King Henry IV Also known as Henry Bolingbroke, Henry IV is the current king of England. He usurped the crown from his predecessor, Richard II. He is aging and sick and suffers from insomnia brought on by guilt, doubt, and fears.

Prince Henry The eldest son of Henry IV and heir to the throne, he is also sometimes referred to as Harry Monmouth (and Prince Hal in *Henry IV, Part 1*). He has a reputation for wasting his life playing wild pranks and hanging out in pubs with a bad crowd. At the end of the play, Prince Henry is crowned King Henry V.

Prince John of Lancaster; Humphrey, Duke of Gloucester; and Thomas, Duke of Clarence Three other sons of Henry IV and brothers of Prince Henry. Prince John is the only one seen acting independently, when he is sent to negotiate the rebels' surrender (4.2).

Henry Percy, Earl of Northumberland Northumberland was the father of Harry Percy, better known as Hotspur, killed by Prince Henry in the rebellion in *Henry IV, Part 1*. Northumberland claimed that he was sick and unable to join his son against the king at that time.

Lady Northumberland and Lady Percy The ladies of Northumberland's household, consisting of his wife and his daughter-in-law, widow of Hotspur.

Lord Bardolph, Travers, and Morton Followers of and co-conspirators with Northumberland.

Archbishop of York Having remained aloof from the earlier rebellion, the Archbishop of York has now declared that the murder of Richard II was a crime against God and raised arms against the king.

Lord Mowbray and Lord Hastings Allies of the Archbishop of York.

Sir John Coleville Another one of the rebels.

Earl of Warwick, Earl of Westmoreland, Earl of Surrey, Sir John Blunt, Gower, and Harcourt Followers of the king.

Lord Chief Justice As the keeper of the king's peace, the Lord Chief Justice is a man of great integrity and honor.

Poins This is one of the brighter of Prince Henry's disreputable companions, who aids him in plotting practical jokes to be played on other members of the group.

Sir John Falstaff A fat, aging rogue, full of his own importance, who has cultivated Prince Henry's friendship by providing constant merrymaking and is convinced that he will reap full benefits of the prince's friendship when Henry becomes king.

Bardolph, Pistol, Peto, Hostess Quickly, Doll Tearsheet, and Falstaff's Page Friends and companions of Falstaff. The Page was presented to Falstaff by Prince Henry. Pistol with his bravado is seen as a reduction of Hotspur and was featured on the bill alongside Falstaff.

Robert Shallow, Silence, and Davy A senile country justice in Gloucestershire from whom Falstaff wishes to cozen money; his cousin and his servant.

Sergeant Fang and Yeoman Snare Officers of the law.

Ralph Mouldy, Simon Shadow, Thomas Wart, Francis Feeble, and Peter Bullcalf Country soldiers whom Falstaff is sent to recruit to fight for the king.

CHARACTER STUDIES
King Henry IV

The title of the play is *King Henry, IV Part 2*, yet King Henry IV does not appear until Act III. He enters the stage in his nightgown, working at one in the morning because he cannot sleep. This arrival without the formal clothes of office and his later appearance carried in a chair because he is too ill to stand (4.4) make it clear that the role of king is a 24-hour, seven-days-a-week job. Even his death is a public event. Being king is not what he does; it is who he is.

Yet, the crown has been troublesome, with those who supported him and encouraged his usurpation becoming his greatest enemies as time goes by. This play shows him as old, sick, and wracked with worries, caused by both his rebellious ex-supporters and his own son's behavior. His enemies believe him to be "like to a fangless lion" (4.1.218), able to threaten but unable to carry through those threats. They see him as "weary / Of dainty and such picking grievances" (4.1.197–198), and indeed, he seems exhausted by life, exclaiming "O God, that one might read the book of fate, / and see the revolution of the times . . . The happiest youth, viewing his progress through, / What perils past, what crosses to ensue, / Would shut the book and sit him down and die" (3.1.45–56). He appears to

The Earls of Surrey and Warwick listen to King Henry muse on his sleeplessness in Act III, Scene I of *Henry IV, Part 2*. Drawing from the Chiswick edition of Shakespeare, 1900 *(Illustration by John Byam Lister Shaw)*

To justify such a sin, he must attribute his success to God's will, setting the precedent that God can change his mind while creating a major headache for himself. Despite his great skill as a politician, the only way to end this situation is to move back to the dynastic tradition; if his son can inherit the throne, it may be possible to sweep this whole thorny issue under the carpet.

Although, at times, he sees in Prince Henry "the noble image of [his] youth" (4.4.55), the king more often sees him through the eyes of fear for the future: "when headstrong riot hath no curb, / When rage and hot blood are his counsellors" (4.4.62–63). This misunderstanding between youth and age is described by Falstaff in Act I, Scene 2: "You that are old consider not the capacities of us that are young; you do measure the heat of our livers with the bitterness of your galls" (1.2.96–97). The king's age, experience, and general health lead to his misinterpreting his son's behavior, although, to be fair, Prince Henry has been putting on a very convincing show.

The king tries to cement the family together, as can be seen in his discussion with Prince Henry's favorite brother, Clarence, encouraging him to exploit that friendship to "prove a shelter to [his] friends, / A hoop of gold to bind [his] brothers in, / That the united vessel of their blood . . . Shall never leak" (4.4.42–47), for the king sees that the only way to protect his dynasty is to form them into a firm unit that can work together. When he dies, he takes the visible sign of usurpation with him, and he hopes to ensure enough of a peace for the new reign to start free of trouble. Toward the end, the king appears to be holding on to life with grim determination just to get to this point. Prince John of Lancaster's destruction of the rebel threat cuts one of the last threads holding him to life.

It is in the scene (4.5) with Prince Henry, however, that the king reveals his most private person. The final discussion with the prince is in private, a time for straight talk and true emotions rather than political euphemisms and half-truths. King Henry hurls angry, hurt invective at the prince, accusing him of tainting his final half-hour of life with the

be expressing some form of regret—the idea that knowing what he knows now, perhaps he would never have taken the throne in the first place—and appears to be superstitiously fearful of Richard's prophecy of Northumberland's rebellion.

Yet, despite his apparently distraught outbreak, he still manages to include the fact that "God knows, I had no such intent / But that necessity so bow'd the state / That I and greatness were compell'd to kiss (3.1.72–74). This is the official story, the public face of the usurpation; Henry Bolingbroke was forced to take the throne, not through personal ambition, but for the greater good to remove a bad king. As king, he is the representative of law and order; however, to become king, he broke the law and sinned by removing the true king, God's chosen representative on earth.

confirmation that Prince Henry does not love him. The violence of "get thee gone, and dig my grave thyself" (4.5.111), "Pluck down my officers; break my decrees" (4.5.118), and his description of his son's future reign where "sage counsellors" will be replaced by "apes of idleness" and villains who "will swear, drink, dance, / Revel the night, rob, murder, and commit / The oldest sins the newest kind of ways" (4.5.121–127) are the words of a man who despairs for the future and is deeply hurt by what seems to be the final insult, proof of ingratitude and demonstrating a lack of any filial affection.

Yet, the prince's penitential tears provide an explanation of his actions, including his desire to "show th'incredulous world / The noble change that I have purposed" (4.5.154–155). This seems to be the turning point in the king's emotions as suddenly he is brought face to face with a son who has his own tendency toward subtlety. Warwick's earlier words: "My gracious lord, you look beyond him quite. The Prince but studies his companions" (4.4.67) suddenly make sense, and the king is comforted as, at last, he comes to know his son and realize that he will be the successor he has hoped for after all. He is finally able to confess some guilt for the "by-paths and indirect crook'd ways" (4.5.185) he came by the crown, and his last concerns about his dynastic succession are put to rest.

Prince Henry

Prince Henry is a "vile politician" (1.3.241) like his father. He has learned the lesson of political necessity over friendship, watching as, one by one, friends who supported the removal of Richard turned into the king's bitter enemies. The prince has spent his youth honing his political skills on companions he can regard without great passion. He is able to remove himself from them and, if necessary, sacrifice them for the greater good.

However, the prince has become a victim of his own plot to throw off the noxious clouds of his companions and confound everyone's expectations. Poins, when he confides his true sorrow at his father's illness, reflects the common man's view

that Henry is "a most princely hypocrite" (2.2.59). His father, his companions, the court, the whole world, in fact, is taken in by his apparent wildness. Falstaff tells the Lord Chief Justice that "The young Prince hath misled [him]" (1.2.164), yet this is mere wordplay. The wily Falstaff is as taken in as the rest. Despite his jests and his attempt with Poins to recapture the pre-Shrewsbury light-heartedness, it is clear that Prince Henry is no longer at ease with his former companions. His bantering tone with Poins is short lived, and in the serious conversation that follows, he speaks to him "as one it pleases me for fault of a better to call my friend" (2.2.44); Poins does not understand the prince's genuine sadness, nor that he is considered simply one of the "vile company" (2.2.52) who will be shrugged off come the coronation.

The prince plays jokes on Falstaff by setting him out with a small page boy for humorous contrast (1.2) and again at the tavern by hiding and overhearing Falstaff's conversation, yet the moment real events intrude, he provides no more than a curt "good night" (2.4.572) to Falstaff before returning to the world of the court. He talks of Falstaff with Poins in terms of contempt (2.2), terming him a "wen" (lump), and an "old boar" (2.2.115, 159). However, Falstaff effectively calls him a brainless performer of rash acts of bravado. This scene shows the prince enjoying Falstaff's position of uncertainty, watching him squirm his way out of it only to catch and pin him again. It also shows how abruptly and apparently easily the prince can turn from a friend and entertainment to taking care of business. This changeability of character is marked by the king, when he describes to Clarence the best way to handle his brother when he assumes the throne: "he is gracious, if he be observ'd, / He hath a tear for pity, and a hand / Open as day for melting charity: / Yet notwithstanding, being incens'd, he's flint, / As humorous as winter, and as sudden / As flaws congealed in the spring of day. / His temper therefore must be wel observ'd" (4.4.30–36). Prince Henry is "moody," (4.3.39) and changes in his mood are "sudden" (4.3.34). However, these are parts of him that the prince will throw off when he matures; after his father's death, the prince says: "My father is gone wild into his grave, / For in his tomb lie my affections" (5.2.123–124). In other words, all his wildness is now buried with his father, and from now on, justice and law will rule his actions.

By choosing the Lord Chief Justice as his new surrogate father, the newly crowned Henry V has made the morality play choice between law and misrule, matching his choice between vanity and chivalry in *Henry IV, Part 1;* he now possesses all the qualities of kingship and is prepared for his new role. He has used his companions to increase his understanding of his subjects, from highest to lowest, and this provides him with the ability to inspire and lead, to be that "little touch of Harry in the night" (*Henry V,* Act IV, Chorus) even in the hopeless night before Agincourt. However, Henry excises the private face that would provide friendship and favoritism, crystallized in the rejection of Falstaff.

The scenes around his father's death are those that offer the most insight. When Prince Henry arrives, he is still clothed in his brash wild-boy personality. He mocks Clarence's tears as "rain indoors" (4.5.9). Alone with his father, although he talks of the crown's effect on his father's life, it is his crown prince's relationship with the crown and his determination to keep it for himself and his heirs that dominates his speech. Yet, there seems no doubt of his genuine sorrow at his father's apparent death, to whom he acknowledges the debt of "tears and heavy sorrows" (4.5.38), and Warwick later finds him "Washing with kindly tears his gentle cheeks, / With such a deep demeanour in great sorrow, / That tyranny, which never quaff'd but blood, / Would, by beholding him, have wash'd his knife / With gentle eye-drops" (4.5.84–88). The prince's grief for his father belongs to the private man, not the public face of the king. Despite the deep sorrow of personal loss, it is the political necessity that rules his mind and actions.

His story of the taking of the crown is suitably edited to make his father the centerpiece, but it is his revelation of the motivation behind his wild behavior, "The noble change that [he has] purposed" (4.5.155), that seems to be key to this scene. He has at last shown his father the inner workings of his mind, a mind built along his father's own lines. By uncharacteristically revealing himself, he releases the father-son deadlock of misunderstanding and disappointment. Father and son share the same dynastic ambitions, for just as his father provided this (small but significant) "canker'd heap of strange-achieved gold" (4.5.72) to pass to his son, so Prince Henry calls the crown "This lineal honour" (4.5.46), and intends to leave it to his heirs.

Sir John Falstaff

Falstaff describes himself as "not only witty in myself, but the cause that wit is in other men" (1.2.9). In their initial encounter, Falstaff refuses to see or hear the Lord Chief Justice until he is forced to. This is symbolic of his entire relationship with the law, which he will dodge, avoid, or even trample unless there is no choice. The Lord Chief Justice says that Falstaff "follow[s] the young Prince up and down, like his ill angel" (1.2.185), reminding us of the morality play struggle between good and evil for a man's soul and casting Falstaff firmly in the evil camp. Falstaff can be seen delighting in his evil like the morality play figure of Vice, yet it becomes clear that this bad angel has already been separated from the prince. Although the rejection scene at the end of the play seems to be the point at which Falstaff and Prince Henry separate, it is merely the symbolic acknowledgment of what has been visible throughout the play: Prince Henry and Falstaff are only on the stage simultaneously in one other scene, in which the prince is an observer and inquisitor and instantly dismisses Falstaff when other business intervenes; the prince talks of Falstaff with contempt; it is "With Poins and other his continual followers" (4.4.53), rather than Falstaff, that he has been dining; the prince has to ask where Falstaff dines; and neither Henry nor Poins knows who Doll Tearsheet is. The prince has already separated from his old friend, but Falstaff is too engaged in his own version of the world to see this.

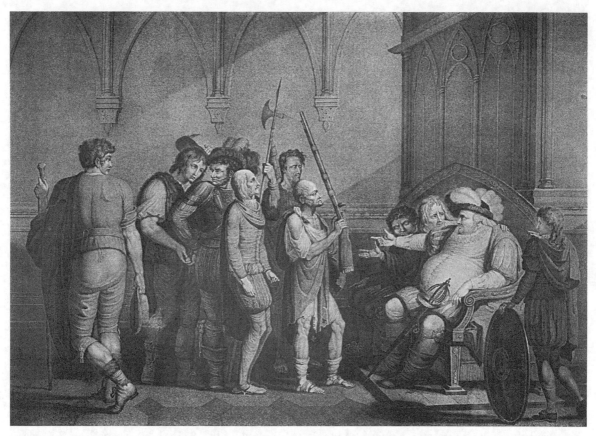

Falstaff speaks to his recruits Mouldy, Shadow, Wart, Feeble, and Bullcalf at Justice Shadow's home in Act III, Scene 2 of *Henry IV, Part 2*. This is a print from the Boydell Shakespeare Gallery project, which was first conceived in 1786 and lasted until 1805. *(Painting by James Durno; engraving by Thomas Ryder)*

Despite possessing "a moist eye . . . a dry hand . . . a yellow cheek . . . a white beard . . . a decreasing leg . . . an increasing belly" and having his "voice broken . . . wind short . . . chin double . . . wit single . . . and every part about [him] blasted with antiquity" (1.2.203–208), Falstaff shows himself to be a man of swift thought and cunning. He has managed to avoid hanging as a robber and paying his debts by going to war in the king's army. This allows him to recruit, taking bribes and probably claiming pay for soldiers who do not exist. He turns up late in Gaultree, yet he is lucky enough to have a rebel surrender to him. He has used the trip wisely to scout out a new person to use, in the form of Justice Robert Shallow. Returning to Gloucestershire, his plans range from jokes at Shallow's expense that will keep the prince laughing so much that "his face be like a wet cloak ill laid up!" (5.1.94) to money, as he notes that Shallow has "here a goodly dwelling, and a rich" (5.3.7).

There has been much said on the subject of Falstaff's cowardice. It has been argued that he does what has to be done when necessity dictates but, otherwise, sees no point in unnecessarily risking death. This could account for the fearsome reputation he has that causes Coleville to surrender to him and Mistress Quickly's comment (if we avoid the obvious sexual innuendo of getting his weapon out, and so forth) that "A cares not what mischief he does, if his weapon be out; he will foin like any devil, he will spare neither man, woman, nor child" (2.1). (To *foin* is to *stab*.)

He has no sense of shame that the Lord Chief Justice can ignite, when Mistress Quickly is trying to regain her money, but his vanity is quite another situation. He is offended by applejohns (a good storage apple) withered from being kept over winter because the prince once compared him to one; it is one thing for Falstaff to make derogatory jokes about himself, and graciously let people laugh with him, but it is quite another for them to make jokes without his sanction, particularly when it is the crown prince, who can not be slapped down with any kind of comeback. Shakespeare highlights his vanity again and again, with the amount of silk he wanted from Master Dommelton, his self-importance in his letter writing, and his fussing about not having time to get new clothes made for the coronation.

In this last instance, however, there seems to be something of the needy lover seeking reassurances from others to bolster his or her self-esteem, the image completed by Falstaff's words "sweating with desire to see him, thinking of nothing else, putting all affairs else in oblivion, as if there were nothing else to be done but to see him" (5.5). Momentary crisis over, Falstaff is fully confident once more that he can get Doll released from prison.

In Gloucestershire his confidence is high. "Let us," he says "take any man's horses," for, (5.3.41) in his eyes, his reward is imminent: The young king is sick for [him], and "the laws of England are at [his] commandment" (5.3.142). When the blow falls, which the audience has been expecting for some time, although Falstaff is unprepared, he demonstrates his resilience, adjusting his worldview sufficiently to incorporate this new experience: from open power to secret councils. As he spoke of Justice Shallow and his servants infecting one another with their attitudes and behaviors, perhaps he believes that this is what will have happened to the prince and himself. In fact, Prince Henry

and Falstaff have traits in common: while Prince Henry has "a hand / Open as day for melting charity: Yet notwithstanding, being incens'd he's flint" (4.4.31–33), Falstaff in good fortune can be very generous to his friends, offering Justice Shallow a lordship and telling Pistol to "devise something to do himself good" (5.3.139), for "Blessed are they that have been [his] friends, and woe to my Lord Chief Justice!" (5.3.143)

Without Prince Henry to draw out his best humor, there is a dark tone to Falstaff in this play. His humorous jests have consequences for those he takes in. We see the pain he causes to Mistress Quickly. There is more hard-edged intent in his money-making schemes. By the time his punishment arrives, the audience is ready to cheer at his incarceration, knowing that it is only a temporary measure. Although the Epilogue promises a return for Falstaff in *Henry V* ("if you be not too much cloyed with fat meat"), having categorically pointed out his unsuitability as a companion for a king, one suspects he would have to change into someone else to be allowed to travel to France. Instead, he has been superseded by Pistol, with whom he shared double-billing on the quarto version title page of *Henry IV, Part 2,* to wit "With the humours of Sir John Falstaff and swaggering Pistol."

Lord Chief Justice

Yet another older man in this play, the Lord Chief Justice seems to be the only one untouched by sickness and decay. He can be contrasted very favorably against Justice Robert Shallow. His speech is direct and to the point, where Shallow's is repetitive and vague. He is totally immune to Falstaff's blandishments, while Shallow falls under his spell to the tune of 1,000 pounds. His delivery of justice is impeccable, while Shallow's is subject to the whims of his servants. Justice, it appears, is variable in the country but very precise in London, where it is the image of the king.

The Lord Chief Justice also exists in opposition to Falstaff, playing the good angel to Falstaff's bad. In very bald morality play terms, he represents law while Falstaff represents anarchy. Apart from

Falstaff's Page, he is the only character who does not have a name. He is called by his function, and perhaps, like the king, he is the Lord Chief Justice 24 hours a day, seven days a week. His clear sight means that Falstaff is not able to get the better of him. For example, when he comes across the brawl with Mistress Quickly, he remains undistracted by Falstaff, saying, "Sir John I am well acquainted with your manner of wrenching the true cause the false way. . . . You have, as it appears to me, practised upon the easy yielding spirit of this woman and made her serve your uses both in purse and in person" (2.1.119–127). He demands that Falstaff sort out the situation and will settle for nothing less. He appears to hold Falstaff in some contempt, ignoring his interjections into his conversation with Gower and calling him simply "a great fool."

After the king's death, Henry V tests the Lord Chief Justice. They have crossed swords before, with the Prince striking the Lord Chief Justice and the justice sending the prince to prison. However, despite his fear that the new king will hold this event against him, the Lord Chief Justice would rather risk imprisonment or death than give up "truth and upright innocency" (5.2). Henry V's test is a good one, and the Lord Chief Justice gives a true measure of his worth in standing his ground. His argument is soundly reasoned: He is "The image of the king whom [he] presented" (5.2.79). Now that the prince has become king, and he represents him, the Lord Chief Justice asks how Henry V would feel "to have a son set your decrees at naught? To pluck down justice from your aweful bench? To trip the course of law, and blunt the sword that guards the peace and safety of your person?" (5.2.85–88) He appeals to the new king's powers of reason, and "After this cold consider-ance sentence [him]" (5.2.98). The king admires his "bold, just, and impartial spirit" (5.2.116) and reinstates him in his office, yet with greater power to influence the king's decisions.

The king has chosen to adopt the wise coun-cillor as his new mentor, leaving behind Falstaff's influences. The Lord Chief Justice, unlike Falstaff, given power over the old fat knight, can be trusted to deal honestly and passionlessly, without petty vengeance.

Mistress Quickly

There are only four women in this play: the Earl of Northumberland's wife, Lady Northumberland, and daughter-in-law, Lady Percy, Doll Tearsheet, and Mistress Quickly. Of them all, it is Mistress Quickly who has the biggest part to play. She keeps a tavern in Cheapside, at which Falstaff is her most salubrious customer. It certainly seems to be at the lower end of the social scale, frequented by rogues and ruffians such as Pistol, in addition to prosti-tutes like Doll Tearsheet.

Yet, the hostess is far from an ignorant woman. She has a wide vocabulary, although she often sub-stitutes one word for another, as in *infinitive* for *infinite, indited* for *invited,* and *exion* for *action* (2.1). She runs her own establishment and has a position to uphold among her neighbors, currently being put at risk by the likes of Pistol making too much noise late at night and not helped by the somewhat drunken Doll.

Mistress Quickly has an "easy-yielding spirit" (2.1.126), and for all her learning, she is no match for a honey-tongued rogue like Falstaff, for although "he hath put all [her] substance into that fat belly of his" (2.1.81), driving her to try to have him arrested out of desperation, within moments he has charmed her into lending him more money, even at the cost of pawning her household goods, and her clothes. The hostess is a sentimental woman. She has known him for 29 years. She gives a misty-eyed, unnecessarily detailed account of Fal-staff proposing marriage to her. The detail lends authenticity to the tale and a strong feeling of domesticity, while also painting a picture of a type of woman who, however nice she may be, annoy-ingly never gets to the point. One can imagine that quick-witted Falstaff might woo her money but would never wed her.

It would be quite easy to have a somewhat senti-mental view of Mistress Quickly, yet she is consider-ably pugnacious when they try to arrest Falstaff, and much more so when she and Doll are being arrested in Act V. Suddenly, the audience is put face to face with the realities of her life. Both women are struggling and abusive to their captor, and it seems likely that they are heading for a flogging or a hanging as Mistress Quickly and Doll and Pistol have been involved in beating a man who has later died. Their lives revolve around drinking, the sex trade, robbery, and casual violence, and however soft she may appear among her friends, Mistress Quickly is deeply embroiled in the less savory parts of her world.

DIFFICULTIES OF THE PLAY

The main difficulty for students in understanding the play is that it is essential to know both the events of the preceding play and some historical background of the period, which Shakespeare would have assumed of his audience. The following is intended to provide useful insight into the events that precede the play and the direction Shakespeare is taking his audience overall.

A brief look at the history of England shows that very few kings died comfortably in the beds from old age or sickness. The country was ruled by the king, but he had to be supported by rich and powerful lords, many of whom were his relatives and most of whom were ambitious, with no other post to aspire to than to become king themselves. Although kings changed frequently, there was usually a direct line of descent from one king to another. Henry IV, however, was a usurper; he had forced his cousin, Richard II, to abdicate and then taken the throne, despite not being next in line of succession.

Shakespeare's sequence of eight historical plays covered the transition of the monarchy from the Plantagenet family through the Lancastrian and York branches to the Tudor monarchy, in the form of Queen Elizabeth I's grandfather, Henry VII. The Plantagenet king, Edward III, had four sons. The three younger sons had flourishing lines of descendants, but the crown prince, Edward, the Black Prince, died before his father, leaving only one living son, Richard. On the death of Edward III, Richard II was crowned; he was only 10 years old. Shakespeare's play *Richard II* portrays Rich-

ard as a vindictive, irresponsible, and cruel king. However, Shakespeare, like all good writers, is selective about what sources he uses and what information he takes from them in the interests of a good story and, in a sequence of stories, in the interests of a cohesive whole. Modern historians are more inclined to believe that Richard was no better or worse than his predecessors but was simply let down by his methods of trying to get what he wanted through favoritism, personal revenge, setting up an opulent court instead of easing taxes, and so on. Students should be careful to keep in mind that Shakespeare's historical characters are his inventions rather than fully faithful representations of real people.

In 1397 (20 years into Richard's reign), turmoil broke out between two powerful men, Henry Bolingbroke, duke of Hereford (son of John of Gaunt, uncle to the king), and Thomas de Mowbray, duke of Norfolk. Bolingbroke accused Mowbray of saying they were next on the king's hit list; Mowbray swore he had not made this statement. To have said such a thing was treason, punishable by death. The two dukes were to fight to settle the argument, but instead, just as they were about to begin to fight, the king exiled them both, Mowbray for life and Bolingbroke for 10 years. When Bolingbroke's father died in 1399, the king extended Bolingbroke's exile for life and seized John of Gaunt's lands for himself. This was the catalyst that would destroy Richard's reign. Bolingbroke returned from Paris, where he had been living with a small group of loyal followers. Men discontented with Richard's reign swiftly joined him, in particular Henry Percy, the earl of Norfolk. Initially, Bolingbroke said he just wanted to reclaim his lands, but it became apparent that he was really intending to take the throne. By the time Richard returned from Ireland, where he had been fighting, popular support made it impossible for him to do anything but negotiate. He was forced to abdicate and was imprisoned in the Tower of London. Bolingbroke now wanted to be crowned, but there was another heir between him and the throne. Although he could claim that Richard's

removal was necessary due to his being unfit to
be king, Bolingbroke's father, John of Gaunt, was
only the third son of Edward III; the next in line
for the throne was Edmund Mortimer, earl of
March (at this point seven years old), a descendant
of Lionel of Antwerp, Edward III's second son.
Mortimer was the grandson of Lionel's daughter,
and by stressing the importance of the male line,
it was therefore possible for Bolingbroke to mar-
ginalize Mortimer's claim to the throne. Shortly
after Henry's coronation, a plot was uncovered
involving several demoted and dissatisfied noblemen. They planned to assassinate the new king and
restore Richard to the throne. This highlighted the
dangers of keeping Richard alive in captivity. He
died shortly afterward, probably murdered, possibly starved to death.

The new king Henry IV had gained the throne,
but keeping it would not be easy. His reign was
spent mostly at war, dealing with rebellions in his
own kingdom, as well as fighting the Welsh, the
Scots, and the French. In reality, it would seem
that Prince Henry (sometimes affectionately called
Prince Hal, at others Harry Monmouth because
he was born at Monmouth Castle in Wales) was
not the hell-raising ne'er-do-well that Shakespeare
paints. He was invested as the Prince of Wales
when his father was crowned King Henry IV. At
the age of 16, he led his own army into Wales to
defeat the self-declared prince of Wales, Owain
Glyndwr (Owen Glendower), in the last great Welsh
uprising against English rule. Prince Henry then
joined forces with his father to defeat Harry Percy
(Hotspur) at the Battle of Shrewsbury. Although
father and son disagreed politically at times, there
is no proof of Prince Henry behaving as depicted
in Shakespeare, and the story of him striking the
Lord Chief Justice appears for the first time in
1531 related by Thomas Elyot. From 1410, as his
father's health deteriorated, Prince Henry took on
a greater share of the government of England with
the assistance of his uncles Henry and John Beau-
fort (legitimized sons of John of Gaunt). There was
some suggestion of persuading Henry IV to step
down in favor of his son, and the defamation of

Prince Henry's youthful character may relate to factions fighting against this. Prince Henry was good
friends with Sir John Oldcastle (who later married
into the title Lord Cobham), who is thought to be
represented in the plays by Falstaff. Oldcastle was a
seasoned campaigner and one of the prince's most
trusted soldiers and was sent as part of a successful
expedition to France in 1411. He appears to have
been very unlike Falstaff in person and was imprisoned for practicing Lollardy. Henry V, crowned in
1413, gave him a 40-day respite on his original sentence in 1413, during which he escaped. However,
Oldcastle was constantly engaged in plots to remove
the king, and as a result, when he was finally recap-
tured in 1417, he was hanged and then burned.

KEY PASSAGES
Act I, Scene 2, 150–231

CHIEF JUSTICE. I sent for you when there
were matters against you for your life, to
come speak with me.

FALSTAFF. As I was then advised by my
learned counsel in the laws of this land-
service, I did not come.

CHIEF JUSTICE. Well, the truth is, Sir John,
you live in great infamy.

FALSTAFF. He that buckles himself in my
belt cannot live in less.

CHIEF JUSTICE. Your means are very
slender, and your waste is great.

FALSTAFF. I would it were otherwise, I
would my means were greater and my waist
slenderer.

CHIEF JUSTICE. You have misled the
youthful Prince.

FALSTAFF. The young Prince hath misled
me. I am the fellow with the great belly, and
he my dog.

CHIEF JUSTICE. Well, I am loath to gall a new-healed wound. Your day's service at Shrewsbury hath a little gilded over your night's exploit on Gad's Hill. You may thank th'unquiet time for your quiet o'er-posting that action.

FALSTAFF. My lord!

CHIEF JUSTICE. But since all is well, keep it so; wake not a sleeping wolf.

FALSTAFF. To wake a wolf is as bad as smell a fox.

CHIEF JUSTICE. What! You are as a candle, the better part burnt out.

FALSTAFF. A wassail candle, my lord, all tallow—if I did say of wax, my growth would approve the truth.

CHIEF JUSTICE. There is not a white hair in your face but should have his effect of gravity.

FALSTAFF. His effect of gravy, gravy, gravy.

CHIEF JUSTICE. You follow the young Prince up and down, like his ill angel.

FALSTAFF. Not so, my lord, your ill angel is light, but I hope he that looks upon me will take me without weighing. And yet in some respects, I grant, I cannot go. I cannot tell—virtue is of so little regard in these costermongers' times that true valour is turned bearherd; pregnancy is made a tapster, and his quick wit wastedin giving reckonings; all the other gifts appertinent to man, as the malice of this age shapes them, are not worth a gooseberry. You that are old consider not the capacities of us that are young; you do measure the heat of our livers with the bitterness of your galls; and we that are in the vaward of our youth, I must confess, are wags too.

CHIEF JUSTICE. Do you set down your name in the scroll of youth, that are written down old with all the characters of age? Have you not a moist eye, a dry hand, a yellow cheek, a white beard, a decreasing leg, an increasing belly? Is no your voice broken, your wind short, your chin double, your wit single, and every part about you blasted with antiquity? And ill you yet call yourself young? Fie, fie, fie, Sir John!

FALSTAFF. My lord, I was born about three of the clock in the afternoon, with a white head, and something a round belly. For my voice, I have lost it with hallooing, and singing of anthems. To approve my youth further, I will not: the truth is, I am only old in judgment and understanding; and he that will caper with me for a thousand marks, let him lend me the money, and have at him! For the box of the ear that the Prince gave you, he gave it like a rude prince, and you took it like a sensible lord. I have checked him for it, and the young lion repents—*[Aside]* marry, not in ashes and sackcloth, but in new silk and old sack.

CHIEF JUSTICE. Well, God send the Prince a better companion!

FALSTAFF. God send the companion a better prince! I cannot rid my hands of him.

CHIEF JUSTICE. Well, the king hath severed you and Prince Harry: I hear you are going with Lord John of Lancaster, against the Archbishop and the Earl of Northumberland.

FALSTAFF. Yea, I thank your pretty sweet wit for it.

Act I, Scene 2 marks Falstaff's first appearance in the play. It opens with Falstaff behaving pretty much how the audience expects and ends with him plotting ways to increase his funds. However, the largest part of the scene is spent with him in dialogue with the Lord Chief Justice. The audience is introduced to a man who is Falstaff's match, who is incorruptible and who can call him to account. The Lord Chief Justice cannot be tricked or joked out of doing his duty. For an audience familiar with *Henry IV, Part 1,* this is a new experience. Despite occasional moments when Prince Henry makes it clear that he will change when he becomes king, there is a sense that Falstaff lives a charmed life and, no matter what, will always come out on top. This scene is significant because for the first time, it is clear that there are serious consequences to the acts of the Cheapside characters and that even Falstaff cannot remain insulated from them forever. Falstaff's initial response to the Lord Chief Justice, pretending he can neither see nor hear him, is symbolic of his entire attitude toward the laws of the land.

The above passage begins with the potential consequences of the Gad's Hill robbery from *Henry IV, Part 1.* (Falstaff and his followers have been supporting themselves by highway robbery and hear of a rich prize. Prince Hal refuses to join them but later holds up the robbers themselves and returns the money to its rightful owners.) Robbery was punishable by death, and the Lord Chief Justice had called him to account. Luckily for Falstaff, he was called up on active duty, ending up at the Battle of Shrewsbury, where he claims to have killed Hotspur, actually only stabbing the corpse after Prince Henry has killed him. The Lord Chief Justice is prepared to allow him some leeway because his "day's service at Shrewsbury hath a little gilded over [his] night's exploit on Gad's Hill," but he makes it clear that it is "th'unquiet time" that has saved Falstaff's neck rather than any belief in his innocence.

The two men are shown to be fairly equally matched. Their initial exchanges are in a stichomythic form, as Falstaff skillfully takes the Lord Chief Justice's negative comments about his relationship with the prince, and humorously turns them back on the prince or the Lord Chief Justice, or into jokes about himself. For example, the Lord Chief Justice implies that he and the powers he wields are best left undisturbed like a potentially merciless but currently "sleeping wolf." Falstaff counters that "To wake a wolf is as bad as smell a fox." Foxes are known for their cunning as well as their rank odor, so Falstaff acknowledges the wily nature of his adversary but simultaneously insults him by implying that he smells.

When Falstaff launches into a full-fledged piece of humor extolling the virtues of youth versus age, and putting himself firmly in the camp of youth, the Lord Chief Justice is incredulous and mockingly points out all the signs of age he shows. He is neither distracted nor impressed by Falstaff's claim to have used his aged "judgement and understanding" to discipline the prince over the ear-boxing incident. It is at the end of this section that we learn two vital things: Falstaff is being separated from Prince Henry and sent north with Prince John to fight the Archbishop, and Falstaff suspects this is due to the influence of the Lord Chief Justice. Shakespeare is clearly telling the audience that Falstaff and Prince Henry are to be separated and demonstrating the importance of the Lord Chief Justice, who has the king's ear, thereby laying the groundwork for his being so high in the regard of the new king at the end of the play. Before the Lord Chief Justice leaves the stage, Falstaff has tried to hit on him for a loan of 1,000 pounds; the Lord Chief Justice is no fool and refuses to lend him anything, setting him up in opposition not only to Falstaff but also to the foolish Justice Shallow.

Act IV, Scene 1, 67–143

ARCHBISHOP. I have in equal balance justly
   weigh'd
What wrongs our arms may do, what wrongs
   we suffer,
And find our griefs heavier than our offences.
We see which way the stream of time doth run,
And are enforc'd from our most quiet there
By the rough torrent of occasion,
And have the summary of all our griefs,
When time shall serve, to show in articles,
Which long ere this we offer'd to the King

And might by no suit gain our audience.
When we are wrong'd, and would unfold our
  griefs,
We are denied access unto his person,
Even by those men that most have done us
  wrong.
The dangers of the days but newly gone,
Whose memory is written on the earth
With yet-appearing blood, and the examples
Of every minute's instance, present now,
Hath put us in these ill-beseeming arms,
Nor to break peace, or any branch of it,
But to establish here a peace indeed,
Concurring both in name and quality.

WESTMORELAND. Whenever yet was your
  appeal denied?
Wherein have you been galled by the King?
What peer hath been suborn'd to grate on you,
That you should seal this lawless bloody book
Of forg'd rebellion with a seal divine,
[And consecrate commotion's bitter edge?]

ARCHBISHOP. My brother general, the
  commonwealth,
[To brother born an household cruelty,]
I make my quarrel in particular.

WESTMORELAND. There is no need of any
  such redress,
Or if there were, it not belongs to you.

MOWBRAY. Why not to him in part, and to
  us all
That feel the bruises of the days before,
And suffer the condition of these times
To lay a heavy and unequal hand
Upon our honours?

WESTMORELAND. O, my good Lord
  Mowbray,
Construe the times to their necessities,
And you shall say, indeed, it is the time,
And not the King, that doth you injuries.
Yet for your part, it not appears to me

Either from the King or in the present time
That you should have an inch of any ground
To build grief on: were you not restor'd
To all the Duke of Norfolk's signories,
Your noble and right well-remember'd father's?

MOWBRAY. What thing, in honour, had my
  father lost,
That need to be reviv'd and breath'd in me?
The King that lov'd him, as the state stood
  then,
Was force perforce compell'd to banish him,
And then that Henry Bolingbroke and he,
Being mounted, and both roused in their seats,
Their neighing coursers daring of the spur,
Their armed staves in charge, their beavers
  down,
Their eyes of fire sparkling through sights of
  steel,
And the loud trumpet blowing them together,
Then, then, when there was nothing could
  have stay'
My father from the breast of Bolingbroke,
O, when the King did throw his warder down,
His own life hung upon the staff he threw;
Then threw he down himself and all their lives
That by indictment and by dint of sword
Have since miscarried under Bolingbroke.

WESTMORELAND. You speak, Lord
  Mowbray, now you know not what.
The Earl of Hereford was reputed then
In England the most valiant gentleman.
Who knows on whom Fortune would then
  have smil'd?
But if your father had ben victor there,
He ne'er had borne it out of Coventry;
For all the country, in a general voice,
Cried hate upon him; and all their prayers and
  love
Were set on Hereford, whom they doted on,
And bless'd, and grac'd, indeed more than the
  King.
But this is mere digression from my purpose.
Here I come from our princely general

To know your griefs, to tell you from his Grace
That he will give you audience;

In this scene, the first of two, back to back, featuring the rebel leaders, the Archbishop of York, Mowbray, and Hastings are approached by Westmoreland acting in the role of a herald for Prince John. This scene shows the rebels' unsuitability to replace the current administration. It should be noted that heralds were more than mere messengers; they were usually members of the nobility and were expected to be diplomatic and politically astute. As a herald carries the reputation of the person he represents, the herald must know how flexible the message he is carrying is. For example, a message may need expanding to cover unforeseen circumstances; at a time when the horse was the fastest form of transport, situations could change drastically while the herald traveled to the recipient. Alternatively, the herald may have need to use psychological tricks in order to influence the decisions of the recipient of the message in the sender's favor.

Prince John's army is outnumbered by the rebels. Westmoreland's job is to separate the rebel leaders from their army by persuading them to enter negotiations. He opens his campaign by attacking the strongest member of the group, whose position as a high-ranking member of the clergy has increased the popularity of their cause, because his presence suggests that this rebellion is backed by God. His cause at first seems valid, for he has a list of their grievances, which the king had not seen for "when [they] were wrong'd, and would unfold [their] griefs, / [They] are denied access" to the King. Yet, when Westmoreland demands particulars of this situation, the Archbishop has to admit that it is not he, himself, who has suffered in this way; it is the "commonwealth," the good of society, for whom the Archbishop is fighting. Westmoreland dismisses the Archbishop's reason.

Mowbray tries to back up the Archbishop, but Westmoreland is ready for him. The lands his family lost to Richard II when his father was banished for life have been restored by King Henry (at that time the duke of Hereford). King Richard stopped

Henry and Mowbray's father (the duke of Norfolk) from jousting. Mowbray contends that, had the joust continued, his father would have won, only Bolingbroke would have suffered, Richard would still be king, and the country would not be in the current mess (a problem he assigns entirely to Henry IV's bad management). Westmoreland smoothly points out Bolingbroke's reputation as a "valiant gentleman," that the outcome of the joust was by no means certain, and that all the country "Cried hate upon" Mowbray's father. Without leaving room for a reply, he then easily moves on to the business at hand.

Westmoreland has successfully intimated that the Archbishop is espousing a cause he has no right to fight for and that Mowbray's actions may well be based on motives of personal revenge rather than on any set of articles. Hastings is given no opportunity to speak, perhaps because his motives are purer, but also his place in this meeting is marginalized; he has only spoken three times so far, and only one line each time. He is the only one who seeks assurances, asking, "Hath the Prince John a full commission, / In very ample virtue of his father / To hear, and absolutely determine, / Of what conditions we shall stand upon?" Westmoreland greets this with a contemptuous affirmative, making his query seem petty and stupid. Of course, this is a very important question, for acting without the king's authority, Prince John could agree to anything they asked, only for the king to retract it the next day; if he has been granted a "full commission," then the king is bound by the agreements he makes.

At the end of the scene, the Archbishop hands over the schedule of grievances to Westmoreland, stating his terms, that each article should be put right and that "All members of our cause, both here and hence, / That are ensinew'd to this action / [be] Acquitted." His terms are clearly made to Westmoreland. However, Westmoreland does not agree to them and merely says he will show the schedule to the prince. As can be seen in the next scene, the rebels never repeat their terms; they simply assume that because the Archbishop has said this to Westmoreland, Prince John of Lancaster is agreeing to all their terms. Their naïveté is fatal, as the prince agrees to undertake only one part of their terms.

Act IV, Scene 2, 53–123

WESTMORELAND. How far forth you do
  like their articles.

LANCASTER. I like them all, and do allow
  them well,
And swear here, by the honour of my blood,
My father's purposes have been mistook,
And some about him have too lavishly
Wrested his meaning and authority.
My lord, these griefs shall be with speed
  redress'd;
Upon my soul they shall. If this may please you,
Discharge your powers unto their several
  counties,
As we will ours; and here between the armies
Let's drink together friendly and embrace,
That all their eyes may bear those tokens hom
Of our restored love and amity.

ARCHBISHOP. I take your princely word for
  these redresses.

LANCASTER. I give it you, and will maintain
  my word;
And thereupon I drink unto your Grace.

HASTINGS. Go, captain, and deliver to the
  army
This news of peaxe. Let them have pay, and
  part.
I know it will please them well. Hie thee,
  captain.
[*Exit Officer.*]

ARCHBISHOP. To you, my noble Lord of
  Westmoreland.

WESTMORELAND. I pledge your Grace;
  and if you knew what

pains I have bestow'd to breed this present
  peace
You would drink freely; but my love to ye
Shall show itself more openly hereafter.

[Lines 77–101 are omitted. The rebels, Prince John of Lancaster, and Westmoreland toast one another as the armies are dismissed. There is irony for those who know what is coming in Westmoreland's comments. Prince John's army remains, as it allegedly will not depart until it receives direct word from him.]

HASTINGS. My lord, our army is dispers'd
  already.
Like youthful steers unyok'd they take their
  courses
East, west, north, south; or, like a school
  broke up,
Each hurries toward his home and
  sporting-place.

WESTMORELAND. Good tidings, my Lord
  Hastings; for the
which I do arrest thee, traitor, of high treason;
And you, Lord Archbishop, and you, Lord
  Mowbray,
Of capital treason I attach you both.

MOWBRAY. Is this proceeding just and
  honourable?

WESTMORELAND. Is your assembly so?

ARCHBISHOP. Will you thus break your
  faith?

LANCASTER. I pawn'd thee none.
I promis'd you redress of these same grievances
Whereof you did complain; which, by mine
  honour,
I will perform with a most Christian care.
But, for you rebels, look to taste the due
Meet for rebellion and such acts as yours.
Most shallowly di you these arms commence,

Fondly brought here, and foolishly sent hence.
Strike up our drums, pursue the scatter'd stray:
God, and not we, hath safely fought today.
Some guard these traitors to the block of
  death,
Treason's true bed and yielder-up of breath.

This section of Act IV, Scene 2 contrasts the political naïveté of the rebels against the pragmatic realism of the Lancasters. Although near the end of the previous scene Mowbray expressed some fears about their future relationship with the king, they all seem content to believe that he is tired of civil war and that their "peace will, like a broken limb united, / Grow stronger for the breaking" (4.1.222). This level of political innocence demonstrates how unfit they are for government. They fail to examine the words they are wooed with, fail to investigate the deal they are being offered, and seem almost unaware of the political reality: Once you have raised an army against your king, however strong your justification, the king cannot afford to set a precedent of mercy. There have to be consequences to armed rebellion against the king, or before much time has passed, there will be many armies supporting various causes, and the rule of law will dissolve into anarchy. Treason is an all-or-nothing situation; you either win and become king (as in the case of Henry Bolingbroke) or lose and live in exile or die. However, the rebels clearly have no plans for ruling the country if they were to win. They compound their stupidity by releasing their own army without making any attempt to ensure their own safety.

This scene shows the amateur nature of their organization. Their army disbands "like a school broke up," suggesting that it is more of a rabble than an army and that, despite being the larger, it may well have lost against an army that was "more full of names than yours, / Our men more perfect in the use of arms, / Our armour all as strong, our cause the best" (4.1.154–156). In Holinshed, the rebels' defeat was managed by Westmoreland. Although Holinshed also quotes another version in which they are persuaded by Westmoreland to sub-

mit to the king's justice by presenting themselves to Prince John, it is still Westmoreland who has made the plan. However, by placing Prince John firmly in control of the situation, Shakespeare has highlighted the Lancastrian trait of subtlety and political necessity, or the greater good over being a nice person. The rebels question his honor and good faith, but, as he points out, he will do as he promised with regard to the articles but has made no promises concerning their personal safety. He contemptuously describes their rebellion as "shallow" and "foolish" and condemns them to "the block of death, Treason's true bed and yielder-up of breath."

His relatively bloodless victory from words and expectations may be seen as a precursor for the victory of Harfleur in *Henry V*. In Act III, Scene 3, Henry V and his troops are besieging the French town of Harfleur, which is holding out in hopes of relief from the dauphin (the crown prince of France). Their hopes are fading, and Henry presents them with a choice: They can either surrender, in which case they will be treated well, or they can make him fight for every street, in which case he "will not leave the half-achieved Harfleur / Till in her ashes she lie buried" (*Henry V*, 3.3.8–9). Henry paints a very frightening and convincing word picture of the consequences of not surrendering using the rhetoric of Christopher Marlowe's heartless Scythian warlord, Tamberlain: "look to see / The blind and bloody soldier with foul hand / Defile the locks of your shrill-shrieking daughters; / Your fathers taken by the silver beards, / And their most reverend heads dashed to the walls; / Your naked infants spitted upon pikes, / Whiles the mad mothers with their howls confused / Do break the clouds" (*Henry V*, 3.3.33–40). This speech wins him the town, and the audience is left to wonder whether this was simply bluff, using more of that Lancastrian subtlety, or if he would actually have carried out his threats if Harfleur had not surrendered.

At the end of his final speech to the traitors, Prince John states that "God, and not we, hath safely fought today." This may be a foreshadowing of Henry V's reaction when, upon winning the

Battle of Agincourt, he learns that the French lost 10,000 men while he lost only 29. Henry V assigns the victory to God, commanding that no one may boast of it or take the glory on themselves that is God's alone. When questioned as to whether they can tell others about the number killed, Henry responds: "Yes, Captain, but with this acknowledgement / That God fought for us" (*Henry V*, 4.8.124–125). There is a strong sense that the Lancastrians believe firmly that God is working for them, providing them with victories, prompting Prince Henry to take the crown so that he and his father's reconciliation will be more joyous. Like Henry VIII and Elizabeth I, they are firm advocates of the divine right of kings, wherein the king is seen as God's representative on earth.

Act IV, Scene 5, 143–225

PRINCE. There is your crown;
And He that wears the crown immortally
Long guard it yours! If I affect it more
Than as your honour and as your renown,
Let me no more from this obedience rise,
Which my most inward true and duteous spirit
Teacheth this prostrate and exterior bending.
God witness with me, when I here came in,
And found no course of breath within your
　Majesty,
How cold it struck my heart! If I do feign,
O, let me in my present wildness die,
And never live to show th'incredulous world
The noble change that I have purposed!
Coming to look on you, thinking you dead,
And dead almost, my liege, to think you were,
I spake unto this crown as having sense,
And thus upbraided it: 'The care on thee
　depending
Hath fed upon the body of my father;
Therefore thou best of gold art worst of gold.
Other less fine in carat, is more precious,
Preserving life in med'cine potable;
But thou, most fine, most honour'd, most
　renown'd,
Has eat thy bearer up'. Thus, my most royal
　liege,

Accusing it, I put it on my head,
To try with it, as with an enemy
That had before my face murder'd my father,
The quarrel of a true inheritor.
But if it did infect my blood with joy,
Or swell my thoughts to any strain of pride,
If any rebel or vain spirit of mine
Did with the least affection of a welcome
Give entertainment to the might of it,
Let God for ever keep it from my head,
And make me as the poorest vassal is,
That doth with awe and terror kneel to it!

KING. O my son,
God put it in thy mind to take it hence,
That thou mightst win the more thy father's
　love,
Pleading so wisely in excuse of it!
Come hither, Harry, sit thou by my bed,
And hear, I think, the very latest counsel
That ever I shall breathe. God knows, my son,
By what by-paths and indirect crook'd ways
I met this crown, and I myself know well
How troublesome it sat upon my head.
To thee it shall descend with better quiet,
Better opinion, better confirmation,
For all the soil of the achievement goes
With me into the earth. It seem'd in me
But as an honour snatch'd with boist'rous
　hand,
And I had many living to upbraid
My gain of it by their assistances,
Which daily grew to quarrel and to bloodshed,
Wounding supposed peace. All these bold fears
Thou seest with peril I have answered;
For all my reign hath been but as a scene
Acting that argument. And now my death
Changes the mood, for what in me was
　purchas'd
Falls upon thee in a more fairer sort;
So thou the garland wear's successively.
Yet though thou stand'st more sure than I
　could do,
Thou art not firm enough, since griefs are
　green;

And all my friend, which thou must make thy
    friends,
Have but their stings and teeth newly ta'en out;
By whose fell working I was first advanc'd,
And by whose power I well might lodge a fear
To be again displac'd; which to avoid,
I cut them off, and had a purpose now
To lead out many to the Holy Land,
Lest rest and lying still might make them look
Too near unto my state. Therefore, my Harry,
Be it thy course to busy giddy minds
With foreign quarrels, that action hence borne
    out
May waste the memory of the former days.
More would I, but my lungs are wasted so
That strength of speech is utterly denied me.
How I came by the crown, O God forgive,
And grant it may with thee in true peace live!

PRINCE. My gracious liege,
You won it, wore it kept it, gave it me;
Then plain and right must my possession be,
Which I with more than with a common pain
'Gainst all the world will rightfully maintain.

This scene is the most moving in the play. It contains the deathbed reconciliation of Henry IV with
his son, Prince Henry, combining a personal and
private familial relationship with the very public
issue of the succession. This passage crystallizes
the way in which the crown can be both a blessing and a curse to the wearer. With good reason,
Henry IV states: "Uneasy lies the head that wears
a crown" (3.1.31). Earlier in this scene, the prince
has mistaken the king's very deep sleep for death
and, taking the crown, places it on his head and
leaves to grieve and contemplate the future. Awak-
ing to discover the crown gone, the king concludes
that his ungrateful son could not wait "Till his
friend sickness" (4.5.82) had ended his father's
life. The prince returns, and the king rails at him.
When finally the prince has a chance to speak, he
is crying as he kneels to return the crown and beg
forgiveness. This is the catalyst needed to reconcile
Henry IV and Prince Henry.

Prince Henry kneels before the king and explains why
he took the crown in Act IV, Scene 5 of *Henry IV, Part 2*.
This is a print from Malcolm C. Salaman's 1916 edition
of *Shakespeare in Pictorial Art*. *(Painting by Josiah Boydell)*

Yet, for all his protestations that God should
strike him down if he showed any pleasure in
receiving the crown, his explanation to the king
of his actions does not sit well with the soliloquy
he made when he took it. Crowning himself, the
prince had claimed that God shall guard and keep
it on his head; indeed, if you "put the world's whole
strength / Into one giant arm, it shall not force /
This lineal honour" from him (4.5.44–46). The
prince also slips into his explanation that he took
up "the quarrel of a true inheritor" when he wres-
tled with the crown (4.5.169), and again, after his
father has delivered his last advice, Prince Henry
stresses that his claim to the crown is "plain and
right" (4.5.223). Prince Henry is highlighting his
position as an inheritor of the crown, rather than

a usurper, like his father. By showing the prince crowning himself earlier in the scene, Shakespeare ensures Henry IV's hope that "all the soil of the achievement [of the crown] goes / With [him] into the earth," for the prince has not received it from his father's tainted hands. The firmness with which King Henry states this may seem at odds with the Bible's often repeated theme that the sins of the father shall be visited upon the sons to the third or fourth generation (Exodus 20:5, Deuteronomy 5:9, Exodus 34:6–7). However, Deuteronomy 24:16 and Ezekiel 18:20 both pose the opposite view, that no one is held responsible for any sin but his or her own, so perhaps Shakespeare here is optimistically cherry-picking the bits of the Bible he wants to be true. A second possibility might be that Shakespeare is writing for Queen Elizabeth I, whose grandfather was a Henry (VII) who killed a Richard (III) to gain the throne. Might Shakespeare be implying that, should Henry VII have incurred any "soil" in taking the throne from Richard III, it went to the grave with him? The queen's father, Henry VIII, and the queen herself would therefore be completely unsullied and "true inheritor[s]."

The king's speech expresses some regrets about the "by-paths and indirect crook'd ways" by which he gained the crown, although he really had little choice once he attempted to regain his lands from Richard II with an army. These are the regrets of the private man, for if the public persona of the king expressed such thoughts, he would appear weak; to maintain his power, a king must be decisive and firm. Asking God's forgiveness (presumably regretting the murder of Richard II), he describes his whole reign as "a scene acting that argument." He has spent his whole reign fighting for the throne against rebels, who initially supported his usurpation but then grew disenchanted with his policies or a lack of influence they felt they deserved. However, he sees his death almost in terms of a sacrifice to ensure that his son has a quieter reign than himself, and he advises the prince to "busy giddy minds with foreign quarrels," redirecting potential troublemakers with hard work. Prince Henry

takes his father's advice, though with France rather than a crusade, for Prince John informs the Lord Chief Justice (and the audience) at the end of Act V that they will bear "civil swords and native fire" to France before the year is out (5.5.112).

Act V, Scene 3, 121–144

PISTOL. Sir John, thy tender lambkin now is
  King;
Harry the Fifth's the man: I speak the truth.
When Pistol lies, do this and fig me, like
The bragging Spaniard.

FALSTAFF. What, is the old King dead?

PISTOL. As nail in door! The things I speak
  are just.

FALSTAFF. Away, Bardolph, saddle my horse.
  Master Robert Shallow, choose what office
  thou wilt in the land, tis thine. Pistol, I will
  double-charge thee with dignities.

BARDOLPH. O joyful day! I would not take
  a knighthood for my fortune.

PISTOL. What, I do bring good news?

FALSTAFF. Carry Master Silence to bed.
  Master Shallow, my Lord Shallow—be what
  thou wilt; I am Fortune's steward! Get on
  thy boots, we'll ride all night. O sweet Pistol!
  Away, Bardolph! *[Exit BARDOLPH.]* Come,
  Pistol, utter more to me; and withal devise
  something to do thyself good. Boot, boot,
  Master Shallow! I know the young King is
  sick for me. Let us take any man's horses—
  the laws of England are at my commandment.
  Blessed are they that have been my friends,
  and woe to my Lord Chief Justice!

Falstaff has shown himself corrupt and sly. He is a glutton and an alcoholic; he holds nothing sacred and cares for nothing and no one but himself and his own comfort. In *Henry IV, Part 1,* he committed a robbery and recruited cannon fodder, letting off those who could bribe him, and then absorbed the pay of any soldiers who died in his service. In *Henry IV, Part 2,* he is found brawling on the streets, swindling Mistress Quickly of her plate, her wall hangings, even her best dress, playing the same recruitment scam and taking Justice Shallow for 1,000 pounds, as well as bringing him to town primarily to be the butt of his jokes for the new king. Yet, in this play, for the most part, he has been without his princely audience, and the aspect has become darker. Prince Hal's detached amusement and occasional involvement provided an indulgent, friendly viewpoint for the audience in Falstaff's schemes; they seemed merely set up for the amusement of the prince and the audience. In *Henry IV, Part 2,* the schemes are more mercenary, the veneer of light humor and ludicrous lies have been stripped away; Falstaff is still entertaining, but now, with his purpose laid bare, there is a nastier edge to his actions, and he starts to soliloquize in a manner reminiscent of Richard III. He invites us to share in his worldview of people as a series of easy marks, and we gasp at his audacity and begin to anticipate his come-uppance.

Of course by the end of Act IV, the audience is a step or two ahead of Falstaff. It has witnessed the moving deathbed scene showing the reconciliation of the prince and the king. The Elizabethan audience would also have been familiar with the story of the redemptive Prince Hal, and Shakespeare has given them clues in *Henry IV, Part 1,* where Hal talks of being like the Sun covering himself in noxious clouds, only to shine the more brightly when they are cleared away (1.2). By the time Falstaff hears that Henry IV is dead, the audience has already seen Henry V confirm his intentions to throw off his old ways and promote the Lord Chief Justice to school him in wisdom.

Act V, Scene 3 is where Shakespeare really drives home two points: first, Falstaff's unsuitability as a companion for a king, and second, the fact that Falstaff has completely misread the times and is riding for a colossal fall. Upon hearing news of the old king's death, Falstaff believes that "the laws of England are at [his] commandment." In his enthusiasm, he has failed to grasp an essential point of kingship; although the king has power, at least a part of that power comes from making and keeping the laws of the land. The king cannot be everywhere, so it is necessary to have approved laws and approved people to practice them. As the Lord Chief Justice has just pointed out to the new king, "the majesty and power of law and justice [are] the image of the King whom [the Lord Chief Justice] presented" (5.2.78–79). When judges are corrupt or wrongdoers make a mockery of the law, it is the king's image, and therefore his power, that is damaged. Falstaff is oblivious to this fact and cannot conceive of a world that will not bend to his whim.

DIFFICULT PASSAGES
Act V, Scene 5, 47–107

FALSTAFF. God save thee, my sweet boy!

KING. My Lord Chief Justice, speak to that vain man.

CHIEF JUSTICE. Have you your wits? Know you what 'tis you speak?

FALSTAFF. My King! My Jove! I speak to thee, my heart!

KING. I know thee not, old man. Fall to thy prayers.
How ill white hairs becomes a fool and jester!
I have long dreamt of such a kind of man,
So surfeit-swell'd, so old, and so profane;
But being awak'd I do despise my dream.
Make less thy body hence, and more thy grace;
Leave gormandizing; know the grave doth gape
For thee thrice wider than for other men.
Reply not to me with a fool-born jest;
Presume not that I am the thing I was;
For God doth know, so shall the world perceive,
That I have turn'd away my former self;
So will I those that kept me company.

When thou dost hear I am as I have been,
Approach me, and thou shalt be as thou wast,
The tutor and the feeder of my riots.
Till then I banish thee, on pain of death,
As I have done the rest of my misleaders,
Not to come near our person by ten mile.
For competence of life I will allow you,
That lack of means enforce you not to evils;
And as we hear you do reform yourselves,
We will according to your strengths and
 qualities,
Give you advancement.
[*To the LORD CHIEF JUSTICE*]
Be it your charge, my lord,
To see perform'd the tenor of my word.
Set on. [*Exit KING with his train.*]
FALSTAFF. Master Shallow, I owe you a
 thousand pound.

SHALLOW. Yea, marry, Sir John, which I
 beseech you to let me have home with me.

FALSTAFF. That can hardly be, Master
 Shallow. Do not you grieve at this; I shall
 be sent for in private to him. Look you, he
 must seem thus to the world. Fear not your
 advancements; I will be the man yet that shall
 make you great.

SHALLOW. I cannot perceive how, unless you
 give me your doublet, and stuff me out with
 straw. I beseech you, good Sir John, let me
 have five hundred of my thousand.

FALSTAFF. I will be as good as my word.
 This that you heard was but a colour.

SHALLOW. A colour that I fear you will die
 in, Sir John.

FALSTAFF. Fear no colours. Go with me
 to dinner. Come, Lieutenant Pistol; come,
 Bardolph. I shall be sent for soon at night.
[*Enter the LORD CHIEF JUSTICE and
PRINCE JOHN, with Officers.*]

CHIEF JUSTICE. Go carry Sir John Falstaff
 to the Fleet;
Take all his company along with him.

FALSTAFF. My lord, my lord,—

CHIEF JUSTICE. I cannot now speak: I will
 hear you soon.
Take them away.

PISTOL. Si fortuna me tormenta, spero me
 contenta.
[*Exeunt all but PRINCE JOHN and the
 CHIEF JUSTICE.*]

LANCASTER. I like this fair proceeding of
 the King's.
He hath intent his wonted followers
Shall all be banish'd till their conversations
Appear more wise and modest to the world.

The scene of Falstaff's rejection is one that causes many critics to struggle. It establishes once and for all that Henry V has cut himself off from his wilder days and is ready to become the great national hero in a way that all the rhetoric at his father's bedside and with the Lord Chief Justice cannot. While everyone agrees that Falstaff is totally unsuitable to be the new king's companion, some critics complain that Henry's tone is preaching and didactic, that after all those years during which Henry had been as much an instigator of wild romps as any of his companions, he should not sit in judgment over Falstaff for behavior that he himself encouraged. They ask why Henry did not simply warn Falstaff. Henry has been as much a "misleader" as Falstaff, but it was choice, not necessity, that led him to Cheapside and kept him returning there.

Of course, Henry has misled his companions in allowing them to believe that they will rise with him, and by not privately warning Falstaff that things will be different once he is crowned. Was this failure to warn Falstaff simply in order to provoke this confrontation, allowing the king to publicly reject his former life, part of that Boling-

King Henry V denies knowing Falstaff after his coronation in Act V, Scene 5 of *Henry IV, Part 2*. Print from the Boydell Shakespeare Gallery project *(Painting by Robert Smirke; engraving by Joseph Collyer)*

Despite the coldness of the delivery, however, the speech does not issue a death penalty. Falstaff is to receive an income, as, according to Prince John, will all the rest of the king's rowdier companions, and the opportunity for promotion, should they prove themselves worthy. Because both Falstaff and Henry have engaged with the Lord Chief Justice earlier in the play, the audience know that he is a man of honor and insight; he is a match for Falstaff and will not be misdirected by his tricks, jests, and lies, but he will carry out Henry's wishes should Falstaff reform.

Falstaff's first line after the exit of the king is hard to interpret. Critics have struggled to work out what his emotional state is. Is he dazedly grasping at the hugeness of his loss and therefore debts? Is he so shocked that his mouth is saying words without engaging with his brain? Is he angry, hurt, crushed? Perhaps the most likely possibility is that he is swiftly rallying and struggling to get control of the situation. The most immediate thing on his mind is presumably the huge amount of money he has just borrowed from Shallow and how to keep hold of it since Shallow has witnessed his rejection and is likely to think him a poor investment now. Falstaff is quick to assess the situation in his favor, and realizing that the king cannot acknowledge him publicly, he believes that he shall be sent for later. In the face of his certainty, Shallow weakly drops his demands for the full 1,000 pounds to 500 and is being swept off to dinner still weakly protesting when Falstaff's hopes are shattered. The Lord Chief Justice returns to have him and all his companions (including the doubtlessly devastated Justice Shallow) taken to the Fleet Prison.

This seems bizarre to the modern audience. The king had rejected Falstaff in no uncertain terms and effectively set a restraining order on him so that he could not come within 10 miles of Henry. Why then would he send him to prison? The restraining order means that the prison sentence could only be a temporary measure. It has been suggested that Henry was angered by the way in which Falstaff had sullied his triumphant return from his coronation, putting a bad taste on what should be one of his

broke tendency toward calculation? An alternative and kinder interpretation might be as follows: Henry did not expect the wily Falstaff to behave so stupidly. He tries to deflect the confrontation via the Lord Chief Justice. When this is insufficient, he is forced to take on the unpleasant task of disabusing his erstwhile friend. The language he uses is stilted and preachy because Henry has just exchanged unofficial foster-fathers, dumping the world, wit, and wisdom of Falstaff to take on the advice and language of the Lord Chief Justice and, as such, is speaking an unfamiliar tongue. His speech to Falstaff is not something he enjoys, but it is necessary.

greatest moments. Henry IV described his son as "being incens'd, he's flint, as humorous as winter" (4.4). Perhaps, in a fit of anger over Falstaff's interruption to the solemn occasion, and once unable to see the face of the man he spent so much time with, the king sent the Lord Chief Justice back to punish him. The Fleet Prison at this time was not that bad a place and, indeed, was the prison the Lord Chief Justice had sent Henry to when Henry challenged his authority and boxed his ears. It was not uncommon for Queen Elizabeth I to send courtiers there for a spell when they fell out of favor, so to the Elizabethan audience this would not have quite the same discordance that a modern audience feels. However, it seems equally probable that, having had one bit of the day spoiled, Henry did not want Falstaff ruining the rest of it by optimistically turning up to see him and causing a scene. He has known Falstaff for many years and has learned how his mind works; it is not impossible to imagine that Henry would anticipate Falstaff's belief that a secret meeting was intended for later. This way, there is no scene, the message is clear, and the distancing process complete.

Epilogue, 1–36

First my fear; then, my curtsy; last, my speech.

My fear is your displeasure; my curtsy, my duty; and my speech, to beg your pardons. If you look for a good speech now, you undo me, for what I have to say is of mine own making; and what indeed I should say will, I doubt, prove my own marring. But to the purpose, and so to the venture. Be it known to you, as it is very well, I was lately here in the end of a displeasing play, to pray your patience for it, and to promise you a better. I meant indeed to pay you with this; which if like an ill venture it come unluckily home, I break, and you my gentle creditors lose. Here I promised you I would be, and here I commit my body to your mercies. Bate me some, and I will pay you some, and, as most debtors do, promise you

infinitely: and so I kneel down before you— but, indeed, to pray for the Queen.

If my tongue cannot entreat you to acquit me, will you command me to use my legs? And yet that were but light payment, to dance out of your debt. But a good conscience will make any possible satisfaction and so would I. All the gentlewomen here here have forgiven me: if the gentlemen will not then the gentlemen do not agree with the gentlewomen, which was never seen before in such an assembly.

One word more, I beseech you. If you be not too much cloyed with fat meat, our humble author will continue the story, with Sir John in it, and make you merry with fair Katharine of France; where, for anything I know, Falstaff shall die of a sweat, unless already a be killed with your hard opinions; for Oldcastle died martyr, and this is not the man. My tongue is weary; when my leg are too, I will bid you good night.

The Epilogue can be confusing, mainly because the introductory line and the first paragraph would not have been spoken together with the following two paragraphs. As Tiffany Stern argues in her article "*A small-beer health to his second day:* Playwrights, Prologues, and First Performances in the Early Modern Theater," prologues and epilogues were temporary additions to the play. They were written for specific occasions or presentations as part of the packaging and then discarded. The printers of *Henry IV, Part 2* appear to have combined two separate epilogues, making for confusing reading.

The speaker of the former paragraph appears to be the author of the play, that is, Shakespeare himself. He (as was common) is asking the audience to treat his play kindly and accept it as an appropriate apology for "a displeasing play" that recently went down badly. There is no way (short of using a time machine) to discover which play this was, but the fact that this statement is made and that the audience is expected to know is good evidence that this epilogue was written for the occasion and not expected to be repeated. Shakespeare plays with his audience by stating that "If you look for a good speech now, you undo me, for what I have to say is of mine own making; and what indeed I should say will, I doubt, prove my own marring." Both he and the audience are well aware that all the grand and powerful speeches in the play they have just witnessed were written by Shakespeare; he presents a humorous false modesty, easily seen through and enjoyed by the audience.

Shakespeare plays with the language of debt in this paragraph; he owes the audience a good play, but if they dislike this one, he has failed to repay his debt. They could beat him up, like loan sharks, in lieu of money, but if they let him off, he will continue to write plays and pay the debt a little at a time. Loan-sharking was a considerable problem for young gentlemen in Elizabethan London. In his book *The Reckoning: The Murder of Christopher Marlowe,* Charles Nicholl discusses this in some detail. The creditor would persuade the young man to sign an agreement for the amount that he wished to borrow but then fail to have enough cash to cover the amount. Instead, the creditor would provide goods that were supposed to cover the value of the missing money (which, of course, they never did), meaning that the borrower never had the full sum he had apparently borrowed and was never able to pay it back. Instead, he would become entangled in the loan shark's web, being let off some payments if he befriended other young men and brought them to the moneylender. Use of "infinitely" suggests the double irony: that debtors always promise to pay, but often lack the means, while creditors are frequently dishonest, finding ways to keep the debtor permanently indebted.

Finally, Shakespeare implies that he is kneeling down humbly to beg forgiveness of his audience, only to unexpectedly switch this into the prayer for the monarch instead. Serious epilogues often ended with a prayer to the monarch. This may be additional proof that this epilogue is separate from the other two paragraphs. (The quarto version of this play was printed with the prayer at the end of the first paragraph, while in the First Folio, it was moved to the end.)

The second paragraph continues with the language of debt, but the speaker, wishing to be released from his debt, intends to pay with the "use of his legs" to dance his way free and concludes that he will leave the stage when his legs are tired. Shakespeare wrote and acted, but dancing was not something for which he was known. It is more likely that this speech was made by one of the boys of the company. In the third paragraph, further proof that the author is not the speaker lie in the words "our humble author will continue the story." The description of the audience as "gentlewomen" and "gentlemen," and the unheard-of lack of chivalry in "such an assembly" suggest this may have been a court performance. The final paragraph provides an advertisement for *Henry V,* which includes Falstaff, whom Shakespeare ultimately excluded from *Henry V,* presumably because to be allowed back in the king's company, Falstaff would have to have rid himself of all the characteristics that made him such a popular character. There is also the reference to Oldcastle who "died martyr" and is not Falstaff: The name was changed after Sir John Oldcastle's relatives, the powerful Brooke family, complained at the defamation of Oldcastle's name after early performances of *King Henry IV, Part 1.* This is further proof that the first paragraph is not related to the latter two.

CRITICAL INTRODUCTION
TO THE PLAY
Style and Language

Henry IV, Part 2 does not have a gripping story. King Henry IV does not himself appear until the third act, and he is ailing and heading toward death. In contrast to *Part 1,* Prince Henry does not engage in vivacious humorous scrapes and jests; he has no nemesis to be compared unfavorably to, and ultimately to defeat, for Hotspur is dead, and although Hotspur's widow describes him once more as "the glass / Wherein the noble youth did dress themselves / [. . . for] in speech, in gait, / In diet, in affections of delight, / In military rules, humours of blood, / He was the mark and glass, copy and book, / That fashion'd others" (2.3.21–32), Hotspur is no more than an after-image, and his time has passed. There are no battles; the rebellion is a damp squib defeated by subtle wiles and the rebels' own naïveté, and neither Prince Henry nor the king takes any active part in it. Even Falstaff's part at Gaultree, although amusing (and possibly foreshadowing Pistol's capture of a Frenchman in *Henry V*) is lacking in excitement. Much of the story could be viewed as padding out the very weak plot: Henry IV dies, and Henry V is crowned and looks as if he will be a good king.

However, as A. R. Humphries points out, it is the way in which Shakespeare writes this play that keeps the audience enthralled. He interweaves a wide variety of styles in *Henry IV, Part 2*, arguably wider than in any other play he wrote. Scenes take on their own separate identity depending on the nature of the mood and tone set by the writing. Contrasts between scenes are deeply illuminating. The flashy verbal sparring between Falstaff and the Lord Chief Justice is set against the hasty planning by the rebels in Act I. The mellow after-dinner glow in Justice Shallow's garden comes just before the harsh arrest of Mistress Quickly and Doll Tearsheet in Act V. Such effects keep the audience pinned to their seats in a way that the story itself does not.

An examination of Act II, Scene 4 and Act V, Scene 3 provides some examples of how Shakespeare achieves this. Both these scenes deal with lower-class characters, both feature Falstaff, and both take place in the evening after the protagonists have enjoyed a substantial and alcoholic supper off stage. The former takes place in Eastcheap (in London), while the latter takes place in Gloucestershire. The Eastcheap scene opens with bustle; the diners are retiring from the table unexpectedly early, and one of the servants has picked up apples that Falstaff particularly hates, while another is dispatched to find musicians. When the diners enter, Doll has been feeling unwell because she has drunk too much wine, and Falstaff announces the chamber pot needs emptying. The conversation is

Falstaff and Doll Tearsheet flirt while Prince Henry and Poins listen in the background in Act II, Scene 4 of *Henry IV, Part 2*. This print is from the Boydell Shakespeare Gallery project. *(Painting by Henry Fuseli; engraving by William Leney)*

swift and full of banter and double entendre. In Gloucestershire, the only servant present is Davy, who looks after them all in a polite manner. Shallow is keen to feed the guests apples he has grafted himself, before they all go to bed, a destination almost unknown to the London crowd. Shallow's frequent repetitions slow the pace of the conversation, as do Silence's songs (there are no professional musicians just hanging around to be employed, as there might be in the city). Although Falstaff might be disposed to be witty, there is no one with whom to exchange barbs, and he is hoping to coax money out of Shallow and, therefore, must not offend him.

Both parties are disturbed by Pistol, whose presence, full of bluster and classical references, is more problematical in London, where Doll will verbally spar with him, while Mistress Quickly needs to keep the noise down. In Gloucestershire, none of the near-somnambulent dinner guests is prepared to fight with him. Pistol has, besides, a purpose for being there: bringing the message that the king has died. This leads to the climax of the scene, for in the country there are few people about and little to do. Master Silence is packed off to bed, and the rest hurry off to London. By contrast, in Eastcheap, the visit from Pistol and his subsequent ejection for "swaggering" are merely part and parcel of a night out. Pistol has no purpose being there, so the scene moves on to its own climax with the late arrival of Prince Henry and Poins. The scene ends, as does the Gloucestershire one, with the intrusion of world events into the small self-enclosed world of the tavern.

These scenes both involve lower class and/or comic characters, and as such, Shakespeare writes their lines in prose, saving the poetry of blank verse, rhetorical devices, and classical imagery for the upper-class characters. Pistol, however, peppers his speech with classical references. He makes a speech in blank verse in the London scene and talks almost entirely in blank verse in the Gloucestershire scene. Prince Henry speaks blank verse with the court, yet with Poins and Falstaff he mostly speaks in prose. When Peto intrudes from the court with word of the return of the king, the prince switches to blank verse, marking an end to his time with the lower characters and a return to the serious business of the world. In the Gloucestershire scene Falstaff, too, switches to blank verse along with Pistol, yet both of them switch back to prose once more, for this is their natural way of speaking. They will not be moving to more hallowed positions.

Shakespeare has thereby formed two distinctly separate environments. The lower-class London scenes always begin with movement and urgency: Falstaff and his Page walking somewhere, Mistress Quickly summoning officers to capture Falstaff, Mistress Quickly and Doll being dragged to prison by beadles, servants laying out dishes, or grooms laying rushes for the king's procession. In Gloucestershire, the pace is slower: Shallow, Silence, and the recruits stand waiting for Falstaff with nowhere else to go, Davy is busy about his master's business, putting that before matters of hospitality, and the figures amble into the orchard.

Shakespeare uses similar techniques to underline the differences between the rebels, between Northumberland's faction and family, and between the scenes of the king with his nobles versus the scene of him alone with his son.

Imagery

The images Shakespeare uses affect not only the tone of a scene but also the mood of a speech, turning what might be a dull report into a sharply visual, almost visceral experience. For example, in Act IV, Scene 5, Henry IV says:

> Stay but a little, for my cloud of dignity
> Is held from falling with so weak a wind
> That it will quickly drop; my day is dim.
> Thou hast stol'n that which after some few
>   hours
> Were thine without offence, and at my death
> Thou hast seal'd up my expectation.
> Thy life did manifest thou lov'dst me not,
> And thou wilt have me die assur'd of it
> Thou hid'st a thousand daggers in thy
>   thoughts,
> Which thou hast whetted on thy stony heart,
> To stab at half an hour of my life.
>
> (4.5.99–109)

This set of images begins with the weather. Shakespeare creates a cloud, held aloft by a wind that will soon weaken, causing the cloud to drop; the light of the day is dim because the cloud blocks the Sun. However, the physical cloud is made up of an abstract notion, the king's "dignity," which will soon be stripped away by death; the king's breath is the weakening wind that supports the cloud, and the day is dim because the king is nearing his end and the darkness that is death. Shakespeare repeats this trick of connecting something physical with something abstract, describing Prince Henry hiding daggers in his thoughts and stabbing at units of time, while his heart, which cannot literally be stone, is transformed in this speech into something hard enough to sharpen daggers on. Shakespeare could have simply written the king telling his son there was not long to wait, that he would shortly be dead, and that by taking the crown the prince had confirmed his belief that his son did not love him. However, the imagery heightens the intensity of the situation.

There is a considerable variety of imagery used in *Henry IV, Part 2*. Time is viewed as water by the rebels who see "which way the stream of time doth run, / And are enforc'd from our most quiet there / By the rough torrent of occasion" (4.1.70–72), while on other occasions it is viewed as the ultimate tyrant who lays "a heavy and unequal hand / Upon [their] honours" (4.1.102–103). Animals figure frequently and often describe something out of control, such as the "blunt monster with uncounted heads" (Induction) that passes on wild rumors, or Prince Henry's future rule imagined by his father as an unmuzzled wild dog "flesh[ing] his tooth on every innocent" (4.5.133). Plants and gardening analogies are used to represent caring for the kingdom or for people: Talking of the Page, Poins wishes that "this blossom could be kept from cankers" (2.2.101); the Archbishop notes that it is impossible for Henry IV to "weed this land" of all his enemies as they are "so enrooted with his friends / That plucking to unfix an enemy / He doth unfasten so and shake a friend" (4.1.207–209). Lord Bardolph uses an image of planning a building properly to ensure that the project is completed well to the planning of the rebellion (1.3)

This variety is exciting, yet there is one set of imagery that Shakespeare uses in this play more than any other type, and that is imagery of disease and sickness. The play is littered with sick old men—Henry IV, the Earl of Northumberland, Falstaff, Shallow, and Silence. However, sickness is different things to different people.

Northumberland is described by Rumour as "crafty-sick" (Induction), but when he hears of his son's death, the bad news is like a medicine, pulling him out of his sickbed like "the wretch whose fever-weaken'd joints, / Like strengthless hinges, buckle under life, / Impatient of his fit, breaks like a fire / Out of his keepers arms, even so my limbs, / Weaken'd with grief, being now enrag'd with grief, / Are thrice themselves" (1.1.140–145). There is no proof that Rumour's slur against Northumberland is true, and his grief at his son's death seems genuine, yet each time he is supposed to fight with the rebels against Henry IV, his feverish determination is as short lived as that of the fever victim to whom he compares himself. Had he added his forces to the rebellions of either Hotspur or the Archbishop of York, the Lancastrians might well have fallen.

As it is, King Henry's usurpation infects the land as described by the Archbishop in Act IV, Scene 1:

> we are all diseas'd,
> And with our surfeiting, and wanton hours,
> Have brought ourselves into a burning fever,
> And we must bleed for it; of which disease
> Our late King Richard being infected died. . . .
> I take not on me here as a physician, . . .
> But rather show awhile like fearful war
> To diet rank minds sick of happiness,
> And purge th'obstructions which begin to stop
> Our very veins of life.
>
> (4.1.54–66)

The usurpation is an illness that has infected the entire nation; it killed King Richard, and by their behavior, the people have made themselves worse. Bleeding was a surgical procedure for bringing down a fever, but of course, in this position it also refers to those who will be wounded and killed on the battlefield. However, the Archbishop says that he is not there as a doctor or a war maker, but instead by putting on the appearance of war, he feels he can lead the king and court back to the correct path. He sees them as bloated with ease and luxury, out of touch with reality, and wishes to remove the "obstructions" that stop the kingdom from operating correctly.

While the Archbishop uses this imagery to provide striking images for serious purposes, Falstaff uses the same vivid imagery for banter. He uses it in the first scene he has with the Lord Chief Justice, primarily entering into the topic in an attempt to distract the Lord Chief Justice from the point at hand. The Lord Chief Justice picks up on his topic, suggesting that he would like to be a "physician" to Falstaff to cure him of his feigned deafness by putting him in the stocks or prison (1.2.143). Falstaff replies: "Your lordship may minister the potion of imprisonment to me in respect of poverty; but how I should be your patient to follow your prescriptions, the wise may make some dram of a scruple, or indeed a scruple itself" (1.2.145–149). Falstaff has no money, so the Lord Chief Justice will have to send him to prison. However, Falstaff feels a particle of doubt as to whether the Lord Chief Justice's remedies would be good for him or that he could afford them. This image also carries the pun on the words *dram* and *scruple,* a dram being an apothecary's measure for 60 grains, while a scruple is a third of a dram.

Falstaff also uses sickness as a humorous way to describe his finances. He "can get no remedy against this consumption of the purse; borrowing only lingers and lingers it out, but the disease is incurable" (1.2.264–266). Anyone who has tried to live on a budget can sympathize with this state of affairs. But, Falstaff has greater expenses than other men, being bigger in every dimension. There is more of him to clothe and more of him to feed, and his lifestyle must be greater than that of other men.

Structure

The play seems to contain three separate plots: 1) the reformation of Prince Henry, 2) the rebellion against King Henry IV, and 3) Falstaff's day-to-day life and search for 1,000 pounds. None of these plots is strong enough to be a play on its own, but together, they contribute toward the prince's reformation. The three plots present three different attitudes toward kingly authority, Falstaff's being to ignore it whenever possible, the rebels to fight against it, and the prince's to slowly come to embrace it. The scenes are skillfully interwoven, more or less evenly divided between the comical and historical worlds, with Falstaff appearing in more than any other character—eight out of the total of 19 scenes. This breaks up the story, keeping the audience alert. Although the two worlds seem to oppose each other—nobility against commoners, poetry against prose, law against misrule—there is a commonality of themes and imagery that links them together. They both contain aspects of the turmoil that results from Henry IV's reign, and the imagery of disease is prevalent throughout the play until the old king is dead, taking it with him to his grave, as he had hoped.

For the prince's reformation, Shakespeare has borrowed the structure of a morality play, placing Henry between two opposite poles, those of misrule and law. However, Falstaff only appears in one scene with Prince Henry; it is to the audience that he demonstrates Falstaff's unfitness as a royal companion, presumably because this is something that the prince already knows. This allows the audience to anticipate Falstaff's come-uppance in the final scene and accept it as his just deserts.

There is a considerable amount of mirroring and echoing of events and characters in the play, often presenting a distorted reflection. Northumberland and Henry IV are two wily, sick old men, and Falstaff is a kind of reflection of them, as a father figure to the prince and in his first scene as a parody of Northumberland's limping, ranting old man. There are two women in the Eastcheap scenes, Mistress Quickly and Doll Tearsheet, reflecting Northumberland's household. Prince Henry and Poins are alike in their hell raising yet totally different in birth and comprehension. Scenes are repeated, the after-dinner scene in Eastcheap reflecting and contrasting with the after-dinner scene in Gloucestershire. The scene that ends with Falstaff pointing out that "the undeserver may sleep, when the man of action is called on" (2.4.406) is immediately followed by one in which the usurping king cannot sleep. The Lord Chief Justice is asked by Falstaff for 1,000 pounds, which he refuses to give; however, though Justice Shallow is not asked on stage, it becomes clear by the coronation scene that he has given the money to Falstaff.

Although the general story lacks tension, for the audience knows what will become of Falstaff and is quick to discover that the rebels will not get Northumberland's support, each scene builds upon and comments on the last one in a satisfying manner.

EXTRACTS OF CLASSIC CRITICISM

Samuel Johnson (1709–1784) [Excerpted from *The Plays of William Shakespeare*, Johnson's landmark 1765 edition of Shakespeare. Johnson was one of the greatest of all English literary critics.]

None of Shakespeare's plays are more read than the first and second parts of *Henry IV*. Perhaps no authour has ever in two plays afforded so much delight. The great events are interesting, for the fate of kingdoms depends upon them; the slighter occurrences are diverting, and, except one or two, sufficiently probable; the incidents are multiplied with wonderful fertility of invention, and the characters diversified with the utmost nicety of discernment, and the profoundest skill in the nature of man.

The prince, who is the hero both of the comick and tragick part, is a young man of great abilities and violent passions, whose sentiments are right, though his actions are wrong; whose virtues are obscured by negligence, and whose understanding is dissipated by levity. In his idle hours he is rather loose than wicked, and when the occasion forces out his latent qualities, he is great without effort, and brave without tumult. The trifler is roused into a hero, and the hero again reposes in the trifler. This character is great, original and just.

Piercy is a rugged soldier, cholerick and quarrelsome, and has only the soldier's virtues, generosity and courage.

But Falstaff, unimitated and unimitable Falstaff, how shall I describe thee? Thou compound of sense and vice; of sense which may be admired but not esteemed, of vice which may be despised, but hardly detested. Falstaff is a character loaded with faults, and with those faults which naturally produce contempt. He is a thief, and a glutton, a coward, and a boaster, always ready to cheat the weak, and prey upon the poor; to terrify the timorous and insult the defenceless. At once obsequious and malignant, he satirises in their absence those whom he lives by flattering. He is familiar with the prince only as an agent of vice, but of this familiarity he is so proud as not only to be supercilious and haughty with common men, but to think his interest of importance to the duke of Lancaster. Yet the man thus corrupt, thus despicable, makes himself necessary to the prince that despises him, by the most pleasing of all qualities, perpetual gaiety, by an unfailing power of exciting laughter, which is the more freely indulged, as his wit is not of the splendid or ambitious kind, but consists in easy escapes and sallies of levity, which make sport but raise no envy. It must be observed that he is stained with no enormous or sanguinary crimes, so that his licentiousness is not so offensive but that it may be borne for his mirth.

The moral to be drawn from this representation is, that no man is more dangerous than he that with a will to corrupt, hath the power to please; and that neither wit nor honesty ought to think themselves safe with such a companion when they see Henry seduced by Falstaff.

Maurice Morgann (1725–1802). [Excerpted from *An Essay on the Dramatic Character of Sir John Falstaff* (1777). Morgann treats *Henry IV, Part 1* and *Part 2* as if they are one play, and therefore, the incidents he reports are a mixture taken from both plays.]

I am to avow, then, that I do not clearly discern that Sir John Falstaff deserves to bear the character so generally given him of an absolute Coward; or, in other words, that I do not conceive Shakespeare ever meant to make Cowardice an essential part of his constitution. . . . What then can be the cause that we are not at all surprised at the gaiety and ease of Falstaff under the most trying circumstances; and that we never think of charging Shakespeare with departing, on this account, from the truth and coherence of character? Perhaps, after all, the real character of Falstaff may be different from his apparent one; and possibly this difference between reality and appearance, whilst it accounts at once for our liking and our censure, may be the true point of humour in the character, and the source of all our laughter and delight. We may chance to find, if we will but examine a little into the nature of those circumstances which have accidentally involved him, that he was intended to be drawn as a character of much Natural courage and resolution; and be obliged thereupon to repeal those decisions which may have been made upon the credit of some general tho' unapplicable propositions; the common source of error in other and higher matters. . . .

We will begin then, if the reader pleases, by inquiring what Impression the very Vulgar had taken of Falstaff. If it is not that of Cowardice, be it what else if may, that of a man of violence, or a Ruffian in years, as Harry calls him, or any thing else, it answers my purpose; how insignificant soever the characters or incidents to be first produced may otherwise appear;—for these Impressions must have been taken either from personal knowledge and observation; or, what will do better for my purpose, from common fame. Altho' I must admit some part of this evidence will appears so weak and trifling that it certainly ought not to be produced but in proof Impression only.

The Hostess Quickly employs two officers to arrest Falstaff: On the mention of his name, one of them immediately observes "that it may chance to cost some of them their lives, for that he will stab."—"Alas a day," says the hostess, "take heed of him, he cares not what mischief he doth; if his weapon be out he will foin like any devil; He will spare neither man, woman, or child." Accordingly, we find that when they lay hold on him he resists to the utmost of his power, and calls upon Bardolph, whose arms are at liberty, to draw. "Away, varlets, draw Bardolph, but me off the villain's head, throw the quean in the kennel." The officers cry a rescue, a rescue! But the Chief Justice comes in and the scuffle ceases. In another scene, his wench Doll Tearsheet asks him "when he will leave fighting . . . and patch up his old body for heaven." This is occasioned by his drawing his rapier, on great provocation, and driving Pistol, who is drawn likewise, down stairs, and hurting him in the shoulder. To drive Pistol was no great feat; nor do I mention it as such; but upon this occasion it was necessary. "A Rascal bragging slave," says he, "the rogue fled from me like quicksilver": Expressions which, as they remember the cowardice of Pistol, seem to prove that Falstaff did not value himself on the adventure. Even something may be drawn from Davy, Shallow's serving man, who calls Falstaff, in ignorant admiration, the man of war. I must observe here, and I beg the reader will notice it that there is not a single expression dropt by these people, or either of Falstaff's followers from which may be inferred the least suspicion of Cowardice in his character; and this is I think such an implied negation as deserves considerable weight. . . .

It will be needless to shew, which might be done from a variety of particulars, that Falstaff was known and had consideration at Court. Shallow cultivates him in the idea that a friend at Court is better than a penny in purse: Westmorland speaks to him in the tone of an equal: Upon Falstaff's telling him that he thought his lordship had been already at Shrewsbury, Westmorland replies,—"Faith, Sir John, 'tis more than time that were there, and you too; the King I can tell you looks for us all, we must away all tonight."—"Tut," says Falstaff, "never fear me, I am as vigilant as a cat to steal cream."—He desires, in another place, of my lord John of Lancaster, "that when he goes to Court, he may stand in his good report." His intercourse and correspondence with both these lords seem easy and familiar. "Go," says he to the page, "bear this to my Lord of Lancaster, this to the Prince, this to the Earl of Westmorland, and this (for he extended himself on all sides) to old Mrs Ursula," whom, it seems, the rogue ought to have married many years before.— But these intimations are needless: We see him ourselves in the Royal Presence; where, certainly, his buffooneries never brought him; never was the Prince of a character to commit so high an indecorum, as to thrust, upon a solemn occasion, a mere Tavern companion into his father's Presence, especially in a moment when he himself deserts his looser character, and takes up that of a Prince indeed.—In a very important scene, where Worcester is expected with proposals from Percy, and wherein he is received, is treated with, and carries back offers of accommodation from the King, the King's attendants upon the occasion are the Prince of Wales, Lord John of Lancaster, the Earl of Westmorland, Sir Walter Blunt, and Sir John Falstaff.—What shall be said to this? Falstaff is not surely introduced here in vicious indulgence to a mob audience;—he utters but one word, a buffoon one indeed, but aside, and to the Prince only. Nothing, it should seem, is wanting, if decorum would here have permitted, but that he should have spoken one sober sentence in the Presence (which yet we are to suppose him ready and able to do if

occasion should have required; or his wit was given him to little purpose) and Sir John Falstaff might be allowed to pass for an established Courtier and counsellor of state. "If I do grow great," says he, "I'll grow less, purge and leave sack, and live as a nobleman should do." Nobility did not then appear to him at an unmeasurable distance; it was, it seems, in his idea, the very next link in the chain. . . .

But as yet we have dealt principally in parole and circumstantial evidence, and have referred to Fact only incidentally. But Facts have a much more operative influence: They may be produced, not as arguments only, but Records; not to dispute alone, but to decide.—It is time then to behold Falstaff in actual service as a soldier, in danger, and in battle. We have already displayed one face in his defence against the censure of Lancaster; a fact extremely unequivocal and decisive. But the reader knows I have others, and doubtless goes before me to the action in Shrewsbury. In the midst and in the heat of battle we see him come forwards;—what are his words? "I have led my Rag-o-muffians where they are peppered; there's not three of my hundred and fifty left alive." But to whom does he say this? To himself only; he speaks in soliloquy. There is no questioning the fact, he had led them; they were peppered; there were not three left alive. He was in luck, being in bulk equal to any two of them, to escape unhurt. Let the author answer for that, I have nothing to do with it: . . . Well might the Chief Justice as we now find, acknowledge Falstaff's services in this day's battle; an acknowledgement which amply confirms the fact. A Modern officer, who had performed a feat of this kind, would expect, not only the praise of having done his duty, but the appellation of a hero. But poor Falstaff has too much wit to thrive: In spite of probability, in spite of inference, in spite of fact, he must be a Coward still. . . . We see him, after he had expended his Rag-o-muffians, with a sword and tar-get in the midst of battle, in perfect pos-session of himself, and replete with humour and jocularity. He was, I presume, in some immediate personal danger, in danger also of a general defeat; too corpulent for flight; and to be led a prisoner was probably to be led to execution; yet we see him laughing and easy, offering a bottle of sack to the Prince instead of a pistol, punning and telling him, "there was that which would sack a city".— "What, is it a time," says the Prince "to jest and dally now?" No, a sober character would not jest on such an occasion, but a Coward could not; he would neither have the inclina-tion, or the power. And what could support Falstaff in such a situation? Not principle; he is not suspected of the Point of honour; he seems indeed fairly to renounce it. "Honour cannot set a leg or an arm; it has no skill in surgery:—What is it? A word only; meer air. It is insensible to the dead; and detraction will not let it live with the living." What then but a strong natural constitutional Courage, which nothing could extinguish or dismay?

William Hazlitt (1778–1830)   [Excerpted from *Characters of Shakespear's Plays* (1817). Although writing in this section about *Henry IV* (here treated as one play), Hazlitt seems to think the only char-acter worth discussing is Falstaff and, indeed, seems to vehemently dislike Prince Henry.]

If Shakesspear's fondness for the ludicrous sometimes led to faults in his tragedies (which was not often the case) he has made us amends by the character of Falstaff. This is perhaps the most substantial comic character that ever was invented. Sir John carries a most portly presence in the mind's eye; and in him, not to speak it profanely, "we behold the ful-ness of the spirit of wit and humour bodily." We are as well acquainted with his person as his mind, and his jokes come upon us with

double force and relish from the quantity of flesh through which they make their way, as he shakes his fat sides with laughter, or "lards the lean earth as he walks along." Other comic characters seem, if we approach and handle them, to resolve themselves into air, "into thin air": but this is embodied and palpable to the grossest apprehension : it lies "three fingers deep upon the ribs," it plays about the lungs and the diaphragm with all the force of animal enjoyment. His body is like a good estate to his mind, from which he receives rents and revenues of profit and pleasure in kind, according to its extent, and the richness of the soil. Wit is often a meagre substitute for pleasurable sensation; an effu-sion of spleen and petty spite at the comforts of others, from feeling none in itself. Fal-staff's wit is an emanation of a fine constitu-tion; an exuberance of good-humour and good-nature; an overflowing of his love of laughter and good-fellowship; a giving vent to his heart's ease, and over-contentment with himself and others. He would not be in character, if he were not so fat as he is; for there is the greatest keeping in the boundless luxury of his imagination and the pampered self-indulgence of his physical appetites. He manures and nourishes his mind with jests, as he does his body with sack and sugar. He carves out his jokes, as he would a capon or a haunch of venison, where there is *cut and come again;* and pours out upon them the oil of gladness. His tongue drops fatness, and in the chambers of his brain "it snows of meat and drink." He keeps up perpetual holiday and open house, and we live with him in a round of invitations to a rump and dozen.— Yet we are not to suppose that he was a mere sensualist. All this is as much in imagination as in reality. His sensuality does not engross and stupefy his other faculties, but "ascends me into the brain, clears away all the dull, crude vapours that environ it, and makes it full of nimble, fiery, and delectable shapes."

His imagination keeps up the ball after his senses have done with it. He seems to have even a greater enjoyment of the freedom from restraint, of good cheer, of his ease, of his vanity, in the ideal exaggerated description which he gives of them, than in fact. He never fails to enrich his discourse with allusions to eating and drinking, but we never see him at table. He carries his own larger about with him, and he is himself "a tun of man." His pulling out the bottle in the field of battle is a joke to shew his contempt for glory accompanied with danger, his systematic adherence to his Epicurean philosophy in the most trying circumstances. Again, such is his deliberate exaggeration of his own vices, that it does not seem quite certain whether the account of his hostess's bill, found in his pocket, with such an out-of-the-way charge for capons and sack with only one halfpenny-worth of bread, was not put there by himself as a trick to humour the jest upon his favourite propensities, and as a conscious caricature of himself. He is represented as a liar, a braggart, a coward, a glutton, etc. and yet we are not offended but delighted with him; for he is all these as much to amuse others as to gratify himself. He openly assumes all these character to shew the humourous part of them. The unrestrained indulgence of his own ease, appetites, and convenience, has neither malice nor hypocrisy in it. In a word, he is an actor in himself almost as much as upon the stage, and we no more object to the character of Falstaff in a moral point of view than we should think of bringing an excellent comedian, who should represent him to the life, before one of the police offices. We only consider the number of pleasant lights in which he puts certain foibles (the more pleasant as they are opposed to the received rules and necessary restraints of society) and do not trouble ourselves about the consequences resulting from them, for no mischievous consequences do result. Sir John is old as well as fat, which gives a melancholy retrospective tinge to the character; and by the disparity between his inclinations and his capacity for enjoyment, makes it still more ludicrous and fantastical.

The secret of Falstaff's wit is for the most part a masterly presence of mind, an absolute self-possession, which nothing can disturb. His repartees are involuntary suggestions of his self-love; instinctive evasions of every thing that threatens to interrupt the career of his triumphant jollity and self-complacency. His very size floats him out of all his difficulties in a sea of rich conceits; and he turns round on the pivot of his convenience, with every occasion and at a moments warning. His natural repugnance to every unpleasant thought or circumstance, of itself makes light of objections, and provokes the most extravagant and licentious answers in his own justification. His indifference to truth puts no check upon his invention, and the more improbable and unexpected his contrivances are, the more happily does he seem to be delivered of them, the anticipation of their effect acting as a stimulus to the gaiety of his fancy. The success of one adventurous sally gives him the spirits to undertake another: he deals always in round numbers, and his exaggerations and excuses are "open, palpable, monstrous as the father that begets them." . . .

The heroic and serious part of these two plays founded on the story of Henry IV, is not inferior to the comic and farcical. The characters of Hotspur and Prince Henry are two of the most beautiful and dramatic, both in themselves and from contrast, that ever were drawn. They are the essence of chivalry. We like Hotspur the best upon the whole, perhaps because he was unfortunate.—The characters of their fathers, Henry IV and old Northumberland, are kept up equally well. Henry naturally succeeds by his prudence and caution in keeping what he has got;

Northumberland fails in his enterprise from an excess of the same quality, and is caught in the web of his own cold, dilatory policy. Owen Glendower is a masterly character. It is as bod and original as it is intelligible and thoroughly natural. The disputes between him and Hotspur are managed with infinite address and insight into nature. . . .

The peculiarity and the excellence of Shakespear's poetry is, that it seems as if he made his imagination the hand-maid of nature, and nature the plaything of his imagination. He appears to have been all the characters, and in all the situations he describes. It is as if either he had all their feelings, or had lent them all his genius to express themselves. There cannot be stronger instances of this than Hotspur's rage when Henry IV forbids him to speak of Mortimer, his insensibility to all that his father and uncle urge to calm him, and his fine abstracted apostrophe to honour, "By heaven, methinks it were an easy leap to pluck a bright honour from the moon," etc. After all, notwithstanding the gallantry, generosity, good temper, and idle freaks of the mad-cap Prince of Wales, we should not have been sorry, if Northumberland's force had come up in time to decided the fate of the battle at Shrewsbury; at least we always heartily sympathise with Lady Percy's grief, when she exclaims,

Had my sweet Harry had but half their
     numbers,
Today might I (hanging on Hotspur's
     neck)
Have talked of Monmouth's grave.

The truth is, that we never could forgive the Prince's treatment of Falstaff; though perhaps Shakespear knew what was best, according to the history, the nature of the times, and of the man. We speak only as dramatic critics. Whatever terror the French in those days might have of Henry V yet, to the readers of poetry at present, Falstaff is the better man of the two. We think of him and quote him oftener.

MODERN CRITICISM AND CRITICAL CONTROVERSIES

Earlier critics inherited their views of drama from the ancient Greeks and Romans. There was a strict set of rules governing what constitutes drama and for categorizing each play into either the comedy or the tragedy genre. Plays on historical subjects of the classical era, such as *Julius Caesar* or *Antony and Cleopatra*, were categorized as tragedies. Yet, Shakespeare's history plays seemed to rest in a category of their own, and indeed, when they were first printed en masse in 1623 in what is now known as the First Folio, the title—*Mr William Shakespeare's Comedies, Histories and Tragedies*—implied that they were one of the three genres of play. Because they portrayed significant historical events of the nation, there was a tendency to view them as patriotic spectacle alone. John Dryden dismissed the history plays as being "rather so many chronicles of Kings" (26), while Charles Gildon stated that they "mix comic and tragic, and, being histories, contain no fable or design" (qtd. in Hunter 229). H. B. Charlton in his 1929 essay, "Shakespeare, Politics and Politicians" challenges this view. While he describes most history plays as tragedies in a historical setting, he argues that the real hero of an English history play is England itself and that such plays are not so much history plays as political plays. He believes that Shakespeare achieved this in *Henry IV,* in which the king suspends all moral considerations except as tools of expediency. He also points out that "Falstaff's principles are Henry's, supplied to the domain of private life" (qtd. in Hunter 87). In recent years, the view of history plays as mere shallow pageantry has undergone considerable revision.

More modern criticism of the two parts of *Henry IV* has focused on whether Shakespeare originally intended to write one play or two. For A. C. Bradley there is no doubt that Shakespeare intended both plays as one unit when he first started to write.

John Dover Wilson considers the story to be in the classic structure of one play stretched out over 10 acts, instead of the usual five, while E. M. W. Tillyard is certain that each play is incomplete without the other. On the opposing side are R. A. Law, who sees the plays as two independent organic units, and George Lyman Kittredge, who categorically states that they are each complete in themselves. Arguments in favor of interdependence include the fact that in *Part 1,* the Archbishop of York is seen preparing for his rebellion, which actually has no place in *Part 1.* Arguments in favor of them being two separate plays all along include the difference in structure between the two plays. Harold Jenkins studies all their arguments in his 1956 essay, "The Structural Problem in Shakespeare's *Henry IV,*" picking up on the critics' use of the words *planned* and *unpremeditated,* and points out that it is impossible to know what Shakespeare's original intention may have been. However, he concludes that Shakespeare began with the intention of writing one play, compressing time sufficiently that the Battle of Shrewsbury would take place in Act IV and then move straight into the death of Henry IV, the coronation, and the rejection of Falstaff. The evidence he cites for this includes the fact that nothing much happens in Act IV of *Part 1;* it is wasted on preparations and heralds going back and forth between the two armies (which he concedes is interesting enough). By moving the battle and the prince's reconciliation to Act V, Shakespeare left no room for the rejection of Falstaff. Jenkins concludes that there is little to talk about regarding *Part 2* as it is completely dictated by what is left out of *Part 1,* making the extra scenes with Falstaff merely filler.

A large part of the criticism of *Henry IV* relates to or orbits the character of Falstaff. Many critics seem to feel a deep personal anger at the newly crowned Henry V's treatment of the jolly fat man and desperately seek ways to explain this without actually committing the cardinal sin of saying "Shakespeare got it wrong." Bradley explores what he thinks the audience is feeling at the point of rejection and why it feels so; he suggests that the audience is carried along by its knowledge of the goodness of the prince and, therefore, experiences shock at his apparent mistreatment of Falstaff. Yet, throughout the play, the prince has been shown becoming more and more grave, while Falstaff's life appears seamier and seamier, with the spotlight on his using and ruining of Mistress Quickly or his intention to gull Justice Shallow. What maintains audience sympathy through this with Falstaff is his brilliant wit. Wilson continues with this theme, adding to it, regretfully, that Shakespeare has failed in his attempt to disenchant his audience. J. M. Stewart holds out another reading of the situation. He approaches the incident through the morality play concept displayed in both *Part 1* and *Part 2,* linking this to folk traditions. He suggests that the rejection of Falstaff is actually a form of symbolic sacrifice to ensure the success of the new king's reign. Falstaff has been a substitute father figure for Prince Henry, even at one point in *Part 1* playing his role in a bit of satirical acting, with the prince kneeling at his feet. Therefore, Stewart posits, Falstaff, "standing for the old king, symbolises all the accumulated sin of the reign, all the consequent sterility of the land." Like the sacrifice of the summer king in old traditions, Falstaff's symbolic

The beadles drag Doll Tearsheet and Mistress Quickly off to prison in Act V, Scene 4 of *Henry IV, Part 2.* Print from Malcolm C. Salaman's 1916 edition of *Shakespeare in Pictorial Art (Painting by William Heath)*

death washes the world clean, as the son kills the father in true Oedipal style and takes the mother (England) to be his wife.

The historical plays mainly exclude women. Valerie Traub believes that "Shakespearian drama and psychoanalytic theory share in a cultural estimation of the female reproductive body as a Bakhtinian 'grotesque body' and that they repress this figure in their narratives of psychic development." She directly compares the process of Hal's progression through the Henriad to Jacques Lacan's "description of the development of subjectivity within phallocentric culture," that is, the infant achieving separation from the mother and taking its place within a male-oriented culture as either a male or female. In such an environment, Falstaff comes to represent the pre-separation mother figure from whom the Prince must tear himself away, while Katharine of France (who appears in *Henry V*)—the defeated, lacking language, the virgin nonreproductive figure—is the essential state of woman to bolster male sexuality. Whereas previous critics such as Ernst Kris, Murray Schwartz, and Peter Erickson had seen Hal's struggle as a fight to choose between two fathers, Traub compares Falstaff to the Nurse puffing her way about in *Romeo and Juliet* and the "spherical, oily kitchen maid" in *The Comedy of Errors,* and focuses on the constant descriptions of what goes in and out of Falstaff's body, concluding that he is grotesque; Falstaff's self-description as a "sow that hath overwhelmed all her litter but one" and the references to his "belly" provide the feminizing element (1.2.11). At the end of *Henry V,* Falstaff, representing the grotesque female reproductive body, has been replaced by Princess Katharine, subjugated and virginally lacking in openings; the opposite (for the time being) of the grotesque other that threatens masculine sexual security.

Bakhtin's grotesque body is also a feature in Graham Holderness's work on Falstaff in 1992. He uses the familiar concept of carnival—a period of holiday often involving the election of a mock king, when the world is turned topsy-turvy, social distinctions are dissolved allowing people in rigidly controlled societies to let off steam—and, in particular, Bakhtin's definition of carnival involving the grotesque (wherein "all that is bodily becomes grandiose, exaggerated, immeasurable") to explain Falstaff. Holderness asserts: "Falstaff clearly performs the function, in *Henry IV, Parts One* and *Two* of carnival. He constitutes a constant focus of opposition to the official and serious tone of authority and power: his discourse confronts and challenges those of king and state. His attitude to authority is always parodic and satirical: he mocks authority, flouts power, responds to the pressures of social duty and civic obligations by retreating into Bacchanalian revelry" (Shakespeare Recycled 138). However, Falstaff represents the body of the people, wherein all the people exist in the form of one gargantuan body. He is not one coherent figure but many, and this is shown not just by his size but by the range of linguistic styles that Shakespeare has culled from popular culture: "the cant of criminals, the accents of anti-Puritan parody and satire, the language of tavern and high-road" (Shakespeare Recycled 139).

Critics such as C. L. Barber and Wilson believe that misrule exists purely to bolster the country's rule; therefore, the wild carnival days must end to ensure that rule continues. Falstaff must be rejected; misrule must go back in its box. This is the natural order of things. Yet, Holderness argues that, in actuality, when he is with Falstaff, the prince becomes part of misrule, that "ever-growing, inexhaustible, ever-laughing principle" (146). His shared fantastical conversations with Falstaff (in *Part 1*) and with Poins (in *Part 2*, Act II, Scene 2) are signs that misrule has become a part of who he is. This causes increasing tension until he has to make the climactic break with misrule in the person of Falstaff at the end of *Henry IV, Part 2*.

Stephen Greenblatt, meanwhile, reads the plays from the perspective of the marginalized characters, colonizers and colonized. He sees in Prince Henry the less pleasant side of the modern state. Greenblatt writes: "the founding of the modern state, like the self-fashioning prince, is . . . based upon acts of calculation, intimidation, and deceit"

(52). He presents Henry as "the prince and principal of falsification," an unscrupulous, manipulative, ambitious man, whose ultimate betrayal of Falstaff marks his absorption into the dehumanizing monarchy (42). He describes him in *Part 1* as a theatrical improvisor wearing a series of masks, "his father, Hotspur, Hotspur's wife, a thief in buckram, himself as prodigal, himself as penitent," and explains that rather than removing these masks when he reforms, Prince Henry simply changes them for another (46). Greenblatt believes that although *Part 1* offered the audience a selection of ways of using power, in *Part 2,* this has been degraded to one version only, "based on predation and betrayal" (47). The Lancastrian state operates on the breaking of oaths, and its system of cruelty and injustice in which a few have power and wealth while the many are poor and starve is justified through the suffering of the ruling class. For this, he refers to Henry IV's soliloquy in Act III, Scene 1, where the king is unable to sleep because of the worries of the state and his guilt over the taking of the crown. Greenblatt concludes that the authority of monarchical power in England "rests upon a hypocrisy so deep that the hypocrites themselves believe it" (55). He suggests that the audience should rebel against this, but like the American Indians of the New World, the audience is "compelled to pay homage to a system of belief whose fraudulence somehow only confirms their power, authenticity and truth" (56).

Brian Vickers, in *Appropriating Shakespeare* (1993), attacks Greenblatt's argument, equating it to similar, long-refuted works by Maurice Morgann, Bradley, and Richard Simpson. He claims that Greenblatt has ignored about 95 percent of the text and what he has used has been taken out of context; in accusing Prince Henry of spying on his people, pretending friendship, compiling dictionaries of their slang in order to betray them, Greenblatt has failed to mention "the widely-understood principle in classical and Renaissance politics that a ruler should get to know his subjects" in order to govern them properly. Vickers believes that Greenblatt, while assigning these sinister intents to the prince, totally misses the point that the prince is enjoying himself, having fun in a way that he cannot indulge in at court or later when he is king. Greenblatt has forced his framework of colonizer-colonized onto the work, presenting Falstaff as betrayed native to the prince's aggressive invasion of his world. Far from betraying him, it is clear from the text that Prince Henry had promised him nothing (and indeed, in *Part 1,* actually said that he would banish him). The prince actually provides more than he needs to, supplying Falstaff with an income and the potential for advancement. In addition, it is equally clear from the text that Falstaff is an unscrupulous scoundrel, cheating Mistress Quickly of all she possesses. Vickers points out what he believes are many misreadings and misrepresentations in Greenblatt's work.

Greenblatt's analysis also comes under attack by Hugh Grady in *Shakespeare, Machiavelli, and Montaigne: Power and Subjectivity from* Richard II *to* Hamlet. Grady comments: "the peculiar and sudden shift in tone . . . from *1 Henry IV* to *2 Henry IV* . . . marks a decisive turning point within the Henriad and within the larger trajectory of Shakespeare's writing. . . . It marks the beginning of a descent from the high point of optimism about the possible compatibility of power and subjectivity, of Machiavelli and Montaigne that was achieved in *1 Henry IV*". He stresses the polarization of the influences of Machiavelli (whose theory involved the subjugation of the subject to supreme power) and Michel de Montaigne (who advocated questioning subjects, communicative discourse more or less independent of the state) and suggests that Greenblatt has underestimated the importance of Montaigne's influences in the first two plays of the Henriad, instead focusing on the denial of free subjective pleasure in *Henry IV, Part 2* and *Henry V.* It should be noted that Montaigne's works were not published in English until 1603, and Machiavelli's *The Prince* was not published in English until 1640. A number of scholars believe, however, that Shakespeare had access to these works, and certainly, the concepts would have been under discussion at the time.

Andrew Hadfield, in *Shakespeare and Renaissance Politics,* argues that Shakespeare's plays through the 1590s and early 1600s are concerned with succession issues and royal legitimacy. He discusses Prince Henry's play acting in *Part 1;* King Henry's comment in Act IV, Scene 5, where the king refers to the troubles of the realm as "a scene / Acting that argument" (198–199); and the fact that, even when Henry IV died, it was in a fake Jerusalem (the Jerusalem Chamber in Westminster Abbey) rather than on a crusade to the real one as he planned. Given that from the death of Richard II, the successive English monarchs have very shaky if not outright illegitimate claims to the throne, Hadfield compares the play acting of Henry IV's kingship to the image building of Elizabeth I. Her grandfather's, and therefore her own, claim to the throne is no more legitimate than that of Henry IV. He points out that "the theatre audience would have also been aware of Elizabeth's desire to play the part of queen, and surround her role as majesty with sacred mystery, providing an obvious topical reference point and significance to the reproduction of English history on stage" (60).

THE PLAY TODAY

Over the last century, *Henry IV, Part 2* has slowly been transformed. Initially, it was seen as a poor copy of *Part 1,* perhaps written to cash in on the popularity of the original. There was criticism of its contradictory elements; for example, Prince Hal at the end of *Part 1* appears reformed by virtue of his martial victory, yet in *Part 2,* he is still in disgrace with his father and peers and is still hanging around with his rowdy low-life companions. In addition, the historical plays were considered to be merely pageants glorifying the monarchy and Englishness.

Nowadays, however, critics have come to accept that the history plays are far more complex than originally perceived, containing much subversive material. It is commonly accepted, for example, that *Henry V* can be read as a glorification of a national hero embodying all the best characteristics of Englishness, or alternatively, a study of a man

who is Machiavellian, cunning, manipulative—just what would have happened at Harfleur if the French had not surrendered? The history plays provide an examination of all aspects of kingship and, in Elizabethan times, were seen to hold up a mirror to current events, on occasion without the writer's intention.

Henry IV, Part 2 provides a different view on the story of *Part 1:* It is darker, dealing with the world of political expediency. Where *Part 1* rendered through Hal the morality tale choice between vanity and chivalry and gave him the contrasting extreme examples of Falstaff and Hotspur, *Part 2* offers the prince the choice between law and anarchy, played by the Lord Chief Justice and Falstaff. To explain the incompatibility between the two parts, and the repetition of the story of wild prince reforms, Prince Henry, himself, has been compared to mythical heroes like Robin Hood, able to successfully appear in different versions of the same story that contradict one another. The two reform stories are explained as two different aspects of the same reform, and both sets of choices are necessary for the prince to become a true monarch.

Henry IV, Part 2 is rarely performed as a play in its own right. It is usually put on as part of a run of the history plays or in conjunction with *Henry IV, Part 1* and/or *Henry V.* There have been some inventive re-imaginings of the play. For example, Orson Welles's 1966 film *Chimes at Midnight* mixes together primarily parts of *Henry IV, Part 1* and *Henry IV, Part 2* but also includes bits from *Richard II, Henry V,* and *The Merry Wives of Windsor.* It is regarded by many as Welles's best work, and he is quoted as saying in 1982, "If I wanted to get into heaven on the basis of one movie, that's the one I'd offer up." Meanwhile, the Shrewsbury battle scene has provided inspiration for movies such as *Braveheart* and *Saving Private Ryan.*

Although written more than 400 years ago about incidents that happened almost 200 years before that, the play holds much relevance to modern-day readers and theatergoers. What relevance, you may ask, does it have to us? Misunderstandings between generations will always abound, and this play shows us that it was no different in Shakespeare's time. When Prince Henry takes the crown, his father makes a bitter speech on the nature of parenting:

> See, sons, what things you are,
> How quickly nature falls into revolt
> When gold becomes her object!
> For this the foolish over-careful fathers
> Have broke their sleep with thoughts,
> Their brains with care, their bones with
>   industry;
> For this they have engrossed and pil'd up
> The canker'd heaps of strange-achieved gold;
> For this they have been thoughtful to invest
> Their sons with arts and martial exercises.
> (4.5.365–374)

King Henry, angry and hurt because he believes the crown prince cannot wait for him to die, sees his son as greedy and heartless. King Henry builds himself a picture in which he is the "over-careful" father who has done everything for his son, who in return is ungrateful and unloving. As is so often the way, the king ignores completely the fact that much of what he has done has been to satisfy his own ambitions. His "canker'd heaps of strange-achieved gold" probably refer to Richard's crown, which he won through shrewd political maneuvering and force of arms, only to find the infection of usurpation damaging his personal health and the peace of England. Although he might be ambitious to have his son follow him on the throne, Prince Henry probably was never asked if he wanted a life of constant danger at the time the king planned his campaign (the prince was about 14 when his father took the throne). For all King Henry knows, the prince may have had ambitions to live quietly on an estate somewhere growing apples and brewing his own beer, but once his father became king, his choices were locked down to one: He would be the heir to the throne and then king. To do anything else would probably result in his being killed; he had seen how well abdication had worked out for Richard II. The prince is taking his own path,

The king berates Prince Henry for taking the crown before his father's death in Act IV, Scene 5 of *Henry IV, Part 2*. This is a plate from *Retzsch's Outlines to Shakespeare:* Henry IV, published in 1828. *(Illustration by Moritz Retzsch)*

forming his own opinions and becoming a man. This is often a time of friction between parent and child.

Another familiar situation is the way in which Justice Shallow talks with Silence in Act III, Scene 2. Anyone who has sat listening to elderly relatives at a family gathering will recognize parts of this conversation. First, there is the query into general family health; next an inquiry into the schooling and career prospects of the younger members of the family, and then the reminiscences start. Trivial incidents of no importance are blown out of proportion (such as the day Shallow fought "with one Samson Stockfish, a fruiterer, behind Grays Inn"), either because nothing else significant happened in their lives or because it is all they can remember at that point. They are each the hero of his or her own tale. Finally, the list of who is dead begins, interspersed at odd moments by current-day trivia.

It is Shakespeare's ability to portray humanity in all its stupidity and glory that keeps this play constantly fresh and relevant to new generations. We share with the prince his discovery that becoming an adult has a price; his games with Falstaff have taught him many lessons, one of which is that one cannot live one's entire life as a jest. Eventually, the time will arrive to take on the mantle of responsibility and be the man his father hopes he will be—but in his own way.

FIVE TOPICS FOR
DISCUSSION AND WRITING

1. **Imagery of disease and decay:** Find some examples of images of disease and decay. Which characters use it, and how do they use it? Does the imagery differ among the different strata of society? How is it tied in with the political situation? What effect does it have on the play as a whole? Are some images more vivid than others? What is it that makes them stand out?

2. **Kingship:** How is the role of kingship portrayed? What is its connection to justice? What imagery is connected with the king? How secure is the throne? How does usurpation affect the country, the usurper, and his descendants? How does this play develop the distinction between the private and the public individual? What pressures does kingship place on the father-son relationship? What qualities make a good king? Is Henry IV a good king? Is it possible to be both a good king and a good man?

3. **Falstaff:** What is his social position? What is his relationship with Prince Henry? Does Falstaff have a social group to which he belongs? Examine his scenes with the Lord Chief Justice. What methods does Falstaff use to handle him? Is he successful? Examine their relationship with each other and with Prince Henry in terms of morality plays. How does Falstaff's character and relationship with the prince differ from that portrayed in *Henry IV, Part 1*? What does the prince learn from Falstaff? Does Falstaff deserve what happens to him at the end of the play? How is the audience meant to feel during the rejection scene?

4. **Rebellion:** What are the reasons for the rebellion against the king? Are they "just and honourable" (4.2.110)? Who is the rebel leader? Why do the rebels fail? How does the Archbish-

op's presence change the nature of the rebellion? What is Northumberland's role in the play? Is his decision not to fight due to the persuasion of his wife and daughter-in-law, or is it his natural inclination? Are Prince John's actions at Gaultree defensible? What is Coleville's place in the rebellion? Why does he surrender? Could Falstaff, arriving late at the battle, rejecting the rule of law, be described as a rebel?

5. **Plot and structure:** Who is the hero of the play? Compare the comic plot with the political plot. Are there actually two or more different plays taking place on stage? Sometimes when plays are performed, certain scenes may be omitted or put in a different order by the director. A commonly removed scene is Act V, Scene 4, where Mistress Quickly and Doll Tearsheet are taken off to jail. What effect does removing this scene have on the preceding and following scenes? Which scenes would you cut or reorder, and what effect would that have on the plot? Are there benefits to the multiple changes of location in the play?

Bibliography

Crystal, David, and Ben Crystal. *Shakespeare's Words: A Glossary and Language Companion*. London: Penguin Books, 2004

Dryden, John. *Dramatic Essays by John Dryden*. London: J. M. Dent & Sons, 1921.

Grady, Hugh. *Shakespeare, Machiavelli, and Montaigne: Power and Subjectivity from* Richard III *to* Hamlet. Oxford and New York: Oxford University Press, 2002.

Greenblatt, Stephen. *Shakespearian Negotiations: The Circulation of Social Energy in Renaissance England*. Oxford: Oxford University Press, 1988.

Hadfield, Andrew. *Shakespeare and Renaissance Politics*. London: Arden Shakespeare, 2004.

Henry IV, Part 2, narrated by Brian Ahern. Vintage Radio Collection, 1937.

Henry IV, Part 2, narrated by Flo Gibson. Classic Books Collection, January 2004.

Holderness, Graham. "Carnival and History: Henry IV." In *Shakespeare's History Plays*, edited by R. J. C. Watt, 128–176. London: Longman, 2002.

————. *Shakespeare Recycled: The Making of Historical Drama.* Hertfordshire, U.K.: Harvester Wheatsheaf, 1992.

Holinshed, Raphael. *The Chronicles* and *The Historie of England.* Available online. URL: http://www.gutenberg.org/browse/authors/h#a5166.

Hunter, G. K., ed. *Shakespeare:* Henry IV Parts I *and* II. London: Macmillan, 1983. [Note: Includes comments by A. C. Bradley, George Lyman Kittredge, R. H. Law, E. M. W. Tillyard, and John Dover Wilson.]

Jenkins, Harold. "The Structural Problems in Shakespeare's *Henry the Fourth.*" In *Structural Problems in Shakespeare,* 96–98. London: Arden, 2002.

Nicholl, Charles. *The Reckoning: The Murder of Christopher Marlowe.* London: Vintage, 2002.

Shakespeare, William. *The Second Part of King Henry IV.* The Arden Edition of the Works of William Shakespeare. Edited by A. R. Humphreys. London: Methuen, 1971.

Shakespeare's Henry IV, Part 2, introduced by Richard Eyre. BBC Audiobooks Ltd., 2006.

Spurgeon, Caroline. *Shakespeare's Imagery and What It Tells Us.* Cambridge: Cambridge University Press, 1971.

Stern, Tiffany. "*A small-beer health to his second day:* Playwrights, Prologues, and First Performances in the Early Modern Theater." *Studies in Philology* 101, no. 2 (Spring 2004): 172–199.

Traub, Valerie. "Prince Hal's Falstaff: Positioning Psychoanalysis and the Female Reproductive Body." *Shakespeare's Quarterly* 40 (1989): 456–474.

Vickers, Brian. *Appropriating Shakespeare: Contemporary Critical Quarrels.* London: Yale University Press, 1993.

Watt, R. J. C., ed. *Shakespeare's History Plays.* London: Longman, 2002.

Weiss, René, ed. *The Oxford Shakespeare:* Henry IV, Part 2. Oxford: Oxford University Press, 1997.

Young, David P., ed. *Twentieth Century Interpretations of* Henry IV, Part Two. Englewood Cliffs, N.J.: Prentice Hall, 1968.

FILM AND VIDEO PRODUCTIONS

Bogdanov, Michael, dir. *Henry IV, Part 2.* With Michael Cronin, Michael Pennington, Francesca Ryan, and Paul Brennan. English Shakespeare Company, 1990.

Branagh, Kenneth, dir. *Henry V.* With Kenneth Branagh, Emma Thompson, Derek Jacobi, Brian Blessed, and Ian Holm. Columbia Tristar, 1989.

Giles, David, dir. *The Complete Dramatic Works of William Shakespeare: Henry IV, Part II* (or *The Second Part of Henry the Fourth Containing His Death and the Coronation of King Henry the Fifth*). With David Gwillim, Michelle Dotrice, Jon Finch, and Bruce Purchase. BBC and Time-Life Television, 1979.

Welles, Orson, dir. *Chimes at Midnight.* With Orson Welles, John Gielgud, Keith Baxter, and Margaret Rutherford. Suevia Films, 1966.

—Julia A. Daly